THE LIBRARY OF LIVING PHILOSOPHERS

THE PHILOSOPHY OF
MARTIN BUBER

THE LIBRARY OF LIVING PHILOSOPHERS

PAUL ARTHUR SCHILPP, FOUNDER AND EDITOR 1939-1981
LEWIS EDWIN HAHN, EDITOR 1981-

Paul Arthur Schilpp, Editor

THE PHILOSOPHY OF JOHN DEWEY (1939, 1971, 1989)
THE PHILOSOPHY OF GEORGE SANTAYANA (1940, 1951)
THE PHILOSOPHY OF ALFRED NORTH WHITEHEAD (1941, 1951)
THE PHILOSOPHY OF G. E. MOORE (1942, 1971)
THE PHILOSOPHY OF BERTRAND RUSSELL (1944, 1971)
THE PHILOSOPHY OF ERNST CASSIRER (1949)
ALBERT EINSTEIN: PHILOSOPHER-SCIENTIST (1949, 1970)
THE PHILOSOPHY OF SARVEPALLI RADHAKRISHNAN (1952)
THE PHILOSOPHY OF KARL JASPERS (1957; aug. ed., 1981)
THE PHILOSOPHY OF C. D. BROAD (1959)
THE PHILOSOPHY OF RUDOLF CARNAP (1963)
THE PHILOSOPHY OF C. I. LEWIS (1968)
THE PHILOSOPHY OF KARL POPPER (1974)
THE PHILOSOPHY OF BRAND BLANSHARD (1980)
THE PHILOSOPHY OF JEAN-PAUL SARTRE (1981)

Paul Arthur Schilpp and Maurice Friedman, Editors
THE PHILOSOPHY OF MARTIN BUBER (1967)

Paul Arthur Schilpp and Lewis Edwin Hahn, Editors
THE PHILOSOPHY OF GABRIEL MARCEL (1984)
THE PHILOSOPHY OF W. V. QUINE (1986)
THE PHILOSOPHY OF GEORG HENRIK von WRIGHT (1989)

Lewis Edwin Hahn, Editor
THE PHILOSOPHY OF CHARLES HARTSHORNE (1991)

In Preparation:
Lewis Edwin Hahn, Editor
THE PHILOSOPHY OF A. J. AYER
THE PHILOSOPHY OF PAUL RICOEUR

THE LIBRARY OF LIVING PHILOSOPHERS

VOLUME XII

THE

PHILOSOPHY

OF

MARTIN BUBER

EDITED BY

PAUL ARTHUR SCHILPP

**NORTHWESTERN UNIVERSITY &
SOUTHERN ILLINOIS UNIVERSITY**

and

MAURICE FRIEDMAN

MANHATTANVILLE COLLEGE

LA SALLE, ILLINOIS • OPEN COURT • ESTABLISHED 1887

Cover and frontispiece photographs courtesy of Department of Manuscripts and Archives, Jewish National and University Library, Jerusalem, Israel.

          THE PHILOSOPHY OF MARTIN BUBER

OPEN COURT and the above logo are registered in the U.S. Patent and Trademark Office.

First printing 1967
First paperback printing 1991

Printed and bound in the United States of America.

The Philosophy of Martin Buber

Library of Congress Catalog Card Number: 65-14535
ISBN 0-87548-129-9
ISBN 0-8126-9152-0 (pbk.)

The Library of Living Philosophers is published under the sponsorship of Southern Illinois University at Carbondale.

GENERAL INTRODUCTION*
TO
"THE LIBRARY OF LIVING PHILOSOPHERS"

According to the late F. C. S. Schiller, the greatest obstacle to fruit-ful discussion in philosophy is "the curious etiquette which apparently taboos the asking of questions about a philosopher's meaning while he is alive." The "interminable controversies which fill the histories of philosophy," he goes on to say, "could have been ended at once by ask-ing the living philosophers a few searching questions."

The confident optimism of this last remark undoubtedly goes too far. Living thinkers have often been asked "a few searching questions," but their answers have not stopped "interminable controversies" about their real meaning. It is none the less true that there would be far greater clarity of understanding than is now often the case, if more such searching questions had been directed to great thinkers while they were still alive.

This, at any rate, is the basic thought behind the present undertak-ing. The volumes of *The Library of Living Philosophers* can in no sense take the place of the major writings of great and original think-ers. Students who would know the philosophies of such men as John Dewey, George Santayana, Alfred North Whitehead, G. E. Moore, Bertrand Russell, Ernst Cassirer, Karl Jaspers, Rudolf Carnap, Martin Buber, *et al.*, will still need to read the writings of these men. There is no substitute for first-hand contact with the original thought of the philosopher himself. Least of all does this *Library* pretend to be such a substitute. The *Library* in fact will spare neither effort nor expense in offering to the student the best possible guide to the published writ-ings of a given thinker. We shall attempt to meet this aim by providing at the end of each volume in our series a complete bibliography of the published work of the philosopher in question. Nor should one over-look the fact that the essays in each volume cannot but finally lead to this same goal. The interpretative and critical discussions of the various phases of a great thinker's work and, most of all, the reply of the thinker himself, are bound to lead the reader to the works of the philosopher himself.

* This *General Introduction,* setting forth the underlying conception of this *Library,* is purposely reprinted in each volume (with only very minor changes).

At the same time, there is no denying the fact that different experts find different ideas in the writings of the same philosopher. This is as true of the appreciative interpreter and grateful disciple as it is of the critical opponent. Nor can it be denied that such differences of reading and of interpretation on the part of other experts often leave the neophyte aghast before the whole maze of widely varying and even opposing interpretations. Who is right and whose interpretation shall he accept? When the doctors disagree among themselves, what is the poor student to do? If, in desperation, he decides that all of the interpreters are probably wrong and that the only thing for him to do is to go back to the original writings of the philosopher himself and then make his own decision—uninfluenced (as if this were possible) by the interpretation of any one else—the result is not that he has actually come to the meaning of the original philosopher himself, but rather that he has set up one more interpretation, which may differ to a greater or lesser degree from the interpretations already existing. It is clear that in this direction lies chaos, just the kind of chaos which Schiller has so graphically and inimitably described.[1]

It is curious that until now no way of escaping this difficulty has been seriously considered. It has not occurred to students of philosophy that one effective way of meeting the problem at least partially is to put these varying interpretations and critiques before the philosopher while he is still alive and to ask him to act at one and the same time as both defendant and judge. If the world's great living philosophers can be induced to co-operate in an enterprise whereby their own work can, at least to some extent, be saved from becoming merely "dessicated lecture-fodder," which on the one hand "provides innocuous sustenance for ruminant professors," and, on the other hand, gives an opportunity to such ruminants and their understudies to "speculate safely, endlessly, and fruitlessly, about what a philosopher must have meant" (Schiller), they will have taken a long step toward making their intentions clearly comprehensible.

With this in mind, *The Library of Living Philosophers* expects to publish at more or less regular intervals a volume on each of the greater among the world's living philosophers. In each case it will be the purpose of the editor of the *Library* to bring together in the volume the interpretations and criticisms of a wide range of that particular thinker's scholarly contemporaries, each of whom will be given a free

---

[1] In his essay on "Must Philosophers Disagree?" in the volume by the same title (Macmillan, London, 1934), from which the above quotations were taken.

hand to discuss the specific phase of the thinker's work which has been assigned to him. All contributed essays will finally be submitted to the philosopher with whose work and thought they are concerned, for his careful perusal and reply. And, although it would be expecting too much to imagine that the philosopher's reply will be able to stop all differences of interpretation and of critique, this should at least serve the purpose of stopping certain of the grosser and more general kinds of misinterpretations. If no further gain than this were to come from the present and projected volumes of this *Library*, it would seem to be fully justified.

In carrying out this principal purpose of the *Library*, the editor announces that (insofar as humanly possible) each volume will conform to the following pattern:

First, a series of expository and critical articles written by the leading exponents and opponents of the philosopher's thought;

Second, the reply to the critics and commentators by the philosopher himself;

Third, an intellectual autobiography of the thinker whenever this can be secured; in any case an authoritative and authorized biography; and

Fourth, a bibliography of writings of the philosopher to provide a ready instrument to give access to his writings and thought.

The editor has deemed it desirable to secure the services of an Advisory Board of philosophers to aid him in the selection of the subjects of future volumes. The names of the seven prominent American philosophers who have consented to serve appear below. To each of them the editor expresses his sincere gratitude.

Future volumes in this series will appear in as rapid succession as is feasible in view of the scholarly nature of this *Library*. The next two volumes in this series will be those of C. I. Lewis and Karl R. Popper.

Through the generosity of the Edward C. Hegeler Foundation, the publication of each new volume of the *Library* is assured on completion of the manuscript. However, funds are still required for editorial purposes in order to place the entire project of *The Library of Living Philosophers* on a sound financial foundation. The *Library* would be deeply grateful, therefore, for gifts and donations. Moreover, since November 6th, 1947, any gifts or donations made to The Library of

Living Philosophers, Inc., are deductible by the donors in arriving at their taxable net income in conformity with the Internal Revenue Code of the Treasury Department of the United States of America.

PAUL ARTHUR SCHILPP
FOUNDER AND EDITOR, 1939–1981

ADVISORY BOARD

ACKNOWLEDGMENTS

by the editors

The editors hereby gratefully acknowledge their obligation and sincere gratitude to all the publishers of Professor Buber's books and publications for their kind and uniform courtesy in permitting us to quote—sometimes at some length—from Professor Buber's writings.

PAUL A. SCHILPP
MAURICE FRIEDMAN

TABLE OF CONTENTS

Frontispiece...*facing page* v

General Introduction to *The Library of Living Philosophers*.................vii

Acknowledgments.. x

Preface.. xv

I. AUTOBIOGRAPHICAL FRAGMENTS: Martin Buber

Facsimile of Buber's handwriting.............*facing page* 3

MARTIN BUBER: "Autobiographical Fragments" 3

   1. My Mother 3

   2. My Grandmother 4

   3. Languages 5

   4. My Father 6

   5. The School 8

   6. The Two Boys 8

   7. The Horse 10

   8. Philosophers 11

   9. Vienna 13

  10. A Lecture 14

  11. The Cause and the Person 16

  12. The Zaddik 19

  13. The Walking Stick and the Tree 22

  14. Question and Answer 23

  15. A Conversion 25

  16. Report on Two Talks 26

  17. Samuel and Agag 31

Appendix I: Beginnings 33

Appendix II: A Tentative Answer 35

Appendix III: Books and Men 37

II. DESCRIPTIVE AND CRITICAL ESSAYS ON THE PHILOSOPHY OF MARTIN BUBER

1. GABRIEL MARCEL: "I and Thou" 41

2. CHARLES HARTSHORNE: "Martin Buber's Metaphysics" 49

3. PHILIP WHEELWRIGHT: "Buber's Philosophical Anthropology" 69

4. NATHAN ROTENSTREICH: "The Right and the Limitations of Buber's Dialogical Thought" 97

5. EMMANUEL LEVINAS: "Martin Buber and the Theory of Knowledge" 133

6. MARVIN FOX: "Some Problems in Buber's Moral Philosophy" 151

7. MAURICE FRIEDMAN: "The Bases of Buber's Ethics" 171

8. FRITZ KAUFMANN: "Martin Buber's Philosophy of Religion" 201

9. MALCOLM L. DIAMOND: "Dialogue and Theology" 235

10. MORDECAI M. KAPLAN: "Buber's Evaluation of Philosophic Thought and Religious Tradition" 249

11. EMIL L. FACKENHEIM: "Martin Buber's Concept of Revelation" 273

12. HUGO BERGMAN: "Martin Buber and Mysticism" 297

13. EMIL BRUNNER: "Judaism and Christianity in Buber" 309

14. MAX BROD: "Judaism and Christianity in the Work of Martin Buber" 319

15. HANS URS VON BALTHASAR: "Martin Buber and Christianity" 341

16. NAHUM N. GLATZER: "Buber as an Interpreter of the Bible" 361

17. JAMES MUILENBURG: "Buber as an Interpreter of the Bible" 381

18. RIVKAH SCHATZ-UFFENHEIMER: "Man's Relation to God
    and World in Buber's Rendering of the
    Hasidic Teaching" 403

19. ROBERT WELTSCH: "Buber's Political Philosophy" 435

20. JACOB TAUBES: "Buber and Philosophy of History" 451

21. HERBERT W. SCHNEIDER: "The Historical Significance
    of Buber's Philosophy" 469

22. JEAN WAHL: "Martin Buber and the Philosophies
    of Existence" 475

23. PAUL E. PFUETZE: "Martin Buber and American
    Pragmatism" 511

24. ERNST SIMON: "Martin Buber, the Educator" 543

25. LESLIE H. FARBER: "Martin Buber and Psychotherapy" ...577

26. CARL F. VON WEIZSÄCKER: "I-Thou and I-It in the
    Contemporary Natural Sciences" 603

27. LOUIS Z. HAMMER: "The Relevance of Buber's
    Thought to Aesthetics" 609

28. CARL KERÉNYI: "Martin Buber as Classical Author" 629

29. HELMUT KUHN: "Dialogue in Expectation" 639

30. WALTER KAUFMANN: "Buber's Religious Significance" 665

III. THE PHILOSOPHER REPLIES

MARTIN BUBER: "Replies to My Critics" 689

    I. Philosophical Accounting. Personal Determination 689

    II. Philosophical Accounting. Against Simplifications 691

    III. Misunderstandings 693

    IV. Some General Matters 700

    V. I and Thou 705

    VI. Theology, Mysticism, Metaphysics 712

    VII. Ethics 717

    VIII. On the Interpretation of the Bible 726

    IX. On Hasidism 731

Conclusion 741

IV. BIBLIOGRAPHY OF THE WRITINGS OF
MARTIN BUBER
(compiled by Maurice Friedman) 747
Index (arranged by Marvin Katz, *et al.*) 789

EDITORS' PREFACE

It is particularly fitting that there should be a *Philosophy of Martin Buber* volume in *The Library of Living Philosophers*. Not only has Buber's philosophy of dialogue won a worldwide recognition that insures him a place among the great philosophers of our time, but the very principle underlying *The Library of Living Philosophers* is one of dialogue. *The Library* gives other philosophers the opportunity to question and criticize the philosopher while he is still alive, and it gives the philosopher the opportunity to respond to their questions. Thus it introduces into the critical dialectic that has traditionally constituted philosophical interchange the basic elements of a dialogue in which really different points of view may come into fruitful contact. The philosopher must endeavor to understand the points of view from which he is questioned while at the same time pointing out to his critics those misunderstandings in their criticism that arise from seeing his philosophy from the outside rather than from within. To object to *The Library* on the grounds that "it gives the philosopher the last word" by allowing him to respond to his critics (as did one distinguished scholar in rejecting our invitation to contribute to the present volume) is to miss the whole point of the dialogue. Criticism of a philosophy is open to anyone whether the philosopher be alive or not. But to find out what a philosopher really *means* by what he says through eliciting his direct response to one's questions is only possible within a framework such as that which *The Library of Living Philosophers* affords.

We began work on the Buber volume of *The Library* in the fall of 1956. A distinguished group of philosophers and scholars have contributed to this volume from a wide range of fields that does justice to most aspects of Martin Buber's thought. The only notable omission is social philosophy. It had been our hope to have an article written from the standpoint of Reinhold Niebuhr's social ethics, which converge with Buber's in the personal I-Thou relationship but sharply diverge in the political and social. Despite this omission our volume is exceptionally rich in the dialogues that it has brought into being—not only between Buber and the contributors but also between Buber's thought and that of such eminent thinkers as Alfred North White-

head, Paul Tillich, and Gershom Scholem. Even the misunderstandings that inevitably enter into such an interchange have proved
fruitful in eliciting from Buber explanations and elaborations which
he would not otherwise have made. The *method* of Buber's thought is
dialogical as well as its conclusions: his thinking does not take the
form of systematic structures and *Weltanschauungen* but of responses
to real situations and real questions. For this reason the contribution
of *The Library of Living Philosophers* is especially great in the case
of Martin Buber.

Buber's "Autobiographical Fragments" differ from most of the
autobiographies in this series in that they tell us not of intellectual
influences and developments but of events that had decisive influence
on Buber's personal life and through this on his thought. This does
not mean that Buber was uninfluenced by the intellectual currents
of his time. On the contrary, he took in a bewilderingly rich variety
of them. But the specifically intellectual contacts were secondary to
the human, or to the experience of listening to Bach sung and played
"as Bach himself wished that it be sung and played." To use the
fifteenth fragment's story of "A Conversion" as an illustration of a
supposed influence of Franz Rosenzweig on the turning-point in
Buber's thought[1] is a pure fantasy which misses entirely the fact that
Buber's existential dialogue can never be reduced to an intellectual
dialectic between "points of view" divorced from the meeting between
actual persons in concrete situations.

The sense in which Buber does and does not regard himself as
belonging to the traditional categories of philosopher and theologian
is made explicit in the "Philosophical Accounting" that he offers at
the beginning of his Responsa. These responsa give us an understanding of another unique form that philosophizing may take in our
age, while still remaining genuine philosophy with its own place
within the central stream of the history of western philosophy. This
bursting of ready-made categories is of great importance in an age in
which it has all too often become customary to limit the boundaries
of "true philosophy" within the methods and analyses of one or
another school and dismiss those who do not fit into those limits as
not "technical" or "systematic" and therefore as not truly philosophers. It is particularly important in the case of a thinker like Buber

[1] Meyer Levin, "Sage Who Inspired Hammarskjold," *The New York Times Magazine*, December 3, 1961, p. 60.

who does not fit into any category, unless it be that of his own dialogical approach to philosophical anthropology.

Our gratification in at long last bringing this volume to press is sadly tempered by the fact that our friend, fellow-contributor, and chief advisor on this volume, Professor Fritz Kaufmann, is no longer with us to share in it. The selection of contributors for our Buber volume was among Professor Kaufmann's last concerns before his untimely death in the summer of 1958. However, long before the *Buber*-volume came into purview, almost from the very inception of *The Library of Living Philosophers*, Professor Kaufmann was personally and vitally involved in this series. He contributed very important essays to both the *Cassirer* and the *Jaspers* volumes and could at all times be counted on for serious help and advice. His passing leaves a great gap, which will not soon nor easily be filled.

Professor Marvin Fox of the Department of Philosophy at Ohio State University also served as advisor during the early stages of this volume. Finally, we should acknowledge the help given us by Professor Buber himself in suggesting contributors, in locating the German originals of the quotations in English, in preparing the Bibliography—all in addition to his work in writing the Autobiographical Fragments and the Replies to His Critics. We wish to express to him here once more publicly our sincerest gratitude.

Apart from the exclusion of items which are in the broad sense not of philosophical interest, the Bibliography of Buber's works in this volume is comprehensive and up-to-date as is no other bibliography of his that has yet appeared.[2]

It is a pleasure to call the attention of our readers to the fact that with the publication of the preceding volume of our *Library* (Volume 11, *The Philosophy of Rudolf Carnap*), this Series is appearing under the imprint of a new publisher. The Open Court Publishing Company of LaSalle, Illinois will publish all future volumes of the *Library*, and has also agreed to keep in print all the volumes of this series.

The Editors also wish to express their gratitude and appreciation to the Hegeler Foundation of LaSalle, Illinois, for a grant covering some secretarial expenses, and to the Graduate Research Council of

---

[2] Moshe Catanne's Martin Buber *Bibliography*, written in Hebrew (Jerusalem: Bialik, 1961) is more comprehensive, but it makes no attempt to discriminate between what is and what is not of philosophical significance, and it is up-to-date only through 1957.

Northwestern University, and specifically to Vice-President Payson S. Wild and Dean Moody E. Prior of the Graduate School for the continuance of a small grant-in-aid to help defray some of the editorial expenses of this as well as of other volumes in our *Library*.

The Editors also wish to express their appreciation to Professor Eugene Freeman of San Jose State College, Philosophy Editor of The Open Court Publishing Company, and Editorial Consultant to the Editors of this volume, for his extensive and painstaking assistance in the preparation of this volume for the press. The Editors also wish to express their sincerely felt gratitude to his wife, Ann Freeman, Managing Editor of *The Monist,* for her able and gracious assistance in the laborious and tedious task of seeing the book through the press.

Paul Arthur Schilpp
Maurice Friedman

April, 1965

Postscript

The passing of Martin Buber, on June 13, 1965, at the age of 87, leaves, as everyone knows, a great and unfillable void. At the same time, we can only be grateful that we were permitted to have this great soul in our midst for so long a time; and grateful too for the fact that we got his "Reply" for this volume before it was too late, and grateful also that he was at least permitted to see this volume in print in his mother-tongue (German). Now it remains for those of us who survive him to carry on the work he left unfinished.

P. A. S. & M. S. F.

June 14, 1965

1991 PREFATORY NOTE

It is good to have the 1967 Volume XII of the Library of Living Philosophers, *The Philosophy of Martin Buber*, edited by Paul A. Schilpp and Maurice Friedman, reissued in more readily available paperback, for it makes a unique contribution to a series the heart of which is dialogue. From Buber's concern with genuine listening and his knack of getting people to really listen and to want to interact with others comes a distinctive form of philosophical dialogue. It is in dialogue that we treat our fellow human beings as persons and not merely as things. Through dialogue we share our insights, attitudes, and feelings and come to think of ideas which otherwise would never have occurred to us.

Both the exchanges with his critics and his "Autobiographical Fragments" exemplify distinctive forms of dialogue, enrich our knowledge of the philosopher, and broaden our philosophical background and our capacity to philosophize. As he put it in his replies to his critics, he witnessed for experience and appealed to experience. But Martin Buber's major philosophical strength was not in making and defending a comprehensive all-inclusive system. Rather it was an affair of seeing in reality as experienced something which had not or had too little been seen and then working imaginatively and persistently to help the rest of us see it too.

LEWIS EDWIN HAHN

DEPARTMENT OF PHILOSOPHY
SOUTHERN ILLINOIS UNIVERSITY AT CARBONDALE
JULY 1991

MARTIN BUBER

AUTOBIOGRAPHICAL FRAGMENTS

Seit ich zu einem Leben aus eigener Erfahrung
gereift bin – ein Prozess, der kurz vor dem
„ersten Weltkrieg" begann und bald nach
ihm vollendet war –, habe ich unter der
Pflicht gestanden, den Zusammenhang
der damals gemachten entscheidenden
Erfahrungen ins menschliche Denkgut
einzufügen, aber nicht als „meine" Erfahrungen, sondern als eine für andere
und auch für andersartige Menschen gül-
tige und wichtige Einsicht. Da ich aber
keine Botschaft empfangen habe, die
solcherweise weiterzugeben wäre, sondern
nur eben Erfahrungen gemacht und
Einsicht gewonnen habe, musste meine
meine Mitteilung eine philosophische

Martin Buber

FACSIMILE REPRODUCTION OF BUBER'S HANDWRITING
(See p. 689, paragraph 3)

AUTOBIOGRAPHICAL FRAGMENTS*

1. *My Mother*

IT CANNOT be a question here of recounting my personal life (I do not possess the kind of memory necessary for grasping great temporal continuities as such), but solely of rendering an account of some moments that my backward glance lets rise to the surface, moments that have exercised a decisive influence on the nature and direction of my thinking.

The earliest memory which has this character for me stems out of my fourth year of life. About a year before that the separation of my parents broke up the home of my childhood in Vienna (still today I see with closed eyes the Danube canal under the house, the sight of which I used to enjoy with a feeling of certainty that nothing could happen to me). At that time I had been brought to my grandparents on my father's side near Lvov (Lemberg), then the capital city of the Austrian "crownland" Galicia. They were both people of high rank, noble persons in the exact sense of the term and, in a special manner, suited to and supplementing each other. They were both disinclined to talk over the affairs of their own existence. Of what had taken place between my parents, nothing, of course, was spoken in my presence; but I suspect that it was also hardly ever a subject of discussion between them, except in practical and unavoidable connection. The child itself expected to see his mother again soon; but no question passed his lips. Then there took place at one time what I have to tell here.

The house in which my grandparents lived had a great rectangular inner courtyard surrounded by a wooden balcony extending to the roof on which one could walk around the building at each floor. Here I stood once in my fourth year with a girl several years older, the daughter of a neighbor, to whose care my grandmother had entrusted me. We both leaned on the railing. I cannot remember that I spoke of my mother to my older comrade. But I hear still how the big girl said to me: "No, she will never come back." I know that I remained silent, but also that I cherished no doubt of the truth of the spoken words.

* Translated by Maurice Friedman.

It remained fixed in me; from year to year it cleaved ever more to my heart, but after more than ten years I had begun to perceive it as something that concerned not only me, but all men. Later I once made up the word *"Vergegnung"*—"mismeeting," or "miscounter"—to designate the failure of a real meeting between men. When after another twenty years I again saw my mother, who had come from a distance to visit me, my wife, and my children, I could not gaze into her still astonishingly beautiful eyes without hearing from somewhere the word *"Vergegnung"* as a word spoken to me. I suspect that all that I have learned about genuine meeting in the course of my life had its first origin in that hour on the balcony.

2. *My Grandmother*

My grandmother Adele was one of those Jewesses of a certain period who, in order to create freedom and leisure for their husbands to study the Torah, managed the business with circumspect zeal. For my grandfather "study of the teaching" had a special significance. Although an autodidact, he was a genuine philologist who is to be thanked for the first, and today still the authoritative, critical edition of a special class of Hebrew literature: the Midrashim—a unique mixture of interpretation of the Bible, wise sayings, and rich saga. In his civil occupation he was a great landowner, in addition a corn-merchant and the owner of phosphorite mines on the Austrian-Russian border. Beyond this he belonged to the number of the leading men of the Jewish community and to those of the town's chamber of commerce, experienced men with a judgment of their own. He never neglected these honorary offices; his own business, however, he left in general to his wife who conducted it all in a splendid and circumspect manner, but made no decision without consulting her spouse.

Among the Jews in the small Galician town where my grandmother grew up the reading of "alien" literature was proscribed, but for the girls all readings, with the exception of edifying popular books, were held unseemly. As a fifteen-year-old she had set up for herself in the storehouse a hiding place in which stood volumes of Schiller's periodical *"Die Horen,"* Jean Paul's book on education, *Levana,* and many other German books which had been secretly and thoroughly read by her. When she was seventeen years old, she took them and the custom of concentrated reading with her into her marriage, and she reared her two sons in the respect for the authentic word that cannot be paraphrased. The same influence she later exercised on me. I learned even before I was fourteen (at that time I moved into the house of my father and my stepmother) what it means really to express something. I was affected in a special manner by the way that this woman handled the large-size, similarly bound copy-books in which she recorded every day income and expenditures: in between these entries she registered, after she had spoken them half aloud to herself, the passages which had become important to her out of her readings. Now and then she set down her own comments as well, which in no way imitated the style of the classic but from time to time stated something that she had to reply in intercourse with the great spirits. The same was true of her oral utterances: even when she obviously communicated the conclusion of a reflection, it had the appearance of something perceived. That undoubtedly came from the fact that with her, experiencing and reflecting on experience were not two stages but, as it were, two sides of the same process: when she looked at the street, she had at times the profile of someone meditating on a problem, and when I found her all alone in meditation, it seemed to me at times as if she listened. To the glance of the child, however, it was already unmistakable that when she at times addressed someone, she really addressed him.

My grandfather was a true philologist, a "lover of the word," but my grandmother's love for the genuine word affected me even more strongly than his: because this love was so direct and so devoted.

3. Languages

I went to school for the first time when I was ten years old. Up till then I received private tutoring, chiefly in languages, both because of my own inclination and talents and because for my grandmother a language-centered humanism was the royal road to education.

The multiplicity of human languages, their wonderful variety in which the white light of human speech at once fragmented and preserved itself, was already at the time of my boyhood a problem that instructed me ever anew. In instructing me it also again and again disquieted me. I followed time after time an individual word or even structure of words from one language to another, found it there again and yet had time after time to give up something there as lost that apparently only existed in a single one of all the languages. That was not merely "nuances of meaning": I devised for myself two-language conversations between a German and a Frenchman, later between a Hebrew and an ancient Roman and came ever again, half in play and yet at times with beating heart, to feel the tension between what was heard by the one and what was heard by the other, from his thinking in another language. That had a deep influence on me and has issued in a long life into ever clearer insight.

My knowledge of languages as a boy also made it possible for me at times to provide my grandfather, whom I went to visit daily from my father's house, with a little help at his work. Thus it happened, for instance, that in reading "Rashi" (Rabbi Shlomo Yizhaki), the great Bible and Talmud exegete of the eleventh century, my grandfather found a text explained through a reference to a French turn of speech and asked me how this was to be understood. I had at times to deduce from the Hebrew transcription the old French wording and now to make this understandable first to myself, then to my grandfather. Later, however, when I sat alone in my room in my father's house, I was oppressed by the question: What does it mean and how does it come about that one "explains" something that was written in one language through something that one is accustomed to say in another language? The world of the Logos and of the Logoi opened itself to me, darkened, brightened, darkened again.

4. *My Father*

From about the ninth year on I spent each summer on the estate of my father, and at fourteen I moved from my grandfather's house to my father's townhouse.

The influence of my father on my intellectual development was of a different kind from that of my grandparents. It did not derive at all from the mind.

In his youth my father had had strong intellectual interests; he had occupied himself seriously with the questions that had been raised in books such as Darwin's *Origin of the Species* and Renan's *Life of Jesus*. But already early he dedicated himself to agriculture and devoted ever more of himself to it. Soon he was an exemplary phenomenon in the East Galician landed property.

When I was still a child, he brought with him from the Paris International Exhibition a great packing of breeding eggs of a type of hen still unknown in the east; he held it on his knees the whole long journey in order that no harm might come to it. Thirty-six years he worked with all kinds of implements whose specific effects he carefully tested in order to heighten the productivity of his soils.

He had mastered the technique of his age in his domain. But I noticed what really concerned him when I stood with him in the midst of the splendid herd of horses and observed him as he greeted one animal after the other, not merely in a friendly fashion but positively individually, or when I drove with him through the ripening fields and looked at him as he had the wagon halt, descended and bent over the ears again and again, in order finally to break one and carefully taste the kernels. This wholly unsentimental and wholly unromantic man was concerned about genuine human contact with nature, an active and responsible contact. Accompanying him thus on his way at times, the growing boy learned something that he had not learned from any of the many authors that he read.

In a special way the relationship of my father to nature was connected with his relationship to the realm that one customarily designates as the social. How he took part in the life of all the people who in one or another manner were dependent on him: the laborers attached to the estate, in their little houses that surrounded the estate buildings, houses built according to his design, the little peasants who performed service for him under conditions worked out with exact justice, the tenants; how he troubled about the family relationships, about the upbringing of children and schooling, about the sickness and aging of all the people—all that was not derived from any principles. It was solicitude not in the ordinary, but in the personal sense, in the sense of active responsible contact that could rise here to full reciprocity. In the town too my father did not act otherwise. To sightless charity he was fiercely averse; he understood no other help than that from person to persons, and he practised it. Even in his old age he let himself be elected to the "bread commission" of the Jewish community of Lemberg and wandered tirelessly around the houses in order to discover the people's real wants and necessities; how else could that take place except through true contact!

One thing I must still mention. My father was an elemental story teller. At times in conversation, just as its way led him, he told of people whom he had known. What he reported of them there was always the simple occurrence without any embroidery, nothing further than the existence of human creatures and what took place between them.

5. *The School*

My school was called "Franz Joseph's Gymnasium." The language of instruction and of social intercourse was Polish, but the atmosphere was that, now appearing almost unhistorical to us, which prevailed or seemed to prevail among the peoples of the Austro-Hungarian empire: mutual tolerance without mutual understanding. The pupils were for the largest part Poles, in addition to which there was a small Jewish minority (the Ruthenians had their own schools). Personally the pupils got on well with one another, but the two groups as such knew almost nothing about each other.

Before 8 o'clock in the morning all the pupils had to be assembled. At 8 o'clock the signal bell sounded. One of the teachers entered and mounted the professor's lecturing desk, above which on the wall rose a large crucifix. At the same moment all the pupils stood up in their benches. The teacher and the Polish students crossed themselves; he spoke the Trinity formula, and they prayed aloud together. Until one might sit down again, we Jews stood silent and unmoving, our eyes glued to the floor.

I have already indicated that in our school there was no perceptible hatred of the Jews; I can hardly remember a teacher who was not tolerant or did not wish to pass as tolerant. But the obligatory daily standing in the room resounding with the strange service affected me worse than an act of intolerance could have affected me. Compulsory guests, having to participate as a thing in a sacral event in which no dram of my person could or would take part, and this for eight long years morning after morning: that stamped itself upon the life-substance of the boy.

No attempt was ever made to convert any of us Jewish pupils; yet my antipathy to all missionary activity is rooted in that time. Not merely against the Christian mission to the Jews, but against all missionarizing among men who have a faith with roots of its own. In vain did Franz Rosenzweig try to win me for the idea of a Jewish mission among the non-Jews.

6. *The Two Boys*

The classroom included five rows with six benches apiece. At each bench two pupils sat.

The furthest bench to the left, at the window, through which one saw nothing else than the almost empty square for play and sports, belonged to me and my best friend. For eight years we sat at this same bench, he to the left, I to the right.

The recesses in the teaching lasted a full quarter of an hour as a rule. When the weather was in some measure favorable, the whole school band used to storm out to the square and stay there in zealous activity until the signal bell. When the weather was all too adverse, we remained together in the classroom, but only on special occasions did a larger group form. Ordinarily the structure was only loose; a few youths stood telling things or discussing together, and the composition of these small groups changed according to the different themes that emerged from one time to the next.

Once, however, in a fall utterly spoiled by rain (in the winter before I had become twelve) a special change took place that continued for some weeks.

In the third bench of the middle row sat two boys who until then had in no wise struck me and probably also had not struck most of the others as unusual. Now, however, they drew all glances to themselves. Day after day they conducted for us, without leaving the bench, mimic games with clownlike agility. They made no sound, and their faces remained unalterably severe. After some time the game took on an ever more penetratingly sexual character. Now the faces of the two looked as I imagined souls in the pains of hell, about which some of my fellow pupils knew to report to me in the tone of experts. All movements were cruelly forced. We stared at the two as long as the spectacle lasted. Shortly before the end of the recess they broke off. In our conversations the occurrence was never mentioned.

A few weeks after the spectacles had taken on this character, I was called to the school director. He received me with the gentle friendliness that we knew in him as something unalterable and asked me at once what I knew of the activities of the two. "I know nothing!" I screamed. He spoke again, just as gently as before. "We know you well," he said to me; "you are a good child, you will help us." "Help? Help whom?" I wanted—so it seems to me—to reply; but I remained silent, I stared silently at the director. Of what else happened almost nothing has penetrated into my memory, only that a great weeping as never before overcame me, and I was led away almost unconscious. A few hours later, however, when I tried at home to remember the last look of the director, it was not a gentle, but a frightened look that met me.

I was kept home for a few days, then I returned to school. The third bench of the middle row was empty and remained so until the end of the school year.

The long series of experiences that taught me to understand the problematic relationship between maxim and situation and thereby disclosed to me the nature of the true norm that commands not our obedience but ourselves, had begun with this convulsion of my childhood.

7. *The Horse*[1]

When I was eleven years of age, spending the summer on my grand-parents' estate, I used, as often as I could do it unobserved, to steal into the stable and gently stroke the neck of my darling, a broad dapple-gray horse. It was not a casual delight but a great, certainly friendly, but also deeply stirring happening. If I am to explain it now, beginning from the still very fresh memory of my hand, I must say that what I experienced in touch with the animal was the Other, the immense otherness of the Other, which, however, did not remain strange like the otherness of the ox and the ram, but rather let me draw near and touch it. When I stroked the mighty mane, sometimes marvellously smooth-combed, at other times just as astonishingly wild, and felt the life beneath my hand, it was as though the element of vitality itself bordered on my skin, something that was not I, was certainly not akin to me, palpably the other, not just another, really the Other itself; and yet it let me approach, confided itself to me, placed itself elementally in the relation of *Thou* and *Thou* with me. The horse, even when I had not begun by pouring oats for him into the manger, very gently raised his massive head, ears flicking, then snorted quietly, as a conspirator gives a signal meant to be recognizable only by his fellow-conspirator; and I was approved. But once—I do not know what came over the child, at any rate it was childlike enough—it struck me about the stroking, what fun it gave me, and suddenly I became conscious of my hand. The game went on as before, but something had changed, it was no longer the same thing. And the next day, after giving him a rich feed, when I stroked my friend's head he did not raise his head. A few years later, when I thought back to the incident, I no longer supposed that the animal had noticed my defection. But at the time I considered myself judged.

[1] Reprinted from *Between Man and Man*, "Dialogue," p. 11, with the permission of the Macmillan Co.

8. *Philosophers*

In that early period of my life, philosophy twice, in the form of two books, entrenched directly upon my existence—in my fifteenth and in my seventeenth year.

The two events do not allow themselves to be inserted into the process of appropriating a philosophical education, which was established in particular on a thorough reading of Plato (Greek was my favorite language). They were events which broke through the continuity—the presupposition of all genuine educational work—catastrophic events. In the first of them the philosophy confronted the catastrophic situation, delivering and helping. In the second the philosopher not only stirred me up but transported me into a sublime intoxication. Only after a long time was I able to escape this intoxication completely and attain to a certainty of the real.

Of the first of these two events I have told elsewhere,[2] but it is of importance to me to interpret still more clearly something of what was reported there.

It says in that passage:

A necessity I could not understand swept over me: I had to try again and again to imagine the edge of space, or its edgelessness, time with a beginning and an end or a time without beginning or end, and both were equally impossible, equally hopeless—yet there seemed to be only the choice between the one or the other absurdity.

Here it must be added above all that at that time the question about time had oppressed me in a far more tormenting fashion than that about space. I was irresistibly driven to want to grasp the total world process as actual, and that meant to understand it, "time," either as beginning and ending or as without beginning and end. At each attempt to accept them as reality, both proved equally absurd. If I wanted to take the matter seriously (and I was ever again compelled to want just this), I had to transpose myself either to the beginning of time or to the end of time. Thus I came to feel the former like a blow in the neck or the latter like a rap against the forehead—no, there is no beginning and no end! *Or* I had to let myself be thrown into this or that bottomless abyss, into infinity, and now everything whirled. It happened thus time after time. Mathematical or physical formulae

[2] Martin Buber, *Between Man and Man*, "What is Man?" "From Aristotle to Kant," trans. R. G. Smith (New York: Macmillan Paperbacks, 1965), p. 136.

could not help me; what was at stake was the reality of the world in which one had to live and which had taken on the face of the absurd and the uncanny.

Then a book came into my hand, Kant's *Prolegomena*. In it was taught that space and time are "nothing more than formal conditions of our sensory faculty," are "not real properties that adhere to the things in themselves" but "mere forms of our sensory perception."

This philosophy exercised a great quieting effect on me. Now I needed no longer, tormented, to inquire of time a final time. Time was not a sentence hanging over me; it was mine, for it was "ours." The question was explained as unanswerable by its nature, but at the same time I was liberated from it, from having to ask it. Kant's present to me at that time was philosophical freedom.

About two years after that the other book took possession of me, a book that was, to be sure, the work of a philosopher but was not a philosophical book: Nietzsche's *Thus Spake Zarathustra*. I say "took possession of me," for here a teaching did not simply and calmly confront me, but a willed and able—splendidly willed and splendidly able—utterance stormed up to and over me. This book, characterized by its author[3] as the greatest present that had ever been made to mankind up till then, worked on me not in the manner of a gift but in the manner of an invasion which deprived me of my freedom, and it was a long time until I could liberate myself from it.

Nietzsche himself wished "the basic conception" of this book to be understood as an interpretation of *time:* its interpretation as "eternal return of the same," that is, as an infinite sequence of finite periods of time, which are like one another in all things so that the end phase of the period goes over into its own beginning. This conception, evaluated by its proclaimer as the most abysmal teaching, is no teaching at all but the utterance of an ecstatically lived-through possibility of thought played over with ever new variations. The "Dionysian" pathos has by no means been transformed here into a philosophical one, as Nietzsche already early had in mind. It has remained Dionysian, as its modern variant, produced by the enthusiasm of the Dionysian man over his own heights and depths.

Kant had not undertaken to solve the sense-confusing riddle that is set us by the being of time; he completed the philosophical limitation of it in that he made it into a problem of we ourselves be-

---

[3] In the book *Ecce Homo*.

ing referred to the form of time. Nietzsche, who wanted to have nothing to do with philosophical self-moderations, set in the place of one of the primal mysteries of time—the manifest mystery of the uniqueness of all happening—the pseudo-mystery of the "eternal return of the same."

Although the boy of seventeen did not and could not accept this conception, there still took place in his spirit a, so to speak, negative seduction. As he appears to me in my memory, after so many years— through Kant, who understood time as the form of "our" perception, the way could open to him to ask the question: "But if time is only a form in which we perceive, where *are* 'we'? Are we not in the timeless? Are we not in eternity?" By that, of course, a wholly other eternity is meant than the circular one which Zarathustra loves as "fatum." What is meant is what is incomprehensible in itself, that which sends forth time out of itself and sets us in that relationship to it that we call existence. To him who recognizes this, the reality of the world no longer shows an absurd and uncanny face: because eternity is. That the entrance to this way long remained closed to me is to be traced to a certain, not insignificant, extent to that fascination by "Zarathustra." [4]

9. *Vienna*

I spent my first year of university studies in Vienna, the city of my birth and my earliest childhood. The detached, flat memory images appear out of the great corporal context like slides of a magic lantern, but also many districts that I could not have seen address me as acquaintances. This original home of mine, now foreign, taught me daily, although still in unclear language, that I had to accept the world and let myself be accepted by it; it was indeed ready to be accepted. Something was established at that time that in later years could not become recast through any of the problematics of the age.

The lectures of those two semesters, even the significant scholarly ones, did not have a decisive effect on me. Only some seminars into which I had prematurely flung myself, rather the seminar as such, im-

---

[4] I was at that time so taken by the book that I decided to translate it into Polish and had even translated the first part. I had just gone to the second part when I received the letter of a known Polish author who likewise had translated several sections of the book and proposed to me to do the work in common. I preferred renouncing in his favor.

mediately exerted a strong influence: the regulated and yet free intercourse between teacher and students, the common interpretations
of texts, in which the master at times took part with a rare humility, as if he too were learning something new, and the liberated
exchange of question and answer in the midst of all scholastic fluency
—all this disclosed to me, more intimately than anything that I read
in a book, the true actuality of the spirit, as a "between."

What affected me most strongly, however, was the Burgtheater into
which at times, day after day, I rushed up three flights after several
hours of "posting myself" in order to capture a place in the highest
gallery. When far below in front of me the curtain went up and I
might then look at the events of the dramatic agon as, even if in play,
taking place here and now, it was the word, the "rightly" spoken
human word that I received into myself, in the most real sense. Speech
here first, in this world of fiction as fiction, won its adequacy; certainly it appeared heightened, but heightened to itself. It was only
a matter of time, however, until—as always happened—someone
fell for a while into recitation, a "noble" recitation. Then, along with
the genuine spokenness of speech, dialogical speech or even monological (in so far as the monologue was just an addressing of one's own
person as a fellowman and no recitation), this whole world, mysteriously built out of surprise and law, was shattered for me—until after
some moments it arose anew with the return of the over-against.

Since then it has sometimes come to pass, in the midst of the casu-
alness of the everyday, that, while I was sitting in the garden of an inn
in the countryside of Vienna, a conversation penetrated to me from a
neighboring table, (perhaps an argument over falling prices by two
market wives taking a rest) in which I perceived the spokenness of
speech, sound becoming "Each-Other."

10. *A Lecture*

My third semester, during which I completed my twentieth year
of life, I spent in Leipzig.

What had the strongest effect on me there was undoubtedly hearing Bach's music, and in truth Bach's music so sung and played—
of that I was certain at that time and have remained certain—
as Bach himself wished that it be sung and played. But it would be
fruitless for me to undertake to say, indeed, I cannot even make clear to
myself—in what way Bach has influenced my thinking. The ground-

tone of my life was obviously modified in some manner and through that my thinking as well. In general I am not at all in the position, in these autobiographical fragments, to report on such great and mysterious things. In its stead I shall tell here of a small incident that took place then and, as it later proved, was not unimportant.

I had for some time occupied myself with the talks and writings of Ferdinand Lassalle and with his biography too. I admired his spiritual passion and his readiness, in personal as in public life, to stake his existence. What was manifestly problematic in his nature went unnoticed; it did not even concern me. When a socialist club whose meetings I had attended a few times invited me to deliver a lecture, I decided to speak about Lassalle and did so. The lecture that I delivered was the image of a hero after the model of Carlyle. I pointed to a destiny that was intended for tragedy from the beginning. This tragedy was manifested in the path of his work—the failure of his undertaking to lay the foundation of a new society—but also in that of his life up till his absurd and yet symbolically significant death.

When I had finished, the applause was great. Then an old man came up to me. He was, as he at once communicated to me, a tailor by trade and had in his youth belonged to Lassalle's most intimate circle. He seized my hand and held it fast for a long time. Then he looked at me enthusiastically and said: "Yes! Thus, thus he was!"

An almost tender feeling came over me: "How good it is to be confirmed thus!" But even at that moment a fright suddenly fell upon me and pierced through my thoughtless joy: "No, it is I who have been the confirmer, the lying confirmer of an idol!"

The true, hidden, cast aside, issue of my Lassalle studies revealed itself in a flash: the knowledge of the unmanageable contradiction that had burned in a bold and vain heart and out of it had been hurled into the human world. I stammered a salutation to the friendly tailor and fled.

In the following weeks I sought, with the most inadequate means and with the lack of success that was its due, to substitute for the smashed hero's bust a kind of analytical representation: this proved to be an only seemingly legitimate simplification. Slowly, waveringly, grew the insight into the problematic reality of human existence and into the fragile possibility of doing justice to it. Bach helped me.

11. *The Cause and the Person*[5]

It was at the Sixth Zionist Congress, 1902, Herzl had just launched the thunder of his denunciation against the opposition; he had answered the criticism of Davis Trietsch, less with factual arguments than with personal counter-criticism in which he dealt with Trietsch's own colonizing activities. The chief thrust was a record that had been taken down from a "victim" of this activity.

(It must be mentioned here that in the days after this incident I was a member of what was virtually a board of arbitration appointed by the Congress. That board decided, by a vote of three to two—I was one of the minority—to issue no detailed statement on the result of its investigations, but some details may be made public to-day.)

Apart from the fact that this thrust was directed against the person rather than against his cause, it was not executed with a correct sword; the "victim" was no victim, and the record—well, it was a record. . . . Herzl swung his weapon in good faith; no doubt existed about that. But he had not examined it closely enough beforehand.

After his speech Herzl retired into his conference room. Berthold Feiwel and I soon followed him there to point out, as friends of Trietsch, the untenable nature of his accusations, and to demand the appointment of a committee to make an inquiry into them. As we walked the short distance to the conference room, I was profoundly perturbed. I had already, indeed, since the previous Congress, stood in decisive opposition to Herzl, but this opposition had been wholly objective, and I had not ceased for a moment to have faith in the man. Now, for the first time, my soul revolted—so violently that I still have a physical recollection of it. When I entered the room, however, my agitation was in an instant transformed by the sight that met me, and the heart that had just been pounding grew numb.

Only Herzl and his mother were in the room. Frau Jeannette sat in an armchair, silent and unmoving, but her face and eyes shining with the most lively sympathetic participation—splendid in sympathy as I had known once in my grandmother. Herzl was pacing up and down the room with long strides, exactly like a caged lion. His vest was unbuttoned, his breast rose and fell; I had never dreamed that he, whose gestures were always mastered and masterly, could breathe so wildly. It was only later that I noticed his pallor, so strongly did his eyes flash and burn.

[5] Translated from *Kampf um Israel*, pp. 171-177.

It became at once compellingly clear to me that here it was impossible to remain inwardly the representative of one side. Outside, in the hall, was a man, my friend and ally, who had been hurt, who had suffered a public injustice. But here was the author of the injustice, whose blow had dealt the wound—a man who, though misled, was still my leader, sick with zeal; a man consumed with zeal for his faith:his faith in his cause and in himself, the two inextricably bound together.

I was twenty-four years of age and this was perhaps the first time that I set foot on the soil of tragedy where there is no longer such a thing as being in the right. There was only one thing to learn that was greater still: how out of the grave of being in the right the right is resurrected. But this is something I only learned many years later.

Our task had become inwardly impracticable: for speaking to this man opposite, one could only essentially appeal from "his cause," which he so lived, to the—truth of his cause, and who could do that? But, of course, we carried out our task: we pointed out, demanded what we were authorized and obliged to point out and demand.

Herzl continued to pace up and down the room, giving no sign that he was listening. Occasionally I glanced at his mother—her face had darkened; there was something there that terrified me, I did not know what it was, but it was there.

Suddenly, however, Herzl stopped before us, and spoke to us. His tone was by no means what we might have expected—it was a passionate but smiling tone, although there was no smile on his lips. "I would have taken him to task in a wholly different way!" he exclaimed. "Wholly differently! But there before the platform, directly opposite me, a girl—his fiancée, I have heard—placed herself; there she stood, her eyes flashing at me. A wonderful person, I tell you! I could not do it!"

And now his mouth, too, smiled, as though liberated. And who could have refrained from smiling with him? The charmer "Told" smiled in his romantic way; I, undoubtedly, smiled too, like a schoolboy who has discovered that Horace meant real friends and real sweethearts, and even on the once more brightened face of the old—no, not old at all—gentlewoman in the armchair there was a smile, such as I have only observed in the Jewish women of that generation. The secret of that smile has been lost.

It was no longer possible to reply. In the light of the non-objectivity of his confession concerning the reason for his forbearance, the non-objectivity of his attack naturally seemed even more grave. And yet

. . .! We discharged our task, everything now going off smoothly, impersonally, without difficulties of any sort and we took our leave. This was the last time that I saw Herzl at such close quarters.

Then I did not want to recollect that image, but since then—after the angel had done his work,[6] the angel whose nameless presence had at that time frightened Herzl's mother and me—I have often thought over that occasion.

What, indeed, was Theodor Herzl's attitude toward the cause and the person? And how is it in general with these two, "cause" and "person"?

That to Herzl his cause was indissolubly bound up with his person—this fact manifested itself clearly enough in his fight against Ahad Ha-am[7] when he summoned us young men, who in that situation stood on the side of his opponent, to "find our way back to *the movement.*" Probably this is the case with most of the men who act in history. His fundamental view was certainly that there was little sense in discussing principles and methods, since, in the final analysis, everything depends not upon them, but upon the person to whom their realization and application is entrusted, in other words: upon the individual that uses them, and by means of them serves. Serves whom? Just the cause that is indissolubly bound up with the person? We appear to be reasoning in a circle.

But let us regard the problem from the other side, from the side of the people. Let us consider, for example, the concept of Max Weber, according to whom genuine democracy means to appoint a leader whom one trusts and to follow him as long as he accomplishes his task, but if he fails, to call him to account, to judge him, to depose him, even "To the gallows with him!"[8] The cause, therefore, is bound up with the person as long as his *charisma,* i.e., his power of leadership, to use Weber's term, proves effective. From this point of view we can understand Herzl's attitude toward his critics; it is charismatic. This is why he does not say: "You are wrong, for matters stand thus and so," but rather: "You are wrong, for you are not the man to do this properly—you lack the *charisma.*"

---

6 Herzl died of a heart attack in 1904.

7 "Ahad Ha-am," i. e., "one of the people," was the pseudonym of Asher Ginsberg, who in opposition to Herzl's political Zionism represented an essentially cultural Zionism.

8 Cf. the report of a discussion of Max Weber with Ludendorff in Marianne Weber's book *Max Weber,* p. 664 f.

But is this concept right or wrong? It cannot be set aside by a cheap idealogy composed of a mediocre policy and a mediocre morality. The "history of the world" so far attests to it. Only our hope for a different leadership and a different following, for a truly dialogical relationship between the two, contests it. In any case, the categories of the objective and the subjective, with which we are so familiar, do not in truth hold for the problem that has opened up to us.

But the fiancée with the flashing eyes! Is this not certainly a dreadful lack of objectivity? I do not know. Perhaps through the impression that his opponent had one, even if only one human being who would take his part *thus,* Herzl had been gripped by the question whether there might not be yet another reality, different from that of obvious world history—a reality hidden and powerless because it has not come into power; whether there might not be, therefore, men with a mission who have not been called to power and yet are, in essence, men who have been summoned; whether excessive significance has not perhaps been ascribed to the circumstances that separate the one class of men from the other; whether success is the only criterion; whether the unsuccessful man is not destined at times to gain a belated, perhaps posthumous, perhaps even anonymous victory which even history refuses to record: whether, indeed, when even this does not happen, a blessing is not spoken, nonetheless, to these abandoned ones, a word that confirms them; whether there does not exist a "dark" *charisma.* The man who acts in history does not allow himself to be overwhelmed by such questions, for if he did so, he would have to despair, and to withdraw. But the moments in which they touch him are the truly religious moments of his life.

12. *The Zaddik*[9]

In my childhood I spent every summer on an estate in Bukovina. There my father took me with him at times to a nearby village of Sadagora. Sadagora is the seat of a dynasty of "zaddikim" (zaddik means righteous, proven), that is, of Hasidic rabbis. There no longer lives in the present-day community that high faith of the first Hasidim, that fervent devotion which honored in the zaddik the perfected man in whom the immortal finds its mortal fulfillment. Rather the present-day Hasidim turn to the *zaddik* above all as the mediator through

[9] Reprinted from *Hasidism and Modern Man,* "My Way to Hasidism," pp. 50-53, 64-67, with permission of the Horizon Press, Inc.

whose intercession they hope to attain the satisfaction of their needs. Even in these degenerate Hasidim there still continues to glow, in the unknown ground of their souls, the word of Rabbi Eliezar that the world was created for the sake of the perfected man (the zaddik), even though there should be only one.

This I realized at that time, as a child, in the dirty village of Sadagora from the "dark" Hasidic crowd that I watched—as a child realizes such things, not as thought, but as image and feeling—that the world needs the perfected man and that the perfected man is none other than the true helper. Certainly, the power entrusted to him has been misinterpreted by the faithful, had been misused by himself. But is it not at base a legitimate, the legitimate power, this power of the helping soul over the needy? Does there not lie in it the seed of future social orders?

At any rate, in a childish fashion, these questions already dawned on me at that time. And I could compare on the one side with the head man of the province whose power rested on nothing but habitual compulsion; on the other with the rabbi, who was an honest and God-fearing man, but an employee of the "directorship of the cult." Here, however, was another, an imcomparable; here was, debased yet uninjured, the living double kernel of humanity: genuine *community* and genuine *leadership*.

The palace of the *rebbe*, in its showy splendor, repelled me. The prayer house of the Hasidim with its enraptured worshippers seemed strange to me. But when I saw the *rebbe* striding through the rows of the waiting, I felt, "leader," and when I saw the Hasidim dance with the Torah, I felt "community." At that time there rose in me a presentiment of the fact that common reverence and common joy of soul are the foundations of genuine human community.

In 1910 or 1911, in Bukovina, not far from Sadagora, after a lecture that I had delivered, I went, with some members of the association that had arranged the evening, into a coffee house. I like to follow the speech before many, whose form allows no reply, with a conversation with a few in which person acts on person and my view is set forth directly through going into objection and question.

We were just discussing a theme of moral philosophy when a well-built middle-aged Jew of simple appearance came up to the table and greeted me. To my no doubt somewhat distant return greeting, he replied with words not lacking a slight reproof: "Doctor! Do you not recognize me?" When I had to answer in the negative, he introduced himself as M., the brother of a former steward of my father's. I invited him to sit with us, inquired about his circumstances of life and then took up again the conversation with the young people. M. listened to the discussion, which had just taken a turn toward somewhat abstract formulations, with eager attentiveness. It was obvious that he did not understand a single word; the devotion with which he received every word resembled that of the believers who do not need to know the content of a litany since the arrangement of sounds alone gives them all that they need, and more than any content could.

After a while, nonetheless, I asked him whether he had perhaps something to say to me; I should gladly go to one side with him and talk over his concern. He vigorously declined. The conversation began again and with it M.'s listening. When another half hour had passed, I asked him again whether he did not perhaps have a wish that I might fulfill for him; he could count on me. No, no, he had no wish, he assured me. It had grown late; but, as happens to one in such hours of lively interchange, I did not feel weary; I felt fresher, in fact, than before, and decided to go for a walk with the young people. At this moment M. approached me with an unspeakably timid air. "Doctor," he said, "I should like to ask you a question." I bid the students wait and sat down with him at a table. He was silent. "Just ask, Mr. M.," I encouraged him; "I shall gladly give you information as best I can." "Doctor," he said, "I have a daughter." He paused; then he continued, "And I also have a young man for my daughter." Again a pause. "He is a student of law. He passed the examinations with distinction." He paused again, this time somewhat longer. I looked at him encouragingly; I supposed that he would entreat me to use my influence in some way on behalf of the presumptive son-in-law. "Doctor," he asked, "is he a steady man?" I was surprised, but felt that I might not refuse him an answer. "Now, Mr. M.," I explained, "after what you have said, it can certainly be taken for granted that he is industrious and able." Still he questioned further. "But Doctor," he said, "does he also have a good head?"—"That is even more difficult to answer," I replied; "but at any rate he has not succeeded with industry alone, he must also have something in his head." Once again M. paused; then he asked, clearly as a final question, "Doctor, should he now become a judge or a lawyer?"—"About that I can give you no information," I answered. "I do not know the young man, indeed, and even if I did know him, I should hardly be able to advise in this matter." But then M. regarded me with a glance of almost melancholy renunciation, half-complaining, half-understanding, and spoke in an indescribable tone, composed in equal part of sorrow and humility: "Doctor, you do not *want* to say—now, I thank you for what you have said to me."

As a child, I had received an image of the *zaddik* and through the sullied reality had glimpsed the pure idea, the idea of the genuine leader of a genuine community. Between youth and manhood this idea had arisen in me through knowledge of Hasidic teaching as that of the perfected man who realizes God in the world. But now in the light of this droll event, I caught sight in my inner experience of the *zaddik's* function as a leader. I who am truly no *zaddik*, no one assured in God, rather a man endangered before God, a man wrestling ever anew for God's light, ever anew engulfed in God's abysses, nonetheless, when asked a trivial question and replying with a trivial answer, then experienced from within for the first time the true *zaddik*, questioned about revelations and replying in revelations. I experienced him in the fundamental relation of his soul to the world: in his responsibility.

13. *The Walking Stick and the Tree*[10]

After a descent during which I had to utilize without a halt the late light of a dying day, I stood on the edge of a meadow, now sure of the safe way, and let the twilight come down upon me. Not needing a support and yet willing to afford my lingering a fixed point, I pressed my walking stick against a trunk of an oak tree. Then I felt in twofold fashion my contact with being: here, where I held the stick, and there, where it touched the bark. Apparently only where I was, I nonetheless found myself there too where I found the tree.

At that time dialogue appeared to me. For the speech of man is like that stick wherever it is genuine speech, and that means: truly directed address. Here, where I am, where ganglia and organs of speech help me to form and to send forth the word, here I "mean" him to whom I send it, I intend him, this one unexchangeable man. But also there, where he is, something of me is delegated, something that is not at all substantial in nature like that being here, rather pure vibration and incomprehensible; that remains there, with him, the

[10] Reprinted from *Daniel: Dialogues of Realization*, "Author's Preface," p. 47, with the permission of Holt, Rinehart, Winston, & Co.

man meant by me, and takes part in the receiving of my word. I encompass him to whom I turn.

14. *Question and Answer*

It was in May of the year 1914 (my wife and I and our two children, now had already lived some eight years in a suburb of Berlin) when Reverend Hechler, whom I had not seen for a long time, called me. He was just in Berlin and would like to visit me. Soon afterward he came.

I had become acquainted with Hechler in the autumn of 1899 in a railroad carriage. The much older man began a conversation with me in which we soon learned that we shared the same views. Through a real eschatological belief in the living Christ, he stood close to the Zionist movement to which I then had belonged for a short time. The return of the Jewish people to their homeland was to him the promised presupposition of the return of Christ. He journeyed just then to the Grand Duke of Baden to whom he had a short time before introduced Herzl. He had been an educator of princes and was highly esteemed in many European courts.

In the course of the conversation I handed to Hechler the manuscript of a "hymn" to the awakening Jewish people which I had written shortly before. This hymn filled him with such enthusiasm (entirely without basis) that he declared that he must read it to the Grand Duke. Soon afterward he had not merely done this but had published the questionable little opus without my knowledge. When I opened the door of my Berlin dwelling to Hechler, I was struck by how aged, but also by how upright he was. After the warm mutual greeting, he drew forth from one of the gigantic pockets of his havelock a bundle of papers wrapped in a blue-white cloth. Out of it, first of all, he pulled forth the manuscript together with the proofs of that poem of 1899, but then a large sheet that he slowly unfolded. It was a graphic representation of the prophecy of Daniel on which he indicated to me, as if on a map of a historical period, the exact point in which we just now found ourselves. Then he spoke somewhat as follows: "Dear friend! I come from Athens (he had earlier been the teacher of the Greek princes, among others). I have stood on the spot where Paul spoke to the Athenians of the unknown God. And now I come to you to say to you that in this year the world war will break out."

The certainty which was expressed in this sentence stemmed, as I have only later understood, out of a peculiar fusion of spheres: the believing interpretation of Daniel had been mixed and concretized with material flowing to it from the courts of Europe, without an awareness of what took place thus in the depths of the soul having penetrated into that consciousness. But what struck me most forcibly in the sentence that he spoke was the word "world war" which I heard then for the first time. What kind of a "war" was that—so I asked myself although still by no means clearly enough—which embraced the "world"? Clearly something essentially different at any rate from what one had formerly called "war"! From that hour dates the presentiment that has from then on grown in me, that the historical time of "wars" was over and something different, only seemingly of that same nature, but becoming ever more different and ever more monstrous, was getting ready to swallow history and with it men.

Hechler stayed a few hours with us. Then I accompanied him to the railway station. In order to get there, one first had to go to the end of the small street of the "colony," in which we lived and then on a narrow path covered with coal-dust, the so-called "black path" along the railroad tracks. When we had reached the corner where the colony street met this path, Hechler stood still, placed his hand on my shoulder and said: "Dear friend! We live in a great time. Tell me: Do you believe in God?" It was a while before I answered, then I reassured the old man as best I could: He need have no concern about me in this matter. Upon this I brought him to the railway station and installed him in his train.

When I now returned home, however, and again came to that corner where the black path issued into our street, I stood still. I had to ponder to the depths of the matter. Had I said the truth? Did I "believe" in the God whom Hechler meant? What was the case with me? I stood a long time on the corner determined not to go further before I had found the right answer.

Suddenly in my spirit, there where speech again and again forms itself, there arose without having been formulated by me, word for word distinct:

"If to believe in God means to be able to talk about him in the third person, then I do not believe in God. If to believe in him means to be able to talk to him, then I believe in God." And after a while, further: "The God who gives Daniel such foreknowledge of this hour of human history, this hour before the 'world war,' that its fixed place in the march of the ages can be foredetermined, is not my God and not God. The God to whom Daniel prays in his suffering is my God and the God of all."

I remained standing for a long while on the corner of the black path and gave myself up to the clarity, now beyond speech, that had begun.

15. *A Conversion*[11]

In my earlier years the "religious" was for me the exception. There were hours that were taken out of the course of things. From somewhere or other the firm crust of everyday was pierced. Then the reliable permanence of appearances broke down; the attack which took place burst its law asunder. "Religious experience" was the experience of an otherness which did not fit into the context of life. It could begin with something customary, with consideration of some familiar object, but which then became unexpectedly mysterious and uncanny, finally lighting a way into the lightning-pierced darkness of the mystery itself. But also, without any intermediate stage, time could be torn apart—first the firm world's structure then the still firmer self-assurance flew apart and you were delivered to fulness. The "religious" lifted you out. Over there now lay the accustomed existence with its affairs, but here illumination and ecstasy and rapture held without time or sequence. Thus your own being encompassed a life here and a life beyond, and there was no bond but the actual moment of the transition.

The illegitimacy of such a division of the temporal life, which is streaming to death and eternity and which only in fulfilling its temporality can be fulfilled in face of these, was brought home to me by an everyday event, an event of judgment, judging with that sentence from closed lips and an unmoved glance such as the ongoing course of things loves to pronounce.

What happened was no more than that one forenoon, after a morning of "religious" enthusiasm, I had a visit from an unknown young man, without being there in spirit. I certainly did not fail to let the meeting be friendly, I did not treat him any more remissly than all his contemporaries who were in the habit of seeking me out about

11 Reprinted from *Between Man and Man,* "Dialogue," pp. 14f., with the permission of the Macmillan Co.

this time of day as an oracle that is ready to listen to reason. I conversed attentively and openly with him—only I omitted to guess the questions which he did not put. Later, not long after, I learned from one of his friends—he himself was no longer alive—the essential content of these questions; I learned that he had come to me not casually, but borne by destiny, not for a chat but for a decision. He had come to me, he had come in this hour. What do we expect when we are in despair and yet go to a man? Surely a presence by means of which we are told that nevertheless there is meaning.

Since then I have given up the "religious" which is nothing but the exception, extraction, exaltation, ecstasy; or it has given me up. I possess nothing but the everyday out of which I am never taken. The mystery is no longer disclosed, it has escaped or it has made its dwelling here where everything happens as it happens. I know no fulness but each mortal hour's fulness of claim and responsibility. Though far from being equal to it, yet I know that in the claim I am claimed and may respond in responsibility, and know who speaks and demand a response.

I do not know much more. If that is religion then it is just *everything,* simply all that is lived in its possibility of dialogue. Here is space also for religion's highest forms. As when you pray you do not thereby remove yourself from this life of yours but in your praying refer your thought to it, even though it may be in order to yield it; so too in the unprecedented and surprising, when you are called upon from above, required, chosen, empowered, sent, you with this your mortal bit of life are meant. This moment is not extracted from it, it rests on what has been and beckons to the remainder which has still to be lived. You are not swallowed up in a fulness without obligation, you are willed for the life of communion.

16. *Report on Two Talks*[12]

I shall tell about two talks. One apparently came to a conclusion, as only occasionally a talk can come, and yet in reality remained unconcluded; the other was apparently broken off and yet found a completion such as rarely falls to the lot of discussions.

Both times it was a dispute about God, about the concept and the name of God, but each time of a very different nature.

[12] Reprinted from *Eclipse of God,* Chap. 1, pp. 11-18, with the permission of Harper & Row, Inc.

On three successive evenings I spoke at the adult folk-school of a German industrial city on the subject "Religion as Reality." What I meant by that was the simple thesis that "faith" is not a feeling in the soul of man but an entrance into reality, an entrance into the *whole* reality without reduction and curtailment. This thesis is simple but it contradicts the usual way of thinking. And so three evenings were necessary to make it clear, and not merely three lectures but also three discussions which followed the lectures. At these discussions I was struck by something which bothered me. A large part of the audience was evidently made up of workers but none of them spoke up. Those who spoke and raised questions, doubts, and reflections were for the most part students (for the city had a famous old university). But all kinds of other circles were also represented; the workers alone remained silent. Only at the conclusion of the third evening was this silence, which had by now become painful for me, explained. A young worker, came up to me and said: "Do you know, we can't speak in there, but if you would meet with us to-morrow, we could talk together the whole time." Of course I agreed.

The next day was a Sunday. After dinner I came to the agreed place and now we talked together well into the evening. Among the workers was one, a man no longer young, whom I was drawn to look at again and again because he listened as one who really wished to hear. Real listening has become rare in our time. It is found most often among workers, who are not indeed concerned about the person speaking, as is so often the case with the *bourgeois* public, but about what he has to say. This man had a curious face. In an old Flemish altar picture representing the adoration of the shepherds one of them, who stretches out his arms toward the manger, has such a face. The man in front of me did not look as if he might have any desire to do the same; moreover, his face was not open like that in the picture. What was notable about him was that he heard and pondered, in a manner as slow as it was impressive. Finally, he opened his lips as well. "I have had the experience," he explained slowly and impressively, repeating a saying which the astronomer Laplace is supposed to have used in conversation with Napoleon, "that I do not need this hypothesis 'God' in order to be quite at home in the world." He pronounced the word "hypothesis" as if he attended the lectures of the distinguished natural scientist who had taught in that industrial and university city and had died shortly before. Although he did not reject the designation "God" for his idea of nature, that naturalist spoke in a similar manner whether he pursued zoology or *Weltanschauung.*

The brief speech of the man struck me; I felt myself more deeply challenged than by the others. Up till then we had certainly debated very seriously, but in a somewhat relaxed way; now everything had suddenly become severe and hard. How should I reply to the man? I pondered awhile in the now severe atmosphere. It came to me that I must shatter the security of his *Weltanschauung,* through which he thought of a "world" in which one "felt at home." What sort of a world was it: What we were accustomed to call world was the "world of the senses," the world in which there exists vermilion and grass green, C major and B minor, the taste of apple and of wormwood. Was this world anything other than the meeting of our own senses with those unapproachable events about whose essential definition physics always troubles itself in vain? The red that we saw was neither there in the "things," nor here in the "soul." It at times flamed up and glowed just so long as a red-perceiving eye and a red-engendering "oscillation" found themselves over against each other. Where then was the world and its security? The unknown "objects" there, the apparently so well-known and yet not graspable "subjects" here, and the actual and still so evanescent meeting of both, the "phenomena" —was that not already three worlds which could no longer be comprehended from one alone? How could we in our thinking place together these worlds so divorced from one another? What was the being that gave this "world," which had become so questionable, its foundation?

When I was through a stern silence ruled in the now twilit room. Then the man with the shepherd's face raised his heavy lids, which had been lowered the whole time, and said slowly and impressively, "You are right."

I sat in front of him dismayed. What had I done? I had led the man to the threshold beyond which there sat enthroned the majestic image which the great physicist, the great man of faith, Pascal, called the God of the Philosophers. Had I wished for that? Had I not rather wished to lead him to the other, Him whom Pascal called the God of Abraham, Isaac, and Jacob, Him to whom one can say Thou?

It grew dusk, it was late. On the next day I had to depart. I could not remain, as I now ought to do; I could not enter into the factory where the man worked, become his comrade, live with him, win his trust through real life-relationship, help him to walk with me the way of the creature who *accepts* the creation. I could only return his gaze.

Some time later I was the guest of a noble old thinker. I had once made his acquaintance at a conference where he gave a lecture on elementary folk-schools and I gave one on adult folk-schools. That brought us together, for we were united by the fact that the work "folk" has to be understood in both cases in the same all-embracing sense. At that time I was happily surprised at how the man with the steel-gray locks asked us at the beginning of his talk to forget all that we believed we knew about his philosophy from his books. In the last years, which had been war years, reality had been brought so close to him that he saw everything with new eyes and had to think in a new way. To be old is a glorious thing when one has not unlearned what it means to *begin;* this old man had even perhaps first learned it thoroughly in old age. He was not 'at all young, but he was old in a young way, knowing how to begin.

He lived in another university city situated in the west. When the theology students of that university invited me to speak about prophecy, I stayed with the old man. There was a good spirit in his house, the spirit that wills to enter life and does not prescribe to life where it shall let it in.

One morning I got up early in order to read proofs. The evening before I had received galley proofs of the preface of a book of mine, and since this preface was a statement of faith,[13] I wished to read it once again quite carefully before it was printed. Now I took it into the study below that had been offered to me in case I should need it. But here the old man already sat at his writing-desk. Directly after greeting me he asked me what I had in my hand, and when I told him, he asked whether I would not read it aloud to him. I did so gladly. He listened in a friendly manner but clearly astonished, indeed with growing amazement. When I was through, he spoke hesitatingly, then, carried away by the importance of his subject, ever more passionately. "How can you bring yourself to say 'God' time after time? How can you expect that your readers will take the word in the sense in which you wish it to be taken? What you mean by the name of God is something above all human grasp and comprehension, but in speaking about it you have lowered it to human con-

13 It was the Foreword to the collected edition of my "Talks on Judaism" *(Reden über das Judentum,* 1923) .

ceptualization. What word of human speech is so misused, so defiled, so desecrated as this! All the innocent blood that has been shed for it has robbed it of its radiance. All the injustice that it has been used to cover has effaced its features. When I hear the highest called 'God,' it sometimes seems almost blasphemous."

The kindly eyes flamed. The voice itself flared. Then we sat silent for awhile facing each other. The room lay in the flowing brightness of early morning. It seemed to me as if a power from the light entered into me. What I now answered, I cannot to-day reproduce but only indicate.

"Yes," I said, "it is the most heavy-laden of all human words. None has become so soiled, so mutilated. Just for this reason I may not abandon it. Generations of men have laid the burden of their anxious lives upon this word and weighed it to the ground; it lies in the dust and bears their whole burden. The races of man with their religious factions have torn the word to pieces; they have killed for it and died for it, and it bears their finger-marks and their blood. Where might I find a word like it to describe the highest! If I took the purest, most sparkling concept from the inner treasure-chamber of the philosophers, I could only capture thereby an unbinding product of thought. I could not capture the presence of Him whom the generations of men have honoured and degraded with their awesome living and dying. I do indeed mean Him whom the hell-tormented and heaven-storming generations of men mean. Certainly, they draw caricatures and write 'God' underneath; they murder one another and say 'in God's name.' But when all madness and delusion fall to dust, when they stand over against Him in the loneliest darkness and no longer say 'He, He' but rather sigh 'Thou,' shout 'Thou,' all of them the one word, and when they then add 'God,' is it not the real God whom they all implore, the One Living God, the God of the children of man? Is it not He who *hears* them? And just for this reason is not the word 'God' the word of appeal, the word which has become a *name*, consecrated in all human tongues for all times? We must esteem those who interdict it because they rebel against the injustice and wrong which are so readily referred to 'God' for authorization. But we may not give it up. How understandable it is that some suggest we should remain silent about the 'last things' for a time in order that the misused words may be redeemed! But they are not to be redeemed *thus*. We cannot cleanse the word 'God' and we cannot make it whole; but, defiled and mutilated as it is, we can raise it from the ground and set it over an hour of great care."

It had become very light in the room. It was no longer dawning, it was light. The old man stood up, came over to me, laid his hand on my shoulder and spoke: "Let us be friends." The conversation was completed. For where two or three are truly together, they are together in the name of God.

17. *Samuel and Agag*

I once met on a journey a man whom I already knew through an earlier meeting. He was an observant Jew who followed the religious tradition in all the details of his life-pattern. But what was for me essential (as had already become unmistakably clear to me at that first meeting) was that this relationship to tradition had its origin and its constantly renewed confirmation in the relationship of the man to God.

When I now saw him again, it turned out that we fell into a discussion of biblical questions, and indeed not of peripheral questions but central ones, central questions of faith. I do not know exactly any longer in what connection we came to speak of that section of the Book of Samuel in which it is told how Samuel delivered to King Saul the message that his dynastic rule would be taken from him because he had spared the life of the conquered prince of the Amalekites. I reported to my partner in dialogue how dreadful it had already been to me when I was a boy to read this as the message of God (and my heart compelled me to read it over again or at least to think about the fact that this stood written in the Bible). I told him how already at that time it horrified me to read or to remember how the heathen king went up to the prophet with the words on his lips, "Surely the bitterness of death is past," and was hewn to pieces by him. I said to my partner: "I have never been able to believe that this is a message of God. I do not believe it."

With wrinkled forehead and contracted brows, the man sat opposite me and his glance flamed into my eyes. He remained silent, began to speak, became silent again. "So?" he broke forth at last, "so? You do not believe it?" "No," I answered, "I do not believe it." "So? so?" he repeated almost threateningly. "You do not believe it?" And I once again: "No" "What . . . what . . .,"—he thrust the words before him one after the other—"what do you believe then?" "I believe," I replied without reflecting, "that Samuel has misunderstood God." And he, again slowly, but more softly than before: "So? You believe that?" And I: "Yes." Then we were both silent. But now something happened the like of which I have rarely seen before or since in this my long life. The angry countenance opposite me became transformed, as if a hand had passed over it soothing it. It lightened, cleared, was now turned toward me bright and clear. "Well," said the man with a positively gentle tender clarity, "I think so too." And again we became silent, for a good while.

There is in the end nothing astonishing in the fact that an observant Jew of this nature, when he has to choose between God and the Bible, chooses God: the God in whom he believes, Him in whom he can believe. And yet, it seemed to me at that time significant and still seems so to me today. The man later came to the land of Israel and here I met him once again, some time before his death. Naturally I regarded him then as the speaker of that word of one time; but in our talk the problem of biblical belief was not touched on. It was, indeed, no longer necessary.

For me, however, in all the time since that early conversation the question has again and again arisen whether at that time I expressed in the right manner what I meant. And again and again I answered the question in the same way: Yes and No. Yes in so far as it concerns what had been spoken of in that conversation; for there it was right to answer my partner in his language and within the limits of his language in order that the dialogue might not come to naught and that the common insight into one truth at times afforded to two men might fulfill itself, in no matter how limited a way. In so far as it concerns that, Yes. But No when it concerns both recognizing oneself and making known that man and the human race are inclined to misunderstand God. Man is so created that he can understand, but does not have to understand, what God says to him. God does not abandon the created man to his needs and anxieties; He provides him with the assistance of His word; He speaks to him, He comforts him with His word. But man does not listen with faithful ears to what is spoken to him. Already in hearing he blends together command of heaven and statute of earth, revelation to the existing being and the orientations that he arranges himself. Even the holy scriptures of man are not excluded, not even the Bible. What is involved here is not ultimately the fact that this or that form of biblical historical narrative has misunderstood God; what is involved is the fact that in the work of throats and pens out of which the text of the Old Testament has arisen, misunderstanding has again and again attached itself to understanding, the manufactured has been mixed with the received. We have no objective criterion for the distinction; we have only faith—when we have it. Nothing can make me believe in a God who punishes Saul because he has not murdered his enemy. And yet even today I still cannot read the passage that tells this otherwise than with fear and trembling. But not it alone. Always when I have to translate or to interpret a biblical text, I do so with fear and trembling, in an inescapable tension between the word of God and the words of man.

Appendix I

BEGINNINGS [14]

The question of the possibility and reality of a dialogical relationship between man and God, thus of a free partnership of man in a conversation between heaven and earth whose speech in address and answer is the happening itself, the happening from above and the happening from below, had already accosted me in my youth. In particular since the Hasidic tradition had grown for me into the supporting ground of my own thinking, hence since about 1905, that had become an innermost question for me. In the language of the writings on the dialogical principle that arose many years later, it appears emphatically for the first time in the autumn of 1907 in the introduction to my book, *The Legend of the Baal-Shem*. This introduction was concerned with the radical distinction between myth in the narrower sense (the myth of the mythologists) and legend. It said:

The legend is the myth of the calling. In pure myth there is no difference of being . . . Even the hero only stands on another rung than the god, not over against him; they are not the I and the Thou . . . The god of pure myth does not call, he begets; he sends forth the begotten, the hero. The god of the legend calls, he calls the son of man: the prophets, the saints . . The legend is the myth of I and Thou, of caller and called, of the finite that enters into the infinite and of the infinite that needs the finite.

Here the dialogical relationship is thus exemplified in its highest

14 Taken from *Die Schriften über das dialogische Prinzip*, "Nachwort," pp. 292-296. Reprinted from "The History of the Dialogical Principle," *Between Man and Man*, trans. Maurice Friedman (with permission of the Macmillan Co.) .

peak: because even on this height the essential difference between the partners persists unweakened, while even in such nearness the independence of man continues to be preserved.

From this event of the exception, of the extraction, however, my thought now led me, ever more earnestly, to the common that can be experienced by all. The clarification took place first of all here too in connection with my interpretation of Hasidism: in the "Preface" written in September 1919 to my book, *Der Grosse Maggid und seine Nachfolge* (1921), the Jewish teaching was described as "wholly based on the two-directional relation of human I and divine Thou, on reciprocity, on the *meeting.*" Soon after, in the autumn of 1919, followed the first, still unwieldy draft of *I and Thou.*

There now followed two years in which I could do almost no work except on Hasidic material, but also—with the exception of Descartes' *Discours de la methode* which I again took up—read no *philosophica* (therefore the works connected with the subject of dialogue by Cohen, Rosenzweig, and Ebner[15] I read only later, too late to affect my own thought). This was part of a procedure that I understood at that time as a spiritual askesis. Then I was able to begin the final writing of *I and Thou,* which was completed in the spring of 1922. As I wrote the third and last part, I broke the reading-askesis and began with Ebner's fragments.[16] His book showed me, as no other since then, here and there in an almost uncanny nearness, that in this our time men of different kinds and traditions had devoted themselves to the search for the buried treasure. Soon I also had similar experiences from other directions.

Of the initiators I had already as a student known Feuerbach and Kierkegaard; Yes and No to them had become a part of my existence. Now there surrounded me in spirit a growing circle of men of the present generations who were concerned, even if in unequal measure, about the one thing that had become for me an ever more vital matter. The basic view of the twofold nature of the human attitude is expressed in the beginning of *I and Thou.* But I had already prepared the way for this view in the distinction presented in my book *Daniel* (1913)

---

15 Hermann Cohen, *Religion der Vernunft aus den Quellen des Judentums* (1919). Franz Rosenzweig, *Der Stern der Erlösung* (1919), Ferdinand Ebner, *Das Wort und die geistigen Realitäten* (1921). Therefore Rosenzweig states in one of his letters *(Briefe,* p. 462) that in December 1921 I did not yet know his book.

16 First I happened to see some of them which were published in an issue of *Brenner* and then sent for the book.

between an "orienting," objectifying basic attitude and a "realizing," making-present one. This is a distinction that coincides in its core with that carried through in *I and Thou* between the I-It relation and the I-Thou relation, only the latter is no longer grounded in the sphere of subjectivity but in that between the beings. But this is the decisive transformation that took place in a series of spirits in the time of the first World War. It announced itself in very manifold meanings and spheres, but the fundamental connection between them, stemming out of the disclosed transformation of the human situation, is unmistakable.

Appendix II

A TENTATIVE ANSWER [17]
(Jerusalem, May 1955.)

Asked about a tentative answer which might then be the chief conclusion expressible in conceptual language of my experiences and observations, I can give no other reply than confess to the knowledge comprehending the questioner and myself: to be man means to be *the* being that is over against. The insight into this simple fact has grown in the course of my life. It has been expressed in divers other theses of like subject and similar construction, and I certainly hold many of them to be not incorrect; my knowing leads to just this, however, that it is this over-againstness which matters.

In this thesis the definite article is fully accentuated. All beings in nature are indeed placed in a being-with-others, and in each living being this enters as perception of others and action toward others in work. But what is peculiar to man is that one can ever and again become aware of the other as this being existing over-against him, over against whom he himself exists. He becomes aware of the other as one who relates to him out of his selfhood and to whom he relates out of his selfhood. By virtue of this characteristic reserved to him, man has not simply entered into being as one species among other species— only just so much more manifoldly endowed—but as a special sphere. For here, and within what we call world only here, does the meeting of the one with the other take place in full reality. Certainly there is nowhere in all world-immanence a self-enclosed unity—this is as

17 Translated from Elga Kern, editor, *Wegweiser in der Zeitwende,* Self-testimonies (Munich/Basel, Ernst Reinhardt Verlag, 1955) , pp. 264 ff.

such transcendence—but each individual is directed and referred to the other. Only in man, however, does this interrelatedness transform itself and issue into the reality of meeting in which the one exists over against the other as his other, as one able in common presence at once to withstand him and confirm him. Where this self-being turned toward the partner over against one is not lived, the sphere of man is still unrealized. The human means the taking place from one time to another of that meeting which is latent in the being of the world.

The insight that I have intimated here encounters ever again an impressive argument—only rarely, to be sure, in an outspoken manner, mostly as the wordless self-emphasis of "spiritual" persons. It is argued through a reference, mostly only just presented, to the alleged essential nature of mental work. This takes place not in a living over-against, ready for give and take, but in a fundamentally impermeable being-in-oneself that is alone accessible to the "spirit," that is, to ideas and images that emerge out of the all-encompassing depths of the self. The thinking of the thinker is said to bear the most unmistakable witness that this is so.

My experiences and observations have taught me to see it otherwise. Out of all the ages of man about whose spiritual work I know, I have become acquainted not merely with no great configuration, but also with no great thought whose origin was not to be gathered from the self-involving contact with existing being over against one. The evolved substance which the spirit brings as a work into the ages has come to it out of the unreserved meetings of its personal bearers with otherness. For as in other respects there is in the world-immanence no self-enclosed unity, so also there is in it no self-enclosed unity of the spirit. Only through opening out, through entering into openness, does the spirit that has descended into the human realm win that coherence in work that has not already passed away in becoming. The fortress into which the self-possessed spirituality retreats before the exacting demand of answering life over against one is a gloriously painted coulisse.

It is the spirit that, having entered into the being of man, enables and fits him to live over-against in distance and relation; the spirit has thereby empowered man to be a special sphere of being. From this primal process has come forth the highest work-treasure of man, speech, the manifest proclamation of existing reciprocity between the one and the other. But the gifts of the spirit have also brought with them the great danger, becoming ever greater, that threatens mankind. It has belonged to the constitution of the human person as the bearer of the spirit that the basic situation of existing over-against also carries over here into the inwardness of the person. Thus there could develop a relationship of the individual to himself foreign to the non-human world, although here there naturally belonged to the situation of "being over-against" nothing of the structural difference and the independence of answer of being over-against in actual dialogue—unless it was in the cases of a sickness that splits the personal coherence. But now at the same time the possibility opened that the dialogic of the soul cut itself off from all real communicating with the otherness outside it and degenerated into a self-enjoying of individual meaning, indeed to a hybris of an All-Self that arrogates to itself the self-enclosed unity of the Godhead existing before all creations and emanations. What was to be found as existing outside of the self was no longer the partner of a genuine reciprocity, but ultimately only the objective knots within a psyche that might certainly have been conceived in theory as more or less universal, but was lived as exclusively individual. By means of the universalizing philosophical positions, this individual self could be identified in practice simply with the Self and was no longer exposed to the claim of otherness.

My experience and observations have taught me to recognize in this degeneration the opponent of mankind, steadily increasing in might during the epochs of history, but especially in our time. It is none other than the spirit itself, cut off, that commits the sin against the holy spirit.

Appendix III

BOOKS AND MEN[18]

If I had been asked in my early youth whether I preferred to have dealings only with men or only with books, my answer would certainly have been in favour of books. In later years this has become less and less the case. Not that I have had so much better experiences with men than with books; on the contrary, purely delightful books even now come my way more often than purely delightful men. But the many bad experiences with men have nourished the meadow of my life

18 Reprinted from *Pointing the Way*, p. 3, with the permission of Harper & Row, Inc.

as the noblest book could not do, and the good experiences have made the earth into a garden for me. On the other hand, no book does more than remove me into a paradise of great spirits, where my innermost heart never forgets I cannot dwell long, nor even wish that I could do so. For (I must say this straight out in order to be understood) my innermost heart loves the world more than it loves the spirit. I have not, indeed, cleaved to life in the world as I might have; in my relations with it I fail it again and again; again and again I remain guilty towards it for falling short of what it expects of me, and this is partly, to be sure, because I am so indebted to the spirit. I am indebted to the spirit as I am to myself, but I do not, strictly speaking, love it, even as I do not, strictly speaking, love myself. I do not in reality love him who has seized me with his heavenly clutch and holds me fast; rather I love her, the 'world,' who comes again and again to meet me and extends to me a pair of fingers.

Both have gifts to share. The former showers on me his manna of books; the latter extends to me the brown bread on whose crust I break my teeth, a bread of which I can never have enough: men. Aye, these tousle-heads and good-for-nothings, how I love them! I revere books—those that I really read—too much to be able to love them. But in the most venerable of living men I always find more to love than to revere: I find in him something of this world, that is simply there as the spirit never can be there. The spirit hovers above me powerfully and pours out his exalted gift of speech, books; how glorious, how weird! But she, the human world, needs only to cast a wordless smile, and I cannot live without her. She is mute; all the prattle of men yields no word such as sounds forth constantly out of books. And I listen to it all in order to receive the silence that penetrates to me through it, the silence of the creature. But just the human creature! That creature means a mixture. Books are pure, men are mixed; books are spirit and word, pure spirit and purified word; men are made up of prattle and silence, and their silence is not that of animals but of men. Out of the human silence behind the prattle the spirit whispers to you, the spirit *as soul*. She, she is the beloved.

Here is an infallible test. Imagine yourself in a situation where you are alone, wholly alone on earth, and you are offered one of the two, books or men. I often hear men prizing their solitude but that is only because there are still men somewhere on earth even though in the far distance. I knew nothing of books when I came forth from the womb of my mother, and I shall die without books, with another human hand in my own. I do, indeed, close my door at times and surrender myself to a book, but only because I can open the door again and see a human being looking at me.

Martin Buber

THE HEBREW UNIVERSITY
JERUSALEM, ISRAEL

DESCRIPTIVE
AND CRITICAL ESSAYS ON THE
PHILOSOPHY OF MARTIN BUBER

Gabriel Marcel

I AND THOU*

I AM particularly delighted that this collective tribute to that great thinker, Martin Buber, affords me an opportunity to express my admiration for the priceless little book, *I and Thou*.[1] A French translation has existed for about twenty years, but it seems to me that outside a small circle we in France have not succeeded in grasping the full importance of this book. In this connection I find myself in a peculiar position. By a striking coincidence, I discovered the particular reality of the *Thou* at approximately the same time Buber was writing his book. His name was quite unknown to me, moreover, as were the names of Ferdinand Ebner and Friedrich Rosenzweig, who appear to have preceded us on this path. Thus, we are faced with one of those cases of spiritual convergence which always merit attention. Generally, they are not easy to interpret. Nevertheless, without calling directly upon that *Zeitgeist* which is always a little too easy to fall back on, we may say the following in this case: At a time when a philosophy which concentrated more and more exclusively upon the world of the *It*, the denotable, upon the *Eswelt*, was leading into technocratic developments increasingly perilous for the integrity of man and even for his physical existence —the current atomic threat representing merely the paroxysm of this trend—it was surely inevitable that here and there men were moved to bring clearly and methodically to consciousness a counterpoise, that is, a consideration of the *Thou*.

Having underscored this convergence of the thought of Buber and my own investigations as these appeared in my *Journal Métaphysique,* I feel bound to stress the fact that the Jewish thinker went much further than I in elucidating this structural aspect of the fundamental human situation.

---

*Trans. from the French original by Forrest Williams.

[1] Throughout I have consulted *Dialogisches Leben (I and Thou* and *Between Man and Man).*

It was a remark by Feuerbach, Buber himself has said, which contributed initially to his orientation. "The individual man," wrote Feuerbach in "The Program Of 1843" which preceded *The Principles of the Philosophies of the Future*, "does not contain in himself the essence of man either in so far as he is a moral being or in so far as he is a thinking being. The essence of man is contained only in the community, in the unity of man and man—a unity which rests upon the reality of the difference between 'I' and 'Thou'."[2] It is interesting to note, moreover, that Feuerbach himself did not succeed in drawing the consequences of this capital discovery, which Buber himself terms Copernican. Yet it was a fundamental event, as Karl Heim has said, which could have signaled a second beginning in European philosophy.

In the last part of *The Problem of Man*, Buber has subjected to a rigorous critical examination the attempts by Heidegger and by Scheler to cope with man's radical jeopardizing of himself manifested since Kant, Kierkegaard, and Nietzsche. Buber then has shown with the greatest possible cogency that only what he calls a philosophy *des Zwischen*—I would say, for my part, a philosophy of intersubjectivity —can rescue us from either the impasse of an individualism which considers man solely in reference to himself or the other impasse of a collectivism which has eyes only for society. These are, indeed, but complementary expressions of a single state of affairs, a humanity uprooted that no longer feels at home in the cosmos, and that has, moreover, seen the circumscribed communities such as the family, of which everyone used to feel himself a member, collapse one after another. It is true that the human personality first attempts to escape its isolation by adding itself to the mass. Yet therein lies an illusion that reflection suffices to dispel. In the midst of a collectivity, man is not *with* man or *alongside* man. The isolation is not surmounted, it is smothered as a sound may be drowned out by noise. As Buber nicely puts it in an untranslatable word, the isolation is *übertäubt*. It is only when the individual recognises the other in his very otherness, as a human being other than himself, and when on this basis he effects a penetration to the other, that he can break the circle of his solitude in a specific, transforming encounter.

At this very hour the era of individualism seems fulfilled. Collectivism, by contrast, is at its apogee. But already there is visible on

2 Quoted by Buber, *ibid.*, p. 365.

the horizon a profound dissatisfaction. Already there is taking shape
the battle against the distortion of man: it is a question of redis-
covering his original stature as once contemplated by generations
inspired by faith and hope. The fundamental datum of human
existence is *man with man*. The specific character of the human
world consists above all in the fact that here is actualised from being
to being something unparalleled anywhere else in nature. A determinate being addresses himself to another, equally determinate being,
but for the sake of communicating in a sphere common to them both
while going beyond their respective domains. Thus, it is definitely
the *Zwischen*, that is to say, the intermediary reality, upon which the
emphasis must be placed. Indeed, it is neither a matter of a
characteristic which could be internal to the individual nor of some
generality which might relate individual beings to one another. We
are really faced with an authentic bond which is in no wise an artificial
construction. If this has not been sufficiently acknowledged, it is
because we are not dealing here with a continuum, as in the case of
what is considered the individual soul and the surrounding world,
but rather with something which reconstitutes or recreates itself all
over again upon each human encounter. If we think, for example, of
true intercourse, each talking with the other with a spontaneity that
gives it an unpredictable character, or of a true class-session which
goes beyond the routine framework, or of a veritable embrace and the
like, we note that in all these situations the encounter does not take
place in each of the participants, or in a neutral unity encompassing
them, but *between* them in the most exact sense, in a dimension
accessible to them alone.

Thus is strictly excluded the rationalistic interpretation, advanced in our times, for example, by a Brunschvicg, according to
which communication between men is based upon a certain impersonal order wherein verification is possible, that is to say, an act
by which a truth is constituted. To be sure, Buber is careful not to
contest the intrinsic validity of this notion, but in his eyes it does
not enable us to penetrate to that which is specific in intersubjectivity, for example, in the look exchanged at a decisive moment by
two individuals who are not acquainted with each other: perhaps
they are both gripped by the beauty of a landscape or by a musical
phrase. Let us not content ourselves here with an emotion. Such

experiences have an *ontic* character which transcends the limits of psychology. We are here on the narrow edge where *I* and *Thou* meet, beyond subjectivity and this side of the object.[3]

Buber has insisted many times, moreover, on the necessity of going beyond affectivity when one tries to conceive intersubjectivity, even love.

> Feelings accompany the metaphysical and metapsychical fact of love, but do not constitute it, and these concomitant feelings may in their nature be quite diverse. The feeling Jesus had for the demoniacally possessed is different from that which he directed toward his favorite disciple: yet love here remains one ... Feelings inhabit man, but man inhabits his love. That is not a mere metaphor, but a reality: love does not adhere (*haftet nicht*) to the 'I' in such a fashion that the 'Thou' would be its content or object, for love is between I and Thou.[4]

We find here once again the *Zwischen,* or what Buber denotes by the term *Beziehung.* He goes so far as to say that it is primordial. But I cannot help wondering whether a difficulty does not exist here which the author perhaps did not fully recognize.

It seems to me rather difficult not to translate the term *Beziehung* as relation. Yet every relation is a connection between two terms, or if you like, between data capable of being treated as terms. But can *I* and *Thou* be regarded in this way? The question is most delicate. It is in effect unavoidable—and Buber himself has forcefully insisted upon it—that each *Thou* become a thing or lapse into thinghood (*Dinghaftigkeit*). But this is still not saying enough: I would add for my part that it is of the essence of language to effect this transformation. When I speak of you [*toi*], even when I expressly declare that you are not a thing, that *you* are the opposite of a thing, I reduce you in spite of myself to the condition of a thing. The *Du* becomes an *Es.* We must therefore recognize that we are confronted by a profound and doubtless essential contradiction. The *Thou* is he to whom I address myself: perhaps we would not be wrong in saying that he is essentially in the dative case,[†] and that I denature him by putting

---

[3] *Ibid.,* p. 457.

[4] *Ibid.,* pp. 26–27.

[†] In the original French manuscript, the contrast between the accusative case and the dative case is easily rendered for the reader by *tu* and *toi,* respectively. There is no parallel in English. Moreover, although a literal translation would employ only

him in the accusative case. Note well that this word 'dative' is certainly to be taken literally: it is a question of a gift, an offering, and thereby an act. But there is room for doubt that the term *Beziehung*, and particularly 'relation', can suit the act considered in itself: one can scarcely keep such a term from expressing rather the objectification of this act.

To be sure, the fundamental intuition of Buber remains to my mind absolutely correct. But the whole question is to know how it can be translated into discourse without being denatured. It is this transposition which raises the most serious difficulties, and therein probably lies the fundamental reason why the discovery of Feuerbach recalled by Buber remained so long without fruit.

In addition, it does not seem accurate to say: in the beginning was the relation. In the beginning, rather, is a certain felt unity which becomes progressively articulated so as to make room for an ensemble involving interrelated terms. It seems to me that on this point Bradley saw more clearly. This transformation, indeed, will not take place without incurring an impoverishment, a kind of drying-up of the realm of experience. But that is only the inevitable price of a major advance—that advance which makes of the realm of experience a place in which verification becomes possible, in which the very word 'truth' acquires a meaning, whereas at the level of felt unity it had none.

But, it will be asked, how could the *Zwischen* fail to be a relation? It is appropriate to reply that this word is not without ambiguity. It is only too clear that if between two terms I interpose a third, I institute new relations. But is the word used in this sense by Buber? It seems to me he has in mind something much more mysterious, which cannot be defined in an arithmetical or geometrical language. He means basically that, in the presence of human beings, there is created among them, let us not say even a field of forces, but a creative milieu, in which each finds possibilities of renewal. The term 'meeting', *Begegnung*, is here far more adequate than that of 'relation'. Of course, it must be understood—and Buber would agree, without any doubt—that the word 'presence' must be taken in its strongest sense, not in the sense of the chemist who puts two bodies in the 'presence' of each other to see how they will react. In such a

thou, you has been used where *thou* would appear awkward and the context clearly indicates that the tone is personal, as in the French writer's use of *tu*. (Translator's note.)

situation, the word 'presence' is so far emptied of its meaning that
one cannot use it without generating grave confusions. Let us note,
moreover, that in daily life each of us, even in the streets or on
public transportation, rubs elbows with an infinity of other beings
without there being any question of "being in the presence of"—
even if one contracts an infectious disease upon contact with some
stranger.

In my *Journal Métaphysique* I attempted to show by a concrete
example how this authentic meeting manifests itself phenomenolog-
ically. It is surely correct to say that within the meeting there is
created a certain community *(Gemeinschaft)*. And, on the other
hand, Buber is absolutely right not to found this community upon
an abstract principle, or on some generality. But I am tempted to ask
myself today if the question is not above all one of a co-belonging
to [*co-appartenance à*] the same history, perhaps one could say,
the same destiny, on condition that too tragic a tone is not put on this
word. The stranger seated beside me in the train or in the restaurant
to whom I say nothing does not belong to my history. The fact
that we eat the same food, for example, is not enough to create a
community among us. But a minute event might be enough to give
birth to this community, for example, an unexpected stop of the
train which threatens to have for both of us existential consequences.
This could suffice for an opening in the sort of barrier which separates
us, in short, for us to make contact. And it is only from the moment
that this opening is effected that we can become *Thou* for each other,
even in a still limited way. It seems to me that in this perspective
one would no doubt be inclined to insist more than Buber has done
on the fact that this community, still embryonic but capable of
growing, of becoming infinitely rich, is created between beings each
engaged in a certain adventure; but this adventure itself may, of
course, be undertaken at a variety of levels, according to whether or
not it touches the *heart* of the matter. Here we verge, I think, on
something essential, but also well protected, well guarded against the
possible assaults of reflection. The *heart* of my existence is what is at
the center of what we might also call my vital interests; it is that by
which I live, and which, moreover, is usually not an object of clear
awareness for me. The community between *Thou* and *Me*, or the
co-belonging, is the more real, the more essential, *the closer it is to
this heart.*

In all the preceding I have wandered from the text of Buber literally interpreted, but I do not think I have betrayed its underlying meaning.

The spirit [*l'esprit*], Buber tells us,[5] in so far as it is humanly manifested, is the response of man to his *Thou*. Man expresses himself in many languages: language in the strict sense, also in art and in action. But the spirit itself is one: response to the *Thou* which shows itself to him and which calls to him in a setting of mystery. Moreover, there is always the danger that the reply, when it is too forceful, may transform the *Thou* into an object. Only silence—and here Buber is close to Max Picard—leaves to the *Thou* its freedom, and subsists with it in unobtrusiveness; then, spirit no longer announces itself, but *is*. The melancholy destiny of man and also his greatness reside in the fact that every reply binds the *Thou* to the world of objects.

Our author is therefore far from minimizing the role of what Hegel called 'Objective Spirit'. Rather, he reminds us, with an insistence which never excludes this notion, of the subtlety that above the world of objects the presence of the *Thou* is suspended like the spirit upon the waters. And the comparison is here called for, because this vapor is not inactive, it puts itself forth as a beneficent rain. Through its agency, man can resist the oppressive force which emanates from the object.

It is wholly apparent that metaphors are here quite insufficient. But they are also indispensable. The problem for the philosophers is to give us access to a dimension which can only be conceived dynamically, but which we perpetually tend to lose sight of, as we succumb to the vertigo of the object.

Moreover, this is the point of departure for a sketch by Buber of a philosophy of history perhaps not lacking in affinity with that of Vico. Every great culture which extends to entire peoples has at its base an original meeting, that is to say, an essential act of spirit. Reinforced by the power of successive generations, it brings to birth in the mind an original interpretation of the cosmos. But as soon as a culture ceases to concentrate upon such a living, continually renewed process, it petrifies into a world of things penetrated only occasionally and eruptively by the fiery acts of great and solitary spirits.

[5] *Op. cit.*, p. 49.

By this vehement pronouncement upon the peril of objectification, it is apparent that Buber rejoins Nicolas Berdyaev, with whom he had, if I am not mistaken, sustained relations. But would the Russian philosopher have subscribed, as I myself would, to the affirmations concerning the eternal *Thou* who, by nature, can never become an *It*, because he admits of no measure, no limit, because he cannot be regarded as a sum of properties, not even an infinite sum? It seems to me the answer is Yes; and it is certain he would have recognized that we constantly tend to make this eternal *Thou* into a *Quid,* a thing, and by a process which is in no wise arbitrary.

To tell the truth, we are indeed confronted by one of those towering mountain ranges of contemporary philosophy, to the extent that contemporary philosophy has resisted both the Marxist temptation and yet another temptation: one which today is generally topped by an existentialism cut from its religious roots, an existentialism which by a strange rejection of itself, moreover, has ended by making peace with the very mode of thought whose contradictions it had originally disclosed so lucidly.

Why not pay tribute to the thinker who has succeeded in our time, as much and more than anyone, in achieving a living equilibrium between reason and that sort of continuous revelation by which man is nourished at eternal sources?

GABRIEL MARCEL

THE SORBONNE
PARIS

2

Charles Hartshorne

MARTIN BUBER'S METAPHYSICS

BUBER has no metaphysics; Buber is one of the greatest of metaphysicians—this, in somewhat paradoxical language, is my feeling about my assigned topic. He does not, formally speaking, have a metaphysics, a general system of ultimate categories, carefully defined and defended against rival systems. He is, I imagine, little interested in such things, and I daresay that what I can offer here will not, for the most part, be much to his liking. Moreover, it appears that in recent decades he has become even less inclined to philosophical speculation than he once was, in *Ich und Du*. Yet there are some pages in *Ich und Du* that seem to me among the most inspired ever written on the relations of the creation and the creator. True, they are couched in the language of piety, of existential response, rather than that of theory and rational evidence. It could be called a kind of poetry—and great poetry. Some similar thoughts can be found in Berdyaev, but mixed with philosophical ratiocinations and polemical attacks, and somewhat marred by an element of Manichean "hatred of reality." The thoughts are also in Whitehead, embedded in a maze of philosophical subtleties. In Buber there is an austere simplicity and centrality, with just sufficient polemical indications to mark off the point of view from some of its most important rivals, and there is no distracting assemblage of arguments or evidences. One feels the sheer force of actual experience, from which, in one way or another, all evidence must come.

I shall now attempt to elicit some metaphysical principles from Buber's words, but without in the least rendering him responsible for the result. It is what I am able to make of these words, when I try to conceptualize them, as I am too strongly habituated to doing to desist, even when reading so eloquent and poetic a writer as he.

First, the supreme principle is not absoluteness or self-sufficiency, but relativity. "Primary words do not signify things, but they intimate relations."[1] This primacy of relatedness is not to be denied even of God. "Let no attempt be made to sap the strength from the meaning of the relation: relation is mutual."[2] " 'Thy will be done,' he [the worshipper] says, and says no more: but truth adds for him 'through me whom thou needest.' "[3] In half a dozen ways this point is driven home: that God, the inclusive Thou, is relative to us, as well as we to Him. Our dependence upon Him is not the whole story. Nor are we merely creature while He is creator. We are "both creaturely and creative,"[4] and this means creative not merely of ourselves or of one another, but of something in God. We have, "in an incomprehensible way, an effect upon God."[5] There is no "God who becomes," as though some situation initially lacking in deity could bring God into existence. But "we know unshakably in our hearts that there is a becoming of the God that is. The world is not divine sport, it is divine destiny."[6] To very many, these are strange, puzzling, or even odious and blasphemous words. To me, an incurable, and, in part of myself at least, an ice-cold, rationalist, they are (assuming a theistic point of view) merely logic, neither less nor more, and those theologians who wonder at them are (to me) wonderfully illogical. For consider: if there is in us any freedom, any power of deciding what otherwise and by other beings is left undecided, then what we decide is not merely something in us, our own act, but on theistic premises, it is something in God. Why? Because in God is knowledge that we act as we do; and this knowledge could not be in God were we to act otherwise (for then it would be error, not knowledge). Thus either we have power to determine something in God, or we have no power to determine anything—unless God is capable of ignorance or error. Furthermore, if freedom is denied to man, then it cannot rationally be attributed to God; since if we experienced no freedom in ourselves, no power of resolving indetermination, we could not even have the idea, unless by sheer mystic insight into the divine nature itself. Besides, even if we could arrive at the idea, there would be contradiction in attributing ideal power or freedom to the supreme

[1] *I and Thou,* p. 3.
[2] *Ibid.,* p. 8.
[3] *Ibid.,* p. 83.
[4] *Ibid.,* p. 82.
[5] *Ibid.,* p. 83.
[6] *Ibid.,* p. 82.

reality, and zero freedom to creatures. The formula for comparing God and ourselves cannot be perfection and nothing, but only perfection and something—it cannot be supreme freedom and no freedom, but only supreme or ideal, compared to inferior or deficient, power or freedom. Not zero and infinity (if that is the right term), but the finite and the infinite.

Thus in Buber's poetry I see the soberest logic. Jonathan Edwards, with his harsh predestinarianism, argued for in cold-blooded and at times downright cruel logic, is really quite illogical. Omniscience is the record of reality; hence, if we have power over anything, we have power over omniscience. To determine any reality is to determine part of the infallible record, is to write in the book from which no jot or tittle can be erased. This book is written in divine ink, for there can be no other which could possess the required indestructibility and infinite subtlety. Yet a book which is not also written in this ink is not written in any!

That God "does not become," in the sense of first coming to exist at a given time, is also sober deduction from theistic premises. That which becomes bears the marks of its origin, and only a perfect or divine source could produce divinity. Besides, omniscience of all the past is not conceivable in a being with a genesis. But nevertheless, that there is becoming in God, or that God does in some respect or aspect become, is likewise the most consistent way of conceiving perfection. For if God is sheer being, devoid of becoming, then all becoming is external to Him, and yet He knows it. Can the perfectly known be external to the knowing? Moreover, if becoming is external, then the total reality is the divine being *and* the worldly becoming, a total of which the divine is a constituent. Is this a promising way to conceive the highest? It has been a popular way, but I deeply believe it is, taken strictly, an impossible way. I think I know the answers which can be made to me at this point, and they seem to me to leave the absurdity intact. Moreover, this is not just a matter of theoretical interest; it has religious significance, in just the way Buber indicates it has. The doctrine of mere Being suggests that the way to find God is to "leave the world behind," to turn from becoming altogether. This is to miss our proper vocation, which is to "hallow this life (and thus) meet the living God." The way to find God is to "leave nothing behind . . . to include the whole world in the Thou, to include nothing beside God but everything in Him."[7]

7 *Ibid.*, p. 79.

This means to find becoming in Him; for becoming is not nothing.

It appears that Buber later had some misgivings about using the term becoming in this manner. I do not know what the misgivings rested upon, and it would be interesting to know. But frankly I am not much concerned. The earlier treatment speaks for itself.

What is the basic logic of the assumption that relativity is primary, not absoluteness? Again, we have the simplest, clearest kind of rationality. The concept of the non-relative is parasitic on that of the relative. Given the concept of relatedness, we can then by negation (itself an example of relativity) arrive at that of non-relatedness. Relativity means that the thing said to be relative depends for being what it is upon some relation to another. It means that if you attempt to assume alternative relations of the thing to alternative relata, you find that the thing itself must be supposed somehow different. Relativity is, to speak somewhat metaphorically, sensitivity to relational alternatives. Absoluteness is neutrality to such alternatives. But neutrality presupposes what we have termed sensitivity. "The alternatives make no difference" (to the absolute) has meaning only in terms of the concept of "making a difference," that is, relativity.

There is another way of reaching the same conclusion. Suppose there is relative reality *and* also non-relative; then what is this togetherness of the two kinds of reality, as indicated by the 'and'? Is it relative, or non-relative? Clearly, it is relative. For if relational alternatives make a difference to one of two elements in a togetherness or totality, they make a difference to the totality, even though none to the other element. Thus relativity, and not absoluteness, is the inclusive conception.

The same argument holds even more obviously of necessity and contingency. Any contingent factor in the whole makes the whole contingent; for had the contingent factor been absent, the whole would have been to that extent a different one.

Let us now look at Becoming. Surely becoming is the relative and contingent factor; therefore, it is logically the inclusive factor. And this too is directly evident. For if a single item in the total becomes, then to that extent a new totality becomes. And if becoming can never reach a final stage, then there is no eternal totality, and only an eternal progression from one totality to another and richer one. The divine life does not begin or come into existence, and in this sense God does not become; but the divine life is a beginningless and endless, and as Schelling said (whatever he meant in his, to me, cloudy language), an eternal, becoming. And there is, once more, a coldly logical reason for denying a final stage of becoming. This is that the possibilities open to creation are "absolutely infinite," and cannot be exhausted. Why stop short arbitrarily when more beauty or richness of life can always be added? The possibilities open to creation are absolutely infinite because it is against this unlimited background of potential creation that all notions of limit and finitude have their meaning. Further, the absolute infinity of the potential cannot be translated fully into actuality; for the simple reason that things possible disjunctively are often impossible conjunctively. Need I elaborate on this truism?

Thus I maintain that the metaphysical framework of *I and Thou* is nothing if not rational and coherent. (This is not a strange view for me to take, since it is my own doctrines which I have succeeded in reading into Buber.)

We must now come to the great saying of Buber that God can be only Thou, not It—with the implication that there can be no science or rational analysis of deity. I believe this to be a one-sided formulation, quite true in a sense, but easily so taken as to be invalid.

I do indeed believe that there is a God who cannot be thought, but can only be addressed, as one who addresses us. But even in saying this, I have spoken about God, not merely to Him. More than that, I have attributed to Him an abstract characterization, that of being so sensitively relative to each individual in the world as to acquire a special, unique quality by virtue of His relatedness to that individual. To know the God who is Thou for you, I must know you in your individual uniqueness, as disclosed to the individual of higher order for whom alone that uniqueness is transparent. In so far as I know my own intimacy rather than yours, I must know my God rather than yours, and I can know my God only so far as my self-knowledge goes, in the act of living in the divine presence—a very limited, largely practical sort of awareness which Buber described in its general features better than most writers have done.

But in my opinion, the secret of our being able to discuss the undiscussible is in the distinction between the abstract and absolute, on the one hand, and the concrete and relative, on the other. Buber does not employ the care I feel to be desirable in using the term 'absolute', or 'the absolute'. The actual Thou cannot be non-relative, for Relation is precisely what is required here. But the general principle of relativity can itself have a sort of absoluteness. That there are relations, some relations or other, is not a relative fact, for to what could it be relative? There is no alternative to relation as such. This is part of Buber's discovery. Hence relativity is absolute. Nor is this a contradiction. For that concrete things are always relative does not mean that the abstraction, "something or other being relative," must itself be relative. This would be a logical-type confusion, a category mistake.

We may now take a further step. Relativity, the absolute abstract principle, has a double character. There is the ordinary form of being relative, such as we exemplify in being dependent upon one another, upon the cells of our bodies, etc. There is also, I hold, the transcendental form, "Transcendental Relativity," which is the divine principle, the divine essence. It is the essence of God; it is not God. The whole discovery of existential theology (as old, however, as Socinus, at least) is that God is super-essential, because He is actual. The divine form of relativity, the divine way of addressing and being addressed as Thou, is not the actual divine Thou itself, as your God now, or mine. Transcendental relativity is what all possible cases of the divine Thou have in common (or that in which all are similar to one another). It is the highest abstraction. Like any abstraction it is It, not Thou. And so one may say: Only Thou, O God, canst exhibit Transcendental Relativity as thine own characteristic, but since Thou dost always exhibit it everywhere and to everyone it can always be referred to without our having to specify any particular instance of thy relatedness.

The contrast between abstract and concrete, or between absolute and relative (I regard it as the same contrast) I take to be an ultimate distinction, valid even for omniscience. Were it otherwise, then all talk about 'omniscience' or divine relatedness would be nonsensical. Had God no abstract essence, He could not serve as the God of rational beings at all. For reason is helpless without the objective distinction between laws and cases, necessities and contingencies, and this, at the highest level, is the same as that between abstract and concrete.

To suppose (as so many have done) that the divine essence is simply God Himself is to talk as though the Mystery were hidden from us merely because we are not clever enough mathematicians to unravel the intellectual structure of deity. Or it is to misuse the word essence, and to imply that God simply has no nature, in rational, i.e., abstract, terms, but only a fullness of actuality concerning which even the general term 'actuality' has no validity. But we do have an abstraction, Transcendental Relatedness, infinite sensitivity or love, which fits nothing unless it fits God. Yet even infinite loving-kindness, or infinite beneficent creativity, is an utterly empty abstraction, by itself. Love for what creatures, how numerous and varied? In what contingent or freely creative way are they embraced in the incomparable Relatedness? (For surely the bare requirement of 'perfection' is not going to prescribe the way, since this would be the contradiction that "perfect freedom," as a fixed essence or universal, could tell the perfectly free being what use to make of his freedom.) Actuality infinitely overflows any essence whatever, including the divine essence. Only the essence, not God, is It, and is precisely the highest It. Hence we can know It, discuss It, without thereby knowing even a finite fraction of the contingent creative and self-creative action and passion which is the actual divine life. We know of the contingent Fullness only that it is in all particular phases contingent and inconceivably full—this truth indeed not being contingent.

Let us now turn to Buber's contention that anything other than God can be dealt with either as Thou or as It. There are at least three senses in which a concrete reality of nature (Buber's example, a tree) can be a Thou for us. (1) It can be imagined, animistically, to have a "soul" of its own, meaning here simply that it can be taken as an at least sentient and perhaps conscious individual. (2) It can be imagined to form a part or manifestation of such an individual, as a man's hand is a part or manifestation of him. (If we personify nature, then all things can be addressed as Thou, in so far as they are members of the cosmic organism. Or, all can be taken as expressions of the divine Thou.) (3) The thing can be imagined as a collection of individuals, each of which, could we deal with it in its uniqueness, would appear as a sentient, perhaps conscious, being. If anyone holds that some things cannot, without falsification, be dealt with as more than mere it's, then he is claiming to know that these things are (a) not sentient individuals, also (b) not composed of sentient members, and (c) not members or manifestations of any sentient whole. To know all of these negative characterizations surpasses, I suspect, any conceivable cognitive power, and hence is probably nonsensical or self-contradictory. I believe Buber is quite safe in his contention. There is in addition a fourth aspect of possible validity in addressing even inanimate things as Thou. They are all social realities in the sense that it is inherent in our concept of their objective presence that they are there for other human beings, and indeed other vertebrate animals, at least, as well as for ourselves. Most inanimate objects which we see in our immediate environment have been to some extent modified by human effort and skill, and this is a fifth sense in which Thou is appropriate to our experience of them.

Buber is clear that science must turn the Thou into an It. The reason, I take it, is that science abstracts from qualitative uniqueness and looks upon the individual as a mere special case of universal structures. The individual is a value of some variable, a value only approximately definable; and it is the variable that is scientifically interesting, not the value. Furthermore, except occasionally in nuclear physics, in clinical psychology, or in life histories of individual animals, science usually studies, not individuals, but aggregates, often with quintillions of members, as in the earth's atmosphere. We must go even farther. The very variables of which individuals are values, as such not exactly knowable, are one-sidedly abstract as science treats them. They are not variables of quality, such as emotional quality, sensory quality, qualities of joy and sorrow and enthusiasm. Rather, they are spatiotemporal structures, types of behavior, as intersubjectively observable in definite terms. We know in our own human case that there are variables of quality not clearly and concretely observable save in one's own psycho-physical system. But these variables are not chosen for scientific generalization. How a man feels, still less how an amoeba or a plant cell might feel, is not even a question for science as it now operates, *perhaps* must always operate, except when translated into how the man or amoeba acts. It is sheer error, as I see it, to try to get negative information out of this methodological exclusion practiced by science. Nothing, and I mean blank nothing, follows as to the objective absence of feeling in any of these cases. Feeling is merely not inquired into. That and that alone is the sense in which science rejects every version of the animistic idea of nature. But we should never forget that in our own case we know that the methodological exclusion really does exclude something actually there! Consequently, there are only two theoretical possibilities: (1) it excludes or neglects something really there only in the case of human beings (or of vertebrate animals, or of all animals, or of all cells and all animals. Draw the line where you wish, no scientist can show that it belongs somewhere else); or (2) the neglect is not a local one at all, but is quite general, and means that any and every reality is known in one-sided fashion by the behavioristic limitation which science has to accept for itself. I am perfectly confident that (1) can never be justified either scientifically or philosophically, and that Buber's basic point will eventually emerge as the only tenable one. In particular, I have the most vivid sense that the relations of a human being with the members of his own bodily organism are in a primitive intuitive sense thou-relations, relations of participation or sympathy. Injure certain of my cells and you injure me. Their injury becomes mine immediately. The well-being of my cells after a good rest flows into my experience from moment to moment as does the good cheer of companions. The cells are precisely my most intimate companions, the ones I cannot ever declare myself indifferent to and continue to be myself. Thus I believe Buber's formula has a literal truth in comparison with which all I-It schemata are mere useful fictions like 'perfect lever', not only not true but incapable of being literally true.

Our account so far has been based chiefly on *I and Thou*. The other work which seems most relevant is *The Eclipse of God*. This is an interesting book for any philosopher to read. I found the treatment of Heidegger helpful; likewise the well-documented critique of that brilliant muddle which is Jung's theory of religion. Apparently Jung's reply reiterated the sort of confusion from which some of us have suffered while reading this strange writer.

However, I am inclined to quarrel somewhat with the basic thesis of the book. Consider the following:

What the philosophers describe by the name of God cannot be more than an idea. But God . . . is not an idea.[8]

The idea of God . . . is only . . . the most lofty of the images by which man imagines the imageless God.[9]

[God] shines through all forms and is Himself formless.[10]

[He is] a being who, though in Himself unlimited and unconditioned, lets other beings, limited and conditioned indeed, exist outside Himself. He even allows them to enter into a relation with Him such as seemingly can only exist between limited and conditioned beings. . . . We are making no statement about the Absolute which reduces it to the personal. . . . We are rather say-

[8] *The Eclipse of God*, pp. 67–68.
[9] *Ibid.*, p. 84.
[10] *Ibid.*, p. 62.

ing that it enters into the relationship as the Absolute Person whom we call God.[11]

Unlimited being becomes, as absolute person, my partner.[12]

To identify God with what is absolute or unlimited, as seems to be done in some of these and many other passages, suggests a confusion of religion with philosophy, and bad philosophy at that. Is there no better philosophical "idea of God" than that He is the formless, unconditioned, wholly independent reality? Whether or not God is more than an idea, He must surely—some philosophers think—be more than *this* idea. What, after all, is the absolute, independent, or formless? It is that which is neutral to all possible alternatives; and this is simply the abstraction which is left when we leave out of account all that is definite. That which would be the same no matter what else might be or fail to be is not the fullness of reality but the very opposite, the empty common denominator of all possible alternative total states of reality. If God is no more than that, He is not only a mere idea, He is the emptiest of ideas, or rather, He is the very idea of emptiness itself. There is surely no logical reason why philosophy must identify this idea of uttermost emptiness with God, and many philosophers, some recent or living, some of earlier centuries, have carefully avoided this identification. (As with many writers of largely German cultural background, Buber seems sometimes to assume that 'philosopher' can only refer to one of the following: (a) someone who lived long ago, (b) a German, or (c) a figure of minor importance. Yet even in Hegel and Schelling one finds at least cloudy glimpses of the notion that absoluteness is only an aspect of what, in its complete nature, must be described in other and indeed contrary terms. In Whitehead and others, this becomes a systematic doctrine.)

The appropriate 'idea' of the divine nature or essence, I have been arguing, and it seems that Buber on his own showing ought also to hold, is the idea of supreme Relatedness—Transcendental Relativity, if we need a name for it—a mode of self-relating to others which is perfect or unsurpassable (beyond all possible rivalry) in its adequacy, the ideal form of self-relatedness. God is indeed Absolute Person; but 'person' not only implies no "reduction" of

11 *Ibid.,* pp. 126f.
12 *Ibid.,* p. 61.

absoluteness, it connotes unspeakably more than does 'absolute'. God loves (which implies relativity or nothing) unsurpassably, perfectly, if you will absolutely, and He is absolutely or unsurpassably worthy of being loved; but to turn this adverbial absoluteness into a self-sufficient adjective, to make independence without qualification applicable to deity (as is suggested by speaking as though 'the absolute' were a synonym for 'God') is, I am deeply convinced, the source of endless confusion, and calculated to compromise Buber's great insight into the primacy of relation. It sometimes appears that he sees this primacy only religiously, not intellectually. But modern logic, in its most coldly neutral aspects, supports the view. Indeed if "philosophers" today are approaching agreement in anything, it may well be in this: that 'the absolute' is not the basic idea, the 'image of images' (as our author puts it); but rather it is "relation" and "relativity" which deserve this status.

If for 'absolute' we substitute 'formless' or 'limitless', the result is the same. Not only can a reality be more than the formless, but almost anything is more than this. We need to regain the Greek insight, properly qualified by our additional intellectual and religious experiences, that the merely unlimited or infinite is totally lacking in beauty or goodness, and cannot be anything actual. "All determination is negation," said Spinoza, but failed to add; "And 'the indeterminate' is the greatest negation of all." Negation is ultimate. It cannot be simply transcended.

Is there not a key to this paradox? What is the unlimited or absolutely infinite but the content of pure or logical possibility? In theistic terms, this is the divine power or potentiality, God's capacity to sustain and possess in His knowledge or love anything whatever, should it exist. This capacity is indeed totally unlimited; for any supposed limit must imply that there could be something which God could not know or love. But it is entirely different to say that God's actual possession of things is unlimited: for what of the things which might exist but do not? He can possess them only as possibilities, but not as actualities; for there are no such actualities to possess. To deny that it makes any difference to the divine reality what possibilities are actualized, and what not, makes a mockery of religion as service of God, and makes Him strictly irrelevant to living. It would mean that to love God with our entire being, and yet care about our neighbor, we must simultaneously devote all our interest to an indifference point between the realization and non-realization of possible weal and woe (our neighbor's) and yet devote some of our interest to the difference between the two. I know well from sad experience that this is just the sort of (to me) hopeless muddle in which some theologians see, or claim to see, sense and truth. But I should not expect Buber to be like them.

If the unlimited is the possible, the divine power—the exhaustive actualization of which is self-contradictory—then God as actual cannot be praised by declaring Him unlimited, for that is the same as denying His actuality. The divine unsurpassability or perfection, which renders Him worshipful by no matter whom, must be otherwise described, with respect not to what God can be, or possess, but to what He is, and does possess. Here we need the concept, not of absolute but of relative perfection. In this aspect (the inclusive one) God is not A-perfect but R-perfect. The meaning of "God is R-perfect" is: God's actual possession, or fullness of reality, must always, in every possible case, be inclusive of all that is actualized in that case in or by any being, and the manner of this inclusion or integration is itself A-perfect, i.e., not even God Himself could surpass it, while no other being could rival it. These requirements guarantee that no conscious being could rightly be in less than a worshipful attitude toward God. This is the religious meaning, I suggest, of perfect. No one can condescend to God, though he might to "God." To demand that we conceive God as perfect in some arbitrarily chosen sense, however traditional and often reiterated, without regard to the religious significance of the term, is one of the bad habits with which theology and philosophy have too long been hampered. That God can acquire enhanced value has nothing to do with any possibility of our condescending to Him. For while He can surpass Himself, it is *He* who does this, and not possibly anyone else. For if X acquires a value which God lacked, God no longer lacks it, and the increment to *His* value is incomparably greater since He embraces the new value in an A-perfect manner, while we possess it in a deficient manner, neither A- nor R-perfect.

Suppose then, for the moment, we substitute Transcendental Relativity or R-perfection for the mere absolute—which, as explained, is only an abstract aspect of R-perfection, the adverb qualifying the basic participial adjective (self-relating, all-integrating). What, then, shall we say about Buber's charge that any philosophical system must render 'God' a name for a human concept, dependent on man for its reality? Several steps are required in attempting to answer this.

First, it is one thing to say, " 'God' stands for an idea," and another to say that the word stands for a merely human idea. For does not God think (or if you will, super-think) and think Himself? If He does, then there is a divine idea (or super-idea) of the divine essence; and our formulations about God are simply our attempts to think, after God, His idea of Himself. Such attempts need no more make God dependent upon us than our attempts to formulate the order of nature make this order dependent upon us.

Second, the essence of God is not necessarily God *tout court*. Indeed, how can it be? The "essence" of an individual, as this phrase may well be used (and no matter how Aristotle used it), is whatever makes that individual himself and not another, whether he experiences this or that. Let us recall that a man, in his deficient fashion, and God in supreme fashion, are free; this freedom (determinists will disagree, but not, I hope, Buber) means that the individual can be himself whether he does this or that instead, and this means that the essence of the individual as defined above does not include the one decision rather than the other. Yet, in so far as the individual is aware of his decision and its results, these will be embraced within the actuality of his experience. Thus actuality transcends the individual essence. How theologians could suppose God to be free and conscious, and yet to have nothing in His actuality besides His essence, is to me a mystery of that strange compound of logic and illogic which is the historical human mind. The Socinians and Schelling were among the first to call attention to the fallacy. God, it seems logical to hold, is vastly greater than any essence, even His own. *A fortiori,* then, God is more than any idea, concept, or image representing Him in a philosophical system, and any good system will make this clear. Even a human individual, in his actuality, is in a sense infinitely more than a mere essence, such as could be grasped in a concept, even a divine super-concept. Conception deals with universals, not actualities. The latter must be sheerly perceived. We should not suppose that metaphysics is tied forever to a primitive theory of signs, such as made possible systems like Hegel's or Fichte's. The concrete or actual individual is referred to by an "indexical" sign (Peirce) which points to, rather than describes, him. Description of any individual in its actuality always falls infinitely short of completeness and accuracy. *A fortiori* God transcends conceptualization. What the best philosophy can do is only to formulate a concept (deficiently realized in any human mind) of the divine essence or R-perfection; but this is an empty universal by contrast with the divine actuality which substantiates it relative to a given stage of the creative process. This actuality is, just as Buber says, pointed to rather than dealt with. This follows from the Essence itself: the supremely relative, less than anything else, can be known in isolation, or by abstraction and reasoning. For it includes all actuality in an actual all-loving comprehension. How can we know this, we who as thinkers must lose sight even of our own concrete fullness of life, not merely that of others!

I earnestly hope that Buber will give some attention to the foregoing argument, the conclusion from which runs: it is not the absoluteness of God, but His relativity, which makes Him for us the abysmal mystery. The mere absolute, the indifference-point of contrasting possible alternatives, is known by abstracting from the differences; on the contrary, the Relative Actuality can be known only by abstracting from nothing, while perceiving everything as embraced in an adequate appreciation. Thus God as actual is known only by sheer perception or encounter, face to face, as Buber says, and not by abstraction or conception. The encountered divine reality is just that from which abstraction abstracts; for it is the concrete of concretes (not at all, the image of images). Obviously we can "perceive everything as embraced in an adequate appreciation" only in an ineffable, non-cognitive fashion; for otherwise we should become instantly omniscient!

But now I may seem to have reached a self-contradictory position. The divine essence, as God's idea of His own individuality, is independent of us, yet since the divine actuality is relative to, dependent upon, all things, hence upon us, and since only an actual deity can think Himself, it appears that the dependence of the essence upon us is not escaped. Yet this is an error. It is not the divine Actuality, relative to us, or any definite set of creatures, which is required if God is to think His own essence, but only the divine Existence. "Actual" is not the same as "existent," even on a commonsense level. I exist as myself whether I actually sit or stand, talk to you or to someone else instead. An individual exists if and so long as his essence or individuality is concretized in some suitable actual "state," experience, or action. So the divine existence involves only that some actuality concretizes the divine essence—what actuality we can know only in the largely non-cognitive encounter. The independence or necessity of God's existence is simply its complete neutrality to contingent alternatives of His own or creaturely actuality; so that, let the creatures be or do what they may, some divine actuality (ideal act of possession) will surely greet them. This cannot fail, for "possibility" itself is the divine capacity to possess diverse creatures in diverse ways.

What then of "the absolute" or "the unconditioned"—a common expression of our author? They denote but an aspect of divine or transcendental Relativity. God is absolutely, unconditionedly (pardon the awkwardness) relative, that is, unfailingly and with utter adequacy self-related to, appreciative ("just judge") of, whatever creatures exist. Transcendental Relativity being an abstraction, the absoluteness which is a mere aspect of this abstraction is in a sense still more abstract; but the abstractness is in neither case due to our human processes of abstracting; rather, it expresses God's own abstractive process. God is aware of the contrast between what makes Him Himself in all possible relationships (the indifference point which constitutes His necessary existence) and what He contingently is in His actual relationships. Only the latter is concrete actuality.

Is there any contradiction in saying that an individual is sensitive, alterable according to circumstances, although his individual mode of sensitivity is not alterable? A man, for instance, responds sensitively to changes in other men and things; but if he has any persistent individuality, there must be something about his responsive changes which does not change. In God, this permanence of individuality is ideal or perfect; here there is a uniquely excellent style-of-being-sensitive which itself, as a style, is sensitive to, alterable by, nothing whatever. In the old phrase, often fatally misinterpreted, this style or law of divine response is "impassible." Herein I see the solution of the riddle of the absolute and the relative. The principle of relativity itself is that which is formless, unlimited, unconditioned. To identify God with this principle, and make Him formless and unlimited, is to limit Him indeed, for it blasphemously denies to Him possession of the wealth of forms which creativity has produced. Is this not an idolatrous confusion between a mere essence and the divine actuality? Absoluteness is a second-order property; it is the adverbial "ideally" in "ideally relative to all things," or "ideally inclusive of all forms, actually, of all actualized forms, and potentially, of all possible forms, in an inconceivably beautiful all-integrating form." The "ideally" is not, in the same primary sense, a form, any more than "formless" is itself, in the primary sense, a form. We say that so and so is adaptive, flexible; but if he is always and equally flexible, then his flexibility is not itself flexible. God is impassible only in that His passivity or receptivity to the creatures is unyieldingly adequate. There are two levels of abstraction here.

Of course I have not shown in the foregoing that, or why, philosophy should accept any idea of God at all. Buber suggests that there can be no proof for God's reality. But for what, of a philosophical or fundamental nature, can there be proof? Are not philosophers such clever people that they can rebut any argument, except in mathematics and perhaps the natural sciences? In the sense in which the reality of God is indemonstrable, everything philosophical is so, for all that I can see. As philosophical arguments go, I hold that the theistic proofs, properly formulated (and thereby hangs a tale of a hundred misses for one bull's eye) are sound and cogent. But this is, here and now, only a declaration of belief.

The doctrine which I have been setting forth for Buber's evaluation (if he can be tempted to evaluate it) is, in its broad outlines, not simply the view of one philosopher, but a trend in modern metaphysics, beginning, say, with Socinus,[13] and including Fechner,[14] Bergson (later phase), Montague, Ward, Whitehead,[15] Berdyaev,[16] Iqbal,[17] and others. What Whitehead calls the "Consequent Nature" of God corresponds fairly closely to Transcendental Relativity; what he terms the Primordial Nature is the absolute aspect, which on his own premises must be included, though he does not perhaps quite say so, in the Consequent or Relative Nature. The divine Actuality, which cannot be known conceptually, Whitehead simply calls "God," but also "the experience of the Supreme Unity of Existence" which "of course we cannot conceive."[18] Berdyaev has a roughly similar scheme, though he, like Buber, seems to think philosophy can conceptualize only the absolute aspect of God, so that the

---

[13] See Hartshorne and Reese, *Philosophers Speak of God*, pp. 225–227. Also Otto Fock, *Der Socinianismus*, pp. 427–31, 438–42.

[14] *Philosophers Speak of God*, pp. 243–57.

[15] *Ibid.*, pp. 273–85.

[16] *Ibid.*, pp. 285–94.

[17] *Ibid.*, pp. 294–97.

[18] *Ibid.* See his lecture on Immortality, sec. xvii, *The Philosophy of Alfred North Whitehead*, pp. 697–98.

truth of the divine relativity to the world is a "mystical" rather than a rational one. I have said enough about my reasons for rejecting this view, if it means we cannot know rationally the abstract truth that Relativity is a (the) divine property.

Both Whitehead and Berdyaev recognize a principle of freedom or creativity in which God and creatures share. This might seem to imply a power behind God, but the inference is, in my judgment, an incorrect reading of either author. The doctrine is not a wholly successful way of saying what Buber also seems to say, that it is the very nature of God to accept decisions from partly free creatures, rather than merely to impose decisions upon them (whatever that could mean). Buber's novel *For the Sake of Heaven* has some fine passages expressing this idea, or at least, suggesting it.

That we are related to God by a meeting, or an I-Thou relation, follows from Whitehead's doctrine that we at all times "physically prehend" or "feel" God, and that God Himself has physical feelings or prehensions of us.[19] 'Physical' merely means having a concrete datum, and 'prehension' means direct intuition, the source of inference or conceptualization, not its result.

One difference between Buber and Whitehead concerns the former's contention that meeting is reciprocal. Whitehead would accept this, in so far as one is speaking of enduring individuals, self-identical through time, as Buber obviously is. But the actual "occasion of experience," the momentary subject or "actual entity," has, according to Whitehead, but a one-way relation to another such subject. Designating my successive momentary experiences as I^{m1}, I^{m2}, I^{m3}, etc., and yours as Y^{m1}, Y^{m2}, Y^{m3} ... then I^{m1} can be prehended not by Y^{m1} but by Y^{m2}, or Y^{m3}, and Y^{m3} only by I^{m4}, or a still later member of my sequence. Does this analysis apply (analogically) to God? Whitehead does not directly say so, and appears at times to deny it, but he is, I think, indirectly committed to such a view. But I cannot see that this makes our relations to God, or to one another, I-It relations. "Objectification is sympathy," "feeling of feeling," says Whitehead; and such participation in the feelings of another is not well described as relationship to a mere "it." (According to both Whitehead and Berdyaev, God participates even in our sufferings. This may be assimilated to what the Yehudi says.[20] Indeed, how could the suffering of creatures be intuited

[19] *Process and Reality*, pp. 523f.
[20] *For the Sake of Heaven*, pp. 230f.

by God except by His feeling these feelings of theirs? Feelings cannot be known in the first instance intellectually; for they are not intellectual entities, concepts, essences, or universals. If I cannot feel your feelings, then I cannot strictly know them either; I can know only what they resemble in the feelings I do feel. But God must know feelings absolutely. Hence a suffering God is not a sentimental or mystical notion, but the only rational one.) Moreover, it remains true that the enduring individual, the sequence or "Society" of experiences, can reciprocally relate itself to another such sequence; and this is what ordinary speech usually refers to by pronouns such as "I" or "You." Yet final conceptual clarity cannot be attained if we remain always on this level.

What, after all, is the logical structure of the contrast between I-Thou and I-It? We are told that the former is a mutual or reciprocal relation, affecting both terms. If this is made a formal requirement, then the only possible relation with anything in the past is I-It. One's own past self, one's ancestors, characters in history, all become cases of It. Does Buber wish to adhere to this? I am not sure. Certainly there is a very significant difference between relating oneself to the life of someone who died before one was born, and surveying the history of a planet. Of course one can express the difference by pointing out that the person of bygone days himself entered into I-Thou relations, while the planet presumably did not. But I am now speaking of the present person's relation, and whereas in the case of the planet he can have no distinct sense of "participation," or of—at least imaginatively—sharing in the experiences and thoughts of another, in the case of the historical person he, of course, can do this. Does Buber do justice to the element of participation? And the point is that, while (apparently) I-Thou is necessarily (by definition?) symmetrical, to the extent that each party possesses relationship to the other, there is reason to suppose that historical characters sustain no joys or sorrows because of what we now feel in regard to them. Nor does my past self enjoy or suffer because of what I now think of it. Buber does not, of course, take I-Thou as symmetrical in an absolute sense; the relation of teacher to pupil, he says, is not the same as that of pupil to teacher. But the point I am making is that bygone teachers have no relation, in terms of their experience, to us as their pupils. Yet our relation to them is not to a mere thing or it.

Asymmetry is also involved in relations to remote posterity. We can love posterity only as an abstractly defined class, but they may love us as individuals. The mere contrast between It and Thou seems to do little justice to these distinctions.

There are reasons of pure logic for supposing that, while relation is indeed "ultimate," the strictly ultimate mode of relatedness is asymmetrical, qualifying A with reference to B, but not B with reference to A. Are not symmetrical relations, like that of "contemporaries" or "brothers," special cases of the fundamental one-way relations, such as "successor" or "descendant of?" Given the asymmetrical or directional relation, the non-directional is derivable by negation, as, for instance, "equal" means "neither being greater than the other;" whereas we cannot define "greater than" by "inequality;" for we should have ambiguity as to the direction of the difference. Directional relations are the truly ultimate ones. This, I suspect, is the final version of the doctrine of relativity. Buber's thought seems hard to relate to this point. Until the matter is worked out, we shall have, I incline to feel, not a theory, but an intuition, a great and important one, but one not yet made into a rational concept. Perhaps there is no wish to make it into the latter. Still, I believe it will have to be done. Even when "I" talk to "you," slight intervals of time intervene, as my speech renders you relative to what I have just thought and felt, and your speech "in turn" relativizes me to your experience in a similar way. The time intervals being very short, simultaneity is achieved for all ordinary purposes.

When we read about the God who addressed Abraham, Isaac, and Jacob, we are, in my belief, not reading about the Thou to which we today can address ourselves. God, as relativized to us, is a new or distinguishable God; the same divine personality or existent, to be sure, but not the same actuality. So long as human beings insist upon the idolatrous requirement that everything be as simple as mental laziness might wish—so long, for instance, as they use "existent" and "actual" as synonyms—we shall be in hopeless confusion about the relations of essence and actuality. That I exist, with my individual character, is one thing; that I exist in a certain actual state, sitting at a typewriter on a cloudy day with a blue jay having just called in my hearing, is logically a quite different matter. To suppose that, in speaking about God, we can forget this obvious distinction is to imply that understanding the term 'God' must be easier than grasping the most elementary differences involved in thinking about ordinary individuals. This notion seems to me idolatrous. Mental laziness is not the road to religious insight. I am criticizing now, not Buber, since he proclaims a faith rather than a theory, but those philosophers and theologians who, after two thousand years, still attempt to operate theoretically with concepts so crude as the dichotomy, essence-existence. All really significant questions must be seen in at least trichotomous terms, as Peirce so well argued. (Existentialism is perhaps partly vitiated by its tendency to rely on "existence" as sufficient alternative to "essence.")

I sum up: Transcendental Relativity, the property of being supremely sensitive or relative, in a definite sense absolutely relative, connotes an abstraction or essence which only God, as actual, can illustrate. Yet the property remains an abstraction. God is the sole individual whose individuality can be conceptualized, instead of the only one whose individuality cannot be! This is not surprising, since God alone is the individual of universal relevance, manifested in everything; and the universally manifested is just what the ultimate universal must be. But Transcendental Relativity remains an abstraction; it is but divineness, not God in His actuality—not our Thou, or anyone else's Thou, but only the universal Form or Essence of Thou. Our God is not of universal relevance, nor is Abraham's; but yet only the God of some definite creature or set of creatures is actual.

What I ask Buber is simply, How far wrong does all this seem to him to be? For alas, I cannot hope that he will find it altogether acceptable. We learn to restrain our expectations in these matters. I shall be happy if he sees some good in my bold, perhaps reckless, analysis.

I do not wish to end on a doctrinal note. In the preface to *For the Sake of Heaven* Buber wrote, "I have no doctrine." What he does have is something perhaps as good or better: wisdom, a sense of the essentials in religion and the good life. His description of the Relationship, which I do believe is the sound kernel in all religions, is something which we should have been immensely poorer without. We are forever in his debt.

CHARLES HARTSHORNE

DEPARTMENT OF PHILOSOPHY
THE UNIVERSITY OF TEXAS

3

Philip Wheelwright

BUBER'S PHILOSOPHICAL ANTHROPOLOGY

I. *The Problem of Philosophical Anthropology*

BUBER'S philosophical anthropology, which is to say his view of the nature of man, is in one sense inalienably at the very heart of his philosophy, although in another sense it does not exist. In so far as the phrase connotes that man is to be understood as constituting a species of potentially isolable individuals, coming together merely for emotional warmth and common utility, then it is fair to say that for Buber no science of man can exist. For the notion of man as in the first instance a solitary ego—*der Einzige*—which by multiplication and induction is expanded into a general notion of mankind—whether in the guise of *homo faber* or of *res cogitans*—looks not to the fulfillment but rather, in Buber's view, to the virtual nullification of man. In practice as a man moves toward essential isolation Buber holds that he does so at the cost of abdicating from his essentially human status, hence of becoming something less than man; and consequently that a theory which sets up some conception of the isolated man, whether primarily as doer or primarily as knower, as its starting-point, is resting upon an unreal abstraction. On this view it follows that if the only possible way of conceiving and discussing man is by an intellectual manipulation of unreal abstractions, then no genuine philosophical anthropology can exist. On the other hand, if there is a way of conceiving and discussing man in his concreteness, then for Buber the first condition of a philosophical anthropology can be met. Buber arrives at his concrete conception of man, in fact, by what may be taken analytically as a double maneuver. It consists, first, in envisaging man not under the category of substance, but under that of relation (*Verhältnis*); secondly, in specifying the kind of relation that distinctively pertains to him as "relationship" (*Beziehung*).[1] In order to understand the precise sense in

1 In order to keep Buber's distinction clear, it is important to use different English words for *Verhältnis* and *Beziehung*. In the present essay, therefore, departing from

which Buber's philosophy is essentially a philosophical anthropology it is necessary to keep in mind this pair of postulates, which distinguishes Buber's doctrine from other doctrines that might well appear to be anthropological or meta-anthropological.

Passing from a logical to a historical way of looking at the problem, we have to consider Buber's remark in "What Is Man?" that philosophical anthropology has reached maturity only in our own time. A classicist might plausibly demur. If philosophical anthropology means the study of man's essential nature and the placing of that study at the very heart and core of philosophy, then there would be some ground for maintaining that the ancient Greeks, particularly Socrates and Aristotle, could be described as philosophical anthropologists. Aristotle's double characterization of man as the animal who is *logikos* and *politikos* (or rather, with the word "animal," a triple characterization) seems to stand pretty much as a basis of all the more serious views that he puts forward. In what sense, then, can philosophical anthropology be said to have come to maturity only in our present age? To discover Buber's answer to this historico-critical question will evidently contribute to a clarification of what philosophical anthropology means for him.

One of Buber's firmest statements on the subject occurs at the beginning of the second main division of "What is Man?": "Only in our time has the anthropological problem reached maturity, that is, come to be recognized and treated as an independent philosophical problem."[2] Two reasons are given at this point for the affirmation. The first Buber describes as sociological, since it is founded on "the increasing decay of the old organic forms of the direct life of man with man." Communities have become "too big to allow the men who are connected by them to be brought together ever anew and set in a direct relationship (*Beziehung*) with one another." There has been a relentless decay of such social forms as the family, the village community, and the work-guild, while such forms as the club, the political party, and the trade union (*Gewerkschaft* as opposed to the older idea of the *Genossenschaft,* or work-guild) have increasingly taken over. Like the older forms these newer ones kindle men's feelings of collective security and thereby give them a sense of larger

the practice of the official translators, I shall always render *Verhältnis* as "relation" and *Beziehung* as "relationship."

[2] *Between Man and Man,* p. 157.

scope and significance in their lives, but they have not been able to reëstablish the sense of permanence and security which was given by the older forms. They operate by dulling man's sense of solitude by immersing him in bustling activities, instead of providing him with the stillness in which "confronted with the problem of his existence" he might learn to "experience the depth of the human problematic" as the ennobling center of his life. To this "sociological" reason for the special importance and maturity of philosophical anthropology in our time Buber here adds a second reason, which he describes as *seelengeschichtlich,* having to do with the soul's history. This shows itself in man's tendency to "lag behind his works;" to his increasing inability to master the world which he himself has brought into being. Jewish mythology supplies the very pertinent figure of the Golem—the soulless monster in the form of a giant man, which an ingenious Rabbi created to help the Jews defend themselves against enemies, but which soon turned its destructive talents against the Jews themselves.

Besides these psycho-sociological factors, which Buber considers to have been largely instrumental in "bringing the anthropological problem to maturity," there is also a noteworthy cause of another kind, to be found in "philosophical development itself, which [has] led to an increasing insight into the problematic nature of human existence."[3] Buber does not immediately explain or elaborate this phrase, but other parts of his writings offer clues to what it evidently means. Two main meanings stand out—a negative and a positive. On the one hand a reason for the rise and clarification of philosophical anthropology in recent philosophy may have been a tendency to react against the traditional over-emphasis upon the rational character of man, whereby, even though the force of his non-rational impulses was of course admitted, it was nevertheless his ability and activity as a reasoner, both contemplative and practical, that were said to mark him off from other animals. Now while Buber does not ever disparage man's rational faculty, and indeed there is plenty of evidence that he prizes it highly, he is unwilling to accept it as the determinative factor in establishing what man essentially is. For, he holds, it is not by his reasoning alone that man differs from his animal cousins: "even man's hunger is not an animal's hunger." Problems of human reason must be seen not simply as contrasted

[3] *Ibid.,* p. 157.

with man's animal nature, but as growing out of it and still bearing a vital relation to it. Consequently the problem of philosophical anthropology is not primarily that of man as rational, in contrast to other beings and to non-rational parts of himself; it is rather the problem of seeing man in his totality—or, in the phrase which Buber applies to Husserl's school (approvingly, it appears), "the problem of a specific totality and of its specific structure."[4]

But the philosophical reason for the emergence and clarification of the idea of philosophical anthropology is not entirely negative and reactive. A more positive explanation is found by tracing the lineage of the idea to Kant. In particular Buber cites Kant's early Handbook to his lectures on Logic, where philosophy in the universal sense (in sensu cosmico) is taken as asking four fundamental questions: (1) What can I know? (2) What ought I to do? (3) What can I hope? and (4) What is man? Kant declares that these four questions find their answers respectively in metaphysics (or what is later to be designated epistemology), ethics, religion, and anthropology. Later, in the Critique of Pure Reason, the first three questions appear without the fourth; but in the earlier version Kant declares that the anthropological question is the most fundamental of them all, since the first three questions may be regarded as phases of it. A germinal idea is implied here, but Kant does not elaborate it. Rather it was Kierkegaard, a generation later, who, as Buber remarks, "was of all thinkers the one who most forcibly indicated that thought cannot authorize itself but is authorized only out of the existence of the thinking man."[5] But although the greater force of insight came from Kierkegaard, it was Kant's critical revolution in philosophy that threw the inquiring individual back with new urgency upon the question, "What am I?" Generalized, the question becomes: What is the nature of the subjects who are the points of transcendental activity, making all this common phenomenal world possible? On its critical side Kant's philosophy established the possibility of knowing a world of objects, but certain problems remained which his critical philosophy could not answer. In his later writings Kant interpreted these residual problems as dealing respectively with God, moral choice, and life after death. The second and third of the problems correspond to the second and third of the four questions in

[4] Ibid., p. 160.
[5] Ibid., p. 161.

Kant's early Handbook; the first problem represents a transformation and transcendence of the first question, after the empirical aspects of it have been formulated in other ways. There is no longer, in Kant's later writings, any problem corresponding to the fourth of the early questions, "What is man?" To be sure, Kant takes the question for granted as presupposed or tacitly involved in all the others. Nevertheless, there might have been a gain in adequacy for Kant's mature philosophy if the question, as formulated, had continued to occupy a central place. As Kant's reputation increased and as the principles of his *Critique of Pure Reason* became formidably influential in academic quarters, it was the first three questions, without any explicit formulation of the fourth, that came to represent Kant's philosophical heritage. The anthropological question was always implicit when the other three questions were asked, but there was the danger that "it would reach, instead of the subject's genuine wholeness, which can become visible only by the contemplation of all its manifold nature, a false unity which has no reality."[6] Nevertheless, granted that "a legitimate philosophical anthropology must know that there is not merely a human species but also peoples, not merely a human soul but also types and characters, not merely a human life but also stages in life,"[7] nevertheless, once the importance of these and other such concretions has been accepted, the Kantian epistemology does supply a framework within which the anthropological question can be newly asked and understood. It does not guarantee by its explicit formulations that man shall raise the question of what, concretely, it is to be man. But it does point to that as the great residual question, which remains to be asked when the categorial analysis of the phenomenal world has been completed.

Consequently it is no accident that it was a neo-Kantian philosopher, Ernst Cassirer, who perhaps more than anyone else contributed to the definition and development of philosophical anthropology in recent decades. Particularly relevant here is Cassirer's conception of man as a symbolizing and mythologizing animal. On the one hand this conception fits into the framework of Kantian epistemology, for man carries on his symbolizing activity—and, by an extension of the same process, his mythologizing activity—not by accident or effort, but as a pre-conscious expression of the apperceptive imagination in

6 *Ibid.*, p. 123.

7 *Loc. cit.*

positing and interpreting the most basic features of the world. On the other hand, this aspect of man is relatively concrete and variable in a way that the categories which Kant had canonized are not. Thus, the category of causality, as Kant interprets it, works identically for all knowers, enabling them to formulate with a priori certitude the judgment of pure reason, "Every event has a cause." In Cassirer's philosophy, by contrast, no corresponding a priori principle is discoverable, for if we seek something more definite than the bare abstraction, "There is meaning," we shall find that the modes of meaning which men posit as belonging to their world show large and lively differences, according to differences of language, tribal and religious traditions, and cognate variables. Thus since, as Buber says, a legitimate philosophical anthropology consists not only of propositions about man in general, but must come to terms with types and characters and stages of human life, we may remark that Cassirer's view of man as a symbolizing animal is at once a development of the Kantian critical outlook and also an approach to the problem of philosophical anthropology.

The symbolical approach is not explicitly Buber's, however. Where Buber differs from Cassirer can be succinctly stated if we accept the general Kantian method, without Kant's restrictive applications; in short, if we undertake to think of the most fundamental characteristics of the world as representing categories of the understanding. We can then say that whereas the most important category that Cassirer sees operating in man's grasp of his world is the pair of correlatives, *sign* and *meaning,* the most important category for Buber can be designated, according to the context in which he approaches the question, as *betweenness, thouhood,* or *relationship.* Such a statement requires only the qualification that in the most recent development of Buber's doctrine the category of relationship is taken to presuppose the category of "primordial distance" (*Urdistanz*), as I shall discuss in Part III. These considerations show, I think, that it is impossible to discuss Buber's, as it is impossible to discuss Kant's, philosophical anthropology without raising the epistemological question as well. Before further pursuing that question in Part III, however, it will be well to face the problem of philosophical anthropology more directly by examining Buber's conception of selfhood.

II. *The Singleness of Selfhood*

Any proper definition of the self must avoid the two opposing errors of mysticism and egoism. The distinguishing mark of mysticism is the notion that man reaches his highest fulfillment through losing his own individuality by becoming merged in a higher reality. Usually in the more explicit forms of mystical philosophy the idea of a mystical goal is backed up by a mystical metaphysic, as is expressed by the Hindu formula, "Atman is Brahman." The logic of mysticism thus runs: We should seek union with the World-Ground (by whatever name it is called) because we are already "really" one with it. Axiology, metaphysics, and semantics are combined, possibly confused, in a rather tricky way in this doctrine, but such problems need not detain us now. Suffice to say that Buber's doctrine of man stands out in sharp opposition to mysticism. No loss or merger of selfhood is involved in the idea of relationship (*Beziehung*). On the contrary, in order to stand in relationship to another I must be myself, recognizing the other as a self too, and through such recognition I become more truly a self, not less so. One way in which Buber has declared the non-mystical character of his doctrine is by referring to man as *der Einzelne*, a phrase which in the English version of *Between Man and Man* is translated "the single one." In the connotations of Buber's term, as in the mysticism which his philosophy stands against, we can detect at once a metaphysical and an ethical sense—a statement of what man essentially is, and a declaration of what he ought to become and be. In the former sense I would think that the official translation is satisfactory; in the latter there seems to me to be a connotation which can perhaps be indicated by the phrase, "the focussed one." Whatever English terminology is chosen, it is important to keep in mind the full meaning of Buber's epithet, which I take to be somewhat as follows: By nature each person is a single being, finding himself in company with other single beings; to be single is not to be isolated, however, and by vocation each one is to find and realize his proper focus by entering into relationship with others.

In short, the idea of focussed singularity, which Buber expresses by the epithet *der Einzelne*, involves an antithesis not only to mysticism but also, in the opposite direction, to egoism. In his essay, "The Question to the Single One," Buber takes Max Stirner as a representative of this latter tendency, and is at pains to distinguish the meaning of *der Einzelne* from Stirner's basic term *der Einzige*. In the published English translation of *Between Man and Man* this epithet of Stirner's is rendered "the unique one" (as if it were *der Einzigartige*); but Buber's meaning would be more aptly conveyed, I think, by such a phrase as "the solitary one" or "the isolated one." Now Stirner is a fairly intelligent type of egoist, and does not assume, as certain more naive egoists often do, that a social life can be entirely motivated by enlightened self-interest that is conscious and deliberate. It is empirically observable that this is not so; for egoism thrives most effectively when watered by occasional self-forgetfulness. Accordingly Stirner recommends "living participation . . . in the person of the other," which is perhaps a valid enough prescription as far as it goes. However, Buber rejects this solution of Stirner's as "unessential" (*wesenlos*), since in the enlightened egoist's eyes the other person has "no primary existence." True, the other may have, for the egoist, a certain relation (*Verhältnis*) to his own self, in which there are certain "magical" possibilities, but he does not stand in genuine relationship (*Beziehung*) to him. The magical possibilities that Buber sees in Stirner's type of living participation are evidently of the sort whereby the ego overcomes the fears and loneliness of its isolation not by forming genuine relationships with other persons, but by merging with them in such a manner as to form "a rigid collective *we*," which is to say, "a group I." Considerable psychic force can often be generated in this manner, but it is altogether different from the genuine relationship which Buber sets as the human goal. The force thus generated is not distinctively human power, for it involves a transference of the power of making decisions from the individual to the group; which is to say that the resultant actions are produced by group impulses and ideological shifts that are the outcome of circumstance, rather than by humanly formed intentions. Consequently the ego as Stirner conceives it is "empty of genuine power," and Stirner is chasing a will-o-the-wisp when he declares that "only the man who belongs to himself, and acknowledges nothing but himself, is free." For in practice this kind of vaunted freedom becomes an epiphenomenon of impulses and circumstances covertly dependent upon pressures of the group and of the environing world. To the egoist a person's need of other persons is of essentially the same order as one's need for food, fresh air, and sexual fulfillment; that is, an accident of man's life in the body and in the world, rather than constitutive of man's very essence.

In contrast at once to the essential superficiality of the egoist's interpretation of man's relationship with his fellow-beings, and to the mystic's virtual negation of the terms that make such a relationship possible, Buber's position involves a certain idea of self-transcendence. There is a general sense, to be sure, in which a principle of self-transcendence holds good at all levels of being; for it is obvious that each thing exists, and must be conceived, in and through its relations with other things. But this abstract truism is not what interests Buber, whose central philosophy hinges upon the form which the principle takes at the human level. For at the human level of being, which is the highest we can know, the principle of self-transcendence manifests itself not in abstract relations, but in relationship. That is to say, a being who stands in genuine relationship with others is not self-enclosed, although neither does he cease to be a single self. Instead of being self-enclosed (which I take to be an essential connotation of *der Einzige*) he is one who achieves a more focussed existence precisely through standing in relationship with others.

On the other hand, granted that the appropriate human condition implies both a certain kind of self-transcendence involving a genuine relationship and also an individual focus of selfhood that is brought to realization thereby, it is important to avoid a certain error that sometimes occurs, especially in strongly religious persons when they attempt to act upon both of these two complementary principles at once. Buber finds the error discernible in the philosophy of Kierkegaard, both as written and as lived. The Danish philosopher, like Buber, recognizes the human person as somehow transcending any strictly empirical categories and relations. Moreover, since both philosophies agree that in essential matters one's contemplative and one's moral reason—that is, one's basic mode of inquiry and one's basic mode of acting and responding—cannot be firmly separated, it follows that both philosophers find themselves immersed in reality in such a way that certain transcendental duties—that is, certain duties which go beyond self-interest even of the subtlest or farthest-reaching sort—become necessary to a person, not by imposition from without (whether by social custom or Deity or bodily impulse or accident) but as determined by and determinative of the person's very nature. This transcendental character of a person, however, shows itself differently according to the views of the two philosophers: for Kierkegaard holds that man's one transcendental relationship that really counts is between himself and God, and that this special relationship may involve a relinquishment of all finite personal relationships or a reduction of them to something quite incidental and secondary, whereas Buber holds that it is only in and through relationships with other finite selves, through having and transcending such relationships, that the relationship with God can be truly realized.

The question takes a particular form with respect to the relationship between man and woman. The central act of Kierkegaard's life, as Buber interprets it, was his renunciation of Regina Olsen, for he made the renunciation not as a separate act nor as attributable to circumstances or preferences, but as an action of concrete universality, as a practical crystallization of his deepest thoughts and convictions. He was acting with conscious reference to the category which Buber takes to be the Danish equivalent of *der Einzelne,* implying a condition of personal focus, solitary yet trans-referential, which Kierkegaard had declared to be the category through which time and history and the race must necessarily pass. Now Kierkegaard understood and chose bachelordom as the ethical expression and outward symbol of a mode of truth, even as Martin Luther in opposing the monastic ideal some four centuries earlier had undertaken marriage as expressive and symbolic of *his* mode of truth. Nevertheless it does not follow that the contrary symbolic actions are of equal validity with respect to the human estate. The limits of Kierkegaard's view are shown plainly in his statement that everyone should be wary of having to do with other persons and "should essentially speak only with God and with himself." Luther, on the other hand, in accepting marriage as a central symbol, was declaring, in effect, that one must speak not only with God and oneself, but quite as necessarily and fundamentally with other persons. Ideally, the sacrament of marriage symbolizes in a special way a readiness to speak and be spoken to, which is to say, a readiness for genuine relationship.

Kierkegaard's view is a "sublimely" mistaken one, Buber declares, adding: "We are created along with one another and directed to a life with one another. Creatures are placed in my way so that I, their fellow-creature, by means of them and with them may find the way to God."[8] In short, God and man are not rivals. Although we are enjoined to love God with *all* our heart and mind, Buber expounds this precept by declaring: "Exclusive love of God is, *because he is God,* inclusive love, ready to accept and include all love."[9] For (the

[8] *Ibid.,* p. 52.

argument continues) it is not himself that God creates, not himself that he redeems, and not himself even that he reveals: he creates the world and especially man, he redeems man, and when he "reveals himself," as we say, he does not reveal himself as an object; what he reveals is unexpected mystery and goodness standing forth in some part of his creation, particularly in human embodiments.

Possibly some light may be thrown upon the point at issue between Buber and Kierkegaard by regarding it as roughly analogous to the venerable dispute between Mahayana and Hinayana Buddhism. Leaving aside historical and geographical factors that may have contributed to the difference, I would say that the essential logic of the situation, recognized explicitly by some Mahayana writers, is this. Whereas Hinayana ("the lesser vehicle") puts the emphasis upon an individual's purity, freedom from action, and consequent emancipation from the wheel of rebirth, Mahayana ("the great vehicle" of the Northern School) takes a further step, which is arrestingly logical. If an individual attains to such perfection that he is ready for release from the wheel of rebirth, he must have overcome, above all, self-attachment. Being perfected he will no longer be disposed to put the concerns of his own self above the concerns of other selves. However, this mode of perfection, if truly attained, is not a cold *ataraxia* or studied imperturbability, which can sometimes serve as a mask for a sophisticated and bloodless kind of egoism. No, the Mahayana doctrine of no-self is characteristically something more. The Christian doctrine of love, if purged of sentimentality and all hope of reward, comes close to it; regarded philosophically it is an awareness of and concern for the other as other. The Mahayana logic takes the form of that most genial myth of the Bodhisattva, wherein it is said that the beings who have attained such perfection that they would naturally pass into the long-desired state of Nibbana (or Nirvana) return voluntarily to earth in embodied form as Bodhisattvas, moved by pure compassion to help their more laggard fellow-beings on the upward way. Of course there is a strong essential difference between Kierkegaard's and Buber's philosophies on the one hand and any form of Buddhism on the other; the difference shows itself succinctly in the contrast between the doctrine of man as *der Einzelne* and the Buddhist doctrine of no-self. But although the *I-thou* relation is fundamentally dissimilar to the

9 *Ibid.*, pp. 51–52.

state of Nibbana, nevertheless there are two ways of seeking to realize the one, as there are of seeking to realize the other. The Mahayana saint, who cares so deeply for his fellow-beings that he makes the supreme sacrifice of returning to the world which he could have left, surely has more in common temperamentally with Buber than with Kierkegaard. Differences of metaphysical theory, however important, should not blind us to this significant similarity and discrimination.

Finally, it should be noted that in insisting upon the practice of relationship in its concrete, which is to say its human embodiments, Buber does not ignore or belittle the need for aloneness in man's spiritual economy. What Nietzsche speaks of as the "passion of distance" is a real factor, more so at some times than at others, in every sturdy soul. To be sure, Buber holds that man's paramount and most intrinsic need is for an "uncurtained" relationship with all fellow-beings, whatever their status; and this must never be lost or compromised, not even in the name of God. On the other hand there is always the danger that our relationships with fellow-beings may become "incapsulated," lapsing into stereotypes. That is to say, such relationships, when left to the accidents of everyday existence, tend to lose their aliveness and fullness of participation, becoming sometimes little more than habitual sets of gestures, words, and attitudes. How is the impoverishment to be avoided? Buber answers that a means of replenishment is available to each of us, and he indicates its nature by a somewhat curious analogy. As the world is sustained in its independent nature as the world (in its *Welthaftigkeit* and its *Selbstständigkeit*) through striving to become closed against God, although at creation *(Schöpfung)* it is open to him, "so every great bond of man—though in it he has perceived his connection with the infinite—resists vigorously against continually debouching into the infinite."[10] The logic of this sentence becomes more evident when we perceive, in the sentence which follows it, that Buber in speaking of "every great bond of man" is referring specifically to the monastic forms *(Klostergestalten)* of life in the world, into which we turn as into temporary shelters, for they "help us to prevent the connection between the conditioned bonds and the one unconditioned bond from slackening." Here, then, is the indispensable paradox that results: that true intercourse and participation with fellow-beings

10 *Ibid.,* p. 54.

require refreshment and fecundation by means of the strength that only an inner acceptance of monastic loneliness, in some sense, can give. By means of self-discipline in loneliness, a man increases his power of self-focussing and thus of participation in "present being" (*das Seiende*). Still, when this has been said, and when the need of "spiritual monasticism" (*Klosterhaftigkeit*) as a basis for essential human participation is recognized, we must always be careful to give sufficient weight to the yet more essential complementary truth and its implied warning. There is a right way of seeking the cloister and a wrong way. Buber is careful to insist that true spiritual monasticism "must never wish to tear us away from fellow-beings, must never refuse to give us over (*entlassen*) to them." For the result of such refusal would be to "close us up," instead of enabling us, as it is the real office (*Amt*) of *Klosterhaftigkeit* to enable us, to "keep open the gates of finitude."

III. *Distance and Relationship*

In what I take to be the most important of his essays since the Second World War[11] Buber has reconsidered the problem of relationship from an epistemological standpoint (although he does not employ Kantian language), and in so doing he has provided a fresh and arresting perspective whereby to reënvisage his conception of the nature of man. The epistemological problem, if conceived with any adequacy, is closely bound up with the problem of philosophical anthropology, as the preceding sections have shown. If in some of its historical appearances it seems to be something less than and distinct from the latter problem, that is because many a given list of categories is inadequate to the full expression of man's intellectual nature. Or, what comes to the same thing, modern philosophy has been impoverished on the whole by its too narrow and abstract concept of intellect. The older Scholastic notion of *intellectus*, as distinguished from *ratio*, had a good deal more adequacy: in the High Middle Ages the word refers to man's basic faculty of beholding and understanding what *is*. Kant, to be sure, was separated from the earlier

---

[11] "Distance and Relation," *Hibbert Journal*, 49 (1951), 105-113; *Psychiatry*, 20 (1957), 97-104. Since the title of the original is *Urdistanz und Beziehung* (published as an individual volume by Verlag Lambert Schneider, Heidelberg, 1951), I am translating the second noun as "relationship," for the reason previously explained. All references in the present section are to this essay.

tradition by the Cartesian dichotomy, then by Berkeleyan subjectivism and Humean scepticism, and his attempt to reëstablish the essential objectivity of reality-as-man-can-know-it therefore took on an aspect of controversiality and even a tinge of the very subjectivism he sought to combat. Still more limiting to the Kantian doctrine, however, was the formal and textbookish way in which the list of categories was constructed, with the result that undue emphasis was placed upon some very trivial distinctions while on the other hand certain categories that are indispensably operative in man's grasping of the world were ignored.

The most important omission in the Kantian list of categories was pointed out by Renouvier, who, working along neo-Kantian lines, supplied personhood (*personnalité*) as the highest and fullest category that man can grasp.[12] Renouvier was right in perceiving that such a category is indispensable in the "total synthesis" that makes up the world for each knower of it, and also in perceiving that the objects of the world to which the category of personhood applies will not merely have the character of objects for one's own consciousness but also that they must be, and be regarded as, subjects of potential consciousness in their own right. Actually this is but a philosophical affirmation of the truism that each of us does and must believe that there are other persons inhabiting the world, inasmuch as it is impossible for anyone to grasp the world as a totality without including such a belief; in short, no man can be a consistent solipsist.

It is along somewhat parallel lines, but with less dependence upon the Kantian outlook and technique, that Buber's inquiry in "Distance and Relationship" is directed. But Buber takes here a significant step beyond such an analysis as Renouvier's on the one hand and beyond his own earlier and more widely known teachings on the other. For the important statement is now made that the category of personhood is not simple but is twofold, representing two complementary movements of the mind. The first of these movements is "the primary setting at a distance" and the second is "entering into relationship." For man, and for man alone, there is "an otherness which is constituted as otherness." Thus the basic otherness of the objects of human experience is the result of a process of distancing on man's part, but the process is primordial and pre-conscious, and

12 Charles Renouvier, *Essais de critique générale: Premier essai* (1854). In the 1912 edition, Vol. 2, pp. 177-184.

consequently the otherness is (to employ Kantian language) transcendental, not empirical—an essential part of man's transcendental
unity of apperception.

An animal forms images of its environment (*Umwelt*), but they
are limited to what is of concern for the animal's bodily being
(*Leibhaftigkeit*) and its activities. Hence the images that the animal
forms are an "unsteady conglomeration," since they pertain only to
its "realm," which draws its character in part from what is given and
in part from the selective process generated by the animal's organic
needs. Man, on the other hand, "reaches out beyond what is given
him" and seeks to know the existent as existent. The realm of an
animal's experience consists of "the meeting of natural being with
the living creature;" it is identifiable with a set of sensations somehow
produced by what lies outside, but selected and interpreted by the
animal's biological needs and tendencies to act. Man, however, has
the unique power of projecting his concern and his questioning
beyond his realm of animal urgencies, and thus he not only reacts to
his environment (*Umwelt*) but also and more distinctively he comes
to orient his thought and actions with respect to an enduring world
(*Welt*) "which comprehends and infinitely transcends his environment." This is shown by the fact that every man, at whatever stage
of development, including the primitive, "always holds over against
himself, to some degree, in some way, that which he does not know
as well as that which he knows, bound up together in one world,
however primitive." Thus man's world (as distinguished from the
environment which belongs to him as an animal) is continually
undergoing enlargement and reënvisagement; he takes up residence
in it as if in an enormous house which he is capable of grasping as a
whole, as a home, although he does not know its ever expanding
limits. Buber's curious simile of a house, which behaves unlike any
house that I have been familiar with, was doubtless suggested to him
by a colloquial connotation of his pivotal word *Beziehung*, which in
suitable context may mean the act (usually of a newlywed) of
entering into residence. Man's fundamental action *qua* man is to
take up residence by positing a world in which he can reside. In
more technical language Buber puts it that man's nature (*Sein*) is
such that he is able to see his "present being" (*das Seiende*) as
detached (*abgerückt*) from himself and thus to recognize it for what
it is and to set over against it a general structure of being (*Seinszusammenhang*). This is what constitutes the process of distancing, and

it is thereby, or rather therein, that man can know an independent world as existing—or (what comes to the same thing) can know that an independent world does exist for man. The process of distancing is epistemologically a priori, in the Kantian sense that it is the basis of our possessing any conception of an independent world and, correspondingly, any conception of ourself. Man's knowledge of his own selfhood and of the world in which he dwells is the result, in both its aspects, of the primordial process of distancing.

The process of distancing implies as its complementary the process of entering into relationship. The two processes are not to be regarded as successive in time; they imply each other mutually. For on the one hand, "one cannot stand in a relationship to something that is not perceived as contrasted and existing in itself." That is to say, there can only be an entering into relationship if there is already an independent other, towards which-or-whom one can take up such a relationship. Yet on the other hand, conversely, it is possible to think of a world standing over against oneself only if that world is conceived as existing independently of one's awareness of it, hence as being in some sense a self in its own right, and hence as standing in potential relationship to one's ownself and as inviting one to enter into relationship with it. To know the world as the world, says Buber, "means the outlines of relationship."

Yet while the categories of distance and relationship are mutually implicative, two qualifications should be noted. In the first place, distance (i.e., *Urdistanz*) is logically prior to relationship. Distance represents the human situation, relationship represents man's becoming in the situation. "It must be firmly maintained," says Buber,

that the first creates the presupposition of the second—not its actuality (*Herkunft*), but its presupposition. With the appearance of the first, therefore, nothing more than room (*Raum*) for the second is given. It is only at this point that the real history of the spirit begins, and this history takes its eternal rise in the extent to which the second movement shares in the intimations (*Kundgebungen*) of the first, to the extent of their mutual interaction, reaction and coöperation.

On the other hand, and this is the second qualification, although such interaction and coöperation are most highly desirable, representing what may reasonably be considered the most natural, because the highest, state of man *qua* man, it must be remembered that there are certainly occasions when the two movements are in mutual

conflict, "each seeing the other as the obstacle of its own realization."
For the distancing process, if left to itself, tends to produce and
encourage an *I-it* relation between the knower and his world. Yet
even in such conflict, it sometimes occurs, "in moments and forms
of grace," that "unity can arise from the extreme tension of the
contradiction, as the overcoming of it." Such moments of grace are
rare, Buber observes, and cannot be counted on; but their occasional
reality (and it is a reality of incomparable intensity when it occurs)
provides a sort of ultimate confirmation of the rightness of the way of
relationship, and perhaps also of what I would deem the basic tenet
of Buber's metaphysic—the potential availability of relationship in
any and all situations, however seemingly unpromising.

IV. *The Finite and the Trans-Finite*

Since personhood essentially involves, both in existence and in
its adequate conception, relationship to other persons, and since
every genuine relationship is a relationship not with the crust of
another's personality but with that other's power of responding and
meeting, which is to say with the divinity that is the very core of that
other person, it follows that the study of personhood necessarily involves a study or at least a questioning of that which transcends the
personal, as the divine does the human. In short, philosophical anthropology implies, without prescriptive dogma, theology. The divinity
of man cannot be understood as something existing all by itself, but
only as the creature, or the reflection or emanation, of the divinity
that is God. For, as Buber has stated the matter, "YHVH is not
only holy but *the* Holy; that is to say, everything in the world which
is to be named holy is so because it is hallowed by Him."[13] What a
threshold study of man involves, of course, is not the changing forms
of God and the doctrines about him, in the manner of Comparative
Religion. To talk about God outside of man's actual relationship to
Him is to mythologize. To speak significantly of God is not to talk
about, but to address Him and (what is more essential) to be addressed
by Him and respond to Him. God, in short, is not he or she or it or
they, but Thou. The mutuality, and therefore, in the most purified
sense, the love that characterizes the *I-thou* relationship are essentially present wherever man's awareness of divinity is more than

[13] *The Prophetic Faith*, pp. 206–207.

mythologizing fancies or pious chatter. Thus it appears that philosophical theology in turn involves philosophical anthropology; in
short, that the two disciplines are mutually implicative.

There seem to be two major phases of man's relation to God.
The one is original, and can most nearly be indicated by the idea
of creation; although this idea, if taken in the context of usual human
associations (and how can it be understood entirely apart from
them?) is strongly metaphorical. The other phase of man's relation
to God is not something that lies outside of man's power, as his
original creation *ex nihilo* obviously does; on the contrary it involves
man's volition, his choice of accepting or rejecting the implications
of divinity within himself. In Buber's terminology it may be said
that this latter phase of man's relation (*Verhältnis*) with God becomes, wherever the affirmative alternative is taken, a relationship
(*Beziehung*). It is the latter phase that directly concerns us, for
here alone we have power to choose. Any metaphysical and theological
theory about original creation has a subsidiary value at best; it will
be valuable so far as it provides a conceptual structure that can help
to demonstrate how central to human nature the fact and need of
relationship must be. Consequently I shall consider first the latter and
for man the more important phase of the human-divine relation, and
shall then conclude the examination of Buber's philosophical anthropology by inquiring what theory of ultimate creation is inter-
involved with his view of man.

How is the right relationship of man to God to be conceived?
Buber, as we have seen, studiously avoids any suggestion of a mystical
solution; at least he has done so ever since his early years when he
was influenced by Hasidism. And if we renounce mysticism on the
one hand and superstitious fancies about a "gaseous vertebrate" and
"the man upstairs" on the other, it seems to me that we shall find two
main concepts that have been most influential and can still be of
especial help in defining such relationship. The one, which has
received the most emphasis in Buber's teachings and which he has
shown to be most deeply embedded in Judaeo-Christian tradition,
envisions the relationship in terms of dialogic, or vocation and
response. The other, which Christian philosophy drew from Greek
rather than from Hebrew sources, is the concept of *imitatio dei*,
the imitation of God. A third idea of great historical importance,
expressed by the ancient Graeco-Jewish formula, "from Light, light,"
I omit, both because it plays no important part in Buber's thinking,

and also because it shows a greater readiness than the other two
concepts to connote and invite a mystical interpretation. Let us look
at the concept of imitation first, and then consider how it can be
drawn into the circle of dialogical thinking.

Ancient Greek attempts at envisioning the man-God relation (one
cannot here call it a relationship) are marked generally by a dispassionate coolness. Aristotle observes that it would be very odd if
anyone were to say he loved Zeus. Well, it would probably have
seemed even odder to an ancient Greek if anyone had suggested that
Zeus might have bothered to love so puny a thing as man. Love of
God, to the Greek, is not love of Zeus but love of the Good, and it is
unilateral. It will be recalled that Plato compares God, or absolute
Good, to the sun, the source of all light, too brilliant to be looked at
directly, but yet clearly knowable to the discerning mind which may
school itself to see the reflections and operations of absolute Good in
all things. Man comes to love the Good more and more adequately
as he discerns its specific manifestations more and more clearly and
is moved by them more and more deeply. But it would be utterly
paradoxical to a Greek to suppose that the Good might be concerned
with him in turn. It is true that Greek philosophy usually regards the
Good as having creative power, and that Plato speaks of it as a
"cause" (*aitia*) of existence as well as of our visual perception of what
exists. But Plato did not think, nor did Aristotle, of the Good (or the
"Something" discussed as the divine ultimate in Book Lambda of the
Metaphysics) as creating the world out of love for the objects of its
creation, but solely as being what It is, and therefore as being loved—
i.e., as being That to which finite beings essentially aspire. The
philosophical God of Plato and Aristotle is the ultimate Final Cause,
eliciting creativity and growth from all things because they all, with
different degrees of adequacy, love It. Thus it is, according to Greek
philosophy, that imitation (*mimesis*) in the primal sense takes place.
One imitates through love, as the *Symposium* declares; but the love
is all on the part of the aspirant, and no trace of active love is ever
supposed to be in the object of one's imitation.

The power and, for many readers, the jolting originality of
Abraham Heschel's *Die Prophetie*[14] results from the sharp contradiction in which his view, and the traditional Jewish view as he

14 Abraham J. Heschel, *Die Prophetie* (Cracow, 1936) ; cf. *The Prophets* (Philadelphia, 1962).

presents it, stand against the classical notion which is likely to appeal to most philosophers today as the more "enlightened." To the modern mind it doubtless seems to show greater enlightenment when we think of God, or when we *think* we think of God, without emotional attributes, on the ground that these are "anthropomorphic"— as if the notion of God as lightning calculator of differential equations (which seems to have been the view of Sir James Jeans) were less anthropomorphic than the notion of God as loving and suffering! It is men who love and suffer, as it is men who formulate and solve mathematical problems, and if we ascribe any such traits to God we do so by analogy and indirection. When we reflect on experience as we actually know it, love and suffering appear to belong quite as fundamentally to existence as mathematical relations do, however vastly different in type. Now the shocking wisdom of Heschel's book consists in the reminder of what should already have been obvious to any unbiassed reader of the Old Testament—namely that God as understood in the early Judaeo-Christian tradition is one who loves and suffers. In particular the God of Israel is one who loves Israel and who suffers whenever His people fall short of the high vocation which He tries constantly and deviously to communicate to them. Putting the same truth in different dress we may remark that the God to whom Jesus cries "Abba!" has the essential attributes of fatherhood, in that He can love and suffer because of and on behalf of His children. Thus the love of God in Judaeo-Christian teaching is a multilateral affair. God is not merely That which is loved; He is also, and more primarily, That which loves. And this difference in one's conception of God profoundly affects one's view of the nature of man.

Nevertheless, the attribution of active love to God does not invalidate the concept of imitation, although it involves an enrichment of its meaning. Buber, in fact, gives explicit attention to the concept in one essay which especially invites consideration.15 He observes that the concept involves a more abrupt paradox for Judaism than for Christianity. The doctrine of the Incarnation brings it about that Christian *imitatio* has reference not to God in His absoluteness but to God as embodied and particularized in a historical human individual. In this context the command to imitate, however for-

---

15 "Imitatio Dei," *Israel and the World*, pp. 66–84. The immediately following quotations are drawn from this essay.

midably difficult in practice, makes fairly plain sense. On the other hand Buber takes it to be the central paradox of Judaism that every worshiper is called upon to imitate, not an incarnation or avatar of God, but God in His stark absoluteness, "the invisible, incomprehensible, unformed, not-to-be-found." The difficulty is evident in the consideration that "one can only imitate that of which one has an idea, . . . but as soon as one forms an idea of God, it is no longer He whom one conceives; and an imitation founded on this conception would be no imitation of Him." How is the difficulty to be met? Two answers, I think, suggest themselves.

The first answer, and the one most plainly indicated by Buber in the essay I am now considering, is that imitation is an inexact way of saying that we perfect our souls "toward" God. Trying to "be like" God is utterly different from trying to be like some human person who is admired. To imitate another finite being is largely a matter of externals, in that it consists in imitating the other's observed or supposed characteristics. *Imitatio dei* is fundamentally different from this. What it means is bound up with the question of what is meant by the statement in Genesis that man is made "in God's image." For Buber interprets the imitation of God as equivalent to the unfolding of the image of God that is one's most essential self. Now no two selves are the same, and yet each of them is "in His image." Does not this paradox furnish the clue? God's infinitude consists in the fact that He, and He alone, can pour His nature into the most diverse individuals and yet thereby make each of them in His image. Does it not follow, then, that man imitates God through seeking to perfect the unique nature that God has stamped upon him? Thus to imitate God means, by this argument, to perfect our souls "toward" God; which means in turn that each one thereby "makes perfect *his* likeness to God, his *yehida*, his soul, his 'only one,' his uniqueness *as* God's image."[16]

A second answer to the Jewish paradox may also be possible; it is an answer which is implicit in a number of Buber's writings, although it cannot be referred to single quotations as easily as the foregoing. A sentence from the brief essay, "In the Midst of History," offers a starting-point. "In creating his creature," Buber there writes, "God, who is Omnipotence, gave it freedom of action, by virtue of which it

[16] *Ibid.*, p. 73.

can turn to or from Him, and act for or against Him."[17] Now God
and man are related not only as creator and creature, they are
related also in "a dialogue of action": do these statements represent
two facts or a single one? The answer has to be that they are
aspects of a single fact, and indeed of the one most basic fact, concerning the relation which is relationship between man and God. In
an older theological language, God not only creates man but also
sustains his existence at every moment, and such sustention can be
considered a continuous and ever-present creation. The ever-con-
tinuing presence of God reveals the meaning of creation; for at
every moment God implants His image in man and yet leaves man
free to accept or reject. It is but a shift from visual to auditory
symbols when we translate this metaphorical statement about God's
image into the language of dialogue, characterizing the relation between God and man as "a dialogue of action."

Thus it is that the concepts of imitation, dialogue, and creation,
which we began by distinguishing, prove to be essentially involved in
one another. If I now look briefly at the concept of creation in the
more usual sense, which is cosmological, or rather cosmogonic, it is
solely by way of confirming the inter-involvement. When we examine
the major myths of cosmic creation we find them to be elaborations
of certain similes by which man has repeatedly tried to draw upon
the familiar as an aid to somehow grasping and expressing the
transcendental. For instance, in the second Judaeo-Christian creation
story, narrated in the second chapter of Genesis, God moulds man
out of the dust of the earth, and afterwards He moulds Eve out of
Adam's rib. Clearly the human analogy here employed is that of the
craftsman. Another widespread creation myth, although it is absent
from the Judaeo-Christian tradition, is that of the primordial love-
coupling. The Jovian seed drops down in the form of rain to fertilize
Mother Earth; or, as in Hawaiian mythology, Father Sky and Mother
Earth had lain in mutual embrace from the beginning, and then
there came a time when Mother Earth was understandably pregnant,
which resulted in her giving birth to the ancestors of animals and
men. I mention these two cosmogonic myths by way of what I think
provides a significant and enlightening contrast. For Buber, too, has
drawn upon a certain aspect of human experience in order to form a
conception of original beginning. (Obviously there is no other way,

---

[17] "In the Midst of History," *Israel and the World*, p. 79.

in the last analysis, for such a conception to be arrived at.) Buber's analogy is a good deal more adequate than either of the two analogies just mentioned, for unlike them it draws upon the most central and distinguishing mark of human experience—the fact that man can respond, can become voluntarily participant in a dialogical situation. Now in any dialogical situation a person not only speaks but listens; he is not only an *I* in the presence of a *thou,* but where such presence is fully realized he thereby becomes a *thou,* recognizing that other *thou* to be an *I* in its (her, his) own right. To be sure, there is no creation in the absolute sense when man thus confronts his fellow-man, for obviously the fellow-man was already in existence before the dialogical situation began. Nevertheless, something further is born in each of the participants in any real dialogical situation; there is thus creation to a limited degree; and so the situation may serve as a model—inadequate, as all human models must be—for the aboriginal act of God. God created and creates by speaking the word (of which "Let there be light" and "Let us make man in our own image" serve as mythic approximations) and then by accepting the independent *I-hood* of what His word has brought into being ("And God saw that it was good," as the first chapter of Genesis remarks). Buber's philosophy of man thus carries over into the farthest reaches of theological speculation, including the unanswerable question of how the world began.

V. *Critical Reflections*

When any great germinal idea enters into the history of thought the right practical and the right critical attitude toward it are sometimes mutually divergent. Whatever ideas come forth to man with power and light demand to be realized in one's living experience and action while the power and the light remain strong. On the other hand, every idea has a history, which is to say a peak of influence, or perhaps a series of peaks, after which it declines. The decline comes about, when it does, not because the truth of the idea was merely specious, but because it was partial, and also because the language through which it was uttered at the time with seeming adequacy has begun to acquire other associations and thus has ceased to arouse the same vision that it once did. A parallel case suggests itself. In certain pieces of nineteenth century literature—of which Maloida von Meysenbug's glowing autobiography, *Memoiren einer Idealistin,* could stand as an apt example and reminder—the language and (as we like to say nowadays) the ideology of post-Kantian idealism testifies to the presence of a real operative force and guiding criterion. But who in our present era of sophistication can speak about "the Ideal" with the freedom, sincerity, and power that Von Meysenbug and many another were once able to do? What seemed profound and important to them and their contemporaries is now, if divorced from its historical and in some instances its autobiographical context, likely to appear as inflated verbiage. It is a critic's duty, even at moments of enthusiasm and acceptance, to note the sad truism that every particular philosophy, though it may come trailing clouds of glory, is marked by historical finitude.

This general reflection suggests the manner, it seems to me, in which we should both accept and critically judge Martin Buber's philosophical anthropology—which is to say, his contribution to man's understanding of man. I regard it as a contribution of high importance, and one that has signally enriched contemporary philosophy. On the other hand, without either blindness or ingratitude we may legitimately observe that other philosophies of man, quite differently oriented, may also claim some validity, in that they too express important although partial sets of truths about the human condition. Furthermore, our very enthusiasm for the dialogical approach may sometimes encourage self-delusion, unless it is tempered by critical restraints produced by other ways of looking at the matter. Let me begin by citing a passage from Buber's own writings where it may be that the danger of self-delusion in applying his principle is unwittingly revealed.

In the essay, "What Is Man?"[18] Buber speaks of the glances exchanged by two strangers meeting in the deadly crush of an air-raid shelter, or perhaps at a Mozart opera where each is responding to the beauty of the music and sees facial evidence that the other person is engaged in a like response. Buber supposes that there is a meeting here, real but momentary; i.e., that there is silent dialogue, although it disperses when the all-clear sounds or when the final curtain falls. Now of this I am sceptical. May not such an appearance of dialogue be illusory? Can a glance between strangers, if unconfirmed by other evidences, be a satisfactory indication that mutuality of response is really present? I presume I am not alone in having had the dis-

---

[18] *Between Man and Man*, p. 204.

illusioning experience of observing a student in a classroom who looks bright, attentive, and responsive, nodding in apparent understanding and agreement whenever the lecturer happens to catch his eye while making some point, and yet who is unable to show, either orally or in writing, that he has achieved any comprehension of what is being spoken about. His behavior, which initially suggested that an *I-thou* relationship was in the making, has turned out to be nothing more than a vague friendly desire to please, roughly on a level with a puppy's reaction to petting. By contrast one might reflect on the case of two collaborators in a scientific experiment. Their awareness of each other's existence has nothing to do with an interchange of glances, but is inferential, as an outcome of their shared activity. Each investigator makes certain observations of his own and verifies their objective truth by listening to what the fellow-investigator reports about *his* observations. By the very logic of their common inquiry each of them accepts and respects the independent existence and mentality of the other. Each listens to the other's speaking, therefore the relation between them is not a mere *I-it*. Yet granted that an *I-thou* relationship is not fully achieved in this situation, is it not at least somewhat fuller and more reliable than in the case of strangers exchanging momentary glances?

The foregoing consideration is by no means intended as refutative of Buber's theory of man. There are possibilities of misapplication in any theory whatever, and it is fair to remark that in attempting to realize the dialogical method we should be on guard against uncritically assuming it to be operative when the only clear fact is that we would like to have it so. However, from a philosophical standpoint there is something yet more to be said. Granted the indispensability of the dialogical method—or, epistemologically stated, of "between" as a category of the understanding wherever other selves are in question —still, should we go to the length that Buber does at the end of "What Is Man?" declaring that the dialogical situation "is not to be grasped on the basis of the ontic of personal existence, or of that of two personal existences, but of that which has its being between them and transcends both"?[19] Does not Buber here overstate his case? It is well to put into language as he does this "realm of the between"; which is "on the far side of the subjective, on this side of the objective,

---

[19] *Ibid.,* p. 204.

on the narrow ridge, where *I* and *thou* meet."[20] But do we not affirm rather than deny the two personal existences when we speak of what lies "between" them? Moreover, passing from the analytic to the practical standpoint, must we not admit, most of us at least, that we do not wish to live so predominantly in the realm of "between"? By rough analogy I may remark that there is a spiritual truth in Hinayana as well as a spiritual truth in Mahayana. Or, ignoring that high comparison, we may reflect that for each of us a central fact is that I live for a short time in the light and then sink back into darkness—a destiny that is given nightly rehearsal. To accept this fact as somehow basic to one's living and thinking is not to be an egoist, for one need not make the mistake of regarding it as the sole relevant fact. The possibility of responding to others and entering into the realm of "between" is also a basic fact, and indispensable to interpretation and conduct while life remains. My reservation with respect to Buber's philosophy is that it strikes me as overplaying the second basic fact at the expense of the first.

But after such qualifications have been duly made, one is still left with a sense of the grandeur of Buber's achievement. Although in a broad sense dialogic is as old as human conversation, and although philosophically (as Calogero's recent studies have emphasized) it was the mode of thought that distinguished Socrates from his predecessors and from most of his contemporaries; yet Buber has established the idea as an essential ingredient in the conception of man, and thus (to paraphrase Kant) he has laid, in one essential respect, the foundations for any future philosophical anthropology. The novelty and substantiality of his contribution can be judged from comparing it with earlier philosophical inquiries into the nature of man, such as those represented in Julián Marías' excellent anthology, *El Tema del Hombre*.[21] In those various discussions of the human situation collected by Marías, man is repeatedly and variously studied in relation to the natural world, in relation to God, and with regard to the connections between impulse and reason within himself. The aspect of man in relation to his fellow-beings, however, is never regarded as a legitimate part of the doctrine of man, but rather as an external corollary of it. The question of fellow-beings does not enter into

20 *Loc. cit.*

21 Julián Marías, *El Tema del Hombre* (Madrid, 1943; Buenos Aires, 1952) ; Guido Calogero, *Filosofia del Dialogo* (Milan, 1962) .

Aristotle's *De Anima*; it belongs to his ethical writings and his treatise on statecraft. Buber's great contribution has been to plant the notion of fellow-beings and the relationship that it involves at the very heart of his philosophical anthropology. Perhaps the next step in modern philosophy should be an attempt at fuller integration of the personal principle and the dia-personal—i.e., of the category of self-hood and the category of betweenness.

PHILIP WHEELWRIGHT

UNIVERSITY OF CALIFORNIA
RIVERSIDE

4

Nathan Rotenstreich

THE RIGHT AND THE LIMITATIONS OF BUBER'S DIALOGICAL THOUGHT

I. *Mutuality*

THE PHENOMENON of "dialogical life" is not only the constant theme in Buber's thought but also his main contribution to what might prima facie be called an ontology of human life. We have to consider in the first place the various details of his findings related to the fact and the character of dialogical life.

Let us begin our analysis by pointing out the fact that through the notion of dialogical life or dialogical form Buber aims at the assessment of the primacy of the relation within the human scope. In the course of his development Buber introduced several terms for the description of the phenomenon, such as, dialogue, essential relation, the "between." Though there is a slight shift in emphasis in these various terms, the main idea has been retained. Following his own description, we may say that the sphere of the interhuman is that of being vis-a-vis one to the other while the explication of this sphere is called the dialogical form (*'das Dialogische'*).[1] To be embedded in the vis-a-vis situation is to be embedded in mutuality or "entering into mutuality."[2] The very partners of a situation of mutuality, those usually described and termed as *I* and *Thou,* are established through the relation of mutuality: "I become through my relations with the *Thou;* as *I* become *I, I* say *Thou.*"[3] Though a possible interpretation of this statement might be that the whole comprising the inter-related human beings is more than its components, Buber actually wants to place the emphasis not just on the independence of the

---

[1] Martin Buber, "Elemente des Zwischenmenschlichen," *Die Schriften über das Dialogische Prinzip,* p. 262. (For a general exposition of Buber's philosophy see Maurice S. Friedman, *Martin Buber: The Life of Dialogue* (Harper Torchbooks 1960).

[2] "Education," *Between Man and Man,* p. 87.

[3] *I and Thou,* p. 11.

whole but on the independence of the relation between the components, as against the individual components. "Each, considered by
itself, is a mighty abstraction. The individual is a fact of existence
insofar as he steps into a living relation with other individuals . . .
the fundamental fact of human existence is man with man."[4] This
sphere of "between" is not simply given and established once and
forever. Though it is created time and again in the course of human
life, it is still not just an outcome of those creating it, because the
very creation of the mutual contact between human beings presupposes a kind of instinct toward this creation, an instinct inherent
in the human beings.

'Between' is not an auxiliary construction, but the real place and bearer of
what happens between men; it has received no specific attention because, in
distinction from the individual soul and its context, it does not exhibit a
smooth continuity, but is ever and again re-constituted in accordance with
men's meetings with one another.[5]

This double face of the sphere of "between," being as it were both real
and atmospheric, is the most characteristic feature of the interhuman
scope and therefore, because of the combination of the two aspects,
very difficult to be conceptually established, let alone analysed. Since
there is, at least in our age, a prevailing tendency towards an analysis
of wholes and relationships, an analysis which amounts to reductions,
the assessment of the independence of the sphere of "between" faces
difficulties connected with the bias of the prevailing systematic forms
of philosophical thought.[6] Since Buber himself uses in this context
the expression of "mysterium" he even admittedly enhances the
difficulty of a morphological, let alone conceptual, establishment of
the sphere of "between."

Yet the essential relationship between two human beings is,
speaking in cosmic terms, the new phenomenon introduced into the
cosmos by the appearance of man. From this point of view, Buber
talks about the primordial chance of being as it comes to appear
through and because of the fact that there are human beings.[7] It
might be proper to add at this juncture that sometimes Buber does

---

[4] "What Is Man?" *Between Man and Man*, p. 203.

[5] *Ibid.*

[6] "Elemente des Zwischenmenschlichen," p. 271.

[7] "Nachwort," *Die Schriften*, p. 287.

not confine his description and analysis to the human sphere proper as for instance when he says, describing the emergence of answer or response: "a dog has looked at you."[8] And yet his main concern is with the nature of relationship within the human sphere proper and the hints at what is beyond this sphere are only in nature or an expansion of his main findings about the character of the human sphere.

Actually, one of the main concrete expressions of the existence of the sphere of "between" is the phenomenon of answer: ". . . a word demanding an answer has happened to me."[9] It might be proper at this juncture to suggest that the fact that Buber takes advantage of the term "dialogue" is related to the experience of an answer as pointing to a dialogical situation, though Buber himself transcends, as we shall see, the sphere of linguistic expressions. Still, it might be said that the experience of being addressed and answering "a word and response"[10] is the focus of the sphere of "between" or, to put it differently, the living appearance of the living essence of the mutual "between." The living contract established in the situation of an address and response to it leads Buber to a further step: that of stressing the phenomenon of responsibility in its two senses—the one sense is that of responding to a call and the other is that of being supposed to respond. The second sense approaches responsibility as it has been discussed in the philosophic and juristic literature, that is to say, responsibility *qua* accountability. Yet because Buber places responsibility even in its second sense not in the narrow field of one's being supposed to account for deeds, omissions and so on, but being supposed to live up to the real and essential level of human life—that of responding to a fellow man—responsibility ceases to have a narrow meaning or a moralistic one, for that matter. He suggests that it is rooted in the fundamental features of human life and manifesting them. To put it differently, responsibility has a broad meaning because it is not put in an impersonal domain of one's acting, on the one hand, and as serving a standard idea of what one is supposed to perform in his actings, on the other; for example, in the case where one is supposed to be honest according to an idea of honesty. Responsibility is put in the realm of responding to an

---

[8] "Dialogue," *Between Man and Man,* p. 17.

[9] *Ibid.,* p. 10.

[10] *Ibid.,* "The Question to the Single One," p. 45.

independent human being or, in Buber's own words: "Responsibility presupposes one who addresses me primarily, that is, from a realm independent of myself, and to whom I am answerable."[11] The fact that Buber uses here the expression "answerable" points to what has been introduced above as a second sense of responsibility, that is to say, that I am supposed to act in a certain way according to what the essence of human life is, and this means according to mutuality focused in responsibility. Taking advantage of the modern idiom, we might say that Buber has to use here the "dispositional" expression in order to stress that one can demand from the human being that he behave in a certain way. Yet he formulates the dispositional aspect through his main idea, that it is in the essence of human beings to respond because responsibility is ultimately rooted in the nature of the human sphere.

It has been said that the dialogue is the focus of the sphere of "between." We may now add that responsibility is the focus of dialogue. As responsibility is rooted in the dialogue, the dialogue is rooted in the very essence of human life. Thus, unless I am wrong, this might be a possible interpretation: Buber strives for an ontological or anthropological warrant for the ethical aspect of responsibility. This is what he actually says: "The idea of responsibility is to be brought back from the province of specialised ethics, of an 'ought' that swings free in the air, into that of lived life. Genuine responsibility exists only where there is real responding."[12] This striving for the ontological warrant for ethics amounts actually to the attempt to ethicise the human sphere altogether. The scholastic idea of "ens et bonum convertuntur" is realized within the human sphere.

It is because of this inherent ethical aspect of the sphere of "between" that the human beings embedded in the relationship of mutuality are persons in the terminological sense of the word. Human beings are unities of their experiences and not only thinking things behind and beyond what they actually experience. This description taken from Scheler can be applied to what Buber says in spite of the differences in his view and that of Scheler: "The *I* of the primary word *I-Thou* makes its appearance as person and becomes conscious of itself as subjectivity."[13] We may suggest an interpretation of this

11 *Ibid.*
12 *Ibid.*, "Dialogue," p. 16.
13 *I and Thou*, p. 62.

by saying that the unity of experience is established only in the actual meeting with a fellow human being, because the unity of experience is established in experience itself, and this is a living actuality only in the sphere of "between." Hence to be a person or a personality is not to be a unity outside experience but precisely within it. Hence the status and character of personality itself is established in the sphere of human mutuality.

Buber himself does not talk the language of the ontological warrant for the ethics of mutuality; yet this idea is implied in various expressions present in his writings which aim at establishing the primacy of mutuality. For instance: "In the beginning is relation— as category of being, readiness, grasping form, mould for the soul, it is the *a priori* of relation, the *inborn Thou*."[14] There is no point in discussing the contamination of two philosophical traditions expressed in the synonymous use of inborn and a priori as we find it in the above quotation. But it has to be stressed that Buber, while searching for a foundation for making mutuality the essence of human existence, takes refuge in epistemological terms like a priori or inborn. What he actually wants to present is the idea that mutual relations between human beings are an irreducible fact or a sphere *sui generis*. He expresses this by saying that "The inborn *Thou* is realised in the lived relations with that which meets it. The fact that this *Thou* can be known as what is over against the child . . . is based on the *a priori* of relation."[15] To be sure, this statement carries with itself some difficulty because of the duality hidden in it: there is the *inborn Thou* and there is the *Thou* as realized. Is there really a duality in Buber's morphology of human existence? Buber wants to escape duality because the actual facts encountered in the human scope are those of mutuality. Mutuality is irreducible, incapable of being analysed in its components. Yet if once it is said that the *Thou* is inborn it is saliently said that the mutuality can be dismembered, that is to say, there is an *I* with his inborn *Thou* on the one hand and the *Thou* on the other, and there is the realization of that relation within the actual sphere of human existence. This hidden duality is but an outcome of Buber's drive to base mutuality on a fundamental datum, sometimes assuming that mutuality itself is this fundamental datum and sometimes rooting it in the inborn

14 *Ibid.*, p. 27.
15 *Ibid.*

capacities of the individual human being. Yet it might be said in spite of this shadowy duality, that the main idea is that in the beginning there is relation and that relation cannot be explained even by an a priori or inborn *Thou*. Even in a later stage of his thought, Buber uses the term "*innate* (italics mine) capacity in man to confirm his fellow man."[16] The oscillation between the primacy of relation and the innateness of the approach to the fellow man has some bearing on philosophical problems implied in Buber's thought; but these have to be dealt with separately in what follows.

A slightly different way of putting the primacy of the relationship with the fellow man is indicated by the employment of the term instinct in this context: "what teaches us the saying of Thou is not the originative instinct but the instinct for communion."[17] Here again one may argue that Buber introduces a term in order to provide justification for the reality of the mutual relationship to human beings as an ultimate fact. The status of an ultimate fact is expressed through the term instinct, but still one may doubt whether the instinct of communion as it is introduced here gives an adequate account of what Buber himself tries to convey. It is not just a given fact or inherited instinct of human nature to communicate or to be in communion. Such an explanation connotes in a way a very subjective approach, that of rooting the factual and even overt reality of human life in an instinctive urge of human beings. If relation is the primary sphere, even the individual human being is created in and through relation. Hence the instinct for communion cannot be independent of the actual communion as a primary fact. If the employment of terms *a priori* and *inborn* was in a way a tribute paid to the epistemological vogue, the introduction of the term "instinct" is in a way a tribute paid to the psychological trend. This can be clearly seen from the following statement:

This instinct is something greater than the believers in the 'libido' realize: it is a longing for the world to become present to us as a person, which goes out to us as we to it, which chooses and recognizes us as we do it, which is confirmed in us as we in it.[18]

The idea of longing conveys again a kind of subjective urge and might be a trace of some romanticism; it might be doubtful whether

16 "Distance and Relation," p. 102.

17 "Education," *Between Man and Man*, p. 88.

18 *Ibid.*

it represents the findings of Buber's own phenomenology of human existence. This can be seen clearly from the fact that Buber wants to show that the sphere of "between" overcomes subjectivity, as he himself puts it: "A transfusion has taken place after which a mere elaboration of subjectivity is never again possible or tolerable to him."[19] As long as we use terms like "longing," we retain the subjective touch. As Buber wants to overcome subjectivity, precisely through mutuality, one may wonder whether traces of a subjective terminology do give an adequate account of what he tries to convey.

Now, surveying the advantages of the primacy of mutuality, according to Buber, one may say that in the first place the dichotomy of collectivism and individualism is overcome, as in parallel fashion subjectivism was supposed to be overcome:

I am speaking of living actions, but it is vital knowledge alone which incites them. Its first step must be to smash the false alternative with which the thought of our epoch is shot through—that of 'individualism or collectivism.' Its first question must be about a genuine third alternative.[20] Individualism sees man only in relation to himself, but collectivism does not see man at all, it sees only 'society.' With the former man's face is distorted, with the latter it is masked.[21]

The third alternative is obviously, according to Buber, that of "between" where man is not related to himself only and still not submerged in an anonymous society. Further still: ". . . as there is a *Thou* so there is a *We*."[22] "Only men who are capable of truly saying *Thou* to one another can truly say *We* with one another."[23] "Marx did not take up into his concept of society the real relation between the really different *I* and *Thou*."[24] It is because of this distinction that in the most recent presentations of Buber's thought he is careful to make the distinction between social life and the sphere of "between." Buber assumes that he transcends the already traditional sociological distinction between Society and Community. The real alternative would not be that between Society and Commu-

---

[19] *Ibid.*
[20] *Ibid.*, "What Is Man?" p. 202.
[21] *Ibid.*, p. 200.
[22] *Ibid.*, p. 175.
[23] *Ibid.*, p. 176.
[24] *Ibid.*, p. 148.

nity but that between Society as the mutual aggregation of particular and isolated human beings and that of the *We,* thus presenting the plurality of human beings through the grammatical form of the first person plural. The point is that *We* is not primarily given as *I* and *Thou* in their mutual relation are. *We* is an outcome of the factual relationship. To be sure, what is traditionally called Community might be considered as a nearer realization of the reality of *We* than society is, but still they are not identical because *We* is ontologically closer to the proper realm of human existence, that of mutual relationship.

Another advantage of the primacy of the dialogical mutuality might be found in the ethical aspect of it, certainly related to the idea of responsibility dealt with before. "Trust, trust in the world, because this human being exists—that is the most inward achievement of the relation in education."[25] Though the notion of trust is introduced here in the context of education it seems to be proper to interpret it as the manifestation of mutuality in general and not only as that in the educational activity or sphere. Buber's is the ethics of trust, trust being in turn a manifestation of responsibility *qua* addressing and being addressed. This conveys an optimistic strain in Buber's thought which has some bearing upon the general trend of his outlook. But in this context it will suffice to say that because mutuality is a primary feature of human existence, displacement as an experience and reality can be looked at only as a deviation from fundamental facts. This being so, the ethical attitude of trust is but an active manifestation of the factual basis and nature of human life.

And ultimately there is an affinity between the phenomenological, ethical and religious view as Buber sees it. Criticising ethics as isolated from morphology of human existence, he says:

Religion, certainly, has this advantage over morality, that it is a phenomenon and not a postulate, and further, that it is able to include composure as well as determination. The reality of morality, the demand of the demander, has a place in religion, but the reality of religion, the unconditioned being of the demander has no place in morality.[26]

Because Buber relates responsibility to somebody calling for response, the ethic of responsibility is amplified by the notion or, in Buber's

[25] *Ibid.,* "Education," p. 98.
[26] *Ibid.,* "Dialogue," p. 18.

own view, by the reality of an ultimate demander, thus pointing to the idea of mutuality not only within the confined human realm but also, and perhaps in the first place, within the scope of the relationship between man and God. The logic of the argument seems to be this: since mutuality is actualized in responsibility and since responsibility presupposes two partners of the dialogue, there is a demand to transcend the human sphere in the confined sense of the word and reach a super-human personality as the partner of the dialogue, as the demander and the super-human *Thou.*

II. *The Quintessence of the Other*

It might be a possible suggestion that Buber's "philosophical intuition" lies in the specific relationship between the human being and God. In terms of a religious approach, Buber aims at establishing the double-faced relationship: the human being is not totally submerged in God and hence stands vis-a-vis God as an independent or semi-independent partner, while God is not just a feature of a subjective experience but is independent as well. This two-way relationship based on an independence of the two partners might be the driving motive for the general view of mutuality. Yet we encounter here, philosophically speaking, a kind of ambiguity while going outside the confined human scope toward the encounter between man and God. It has been shown in our previous discussion that the mutuality within the human sphere is a fundamental feature of that sphere and hence it has been suggested to look at it as the ontological basis of human life. This mutuality was clearly one within the human sphere. As against this, the mutuality of the relationship between the human being and God is asserted as well, and hence the question cannot be avoided as to the relationship between the two mutualities. Does Buber want to assert that besides the mutuality in the human sphere there is an independent mutuality between man and God, or does he want to establish the idea of mutuality in general, which finds its double realization within the confined human sphere on the one hand and within the meeting between man and God on the other? It has to be shown now that perhaps Buber himself has not said a definitive word on that issue.

In one of the versions of his view he says: "The extending lines of relations meet in the eternal Thou."[27] Now, this rendering might suggest the idea of projection from the human sphere toward the meeting with God. According to this suggestion the primary fact is the meeting between the two partners within the human scope and this meeting is extended outside the human scope through the approach of God in His position as the eternal *Thou*.[28] Yet on the other hand, Buber says that "in each *Thou* we address the eternal *Thou*" and from this point of view it has to be said that the eternal *Thou* is present, inherent or hidden within the human scope and the extension of the lines is rather in the nature of an explication of what is inherent or implicit and not a real extension in the sense of going outside a confined sphere. Further still, "the relation with man is the real simile of the relation with God."[29] This version, if interpreted, may suggest that the relation with God is the primary fact while the relation with man is but the expression or human manifestation of the primary relation with God. Still, there is a different rendering as well, when it is said that the same *Thou* encountered in the relation between man and man is that which comes down to us from God and steps up from us to God.[30] According to this version, the idea of *Thou* is the primary idea, as it has been hinted before, and it finds its twofold realization within the human sphere on the one hand and in experience of God on the other. The variety of renderings might be understood, and rightly so to some extent, as Buber's own struggle for the most adequate expression of his main intuition. And yet there is a philosophical problem implied in the variety of renderings: because Buber does not want to establish just the abstract notion of the *Thou* which can be differently realized as a Platonic *Thou*, as it were, appearing in various experiental phenomena, he has to point to that unity of the essence of the *Thou* and his reality which is a fundamental irreducible fact of human experience. And here his trend toward a unification of what he himself calls theological anthropology and philosophical anthropology faces its inherent difficulty. Buber is eager to maintain the metaphysical presupposition of the concrete man's bond with the ab-

27 *I and Thou*, p. 73.
28 *Ibid.*, p. 6.
29 *Ibid.*, p. 103.
30 "Nachwort," *op. cit.*, p. 299.

solute,[31] as he himself puts it, and still deal with human existence as it is experientially realized in the mutuality of "between." The trend toward unification of the two possible experiences leads him to the systematic oscillation between the two views: either to assert the semi-independence of the human sphere on the one hand and man's vis-a-vis God experience on the other, or to establish a synthesis of the two experiences. Maintaining the former view might ultimately lead him to a duality which amounts to a hesitation whether mutuality within the human sphere is actually a primary ontological fact as he wants programatically to assert. Maintaining the latter view might bring him close to the problem whether the relationship to God is an extension of the human sphere or the other way round, whether the human sphere is a confinement or a limited realization of the relationship with God.

It seems that the ontological problem facing Buber's view on this point is not dealt with sufficiently extensively and systematically to make possible a conclusion as to his main position. Possibly here again the shift toward experience permits him not to raise the ontological problem and to remain within the experiential encounter itself. Here is what he says:

All the enthusiasm of the philosophers for monologue, from Plato to Nietzsche, does not touch the simple experience of faith, that speaking with God is something *toto genere*, different from 'speaking with oneself'; whereas, remarkably, it is not something *toto genere* different from speaking with another human being.[32]

The ontological problem as to which of the meetings is the primary one, whether that between human beings or that between man and God, is left, as it were, aside, while the similarity of the experiences in the two fields is brought to the fore. Yet even here, granting for the sake of this discussion, that there is a possibility of dealing separately with the experiental aspect outside the ontological one, the question has to be raised whether this similarity can be really maintained. Even within the human sphere the problem of interpretation, the problem of whether or not we actually encounter a *Thou*, can be raised, as has been done in the various discussions of the epistemological question of the *Thou*. But if the problem of interpretation arises

[31] "What is Man?" *Between Man and Man*, p. 163.
[32] *Ibid.*, "The Question to the Single One," p. 50.

within this human sphere, it certainly arises within the sphere of the experience of God *qua* the Other, or the absoluteness of the Other, to use Buber's own words.[33] "Human life—Buber says—touches on absoluteness in virtue of its dialogical character."[34] Can this be said to be just a feature of human experience or intuition or is this precisely an interpretation of human experience, and perhaps an interpretation towards a total systematisation of it as is usually found in philosophical systems? If God is the absoluteness of the other, then the idea of otherness is introduced into the system either as an amplification of the encountered other within the human sphere or as an absolute warrant for the independent position of the other in this field. If a philosophical analogy might be permitted here, then the absolute otherness as a warrant for the independence of the other being, occupies a parallel position to that of "thing in itself" in Kant's view, at least one of the functions of which is to safeguard the reality of the appearances, or to ascertain their givenness vis-a-vis reason or intellect.

Again, we find in the idea of God as understood by Buber a combination of the two aspects characteristic of the otherness in the human sphere: independence, on the one hand, and relation, on the other, God being a reality independent of man and having a relation with him. Here there is a parallelism of structures between the human sphere where the fellow man is both independent and related and the sphere of the experience of God where God is both independent and related. But even here, assuming the parallelism of structures, the problem of primacy of either structure has to be raised precisely because of what Buber says about mutuality as a fundamental feature of human life.

In one point there seems to be a limit to the parallelism between the human sphere in the narrow sense of the word and that between man and God. Within the human sphere the deterioration of the relationship between *I* and *Thou* to that between *I* and *It* is possible, understandable, though not ontologically and ethically permitted. Yet within the sphere between man and God the introduction of the category, or as Buber puts it, primary word *I* and *It* is not justifiable at all. "If God is addressed as He or It, it is always allegorically. But if we say *Thou* to him, then mortal sense has set the unbroken truth

---

33 "Religion and the Modern Thinking," *Eclipse of God*, p. 90.
34 "What is Man?" *op. cit.*, p. 168.

of the world into a word."[35] It would be very difficult to say that
within the confined human sphere the status of *He* or *It* is but an
allegory. Yet this can be said within the sphere of the relation between
man and God. Since God is the otherness in its absoluteness, it cannot
be, ontologically speaking, reduced to the level of an *It*. From this
point of view a possible interpretation might be suggested: that the
position of God as the absolute other is not only a warrant for the
position of the fellowman as an independent and related other, but
is also the guiding idea of the otherness of the fellowman, or, put
differently, the ideal of otherness in the personalistic and ethical
sense of the word. But Buber would be very hesitant to accept this
interpretation because it sounds like an idealistic interpretation of
the otherness of God, being both an idea and an ideal. Yet the paradoxical thing about Buber's view of God is that he touches very
closely on an idealistic position and one may encounter here a gap
between his "philosophical intuition" on the one hand and its exposition on the other. One can agree that the objective of Buber's
thought was to establish the unity of religious experience and anthropological philosophy and wonder whether this objective has been
attained.

III. *Groundwork of the Relationship*

The immanently religious trend of Buber's thought leaves us with
an oscillation as to the primacy of the sphere between man and God.
The later stage of Buber's thought expressed in his idea of distance
and relation leaves us with a doubt whether relationship within the
human sphere is actually as primary as it has been formulated in his
former and most known writings. To be sure, even in the later stage
of his thought, Buber uses expressions reminding us of the texture
of his basic views as, for instance, the expression "becoming a-self
with me."[36] And yet there is a kind of second thought inherent
in his later view as to the primacy of the relationship as an independent, self-contained form of human existence. The traces of a
revision or second thought of his view are indicated in the very fact
that he is talking now about the "primal setting at a distance" being

[35] *I and Thou*, p. 99.
[36] "Distance and Relation," *op. cit.*, p. 104.

"the presupposition of the other (entering into relation)." He continues, saying:

> that the first movement is the presupposition of the other is plain from the fact that one can enter into relation only with being which has been set at a distance, more precisely, has become an independent opposite. And it is only for man that an independent opposite exists.[37]

The notion of the independent opposite is retained from the previous writings of Buber as the fellowman, and God as well, is still viewed as independent opposite. But the new approach comes into relief in the fact that Buber seems to think now that the position of being an independent opposite is not originally given or encountered within the human context. The position of an independent opposite is established through a specific attitude, that of setting at distance. Now, formally speaking one may still argue that the setting at a distance is a sort of relation. But relation as it has been used by Buber was fundamentally a mutual relationship and its expression was a contact of responsibility. From this point of view, relationship had from the outset a humane and even an ethical connotation. But the relation of distance, to keep to the formal aspect, has a different feature because Buber explicitly transcends, as it were, the human situation asking now the question where the human situation is placed or where does the mutual relationship come into existence. This question is answered: "Distance provides the human situation, relation provides man becoming in that situation."[38] If one may introduce here the difference between framework and the picture within the framework, one may say that in his later stage Buber asks the question of the framework of the picture of human life. The picture itself is still that of mutuality but it has to be explained through its placement in the context of the universe, and for the sake of this placement Buber introduces the notion of setting at distance. But if this is the case, then mutuality within the human sphere is only a *prima facie* ontological primacy because ultimately it presupposes the setting of distance as the ontological presupposition of the sphere of relationship. The fact that Buber enlarges, in a way, the locus of the human situation is expressed in the fact that he now uses the expression—following biological distinctions—that a world

37 *Ibid.*, p. 97.
38 *Ibid.*, p. 100.

exists as an independent opposite through the setting of distance.[39] Mutuality of human relations is thus placed in the world. This being so, the world ceases to be a neutral, impersonal fact to be understood according to the category of *It*. If the world set through the distance is the presupposition for mutual relationship, we are actually going beyond the former rigid distinction between the primary words *I* and *Thou* on the one hand and *I* and *It* on the other. The world is not just an *It* and the relationship between *I* and *Thou* is not merely primarily given. The world has a human meaning, being the presupposition of relations because the setting of it is a presupposition of relations.

Moreover, while introducing the idea of setting at a distance, Buber actually presupposes the fundamental position of reflection even for the sake of mutuality of the human relations. To set at a distance is to maintain a reflective attitude, as Buber himself says: "it is only the realm which is removed, lifted out from sheer presence, withdrawn from the operation of needs and wants, set at a distance. . . ."[40] All these expressions point to a reflective attitude because to be removed from needs and wants and so on is to maintain a kind of sovereignty toward the basic situation and this sovereignty can be maintained only through reflection. Clearly, when Buber talks about setting a distance he is not talking in spatial terms but in terms of release, the latter being a kind of freedom, maintained through the position of a spectator. But the position of a spectator is that of a reflective attitude. If this interpretation is correct, then in his later stage Buber actually becomes aware of the fact that the experiential view, as he maintained in his main writings, is again not independent and self-contained but is rooted in a reflective attitude. The experiential attitude of Buber's is, in a way, broken already in terms of the religious trend of his thought. There the direction was toward a combination of an idea within an ideal, as has been stated before. Now the experiential texture of his thought is broken not because of the religious trend but because of his anthropological trend, that is to say, because of the fact that he asks himself the question as to the presupposition for mutuality, thus questioning the primacy of mutuality if not from the point of view of the genesis of our experience, then from the point of view of its ontological and

---

[39] *Ibid.,* pp. 98f.
[40] *Ibid.*

ιogical foundations. The reflective attitude creeps up and thus Buber, perhaps unconsciously, touches upon the question of the transition from the reflective attitude to mutuality of relationship, the question dealt with in Hegel's chapter on the master and the slave. Here we find one of the most important critical points of Buber's thought which has to be picked up later on in our analysis. In the meantime the inner development of Buber's thought itself had to be stressed.

IV. *Background and Motives*

In his analysis and discussions, Buber usually omits historical references and is not very aware of the position of his trend of thinking within an historical-philosophical context. Yet in our analysis of the structure of his thought we cannot omit, to some extent, an attempt at placing it in the philosophical situation, mainly in order to throw some light on the meaning and trend of his thinking. Let us begin with some individual philosophers.

Among philosophers referred to in Buber's writings, perhaps the most-quoted is Feuerbach. Though Buber criticises Feuerbach on two points—because of putting the human relation between *I* and *Thou* in the place of God and because of what he calls the postulative trend in Feuerbach's thinking[41] he is aware of his relationship and indebtedness to Feuerbach. The main point seems to be that expressed by Feuerbach, about man in his relation with his fellowman, and perhaps also a further point not stressed by Buber—that even in one's thinking, that is to say in one's position as a philosopher, one remains a concrete human being—a man with man.[42] Yet it seems to some extent doubtful whether Buber is correct in stressing his relation to Feuerbach, and this not because of the postulative character of Feuerbach's thinking (Does Buber's thinking lack postulates?) and not even because of the anti-theological character of Feuerbach's thought, but because of the main metaphysical position. The difference between Buber and Feuerbach can perhaps best be put this way: Buber attempts to be *concrete* while Feuerbach identifies concreteness with *sensuality;* as Feuerbach himself puts it: the secret of immediate knowledge is sensuality.[43] The main point in Feuerbach's

41 "Nachwort," *op. cit.,* pp. 288, 289, 305.

42 L. Feuerbach, *Philosophie der Zukunft,* para. 60.

43 *Ibid.,* para. 38.

philosophy seems to be the shift from philosophical distinctions, including that of subject and object, to what he considers to be sensual distinctions, the main one of them being that between *I* and *Thou*. Hence the frontal attack of Feuerbach is against the philosophy of identity which nullifies, according to his view, the immediate distinctions; this is not unlike Buber's attack against doctrines and philosophies which do not put in the centre of their systems the relation between concrete human beings. We may sum up this point of difference by saying that Feuerbach puts into relief the relation between *I* and *Thou* because he objects to idealism while Buber puts into relief this relation because he is interested, in the first place and even mainly, in the scope of human relations. Hence Feuerbach's is a comprehensive system of thought whilst Buber deliberately presents variations on one theme—that of *I* and *Thou*—and does not intend to create a system.

Buber said once that in spite of the difference between the trend of his thought and Kant's philosophy there is an affinity between them.[44] He sees the difference in the fact that Kant deals with the human being as with an end in itself, that is to say that Kant confines his outlook to the ethical position. We have seen before that Buber is critical of any abstract ethical position though his own view is certainly to a very large extent coloured by ethical considerations; yet he seems to think that he provides a foundation for the ethical view: since the human being is in the first place embedded in a dialogical situation he is bound to be considered as an end and not a means. But precisely here one may doubt whether the suggested philosophical foundation for the position of an end is sufficient, as Buber is inclined to think. According to Kant, the position of man as an end is grounded in the very relationship between the human being and the ethical sphere, that is to say in the very fact that the human being is a rational one and hence responds to the imperative. Actually Buber cannot avoid the idea of the rationality of man, as we shall see in a later part of our discussion, though he presents this idea through its realization within the human scope, that is to say, within the texture of the relation between *I* and *Thou*.[45]

---

44 "Elemente des Zwischenmenschlichen," *op. cit.*, p. 276.

45 Buber himself does not refer to Fichte. His affinity to some friends in Fichte's doctrines has been brought up in H. Bergmann, "Begriff und Wirklichkeit, Ein Beitrag zur Philosophie, Martin Buber and J. G. Fichte," *Der Jude* (Berlin, 1928).

In his later writings, Buber stresses his affinity to Hermann Cohen, saying that only the discovery of the *Thou* leads oneself to the consciousness of his self. At this point he sees the close affinity between the trend of his analysis and that presented by Hermann Cohen in his later period.[46] Yet one may doubt whether this affinity really exists, because Hermann Cohen has not said that the meaning of the relationship between *I* and *Thou* is primary, immediate and given. On the contrary, Hermann Cohen, even in his later period, remains in what can be called the objective trend, stressing that though *I* and *Thou* are given in experience and from this point of view are natural data, their religious value depends upon their being lifted up to the moral sphere. Actually, even in his later writings there is a kind of deduction in Cohen's view of the moral and religious position of the *Thou*, though there is no deduction of the givenness itself. This can be shown by the fact that Cohen stresses so much in his later writings the importance and guiding principle of pain and poverty for the position of the *Thou*. Pain is the bridge between *I* and *Thou* and the concrete manifestation of pain is poverty or, as Cohen has it, poverty is the optical means for putting into relief the human being as a *Thou* and thus as a natural object of man's love.[47] Buber does not stress either the importance or any specific embodiment of the encounter between two human beings in order to perform, as it were, a philosophical deduction, though not in a logical or transcendental field, of the position of the *Thou*. Buber is certainly more immediate, more experiential and even intuitive, as we shall see, than Cohen was even in his later writings. To sum up this point: one may say that as with Feuerbach, so with Cohen, the trend of Buber's presentations is different though here and there he meets some renderings or focuses of previous philosophers. Yet, as is well-known, in a philosophical discussion not only renderings and results shape the picture but also the ways of reasoning, and it seems that these are different with Buber if compared with that of the philosophers he explicitly mentions.

If one may point to the philosophical tradition where Buber's thinking is rooted, one has to mention some kind of "Lebensphilos-

[46] "Nachwort," *op. cit.*, p. 290.

[47] See Hermann Cohen, *Der Begriff der Religion im System der Philosophie* (Giessen, 1915), p. 79. With Hermann Cohen's approach I dealt at length in the second volume of my book (in Hebrew), *Jewish Thought in Modern Times* (Tel-Aviv, 1950), pp. 54ff.

ophie,"—though not in the technical sense of the term—and some
kind of intuitionism and here again not in the technical sense of the
word. In order to show how Buber belongs to the general atmosphere
of "Lebensphilosophie" it might be sufficient to point to one quotation, and this is taken from one of his main writings: "Lived life is
tested and fulfilled in the stream alone."[48] This short saying may
throw light on Buber's intention to remain, as it were, in the stream
of life and to give a philosophical account of the experiences of
human life from within, that is to say, from the position of life itself.
This being his intention, one will not be surprised to find a kind of
scepticism, not only toward philosophical systems, but toward the
philosophical attitude in general. Here is what he says against the
system: "I wanted to express that I did not rest on the broad upland
of a system that includes a series of sure statements about the absolute,
but on a narrow rocky ridge between the gulfs where there is no
sureness of expressible knowledge but the certainty of meeting what
remains undisclosed."[49] This is still a sceptical or reserved expression
against the philosophical system though, as is known, utterances
against systems were common in the philosophical tradition of
"Lebensphilosophie." But what is more important is that speaking
about philosophising and philosophy, Buber stresses strongly that
these are primarily acts of abstraction.[50] This is not only a descriptive
statement; it is a statement connoting a criticism of an abstract attitude because of its character of removing us from the stream of life.
Because of criticising the attitude of abstraction, Buber says: "Here
you do not attain to knowledge by remaining on the shore and
watching the foaming waves, you must make the venture and cast
yourself in . . . in this way, and in no other, do you reach anthropological insight."[51] What is called here anthropological insight
is opposed to abstraction; anthropological insight is grasping the
stream of life from within. Yet it is only proper to mention here
that the same argument against remaining on the shores and watching
as an outside spectator is an argument of philosophy of intuition
which presents intuition as participation in the stream of life, while
conceptual knowledge is viewed as an expression of a position of an

[48] "The Question to the Single One," *op. cit.,* p. 12.
[49] *Ibid.,* "What is Man?" p. 184.
[50] "Religion and Philosophy," *Eclipse of God,* p. 53.
[51] "What is Man?" *op. cit.,* p. 124.

outsider removed from concrete life or stream. Hence, it might be correct to assume that Buber is very strongly connected to the intuitionist trend and more so than he himself is aware.

To be sure, Buber deals explicitly and, in a way, critically with Bergson's interpretation of intuition because Bergson does not stress, as Buber has it, the special position of the *Thou* as a primary reality. He says that, without acknowledging the primary reality of the *Thou*, intuition is merely patchwork. Buber stresses the importance of this notion of the primacy of the reality of the *Thou* because he rightly sees the danger of intuitionism, that is to say, that in an act of intuition, one may get submerged in the moment of intuition without reaching the true reality of the intuited object which is beyond the moment of presence, i.e., the moment where intuition is performed. He says rightly that the tension between the image of a personality we are directing ourselves to and the personality as it appears in the moment of presence contributes greatly to the dynamics of inter-human relations. For this reason Buber criticises intuitionism as it is presented by Bergson.[52] If one may be allowed to put the difference in a systematic way one might say that Buber shares the intuitionist view as to the non-cognitive or non-conceptual attitude that exists between two human beings in establishing their relationship. Yet he criticises intuitionism because of the "cognitive atomism" that threatens intuitionism, that is to say, that every act of intuition might be unrelated to the former act or to the subsequent act. Secondly, he criticises it because of the lack of clear realism in at least some of the intuitionist views: the contact established in and through intuition may lead to the blurring of the independence both of the *I* and *Thou* while Buber is very strongly interested in stressing the independent, i.e., realistic position of both partners in the dialogical situation. A word about Buber's realism will be said in what follows.

Yet, in spite of this difference between Buber's view and intuitionist philosophy, we have to point to the very many and different expressions to be found in his writings revealing the intuitionist character of his thinking. There is a vacillation in terminology, mainly round the word experience. For instance, in *I and Thou,* he places experience proper within the scope of the relation between

[52] On this—his Hebrew article "Bergson and Intuition," introducing the selection of Bergson's writings—*Spiritual Energy* (Tel-Aviv, 1944). Partially translated in "On Bergson's Concept of Intuition, *Pointing the Way,*" pp. 81–86.

I and *It,* stressing the difference between experience and relation.[53] Yet in a different context he speaks explicitly about one person experiencing another;[54] but this is a minor terminological issue—there are several other renderings which do not leave us in any doubt as to their intuitionist connotations. Let us mention several of these terms and renderings.

One of them is *"personale Vergegenwaertigung."*[55] This kind of "personal making present" is but a summing-up of various descriptions present in Buber's writings, pointing to an immediate knowledge of the *Thou.* "The world of *Thou* is not set in the context of either of these (i.e., space and time) ,"[56] and even stronger; "what does he now 'know' of the other? No more knowing is needed. For where unreserve has ruled, even wordlessly, between men, the word of dialogue has happened sacramentally."[57] Because the immediate nature of the approach to the fellowman is stressed, Buber even says: "Only when every means has collapsed does the meeting come about."[58] This direct relation to the *Thou* is called essential relation; this essential relation is described: "The two participate in one another's lives in very fact, not psychically but ontically."[59] Buber himself seems to avoid the term intuition but still he has some terms which strongly remind us of the usual descriptions of intuition, for instance, *participation,* speaking about "participation in the existence of living beings,"[60] or *inclusion,* speaking about "through inclusion of one another by human souls."[61] Here he even finds a difference between empathy and inclusion, and it might be not out of place to quote him on the difference as he sees it:

Empathy means, if anything, to glide with one's own feeling into the dynamic structure of an object . . . as it were, to trace it from within . . . it means to 'transpose' oneself over there and in there.

[53] *I and Thou,* p. 6.
[54] "Dialogue," *op. cit.,* p. 3.
[55] "Elemente," *op. cit.,* p. 270.
[56] *I and Thou,* p. 33.
[57] "Dialogue," *op. cit.,* p. 4.
[58] *I and Thou,* p. 12.
[59] "What is Man?" *op. cit.,* p. 170.
[60] *Ibid.,* pp. 193, 197–98.
[61] *Ibid.,* "Education," p. 101.

Thus it means the exclusion of one's own concreteness, the extinguishing of the actual situation of life, the absorption in pure aestheticism of the reality in which one participates. Inclusion is the opposite of this. It is extension of one's own concreteness, the fulfilment of the actual situation of life, the complete presence of the reality in which one participates. Its elements are, first, a relation, of no matter what kind, between two persons, second, an event experienced by them in common, in which at least one of them actively participates, and third, the fact that this one person, without forfeiting anything of the felt reality of his activity, at the same time lives through the common event from the standpoint of the other.[62]

The argument against empathy is similar to that pointed out before in our interpretation of the difference between what Buber suggests and what ordinary intuition does. Empathy for Buber is not realistic enough because it tends to blur the independent position of the two human beings meeting each other in a dialogical situation. What Buber intends to stress is that the meeting takes place against the background of the distinction between the two human beings and therefore he points to the danger inherent in empathy as an exclusion of one man for the sake of his partner. Stressing this danger of exclusion, he introduces his own term *inclusion*. Still the term inclusion, like similar terms introduced by Buber, intends to stress the immediate relation between the two human beings: "Opinions were gone, in a bodily way the factual took place."[63] Because of the stress laid on the immediacy of the awareness, Buber, like intuitionists, speaks of knowing with one's whole being: "The primary word *I-Thou* can only be spoken with the whole being. The primary word *I-It* can never be spoken with the whole being."[64]

In a different context Buber introduces the term "real imagining" ("Realphantasie"),[65] which again calls for a stress laid on the first part of the term "real" and yet transcends knowledge in the discursive sense of the word.

The stress laid on the intuitionist trend of Buber's thinking—in spite of all due reservations—leads us to an historical observation. Buber is here close to his teacher, that is to say to Dilthey. When in a later writing Buber talks about the penetration into a human being

---

[62] *Ibid.*, p. 97.
[63] *Ibid.*, "Dialogue," p. 6.
[64] *I and Thou*, p. 3.
[65] "Elemente," *op. cit.*, p. 272. "Elements of the Interhuman."

he speaks about perceiving the wholeness of the human being through perception of his dynamic centre and being aware of all the manifestations of this human being in his attitude and in deeds.[66] This penetration to the centre of the human beings brings us near to what Dilthey called the structural context of the life of the soul or the awareness of the living context of action. To be aware of the living context, of the structural context of the soul calls for a specific cognitive medium, that of insight or "Verstehen" according to Dilthey's view. To put the relationship between Buber and Dilthey in a formula, one may say:[67] Buber materializes the situation which calls for "Verstehen," the relation of mutuality between human beings is not only a situation of "Verstehen" because it is not only a cognitive situation, cognitive though supra-conceptual; it is a living situation where the cognitive approach called participation, inclusion, etc., is submerged or embedded. What has been the front of Dilthey's attack, that is to say, a causal or descriptive attitude toward psychic life, is again materialized in Buber in the "primary word of *I* and *It*" which calls for a different cognitive attitude than that of the primary word *I* and *Thou*. Thus Buber intends, historically speaking, to provide an ontology of human relations which will make "Verstehen" not only permissible but necessary and exclusively adequate.

With the intuitionist strain in Buber's thinking, a realistic approach is tied up. He expresses his realism in two ways: in the ordinary sense of it while speaking about the mutual communication of human beings as they really are.[68] In this sense he is anxious to state that the immediate approach between human beings carries with it the knowing and awareness of them without the epistemological distinctions between appearance and reality, thus penetrating, as it were, the walls of mediation and discursive thinking. From this point of view it can be said that Buber tries, through the device of the philosophy of the dialogical situation, to overcome the solipsistic predicament. He presents the idea that the human being is primarily interwoven in the situation of meeting his fellow-man, and this meeting is not opaquely given, but at the same time, also understood. Thus the ontological situation of the dialogue is *ipso facto* an

---

[66] *Ibid.*, p. 270.

[67] See Wilhelm Dilthey, *Werke*, 5 (1924), 206.

[68] ... mitteilen als das was sie sind. "Elemente," *op. cit.*, p. 266.

epistemological situation of mutual knowledge and adequate knowledge in that matter.

Yet the realistic strain has another meaning as well, realism amounting to every-day life and every-day knowledge. As Buber himself puts it: "I possess nothing but the every-day out of which I am never taken."[69] And sometimes, criticising modern trends in philosophy, he says that "the man of modern philosophy who pretends to think in a reality and not in pure ideation, does he think in reality?"[70] The fact that Buber appeals to everyday life as an authority for knowledge and as a field which has to be accounted for in a philosophical analysis is, of course, not detached from the intuitionist trend analysed before. It only gives another emphasis to the intuitionist trend or, to put it differently, Buber, like Franz Rosenzweig, appeals to everyday knowledge as against ideation, though unlike Franz Rosenzweig he does not appeal to common-sense but to what he calls "everyday." Yet this might only be a slight terminological difference. He, like Franz Rosenzweig, seems to think that what is everyday, or common sense for that matter, carries with itself an unambiguous meaning and thus has only to be stated and as such does not call for, or even preclude, philosophic interpretation.

Proceeding in our analysis of the motives of Buber's thinking, we have to deal now not with epistemological motives but with what might be rather looked at as an optimistic trend in Buber's thought. By optimism is meant here Buber's philosophical intuition that in the last resort man is not lonely in the universe. Hence Buber's view can be coined not only as a dialogical view but as a dialogical cosmism. Let us deal with this trend in his thought in some detail:

In the first place, polemically speaking, this is one of the main points of criticism sounded by Buber against Kierkegaard. Here is what he says:

A God in whom only the parallel lines of single approaches intersect is more akin to that 'God of philosophers' than to the 'God of Abraham and Isaac and Jacob.' God wants us to come to him by means of the Reginas he has created and not by renunciation of them.[71]

The meeting between God and man, according to what might be

---

69 "Dialogue," *op. cit.*, p. 14.

70 *Ibid.*, p. 27.

71 *Ibid.*, "The Question to the Single One," p. 52.

stated as a positive conclusion from this polemic observation, is performed in the togetherness of human beings and not in their lonely or solitary position. Buber even says very strongly here that God wants us to affirm the living creatures we are interwoven with and not to renounce them.[72] According to Buber, the immediate meeting of a single human being with God would amount to an a-cosmism, that is to say to an annihilation of the creation as it has been granted by God. The affirmation of God seems to lead him to the conclusion that we are called to affirm the human beings we are living with and this affirmation is decisively and, even primarily, expressed in a dialogical situation. It seems to me that the motive of cosmic optimism is further developed in Buber's writings.[73]

"An education based only on the training of the instinct of origination would prepare a new human solitariness which would be the most painful of all."[74] What Buber is afraid of here is to leave the human being in his solitariness, which amounts to the fear of the infinite space, to quote Pascal. In his anthropological writings Buber sees the connection between anthropological awareness and solitariness, the former being the ontological and philosophical expression of the existential situation embodied in the latter. He explicitly wants to combine anthropological awareness with the habitation in the universe or with what he calls a "new house in the universe,"[75] and he seems to think that the philosophy of the dialogical situation is the adequate solution of the problem he posed for himself, that is to say, for the problem of assessing the specific human situation and still allowing for its being rooted to the universe. The dialogical situation is, as it were, the microcosmos of habitation within the cosmos in its totality. It mediates between the individual human life and the cosmos at large, or to put it differently, it overcomes from the very beginning the loneliness of the human being.

To be sure, Buber is aware of what might be an alternative view; the view of Spinozistic or Hegelian philosophy, that is to say, of asserting a link between the human being and the universe through the medium of thinking. Yet against the Hegelian view he says: "The

[72] "Nachwort," *op. cit.*, p. 289.

[73] Incidentally, here we find the explanation of Buber's rejection of mysticism because mysticism amounts, in his view, to a cosmism.

[74] "Education," *op. cit.*, p. 87.

[75] *Ibid.*, "What is Man?" p. 137.

Hegelian house of the universe is admired, explained and imitated, but it proves uninhabitable. Thought confirms it and the word glorifies it, but the real man does not set foot in it."[76] This criticism of Hegel is very close, of course, to the criticism expressed by Franz Rosenzweig, but this is not our point here. What has to be stressed is that Buber seems to think that to be related to the universe in a positive and affirmative sense is to live in it in the simple sense of the word, and to live in a situation is to live with other human beings. Thus he seems to think that a cosmic attachment can be provided in and through the medium of the situation of *I* and *Thou* and not through the medium of speculative thinking as expressed, for example, by Spinoza and Hegel. To put it differently: Buber sees the inner connection between what he calls cosmic and social homelessness.[77] He seems to think that the overcoming through dialogue of the social homelessness, that is to say, of what is the nearest homelessness to the concrete human being, leads, *ipso facto,* to the overcoming of the cosmic homelessness or, vice versa, the overcoming of the cosmic homelessness in the dialogical situation between man and God leads to the overcoming of the social homelessness in the dialogical situation between man and man. Here we encounter the optimism inherent in Buber's thought because the very fact that Buber thinks that the same device can overcome both social homelessness and cosmic homelessness is an indication of his optimism. Or to put it differently: Buber thinks that the overcoming of the homelessness of the modern man is inherent in the primary human situation and thus homelessness is but a deviation from the primary situation which has been forgotten or abandoned and has to be re-instituted. Buber's optimism is clearly rooted in his idea that the primary human situation is also the normative principle and guide for what human life ought to be. The problematic situation of modern man or the sickness of time, as he puts it, is an indication of a melancholic development inherent in the fact of our alienation from the basic and normative human situation.

One of the roots of Buber's thinking is to be found in his criticism of the contemporary situation, of our "times of sickness."[78] He himself tells us that in the period of the first world war or, as he calls it

---

[76] *Ibid.,* p. 140.

[77] *Ibid.,* p. 200.

[78] *I and Thou*, p. 53.

the period of the volcanic hour, he had the urge to do justice to existence by thinking.[79] Thus, for instance, he sees in the separation
between spirit and instincts, the separation found, according to his
interpretation, both in Freud's psychology and Scheler's anthropology, only an indication of the more fundamental separation, that
between man and man, man and God, or man and the cosmos.[80] Or,
to take another instance, he considers Heidegger's philosophy to be
based on the isolation of one realm of man from the wholeness of
life.[81] Briefly, the contemporary spiritual situation seems to be that
of the abolition of the dialogical forms in its narrower human and in
its broad religious sense. The analysis of the contemporary situation
is, on the one hand, performed by means of the dialogical philosophy
and is, on the other hand, one of the driving forces for the formulation
of the dialogical philosophy. The question is whether or not Buber
really puts his finger on the fundamental features of the human situation. This will be the object of some of our critical observations.

V. *Ontology or a Postulate*

Starting a critical examination of some of Buber's ideas, it has to
be said in the first place: it is not our task to deal with the factual
importance of the relation between man and man. Our problem is to
elucidate the ontological position of this fact in terms set by Buber
himself, that is to say, that he is enquiring into the basic stratum of
human existence. Even when one does not question the importance
of human mutuality on the factual level, one may doubt whether
the factual level is self-contained, metaphysically independent, or to
put it differently, that it reveals the most fundamental level of
human existence. It might be proper to express some doubts about
this taking-for-granted of identity between the factual importance
and ontological relevance.

In the first place, it has to be said that Buber identifies from the
outset reality with either the reality of the relation between *I* and
Thou and or with the reality of the relationship between *I* and *It*.
He deals with reality as realized in the two material fields of the

79 "Nachwort," p. 290.
80 "What is Man?" *op. cit.,* p. 198.
81 *Ibid.,* p. 168.

relation of the *I* with the *Thou* and the relation of the *I* with the *It*. As he himself puts it: "*Real* existence, that is real man in his relation to his being, is comprehensible only in connection with the nature of the being to which he stands in relation."[82] Yet as a matter of principle there is a distinction between the concept of reality and reality as it is materialised in this or that field. We have to retain this duality and not to assume in the first place that the concept of reality, divorced from its realization in a material field, is but an abtraction; this is tacitly, at least, assumed by Buber. To be sure, Buber shares here the realistic and even existentialistic bias because of his very tendency to give an account from within or to assume that there is no way and no justification for a dealing with reality other than that of pointing to a specific field understood as reality, as he says, for example, in his discussions about the reality of the external world. But here a very simple philosophical consideration cannot be avoided: in order to identify as reality any field of material data, like that of the external world or of mutuality between *I* and *Thou*, one has to use the concept of reality; the concept as such is not given with and in the field of the material data. Hence, the concept of reality is broader than that of a material realization of it, be it the external world or the setting between *I* and *Thou*. In order to know about the reality of *I* and *Thou* we have to know more than about this reality.

Mutatis mutandis, the same can be applied to the concept of relationship, granting the existence and relevance of the relationship between *I* and *Thou*. Can it be assumed as self-evident that relationship is automatically realized either in the sphere of *I* and *Thou* or in the sphere of *I* and *It*? It seems to be correct to say that in order to identify this or that field as a field of relationship, we have to presuppose the concept of relationship and read it into a field of concrete realization of relationship. We can not just decipher it as this or that field inherent in it, that is to say, ultimately, extract it from reality.

This might sound like a scholastic-epistemological consideration rather in a Kantian line; but this is not the purpose of this observation. The purpose is to show Buber's own oscillation with regard to the reflective attitude. It is our purpose to show that Buber himself is not clear on the status of reflection within the human scope: Whether

---

[82] *Ibid.,* p. 165.

reflection itself is but an extraction from the primacy of mutuality or whether mutuality presupposes reflection. It has been shown in a previous stage of our analysis that Buber, in one of his later writings, decides for a reflective attitude as a pre-supposition for relationships. But even in his former writings we may find some kernels of the later development though not a clear conclusion as to this very decisive point.

We have to show that in a very fundamental question Buber holds a two-fold view: he assumes on the one hand that "through the *Thou* a man becomes *I*"[83] or, as he says differently; "the *I* emerges as a single element out of the primal experiences, out of the vital primal words *I—affecting—Thou* and *Thou—affecting—I*, only after they have been split."[84] According to this view, there is a primary wholeness of *I* in his relation to the *Thou* and vice versa and the particular *I* is but an outcome of an isolation from the comprising wholeness. It has to be asked here immediately, what kind of isolation is here performed and by what means is it performed? Is it an isolation like the falling apart of one piece of stone from the conglomerate sand, that is to say, an isolation in space? Or is it a self-realization of the *I* through his awareness, that is to say, reflection, that he is different from the *Thou*, from the whole of the relationship, that is to say he is a self because of the inner centre of his existence rooted in his reflection? But Buber, while holding the view of the primacy of the relationship versus the independence of the *I*, does not seem to share the notion of the basic importance of the reflective attitude as a condition of the self-awareness of the *I* as an independent entity. Here is what he says:

> ... man's essential life is not to be grasped from what unrolls in the individuals inner life, nor from the consciousness of one's own self, which Scheler takes to be the decisive difference between man and beast, but from the distinctiveness of his relations to things and to living beings.[85]

But precisely at this point it has to be asked whether the distinctiveness of the fields of relations can be assumed without pointing to the status of the consciousness of one's own self, and this for a decisive reason: if we do not grant the status of consciousness of one's

[83] *I and Thou*, p. 28.
[84] *Ibid.*, p. 22.
[85] "What is Man?" *op. cit.*, p. 199.

own self we are facing the riddle how could a human being realize that it is he as a human being who maintains relations to things and to living beings and is not just submerged but amounts to a two-fold attitude of detachment and attachment and to a simultaneity of the two aspects of the two-fold attitude. Now, how is it possible to be both detached and attached without the consciousness of oneself as a constitutive feature in the total situation, as Buber himself later recognized in his idea of setting a distance as an outcome of a reflective attitude? What Buber himself says in a metaphoric way, hardly contributes to a conceptual elucidation of his objective: "Life is not lived by my playing the enigmatic game on a board by myself, but by my being placed in the presence of a being with whom I have agreed on no rules for the game and with whom no rules can be agreed on."[86] One may wonder whether this is the real dichotomy —being placed on the board by myself or being placed in the presence of another fellowman. This is not a dichotomy, because the position of being placed in the presence of another being does not abolish the position of myself. It is myself who is placed in a certain position and, as self, one has ultimately to call for one's own consciousness as a basic foundation for one's awareness as "myself." Further still, there is no real dichotomy between being placed in the presence of another human being and playing the game according to rules. Granting that rules are secondary because they are confined or because they do not exhaust the total field of relationships, there is still a fundamental difference of roles, that between *I* and *Thou*, and this division is not an outcome of a rule of games but just a manifestation of the self-consciousness of each of the two human beings who is focussing the relationship on himself by virtue of his self-consciousness.

Hence one may doubt whether Buber is doing justice to Heidegger's view and this can be said even if one holds a critical attitude toward Heidegger's philosophy. Buber says about Heidegger:

. . . the anthropological question, which the man who has become solitary discovers ever afresh, the question about the essence of man and about his relation to the being that is, has been replaced by another question, the one which Heidegger calls the fundamental-ontological question, about human existence in its relation to its *own* being.[87]

[86] *Ibid.*, p. 166.
[87] *Ibid.*, p. 167.

The critical question has to be posed again whether this is a real dichotomy: the relation to one's own being and the relation to the fellowman. The two relations can be considered as lying on two different levels. Heidegger's ontological question refers to the position of self-consciousness; hence Heidegger talks about the ontological sphere as different from the ontic sphere. Yet Buber identifies the question related to one's own being with solitariness as if the two were identical. The basic stratum of self-consciousness does not make human beings solitary; it only points to the centre and focus of all his relations including his relation to the fellowman or to the world in general. Without the presupposition of self-consciousness, all relations would split up or dissolve in atomic moments of relations and would not create the continuum of human relations. To be sure, Buber himself is aware of the fact that human relations, as he describes them, are difficult to grasp because they might be atomic, exhausting themselves in the present flowing and disappearing acts of relationship. Though this impressionistic trend is implied in Buber's view, he still tends to the idea of a perpetual creation of the field of human relations. Yet there is no other condition for a perpetual creation than the fact that human relations have their centre in the self-consciousness of the partners involved in them.

Our point until now was to show that Buber assumes the primacy of relations over the independence status of the *I*, but precisely on this point he holds the contrary view as well. Let us support our contention with a few quotations from his writings: "Certainly in order to be able to go out to the other you must have the starting place, you must have been, you must be with yourself."[88] And he even makes a distinction between the psychological primacy of the relation with the *Thou* and the status of the *I* as an independent being. What Buber says is: "It is true that the child says *Thou* before it learns to say *I*, but on the height of personal existence one must truly be able to say *I* in order to know the mystery of the *Thou* in its whole truth."[89] Though there is no explication of the mystery in this context, one might guess that the mystery of the *Thou* is not unrelated to the existence of the *Thou* as an independent human being and thus centred in his own consciousness. What Buber calls here "height of personal existence" in distinction to the psychological

[88] *Ibid.*, "Dialogue," p. 21.
[89] *Ibid.*, "What is Man?" p. 175.

process of the development of one's own consciousness, points to the distinction which has to be made between the psychological and factual level and the ontological and logical roots and conditions of human existence. Buber's own oscillation between the two views, i.e., the primacy of the relationship on the one hand and the primacy of the *I* on the other, reflects his own hidden oscillation between a factual description of human life and the intended ontology of it.

But even factually one may wonder whether Buber's account of the emergence of the consciousness of the *I* within the setting of the relation with the *Thou* is fully adequate. Let us quote an outcome of a psychological or psychopathological examination:

The need for nature was strongly anchored in her. After the walk (and the following imposed rest) she usually occupied herself more readily and in a better way. It even made her more sociable, while curiously enough, forced contact with people caused her to withdraw within herself. Apparently the pleasure found in nature gave her narcissistic strength. . . .[90]

Now it can be argued that the above quotation points to forced contact with people. But it seems that the main question is whether the real background and reservoir of forces for the emergence of a stable *I* is to be found within the scope of the mutuality between human beings or whether it has to be grounded in the relationship between man and nature or man and the universe, as A. D. Gordon perhaps assumed. To be sure, this is a psychological-factual consideration, but since Buber certainly draws from psychological-factual insight, the psychological question might be considered as not being out of place in the context of our discussion.

Let us now make a further critical observation, not unrelated to the former one; it has to be asked whether the outcome of Buber's thinking is a philosophical description of the human situation or rather an establishment of postulates and imperatives of what human life has to be. Buber certainly cannot avoid the postulative bias, though as has been mentioned before, he criticises Feuerbach slightly for his postulative attitude. Buber says:

We should not live towards another thinker of whom we wish to know nothing beyond his thinking but, even if the other is a thinker, towards his bodily

90 Margaret A. Sechenhaye, *Symbolic Realization* (New York, 1951), p. 113.

life over and above his thinking—rather towards his person, to which, to be sure, the activity of thinking also belongs.[91]

This is certainly, even stylistically, a postulate. Yet in this context a broader issue arises: we may grant that the fulfilment of human existence is to be found in the mutuality of human relations, though this fulfilment, as any other, is certainly not without intrinsic problems. Let us suppose that the mutuality of human relations is a kind of *entelecheia* of the human features; but it still does not follow from this view that fundamentally the human being has to be defined as a creature of mutuality. There is no contradiction—as seems to be supposed by Buber—between one's relation to himself in terms of a reflective attitude and one's realization in terms of the mutuality of human relations.

It has been said before that human relations, if not rooted in the focus of self-consciousness, may become atomic, momentary and even ephemeral. Only by virtue of their grounding in reflection or self-consciousness do we step beyond the factuality of the flow of changing relations. Buber is very anxious not to root the level of relations in a realm which might overstep them, neither in self-consciousness on the one hand nor in any specific content on the other. Even the relationship with God does not overstep the confined scope of relationships proper in order to establish something which is substantive, being a content of relations and not just the dynamics of relationship. Though Buber talks about dialogue and dialogical situations, actually the dialogue as a dynamic occurrence in the plane of linguistic expressions is but a metaphoric description for Buber: "Real faith . . . begins when the dictionary is put down, when you are down with it."[92] It is not by chance that Buber stresses the overcoming of the linguistic expression because in a linguistic expression there is something that refers to a reservoir of contents which is actually conveyed. The doctrine of dialogical mutuality as propagated by Buber is not based in the notion of a substance or a content which is conveyed in the dialogical meeting. The very dialogical meeting is, as it were, its own content according to Buber, as he himself puts it: "Consider man with man, and you see human life, dynamic, twofold, the giver and the receiver, he who does and he who endures."[93] In this

[91] "Dialogue," *op. cit.*, p. 28.

[92] *Ibid.*, p. 12.

[93] *Ibid.*, "What is Man?' p. 205.

dialogical situation there is a giver and a receiver, but there is nothing which is given or received as a realm of content, because the very situation is considered to be self-contained or, as Buber has it, "the Eros of dialogue has a simplicity of fullness."[94] This seems to be a very decisive point: it can be clearly understood why Buber tries to avoid the world of the substantive content; he seems to think that the assumption of a realm of content would amount to an introduction of what is a screen between the two human beings meeting each other and thus would abolish the immediacy of their meeting and living together. Hence he says: "Spirit is not the *I*, but between *I* and *Thou*, Man lives in the spirit, if he is able to respond to his *Thou*."[95] But here again one may doubt whether this is a real dichotomy; either spirit inherent in the *I* or spirit inherent in the relation between *I* and *Thou*. The assumption that we are referring to some principles, like that of the truth or of the good, leads us to a transcendence of both the *I* and the *I* and *Thou*. But Buber is anxious to avoid precisely this transcending of the scope of relations for a third realm of contents. "Man receives and he receives not a specific content but a Presence, a Presence as power"[96] or, in a different context, "Divine Presence, for this Presence's becoming dialogically perceivable."[97] This statement is greatly relevant for Buber's religious thinking because actually there is no revelation in Buber which expresses itself in content but only in the givenness of the Presence or in the meeting with the Presence without the medium of a content and without the crystallization in a content. But leaving aside the religious aspect of his thinking, one may wonder whether there is any human situation or any situation at all which is self-contained in the dynamics of active relations without being included in a framework of content or without having as its constitutive factor a kernel on content, as Buber seems to think. And this is so not only because neither ideas nor interpretations can be avoided but precisely because in a dialogical situation one acknowledges a human being in his position as a human being and this acknowledgement itself is not immediately given or evidently imposed upon us; this acknowledgement presupposes the idea of human existence

94 *Ibid.*, "Dialogue," p. 29.
95 *I and Thou*, p. 39.
96 *Ibid.*, p. 110.
97 "God and the Spirit of Man," *op. cit.*, p. 163.

or the notion of man as man, this notion being only partially realized in the partners meeting each other. To put it differently: the notion of man as man is bound to accompany any meeting between human beings, if this meeting carries with itself the acknowledgement of oneself and one's fellow as concrete human beings. In analogy to what has been said before, it can be now said: as the identification of a field of reality presupposes the idea of reality, so the identification of a dialogical situation presupposes the idea of man as a content, hence as a third realm.

In a way, Buber deals with this problem when he says: "Appeal to a 'world of ideas' as a third factor above this opposition will not do away with its essential twofold nature."[98] But the purpose of our critical observations is not to do away with any justified twofold nature but only to point out that the scope of relations is not self-contained but refers to a factor which is not in itself in the nature of relations, like principles, ideas, etc. Precisely this conception is criticised by Buber when he says:

The fictitious responsibility in face of reason, of an idea, a nature, an institution, of all manner of illustrious ghosts, all that in itself is not a person and hence cannot really, like father and mother, prince and master, husband and friend, like God, make you answerable.[99]

Paraphrasing Hegel's saying, one might say: the realm of reason, ideas, etc. is considered to be fictitious, not because of its own intrinsic nature but because one considers it to be so. Only an assumption that human existence exhausts itself in personal relations can lead to a view that what transcends personal relations is actually fictitious. But here too one may question the dichotomy; either personal relations or fictions. There is a reality in reason and we are answerable to it, though reason is not a personal factor, being a principle or the level for awareness of principles. We are answerable to the principle of truth, though the principle of truth is not like father and mother and even not like God. We are answerable to the principle of truth or to reason because, on the one hand, reason is a pre-condition even for relations and on the other, the dynamics of relations are not unguided. They are, or at least may be, restrained, shaped, channelized and the tension between dynamics and their

[98] *I and Thou,* p. 13.
[99] "The Question to the Single One," *op. cit.,* p. 45.

guidance refers to the relation between our spontaneous activities and the principles we are answerable to.

The abolition of a third realm, be it that of concepts like reality, relation or spirit and principles, leads Buber to a metaphysical impressionism. This can be shown at least in one point: "The present arises only in virtue of the fact that the *Thou* becomes present."[100] If this statement might be interpreted without distorting it, one might say that Buber acknowledges in the span of time presence only; the presence in the temporal sense of the word is but an expression of the presence in the existential sense of the word, be it the presence of the human being or the presence of God, who does not convey any substantive content. Yet human existence, though flowing and actualizing itself in the present moment, is not just a collection of these moments but has some continuity in itself because human existence is delimited between reflection on the one hand and principles on the other. The fact that Buber is in a way oblivious of the two realms, that of reflection and that of spirit in the substantive sense of the word, is an outcome of the postulative nature of his thinking: he sees the remedy of the human predicament implied in the sickness of our time in the fulfillment of the relationship between *I* and *Thou*.[101] Because of the stress laid on the remedy of the sickness of time, he reaches a point where ontology is as a matter of fact replaced by imperatives.

[100] *I and Thou,* p. 12.

[101] See the present authors; *Spirit and Man* (The Hague, 1963).

NATHAN ROTENSTREICH

THE HEBREW UNIVERSITY
JERUSALEM, ISRAEL

5

Emmanuel Levinas

MARTIN BUBER AND THE THEORY
OF KNOWLEDGE*

I. *The Problem of Truth*

THE THEORY of knowledge is a theory of truth.[1] Like the Parmenides of Plato it poses the question: how can the absolute being manifest itself in truth? For to be known, it must manifest itself in the world where error is possible. How can a being, subject to error, touch the absolute being without impairing its absolute character? It is reasonable to suggest that the efforts of ancient Greek philosophy were largely devoted to this question of how to mediate between appearance and reality. For in a universe conceived as a single whole, the gap between the two had to be bridged; and it was assumed that the mind need only reflect on itself to discover the One from which it derived.

The problem of the subject-object relation which arises in modern discussions on theory of knowledge, is an extension of this preoccupation of antiquity with the problem of truth. But it is no longer assumed that the agent of knowledge occupies a distinctive position in the hierarchy of beings which constitute the universe. The individual existent who aspires to the truth is radically separated from being as such. But if the implications of this separation were made clear, we would have to ascribe the metaphysical source of his being to the individual himself. For the latter is posited on the basis of an inferiority which is not directed to anything *other*, i.e., the individual is fixed in a dimension where it has only itself as term. The individual is subsequently identified with the subject of knowledge or consciousness. Hence understanding is construed not as one of

*Trans. from the French original by Robert Rosthal.

1. Textual references are to the *Dialogisches Leben*, containing the collected philosophical works of Buber published up to 1947. The numbers in parentheses appearing in the text of this essay refer to the appropriate page of the *Dialogisches*; reference to the relevant work is omitted.

the many activities of mind or as the superior function of mind, but as its very nature, i.e., that which constitutes its existence as parted, as breaking out from himself. Thus for awareness or for the consciousness which accompanies our acts, nothing, in fact, is external. Every movement of mind, including that which relates it to an external reality such as the acts of affirming, negating, willing, and even acts such as sensation which indicate a dependence on an external reality, is construed as a *pensée* in the Cartesian sense of the term. The consciousness where finally the existence of those movements is acted—the knowledge included in it—is in the origin of all that comes from the exteriority. If one identifies the subject with consciousness, therefore, any event which occurs, including shock or injury which disrupts the continuity of consciousness, has its source in a subject of awareness which exists in and by itself, i.e.: is separated. Philosophy, to employ Husserl's term, is an egology. But if the phenomenology of Husserl which has contributed to the repudiation of the idealist notion of the subject, is an egology, i.e., rediscovers the universe within the subject which constitutes it, it is still an egology which has always interpreted the self in terms of a consciousness which conceptualizes reality.

Theory of knowledge, then, in the contemporary sense of the expression, acquires a peculiar significance for it leads us to *original being*. The subject has that function precisely because it is a subject of knowledge. Thus theory of knowledge is prior to all other types of philosophical inquiry not only as a propaedeutic of knowledge but also as a theory of the absolute. Understanding which is the very life and essence of being, implies a relationship to the object. The object is constituted by the subject as opposed to subject. But that opposition remains in the power of subject.

Both ontology and the theory of the subject-object relation have in common a notion of the truth as an expressible content, regardless of the particular structure of being revealed by that content. Hence the truth is expressible in words but the original function of truth on which such expression depends, is to signify an inner meaning, of a solitary mind, which appeals to no interlocutor. The monumental solidity of being hinges on this possibility of expressing the truth and of conceiving it as an achieved result although being has in fact been interpreted from the time of the Parmenides and Sophist of Plato, as a relation, or since Descartes, as thought, while the object in turn has been interpreted as the intelligible though irrepresentable object of the physico-mathematical sciences. One of the most interesting facets of Buber's thought consists in his attempt to show that the truth is not a content and that words cannot summarize it in any way; that it is more subjective, in a sense, than any other type of subjectivity; yet, as distinct from all purely idealist conceptions of the truth, it provides the only means of access to what is more objective than any other type of objectivity, i.e., to that which the subject can never possess since it is totally *other*. It is this aspect of Buber's philosophy which is closely related to certain main tendencies in contemporary philosophical thought.

II. *From the Object to Being*

For contemporary thought, the history of the theory of knowledge is synonymous with the history of the vanishing of the subject-object problem. The subject, closed upon himself, once the metaphysical source of both the self and the world, is held to be an abstraction. The consistency of the self is resolved into intentional relations as for Husserl, or into the being-in-the-world or *Miteinandersein* of Heidegger, or else it is identified with a continuous process of renovation, typified by Bergson's duration. The concrete reality is man already entering into relations with the world and already projected beyond the present moment of his existence. Such relations are incapable of being characterized as representation, for the theoretical representation would only tend to confirm the autonomy of the thinking subject. But to combat successfully this view of an autonomous subject, analysis must discover underlying the objective representation, the wholly different relations: man is *in* a situation before he takes his place, but this is not to say that this adherence* to being is reducible to a certain status in a hierarchically organized universe or to the performance of a specific function as part of a physical mechanism without any recourse to any truth. What must be insisted on is that a relation with the object is not identical with a relation to being, and objective knowledge, therefore, does not trace the original itinerary of truth. Objective knowledge is already bathed in a light which illuminates its way, and a light is required to see the light, for the philosopher as for the psalmist. It is in this sense, then, that we must reject the propaedeutic and ontological

*"Appartenance." Lit. "belonging" (trans. note).

privileges possessed by a theory of knowledge solely concerned with the way in which a subject may be said to know an object.

Our critique leads us, therefore, to a knowledge of being and to a theory about this knowledge. But the knowledge of being does not resemble an object-relation with the difference that it is concerned with an object of a greater density and impenetrability, so to speak, an object more vast than the object of scientific knowledge. The original meaning of truth as a communication with being consists in not being truth about anything. It consists in not being a discourse about being. Being is not a theme of discourse.† But in the original communication we have with being, the possibility of such discourse is revealed, and the context within which objective propositions may be meaningful is delimited. For Heidegger, revelation of the truth diffuses that light which is necessary to see the light, and one must first react to the light before one can speak *of* it. For Bergson, truth is synonymous with choice, invention, creation, and is not a mere reflection of being.[2] And Bergsonian intuition does not merely imply a union with being which extends beyond any purely external perception of being: Unity with being *is* invention and creation, i.e., truth is the essential act of being itself.

Thus knowledge for contemporary philosophy is directed beyond the object towards being but it does not seek being in the same way as it does the object. Our problem is to provide a positive description of this new orientation, of the search for a theory of more ultimate knowledge. The philosophy of Buber should be envisaged in this perspective.

III. *Experience and Meeting*

Consistent with contemporary views, the self, for Buber, is not a

---

† "Thematisation." An alternate translation might be "problematic" in Marcel's sense of the term (trans. note).

[2] Maurice Friedman's article, "Martin Buber's Theory of Knowledge," *Review of Metaphysics* (Dec., 1954), gives a penetrating analysis of the essential features of Buber's epistemology without, however, showing the narrow connection of the latter with current philosophical tendencies. Although the I-Thou relation may not be specifically stressed, the subject-object relation together with its supporting ontology has everywhere been abandoned. Further, we may remark that Bergson was not the theoretician of the It, as the author suggests. See the excellent bibliography which exhibits the extent of Buber's influence or suggests the theme of the I-Thou relation independently of that influence.

substance but a relation. It can only exist as an "I" addressing itself to a "Thou," or grasping an "It." But it is not to be construed as the same relation with two different terms. The relation itself, as for phenomenology, is related to each of these two terms in a different way.

The sphere of the It coincides with everything which the I comes into contact with in its objective and practical experience. Experience and practice are here associated (45) without consideration being given to the *non-objective* structure of practice which, it is now perceived, already anticipates the commitment of the self to being. For Buber, as for Bergson, the sphere of utilization implies the most superficial type of relation and is identifiable with the objective cognition of things. In effect, the sphere of the It is posited as the correlate of all our mental acts whether willed or felt, in so far as they are directed to an object. "I perceive something. I have a sensation of something. I conceptualize something for myself. I think of something. . . . All this and anything similar to it, constitutes the sphere of the *It*." (16) The It is described, in this connection, in the same terms as those used by Husserl to denote the intentional object. Thus in the measure that the I-Thou relation is distinguished from the I-It relation, the former designates what is not intentional but what for Buber is rather the condition of all intentional relations. Prior to Heidegger's, yet compatible with Bergson's views, Buber, then, pursues his inquiry into ontological structures anterior to those which characterize the objectifying intellect.

Human beings when we speak of them in the third person, "he," "she," "they," as well as my own private psychological states, belong to the sphere of the It. The I experiences these; but only explores their surface without committing its whole being (15-16), and its experiences do not extend beyond itself. (17) The It is neutral. The neuter gender suggests, moreover, that in the It, individuals do not enter into the type of unifying relation in which their otherness is distinctive, where they are, so to speak, other than the others. The individual is rather regarded as that which one may dispose of, what is significant only with respect to the actions of its physical being. Thus the actual purpose of all knowing, i.e., the effort to grasp what is independent of it, what is completely other, is not fulfilled in this case. Being is cast in the role, as the need may be, of an anonymous article of exchange, a funded past, or else is experienced in the actual moment of enjoyment, and cannot be properly interpreted as a real presence. (25)

The I-Thou relation consists in confronting a being external to oneself, i.e., one which is radically other, and to recognize it as such. This recognition of otherness, however, is not to be confused with the *idea* of otherness. To have an idea of something is appropriate to the I-It relation. What is important is not thinking *about* the other, even *as* an other, but of directly confronting it and of saying Thou to it. Hence a real access to the otherness of the other does not consist in a perception but in thou-saying, and this is at once an immediate contact and an appeal which does not posit an object, (30) but of which the object-relation is, in fact, a distortion. This does not mean that the Thou is some unknown sort of object but rather that the movement which relates the Thou is not like one that sets any theme of discourse. The being who is invoked in this relation is ineffable because the I speaks *to* him rather than *of* him and because in the latter case all contact in broken off with the Thou. To speak *to* him is to let him realize his own otherness. The I-Thou relation, therefore, escapes the gravitational field of the I-It in which the externalized object remains imprisoned.

The I-Thou relation is one in which the self is no longer a subject who always remains alone and is for this reason Relation *par excellence*, for it extends beyond the boundaries of the self (404-409) (although it is questionable what these boundaries mean for Buber, for he never described positively the isolation and the limitation of the I). The relation is the very essence of the I: whenever the I truly affirms itself, its affirmation is inconceivable without the presence of the Thou. (23, 40, passim) The Thou, as index of the dimension in which the I seeks (and therefore in a measure already finds) another being, the Thou as the indeterminate horizon of the encounter, is a priori or innate. (39) The I is the term of a relation which cannot be expressed in terms of thought, for the latter only acts to dissolve the relation. Furthermore, I, in the relation, rediscovers "its original community with the totality of being." (443-445) The allegiance of the primitive mind to the law of participation, according to Buber, testifies to the original nature of the relation and the primacy of the I-Thou to the I-It. (30-33)

The distinction between the experience of an object and a meeting in which one being confronts another—a difference which concerns the nature of the relation itself and not merely of its terms, and which implies consequences whose scope Feuerbach, the first to formulate the I-Thou relation, could not foresee; a concern to base human experience on the meeting—these are the fundamental contributions of Buber to theory of knowledge. It is of spiritual significance that this relation to being underlying all of our objective knowledge does not involve an impersonal, neutral unity—the *Sein des Seiendes* of Heidegger—but a *Seiendes* which is the being of the other, and hence implies a social communion considered as the primary act of being.

Finally, we may observe the phenomenological character of Buber's descriptions: they are all based on the concrete reality of perception and do not require any appeal to abstract principle for their justification; the non-theoretical modes of existence are themselves ascriptive of meaning and the ontological structures with which they are associated, are not separable from these.

IV. *The Ontology of the Interval, or the "Between"*

The Relation cannot be identified with a "subjective" event because the I does not represent the Thou but meets it. The meeting, moreover, is to be distinguished from the silent dialogue the mind has with itself (204-205); the I-Thou meeting does not take place in the subject but in the realm of being. (26-27) However, we must avoid an interpretation of the meeting as something objectively apprehended by the I, for the ontological realm is not a block universe but an occurrence. The interval between the I and Thou, the *Zwischen*, is the locus where being is being realized. (27)

The interval between the I and Thou cannot be conceived as a kind of stellar space existing independently of the two terms which it separates. For the dimension itself of the interval opens uniquely to the I and to the Thou which enter into each meeting, (458) and the utmost transcendence is bound to the utmost particularity of the terms. Buber has made an effort to do more than merely define a kind of being which may be distinguished from the being of nature or of things, as, for instance, the process of becoming is distinguished from the Eleatic being. The interval between the I and Thou is inseparable from the adventure in which the individual himself participates, yet is more objective than any other type of objectivity, precisely because of that personal adventure. The *Zwischen* is reconstituted in each fresh meeting and is therefore always novel in the same sense as are the moments of Bergsonian duration.

If the notion of "betweenness" functions as the fundamental category of being, however, man is the locus where the act of being is being acted. (455) Man must not be construed as a subject constituting reality but rather as the articulation itself of the meeting. The personality is for Buber not merely a being among other beings, but is a category, in Kant's sense of the term, and it is Nietzsche who has compelled our acceptance of this. (387) Man does not meet, he is the meeting. He is something that *distances* itself and in this distancing the anonymous existence of the world of things affirms itself by the various uses we make of it, and in that distancing we can also enter into relations with this alien world.[3] By this double movement, Man is situated at the center of being and philosophy is identifiable with anthropology. But he is not at the center in so far as he is a thinking subject, but with respect to his whole being, since only a total commitment can be the realization of his fundamental situation. That situation underlies his thought and already implies a transcendence. "Only when we try to understand the human person in his whole situation, in the possibilities of his relation to all that is not himself, do we understand man." "Man can become whole not by virtue of a relation to himself but only by virtue of a relation to another self."[4]

Man, construed as the possibility of both distancing and relatedness, is not a subject confronting the natural world nor is he a part of the latter. To affirm that the I-Thou relation is not psychological but ontological, does not mean that it is a natural relation. The interval in which the act of being is being acted and which the individual at once creates and bridges, compels us to abandon the notion of a being-content, an already actualized being, or a being as theme of discourse. It is the abandoning of this notion which is the principal feature of present-day ontology.

V. *Communication and Inclusion*

What is the structure of this encounter which is both a knowing relation and an ontological event?

The I-Thou relation is a relation of true knowledge because it

---

[3] Cf. "Distance and Relation."

[4] "What is Man?" *Between Man and Man*, pp. 168, 181.

preserves the integrity of the otherness of the Thou instead of relegating the Thou to the anonymity of the It. It should be observed
that the act whereby the I withdraws and thus distances itself from
the Thou or "lets it be," in Heidegger's terms, is the same act
which renders a union with it possible. In effect, there is no union
worthy of the name except in the presence of this sort of otherness:
union, *Verbundenheit,* is a manifestation of otherness. (44) The
presence of the Thou, of the other, *ipso facto* implies a 'word'
which is addressed directly to me and which requires a response.
"Whoever refuses to reply, no longer perceives the 'word'." (196)
It is impossible to remain a spectator of the Thou, for the very
existence of the Thou depends on the 'word' it addresses to me.
And, it must be added, only a being who is responsible for another
being can enter into dialogue with it. Responsibility, in the ety-
mological sense of the term, not the mere exchange of words, is what
is meant by *dialogue,* and it is only in the former case that there is
meeting. The futility of remaining a spectator is not due to our tragic
participation in a situation which is not of our choice, to our derelic-
tion, but to the necessity of responding to the 'word.' There is a
transcendent reality to which I am somehow committed which "tells
me something," (143-144) nor is this phrase a metaphor, for it
expresses the very essence of language.

Truth, therefore, is not grasped by a dispassionate subject who is a
spectator of reality, but by a commitment in which the other remains
in his otherness. Although the Absolute could not be attained for the
philosophers of antiquity except by means of contemplative detachment, and *the impossibility of the latter is precisely what led to the
separation of being and truth in the Parmenides of Plato,* commitment, for Buber, is what gains access to otherness. For only what is
other can elicit an act of responsibility. (197) Buber attempts to
maintain the radical otherness of the Thou in the Thou relation:
The I does not construe the Thou as object, nor ecstatically identify
itself with the Thou, for the terms remain independent despite the
relation into which they enter. Thus the problem of truth raised by
the Parmenides is resolved in terms of a social or intersubjective
relation.

Commitment is a strictly personal relation. Truth does not consist
in a reflection on that commitment, but is the commitment itself. The
category of man, moreover, is each one of us (349) and not man in
general which is typical of the I-It relation. We may recognize this as

one of the prominent themes of the philosophy of existence, viz., the singularity of existence as forming the basis of knowledge, without, however, implying relativism. (328)

Unlike Bergson and certain themes of the philosophy of existence, however, it is not held here that, as opposed to the representation of being, knowledge by commitment coincides with being. In order to know pain, "the mind must cast itself into the depths of a felt pain," (436) instead of contemplating it as a spectacle; this is equally the case with "all the events of the soul, which resemble mystery rather than spectacle, and whose meaning remains hidden to whoever refuses to enter into the dance." But even for pain which has a privileged status and presupposes a coincidence with being, Buber requires a relation of a different kind which is dialogical in nature, a communication with the "pain in the world." (438)

The relations implied by responsibility, by the dialogue or the original relation with the being is reciprocal. The ultimate nature of dialogue is revealed in what Buber calls *Umfassung*, or inclusion, and which is one of the most original notions of his philosophy. In the I-Thou relation, the reciprocity is directly experienced and not merely known about: The I in its relation with the Thou is further related to itself by means of the Thou, i.e., it is related to the Thou as to someone who in turn relates itself to the I, as though it had come into delicate contact with himself through the skin of the Thou. It thus returns to itself by means of the Thou. This relation should be distinguished from the psychological phenomenon of *Einfühlung* where the subject puts itself completely in the other's place, thus forgetting itself. In the case of *Einfühlung*, then, the I forgets itself, and does not feel itself as a Thou of the Thou, whereas in the *Umfassung* the I sharply maintains its active reality. (280)

VI. *Truth*

Verbundenheit characterizes the reciprocity of the I-Thou relation and of the dialogue where I commit myself to the Thou just because it is absolutely other. The essence of the 'word' does not initially consist in its objective meaning or descriptive possibilities, but in the response that it elicits. The assertion is not true because the thought that it expresses corresponds to the thing or because it is revelatory of being. It is true only when it derives from the I-Thou relation identical with the ontological process itself. The assertion is true when it realizes the reciprocity of the relation by eliciting a response and singling out an individual who alone is capable of responding. This conception of the truth has nothing in common with the static notion of truth as an expressible content. But it is not to be assumed that a Heraclitian or Bergsonian becoming, also inexpressible because the word is necessarily a changeless entity and cannot apply to what is always changing, is the sole reality that may be opposed to immutable being. For Buber describes a sphere of being which cannot be told because it is a living dialogue between individuals who are not related as objective contents to one another: *one individual has nothing to say about the other.* The sensitivity of the I-Thou relation lies in its completely formal nature. To apprehend the other as a content is tantamount to relating oneself to him as an object and is to enter into an I-It relation instead.

The notion of truth (with respect to which Buber's language is insufficiently didactic) is determinated by the I-Thou relation construed as the fundamental relation to being. We must distinguish Truth possessed, Truth as an impersonal result, called also objective Truth (283) from the Truth as a "way of being," a manner of truly being which denotes God. But truth also signifies a "concrete attitude towards being," *"Realverhältnis zum Seienden"* (198-199) and the living test which verifies it (Bewährung). "To know signifies for the creature to fulfill a relation with being, for everyone in his own particular way, sincerely (wahrhaft) and with complete responsibility, accepting it on faith in all its various manifestations and therefore open to its real possibilities, integrating these experiences according to its own nature. It is only in this way that the living truth emerges and can be preserved." (283)

Citing Kierkegaard, Buber asserts that the particular is a verification when it "expresses what has been said (das Gesagte) by the personal existent;" thus truth does not consist in a correspondence with being, but is the correlate of a life authentically lived. Buber however, finds that a correction is necessary here: "I should have said," he writes, "that the particular verifies by expressing what has not been said (das Nicht-Gesagte) by the individual being." (201) Thus Buber wishes to remove from his conception of the truth any association with an assertion or objective content. The truth is wholly an attitude *towards,* an inquiry *into,* a struggle *for,* the truth, (213) i.e., the authenticity of a particular existence rather than an agreement between appearance and reality: "Eine menschliche

Wahrheit, die Wahrheit menschlicher Existenz." (297) The expression, "living truth," so frequently employed by Buber designates an existence which can be understood only: in terms of its authenticity and non-authenticity, rather than an existence directed by any "true idea."

However, within that sphere of responsibility which relates the I to the Thou, there is an "inquiry into the truth" which gives authenticity to the personality of the I, liberating it from the strictures imposed by an anonymous collectivity and from the activities of the unconscious whose instrument it would otherwise be. (251 ff.) The I-Thou relation becomes a personal commitment through its inquiry into the truth, which is not determined by the authenticity but determines it. From this point of view, the truth again seems to assume an intellectualistic physiognomy, and the I-Thou relation, without which the I can have no being, presents once again the spectre of a discarded subjectivity of philosophical idealism.

VII. *The Formal Nature of the Meeting*

The I-Thou relation is nothing but a realization of the meeting. The Thou has no qualities which the I aspires to have or know. The privileged examples of this relation are selected in "Dialogue" from beings who do not *know* one another in this sense of the term. (134) "Between the I and the Thou there is no conceptual structure, no prediction, fantasy, purpose, desire or anticipation. All intermediaries are obstacles. It is only when these vanish that the meeting occurs." (23-24) A content would imply mediation, and therefore would compromise the integrity and simplicity of the act. Buber denotes by the use of the term *Geschehen* (133) ("happening"), this transparent act of transcendence which is incapable of being described. Each encounter must be considered as a unique event, a momentary present which cannot be connected to other temporal instants in order to form a history or biography; each is a spark (234) like Bergson's moment of intuition or the "almost nothing" of his disciple Jankelevitch, where the relation of awareness to its content becomes progressively more attenuated and finally touches on the limit where consciousness no longer has a content but is a needle point penetrating being. The relation is a fulguration of moments without continuity, not a coherent connection of parts nor a final possession. (118; 232; 456-457) Perhaps this conception of being springs from Buber's

religious liberalism, from his religiosity as opposed to his religion, and is a reaction against the rigid, ossified forms of a
spiritual dogmatism, placing contact above content and the pure and
unqualified presence of God above all dogmas and rules. The question
remains however, whether Transcendence without any dogmatic content can receive a content from the dimension of height which Buber
does not take in consideration. As we shall see, the *ethical* aspects of
the I-Thou relation, so frequently evoked in Buber's descriptions are
not determinant, and the I-Thou relation is also possible with respect
to things.

Although Buber accords a privileged status to the purely intersubjective aspects of the I-Thou relation, the reciprocity of which
may be expressed in language, the meeting is also construed as a
relation with God as well as with things. For we can behave towards
God too, as if we were called (18), and the tree, too, instead of being
of use to me or dissolving into a series of phenomenal appearances,
can confront me in person, speak to me and elicit a response. For
Husserl, the presentational immediacy of the thing is merely one
mode of its representation; for Buber, the former alters its representational character and commits me; the thing in this case is not given,
for I am in a measure obligated by it, and the commitment is even
reciprocal. (20-28; 44, passim) The thing which is merely given and
which I can dominate belongs to the sphere of the It. But the
specific way in which the artist, for example, confronts the thing in
creating a work of art, may be construed as a response to an appeal,
and therefore, as a meeting.

In one of his later works, *Der Mensch und Sein Gebild,* Buber
indicates that the empirical world, offered up for our use, and for
the satisfaction of our needs, the world, in short, of the It, is itself
conditioned by the encounter and therefore by the intersubjective
I-Thou relation as well as the I-Thou relation which relates us to
God and to Nature. Thus even perception which lies at the source of
all human behavior (*Der Mensch und sein Gebild*), is not a purely
subjective reality. Perception is the response of man to a meeting
with the unknown object x of science what, inaccessible to representation, awaits Man. *(Ibid.)* Man's response is a formative vision
(Schau), a "formative fidelity dedicated to what is unknown and
which collaborates with the latter; the fidelity is not devoted to the
phenomenon but to the inaccessible being with whom we are in
communication." *(Ibid.)* Buber makes use of Gestalt psychology,

in this connection, but he does not revert to the conception of things as constituted out of sensations: for what is realized is done in the *Zwischen*, and the latter belongs to being, i.e., what is neither subject nor object. Buber has continued to affirm this dating from the *Ich und Du* (102): "The formation of the world and its vanishing are neither internal nor external to me; they have no being at all for they forever recreate themselves (Geschehen) and this creation depends on my own life." In *Der Mensch und sein Gebild*, Buber includes the meeting as a part of nature so that perception is exercised to the same purpose as other vital acts. "Man does not belong to the natural order solely by virtue of his (other) vital activities or in so far as he is responsible for his acts, but also as a perceiving being. My perceptions are acts in the natural order in which both the self and the object participate, without derogation from the spiritual nature of subjective existence." (*Der Mensch und sein Gebild*) Nature aspires to a state of totality, that is, to what is perceived." (*Ibid.*)

What these assertions are designed to show is that Nature is neither subjective appearance nor objective existence, for both are abstractions. The true notion of being is that of the meeting between beings who are abstractions when considered in themselves. If perception is the original act of being, then we may say that the empirical world is more "objective" than objectivity. Perception is the primordial act of being: the being is an act. However, it is typical of Buber's theory of knowledge that both the relation to things and the relation to man have something in common. Thus responsibility which we noted is at the basis of language, never assumes a strictly ethical import, for the response that the self makes to the unknown object *x* of perception, is construed by Buber, as an imperfect form of the I-Thou relation. (*Der Mensch und sein Gebild*) The intersubjective relation, on the other hand, with its ethical overtones based on the mediation or imitation of God (and a theology somewhat too well-informed on the nature of God) (214-215; 221), is only a special case of the encounter. Buber, of course, admits that the perceptual meeting is transcended by four other kinds of meeting: Knowledge, love, art and belief. But none of these can be logically inferred from the purely formal structure of the I-Thou relation. Thus the meeting preserves its formal nature apart. Does this imply a vacillation in Buber's thought? Dating from the publication of *Ich und Du*, Buber admitted that things too can enter into the I-Thou relation, yet it frequently seems that the relation between humans—as soon as the Thou has a human face—has a privileged status and even conditions all other relations: "everything else lives in its light." (20) Furthermore: "one can have confidence, confidence in the world because this man exists." (281) Consequently the light of the Thou—just as the intelligible sun in Plato, the idea of the Good, and the phosphorescence of the *Sein des Seienden* later on in Heidegger—would be the primal truth which is the source of all other truths.

VIII. *Some Objections*

How are we to preserve the specificity of the intersubjective I-Thou relation without ascribing a strictly ethical import to responsibility, and conversely, how ascribe an ethical meaning to the relation and still maintain the reciprocity on which Buber insists? Does not the ethical begin only at the point where the I becomes conscious of the Thou as beyond itself?

We shall direct our criticism mainly to the reciprocity of the I-Thou relation. Ethical themes frequently occur in the writings of Buber, but with respect to the I-Thou relation, a more formal structure involving distance and relatedness is underlying the I-It relation. But it is questionable whether the relation with the otherness of the Other which appears as a dialogue of question and answer can be described without emphazing paradoxically a difference of level between the I and the Thou. The originality of the relation lies in the fact that it is not known from the outside but only by the I which realizes the relation. The position of the I, therefore, is not interchangeable with that of the Thou. But how can we characterize this ipseity? For if the self becomes an I in saying Thou, as Buber asserts, my position as a self depends on that of my correlate and the relation is no longer any different from other relations: it is tantamount to a spectator speaking of the I and Thou in the third person. The formal meeting is a symmetrical relation and may therefore be read indifferently from either side. But in the case of ethical relations, where the Other is at the same time higher than I and yet poorer than I, the I is distinguished from the Thou not by the presence of specific attributes, but by the dimension of height, thus implying a break with Buber's formalism. The primacy of the other like his nakedness, does not qualify what is a purely formal relation to the other, *posterior* to the act of relating, but directly qualifies otherness itself. Otherness is thus qualified, but not by any attribute.

Thus the relation is more than an empty contact which may always be renewed and of which spiritual friendship is the apogee. (285) The reiteration of these "spirituel" themes (compensated for by a fruitful analysis of the connection between the I-Thou relation and the crowd which is opposed to the views of Kierkegaard and Heidegger, and a correction of earlier texts which relegated the third person plural, "they" to the sphere of the It), and the "spirituel" language employed by Buber, are limitations in a work which is otherwise rich in insight. Like the simplified materialism of bodily contact, however, the pure spiritualism of friendship does not correspond to the facts. Buber strongly protests against Heidegger's notion of *Fürsorge*, or care for the other, which for Heidegger, permits access to the other. (401-402) Of course, we need not turn to Heidegger for insight into the love for humanity or for social justice. However, *Fürsorge*, in-as-much as it is a response to the essential misery of the other, *does* give access to the otherness of other. It accounts for the dimension of height and of human distress to a greater degree than *Umfassung*, and it may be conjectured that clothing those who are naked and nourishing those who go hungry is a more authentic way of finding access to the other than the rarefied ether of a spiritual friendship. Is dialogue possible without *Fürsorge*? If we criticize Buber for extending the I-Thou relation to things, then, it is not because he is an animist with respect to our relations with the physical world, but because he is too much the artist in his relations with man.

The transition from the subject-object relation to that of the I-Thou implies the passage of consciousness to a new sphere of existence, viz., the interval, betweenness or *Zwischen*; and this is a passage from thought to *Umfassung*. Buber forcefully affirms in this connection the radical difference between the silent dialogue of the mind with itself and the real dialogue it has with the other. (204-205; 418) But is it not, after all in consciousness that *Zwischen* and *Umfassung* are revealed? Buber himself admits that "all dialogue derives its authenticity from consciousness of *Umfassung*;" (281) it is *only* in consciousness that we can know the latter. A theory of ontological knowledge based on the nature of the "space" existing in the sphere of betweenness should indicate how the Relation by itself, apart from its term, differs from consciousness. It should also be shown how that "space" "deforms," transforms and inverts the act of immediate awareness as it does the act of knowledge itself, once we admit that the I-It relation does in fact corrode the I-Thou. (45)

Finally, we may turn to a problem of more general concern, not restricted therefore to Buber's particular philosophy. It is one which confronts any epistemology which bases truth on a non-theoretical activity or on existence. And it places in question the existence of epistemology itself for it concerns "the truth about the truth," i.e., it asks about the nature of the knowledge epistemology itself claims to have when it communicates the truth. It is here that the theoretical nature of philosophy becomes evident. But perhaps this is due only to the practical exigencies of teaching, and merely corresponds to the return of the philosopher to the Cave where he is compelled to employ the language of enchained slaves?[5] If this is the case, then to philosophize is to live in a certain manner and, according to Buber, to practice to a greater extent than the others, in one's capacity of artist, friend or believer, the dialogue with the real. Is not philosophy then, an attitude distinct from all others—is not *philo sophari* essentially different from *vivere?* If this is so, then perhaps theory of knowledge is not based on any dialogical step that we need take. The truth is rather obtainable in a wholly different kind of dialogue which does not manifest its concern for Relation so much as it does a desire to assure to the I its independence, even if this independence is only possible in a union (Verbunden). Philosophy, then, is definable in terms of a rupture of the individual with the whole, and it is for this reason that it is abstract or critical in nature and implies a full possession of oneself. We need not insist at this point on Buber's indifference to the approximations of scientific knowledge which are hastily classified with our visual observations of reality, without his offering any explanation for the scope of our physico-mathematical knowledge. Although Buber has penetratingly described the Relation and the act of distancing, he has not taken separation seriously enough. Man is not merely identifiable with the category of distance and meeting, he is a being *sui generis,* and it is impossible for him to

---

[5] As Bergson undoubtedly assumed when he began his essay in 1888 with the words: "We must express ourselves in words . . . ."

ignore or forget his avatar of subjectivity. He realizes his own separateness in a process of subjectification which is not explicable in terms
of a recoil from the Thou. Buber does not explain that act, distinct
from both distancing and relating, in which the I realizes itself without
recourse to the other.

EMMANUEL LEVINAS

UNIVERSITÉ DE POITIERS

6

Marvin Fox

SOME PROBLEMS IN BUBER'S
MORAL PHILOSOPHY

MAURICE FRIEDMAN begins his excellent study of Martin Buber with a characterization of Buber's thought as proceeding along a "narrow ridge," a ridge which Buber himself tells us is located "between the gulfs where there is no sureness of expressible knowledge." Many philosophers have had as their aim the building of a complete system which would provide certain and unambiguous answers to the fundamental questions which concern men. Buber thinks of Aristotle, Aquinas and Hegel as the three classic instances of philosophers who aimed at security. In these philosophies "all insecurity, all unrest about meaning, all terror at decision, all abysmal problematic is eliminated."[1] But such security is not possible today when "the question about man's being faces us as never before in all its grandeur and terror—no longer in philosophical attire, but in the nakedness of existence."[2]

In his treatment of the problems of ethics, in his analysis of the phenomenology of moral decision, Buber avoids rigorously any easy security. Walking along the "narrow ridge" he tries to account both for the absolute moral demands which are made on every man and the flexible open way in which we must meet those demands. Every moral decision is a moral risk, because there are no final answers available to us. Yet we have no choice but to take the chance, else we reduce ourselves to mechanical automata and destroy our humanity.

And if one still asks if one may be certain of finding what is right on this steep path, once again the answer is *No;* there is no certainty. There is only a chance; but there is no other. The risk does not ensure the truth for us; but it, and it alone, leads us to where the breath of truth is to be felt.[3]

[1] *Between Man and Man,* p. 139.

[2] *Ibid.,* p. 145.

[3] *Ibid.,* p. 71.

Buber believes that moral values must be absolute and must be related to an absolute else they cannot be binding at all. When a man is concerned to know what it is that he really ought to do there is no possible answer except in terms of an absolute demand. Like Glaucon in Plato's *Republic* Buber denies that anything less than an absolute can be binding. Social conformity, personal interest, fear of punishment are only considerations of expediency, not of morality. Man has to make his decisions as if he were in possession of the ring of Gyges, as if he could do whatever he likes without fear of being found out.

We find the ethical in its purity only there where the human person confronts himself with his own potentiality and distinguishes and decides in this confrontation without asking anything other than what is right and what is wrong in this his own situation.[4]

Ethics is concerned with the "radical distinction" between human actions which makes choice depend not on "their usefulness or harmfulness for individuals and society," but on "their intrinsic value and disvalue."[5] If man wants to know what is right and what is wrong, if he seeks to discover what is intrinsically valuable, then, Buber believes, he must appeal to the Absolute.

In this commitment to absolute values we see one side of Buber's moral philosophy, namely the conviction that the Absolute (i.e., God) exists, that He is the source of values and of moral obligation, and that all men are accountable to Him. "Over and above all the countless and varied peoples there is an authority . . . to which communities as well as individuals must inwardly render an account of themselves."[6] Without such an authority man could not possibly make basic value distinctions, for "only an absolute can give the quality of absoluteness to an obligation."[7] And every genuine obligation is absolute. When a man affirms that he is duty-bound to act in a certain way he is affirming that he is bound absolutely. Duty is not an arbitrary matter, nor is it merely a name for a psychological state. Kant was right in seeing the awareness of duty as the key to morality because each man does experience as real the fact of obliga-

[4] *Eclipse of God* (Harper Torchbook edition), p. 95.

[5] *Ibid.*

[6] *Israel and the World,* p. 220.

[7] *Eclipse of God,* p. 18.

tion. Every moral decision (as distinct from prudential choice) presumes the absoluteness of the claim which is made on us, the absoluteness of our duty. This absoluteness does not derive from ourselves. It is not a feeling within us. It is an ontological reality which we discover when we allow ourselves to face our duty and to hear that which is addressed to us. "I am constitutionally incapable," says Buber,

of conceiving of myself as the ultimate source of moral approval or disapproval of myself, as surety for the absoluteness that I, to be sure, do not possess, but nevertheless imply with respect to this yes or no. The encounter with the original voice, the original source of yes or no, cannot be replaced by any self-encounter.[8]

Only in relationship to the Absolute can man discover true values.

One must stress Buber's view that values are discovered and not freely chosen. No man would feel bound by any value-claim if he were convinced that it was only his own invention. Neither would a man feel bound if he had made a free choice from among a range of possibilities. What is demanded of me here and now in this particular situation is not chosen arbitrarily. If it were it would not bind me absolutely. Buber distinguishes himself from Sartre, who declares that "someone is needed to invent values," else life will be meaningless. Sartre, therefore, understands by value "nothing else than this meaning which you choose." To this Buber replies,

One can believe in and accept a meaning or a value, one can set it as a guiding light over one's life if one has discovered it, not if one has invented it . . . not if I have freely chosen it for myself from among the existing possibilities and perhaps have in addition decided with some fellow-creatures: This shall be valid from now on.[9]

For Buber our moral decisions and our relationship to God derive from revelation. A detailed examination of Buber's views concerning revelation would take us beyond the subject of this essay. Moreover, the problem will undoubtedly be treated in other essays in this volume. For our purposes it is sufficient to draw attention to Buber's passionate assurance that revelation means real meeting between man and God. It cannot be adequately understood from

[8] *Ibid.;* cf. also p. 98.
[9] *Ibid.,* p. 70; cf. also, *Between Man and Man,* p. 108.

without but must be known directly and from within. There are some who try to reduce revelation to symbolic meanings and others who seek to dilute its breath-taking immediacy by speaking of it as a vague cosmic process. Either such men have not truly encountered the divine or else they have failed to reflect on the inner character and the profound effects of that meeting.

What is the eternal, primal phenomenon, present here and now, of that which we term revelation? It is the phenomenon that a man does not pass, from the moment of the supreme meeting, the same being as he entered into it . . . rather, in that moment something happens to the man. At times it is like a light breath, at times like a wrestling-bout, but always it *happens*. The man who emerges from the act of pure relation that so involves his being has now in his being something more that has grown in him, of which he did not know before and whose origin he is not rightly able to indicate. However the source of this new thing is classified in scientific orientation of the world, with its authorised efforts to establish an unbroken causality, we whose concern is real consideration of the real, cannot have our purpose served with subconsciousness or any other apparatus of the soul. The reality is that we receive what we did not hitherto have, and receive it in such a way that we know it has been given to us.[10]

Revelation transforms man by introducing into his being new dimensions of insight and awareness. It is in the meeting with the eternal Thou that man becomes what he is; here alone does man become truly human.

Revelation is not restricted to a few isolated and spectacular moments in history. "The mighty revelations which stand at the beginning of great communities and at the turning point of an age are nothing but the eternal revelation."[11] Man encounters God not only in the events of the Bible or in the ecstatic moments of mystical union. Each moment of human existence, the quiet as well as the dramatic, is a possible moment of revelation. We have only to open ourselves to the voice which addresses us. Thunder and lightning and the cloud of darkness overhanging Sinai are no guarantee of revelation. It becomes revelation only when he who is addressed "listens to that which the voice, sounding forth from this event, wishes to communicate to him, its witness, to his constitution, to his life, to his sense of duty."[12]

[10] *I and Thou*, p. 109.

[11] *Ibid.*, p. 117.

[12] *Israel and the World*, p. 98.

It is in revelation that we are confronted with the Absolute; it is through revelation that we discover absolute values and that we know what is asked of us.

However, the matter is not quite so simple. There are two problems which each moment of revelation poses for us, problems to which Buber is deeply sensitive. The first is the question which plagues every man who wonders whether he has truly heard the voice of the Absolute. Surely, we always risk being mistaken. Buber, himself, cautions that whenever we feel ourselves directed to act in a way which is radically different from the established ethical norms we must be very cautious. When we believe ourselves to be commanded by the Absolute to a "suspension of the ethical" then "the question of questions which takes precedence over every other is: Are you really addressed by the Absolute or by one of his apes?" Buber admits, moreover, that "in our age especially, it appears to be extremely difficult to distinguish the one from the other."[13]

Professor Buber seems to feel that the problem is especially acute in our own time, because now more than ever, "False absolutes rule over the soul, which is no longer able to put them to flight through the image of the true."[14] In other ages of human history men were also subject to the danger of confusing the one true voice with crude imitations. Yet they had, according to Buber, some more-or-less valid image of the Absolute to which they could appeal and which could serve as a control. In our day we have lost this capacity to form even crudely valid images of the Absolute; "the image-making power of the human heart has been in decline so that the spiritual pupil can no longer catch a glimpse of the appearance of the Absolute."[15]

Out of this view of Buber's arise a number of specific questions which I would like to pose. If we admit that individuals can be mistaken when they believe that they have been addressed by God, must we not have some reliable criterion for distinguishing between the false and the true address? But what criterion can there be? So long as man judges revelation by his inner light, is not every claim to revelation equally valid? Nor does it help to distinguish on the basis of the spiritual sensitivity which varies during the various ages of human history, since exactly the same problems which we

[13] *Eclipse of God,* pp. 118–119.
[14] *Ibid.*
[15] *Ibid.*

find as we try to evaluate individual claims are present when we try
to evaluate the claims of nations or religious groups who appeal
to the superior validity of great moments in their past. Admittedly,
the man who is completely convinced that the Absolute has addressed him directly needs no further evidence even if what he hears
violates ethical convention. But such men, at least in our society,
are a small minority. What of the vast numbers who experience claims
and counter-claims, who hear many conflicting voices, how are they
to distinguish the true from the false, the voice of God from the
voices of those who mimic the Divine? Can any genuine guidance be
given to such men? Can a way be opened to them?

The problem grows more aggravated when we consider a second
aspect of Buber's view of revelation. The man who encounters God is
not a *tabula rasa*. He is not a blank neutral tablet on which the
divine finger writes its message. What he is conditions what he
receives, for revelation is a "mixture of the divine and the human."

**The revelation does not pour itself into the world through him who receives
it as through a funnel; it comes to him and seizes his whole elemental being
in all its particular nature, and fuses with it. The man, too, who is the 'mouth'
of the revelation, is indeed this, not a speaking-tube or any kind of instrument, but an organ, which sounds according to its own laws; and to sound
means to *modify*.[16]**

No revelation is pure and wholly divine, according to Buber. What
a man hears reflects, in part, what he brings to his meeting with God.

This raises some further questions. Why is a man's own modification of revelation binding on him? We said earlier that man requires
the absoluteness of absolute values in order to give ground to his
moral decisions, that values cannot bind us if they are our own
inventions. But to the extent that we modify revelation is not the
result our own invention? We cannot hope to disentangle the divine
from the human elements because they are forged together in the
meeting between man and God. How then can we rely on the results
of that meeting? It is not sufficient to answer that a man who has
been seized with the divine fire *does* feel bound, that each revelation
is a "summons and a sending." For one can easily adduce instances
of equally deep commitment without any claim to revelation, and
Buber, himself, cautions us against the allurements of false Gods
who so readily command our loyalty and win our devotion.

[16] *I and Thou*, p. 117.

The "narrow ridge" which Buber walks with respect to problems of moral decision is a result of his denial that the meeting with the Absolute yields a clear and certain moral program. On the contrary he believes that, "As no prescription can lead us to the meeting, so none leads from it."[17] A set of moral rules which is proclaimed to be absolute and permanently binding on all men is most probably a falsification of revelation. "God has truth, but he does not have a system. He expresses his truth through his will, but his will is not a program."[18] So certain is Buber of this that he believes that any other way trivializes both the meeting with God and man's moral struggle. His comments on a verse in the book of Psalms are most revealing. Speaking of the verse, "Thou dost guide me with good counsel," Buber insists that it cannot mean that the speaker expects to receive from God direct and explicit moral instruction. The Psalmist does not believe that God is an oracle who will guide his every action. Buber tells us, "Just because I take this man so seriously I cannot understand the matter in this way."[19]

In Buber's analysis of the phenomenology of the moral decision he has become convinced that to know the right way is almost never an easy or simple matter. Each genuine moral decision is the result of great struggle and searching. There are no cheaply won answers to our perplexities about right and wrong. Men,

who are seriously laboring over the questions of good and evil, rebel when one dictates to them, as though it were some long established truth, what is good and what is bad; and they rebel just because they have experienced over and over again how hard it is to find the right way.[20]

If one takes the moral struggle seriously then he must recognize that it is a struggle. Revelation does not alleviate the struggle by providing us with a set guide to moral practice.

Even the great historic revelations which are set down in such books as the Bible cannot be properly understood as presenting us with finished and set programs of action. The laws which are recorded in the sacred writings of the great religions are interpreted by Buber as human rather than divine. They are the record of

[17] *Ibid.*, p. 110.
[18] *Israel and the World*, p. 114.
[19] *Good and Evil: Two Interpretations*, p. 43.
[20] *Between Man and Man*, p. 105.

what men have done with and to revelation, but they are not the literal text of revelation. In his correspondence with Franz Rosenzweig Buber expresses this view with great clarity, "I do not believe," writes Buber, "that *revelation* is ever a formulation of a law. It is only through man in his self-contradiction that revelation becomes legislation. This is the fact of man."[21] Whatever it is that we derive from revelation it is not a set code of practice.

The reason for this view lies, in part at least, in Buber's understanding of man's moral situation. He sees every instance of moral trial as unique. It has to be decided in terms of the particular circumstances and the particular demands. To decide for the right and the good is an act which can never be performed mechanically, nor can it be accomplished by implementing long-established rules of behavior. There can be no rules to cover the unique and the particular, since rules always are generalizations which must ignore specificity and particularity. A man must know what is asked of him here and now. No set course of action which has been chosen in advance can serve as a guide when the moment of decision is upon us.

Every case, if it is taken seriously in its unique character and situation, proves itself to be something that cannot be anticipated, something withdrawn from planning and precautionary measures. No traditional formulae and rhythms of any kind, no inherited methods of exercising power, nothing which can be known, nothing which can be learnt, are of any use to the man of sacramental existence; he has ever to endure through the moment which is not and cannot be foreseen. . . .[22]

Though these words are spoken of the "man of sacramental existence" they find their echo in many places in Buber's writings and can be fairly taken as an expression of the moral situation of every man.[23]

Buber's attitude toward supposedly revealed legislation is clear in the light of his insistence on the uniqueness of each case of moral decision. If the only question I may properly ask is, "What is demanded of me?" then no law as such binds me. Only when the "Thou shalt" or the "Thou shalt not" speaks personally to me does it command my loyalty and submission. As a general formula it does not

---

[21] Letter to Franz Rosenzweig, June 24, 1924. Contained in Franz Rosenzweig, *On Jewish Learning* (New York, 1955), p. 111.

[22] *Hasidism*, p. 135.

[23] Cf., e.g., *Between Man and Man*, p. 68; *Israel and the World*, pp. 163, 216.

touch me at all. With this attitude Buber, the Jew, rejects much of the legislation of the Hebrew Bible. About this Buber is completely unambiguous when he writes to Rosenzweig, "for me, though man is a law-receiver, God is not a law-giver, and therefore the Law has no universal validity for me, but only a personal one. I accept, therefore, only what I think is being spoken to me. . . ."[24] And Buber believes that when the law is addressed to me it binds me, not because it was set down in ancient days, but because in the uniqueness of the present moment the one true voice speaks through it. For the most part, however, we must find our way without the law which has been set down. We must, rather, keep ourselves open to whatever way may be opened to us as we meet in true relationship with God.

What then does revelation achieve, according to Buber? In man's meeting with God something happens which Buber believes to be far more significant than the receipt of specific instructions about how to act. In this meeting a man becomes bound to God and this fact transforms the man in a radical way. For, though he has not been told explicitly what to do, he has discovered that man is responsible for what he does, that he is held accountable and that he must give an account of himself. When man and God meet

the human substance is melted by the spiritual fire which visits it, and there now breaks forth from it a word, a statement, which is human in its meaning and form, human conception and human speech, and yet witnesses to Him who stimulated it and to His will.[25]

No act can be right, Buber teaches us, unless it arises from our bond with God. No act can be morally significant unless it is linked to God. Whatever we do must be done in and through the burning reality of our relationship to the Absolute. "To do the right thing in the right way, the deed must spring from the bond with Him who commands us. Our link with Him is the beginning, and the function of the teachings is to make us aware of our bond and make it fruitful."[26] This is what comes out of revelation—not codes and not rules, but the reformation of the human spirit. Through revelation man knows that he is commanded, that demands are made of him.

24 In Rosenzweig, *op. cit.*, p. 115.
25 *Eclipse of God*, p. 135.
26 *Israel and the World*, p. 145.

But only the man himself can decide what specifically is asked of him; he alone knows how to respond.

It is no wonder, then, that Buber repeats so often his caution against supposing that we can ever be certain that we have done what is right. Men usually find moral assurance by depending on established moral codes to which they try to conform, or by developing independent but convincing theories about the nature of moral duty which they then live by, or by appealing directly to a conscience which they are certain does not mislead them. As we have seen, Buber denies that any of these ways is absolutely reliable. Nor does revelation itself give me any clear course or program of action. This is why Buber is forced to conclude that "there is not the slightest assurance that our decision is right in any way but a personal way."[27] All we can do is to decide in the light of what we feel is being asked of us, in the light of what the particular circumstances demand. We do so with the consciousness that we are running a risk, but that this is the most and the best that is open to us. A morally sensitive man "knows that he cannot objectively and reliably know whether that which he intends to do is the correct answer to the problem presented to him." This is why he "lives through these moments daringly, in fear and trembling."[28]

In summary, we can say that Buber sees man as obligated by revelation to make a decision in a set of circumstances so unique that only he alone can decide what it is that he ought to do. This seems to place Buber almost at the opposite extreme from his position that values must be absolute. Does he not violate his own doctrine of the absoluteness of the moral demand by making each individual man the sole, but uncertain, judge of what he ought to do? Does he not substitute the privacy of the individual decision for the absolute value? Revelation which does not communicate with man directly seems to make God's word dependent on man's response. But is this not a reduction of the divine to the human? Even if a man believes that a recorded revelation, such as the Pentateuch, is to be understood literally, he still does not have final certainty in every act. There are always conflicts of equally pressing duties and equally just claims. No man can be certain that he has always given priority to the right duty or that he judged correctly in deciding in

[27] *Between Man and Man*, p. 69.
[28] *Hasidism*, p. 162.

favor of a given claim. However, if he believes that he is bound by God's word and that that word is known with much explicitness he can feel secure in many (if not in all) of his decisions. For he does not substitute his opinion for God's commandment. Is this not what Buber would have us do? Does Buber's kind of revelation reveal anything more than the views of individual men?

There is still another difficulty that arises out of this aspect of Buber's moral philosophy. If I understand him correctly he takes the position that there can be no general moral rules or codes which are binding, that each moral situation is unique and requires its own unique solution, that this solution is made responsibly only when the individual man responds to the divine voice with his own act of decision, and that, therefore, there is in the last analysis a kind of complete privacy to each moral decision. Moreover, it would follow from this that we can make no moral judgments of men or societies, and, perhaps, not even of ourselves. But does this not in effect make any kind of human society impossible? We are forced in the ordinary circumstances of our lives to judge men and societies, to throw in our lot with those whom we believe to be good and to oppose those whom we believe to be evil. Can we ever make such judgments without some general principles by which we are guided? Even individual action and decision would become almost impossible. Is each man really expected to be a prophet speaking with the assurances of the divine word, or a creative moral genius who carves his own way out of the dark forest of moral doubt and uncertainty? Most men (perhaps even all men) do need guidance and direction, and without such guidance they would be completely paralyzed. Is it not enough that a man decides for the good? Must he also create out of himself an understanding of what constitutes the good?

Buber partially admits the justice of these objections when he says,

I do not in the least mean that a man must fetch the answer alone and unadvised out of his breast. Nothing of the sort is meant; how should the direction of those at the head of any group not enter essentially into the substance out of which the decision is smelted?

However, he adds immediately that "direction must not be substituted for decision."[29] Yet if there is to be direction at all what role does it play, and what am I to decide? Is each man to decide

29 *Between Man and Man*, p. 69.

only whether to accept that direction which he already acknowledges leads to the good, or must he decide also whether the direction does as a matter of fact lead to the good? In the latter case what principles or criteria shall he invoke? Does he not, in spite of Buber's disapproval, have to "fetch the answers alone and unadvised out of his breast"?

Apparently Buber wants to meet this problem by admitting that the existence of society does require norms of behavior, but that adherence to these norms is not to be confused with genuine moral decision.

Provided society does not insist that the moral and legal forms into which it has transformed the Ten Commandments, that that product which is an I-and-Thou deprived of the I and the Thou, is still the Ten Commandments its activities are unobjectionable; it is as a matter of fact impossible to imagine how society could exist without them.[30]

Though these rules of behavior are necessary conditions of social existence Buber hastens to add that there could be no greater calamity than that which would befall us "if society were to have the temerity to pretend that its voiceless morals and its faceless law are really the Word," if we were to substitute, that is, conformity with social rules for the sense of being personally commanded. And what is to be done with the man who knows only the rules of his society, or the man who accepts on faith the Ten Commandments without feeling any immediate personal address? Or, what is even more troubling, what shall we do with the man who chooses a way in opposition to the norms of society or to the Ten Commandments? Shall we condemn him as evil? But we cannot for he may be acting in accordance with what he is convinced is the voice of God. Neither is Buber prepared to accept such men and to approve of them. For we discover that Buber himself, in spite of his theories, makes many moral judgments, establishes general rules of approved conduct, and appeals to those rules frequently. He, too, seems to acknowledge that without such rules there would be moral chaos. It would be illuminating, indeed, if Professor Buber would help us to see how he reconciles his setting down of such moral norms with his insistence on the uniqueness of each moral situation and the exclusive prerogative of the individual who is called upon to choose a way of acting.

[30] *Israel and the World*, p. 87.

Let us first cite the evidence in order to make certain that we have not misunderstood or misrepresented Buber's intentions. We must first take note of the fact that there are passages in which Buber speaks of revelation as having specific content. In explicating the view of Hasidism, for example, he states that "the Torah [i.e. established Jewish law] marks the circumference of revelation as it is up to the present."31 This seems to imply that this is a valid revelation and that those who accept it are bound by the norms of behavior which are contained therein. Buber adds that "it depends on man whether and to what extent this expands," how far the act of hallowing the world is to go. But one thing is eminently clear, namely that men have no authority to contract the sphere which is under the revealed commandments—not even the man who does not feel that they are spoken directly to him. (It cannot be argued that this is not Buber's own view, but only his explanation of Hasidism. For in his foreword to the book from which these sentences are taken Buber tells us that he considers "Hasidic *truth* vitally important for Jews, Christians, and other," and that "because of its *truth*" he is carrying Hasidism "into the world against its will.") It appears, then, that Buber also admits that revelation involves specific commandments and commandments which are set down as general rules.

He even seems to believe that there are times when we can and should give concrete moral instruction, when it is a moral failure to shirk a request for moral guidance. One such situation is that of the teacher in relationship to his pupils.

The teacher who is for the first time approached by a boy with a somewhat defiant bearing, but with trembling hands, visibly opened-up and fired by a daring hope, who asks him what is the right thing in a certain situation—for instance, whether in learning that a friend has betrayed a secret entrusted to him one should call him to account or be content with entrusting no more secrets to him—the teacher to whom this happens realizes that this is the moment to make the first conscious step towards the education of character; he has to answer, to answer under a responsibility, to give an answer which will probably lead beyond the alternatives of the question by showing a third possibility *which is the right one*. To dictate what is good and evil in general is not his business. His business is to answer a concrete question, to answer what is right and wrong in a given situation.32

31 *Hasidism*, p. 27.
32 *Between Man and Man*, p. 107. Italics mine.

But how on Buber's own ground can or ought any man answer such a question for another? And how can he know "what is right and wrong in a given situation" without having some general principles to which he can appeal?

Let us note further that Buber makes specific judgments of men and of peoples. He speaks disapprovingly of Hitler as "the sinister leading personality" of his time and is convinced that we can distinguish qualitatively "between the charisma of Moses and that of Hitler."[33] In a moving and courageous statement made in Germany in 1953 Buber condemns with the deepest bitterness those of the Germans "who killed millions of my people in a systematically prepared and executed procedure whose organized cruelty cannot be compared with any previous historical event." Of these Germans Buber says, "They have so radically removed themselves from the human sphere, so transposed themselves into a sphere of monstrous inhumanity inaccessible to my conception, that not even hatred, much less an overcoming of hatred, was able to arise in me."[34] It is hardly necessary to say that we share Buber's sentiments. What we are moved to ask, however, is how even such men can be condemned as evil unless there are general moral rules which bind all men. If there are no such rules, then what is the ground for our judgment? May not even such men also be acting in response to their own understanding of the divine voice? Surely Buber meant his statement to be a true and correct moral judgment and not merely an expression of arbitrary personal feelings.

Buber also makes a considerable number of moral pronouncements which take the form of general rules. He rules that lying is evil. "The lie is the specific evil which man has introduced into nature. . . . In a lie the spirit practices treason against itself."[35] From the standpoint of biblical faith, which is Buber's own standpoint,

deceit is under all circumstances regarded as disgraceful . . . even if it is prompted by a desire to promote the cause of justice; in fact, in the latter case, it is the more pernicious, since it poisons and disintegrates the good which it is supposed to serve.[36]

[33] *Eclipse of God*, pp. 77–78.
[34] *Pointing the Way*, p. 232.
[35] *Good and Evil*, p. 7.
[36] *At the Turning*, p. 53.

In fact, in revelation, Buber believes, God "distinguishes between truth and lies, righteousness and unrighteousness," and "He challenges us to make such distinctions within the sphere of our life."[37]

Not only is lying evil, violence is also evil.

What is accomplished through lies can assume the work of truth; what is accomplished through violence, can go in the guise of justice, and for a while the hoax may be successful. But soon people will realize that lies are lies at bottom, that in the final analysis, violence is violence, and both lies and violence suffer the destiny history has in store for all that is false.[38]

If violence is evil then murder must surely be judged evil. And Buber does make precisely this judgment. "In the realm of Moloch," he says, "honest men lie and compassionate men torture. And they really and truly believe that brother-murder will prepare the way for brotherhood! There appears to be no escape from the most evil of all idolatry."[39] Not only such outright violence, but the drive for power itself is condemned by Buber. "A will-to-power, less concerned with being powerful than with being 'more powerful than,' becomes destructive. Not power but power hysteria is evil."[40] In another passage Buber adds the seduction of women to those acts which decent men must reject. It is an evidence of their diseased moral condition that "Don Juan finds absolute and subjective value in seducing the greatest possible number of women, and the dictator sees it in the greatest possible accumulation of power."[41] No man with correct moral perception, Buber believes, would judge these as absolute values.

Just as he makes strong general pronouncements about which things are morally evil Buber also takes a stand with respect to what is good. So, for example, he asserts that the social legislation in the Pentateuch, which seeks to bring about a basic equality of persons and possessions, is good, and, what is even more important, that these laws were explicitly revealed by God.

Communal ownership of the land, regularly recurrent leveling of social distinctions, guarantee of the independence of each individual, mutual aid, a

[37] *Israel and the World*, p. 209.
[38] *Ibid.*, p. 238.
[39] *Eclipse of God*, p. 120.
[40] *Israel and the World*, p. 216.
[41] *Between Man and Man*, p. 108.

general Sabbath embracing serf and beast as beings with an equal claim to rest, a sabbatical year in which the soil is allowed to rest and everybody is admitted to the free enjoyment of its fruits—these are not practical laws thought out by wise men; they are measures which the leaders of the nation, apparently themselves taken by surprise and overpowered, have found to be the set task and condition for taking possession of the land.[42]

That Buber should feel such enthusiasm for the social legislation of the Bible is understandable in the light of the conviction which he shares with Hasidism that all men are equal and that discrimination between men, especially discrimination in favor of myself is evil. "Nothing disturbs the unity of God's work, the foretaste of Eternity, as much as . . . overbearing discrimination between myself and my neighbour, as if indeed I excelled in one way or another above someone else."[43] From this rejection of discrimination between men follows the positive need to extend our love to every man. We must love the world if we are to love God; this must be the aim of every good man.[44]

If we open ourselves to this commandment we will discover, Buber assures us, still another duty. We will know that we must seek peace. This is one demand which God makes of all men without exception. For we are told by Buber that "if we consult our deep inner knowledge about God's command to mankind, we shall not hesitate an instant to say that it is peace."[45] "There is a purpose to creation; there is a purpose to the human race, one we have not made up ourselves. . . . No, the purpose itself revealed its face to us and we have gazed upon it. . . . Our purpose is the great upbuilding of peace. . . . The world of humanity is meant to become a single body."[46]

I have quoted so extensively from Buber in the last several pages because I wanted to allow him to speak for himself without the possibly distorting mediation of paraphrases and explanations. From these quotations it seems to me to be clear, beyond any doubt, that Buber does make numerous positive and negative moral judgments which he intends to be universally and permanently binding. My

---

[42] *Israel and the World*, p. 229; cf. *Pointing the Way*, p. 143.

[43] *Hasidism*, pp. 181–182.

[44] *Ibid.*, pp. 157–8, 165; *I and Thou*, pp. 107–109.

[45] *Israel and the World*, pp. 236–237.

[46] *Ibid.*, p. 186.

question has been stated before and can now be restated. How does Professor Buber reconcile such universal moral judgments with his view that even in revelation there are no set moral principles, and that men can only come to moral decisions in the light of the uniqueness of their particular circumstances? Does this not make impossible judgments and the proclamation of principles of the kind that Buber has so frequently offered us in his writings and in his speeches?

Buber's readiness to take so firm a stand in favor of certain kinds of actions as good and against certain others as evil is even more puzzling when we consider his analysis of the nature of the good and the evil. He repeatedly defines the good as "direction" and the evil as "lack of direction."[47] This direction may either be understood as the movement toward becoming that which I am uniquely intended to be, or else it is understood as the direction toward God.[48] In the former meaning Buber's intention is most beautifully expressed in the Hasidic tale which he has recorded and which has been very widely quoted. "Before his death, Rabbi Zusya said 'In the coming world, they will not ask me: Why were you not Moses? They will ask me: Why were you not Zusya?' "[49] Man's only duty is to become what he uniquely is. All that is asked of a man is that he realize his own particular nature.

In substance, moving in the direction of self-fulfillment is thought by Buber to be the same as moving in the direction of God.

In decision, taking the direction thus means: taking the direction toward the point of being at which, executing for my part the design which I am, I encounter the divine mystery of my created uniqueness, the mystery waiting for me. . . . Every revelation is revelation of human service to the goal of creation, in which service man authenticates himself.[50]

What is demanded of man, above all else, is that he recognize his responsibility, that he make a decision. When the decision is made with the whole strength of a man's being and in the full awareness of the depth of his responsibility then the decision is upright; it is

---

[47] Cf. *Between Man and Man,* pp. 74–75, 78–79, 114; *Hasidism,* p. 105; *Good and Evil,* pp. 125–128.

[48] Cf. *Good and Evil,* p. 140.

[49] *Tales of the Hasidism,* 1, 251.

[50] *Good and Evil,* p. 142.

in the right direction. The only real evil is to fail to come to any
decision. "If there were a devil it would not be one who decided
against God, but one who, in eternity came to no decision."[51] For a
man cannot truly make a decision with less than his whole being and
when he has so unified himself that his entire being moves in a single
direction he has done all that can be asked of him. Buber, in one
place, defines sin as "what a man cannot by its very nature do with
his whole being."[52] On the other hand, when a man has made a
genuine decision, i.e., a decision with his whole being, he is assured
of doing good. For "man can decide only for the direction of God."[53]

Consistently with the rest of his doctrine Buber adds no more
content to his definitions of good and evil than that which we have
set forth. A man must decide. He must direct his entire being
toward an end. That end is the realization of his own uniqueness.
And this is simultaneously a movement in the direction of God. There
is, as there must be, a studious avoidance in all of this of any more
specific identification of the good. But this raises again the very same
questions which troubled us before. First, how does Buber explain,
in the light of these definitions, the many specific statements he
makes about good and evil? Secondly, are we not forced to do
exactly what Buber has done, namely to add content, rules, prescriptions and prohibitions? Otherwise would not every kind of act possibly be one which was in the direction of some person's true self-
realization? Can men not murder or lie with their whole being?

There is still one more dimension of Buber's moral philosophy that
we must examine. We have defined the good as direction and have
understood this as a dedication of man's being to his own fulfillment.
However, Buber is deeply committed to the view that true humanity,
and hence true morality, is only possible when men are related to
each other in a living community. Every true culture is such a community, and the same man who, we were told, must make his own
decision and find his own way must also act as a member of his
culture. At least this is the case so long as the culture is live, integrated, and effective. Cultures express morally valid ways of living
and morally valid ideals. These ideals are not arbitrary, nor are
they the inventions of men or the results of some sort of general

[51] *I and Thou*, p. 52.
[52] *Hasidism*, p. 59.
[53] *Israel and the World*, p. 18.

agreement. "The patterns familiar to us from the history of culture are never personal or arbitrary . . . from the *polites* pattern of classical Greek antiquity to the 'gentleman' of the great era in English history."[54] Such patterns arise from the deepest levels of the life of a people and embody a valid ideal within the history and civilization of that people. Even if we grant Buber's contention that when a culture breaks down man has no choice but to seek his own direction, we should still be disturbed by his claims about the status of men in vital and integrated cultures. Surely Buber would not have us believe that the ideal of every culture is morally acceptable! Must we not distinguish between the moral worth of cultures? What principles, what general criteria shall we employ if we follow Buber's guidance? Buber may well be correct when he teaches us that "though something of righteousness may become evident in the life of the individual, righteousness itself can only become wholly visible in the structures of the life of a people."[55] This does not mean that the institutionalized life of every people is righteous. How, then, can we judge?

Buber is aware of the problem, but his answer leaves us somewhat unsatisfied. He stresses the fact that each man belongs to his community. Yet at the same time we must note "that true membership of a community includes the experience . . . of the *boundary* of this membership." However, this boundary "can never be definitively formulated."[56] We must be critical of our community, recognizing its limits and knowing its evils. Yet, Buber says, there are no external criteria that we can call on. Only one way is open to the man of moral concern, and that is to stand before God in a completely open and receptive way. In so doing he will discover, in pain and agony, where the boundary lies. Again we are turned back to the inner life of man and to the problems which this generates.

In this essay I have not attempted to set forth in all of its detail and richness the whole of Buber's moral philosophy. Some topics have been dealt with sketchily. Some topics, e.g., freedom, the dialogical relationship, the moral implications of I-Thou and I-It, have not been dealt with at all. It is my belief that the basic problems which have been raised here would not be materially affected by Buber's treatment of these topics. For we have seen in Buber's moral

[54] *Ibid.*, p. 150; cf. *Between Man and Man*, pp. 102–103.
[55] *Israel and the World*, p. 210.
[56] *Between Man and Man*, p. 66.

philosophy an attempt to defend moral anarchy while pleading for moral order. It is my hope that Professor Buber will favor us with a clarification of his position.

MARVIN FOX

OHIO STATE UNIVERSITY

7

Maurice Friedman

THE BASES OF BUBER'S ETHICS

I

WHETHER one is concerned with general questions of the relation of the "is" and the "ought" or particular questions such
as "How do I know what I ought to do in this particular situation?,"
the fundamental question of moral philosophy is the basis of moral
value. The basis of Martin Buber's ethics, all, including Buber, would
agree, is religion—whether this be understood as his philosophy of
religion, his interpretation of the Biblical Covenant, his re-creation of
Hasidism, or the "Single One's" unique relation with the "Eternal
Thou." In "Religion and Ethics" Buber himself gives this view the
strongest support: "Always it is the religious which bestows, the ethical which receives." Yet one who tries to analyze the implications of
Buber's "I-Thou" philosophy for contemporary ethical theory and
concrete ethical action[1] is struck by the fact that Buber's philosophical anthropology is as important for his ethics as his philosophy of
religion. What is more, the question must even arise whether the philosophy of dialogue, the I-Thou relation between man and man,
cannot stand by itself as an autonomous ethic, grounded in Buber's
anthropology but not necessarily tied with the relation between man
and God. Could not a case be made for an independent non-religious
ethic that need only be lifted out of the larger context to take on
contour and come into its own?

In Buber's philosophy and interpretation of religion, the source
of the "ought" is the command and will of God; in his philosophical
anthropology, the "ought" is grounded in a conception of "authentic existence." This seeming divergence appears reconcilable
through the fact that Buber's philosophy of religion, like his anthro-

---

[1] As I have done in Chapter XXII, "Ethics," in my book *Martin Buber: The Life
of Dialogue* (Chicago: The University of Chicago Press, 1955; New York: Harper
Torchbooks, 1960).

pology, is centrally concerned with authentic existence while his philosophical anthropology, like his philosophy of religion, is essentially concerned with hearing and responding to what is over against one. Yet "authentic existence" in Buber's religion is found through the individual's and the people's relation with God, whereas in Buber's anthropology it is found in the relation between man and man. In the one case it is God, in the other man who is over against man. Now, of course, we shall appeal to *I and Thou* to show that man meets the "Eternal Thou" in meeting the human Thou and to *Images of Good and Evil* to show that the decision for the good which one makes in meeting man is equally the decision for God, that one's unique personal direction realized in one's relation to the world is one's direction to God. Yet this does not change the essential fact that Buber's philosophical anthropology and the ethic based on it seem to subsist without the need for "revelation" in the special religious sense of the term, while his understanding of religion and of the ethic that grows out of religion cannot.

If then we take the question of an "autonomous" ethic as our starting-point, we must explore more deeply the relation between Buber's anthropology and his philosophy of religion.

II

Martin Buber defines the ethical as the affirmation or denial of the conduct and actions possible to one "not according to their use or harmfulness for individuals and society, but according to their intrinsic value and disvalue."

We find the ethical in its purity only there where the human person confronts himself with his own potentiality and distinguishes and decides in this confrontation without asking anything other than what is right and what is wrong in this his own situation.

He goes on to explain that the criterion by which the distinction and decision are made may be a traditional one or one perceived by the individual himself. What really matters "is that the critical flame shoot up ever again out of the depths" and the truest source for this critical flame is "the individual's awareness of what he 'really' is, of what in his unique and nonrepeatable created existence he is intended to be."[2]

One foundation of this definition of ethics is Buber's philosophy of dialogue with its emphasis on wholeness, decision, presentness, and uniqueness. Another is his philosophical anthropology with its emphasis on the potentiality which only man has and on the direction which each man must take to become what only he can become. In both Buber's philosophy of dialogue and his philosophical anthropology, value is bound up with the question of authentic existence. Valuing to Buber must always remain attached to the full concrete situation of the human being. Responsibility must mean responding to the address of the "lived concrete." It cannot simply float above. This means that the understanding of *authentic* human existence must grow directly out of the understanding of human existence itself. The *description* of human existence—the twofold relationship of I-Thou and I-It—is only the base and the first aspect of what, considered more fully, includes the *normative*—the question of what is authentic in human existence. To Buber one becomes a self, a person, in entering into the relation with the Thou. The problem of authentic existence arises in the difference between becoming *something* of what you can be and becoming more fully what you can be. This is the difference between a "self" for practical purposes, that is, someone who is able to hold the fragments together enough to get by and get business done, and a self in the fuller sense of a person who again and again brings the conflicting parts of himself into an active unity. It is the difference between a person who has partial, fragmentary relations with others and a person who is able ever more fully to enter into relations with others, the difference between a person who only very partially realizes his uniqueness and one who more fully realizes his unique potentialities. One cannot be human at all except in the I-Thou relation. But it is quite possible to be human without being fully human, to fall short of realizing what we might, of authenticating one's own humanity, and that is where the normative grows imperceptibly out of the descriptive. Valuing is the growing point of human existence because we live in the present pointed toward the future, aware of possibilities, having to make decisions between "better" and "worse," having to create our own future through our response to the day-by-day address of existence. So the

---

[2] *Eclipse of God*, "Religion and Ethics," p. 125f.

ontological—the "is" of human existence—must include the dimension of authentic human existence as well.

Man sets man at a distance and makes him independent, writes Buber in the basic statement of his anthropology. He is therefore able to enter into relation, in his own individual status, with those like himself.

> The basis of man's life with man is twofold, and it is one—the wish of every man to be confirmed as what he is, even as what he can become, by men; and the innate capacity in man to confirm his fellowmen in this way. That this capacity lies so immeasurably fallow constitutes the real weakness and questionableness of the human race: actual humanity exists only where this capacity unfolds.

This mutual confirmation of men is most fully realized in what Buber calls "making present," an event which happens partially wherever men come together but in its essential structure only rarely. Making the other present means to imagine quite concretely what another man is wishing, feeling, perceiving, and thinking. It is through this making present that we grasp another as a self, that is, as a being whose distance from me cannot be separated from my distance from him and whose particular experience I can make present. This event is not ontologically complete until he knows himself made present by me and until this knowledge induces the process of his inmost self-becoming.

> For the inmost growth of the self is not accomplished, as people like to suppose today, in man's relation to himself, but . . . in the making present of another self and in the knowledge that one is made present in his own self by the other.[8]

The fundamental fact of human existence, according to Buber's anthropology, is man with man. When two individuals "happen" to each other, then there is an essential remainder which is common to them but which reaches out beyond the special sphere of each. That remainder is the basic reality, the sphere of "the between," of "the interhuman" (das Zwischenmenschliche).[4] The unfolding of this sphere Buber calls the "dialogical." The psychological, that which happens within the souls of each, is only the secret accompaniment

[8] *The Knowledge of Man*, pp. 67f., 71.

[4] *Between Man and Man*, pp. 202–205; *The Knowledge of Man*, pp. 72–75.

to the dialogue. Genuine dialogue can be either spoken or silent. Its essence lies in the fact that "each of the participants really has in mind the other or others in their present and particular being and turns to them with the intention of establishing a living mutual relation between himself and them." The essential element of genuine dialogue, therefore, is "seeing through the eyes of the other" or "experiencing the other side." "Experiencing the other side" is the full development of "making the other present." It means "imagining the real"—a "bold swinging" into the life of "the particular real person who confronts me, whom I can attempt to make present to myself just in this way, and not otherwise, in his wholeness, unity, and uniqueness."[5] One must distinguish here, accordingly, between that awareness, essential to the life of dialogue, which enables one to turn to the other and that reflexive, or "monological," awareness which turns one in on oneself and lets the other exist only as one's own experience, only as a part of oneself.

Dialogue not only means awareness of what addresses one, but responsibility. Responsibility, for Buber, means responding—hearing the unreduced claim of each particular hour in all its crudeness and disharmony and answering it out of the depths of one's being. This responsibility does not exclude a man from membership in a group or community, but it means that true membership in a community includes a *boundary* to membership so that no group or person can hinder one's perception of what is spoken or one's answer from the ground of one's being. This perception is not an "inner light" from God that presents one the answer at the same time as the question. God tenders the situation, but the response comes from the "conscience"—not the routine, surface, discredited conscience but "the unknown conscience in the ground of being, which needs to be discovered ever anew." " 'Conscience' is human and can be mistaken."[6]

Conscience, to Buber, is the voice which calls one to fulfill the personal intention of being for which he was created. It is "the individual's awareness of what he 'really' is, of what in his unique and non-repeatable created existence he is intended to be." This presentiment of purpose is "inherent in all men though in the most

[5] *Between Man and Man*, pp. 20–24, 27, 29f., 36–39, 96f.; *The Knowledge of Man*, pp. 79–81.

[6] *Between Man and Man*, pp. 61–69; letter of August 18, 1952 from Professor Buber to writer.

varied strengths and degrees of consciousness and for the most part stifled by them." When it is not stifled, it compares what one is with what one is called to become and thereby distinguishes and decides between right and wrong. It is partly through this comparison that one comes to feel guilt.

Each one who knows himself . . . as called to a work which he has not done, each one who has not fulfilled a task which he knows to be his own, each who did not remain faithful to his vocation which he had become certain of—each such person knows what it means to say that 'his conscience smites him.'[7]

Ethical decision, for Buber, is thus both the current decision about the immediate situation that confronts one and through this the decision with one's whole being for God. Direction is apprehended through one's inner awareness of what one is meant to be, for it is this that enables one to make a decision. This is a reciprocal process, however, for in transforming and directing one's undirected energies, one comes to recognize ever more clearly what one is meant to be. One experiences one's uniqueness as a designed or preformed one, intrusted to one for execution, yet everything that affects one participates in this execution. The person who knows direction responds with the whole of his being to each new situation with no other preparation than his presence and his readiness to respond. One discovers the mystery waiting for one not in oneself, but in the encounter with what one meets.[8] The goal of creation that we are intended to fulfill is not an unavoidable destiny, but something to which we are called and to which we are free to respond or not to respond. Our awareness of this calling is not a sense of what we may become in terms of our position in society nor is it a sense of what type of person we should develop into. Direction is neither conscious conception nor subconscious fantasy. It is the primal awareness of our personal way to God that lies at the very center of our awareness of ourself as I.

As it is only in genuine relation that we find direction, so it is only in relation that true ethical decision takes place. Only he who knows the presence of the Thou is capable of decision. True decision is not partial but is made with the whole soul. There can be no wholeness "where downtrodden appetites lurk in the corners" or

7 *Eclipse of God,* "Religion and Modern Thinking," pp. 115f., 125f.

8 *Good and Evil,* pp. 127, 140–143; *Between Man and Man,* p. 78f.

where the soul's highest forces watch the action, "pressed back and powerless, but shining in the protest of the spirit."[9] If one does not become what one is meant to be, if one does not bring one's scattered passions under the transforming and unifying guidance of direction, no wholeness of the person is possible. Conversely, without attaining personal wholeness, one can neither keep to direction nor enter into full relation.

Buber's discovery of the source of the moral "ought" in dialogue must not be confused with Jean-Paul Sartre's "invention" of values. Such a self-created morality means freedom without genuine responding and responsibility, just as a "moral duty" imposed from without means "responsibility" without either freedom or genuine responding. The narrow ridge between the two is a freedom that means freedom *to* respond, and a responsibility that means both address from without and free response from within. Sartre's definition of value as the meaning of life which the individual chooses, Buber points out, destroys all meaningful notion of value:

One can believe in and accept a meaning or value . . . if one has discovered it, not if one has invented it. It can be for me an illuminating meaning, a direction-giving value, only if it has been revealed to me in my meeting with being, not if I have freely chosen it for myself from among the existing possibilities and perhaps have in addition decided with a few fellow creatures: This shall be valid from now on.[10]

Buber's concept of the responsibility of an I to a Thou is closely similar to Kant's second formulation of the categorical imperative: Never treat one's fellow or oneself as a means only but always also as an end of value in himself. But even here there is an essential difference. Kant's sentence grows out of an "ought" based on the idea of human dignity. Buber's related concept of making the other present is based on the ontological reality of the life between man and man.[11] To Kant the respect for the dignity of others grows out of one's own dignity as a rational being bound to act according to universal laws. For Buber, the concern for the other as an end in himself grows out of one's direct relation to this other and to that higher end which he serves through the fulfillment of his created uniqueness. Thus Kant's

[9] *Good and Evil*, pp. 125–32, 139f.

[10] *Eclipse of God*, "Religion and Modern Thinking," p. 93.

[11] *The Knowledge of Man*, p. 84.

imperative is essentially subjective (the isolated individual) and objective (universal reason) whereas Buber's is dialogical. In Kant the "ought" of reason is separated from the "is" of impulse. For Buber, in contrast, "is" and "ought" join without losing their tension in the precondition of authentic human existence—making real the life between man and man.

Buber's philosophy of dialogue radically shifts the whole ground of ethical discussion by moving from the universal to the concrete and from the past to the present—in other words, from I-It to I-Thou. Buber does not start from some external, absolutely valid ethical code which man is bound to apply as best as possible to each new situation. Instead he starts with the situation itself.

The idea of responsibility is to be brought back from the province of specialized ethics, of an "ought" that swings free in the air, into that of lived life. Genuine responsibility exists only where there is real responding.[12]

Most of the traditional ethical values—not killing, stealing, commiting adultery, lying, cheating, and so forth—are in fact implied in the I-Thou relation, but not as an abstract code valid in advance of particular situations. Rather one must move from the concrete situation to the decision as to what is the right direction in this instance, one does not go directly from a conscious precept to a moral action, for no action in which a person involved himself merely on a conscious level could really be moral in a meaningful sense of the term. Rather one goes from deep-seated attitudes, of which one is perhaps not fully aware, to the response to the present situation which produces the moral action. The precept and teaching may, of course, have influenced those attitudes: the person may have taken them in at some point and mixed them with himself in such a way that at some time in the future he may indeed act in a manner corresponding to the precept; but it is not by his having memorized the precept and recognized it as a universal moral injunction that this takes place. What Buber writes of the 'great character" also holds true, to a lesser extent, of any responsible person's relation to moral norms.

No responsible person remains a stranger to norms. But the command inherent in a genuine norm never becomes a maxim and the fulfilment of it never a habit. Any command that a great character takes to himself in the

12 *Between Man and Man*, p. 16.

course of his development does not act in him as a part of his consciousness or as material for building up his exercises, but remains latent in a basic layer of his substance until it reveals itself to him in a concrete way. What it has to tell him is revealed whenever a situation arises which demands of him a solution of which till then he had perhaps no idea. Even the most universal norm will at times be recognized only in a very special situation . . . . In moments like these the command addresses us really in the second person, and the Thou in it is no one else but one's own self. Maxims command only the third person, the each and the none.[18]

III

What then are we to conclude about the relation and relative importance of Buber's philosophical anthropology and his philosophy of religion as sources of his ethics? First, that Buber's ethics is directly based on and informed by his philosophical anthropology—that these two are, in fact, inseparable since the problem of what man is includes the question of authentic existence, what it means to be really human, while ethics must be grounded in a descriptive as well as normative definition of what man "is" if its "ought" is to have any meaning or force. Certainly, it is in Buber's philosophical anthropology that one can see the main categories of his ethics spelled out. Yet these very categories—awareness and response, responsibility, uniqueness, decision, direction, personal wholeness—imply, as we have seen, Buber's philosophy of religion. If man becomes authentic, if the person becomes what only he can and should become, it is through responding with his whole being to the address of the unique situation which confronts him, through becoming whole and finding his true personal direction—the direction to God. Inauthentic existence, conversely, is the failure to enter into dialogue, to attain personal wholeness, to find direction, to make true decision, to direct one's passion through making his casual relations essential ones. In what Buber calls the second stage of evil, further, a course of decisionlessness ends in an absolute affirmation of oneself and the denial of God—of any order and reality over against one that might stand in judgment of one's existence.

Buber's answer to the question of the Euthyphro, if implicit, is quite clear: God does not will in accordance with some independent order of the good; on the contrary, the very meaning of "good" and of any order of good that exists is derived from our relation to God

[18] *Ibid.*, p. 114.

and his demand that we make real our created existence by becoming human, becoming real. The choice for Buber is not between religion and morality, as it is for Kierkegaard, but between a religion and morality wedded to the universal and a religion and morality wedded to the concrete.

Only out of a personal relationship with the Absolute can the absoluteness of the ethical co-ordinates arise without which there is no complete awareness of self. Even when the individual calls an absolute criterion handed down by religious tradition his own, it must be reforged in the fire of the truth of his personal essential relation to the Absolute if it is to win true validity. But always it is the religious which bestows, the ethical which receives.[14]

The reason why it is always the religious which bestows and the ethical which receives is to be found in the nature of good as Buber understands it. The good for Buber is not an objective state of affairs or an inner feeling, but a type of relationship—the dialogue between man and man and between man and God.

Every ethos has its origin in a revelation, whether or not it is still aware of and obedient to it; and every revelation is revelation of human service to the goal of creation, in which service man authenticates himself.[15]

This means that the good cannot be referred back to any Platonic universal or impersonal order of the cosmos, nor can it be founded in any general system of utility or interest. It grows instead out of what is most particular and concrete—not the quasi-concreteness of the "empirically verifiable," but the actual present concreteness of the unique direction which one apprehends and realizes in the meeting with the everyday.

At this point, then, Buber's philosophical anthropology and his philosophy of religion converge. We are still left, however, with our original question of whether Buber's philosophy of religion implies "revelation" in a special, specifically religious sense that is not implied by his anthropology. Is the "personal relationship with the absolute" out of which the ethical receives its absoluteness and each man achieves his awareness of self the same as the "revelation" in which "every ethos has its origin," the revelation of "human service to the goal of creation . . . in which man authenticates himself"?

[14] *Eclipse of God*, "Religion and Ethics," p. 129.
[15] *Good and Evil*, pp. 143f.

"The mighty revelations at the base of the great religions are the same in being as the quiet ones that happen at all times," writes Buber in *I and Thou*. And this view is carried forward: "What is given to an individual in this present moment leads to the understanding of the great revelations, but the vital fact is one's own personal receiving and not what was received in former times."[16] In his latest statement on revelation, Buber distinguishes between historical revelations, which are objectifiable and communicable precisely because they are historical and have entered into the life of a group in a given hour of history, and personal revelations without known historical results. These latter cannot be dealt with or communicated, for they do not exist at all "objectively."

But every person open to the influx of the message conveyed by everyday events could and should know that there is no *absolute* difference between such a message and what we call by the name of revelation. What differs, essentially, is the degree of certainty.

Even this difference in certainty is not a great one for the modern man who, like Buber himself, cannot go back on his knowledge of the inmixture of human substance in the historical revelation in which the divine flame nonetheless dwells, never to be distinguished from it. But neither can such men "renounce the historical tradition that has moulded them religiously."

What they can and must do, is to listen again and again, in order to learn which of the commandments of tradition can be heard by them as being commanded by God to them, and of course to live consequently. This can be done only in the stern responsibility of faith.[17]

We must conclude, therefore, that Buber's own working attitude toward the relation between religion and ethics is closer to the "fear and trembling" of the "Single One," as he describes him, than to the essential certainty of the Hasidic community in whose highest hours the separate spheres of religion and ethics merge into human holiness.[18] In "The Question to the Single One" Buber

---

[16] *I and Thou*, pp. 116f.; *Israel and the World*, pp. 94f.

[17] From a statement on Revelation written by Buber in the fall of 1955 in response to questions of the present writer.

[18] Or rather, as Buber himself puts it in response to this passage, in a letter to the present writer of October 7, 1958, "The first is necessarily my point of departure, the second is my hope that, as history tells me, can be fulfilled.'

modifies Kierkegaard's conception by insisting that the Single One must have essential relations to the creature as well as to the Creator, that he must belong to the group while preserving a boundary-line to his membership in the group. Yet he preserves the individual responsibility before God and the "fear and trembling" with which man dares his stammering answer to God's address. In his Hasidic essay, "Love of God and Love of Neighbor," Buber refers to this same position as that of a type of man "especially significant for our age . . . the man who does not have the faith that he knows with assurance through a tradition what God commands him to do in his life."

He regards the traditional revelation as a fusion of the divine and the human . . . . Certainly, he receives from all things and events a divine claim on his person, but in general no indication is thereby given to him as to what he should do for God in this hour, in this situation; rather at most, so to speak, a question is directed to him that he must fill in with his own doing and not doing. . . . No matter how powerful the concentration of the innermost forces, the conscience at no time has any certainty. . . . There are, certainly, hours in which he acts as with full authority, but, also those in which he experiences complete abandonment, and between the two runs his life.[19]

What this means in practice is seen in Buber's incisive criticism of Kierkegaard's conception of "the suspension of the ethical." Buber does not deny Kierkegaard's starting point: that God's command to Abraham to sacrifice his son Isaac was a unique revelation by God that could not be put into any framework of universal morality. But Buber does deny the consequences that Kierkegaard draws from this. Kierkegaard turns the unique situation of Abraham into a more general and equivocal one in which the "knight of faith" must decide for himself who is the "Isaac" whom God wants him to sacrifice. More important still, Kierkegaard takes for granted what even the Bible could not: that the Voice one hears is always the voice of God, that the only right response is obedience.

Abraham, to be sure, could not confuse with another the voice which once bade him leave his homeland. . . . It can happen, however, that a sinful man is uncertain whether he does not have to sacrifice his (perhaps also very beloved) son to God for his sins (Micah 6:7). For Moloch imitates the voice of God. In contrast to this, God Himself demands of this as of every man (not of Abraham, His chosen one, but of you and me) nothing more than justice

---

[19] *Hasidism and Modern Man*, pp. 227ff., 232.

and love, and that he 'walk humbly' with Him, with God (Micah 6:8) —in other words, not much more than the fundamental ethical.[20]

Ours is an age, says Buber, in which the Kierkegaardian suspension of the ethical for the sake of the religious fills the world in a caricaturized form. Everywhere, over the whole surface of the human world, false absolutes pierce unhindered through the level of the ethical and demand "the sacrifice" of personal integrity in order that equality may come, that freedom may come, or that the Kingdom may come. "In the realm of Moloch honest men lie and compassionate men torture. And they really and truly believe that brother-murder will prepare the way for brotherhood!" The cure for this situation is not returning to some objective, universal order of ethics but the rise of a new conscience which will summon men to guard with the innermost power of their souls against the confusion of the relative with the Absolute. The limits, the limitedness of the false Absolute must be discovered by that "incorruptible probing glance"[21] which comes to those who stand their ground in each situation anew and meet it in all its uniqueness. If the "fundamental ethical" thus remains a part of the life of dialogue, this does not imply the special revelation that God makes to Abraham, "His chosen one," but only that dialogue between man and man which is at the same time a dialogue between man and God—a personal revelation, but not necessarily a historical one.

It is misleading, therefore, to overemphasize the part which revelation plays in Martin Buber's ethics unless one keeps in mind that he is here referring primarily to the "everyday revelation" of Micah rather than the exceptional historical revelation of Abraham. The life of the individual, of course, is set in history, and history cannot be understood apart from the historical revelation in the Bible and elsewhere. Buber's moral philosophy, however,—in so far as we may delimit such a sphere within the totality of his thought—does not depend decisively on this latter.

IV

There are two other sources which we must look at in connection with our problem of the bases of Buber's ethics—both late develop-

[20] *Eclipse of God,* "On the Suspension of the Ethical," p. 153.
[21] *Ibid.,* pp. 154ff.

ments in his philosophical anthropology. The one is his essay, "What Is Common to All"—a study of Heraclitus that sets Heraclitus' injunction, "One should follow the common," in contrast with Taoist, Hindu, and modern mystical teachings which Buber characterizes as a flight from "the arch reality out of which all community stems—human meeting." By denying the uniqueness of the human person, these teachings annihilate it, one's own person as well as the other; for human existence and the intercourse of men that grows out of it is the chance for meeting in which each says to the other, not "I am you," but "I accept you as you are." "Here first is uncurtailed existence."

That Buber's basis for this distinction between Heraclitus and the Eastern teachings is, in the first instance, his anthropology, with its conception of authentic existence, rather than his philosophy of religion as such, is made clear by his criticism of Aldous Huxley's counsel to the use of the mescalin drug:

Man may master as he will his situation, to which his surroundings also belong; he may withstand it, he may alter it, he may, when it is necessary, exchange it for another; but the fugitive flight out of the claim of the situation into situationless-ness is no legitimate affair of man. And the true name of all paradises which man creates for himself by chemical or other means is situationless-ness.[22]

While man has his thoughts and experiences as "I," it is as "We" that he raises these thoughts and experiences into being itself, into just that mode of existence that Buber calls "the between." Nor is this We, in any sense, of a secondary or merely instrumental importance. It is basic to existence as such, and in an age such as ours "in which the true meaning of every word is encompassed by delusion and falsehood and the original intention of the human glance is stifled by tenacious mistrust," man is threatened with ceasing to exist at all if he does not recover the genuineness of speech and existence as We. Even the mystic who turns away from the We to a deepened contemplation of existing being is still fleeing from the "leaping fire" with which, in his seventh epistle, Plato describes the dynamics between persons in the We.

The flight from the common cosmos into a special sphere that is understood as the true being is, in all its stages, from the elemental sayings of the ancient

22 *The Knowledge of Man*, p. 100.

Eastern teachings to the arbitrariness of the modern counsel to intoxication, a flight from the existential claim on the person who must authenticate himself in We. It is a flight from the authentic spokenness of speech in whose realm a response is demanded, and response is responsibility.[23]

It is particularly remarkable that Buber rests his case against the Taoist, Vedantist, and modern mystic primarily on anthropological grounds since we are confronted here with basic differences in the understanding of reality, meaning, and value that are in the last instance religious in nature: no nondualist Vedantist would be troubled by Buber's criticism since for him true "personal" existence and the true We are found precisely on the road that Buber holds annihilates them. On the other hand, the common "logos" of speech and response is not merely a similarity between Heraclitus and the Biblical prophets, as Buber points out: it is grounded much more securely in the Biblical view of existence as the dialogue between man and God than in Heraclitus' concept of a reality that "was and is and ever shall be ever living Fire." And Buber himself recognizes this limitation to the possibility of enregistering Heraclitus' teaching of the common in the "life of dialogue":

What he designates as the common has nothing that is over against it as such: logos and cosmos are, to him, self-contained; there is nothing that transcends them. . . . No salvation is in sight for us, however, if we are not able again "to stand before the face of God" in all reality as a We—as it is written in that faithful speech that once from Israel . . . started on its way.[24]

Unhappily, Buber concludes with this paragraph. He does not, as we should have liked, explain to us wherein the common logos and cosmos of Heraclitus was lacking—as dialogue? as authentic existence itself, in its historical dimension? or in the dimension of religious revelation? However, we can in any case conclude that Buber is here recognizing that the ultimate, even if not the immediate base, for his view of authentic existence and for the anthropology in which it is set is religious. Whether this religious base implies, further, a special historical revelation generically different from the revelation that comes in the common speech-with-meaning that makes us a We—about this we cannot reach a conclusion. We

23 *Ibid.*, pp. 107f.
24 *Ibid.*, pp. 108f.

can retain our original hypothesis, nonetheless, if we interpret this final disclaimer to mean, first, that real existence as a We is not possible in a self-contained cosmos but only in ever-renewed dialogue with what is over against one and, second, that although one stands in a We through actual or potential relations between person and person, the We too must sometimes be like an I: to find its own true existence, it too has to enter into relation with the Thou that confronts it—the Thou of other nations, of history, of God.

Buber's treatment of guilt takes us a step further still in understanding the relation between his anthropology and his philosophy of religion. "Original guilt consists in remaining with oneself," Buber says in "What Is Man?" But in "Religion and Ethics," as we have seen, guilt arises from not becoming what one is called to become, not remaining faithful to a task or vocation one has become certain of. Guilt in this case is the product of not taking the direction toward God. But since the direction toward God is found in the meeting with what one encounters in each new hour, we can say at one and the same time that the guilty man is he who shuns the dialogue with God and he who does not enter into the dialogue with man and the world.

In "Guilt and Guilt Feelings," however, Buber distinguishes between three interrelated levels on which one must deal with guilt and reconciliation—the legal, the personal, and the religious. These levels can only be understood in the context of the basic distinction of the essay—that between "groundless" neurotic guilt which is a subjective feeling within a person and "existential guilt" which is an ontic, interhuman reality in which the person dwells. The standpoint from which we must apprehend existential guilt is not that of the repression of social or parental reprimands but "the real insight into the irreversibility of lived time, a fact that shows itself unmistakably in the starkest of all human perspectives, that concerning one's own death." This insight shows us the impossibility of recovering the original point of departure or repairing what has been done. Swept along in the torrent of time, the self in guilt shudders with the realization that he, who has become another, is nonetheless identical with himself, the man whose action or failure to act has burdened him with guilt. The existential discovery of time as a torrent is identical, therefore, with the existential discovery of personal responsibility as extending over time. Existential guilt is "guilt that a person has taken on himself as a person and in a personal situation." But this personal guilt is at the same time and by the same token objective, or rather dialogical, guilt which transcends the realm of inner feelings and of the self's relation to itself: "Existential guilt occurs when someone injures an order of the human world whose foundations he knows and recognizes as those of his own existence and of all common human existence." This "order of the human world" is not an objective absolute existing apart from man: it is the interhuman itself, the genuine We, the common logos and cosmos in Buber's interpretation of Heraclitus. The objective relationship in which each man stands toward others and through which he is able to expand his environment (*Umwelt*) into a world (*Welt*) "is his share in the human order of being, the share for which he bears responsibility." This objective relationship can rise through existential participation into a personal relation; but it can also be merely tolerated, neglected, or injured, and the injury of the relationship is an injury at this place of the human order of being. Buber indicates, correspondingly, a threefold response to existential guilt:

first, to illuminate the darkness that still weaves itself about the guilt . . . ; second, to persevere . . . in that newly won humble knowledge of the identity of the present person with the person of that time; and third, in his place and according to his capacity, in the given historical and biographical situations, to restore the order-of-being injured by him through the relation of an active devotion to the world.[25]

Now, however, Buber distinguishes between three different, though related, spheres in which the reconciliation or reparation of guilt can take place: first, the sphere of the law of society in which confession of guilt is followed by penalty and indemnification; second, the sphere of conscience with its three stages of illumination, perseverance, and reconciliation; and "the third and highest sphere, that of faith." In this last sphere "the action commences within the relation between the guilty man and his God and remains therein," and it is likewise consummated in three events: confession of sin, repentance, and penance. The sphere of conscience is the sphere of real existential guilt which arises out of man's being "and for which he cannot take responsibility without being responsible to his relationship to his own being." Buber does not speak of guilt here, as he does in "Religion and Ethics," as the denial of the created task to which one is called. All the more significant, therefore, is the relationship which

25 *The Knowledge of Man*, pp. 125f., 132–136.

Buber indicates between the separate spheres of conscience and of faith.

This relationship is already implicit in reconciliation, as Buber understands it: reconciliation is only valid, he writes, if it happens "out of the core of a transformed relationship to the world, a new service to the world with the renewed forces of the renewed man." Although, we may suppose, such transformation can take place outside the sphere of faith, it is preeminently in that sphere that man's whole existence becomes involved and renewed. Man is never guilty toward himself alone. He "is always guilty toward other beings as well, toward the world, toward the being that exists over against him." Reconciliation, accordingly, must mean reconciliation with others, with the world, and with the reality that he meets ever again, the "Eternal Thou." Not as if the sphere of conscience is swallowed by the sphere of faith, but the two exist separately and together at once:

For the sincere man of faith, the two spheres are so referred to each other in the practice of his life, and most especially when he has gone through existential guilt, that he cannot trust himself exclusively to either of them.[26]

Both spheres can err, both—conscience not less than faith—must place themselves in the hands of grace. And if Buber will not speak "of the inner reality of him who refuses to believe in a transcendent being with whom he can communicate," he does report the way in which existential guilt, hence the sphere of the conscience, leads to a personal transformation in which the sphere of the conscience and that of faith are indistinguishable:

I have met many men in the course of my life who have told me how, acting from the high conscience as men who had become guilty, they experienced themselves as seized by a higher power. These men grew into an existential state to which the name of rebirth is due.[27]

V

Can we say, then, that it is possible to carve out of Buber's philosophy an autonomous ethics, free from a necessary connection

[26] *Ibid.*, pp. 146-148.
[27] *Ibid.*, p. 148.

with religion? Yes and no. Yes, if we mean by religion a separate sphere of special, specifically religious revelation and command; no, if we understand God's "Where art thou, Adam?" to be addressed to every man at every hour through each everyday event that confronts him, for then "religion" is just man's listening and responding to this address. But it is precisely here that the problem of the bases of Buber's ethics becomes most acute. For if I find authentic existence in the meeting with the Thou over against me, I cannot make that meeting a means to the end of attaining authentic existence without reducing my partner to an It and robbing the meeting of all its genuineness, including its beneficial effect on my own existence. "What humanity is," and hence what I am, "can be grasped only in vital reciprocity." "There resides in every man the possibility of attaining authentic existence in the special way peculiar to him," writes Buber. This basic assumption of Buber's anthropology is clearly founded on his understanding of creation, and attaining authentic existence means here fulfillment of the unique task given one in one's very creation. Here, at its deepest point, therefore, Buber's anthropology clearly rests on a philosophy of religion which is itself nothing other than a pointing to an individual and historical relation to the Eternal Thou, a pointing to that *emuna,* or trust in the relation with God, which is the basic reality of Biblical faith. The concern for authentic personal existence, hence, can never mean that the self is its own goal:

The self as such is not ultimately the essential, but the meaning of human existence given in creation again and again fulfills itself as self. . . . The dynamic glory of the being of man is first bodily present in the relation between two men each of whom in meaning the other also means the highest to which this person is called, and serves the self-realization of this human life as one true to creation.[28]

Thus we are pointed back to the concrete, particular I-Thou relationship both for the general source of value and the specific answer to the question, "What ought I do to do in this situation?"

It would be a mistake to understand the "ought" that arises out of this ethic to mean that one ought every moment to be in an I-Thou relationship, as if that were an ideal to aim for. The "ought" that is asked of one is the *"quantum satis"*—what one is capable of at any

---

[28] *The Knowledge of Man,* p. 85.

moment. And only the person himself can know what this is and then only in the situation itself, not before.

One does not learn the measure and limit of what is attainable in a desired direction otherwise than through going in this direction. The forces of the soul allow themselves to be measured only through one's using them.[29]

Sometimes one is capable of very little indeed, sometimes more than one dreamed possible, for what one is able to do, his potentiality, is called out of him by his response to the situation. This means that the "ought" grows out of the particular interrelation of I-Thou and I-It in that situation.

In *I and Thou* Buber defines "love" not as a feeling within each partner, but as a supra-individual reality *between* the two. This betweenness, however, is the responsibility of an I *for* a Thou and not just *to* him. "Dialogue" means "our entering . . . into the situation which has at this moment stepped up to us, whose appearance we did not know and could not know, for its like has not yet been." Yet there must also be the continuity of being responsible *for* what we have responded *to:*

A situation of which we have become aware is never finished with, but we subdue it into the substance of lived life. Only then, true to the moment, do we experience a life that is something other than a sum of moments. We respond to this moment, but at the same time we respond on its behalf, we answer for it. A newly-created concrete reality has been laid in our arms; we answer for it. A dog has looked at you, you answer for its glance, a child has clutched your hand, you answer for its touch, a host of men moves about you, you answer for their need.[30]

Our responsibility for another does not prevent our having an I-Thou relation to someone else than he. Nonetheless, it is a commitment that in some way limits our possibilities of new response, a "fidelity," as Gabriel Marcel would put it, that binds the past and the present with the future. This continued responsibility is implicit in Buber's treatment of existential guilt: the first response to it, as we have seen, must be the illuminating recognition of the fact of guilt and of the fact that I, who am so different from what I was, am nonetheless identical with the person who injured the common exist-

[29] *Between Man and Man,* pp. 36ff.; *Pointing the Way,* p. 206.
[30] *Between Man and Man,* p. 17.

ence in the past and caused the guilt that I carry; the second stage is the perseverance in this self-identification; and the third the reconciliation with the injured order of being at whatever point is possible to me, including, if it can still be done, approaching the man toward whom I am guilty in the light of my self-illumination, acknowledging to his face my existential guilt, and helping him, in so far as possible, to overcome the consequences of my guilty action.[31]

The continuity of being "responsible for" a Thou as well as responsive to him is essential for an ethic of personal relations that includes continuing, committed relationships such as friendship, love, marriage, the relationship between teacher and student, therapist and patient, pastor and congregant. Spontaneity does not mean gratuitous, arbitrary action; for response with the whole being includes all that one has been, including one's past I-Thou relations with this person and others. Although it is true, moreover, that it is only in an I-Thou relationship that I apprehend the unique value of the other and am able to experience his side of the relationship and know what can help him, still I do not necessarily cease to deal lovingly with him even when he is no longer Thou for me in any but a formal sense.

Since the human Thou must constantly become an It, one is ultimately responsible to the Eternal Thou who never becomes an It. But it is just in the concrete that we meet the Eternal Thou, and it is this which prevents dialogue from degenerating into "responsibility" to an abstract moral code or universal idea. Man is created in the image of God. But I do not respect my fellowman as a deduction from this premise. On the contrary, I realize him as created in the image of God only when I meet him in his concrete uniqueness as Thou. What is meant by love thy neighbor, if it is to become real and not just remain a warm glow in one's heart, can only be discovered in the situation. The I-Thou relation, similarly, is the only relationship in which I discover that men are equal in the only way that they really are equal—that each is of unique value, of value in himself, and that in the meeting with this unique other my own existence is authenticated.

In that relation which claims my whole being, which I must enter as a person, and in which I find the meaning of my existence, in that relation which calls me forth and to which I respond, in that

31 *The Knowledge of Man,* pp. 125–127, 136.

relation of freedom, direction, mutuality, and presentness, there is no room left over to speak of a separate relationship with God. No matter how "inward" he may be, the "religious" man still lives in the world. If he does not have an I-Thou relation with the world, therefore, he necessarily makes the world into an It. He treats it solely as a means for his sustenance and an object for his contemplation. "He who knows the world as something by which he is to profit, knows God also in the same way."[32]

This does not mean, however, that there is a relation to the Eternal Thou only at the moments when there is an *actual* relation to the human Thou. Then our moral responsibility might seem to be subject to the same discontinuity and fragility as our human relationships themselves. In *I and Thou* Buber speaks of the meeting with the temporal Thou as at the same time a meeting with the Eternal Thou: "In each process of becoming that is present to us . . ., in each *thou* we address the eternal *Thou*," "the *Thou* in which the parallel lines of relations meet." But he also speaks of the relation to the Eternal Thou as summons and sending and of the primal twofold movement of "estrangement from" and "turning toward" the primal Source.

Every real relation in the world is consummated in the interchange of actual and potential being, but in pure relation—in the relation of man to God— potential is still actual being. . . . By virtue of this great privilege of pure relation there exists the unbroken world of Thou which binds up the isolated moments of relation in a life of world solidarity.[33]

Does not this mean that we relate to the present and actual Eternal Thou even when the temporal Thou has again become only past and potential, that is, when it has again become It? This does not mean that we have a relation to the Eternal Thou apart from our relation to the temporal Thou, but that our relation to the Eternal Thou is the very foundation of our relation to the temporal Thou if the latter is understood deeply enough. That we are able ever again to meet as Thou either the person who was Thou for us but is now It or some other whom we have never before related to as Thou already implies a continuing, even though not continuous, relation with the Thou that does not become It. It is this potentiality of his

[32] *I and Thou*, p. 107.
[33] *Ibid.*, pp. 100f.

being or again being a Thou for us that ultimately prevents—if anything does—our treating the man whom we do not know as Thou, purely as a dispensable It. And this "potential Thou" rests not only on the "actual Thou" of remembered I-Thou relationships but on the "Actual Thou" of Present Reality—the relation to the Eternal Thou "in which potential is still actual being."

The key difference between the Eternal and the temporal Thou in this respect is that within the very meaning of the former, I-It is also real—that no existent is so God-forsaken that it is cut off from reality, no existence so God-forsaken that it is by its very nature cut off from *real* existence. Even the movement away from relationship is a part of the reality of relationship itself. Trust is trust that there is meaning in the world: it is trust in the world as a world of *potential* Thou. Although again and again in particular situations the Thou and the It are opposed, this trust implies the conviction that ultimately they stand in a dialectical rather than a dualistic relation to each other, that they are, as Buber himself puts it, "two world aspects" rather than "two worlds."[34]

We can understand the problematics of this trust more fully if we turn from the general questions that arise concerning Buber's moral philosophy to the very real problems that confront us as soon as we have to make a difficult moral decision, sacrificing one person or another, one value or another, one goal or another. How do we arrive at a moral decision when we are responsible to more than one Thou and these responsibilities seem incompatible? How are we to distinguish within a particular relationship between I-Thou and I-It relations, how can we know which in fact dominates and when I-Thou may really be a front for I-It? How do we know when a friendship is a true one? How are we to distinguish between that element in a guilt feeling that is based on "existential guilt" and that which is "groundless" and neurotic? How do we know when we are responding with the whole being? How do we know that what we take to be a whole response is not really so intense a partial response that we are unaware of the parts that are suppressed?

These problems point us back in turn to a special problem in the interrelation and interaction of I-Thou and I-It. Since "evil" is defined by Buber as the domination of the Thou by the It and since such evil does exist and again and again vitiates human relations, we

[34] From a letter to the author of October 7, 1958.

cannot take it for granted that any particular I-It relation is a potential I-Thou in the sense of a direct movement being possible from
that situation to an I-Thou relation. It is necessary to distinguish
here between two stages in the transition from I-Thou to I-It: first,
that which as social structure, convention, or agreement, or,
in the case of knowledge, as word, symbol, or image, points back
directly to the unique reciprocal contact and knowing of particular
I-Thou relationships and, second, that which, because it takes the
form of self-perpetuating structures or abstract and general categories, no longer leads or points back to the meeting with the concrete and the unique but instead takes its place and blocks the return.
The first stage of I-Thou relation or knowledge is a primary level of
abstraction and objectification that derives directly from the concrete
meeting with the Thou and may lead back to it again. It may also
serve, however, as material for still further objectification and structuring. Once this second step is accomplished, it cannot so easily lead
directly back to the particular I-Thou meeting even though it may
originally derive from it. An operationalist description of interpersonal relationships from the standpoint of a behaviorist observer, for
example, though it be based on the observation of relationships
many of which were genuinely I-Thou, can never point back to the
concreteness and uniqueness of an I-Thou relationship in the way a
poem or novel could because it has extracted only the general categories through which these relationships could be compared. But in
direct and reciprocal relationships themselves, what may once have
been genuine mutual relation may become a formality or a pretense
from which position a direct return to the I-Thou may be impossible.
The trust in the potential Thou, accordingly, cannot mean the trust
that any particular relationship will ascend or reascend from It to
Thou, but only the refusal to exclude any relationship in principle
from that possibility.

The very limits of our existence make it necessary for every temporal Thou to become an It. Where then is the meaning, the reality
that I find in the meeting with the particular Thou who becomes an
It? Through each Thou I meet *the* Thou—I do not meet the same
Thou, in the sense of an "essence of Thou" or a particular form
of Thou, but once again I find present meaning, present reality.
Ultimately we can find no continuity or security beyond this. The
trust in existence that enables us to live from moment to moment
and to go out to meet what the new moment brings is the trust that

somehow or other in this new meeting we shall again become whole, alive, present. If I trust in a person, a relationship, this means that despite what may and will happen, I trust that I will find a new moment of presentness, I shall enter relationship again and bring all the past moments of Thou and the moments of It too into present meeting. The particular person to whom I now say Thou may die, become sick, become disturbed; he may betray me, rupture the relationship, or simply turn away and fail to respond. And sooner or later something of this does happen for most of us. When it does, it is trust too which enables us to remain open and respond to the new address of the new situation. To relate to the Eternal Thou means that, despite the fact that we cannot possibly preserve a smooth continuity of relations with the temporal Thou, we find the full meaning of our existence by again and again bringing the world into our relationship with the Thou. If we lose our trust in existence, conversely, we are no longer able to enter anew into relationship. The "existential mistrust" between man and man stems from the destruction of trust in human existence itself. "At its core the conflict between mistrust and trust of man conceals the conflict between the mistrust and trust of eternity."[35]

Trust means trust in this present which I am never going to grasp fully with my mind since there are always at least two points of view, two realities which can never be included in any single perspective—my own existence and what is over against me. It also means trust in the future—trust that we shall meet the Thou again in a new form and a new situation. These two trusts supplement each other. If we had no trust in the present Thou, then neither could we trust in the future one. But if we had no trust in the future, then we would lose even what we did have in the present: the mistrust of existence itself would enter as a corroding force into every relationship making impossible full acceptance of the present and going out to meet it with our whole being. Then the present would indeed become nothing but a vanishing moment in which the future is forever going over into the past. Ultimate trust—trust in existence itself—is trust in the present and future at once. It is trust in the God who will be there even as he will be there, who will be with us even when we walk, as we will, in the valley of the shadow of death.

[35] *Pointing the Way,* pp. 224, 229.

It is this God who is *re*-cognized in each genuine meeting with the utterly new, the utterly unique.

It is, then, our trust in the Eternal Thou, our trust in existence itself, that ultimately gives actuality and continuity to our discontinuous and often merely potential relations to the human Thou. And it is this trust, too, that gives continuity and reality to our own existence as persons; for in itself personality is neither continuous nor always actual. If it is the confirmation of others and our own self-confirmation that gets us over the gaps and breaks in the first instance, it is our trust in existence itself that enables this individual course to become a personal direction rather than a meaningless flux. Without a personal relationship with the Absolute, as Buber hast said, "there is no complete awareness of self."

The word person really bridges over and unites three separate realities in the life of the person: on the one hand, when one speaks of person and personality, one speaks of that mysterious imprint of the person, the whole, the I, on an incessantly changing, varying process which could have no essential unity if it were not for this imprint.

To be aware of a man . . . means in particular to perceive his wholeness as a person determined by the spirit; it means to perceive the dynamic center which stamps his every utterance, action, and attitude with the recognizable sign of uniqueness.[36]

Secondly, however, the person finds his full reality in the present, and personality exists in an actualized form only in the present. When we speak, as we must, of personality extending over time, it is the alternation between actual and potential personality of which we speak. Everything that we use to define the term person manifests itself only in presentness, but sometimes there is a present reality of the person and sometimes it does not exist in an actualized form. The existence of the person in time is not a smooth process but an alternation between moments of real presentness and other moments when a person falls from presentness.

A person finds himself as person, thirdly, through going out to meet the Thou, through responding to the address of the Thou. This means, on the one hand, that he remains a person, a Single One: he does not simply lose his borders in an amorphous meeting

---

[36] *The Knowledge of Man*, p. 80.

with the other. He does not lose his standpoint, his center, his personal core; if he sees through the eyes of the other and experiences the other side, he does not cease to see through his own eyes and experience the relationship from his side. Yet at the same time, he does not find his wholeness simply through remaining shut or closed within himself, through going inward, or through using his relations with others as means to his own self-realization. He realizes himself as an I, a person, through going out again and again to meet the other. The Thou "teaches you to meet others and to hold your ground when you meet them."

We meet the Eternal Thou only in our existence as persons, only in our meeting with the other: we cannot know it as if from outside this existence. The philosopher who recognizes this "must renounce the attempt to include God in his system in any conceptual form." He must "point toward God, without actually dealing with him."[37] The philosophy of dialogue precludes, therefore, even the most creative and organic of process philosophies and on this account alone invalidates the attempt which some have made to subsume Buber's philosophy of religion under Whitehead's metaphysics.[38] One meets the God who transcends one's self. This does not mean that the other one meets is "supernatural." The term "natural," however, leads us to forget the reality over against us and to see our existence as entirely included in a conceptual totality which we call "nature," "world," or "universe." In our actual experience, reality, including all other selves, is over against us and not included along with us in some common reality that may be seen from the outside. Much modern thought confuses the subjectivity of the person and the subjectivity of man: it treats man as a totality and what is immanent in him as if it were in a single self. In our concrete existence, however, there is no such totality. The Thou confronts us with the unexpected, takes us unawares. We must stand our ground yet be prepared to go forth again and again to meet we know not what. It is not insight into process but trust in existence that enables us to enter into any genuine meeting with the unique reality that accosts us in the new moment.

There is often a correlation between a thinker's approach to ethics and his approach to philosophy of religion. Those thinkers

[37] *Eclipse of God,* p. 68f.

[38] Cf. Paul E. Pfuetze, *The Social Self* (New York: Bookmans Associates, 1954), pp. 280f., 296n. 152.

who feel that religion is solidly founded only when it rests on proofs
of the existence of God that put God into a rational framework of
universal order or law stand in opposition to the Biblical trust (*emuna*) that receives only what it receives without demanding that
God, man, and world be installed in any objective, comprehensible
totality. The security of the former rests on the cosmos that human
understanding has opened to it, the "holy insecurity" of the latter
on the trust in the reality over against one "that can only properly
be addressed and not expressed"—in the meeting with the God whom
one can talk *to* but not *about*. Similarly, those who demand a logical,
ordered ethics often do so not because they have reason to believe
in the objectivity of the moral order, but because they have an almost
magic belief that what they posit as fixed, objective, and universal
provides security and solidity and protects us against the threat of
the irrational and the demonic, the romantic and the Hitlerian.
Those who criticize Buber's ethics on this basis complain that if one
leaves ethics to the moment and has no a priori values there will be
no guide, but they usually leave to one side the all-important problem
of the *basis* of moral obligation, the question of whether in fact such
an objective moral order exists.

Buber's moral philosophy implies that one ever again finds the
absolute in the relative—not as a timeless essence or universal, but
just in and inseparable from the unique, the unrepeatable, the new.
The reason that the first principle of morality for Buber is hearing
and responding is not that the other person is God or contains the
essence of God, or "that of God in him," but that he is the creature
of God, that the world is God's creation. One's antagonist may, indeed, be the devil or Hitler, but even such a one must be faithfully
answered, contended with. This is the crucial link between Buber's
ethics, his philosophy of religion, and his interpretation of the Bible;
for this faithful hearing and responding has only one basic assumption that is not given in the ethics itself—the assumption implicit
in creation: reality is not given in me alone or in some selected part
of reality with which I identify myself. Just everything that confronts
me demands my attention and response—whether of love or hate,
agreement or opposition to the death—just because it is the reality,
and the only reality, that is given me in that moment. The corollary

of this presupposition is that there is no thing and no event that is absolutely meaningless or absolutely evil, even though meaninglessness and evil are inescapable components of all human existence. This is the *emuna*, the Biblical trust, underlying Buber's ethics. It is the trust that dialogue is the basic and encompassing reality, I-It the secondary and partial one. The ultimate check of the authenticity of an I-Thou relationship is the verification that comes in dialogue itself. Buber does not *prove* his moral philosophy, correspondingly. Rather, he points to the concrete meeting with the situation in which alone it can be tried and tested. Not only the content of ethics, but also the formal nature and basis of ethics itself must be validated, verified, and authenticated in "the lived concrete."

The name Satan means in Hebrew the hinderer. That is the correct designation for the anti-human in individuals and the human race. Let us not allow this Satanic element in men to hinder us from realizing man! . . . Let us dare, despite all, to trust![39]

The traditional approach to ethics is Greek; Martin Buber's is Biblical. In the Crito and The Republic the good is intrinsic to a person's being but not to the relations between man and man themselves: one is just not for the sake of justice but in order not to injure one's soul; justice is primarily a reality of the soul rather than of the interhuman. In the Psalms, in contrast, man's very existence is set in relationship with reality that confronts him, and this relationship transcends "ethics" in the usual understanding of the term:

The Psalmist has . . . another purpose than the philosopher, who tells us that virtue is its own reward. . . . What he really means is completely untouched by what the philosopher could say to him about the "self-enjoyment" of the moral man. What he means about the life of the man of whom he speaks cannot be grasped by means of moral values; and what he means about his happiness has its home in another sphere from that of a man's self-satisfaction. Both the conduct of the man's life and his happiness in their nature transcend the realm of ethics as well as that of self-consciousness. Both are to be understood only from a man's intercourse with God.[40]

[39] *Pointing the Way*, p. 239.
[40] *Good and Evil*, p. 54f.

Here the question of the source of moral obligation is identical with the question of authentic dialogical existence. In this identity all the bases of Buber's ethics join.

MAURICE FRIEDMAN

MANHATTANVILLE COLLEGE

8

Fritz Kaufmann

MARTIN BUBER'S PHILOSOPHY OF RELIGION

I. RELIGION AND PHILOSOPHY

A. *Dialectic and the Dialogical*

T HE TITLE of this essay stands subject to all reservations to which Buber exposes the words "religion" and "philosophy" as well as the name of God: this most deeply degraded, most highly hallowed word, which is after all the "celestial air" of religion but supposedly has no place, not even the highest, in a philosophical system, since it is said to refer to no object, no "idea" of philosophy.[1]

It is, of course, a characteristic of the "new thinking," to which Buber pledged himself in community with Rosenzweig, that it turns back from the *philosophia perennis,* the *via regia* of Greek philosophy, the doctrine of the eternal essences—back to an even older tradition, in which the eternal being is not the object of thinking but the true subject of life, the great I, that I am, the partner we face. His call we must heed, as it comes to us in this, our temporal existence; to Him we must account in the responsible present of each particular moment. In our experience of and response to this call we experience and fulfill our calling—a personal definition that can no more be defined objectively than can, on His side, the master of the call and His name.

The reality of religion is the act of proving true *(tsedakah)* in this coexistence and communication, 'thanks' to which 'thinking' becomes possible. The accounting rendered by thought thus becomes a historical report and witness of what has happened at every particular moment to man in the community of being, and the memorial of

---

[1] The discussion in this section is based particularly on Buber's *Eclipse of God.*

that which was intended (German: *zu-gedacht*) for him at every particular moment in the meetings of life.

In the dynamics of the presence—a presence constantly demanding renewal, not constantly there—of a partner, whom we must look in the eye: in this dynamics there is no room for religion as a matter of sentiment or sentimentality to swell the lonely breast, and as little room for religion as a system of regulations and ceremonies instituted to govern public intercourse with the Highest.

In *world history*, this turning away from a monism of mystical inwardness, in which God and the soul are one, is a product of the period of the first World War, which, catching man in its rough grip, hammered into him his own finiteness—and that means his actually infinite distance from the infinite; taught him a new sym-pathy with his human fellow-creature and at the same time forced him to account for his relationship with him and his guilt toward him before a judge's seat—the court of the Covenant.

In the *history of philosophy*, this departure is a polarization of the "life"-philosophy (*Lebensphilosophie*) current around 1900, which still saw even in the act of transcendence, in the "turning toward the idea" (Simmel) a dialectic process immanent to life: here the idea, too, was nothing but an objectivization of the self, a not-I projected from the I, no Thou of equal rank or even superior to it. Here there was no move and counter-move of two independent entities. In Buber's return from the dialectic to the dialogical, a bipolar middle is found equidistant from subjectivistic and objectivistic monism. Holding to it makes equally impossible a vaporous indulgence in feeling and a petrification in tablets of an enshrined law.

We do not have the word at our disposal; it disposes of us as the commandment of the hour, which is addressed to us and demands our response. The responsible historical consciousness that was alive in the Jewish tradition, and under whose banner Buber overcame the Greek-Nietzschean doctrine of the wheel of eternal recurrence—this historical consciousness fosters understanding of existence not as a condition in which man takes his place in a harmonious cosmos, but as one in which he is sent forth into a future that is always left open. It is a constant being on the way that is always first laying out the way. The past becomes destiny (*Schicksal*) only as it is defined out of a sense for this sending *(Schickung)*, and re-corded (taken to heart) by the self, made its own, made a part of the present. And the future itself is the ad-vent of a present which we on our part are always coming to meet.

B. *"Conservative Revolution"*

Buber's definition of the relation between past, present, and future is reminiscent of a formula suggested by another disciple of Dilthey's —Hugo von Hofmannsthal—of history as "conservative revolution." In this there is a part truth, which for Buber has its consequences with respect both to religion and to philosophy of religion. In religion, it is responsible for his opposition to a merely conservative tradition, his taking his stand on the barricades of religious revolution, his awaiting an ever new, ever more insistent theophany. This is not simply an expression of Buber's early awakened revolutionary temperament nor of a philosophy of life that lacks the sense for well-ordered forms—"to respect and cultivate what is well defined and faithfully interpret what is well established" (Hölderlin). Rather it expresses Buber's great, often compelling integrity (*Redlichkeit*) which is stronger than the temptation inherent in his drive to exert influence—a drive that, to be sure, also has its rightful place in Buber's life task. In the service of this honesty Buber has, in the Jewish realm, taken on his shoulders a deeply tragic fate—an alienation from those nearest him, for which the accord of the peoples, the universality of his Jewish message offer no full compensation.

What he has experienced as religious reality, is just this very "accountability," which—in presence of mind and human readiness—gives an account of itself in response to the absolute, the unconditionable claim addressed to me by the always unique moment—to me, who have a part in the continuity of historical communal life in which there is no substitute for me. The consciousness of the *ego-cogitor*—that I, just as I am, in all my nothingness, am counted on; that in the end something does depend on man—yes, just on this very man, on myself: this may well be the fundamental religious experience that extends into our own days and is as alive in Buber as it was, for instance, in Baader and William James.

That religious truth exists only in such a proving-true in the reality of a full instant, in which an absolute accosts us as in personal presence: this is the immovable point in Buber's thinking. On this point he knows no compromise, in spite of all the difficulties that are bound up with it theoretically and in practice and with which he is still contending. From this standpoint he must question, as fictive, all religious practice that is not tra-dition in his sense: i.e., "Kab-balah" as a communication in which we receive the truth of reality, partake of it together, and bring about the reality of truth in the community.

This genuine community of tradition is not guaranteed by the building of some domed temple, nor is the temple its exclusive home. And yet the way toward God presents itself to the Jew in the renewal of Jewish tradition, as *His* way. Did not the Jewish people come into existence through its acceptance of this teaching, the Torah, which thus becomes for every individual Jew his birthright and his duty? Therefore the proving oneself true (at the present moment) and the keeping troth (to tradition) belong together.

Buber preserved (the German word *"aufheben"* also has two other meanings: to suspend, e.g., a law; and to raise to a higher level) this teaching in that he—together with Rosenzweig—trans-lated it into the realm of the German language, and thus confronted with it the man of today. The original reality, the reality in which a new humanity had its origin, was to find its voice in this Bible translation that should pro-claim the order to be presented to us at this present hour. And in the same way, Buber's communication of the Hasidic message—whether or not it is a strictly correct rendering of the original—is the ever purer and simpler resonance of that original in the attentively listening heart of a man of our days, its re-petition, resumption, into changed time.

To be sure, we are not after all dealing here altogether with a conservative revolution along the lines of Hegelian dialectic or of a historicism that stresses permanence in the midst of flux as much as flux in the midst of permanence—a view of the stream of life in which everything flows away and yet everything flows together into a murky oneness. The continuity of the flow gives way to a discontinuity of meetings, which are not, perhaps, unrelated to one another but in each of which the "ever-moving wave" rounds itself into the "crystal globe" of the fulfilled moment.

The philosophy that lives in all these intellectual aspects and actions cannot, of course, be the philosophy of a systematic order which can be represented in an objective and definite form. Can Buber therefore not be considered a philosopher in the real sense of the word?

The answer depends on what we understand by philosophy and philosophy of religion "in the real sense." Buber has, first of all, an element of negation in common with modern philosophy. He surely would rank himself—and precisely as a religious man—with those philosophers whose radicalism, more and more consciously, carries on the destructive business of digging the grave of the old religion. Their activity bears the stamp of our age: they can speak only of a God who has become an object of thought—a God who has again become unknown, who is dead. The working out of a philosophy so closed up within its own walls is itself an expression of a life estranged from the living God. The despair of this situation leads to iconoclasm, to the rejection of religious trappings and outworn fictions; but it also leads to the soulful wrestling for the one God, while waiting, with the patience of faith, for His flame to spring up in the night of our existence.

Buber is a son of Israel, of him who fought with God, and knows of the dark wrestling of the soul; knows, that the breakthrough of God and the breakthrough of the new man, God's revelation to man and man's turning back to God, are but two sides of an unending process that hallows us and makes us whole, even as it sears us. It marks a station on Buber's own way of faith when in 1912 he speaks of his belief that the ground of religious renewal can only be "the terrifying laceration, the limitless despair, the infinite longing, the pathetic chaos of many of today's Jews." And the "narrow ridge," along which he sees the genuine human being wandering in our own day—this ridge, which appears illumined from moment to moment by lightning flashes of God's presence—it is, lacking all external securities or any unquenchable inner security, no less perilous than was, then, the look into God's abyss, the suspension over the bottomless deep. Buber's human being still is as bare and penniless as the beggar on the street corner, who waits that his "helper come" (1918).

C. Buber Among the Philosophers

1. Existential and objective thinking: Plato and Buber

Buber's relationship to philosophy, insofar as it speaks of God, is, however, not limited to the rejection of the God of the philosophers, the God of an outworn past, in favor of the God of our fathers—and our sons. His own thinking represents a counter-instance to such a purely negative definition. If he denies the competence of philosophy to make the living God the object of its examination (because, according to him, God in this objectification ceases to concern us as a Thou) ; if he allows philosophy only the right to point beyond itself toward God—then a number of things may be brought up in reply.

One is that Buber's own, positive efforts may be subsumed to no small degree under the title of one of his volumes, *"Hinweise"* (Pointers).* That is so not only because Buber in his passionate involvement often lacks the patience for analysis;† nor does it merely reflect—in Buber's quite individual, and, in contrast to Kierkegaard, world-affirming way—the latter's distinction between objective and indirect communication. Beyond this it is a mark of a form of contemporary philosophy in general—not only in relation to God. From Hamann and Jacobi to Husserl, Scheler and Heidegger there runs a line that sees the function of philosophic thinking rather in the Deixis (the pointer), the striking example, than in the Apodeixis, (the demonstration), and takes cognition as recognition, knowledge as acknowledgment.

Moreover, it is after all not the case that objectification through thinking amounts to the same as the devaluation of the subject *kat'exochen* into an object, a thing—and a thing conditioned *(bedingt)* by our thinking. As such, the "he" is not yet degraded to an "it." A position at the objective pole of existence does not necessarily prejudice the character of what is thought; it does not modify its mode of existence in the same way that a painted landscape fails to be the real one. The contrary impression arises only from an idealistic perspective that sees in the object nothing but a product of thinking and takes the objective content only for a content of thought. In reality, that which stands before our eyes in thinking can arrive there from quite a different derivation, and bear witness to derivation and destiny *(Zu-kunft)* still in its present position.

In actuality, Buber's protest against the change of the position of an existential factor into an objective fact strikes not so much at the idealistic positing of the subject as object as at its positing of the object as product of thought and at the impersonal, non-committal objectivity of the theoretic approach and the thinking in terms of mere instrumentalities. Whereas a religious confession does not have the distance of objective statement, but is the passionate expression of a concrete situation "in which the person participates as a person" and

*In English, *Pointing the Way*—Ed.

† One of the exceptions is the essay on "Guilt and Guilt Feeling."

into which enters "the meaning of existence in all the 'concreteness' in which it is lived and enacted at each particular moment": philosophy, on the contrary, grows, according to Buber, out of an "elementary act of abstraction" in which one decisively disregards one's concrete situation. What has once been excluded from philosophy by such methodical abstraction cannot be brought back by any analytical labor and reconstruction (for instance along the lines of Natorp).

The question is, of course, whether the attribution of this impersonal objectivity corresponds to the reality of philosophy as a historical phenomenon. Is it not rather the attitude that gives rise to theories in natural science, while the attitude already of the historian, as Buber himself sees it, is one that strives for impartial, but not impersonal objectivity? Every philosophical truth has a personal kernel. It is "the choice of one who is true on earth" (Werfel). It presents us with a "universal metaphor," which describes how we personally approach the world and how it approaches us. It is a total reaction of our whole being to questions as they face us. Beyond all objective determination, it is at once expression and discovery. In the mental act of seizing (*Ergreifen*) there is a compelling affection that seizes us (*Ergriffensein*). Personal accounting and world-shaping projection are here one. The tuning of our feelings by the affective nature of things is brought into conceptual comprehension.

The question is, therefore, whether and how far it is fair to say that all philosophy "is based on the assumption" that the absolute is to be perceived only in the universal as the proper object of thinking. That is Kierkegaard's charge against Hegel (in his later period). Yet it seems hardly feasible to present the debate over universals, their reality or unreality, as a "philosophical duel" between religion and philosophy, and thus, to put it in a somewhat exaggerated way, to make of the Ockhamites the only *defensores fidei*. But how can such a duel be philosophic at all, if Buber's alternative rightfully exists? In both cases—that of the realists as well as that of the nominalists— are not religious interests as well as philosophic ones at stake: there a verification of the unity of the human race from Adam to Christ and the *Corpus Christi*; here, an insistence on individual responsibility and immortality? And can the great forefather of universalism, can Plato himself be simply checked off as the author of the philosophy of Ideas, to which, to be sure, he is said later to have attached a— not really quite consistent—correction with the introduction of the

Demiurge in the *Timaios*? Does he not already in the *Politeia* pro-
claim the Idea of Ideas as the force of good and the principle of
unity, that is, as the unifying, directing power that as *forma formans,*
as Phyturge, high above the Demiurge of *Timaios,* projects the
formae formatae, the world of the ideas?

If one characterizes the history of philosophy as a series of
glosses on Plato, it is of *this* Plato that one must think. Then there
is a place in this history—though, to be sure, a place apart—for
Augustine as for Pascal (who was, it must be remembered, not only
a mathematician and besides that a Christian writer—as in Buber's
description—but also a philosopher of the first rank); a place, also, for
Kierkegaard, for Schelling—and for Buber.

2. *Existential Concepts*: *Augustine and Buber*

Augustine's *Confessions,* his confessions of guilt and of thanks
before God and men, belong in their dialogic character no less—
though in a different sense—to philosophical literature than do the
Soliloquia and *Monologia.* The *contra se ipsum* of this testimony of a
life, though it may lack system, does have a method in its constant
leaping from the periphery of the external happening to the center
of divine providence, which takes the place of an inborn entelechy.

The duet between the music of eternity, ever loftily and immutably
the same, and the song of yearning sung by the straying, aspiring
soul: this duet is already pre-figured in Plato's and Aristotle's teaching
of *Mimesis* and *Orexis,* although in the context of the Christian life
on earth the accent has shifted from the flightiness of sense data to
the flight from God into sensuality, the *concupiscentia.* Augustine's
analysis does not cease to be an incomparable philosophic achievement
just because it takes its orientation from a Bible verse. Conversely,
the analysis of time and memory in the *Confessions* does not only
owe it to Plato and Aristotle that it has had a deep philosophical
influence down to our own times; rather, it is two things in one:
existential phenomenology and an act of religious faith. Memory is
here regarded not merely in its general nature, but is, beyond that,
bent inwards to become *recordatio,* a taking to heart, in which the
decisive turn of life, the moment of conversion, is loyally held fast.

In this context, the context of a life that has grown reflective,
there are worked out those categories of the personal-historical
dynamics of being that are so wholly different from the attributes of
things in Aristotle as in Kant. But these categories stood at the

cradle of Heidegger's existentiala and have certain parallels already in Plato—especially the Plato of the myths—as well as in Aristotle and even in Kant. In Augustine they are called *aversio* and *conversio, diversio* and *perversio, distentio, intentio* and *extensio,* to mention only a few that already by the relationship of the words indicate the reciprocal oneness of the life that they are meant to explicate, a oneness in which all things are turned toward one another.

Buber tried to articulate the correlational structure of life in a similar way with the aid of primal words like those of God and with primary words taken from the context of Jewish life, the text of the Bible and post-Biblical literature. They have a characteristically Jewish tone, even when they appear in tune with the equivalents of Greek or Latin concepts. I shall mention only *"Umkehr"* (*teshuvah*) as *conversio* and not only as *metanoia*—a "turning" which, however, is also expected of the people in Plato's metaphor of the cave; "world" (*olam*) as creation, a mysterious process, no transparent cosmos; *"Bund,"* "covenant" (*b'rit*) in the joining of I and Thou, seen as the heart of the Old Testament; *"Gegenwart,"* "presence" or "meeting" (as in "tent of meeting") as responsible correlation: a correspondence, then, that is more than aesthetic harmony; *"Bewährung,"* "proving true," in the three-fold sense of *tsedakah*: that of piety, of justice, and of mercy; *"Lehre,"* "teaching," as *"Weisung,"* "direction" (*Torah*) in which life is given its meaning, i.e., is directed to the right path and sent forth to do justice to the concrete demands of each particular situation.

These are guideposts on the way of life, not pillars in the structure of being as with the Greeks. We should not expect a system of categories where no conceptual reconstruction of the universe is intended but where what is at stake is man's proving true in his concrete "now." When Buber occasionally speaks of his "ontological interest," he has in mind something that stands in sharp contrast to all theory of objects. It is a question of the incomparably more difficult construction of key concepts that may give access from the past of our life into the future, by teaching us to realize, and to make real, the present in the ever-new modes in which the absolute presents itself. The task is not to make transparent the structure and totality of being, but to teach the historical humanity that lives in us to comprehend itself in its origin, formation and mission. This concrete concept of man, in which we have understanding for ourselves and in which the past and future of our life join hands—in an instant

that must always be seized anew—this concept is, even with Buber,
more a desideratum than a tangible attainment. It can really, after
all, be developed only in action—in man's acting and suffering and
the self-consciousness expressed in his bearing; the word of direction
can only be a guide to which we entrust ourselves while we interpret
it and work it out in our own way and in our own situation.

One of the ways, however, in which we work it out is in thinking
through and speaking out that which really happened to us at the
decisive turning points of our life. Often it is only in this assimilation
by thought, this communication and communion through language,
that the event reveals at last its full meaning, which at first we may
have not quite grasped or even altogether mistaken. The conversion
of Augustine, for instance, ripens but slowly to the point where it
takes on the form of the conversion scene which it has in the
Confessions. And is it not true also of Buber that the presence of
that which impels him and to which he testifies is completed in the
compelling tone of his expression of it, in the strict weighing of
gesture and word which he stamps and presents like an offering of
pure and beaten gold?

3. Life and Scripture: Pascal and Buber

Every source and form is proper, if such a presence reveals itself
through it. A kind of "double bookkeeping," the mutual confirmation
of choosing and being chosen, provides a fairly adequate safeguard
against merely willful assumptions. Buber, the Jewish "Protestant,"
is hearer as well as doer of the Word: he hears the Bible's claim in
that, and only in that, which it has to say to him, in that which is
specially imparted to him and given to him as his part, in that
which calls upon him here and now to prove true (such a proving
true is not that of an idea, but of the human being); and in turn
he recogni es the calling which was imparted to him personally in
that clair to which the men of the Bible submitted.

This back and forth of mutual illumination and verification is to
some degree related to the conduct of Pascal, though not to his
Jansenist doctrine. In both cases we have an analysis of man that
follows up what already was pre-enacted and pre-figured in the Bible.
But for Pascal life merely presents riddles which historiography then
solves through the interpretation of Christian dogma, whereas for
Buber it is a matter of recognizing God's identity in His old and in
His new presence; and Pascal's analysis is that of introspection into

the *moi haïssable*, not that of correlation, in which the I constitutes
and affirms itself in its relation to the Thou.

4. *The God of the Philosophers: Descartes and Buber*

Buber's inner affinity for Pascal is mirrored in his sharp criticism
of the philosophical position of Descartes. It has long been customary
to see in the one the antithesis of the other; and Buber too is not
free of this tendency, which is partially justified. It would be over-
compensation to wish to make of Descartes a *philosophus Christianis-
simus*. Nor is it my intention to sweep aside the whole problem
"Descartes-Buber" or to deny the doubtful points which Buber sees.
What is required is only to bring into the picture that which Buber
apparently does *not* see but which softens the strict and simple
antithesis of the religious and philosophical positions even in this
exemplary case, in which the philosopher allegedly philosophizes
"in his concrete situation"—only to show thereby that just that is what
he cannot do.

That the "Ego" in the "ego cogito" is not "the living, breathing
person" is of course true only of the I that occurs in the *Epoché*,
not of the I that actively carries out the *Epoché*. The latter merely
enters through this operation into a particular condition, just as,
conversely, the operation is favored by a particular condition, that
of leisure. All this is still within the horizon of Descartes the philosopher, and indeed Husserl, in Descartes' succession, gave his attention
increasingly to this phenomenological point of departure. The act
of "thinking" itself is of course something that the one I has in
common with the other. But the Cartesian *Cogitatio* is not simply
thinking consciousness, but a free and full actuality of consciousness
by which man is distinguished and through which he participates in
the will of God as in the *intellectus ipse*. This becomes quite clear
in the act of universal doubt that is here in question, which represents a possibility freely undertaken, not one that is forced on or
even expected of us. To be sure, this very process reveals not only
the freedom of the children of God, but also the ambivalence of our
existence, the finiteness of our knowledge. In our hovering between
knowledge and ignorance, in our participation in bottomless non-being
as in foundation-erecting being: hovering thus, we are, like all that
is created, not independent with respect to our being: only through
the miracle of a *creatio perpetua* are we borne along from moment
to moment, even as we are about to vanish. But of all that is created,

we, and we alone, have in all our finitude also the idea of the infinite, the absolute and unconditioned by which we are conditioned:
an idea that in a manner defines us as human beings, in the dignity
of being human. That already comes close to the ambivalence, the
greatness and the lowliness of human existence of which Pascal
speaks. And seen thus, the *Ego Cogito* is the expression of quite a
concrete experience, not the formula for a general concept, a philosophical axiom. This Descartes made quite clear in refuting the objections of Gassendi. Certainly it is true that the singular act of introspection which Descartes' readers have to carry out after him, each for
himself, is subsequently expanded—but in an eidetic, not an empirical
generalization—not unlike that which Buber himself demands of his
reader when he uses the communication with tree and horse to
describe the contact of being and being.

True, in the Cartesian thought-experience we are not dealing with
a meeting of I and Thou; nevertheless there is here the recognition of
a being *with*, a recognition that has a validity and value of its own.
The existential relation may indeed reach its culmination in this
meeting face to face; but it is not limited to it. It reveals itself not
only in the act of con-frontation but also in the formation of a
common front, in the following after of the *imitatio* and also in
thinking after, reflecting, when this thinking is a thinking existence,
i.e., when the movement of a whole life issues in it and when in the
thinking itself there takes place a communication with Being as well
as with that which is.

Descartes' *Meditationes*, even by their title, still belong to a class
of religious literature that represents a different (and nevertheless
perhaps legitimate) type or phase of religiosity from the ecstatic
confession or prophetic testimony. Such meditations issue from a
state where we lose ourselves in thought, a state which is a human
possibility and in which we open ourselves for the opening of depths
that are not within our self-willed grasp. It is in this sense that the
Plato of the Seventh Letter, in the passage to which Buber alludes,
speaks of a "living together" which seems after all to signify an
intimacy rather with ideas than with intellectual companions, and
from which, as from a fiery wheel, an inextinguishable spark falls
into our receptive soul—a dawning of the light, a gift of grace that is
granted to our toil in the dark; a turning toward us of the luminous
power of formless unity, from which flow all unities of form, and

toward which aim, in Plato, all formations of unity, from feeling to idea.

This is the final and highest step on the way of religious specula-tion—a falling together of all the threads in a structure of thought or, it may be, of art, which (in the language of Stefan George) —some day, and not in obedience to our will—seems to bring the solution on which we were meditating. In its supra-objective nature, "the form affects me as I affect it."[2]

But in all such meditation there is the foretaste or the aftertaste of actual meeting with the One, the preservation through memory of something that once became presence for us or a groping into the future for a reality which, to speak with Buber as with the Greeks, we cannot yet touch (διγγάνειν). In theosophy, the speculative attempt to feel oneself into the "psychic life of God," as Thomas Mann calls this, may, in spite of all the attendant reverence, too often have shown itself over-bold; but it still is a putting out of feelers, a "trying" in the posi-tive as in the negative sense, in which man interprets the call that goes out to him and that after all transcends all human power to grasp; or it is a speaking, in which his dumbness in face of the "absolutely other" explicates itself.

In the one case as in the other, and in the one sense or the other, man may commit an "ir-responsibility" in the face of the Transcendent, an irresponsibility which is for all that his fate; he falls into it, yet nonetheless must take responsibility for it. In just the same way, there is much that plays into our life from below, that concerns us only insofar as we are creatures and for which we nevertheless stand responsible as persons—as though we let a ball slip from our hands, which we then must nevertheless catch hold of again. Thus one must distinguish between this infrapersonal element of the creature and that transpersonal element which is, in a manner of speaking, the *essentia formalis* of God: but that is a matter that calls for separate treatment.

II. GOD, MAN, AND WORLD

A. *The Primacy of the Practical: Kant and Buber*

The meditative movement toward God, which Buber himself practices and from whose authenticity my essay, too, must derive its

2 *I and Thou*, p. 10.

justification as a human endeavor—this meditative movement he consciously pushes into the background in favor of an evocative movement that emphasizes the "primacy of practical reason."

I use this expression purposely in order to call attention to the affinity (in spite of all differences) between Buber's thinking and Kant's. Buber himself may have occasionally failed to see this, because he got his own thrust forward through a counter-thrust against the neo-Kantianism of Hermann Cohen.

True, the word "reason" is for Buber—in distinction from Kant, and as in the circle of Hamann, Herder and Jacobi—the principal noun that goes with "perception," so that reason forms the bridge between I and Thou. But we must immediately add that for Kant also reason establishes, in practical use, a realm of community in which commandments (imperatives) take the place of the laws in the realm of scientific experience. These are categorical imperatives; and with them, something absolute enters into human relationships which are ruled by this spirit.

What Kant here has in mind is not far removed from the Biblical verse which Buber paraphrases thus in his preface to *Eclipse of God*: "Where two are truly together, it is in the name of God." The formalism of Kantian ethics prescribes the spirit of this being together: it does not determine, or at least not primarily, the material content of our duties; thus it does not, to be sure, do justice to any particular situation, but indicates in what spirit we are to do justice to each and every one. It teaches us the right attitude to our fellow man as an attitude of respect for the other as an individual, as the subject of free, self-initiated action, not as the object of external manipulations. Thus this attitude obtains an absolute sanction, comparable to that which allows Kafka to speak of it as the attitude of prayer. The absoluteness that thereby enters into the soul and rules between thee and me is what Kant in his *Opus Posthumum* meant by the *Deus in nobis*, by God as "a moral relation in me." This is no more subjectivistic than Augustine's discovery of God as the "lord of the soul." Kant, to be sure, speaks the language of the Enlightenment, a language foreign to religion. But he intends to see God respected as the holy spirit of the bond between men, the ruler of an "ethical community" (respect is, after all, a practical attitude, no mere stirring of emotion). For all His unknowability, God is not merely to be enthroned in unapproachable majesty, in cold transcendence.

These ideas are an integral part of Kantian doctrine; they are not intentions that the system does not admit, as Buber maintains in his "The Love of God and the Idea of Deity."* Much as we are moved by the ceaseless circling around the question of God in *Opus Post-humum,* it nevertheless is not quite the dramatic picture of an "existential tragedy beyond compare" which Buber makes of it. But there is no doubt that in the "I-Thou" doctrine Buber has not only created a terminology more closely adapted to the relation between man and man, but that he has also shifted the center of gravity from Kant's intelligible order to the concreteness of the situation, and from a system of human actions to the never-to-be-systematized life of dialogue. The concept of the process of life is for Buber, as for Kafka, that of a process which does not run back into itself but is carried out here, in this questionable and nevertheless beloved world, between two centers.

Belonging together even in polarity—that is the secret of existence, just as infinite nearness with infinite distance is the secret of the God who is addressed in the same blessing as Thou, my Lord, our God, King of the universe. Here are regained a new fervent inwardness and a new distance, compared with Kant. Not the realm of ends, for which all rational beings are to unite, an intelligible world above that of the senses; not that, but the one great reality of the co-venant in which God, man, and world turn toward and find one another— in that, which Buber calls *"reine Beziehung,"* and Rilke *"reiner Bezug"* and which in English might more nearly be rendered by "relationship" than by "relation." Without losing their independence, God, man, and world cease to have their meaning and direction in themselves alone; they are raised from the state of Schelling's potences to the actuality of the three great essences in Rosenzweig's star configuration, in which creation, revelation and redemption work together.

The many-rayed unity of this figure is made structurally possible by the unity in duality of I and Thou. But the Thou has its essential being not as an object of thought but in its confrontation with the I—wherever one being inclines itself toward the other in all its fulness and gives itself to it. This definition of the Thou is broad enough to embrace not only our fellow man but equally God and

Eclipse of God—Ed.

the world. But in this breadth it must be justified. Has Buber succeeded in this justification?

To expect a simple yes to this question would be to demand too much of any person, even of Buber's power of thought and expression. On the other hand, a denial would be primitive if it based itself on the naive distinction between real and figurative speech and admitted a genuine dialogue only with our fellow man, while claiming that to speak of a dialogue with the natural world, which after all cannot answer for itself, is only a *quid pro quo*. All that Buber can do—and what only he can do in just that way—is to draw us on, here too, to the edge of a meeting in which the word Thou has a convincing ring and forces itself to our own lips.

B. *The Human and the Divine Thou*

Kant had already spoken, "only in slightly different words," of the 'appresentation' of God in the perception of and respect for a human reality, of this presence of an Absolute in the handclasp between man and man. We see this *parousia* ruling for example in the sacrament of love that unites two lovers and in which they dwell—an *amare in Deo*. This divine presence may appear in the act of infinite love even of human beings who are finite and feel each other as finite—in this act which always contains something of the compassion, the shared suffering of finiteness. But that, after all, signifies also that we here feel a universal presence whose all-embraciveness reveals itself in this one embrace for this unique instant. The latent "Primal Presence" again and again becomes fulfilled present. In the unconditional devotion to our fellow man, this creature subject to such manifold conditions, there springs up, in the very midst of this human world of ours, the world of the unconditioned, of God. And life can be so veined with the lightning flashes of these relationships that their ever-repeated coruscation from pole to pole creates a brightness that makes it possible to compare "the moments of supreme meeting" to "the rising moon in a clear starlit night."[3]

This is a matter that always will require explanation: how Buber's religious actualism can make the Jewish *emunah*—the trust that we are standing on firm ground—genetically into a function of the meeting in which man is made to stand by God and before God, so that the Thou-relationship builds itself up on a sort of salvo of acts of

[3] *I and Thou,* p. 115.

relating so that pure relationship coincides with present actual meeting.[4] It is hardly possible to sound this question exhaustively. Too many elements have worked together here. The derivation of the concept of the meeting from the concept of the temporally-limited experience and from an impressionistic *Lebensphilosophie* is noticeable in spite of all the contradictions between them. The Hasidic cult of *kavanah*, the intention beyond all intentions that achieves gathering of forces and highest tension in the moment, joins with the praise of the *kairos*, derived from Kierkegaard: the unique moment filled with eternity. The *romantic* temper probably sounds through in the tendency to equate original being with that which was in the beginning, and to see in all process already a falling-away. But at the same time the *reform* temper is at work here, attacking the degeneration into worldliness which indeed threatens all religious development and which also led thus to the ossification of the Hasidism which Buber so loves and which he has called back to life in his works. The genuineness, the authenticity of the actual consummation in the seizing and the being seized of the instant is meant to assert itself generally against the irresponsible trot of life today and against the routine of drilled-in regulation. Original life, after all, consists in the responsible real-ization of the instant, a realization in which the future of our life struggles forth from the *origines*, the roots of our natural-historical existence. Such a moment therefore gains its proper meaning and its whole fulness to the extent in which man's presence of mind proves itself in it—the presence of mind that ever anew satisfies an ever new claim—and, at its highest, the highest claim, the claim that demands ultimate unity. (Conversely, the void of despair opens out in the failure to meet the claim of God and man, in man's forlorn condition and in the brokenness of the poor soul which again and again from its abandoned state cries out to God—now as in the past, then as now.) Thus there is here an interplay of the historical experience of our times and our experience of the historical temporality of our personal being. But even a generation whose life—corresponding to a different historical situation—is centered partly about other motives: even such a generation can and should never-

---

4 Cf. "Elements of the Interhuman" or *Die Schriften über das dialogische Prinzip*, p. 261. A Protestant parallel in Paul Yorck von Wartenburg, *Bewusstseinsstellung und Geschichte*, p. 179: Faith has "its certainty in the power of proving-true, [is subject to] the constant excitation of the postulate . . . [is] never something finally acquired, a settled result, a property, but always a living force."

theless perceive and honor the urgent force of the impulses that became Buber's fate and estranged him from the shelter of the orthodox community.

"But when/ a God appears, o'er Heaven and earth and sea/ spreads all-renewing clearness."[5] The radiance which pours into life from a "highest meeting," a meeting with the Highest, unites in itself two extremes. On the one hand it is the charisma, the gift of grace of the one only moment and of its God—the God of a moment, even if not quite in Usener's sense, still in the sense of the *Keraunos*, the God of the one lightning flash, the fortune of the one day, the *Fortuna huiusque diei*. "Thus all heavenly things pass speedily away; but not in vain."[5A] But not in vain. For on the other hand this radiance is not merely of the one moment; even if it should be extinguished with the moment (as so often it is), nevertheless for this moment it immerses the whole of life in a unity of meaning, thanks to the presence of the One, who is the one and only one, as He bestows unity in the peace of His covenant.

Buber thus shifts the accent from the uniqueness of God to God's speaking to us and our ability to speak to Him, as the foundation of religious community. In this shift there may be an echo of Buber's early sympathy with William James, in whose pluriversum, as we know, there opened up again a way of communication with a plurality of gods; this pluralistic perspective at one time "strongly affected" Buber. But equally it is an expression of protest against Lagarde's ill-willed phrase about Jewish henotheism as well as against the complementary stupidity that denies Amos' monotheism because he allegedly recognized other gods at the side of and under Yahweh. At one with the Jewish tradition, as it was last represented by Rosenzweig, Buber too sees in God—Elohim—the power that is real to the highest degree, over other powers that yet are also real. Thus Buber finds the original and moving force that lives in Judaism above all in its turning to the Thou of a common devotion, a devotion whose undividedness already carries within itself the oneness and uniqueness of God. This is a placing of the accent which, to be sure, does not always seem compatible with that of the community of believers,

---

[5] Hölderlin, "Versöhnender, der Du nimmer geglaubt . . ."
[5A] *Ibid.*

with the role of the *Shema*, the constantly repeated profession of the One God.[6]

Underlying all this, however, is the recognition of the problem that is posed by monotheism, just from Buber's standpoint—posed not so much with reference to God as with reference to man. Monotheism requires the power of historical anamnesis, of recurrent personal re--cognition and bestowing of recognition (*Wiedererkennung und -Anerkennung*). Just as polytheism is rooted in the experience of many different, even contradictory demands which come to us from different spheres of life, of which each has its own spirit and its own shimmer; so monotheism is rooted in active faith in a unity of life, a unity that holds all spheres and values of life together.

Actually this recognition of the one and unifying power is already present in man's nature, in the consciousness and the dynamics of the formation of ever higher unities, which we meet already in Plato and Aristotle and still see in the unity of Kant's transcendental synthesis. But it is a difficult recognition wherever there is a failure of *con-scientia* —the covenant of knowledge—and where, as with the daemon Eros in Plato's *Symposium*, unity of original knowledge must fight against forgetfulness and scatteredness of existence so that it is achieved only in an act of collection.

In the schizophrenia of today's humanity the whole and hallowing spirit of unification is threatened; on such a crossroads there is "no temple to Apollo." There are times of "eclipse of God," in which a life of faith can show itself only in *Hypomené*, as for instance with Kafka—that is, in waiting expectantly for a meaning that here and now is perverted and desecrated into meaninglessness; a meaning to which we nevertheless hold fast, aware of a message which may be the message not of a dead but—already in that it concerns us—of a living God. God is present (*west an*) even in the pain of His absence. And, to use Buber's own metaphor, the lightning flash of the meeting can break through even this darkness of human estrangement. Again and again there lights up in moments of love, a deep certainty:

> ... *aus seinen Finsternissen*
> *Tritt der Herr, soweit er kann,*
> *Und die Fäden, die gerissen,*
> *Knüpft er alle wieder an.*

[6] Cf. *The Origin and Meaning of Hasidism*, "Spinoza," p. 91; *The Prophetic Faith*.

> (From the dark in which He's wrapped
> God steps forth where'er He can;
> And the threads which He finds snapped
> His careful hand ties up again.)

These words might be appended to Buber's philosophy of faith as a motto rich in consolation.

The difficulty of recognizing the One again comes out in Buber so strongly—with such truly fear-ful strength—not only because his God is, after all, always only—and always really—the God of the hour, but also because in this turning toward us, and even in His turning away, He always remains the God who comes—the God who reserves to Himself both His coming and the how of His coming and wants to be recognized as the same through the greatest intervals of His appearances, in giving as in taking. Should His voice come "from the whirlwind or from the stillness that follows it;" "though His coming appearance resemble no earlier one, we shall recognize again our cruel and merciful Lord."[7] But—will we?

Buber's example from literature, which he offers with all due reservation—namely how in different poems we remain aware of the handwriting of the same poet[8]: this example does not do justice to the awesome discrepancy that yawns chasm-like between God's different manifestations, for instance toward Job. Buber knows this, as in some way all know it who have gone through this life. The curse of its grace is a riddle not to be solved; it must be borne out in existence. This means that though we stand ever again, ever anew, in the absolute confrontation in which we must speak our "Here am I" (*Hineni*) so that we are certain of the Thou (for only in the devotion of response and responsibility are we I, and do we find ourselves); nevertheless we shall never succeed and must never succeed in making an image of the Lord in whose sign every such constellation stands. He disposes of us; but He does not dispose Himself into the framework of our imag-ination. We can, to be sure, speak of Him only as *our* God; He, however, is, above and beyond all presence, and still in all absence, just He—purely and simply God. We can be sure of Him, but we cannot possess Him.

All this is far from being a peculiar opinion of Buber's, a mere construction that follows from a pointillistic approach which attempts

---

[7] *At the Turning*, p. 62.

[8] "Dialogue," *Between Man and Man*, p. 15.

to make life a set of experiences. To see reigning in the very ground of life not only the unifying power but also those predicates which for us are irreconcilable: this corresponds to the rent condition, the soul-rending experiences of our fearful and grievous time. From this viewpoint certain Biblical and post-Biblical representations of God gain new meaning: the duality of the names YHVH and Elohim, the antithesis of mercy and wrath in the kabbalistic Sefirot—these forces which in God nevertheless are one—and so forth. If we may still properly speak of God at all without falling into Manicheeism, then we are speaking of a creative being in whose omnipotence the forces of construction and destruction work together in some such manner as they do in the Indian Trimurti or in Nietzsche's Dionysos.

In spite of its omnipresence, the divine presence remains appresentation. The light of the Infinite flashes out only in the finite. God does not meet man, as He did for a while with Rilke, in a flight that leaves the earthly behind and, "startled, halts in the Heavens." With Buber, He steps into life, whereby the earthly gains infinite significance, and seizes hold of a human being who was destined from the beginning to love life.

As with Plato, the "between" is the specific human situation in this type of thinking, which itself has its place in a "between"—"between religion and philosophy." The suprapersonal thus finds its central support and contents in the personal sphere "between man and man." "It is from one man to the other that the heavenly bread of self-being is passed."[9] The finite does not become a mere substitute for the eternal Thou. Service to man, freeing of his self to become God's image, is service of God. The solitary one, the single one hears—like Moses, differently from Kierkegaard—the voice of God in his mission to the community. "The individual is needed"—all contact with the creative occurs in the depth of solitude—but only, after all, so that that which the community has in common may have its original wellspring.[10] That is why sin consists in debt, and the debt in this, that we fail to give the response we owe to our fellow man. The irredeemable in a life is not that it does not round itself to a whole in itself, but that it does not join effectively in the round with the others and the Other.

One has sometimes reproached Buber with not carrying through

[9] "Distance and Relation," p. 104.
[10] "The Question to the Single One," *Between Man and Man,* p. 82.

in full seriousness the dialogue of coexistence for which he calls. As against this reproach I may here bear grateful testimony to his ability to give of the aid of his presence which has proved itself toward me as toward others. But even where he may occasionally have failed, he has thereby only paid the penalty of all that is human. As in the noble definition of Aristotle, being human must be defined by its highest potentialities. The other aspects do not remain absent. It is characteristic equally for human nature and for Buber's integrity that he questions his own existence and that he reports about his own, unconditional concern for man in a chapter of self-accusation in "A Conversion," under a religious title therefore: in a confession of how he failed properly to meet a fellow human being and how this failure became fateful for both.[11] In the failure to find the way, man is directed aright; the way reveals itself to the conscience. Thus the way to God becomes the way in the workaday, everyday world—an everyday that is ever new, ever anew to be consecrated. "If that is religion then it is just *everything*, simply all that is lived in its possibility of dialogue."[12]

May I be permitted in this spirit, and in a serious play on words, to speak of Buber—the philosopher, not only the translator of the Torah (*Weisung*: instruction, direction)—as a *Weltweiser* (sage of the world); where I lend this name used by the Enlightenment a new meaning. Philosophizing has here become direction for the world ("*Weltweisen*")—direction on the right way, rejection of human and national straying. As a philosopher in this doubly weighty sense, Buber, though without prophetic claims, has nevertheless taken on himself the exacting office of the succession of the prophets—that is, of that which they were for their people, and even against their people for humanity.

C. Consecration of the World

He is a "*Weltweiser*" also in the sense that he points the way into the world—this earthly world—which is not only the world of man but also that of nature. Here, too, an inclining of the whole being is possible which corresponds to the claim of something like a Thou in things, their affective quality, the way they present themselves to our concern. Nature, after all, is not only an object of observation and

---

[11] "Dialogue," *Between Man and Man*, pp. 13f.
[12] *Ibid.*, p. 14.

use, but also (for us as for the child and the so-called "primitive") a realm of the elemental, from which we still—for instance in a period of outdoor living—derive new strength as Anteus did whenever he touched Mother Earth. Here there is still in a hundred places the source, "the play of pure forces which no one touches who does not kneel and admire" (Rilke). The being (*Wesen*) of things—"being" understood as a verb—is not only known or unknown to us as is the being (*Wesen*: essential nature) of things in the substantive sense: it is familiar or eerie, tempting or frightening, beneficent, demonically mischievous, mocking us or remaining sometimes stolidly, sometimes grandly, indifferent.

In our present undertaking we are not concerned with the scientific validity of these speculations, but only with this: what role they play for Buber and in the religious relationship as he sees it, namely in sacramental existence. This goes beyond primitive pansacramentalism with its mythology and with the magic that vainly presumes to master the divine in the earthly—beyond all this to the attitude of kneeling devotion in Hasidism.[13] It not only trembles in deep emotion before the "tremendous," but devotes itself to the holy observance of daily duties, to the redemption even of evil, the consecration of the "evil impulse." This is the rung which Buber thought he had reached in *I and Thou*, where the Thou relation can say its "yes" toward all, even in the realm of the elements. From the lips of the drowsy cup-bearer in the *Westöstliche Divan*, Buber in the motto to *I and Thou* accepts the blessing of the deep:

'So hab' ich endlich von Dir erharrt:
In allen Elementen Gottes Gegenwart.

(So, waiting, I have won from you the end:
God's presence in each element) —

from you, from my beloved fellow man, in a love in which the divine becomes present (*anwest*) and all that is in the world can become essential being (*wesenhaft*) and bear witness to the primal Being.

Life in this consecration of the world is conjured up for us and in our day in *Tales of the Hasidim*—and the tales must be understood and honored as such evocation.

13 Cf. *Origin and Meaning of Hasidism*, p. 174.

The idea of this consecration is for Buber bound up with that
of the redemption of the world—the liberation from their dark shells
of the sparks of the divine splendor which are scattered in the world;
the restoration of the divine Glory, the *Shekhinah,* from its exile, its
indwelling in this world of suffering, in which it shares in divine
com-passion. That is a doctrine whose first formation and whose images
come from Gnosis and Kabbalah, which has its Christian parallel in the
dogma of incarnation, but which Buber takes over from Hasidism as
this is bespoken for him and speaks to him: as the partnership between
the absolute and the concrete in the ever newly to be realized contracting of life, not in a contract completed once and for all. Thus
this redemption is a divine-human process, for which God wills
to use man in such a way that the redemption of God and that of
man and of the world, religious promise and ethical demand are
one.

Fulfillment of the ethical demand is the human calling. And this
calling and responsibility intone a dialogue of existence which does
not limit itself to the response that an individual man makes to another
individual man and through him to God, but which swells to a
universal antiphony of responses in which each and every being must
speak to the other and each one proclaims to the other his vocation.
The dialogical life of man plays a part all its own, and an eminent
one, in this universal discourse, in which man is assigned a responsibility that is not demanded of animal, plant, or stone.

That this is a case of communication in a genuine dialogue, and
to what extent it is so: this—the suspicion voiced on p. 211 to the
contrary—we learn in every one of our dealings with things, in which,
perhaps with loving devotion, but in any case with our whole being,
we enter into a response to something experienced as speaking to us.
To the examples which Buber gives from everyday life (tree, cat,
horse), or as we find them, for instance, in Tolstoy's "Master and
Servant," it would be easy to add others from our life with the
elements—the experience of drinking from the living spring that
bubbles up to meet us from the hot bare mountainside, and so on.
In such an inclining toward the Thou, everything can become a sign
and a wonder, a creature that—in contrast to the factory product—
always draws its being from its own source and bears witness to the
creation, a creature from which a creative principle, the eternal
primal spring, wells toward us.

This attitude—in contrast to specialized scientific observation and dissection—is still at work in the contemplative devotion, the *intu-itus* of philosophers of the strain for instance of Scheler or William James; but above all in art and in the artist's knowledge of it, as it was alive for instance in Hopkins and Proust, in Cézanne and Rilke.

Buber is himself so much the artist that he almost necessarily is led to a religious metaphysics of art, which can serve as a support to his philosophy of religion and give it the color of a specific experience. Strangely enough, so far as I can see, this has not yet come about. The philosophy of art developed in the lecture *Der Mensch und sein Gebild* is, in intentional abstraction from faith, a revision of Fiedler's thought (which for me too has been significant) in the spirit of a realism influenced perhaps by Bergson and Scheler, for which the process of perception is one of practically determined selection. This epistemology and the theory of art that follows from it, the procedure from perceptibility to vision, from vision to figure, is not our concern here. But when the whole question is treated as a problem of philosophical anthropology, as a question "into the connection between that which is essentially characteristic of man, and that which is essentially characteristic of art"—then the genius of Buber's own thought presses for an amplification and an intensification, for an inquiry into the *vocation* of man in art. For the essential being of man lies in his vocation.

What there is to say here can only be suggested in this essay. It is to find its proper place in a philosophy of art that is conceived as a contribution to a final idealism; i.e., to a philosophy that does not set out from an idealistic position but lands in it. But Buber himself gives the hint to utilize the doctrine of the sparks which it is man's task to liberate from their shells, for a metaphysics of the artistic experience, and to combine it for example with Cézanne's conception of the artist as the "redeemer of the wavering universe."

Just as, according to the apostle, the earnest expectation of the creature waiteth for the manifestation of the sons of God, so Buber writes: "The creature, the things seek us out on our paths; what comes to meet us on our way needs us for its way."[14] That everything in this world needs us, that all things strangely appeal to our concern, was also, as we know, a perception of the poet of the *Duino Elegies*. This "concern" is not to say that we concern ourselves about the things in our own interest. Rather it means a communion with the

[14] *Origin and Meaning of Hasidism*, p. 181.

things in which we let the "outpourings of their hearts" (Cézanne) go to our hearts. It tells of the mute pleading with which they seem to appeal to us to lend them a new, higher, lighter mode of existence, by forming their affection into our impression, our impression into the expression of their essential being.

It is this movement, not a spatial-temporal but an ontological one, which man must bring about, and which the artist must set to working. *"O monde épars, monde ephémère et éternel qui pour se survivre au lieu de se répéter, a tellement besoin des hommes!"*[15] And Gerard Manley Hopkins is even closer than Malraux to Buber's idea of sacramental life, the glorification of things by returning them to the dominion of the Lord (*Verherrlichung*), restoring them to the ground of their being. According to Hopkins, man is wanted as a "beholder" to make the "being there" of things a full presence. In their service, as the fulfillment of his true vocation, he attains to a proper service of God. " 'The heavens declare the glory of God.' They glorify God, but they do not know it. . . . But man can know God, can mean to give Him glory. This then was why he was made."[16] In devoted vision and reverent forming too there can occur a movement of love, in which, to speak with Proust, we bend toward an individual thing so that we not only "observe it as a show, but believe in it as in a created being without a like." A spark of light is liberated, in which there shines the eternal splendor of His majesty.

D. *The Absolute Person*

Finitum non capax est infiniti. In His fullness beyond human comprehension, mysteriously revealed in His transcendence, God is above all categories of human judgments. Man can, to be sure, contend for justice with the lord of the covenant—as do Abraham and Job—but he cannot judge Him. One can only submit to the incomprehensible. And yet God's presence is experienced as indwelling in that responsive-responsible bending of the person toward the other being, which occurs—in answer to an absolute claim—as it were in God's name, and through which we become His partners.

Buber has tried to hold fast the contradiction which enters in this way into all speech about God, in the paradoxical expression "the

---

[15] André Malraux, *Les Voix du Silence*, p. 464.

[16] G. M. Hopkins, *Poems*, ed. W. H. Gardner, p. 75; *Notebooks*, ed. Humphrey House, pp. 302f.

absolute person."[17] In its one part, this term recognizes God as the absolute, the absolute substance. For history of philosophy, this signifies Buber's partial agreement with Spinoza. Indeed, God bursts through the limits of personal individuality. Buber honors the religious restraint by which Spinoza denies us the possibility of understanding the unity of the attributes in the One God, and by which he lets us have access to only two of the infinitely many, inwardly infinite attributes of the divine being. In contrast to Jaspers, Buber sees as one such attribute God's mode of being as a person *(Personhaftigkeit)*.[18]

But an attribute of God is, for Buber, not only "what the intellect perceives of God" (Spinoza). As it gives itself to us, the Absolute is to be experienced only in the devoted giving of self, its own and ours; not merely in the *amor intellectualis,* but in the love of our whole corporal-spiritual nature; not only as a substance sufficient to itself, not only as *natura naturans,* the absolute power, which according to the nature of power externalizes itself, and must externalize itself, if only because nothing can stand in its way; nor, really, as a subject; rather it is to be experienced as the Thou of man, the second—or more properly, by its rank, the first—person, to whose claims we are subject and which first gives us, ourselves, the rank of person.

In the fact that in our turning to the Thou, God *in persona* approaches us and speaks to us and our soul catches fire from Him; in this, transcendence as well as immanence are transcended. This act of the Absolute becoming person surely remains, for Buber also, a miracle, but one that can happen to us at any time in the everyday. It signifies, to use Maimonides' term, an "attribute of effects" which we experience on ourselves—not, therefore, a dogma of faith like the Incarnation, which identifies a mortal human being substantially with one Person in God. The absolute person reveals itself through this, that we are ruled through and through by the spirit of a love that is true to the earthly and of which love in the spirit is only a legitimate progeny.

The miracle of superterrestrial revelation in the terrestrial present can only be attested to belief through its actuality; as a miracle it cannot be proved. But it becomes believable in the testimony and interpretation that derive from it. For this reason Buber took part in

17 Cf., e.g., *Eclipse of God,* pp. 45, 96f.
18 Cf. *Die Schriften über das dialogische Prinzip.,* p. 301.

the work of transmission of the "Word of God," although he knows that every manifestation of God in the Bible is always also a transmutation of that manifestation by human beings; and—like the individual, the "isolated and exposed one," of whom "The Love of God and Love of Neighbor" speaks—he accepts and passes on help from "any good helpful spirit that has been touched by the spirit of God":[19] especially from German and Jewish mysticism, from Eckhart and probably also Scheler, as well as from Kabbala, and Hasidism (not to speak of the comparisons with Indian and Chinese teachings).

Thus he illuminates the paradox of the "absolute person" by going back to the duality of the Biblical names of God: to Elohim, the power of powers; and to YHVH, the God who gives and demands love, the God who—in love—guides us on His way. He relates these two visions of God to Eckhart's distinction between God and Deity—though, to be sure—and very significantly—with an almost contrary meaning. He does this by applying the Kabbalistic doctrine of *tsimtsum,* God's self-withdrawal, to the Lord of Creation, Elohim, who makes room for the universe in His place and thus dispossesses *(entäussert)* Himself to become *natura naturans,* the Lord of Creation. But this, the creation, flows forth in deepest truth from the primal deity itself, from YHVH, the Lord of the Covenant, the giver of the Revelation, the spirit of love who takes pleasure in our love.[20]

This confession of allegiance to the great lover, who in the community of man creates for Himself beings who may love in return, may be considered as a bending inward of Bergson's dictum that God wished, in the *évolution créatrice* that leads upwards to the Holy, to create Himself as creator in the creation: but it is born of the spirit of Hasidism, as that spirit grasped Buber, and Buber it; and as it finds echoes in the mystical philosophy of the West that was approximately contemporary to Hasidism, up to the love philosophy of the young Schiller and Hegel.

In revelation, the loving communication of being is the expression *(Äusserung),* not the self-dispossession *(Entäusserung)* of the divine being; limitation not as self-alienation, but as a measuring of the proclamation, the claim, *secundum modum recipientis,* according to the power of comprehension of the recipient. In this revelation God

---

[19] *Hasidism and Modern Man,* p. 229.

[20] *Origin and Meaning of Hasidism,* pp. 188–193.

walks through His creation, without transforming Himself into world and worlds.[21] Nor does He thereby become dependent on the creation without which He would not be creator, nor on man, whom He requires as the recipient of His revelation. He sacrifices His unconditionedness just as little as the friend is conditioned by the friend, or the artist by the spirit of the audience which he "makes" for himself. This may be said against the formalistic arguments for the doctrine of the Trinity, as one finds them for instance in Edith Stein.[22]

Martin Buber himself has brought this idea to bear against Jaspers, who had seen in the devout turning to the eternal Thou a degradation of transcendence and a danger to man's relation to his fellow. Actually it is only in this relation that the eternal—the Eternal One—really breaks through into the finite; and that the idea that "God created man for Himself for the sake of communication" seems at least "not unworthy" of the divine transcendence.[23] In prayer, man bares only his own neediness. The covenant *(Bund)* creates a bond that unites, not a bond that fetters its members in the *syndesmos* of being; neither "absolute dependence" of man nor a limitation of the sovereignty of God. The causal concept of dependence has no place here.

The epochal significance of the YHVH concept may justify a supplementary reference to the fact that the duality of our vision of God is expressed not only in the duality of concepts of Him; since Philo it has also appeared in the twofold interpretation which tradition has given the name by which God revealed Himself in the thornbush.[24] In a vision that is literally world history, there is drawn here the pure outline of a new world, illumined by the light of a new idea of God. Metaphysically the conception is fundamental, not only because

---

[21] *Ibid.,* pp. 194ff—three pages that are worth whole books. Quietly, they carry through a complete reversal of the usual scale that sets absolute transcendence, e.g., that of Nirguna Brahman, over the personally qualified transcendence, e.g., of Sargana Brahman. The deity is fully itself only in the free sway of personal revelation, not in the necessary world-producing externalization of the impersonal *natura naturans;* just as it is fully itself only in the living relationship, not in the isolation of the absolute. It is fully itself only as YHVH, the God of our fathers, not as Elohim, the almighty King of the universe. Power is in the service of Providence.

[22] Cf. Edith Stein, *Endliches und ewiges Sein,* p. 324.

[23] *Die Schriften über das dialogische Prinzip,* p. 302. Cf. my essay in the Jaspers volume of *The Library of Living Philosophers.*

[24] I cannot here trace the paths of this double tradition. This I will do in a separate essay, to show where they lead us.

the deepest basis of the Jewish idea of God can be achieved only by plunging into that word by which God revealed Himself to Moses, 'I shall be there,' which has for all times determined the contents of this idea;[25]

but also because on the part of Christian thinkers this name-phrase has been declared the cornerstone of all Christian philosophy.[26]

But the meaning of the phrase itself is in dispute—and this in a way by which the ground of man's soul reveals itself in its double relation to the Highest. For this reason we want to try to understand the two interpretations, and in this quest we may count on Buber's consent. It will not do to play off against each other the *Eheyeh asher Eheyeh* in the interpretation, say, of Judah Halevi and its translation in the spirit of Platonic tradition, the *Sum qui Sum*. Both have their rights; and Buber's conception, though closer to the former interpretation, nevertheless represents, in a wisdom become simple, a masterful compromise between both.

The *Sum qui Sum*—"I am that I am"—it too can make the heart beat faster. We feel it in Augustine and still in Descartes. The being that reveals itself in this magnificent tautology is that of a constant presence transcending all objects, not a timeless object of thought as with Parmenides. "I am he, who is" means also: "Being is always present in the first person." Descartes' idea, that this being in its unchangeable existence guarantees the constancy of nature, is disavowed neither by the misplaced physicalism that crept into Descartes' thought, nor by the consideration that the main weight after all is on the personal and quasi-moral constancy and reliability that constitute "that which stands fast in the earthly days" of man and gives us a firm standing-place (that of *emunah*) on such a foundation. The immutable, the unconditionable, the enduring counterpoise to all human proposals, the silent contradiction to our ambitions: this too after all is part of the reality of our life; without this resistance our impulses would strike into the void. We are forcibly reminded of Kant's figure of the dove, whose flight requires something against which it can support itself. That is the one aspect. The other is man's exposure to the distress and sorrow of finite existence, his never ending outer and his increasing inner dependence on the material sphere, which threatens also to destroy all interhuman relations. The rule of

---

25 *Eclipse of God*, pp. 61–62.

26 Étienne Gilson, *L'Esprit de la Philosophie Médiévale*[2], p. 51.

the It is just as much human fate as service to the Thou is human vocation. The same world that we love in the name of God, for His sake, is also what, as the world of the It, lies between Him and us.

Something of the ambivalence of human life and its highest relationship enters even into that interpretation of the Eheyeh concept which comes forward in the translation *Adero qui Adero,* and which at first sounds like pure promise. (Just as, conversely, El Shaddai has been construed as the God who—at the first—is enough unto Himself; but, beyond this, means the God who satisfies, gives enough, to all our needs.) For God is here conceived in trust in the pledge in which He pledges His future coming (German: *Zu-kunft*) to those who call to Him from the depth of their momentary need (yes, even to those who do not seek Him[27]) —that ever new coming in the future that has already proved itself true in the past, for the fathers. He is defined not as a fixed object of thought, but as a free helper of historical man—and thus not properly defined at all, not held to a set manner of behaving or confined to a set image, a well-delineated appearance; but it is for us to recognize Him again and to give Him recognition in every appearance that He may assume: a tremendous charge is imposed on us and an enterprise of high daring.

Of a set of contradictory claims, cannot each one bear the stamp of absoluteness? This question is not a psychologistic one and cannot be dismissed as such. It is not a matter of a mere feeling of evidence which can attach itself to various experiences and from which one can appeal to the true evidence, in which the things themselves shine out in full clarity. Rather, the situation here seems similar to that of the tragic conflict of unremissible duties, an undeniable possibility for which there seems to be no place in Kant's philosophy of practical reason. And yet (so I construe Buber for my purpose), according to the innermost sense of that which happens to us in the decisive meeting, the answer metaphysically must be after the manner of Spinoza: there can exist only *one* Highest, *one* Absolute, just as the unification which we experience can come only from the One.

But this unification must redeem us ever anew from disunion, must "come to" us in ever different guise. Thus this ever new "advent" of God must find us ever anew ready. This is a readiness *in via,* on a way that is always the way back, that comes out of scatteredness toward unity. The one advent (*Zukunft*) cannot be without the other.

[27] Isaiah, 65:1.

The full sovereignty which God reserves for Himself and His revelation leaves man in the unassuredness of his future (*Zukunft*), of God's coming—to act, to hang in suspense and to wait out his time. The promise contained in the proclamation of the divine name (Exodus 3) has always been juxtaposed with the passage, heavy with historical fatefulness, Exodus 33:19: "I will be gracious to whom I will be gracious and will shew mercy on whom I will shew mercy." This means first of all, before all dogmatic hardening, that God reserves to Himself the when, where, and how of His grace. To such freedom on the part of God there corresponds the freedom of the pious man's consent to the will of the Highest, as he treads the "narrow ridge" which leads Buber's man not, to be sure, out of the covenant, not without the strength drawn from the substance and "merit of the fathers," but without support from the guard-rails of the past, into the untrodden, the unprotected—perhaps toward a new theophany, but nevertheless also into darkness and silence.

What then is faith? It is absolute trust that holds fast to the hope (*espérance*) that is above all hope (*espoir*); to the meaning that seems to be lost in the meaninglessness of this world; to the unifying power of healing and of hallowing that reaches through disunion and doubt and carries us over the abyss of despair. It is the devoted giving of self that demands commitment and makes possible acceptance; the strength to give oneself up for the sake of future possibilities; it is the vicarious sacrifice of the "servant of God," in whose mystery Buber has again and again become absorbed. In faith —and just in the faith of which Buber speaks—suffering becomes the sacrament that is presented to us and that we take to ourselves. He who is capable of this is made by it not only richer and deeper; in suffering there also is unveiled to him the countenance of God. This means, in the spirit of Buber's philosophy: in suffering itself is the testing and—perhaps—the rendering of that full devotion which harbors salvation within it, because it is in this devotion that the light of the absolute falls even into the darkest depth of our existence and ever anew renews our life. Such suffering ceases to be the tormenting, unsolvable riddle of life; in it is redemption; in suffering itself is given the solution to the riddle of life. We do not seek this solution; it falls to our lot as an act of bitter grace.

It is probably in this sense that Buber has repeatedly insisted that in the religious sphere there is no seeking. We may connect this with the insight that one cannot ask for the fulfillment of prayer. To be able to pray is already the achievement and fulfillment of life. To break through the walls that shut us in and through our isolation, to open ourselves to the other, to his speech of heartening, of demand, of contradiction: that is truly prayer, and in that we have reality. That is why Buber's representation leaves room also for the painful words of comfort of Bernard of Clairvaux, that He alone is God who can never be sought in vain, even then, when one cannot find Him.

There has been and there is religious apathy; but there is no suffering from religious hunger. How far it is possible under the conditions of life today, its alienation and fostering of antagonism, for anyone to satisfy his hunger fully by reaching out to others "the heavenly bread of self-being;" how far the absolute can become pure presence among us—how far even the mere mention of it may, from the depth of the soul, bear witness to this possibility: this we do not know. But we feel that Buber fights for such simple attestation by our belief in what he has to say. We sense that in his word a heartening call struggles through to us, to which our knowledge need not deny itself. And we thank him that in all the evil suffering that has come upon us, he yet gave us to taste also of the suffering of God—the wine, pressed in pain, of communion among men of good will.

FRITZ KAUFMANN

DEPARTMENT OF PHILOSOPHY
UNIVERSITY OF BUFFALO

9

Malcolm L. Diamond

DIALOGUE AND THEOLOGY

BUBER'S *I and Thou* has been called a "philosophical-religious poem." The phrase is awkward, but with it, Ronald Gregor Smith, who translated the book into English, captured the flavor of the work. It is a unique blend of the imperative of religious utterance and the reflective character of philosophical discourse. While some dismiss it as specious emotionalism, a major source of Buber's powerful impact upon contemporary religious discussion is his refusal to be apologetic about the existential, non-objective character of his thought. He insists that all language which speaks meaningfully about the ultimate questions of human destiny must be of this character and, therefore, will be considered meaningless by the criteria of positivism.

In *I and Thou* Buber develops two modes of discourse which reflect the two, and only two, basic attitudes which man can adopt towards the beings with which he has commerce. These attitudes determine man's posture towards the world and elicit different responses and modes of expression from him.

The first is that of the self-absorbed individual who confronts beings as objects which he considers more or less significant in terms of their usefulness to him. In holding this attitude, the individual may adopt any role known to man. He may be philosopher, artist, scientist, doctor or businessman, but in all these roles an overacute awareness of his own desires and concerns interposes a barrier between himself and others. Nevertheless, this barrier serves as the source of a reliable, reproducible perspective which men can achieve towards the world—for it keeps the world at a distance and enables it to be measured and surveyed. This response, the I-It attitude, is often misconstrued. People regard it as appropriate only to man's relation to things, since it is thought that they alone may properly be treated as objects of man's utility. But actually, insofar as it is an appropriate attitude for man to adopt, it is also appropriate as a response toward other persons, for the reliability of this perspective enables men to make themselves understood to one another. Man cannot live without this world; it is the world of objective space-time in which he can continually locate himself and others.[1]

The language reflected by this attitude is objectifying language. It is language whose meaning can be verified empirically or logically, according to the strictest canons of positivism. While this attitude and its linguistic modes are necessary to human existence, they are not sufficient for it. Beings elicit a deeper response from man, the I-Thou relation which is grounded in encounter and engagement. As in the case of the I-It attitude, the I-Thou attitude may be manifested towards any being, human or non-human, and it may be fulfilled in any role which man adopts.

Buber develops the difference between these two attitudes by describing three ways of perceiving another man. One is that of the *observer* who intently dissects a man and records his traits. To him a face is nothing but physiognomy. This role may be adopted by scientists when they are completely detached. Then there is the *onlooker* who, in comparison with the observer seems to be related to the person he perceives. He is not intent but relaxes while awaiting the impressions which the other person will make upon him. The onlooker does not dissect the other, but allows the full play of his own unconscious to absorb the essence of the other so that he can project it in a vivid synthesis. He is the artist gaining impressions.

The artist in this role is no closer to engagement than is the detached scientist. Buber's thought cuts across the usual distinctions between the artistic and the scientific approaches to reality. In the instances cited, both regard separation between themselves and the other as necessary to proper perception. But there is another mode of perception which is possible to man. He may *become aware* of the other person in such a way that he feels himself addressed by the other, feels himself bound up with the other in a relation of mutuality. Detachment is broken through to be replaced by the sense of the other as a Thou who stands in his own right.[2] Here the normal I-It nexus of space-time fades away and the perceiver becomes absorbed in an exclusive relation to the other. Throughout its duration the relation suffuses his entire being so that all else is seen in its light.

---

[1] *I and Thou*, pp. 31ff.

[2] "Dialogue," *Between Man and Man*, pp. 8ff.

The paradigm of the I-Thou relation is love fully manifest between man and wife.

Yet man can be engaged in an I-Thou relation by any being whatsoever, by a work of art, a philosophical idea, by animal life or by objects of nature. Perhaps the most famous instance of this is Buber's description of his own I-Thou encounter with a tree. After considering a number of I-It modes of relating to the tree he says, "It can however also come about . . . that in considering the tree I become bound up in relation to it. The tree is now no longer *It*. I have been seized by the power of exclusiveness."[3] Buber is invariably challenged on this, for the mutuality that pertains between man and woman in the relation of love does not obtain here. This criticism only calls attention to the fact that the fundamental mark of the I-Thou relation is not the full blown mutuality of speech and answering speech, but the intuition on the part of man, of the full ontological dimension of the other. While the tree is not a self which can be consciously aware of him, Buber declares:

The tree is no impression, no play of my imagination, no value depending on my mood; but it is bodied overagainst me and has to do with me, as I with it—only in a different way.[4]

The I-Thou relation alone is the bearer of meaning. The immediacy of the dialogic encounter provides its own rationale. When we are totally engaged in an encounter with a Grecian Urn, " 'Beauty is truth, truth beauty,'—that is all ye know on earth and all ye need to know." We have neither the desire nor the need for aesthetic theory or the history of ceramics. These ordered disciplines are derivative— they help us to control beings, but can never proffer grounds for relating to them.

"The *It* is the eternal chrysalis, the *Thou* is the eternal butterfly." If you wish to make the world encountered in the I-Thou relation subject to measurement and comparison you lose it. It cannot be surveyed. The attempt to compare the given urn with other specimens, the attempt to analyze its form and trace its history introduces the element of distance that is the fundamental constituent of the I-It attitude. When the Thou has, according to the exalted melancholy of our fate, again become an It, we are in the position of the

[3] *I and Thou,* p. 7.
[4] *Ibid.,* p. 8.

mystic who knows the dark night of the soul after the moment of ecstatic union. From the standpoint of the I-It perspective the I-Thou relation always claims too much.

I-Thou language cannot be translated into I-It terms. Like poetry it refracts the experience in a way that is *sui generis*. To state the meaning of Buber's encounter with the tree in the form of proposi-tions that could be empirically verified would be to violate the char-acter of the encounter. "A poem should not mean but be"; however inadequate Buber's own philosophical-religious poem may be to the reality he would convey, he cannot change the mode of it—"He that has ears to hear let him hear."

There are obvious criticisms that may be directed against this philosophy of dialogue. In this scheme it is precisely the most signif-icant issues that are least manageable. Man can attain certain knowledge only in those matters which do not concern the funda-mental problems of human nature and destiny, for these fundamen-tal problems are immersed in the waywardness of ephemeral en-counters. Loyalty, love, commitment to God, man and country are incapable of empirical validation. And this, it develops, is precisely the radical challenge of Buber's thought. The distinction between the I-Thou and the I-It attitudes is that in the latter, regardless of the extent to which its attention is directed at other beings, the "I" of the relation is self-absorbed, concentrating upon its own concerns and purposes. However much it may "observe" the others and "look upon" them, the basic context is an "inner" one, the central purpose is egotistical. By contrast, the I-Thou relation ". . . is fulfilled not in the soul but between I-Thou."[5] That is why Buber is so critical of traditional epistemology whenever it seeks an objective criterion, an infallible point of vantage which the self can employ in testing the validity of the judgments it forms about experience. There is no way of validating the judgments of the encounters other than reen-tering them, and this involves acting with the risk that one's judg-ment may be mistaken. There is no criterion which removes the risk. Only the total participation of the self in the full presentness of the encounter can serve as a source of verification, and when the presentness has faded and the self is again in the I-It realm, questions regarding the validity of the I-Thou encounter emerge once again.

According to Buber's critics, he cannot answer their charges by

5 *Ibid.,* p. 81.

pointing to dimensions of reality like love which can only be known through participation, for the greatest need for man today is to reason about precisely these dimensions. Nationalism is an excellent illustration of this. Uncurbed by the cold light of detached I-It knowledge, it runs rampant, wreaking havoc through the world. Therefore, Buber is accused of espousing a philosophical perspective that encourages precisely the kind of unreasoned emotional fanaticism that mankind must outgrow. We need to reason objectively about reality, rather than wallowing in the passions induced by our commitments.[6]

However, the I-Thou relation involves the whole man. Buber does not advocate an intuitive approach to reality that would render all forms of non-intuited apprehension superfluous. Of his I-Thou encounter with the tree he writes:

To effect this it is not necessary for me to give up any of the ways in which I consider the tree. There is nothing from which I would have to turn my eyes away in order to see, and no knowledge that I would have to forget. Rather is everything, picture and movement, species and type, law and number, indivisibly united in this event.[7]

The I-Thou encounters are enriched by the store of I-It experience one has accumulated, as in the case of the man who is aesthetically cultivated. He may find it increasingly difficult to be totally engaged by a work of art, but his responses are truer and far more perceptive when he is so engaged. The beauty he perceives, like the vision of the community of peace and justice, are the deepest realities men know and they cannot be encountered apart from dialogic relations.

The question left in the minds of Buber's readers is directed to the heart of this philosophy. If the "I" of the I-It attitude is characterized by excessive self-absorption and a utilitarian approach to beings, one which orients it in a solipsistic direction, how can it be the ground of an objective verifiable, transubjective world order? Does not the scientist, patiently observing reality with genuine humility and concerned to transmit his findings to others, have the others at least as much if not more in mind than does the subject of the I-Thou relation? Furthermore, there is no validity to Buber's claim that in moments of creative illumination the scientist himself is really in the

[6] For an example of this sort of criticism see Jacob B. Agus, *Major Philosophies of Judaism* (New York, 1941), pp. 276ff.

[7] *I and Thou*, p. 7.

I-Thou realm, since the scientist does not distinguish between the moments of vision and the job of meticulous research and transmission. They are but phases of the ordered cloth of his task, and verifiability and detachment are also necessary parts of it. It is rather commitment and engagement, the characteristics of the I-Thou realm, which introduce distortion into our perspectives. This is why we seek non-partisan judges.

This is a more telling criticism and Buber's discussion of the ontological character of dialogue is relevant to it. The fact that no objective criterion can validate a love relation or any other relation of total engagement (to attempt to validate it is to qualify its totality, to end its full presentness) does not mean that the relation is nothing more than a capricious manifestation of the individual psyche. It involves the real world in which we live—whereas feelings dwell in man, man dwells in his love.[8] This world of the I-Thou relation is in Buber's view ontological not psychological. "Feelings are a mere accompaniment to the metaphysical and metapsychical fact of the relation."[9] He constantly rejects psychological categorizations of the phenomena he describes: ". . . . we whose concern is real consideration of the real, cannot have our purpose served with the subconscious or any other apparatus of the soul."[10] It is part of the intuited reality of the encounter that what is discerned therein is the deepest reality man can know, a reality which is over against him. To attempt to remove it to the soul is to annihilate it.[11] Since Buber cannot recognize any objective criterion of knowledge that can be affirmed independently of the full presentness of the dialogue, he is also unable to regard any ontological concept as an objective description of reality independently of the encounter. He affirms dialogue—the immediate intuited presence of the other over against one—as the only mode of contact with reality in which value and purpose are manifest.

The real boundary for actual man cuts right across the world of ideas . . . to be sure many a man who is satisfied with the experience and use of the

---

[8] *Ibid.,* p. 14.

[9] *Ibid.,* p. 81. See also pp. 14 and 46.

[10] *Ibid.,* p. 109. See also "The Foundation Stone," *Hasidism,* p. 54f.; "Images of Good and Evil," *Good and Evil,* pp. 116f., 123; "The Faith of Judaism," *Israel and the World,* pp. 19f.

[11] *I and Thou,* p. 81.

world of things has raised over or about himself a structure of ideas, in which he finds refuge and repose from the oncome of nothingness . . . and regales himself with the spectacle of primal being or necessary being; but his life has no part in it.[12]

This dialogic way of thinking has a wide range of theological implications. We shall confine the discussion to a contrast between its procedures and those of ontological theology. Just as there is no vantage point outside the immediate presentness of the I-Thou relation from which objective reality can be seen, so too, Buber insists, there is no such vantage point for viewing God. Theologians try to present a God who is more than an idea but while the God of the theologians ". . . is not the God of the philosophers . . . neither is it the God of Abraham, Isaac and Jacob."[13] Theology must, to some extent, conceptualize God and this is to limit God. Although Buber acknowledges the fact that we must use concepts if we are to talk of God at all, he adds a strong note of protest: "Even though I must of necessity use theological concepts when I speak of . . . faith, I must not for a moment lose sight of the nontheological material from which I draw these concepts."[14] Of course, this could be said by any theologian who takes his task seriously, but for Buber it involves a significant methodological consideration. Since there is no objective criterion of theological truth, there can be no objective mode of theological procedure. He is not concerned with systematic consistency in developing his view of God. His main concern is to evoke the memory of past encounters and to point the way to future ones. Here paradox and poetry take precedence over logic and reason.

In every sphere in its own way, through each process of becoming that is present to us, we look out toward the eternal *Thou;* in each we are aware of a breath from the eternal *Thou;* in each *Thou* we address the eternal *Thou.*[15]

The eternal Thou is a singular Thou indeed. It is the symbol for God in Buber's philosophy of I and Thou. He has no intention of using it to replace the word God, which is, in his view irreplace-

---

[12] *Ibid.,* p. 13.

[13] "The Question to the Single One," *Between Man and Man,* p. 57.

[14] "The Faith of Judaism," *Israel and the World,* p. 13.

[15] *I and Thou,* p. 6.

able.[16] Rather, he would speak of the eternal Thou in the hope of clarifying what centuries of the faithful have meant in using the term God. The eternal Thou is addressed in each I-Thou encounter because it is the power that enables each and every dialogic encounter to occur, a relation which gathers up and includes all others.[17] Here we see one reason why man can have I-Thou encounters with non-conscious beings like a tree—the tree is grounded in God, who as the eternal Thou, is the ground of all I-Thou encounters. However, the eternal Thou is not merely an abstract power that enables concrete encounters to take place, it is ". . . the *Thou* that by its nature cannot become *It* . . . which cannot be limited by another *Thou* . . . the Being that is directly, most nearly and lastingly over-against us, that may properly only be addressed not expressed."[18] The Platonic anology of the sun is useful here. As the sun is the most luminous of objects and the source of luminosity in all other objects, so the eternal Thou is the consummate instance of a Thou and the source of the dialogic power of relation in all beings.

Buber's presentation of the eternal Thou reflects a traditional problem of theism. If the personal character of God is emphasized, as Buber emphasizes it in speaking of God as " . . . the Thou that by its nature cannot become It," there is the danger of reducing God to the order of a finite being, a person among persons. If, on the other hand, the transcendent character of the Absolute is emphasized, as when Buber stresses God as the eternal Thou in which the extended lines of relations meet, there is the danger of reducing God to the status of an idea in which the personal dimension of the experience of faith is lost. And Buber emphatically rejects the view that God is merely an idea, even the most sublime of ideas.[19] He combines the personal element with the transcendent one by speaking paradoxically of the " . . . *absolute personality* we call God."[20] He claims that this paradoxical combination is the basis of all religion.

Philosophy is grounded on the presupposition that one sees the absolute in universals. In opposition to this, religion, when it has to define itself philosophically, says that it means the covenant of the absolute with the particular,

---

[16] *Ibid.*, pp. 75f. See also "Report on Two Talks," *Eclipse of God*, pp. 17f.

[17] *I and Thou*, p. 80.

[18] *Ibid.*, pp. 75, 80f.

[19] "The Love of God and the Idea of Deity," *Eclipse of God*, pp. 68f., 78ff.

[20] *Ibid.*, p. 81.

with the concrete . . . I-Thou finds its highest intensity and transfiguration in religious reality, in which unlimited Being becomes, as absolute person, my partner.[21]

Since he does not begin with theology, but with " . . . the actual attitude of faithful Jews from the earliest days down to our own time," Buber finds "the unity of the contraries . . . at the innermost core of the dialogue," a unity in which the logical contradictoriness of A and non-A is transcended in the dialogic character of the lived experience. It is a quality that simply cannot be expressed in rational terms. It can be expressed only in the language of paradox.[22] This is an operative assumption that is fundamental to Buber's thought. He holds that there is a correlation between language and experience, but that the correlation is twofold in accordance with the twofold character of the I-It and the I-Thou attitudes. Whereas rationally coherent language is adequate to I-It experience it radically distorts the deepest dimension of reality, namely, that disclosed in the I-Thou encounters. Thought can accurately reflect this dimension only by recognizing that it is transcended within it. It must therefore allow seemingly irreconcilable propositions to be reconciled in the language of paradox.

The paradoxical approach governs Buber's treatment of many traditional theological problems. Grace and freedom is paramount among these. From the standpoint of reason, either God is sovereign and controls all human actions or man is free to control his own will.

But if I consider necessity and freedom not in worlds of thought but in the reality of my standing before God, if I know that "I am given over for disposal" and know at the same time that "It depends on myself", then I cannot try to escape the paradox that has to be lived . . . but I am compelled to take both to myself, to be lived together, and in being lived they are one.[23]

Buber's paradoxical assertion in *I and Thou* that "Of course God is the 'wholly Other'; but He is also the wholly Same, the wholly Present,"[24] is buttressed in "The Faith of Judaism" by his appeal to

[21] "Religion and Philosophy," *Eclipse of God*, pp. 56, 61.

[22] "The Faith of Judaism," *Israel and the World*, pp. 13, 17.

[23] *I and Thou*, p. 96. See also, "Spinoza, Sabbattai Zevi and the Baalshem," *The Origin and Meaning of Hasidism*; "The Faith of Judaism," *Israel and the World*, pp. 16–21.

[24] *I and Thou*, p. 79.

the actual attitude of faithful Jews from the earliest days to our own time. Thus the wise man who said "My God, where can I find you, but where can I not find you?"[25] From this continual appeal to the life of dialogue as it is actually experienced in the intuited presence of the other we learn that " . . . meaning itself does not permit itself to be transmitted and made into knowledge generally current and admissible . . . it is not prescribed, it is not specified on any tablet to be raised above all men's heads."[26]

The fact that God can be truly apprehended only in man's ephemeral encounters with the eternal Thou, has important implications for Buber's use of religious language. Since the encounters must be lived rather than thought, the paradoxical formulations which alone can do justice to the encounters must remain as close as possible to the biblical language. For example, Buber holds that God, because of His infinite transcendent character, remains hidden even when He discloses Himself to man in revelation. Yet, since man cannot know the true nature of God apart from the dialogic encounters Buber insists that He cannot be called a "hidden" God, for "hidden" is a static non-dialogic term that implies objective conceptual knowledge of God. Buber remains closer to the language of Second-Isaiah— "Truly, thou art a God who hidest thyself, O God of Israel, the Savior" (Isaiah 45:15)—by speaking in dialogic, that is, relational terms of God as One who is self-concealing as well as self-revealing.[27] Buber is quite consistent in this—the paradoxical language of encounter is a truer expression of man's relation to God than is the language of rational coherence.

At this point it would be fruitful to compare Buber's procedure with that of Paul Tillich, the eminent theologian with whom he has much in common in the way of background and perspective.[28] Tillich's concern as a theologian is indicated by the title of his major work *Systematic Theology*. Consistency and rigor are central preoccupations which Tillich holds to be unavoidable for the theologian. For the task of theology is to correlate the biblical perspective with the questions that arise in each age. These questions are posited

[25] *Israel and the World,* p. 15.

[26] *I and Thou,* p. 111.

[27] "Religion and Ethics," *Eclipse of God,* p. 139.

[28] Paul Tillich, "Martin Buber and Christian Thought," *Commentary,* 5 June, 1948), 516.

in philosophical terms, and they must be answered in these same terms. There can be no purely "biblical theology." The Bible does not speak philosophically and the task of theology is to cast its message into a philosophical form that will render it authentically while refraining from arbitrarily imposing supernatural categories upon philosophical discussion.

Using a reason that is quickened by the non-rational depths of being that lie at the ultimate level of the self as well as at the ultimate level of reality (the formulation is strikingly Augustinian), Tillich finds an unassailable objective point of departure for theology in the notion of "being-itself." Being-itself is the *prius* of thought, the rock of existence which emerges when one is engaged by the ultimate metaphysical question "Why is there being rather than nothing?" Being-itself is the ultimate ground or power of being that has been the point of departure for mystics throughout the ages; it is the ultimate destination of the *via negativa*. Of it Tillich says:

The statement that God is being-itself is a nonsymbolic statement. It does not point beyond itself. It means what it says directly and properly; if we speak of the actuality of God, we first assert that he is not God if he is not being-itself. Other assertions about God can be made theologically only on this basis. . . . However, after this has been said, nothing else can be said about God as God which is not symbolic.[29]

The end result of this unambiguous use of being-itself is that Tillich's thought is always in danger of losing its theistic character. Indeed, this is the most common criticism of his theology. In *The Courage To Be* the concluding section presents "the God above God" as the only point at which the man of today, struggling with the problem of despair, can be engaged.[30] The living God of the Bible becomes a penultimate symbol whose significance can be appropriated only after the individual has transcended this God of theism, by encountering "the God above God."

It is precisely this sort of transtheistic position that Buber seeks to avoid. Because of his concern for an objective criterion and for systematic rigor Tillich ultimately subsumes the God of the Bible in an ontological framework that, for all Tillich's protestations to the contrary, is as impersonal as the "necessary being" of Saint Thomas Aquinas.

29 *Systematic Theology*, 1 (Chicago, 1951), 238f.
30 Pp. 82–90.

As we have noted, Buber is not unmoved by the considerations which impress Tillich. He recognizes the danger of speaking of God as a person and thereby reducing Him to the finite level as a person among persons—hence the aspects of his thought which present God as the eternal Thou, the Thou which is the ground of all I-Thou relations. Buber is so much aware of the danger of reducing God to a mere person that some critics have insisted that he, like Tillich, represents God in impersonal non-theistic categories.[31] But Buber walks the "narrow ridge" between an ontological transpersonal ultimate, and the Living God of Abraham, Isaac, and Jacob. Hence his answer to Spinoza:

Spinoza's fundamental mistake was that he imagined the teaching of Israel to mean that God is also a person; and he turned against this as a lessening of the Godhead. But the truth of the teaching lies in its insistence that God is *also* a person; and that stands over against all impersonal unapproachable "purity" on the part of God as a heightening of the Godhead.[32]

Tillich might agree that the God who as being-itself transcends all categories is *also* a person, but the difference between his methodology and Buber's is crucial. Tillich has established being-itself as an objective island in the midst of the sea of existential encounter. He then proceeds to develop his theology with rational consistency. As a result his setting of the God above God as his ultimate must be unambiguously transtheistic. As we have seen, Buber sees no point of reference which stands beyond the engagement of dialogue, the eternal Thou is a symbol for the ultimate and not a literal statement of it, as being-itself is for Tillich. Furthermore, we have commented upon Buber's distrust of theology, a distrust which leads him to express himself in evocative language, language which is similar in tone to the passionate utterance of the Bible. This distrust of theology also leads him to proceed paradoxically without concern for the principle of contradiction which he regards as a necessary limit of logic but not of lived dialogue.

The contrast between the ontological theology of Tillich and the dialogic thought of Buber reflects a difference in their traditions as well as a difference in temperament. Christianity represents a synthe-

---

[31] Edmund La B. Cherbonnier, "The Theology of the Word of God," *Journal of Religion*, 33 (January, 1953), 28f.

[32] "Spinoza, Sabbattai Zevi and the Baalshem," *Hasidism*, p. 97.

sis between the biblical tradition of Israel and the philosophical tradition of Greece. Judaism on its native soil did not develop a theology that was directed toward the philosophically oriented nonbeliever. Only in the diaspora, at periods of Jewish history when there was cultural interchange between Jews and gentiles, did Judaism produce apologetic theology, the defense of the faith in philosophical terms. Furthermore, another theological tradition has always existed alongside the apologetic one, often in the same thinker. This is confessional theology which does not aim to find an objective point of contact with the non-believer, but does attempt to reformulate the faith in contemporary terms for those who are already passionately engaged. It is this latter task that Buber has performed with surpassing power, and it is a task which is more authentically Jewish than is the task of apologetics.

When this has been said, some fundamental questions remain. We have noted that Buber admits that he cannot dispense with the theological conceptualizing of which he is so suspicious. Does this suggest that Tillich is right in claiming that since all theologians must, of necessity, be conceptualizers, they had best be systematic, that attempts to remain closer to the emotive language of the Bible lead only to poor conceptualizing and to bad systems?

Finally, we return to the problem of the limitation of the divine through language. Buber distrusts the systematic approach to theology because it limits God to the categories of human conceptualizing. Tillich, by contrast, claims that ultimately thought and being correspond, that beyond all the existential distortions of reason there is a point where the *Logos,* the structure of human reason, mirrors the structure of reality. That is why he can employ being-itself as a *prius* of thought which can be univocally affirmed of the absolute. From this standpoint we may ask Buber why he insists that paradoxical expressions, which are also of human construction, limit God less than ontological concepts? Is it not a severe limitation of the divine to insist that it does not truly disclose itself in the structure of human thought?

MALCOLM L. DIAMOND

DEPARTMENT OF RELIGION
PRINCETON UNIVERSITY

10

Mordecai M. Kaplan

BUBER'S EVALUATION OF PHILOSOPHIC THOUGHT AND RELIGIOUS TRADITION

I

B UBER does not profess to be the creator of a philosophic system. He, in fact, questions the very possibility of embodying living truth, or reality, as it actually exists and operates, in any systematic hierarchy of ideas. His main contribution to the ordering of thought consists fundamentally in his proposal of a new method in the art of living, a method he came to designate as "the life of dialogue." The numerous essays, lectures and short works in which his thoughts find expression possess the unique quality of being designed, as he puts it, "to meet the needs of particular moments, and bear the mark of time." In another writer, such a quality might give those thoughts a journalistic and transitory value. Not so in the case of Buber. Whatever idea he has occasion to expound emerges from the very depth of his character and his innermost being. The wide range of his intellect and its highly integrated power are a guarantee for the viability of his pronouncements. There is such a decided consistency and coherence in the multitude of his writings that it is possible to identify the well-integrated pattern of his thinking.

The pattern is not, I believe, adequately characterized by the central approach which Maurice S. Friedman places at the head of his work on *Martin Buber: The Life of Dialogue.* He there quotes Buber as describing his own standpoint as the "narrow ridge." Friedman interprets that standpoint as "the paradoxical unity of what one usually understands only as alternatives—I and Thou, love and justice, dependence and freedom, the love of God and the fear of God, passion and direction, good and evil, unity and duality." Friedman's statement is, indeed, a comprehensive summary of virtually everything that Buber has written, but it fails to furnish the key to an understanding of "the quality and significance of Martin Buber's life and thought." In my opinion, the one piece of writing that provides the key to that understanding is the essay entitled "The Demand of the Spirit and Historical Reality"[1] which was de-livered by Buber as an inaugural lecture at the Hebrew University in 1938, when he was in his sixty-first year. It sounds a note which justi-fies Friedman's characterization of Buber as "spokesman for Judaism before the world."[2] But, in order to derive from that address the key-principle of Buber's interpretation of Judaism, we need to know some of the main facts and factors which form the background of that address.

A knowledge of that background is indispensable particularly to an insight into Buber's attitude toward philosophy and tradition. That attitude was not arrived at as a result merely of intellectual exploration. It was definitely a response, or, to use the formula Buber recommends as a principle of true living, "a responsible decision," in answer to the concrete situation in which he found himself. Rather than detracting, therefore, from the validity of Buber's attitude to-ward philosophy and tradition, it confirms its validity, at least within the framework of that concrete situation. For that reason none of the details in the following description of Buber's early background should be considered irrelevant to our main theme.

As a young lad, Buber grew up in the home of his grandfather, Solomon Buber, who, in addition to being a well-to-do merchant was a Midrash scholar, one of the last great masters of the Haskala, or Hebrew enlightenment movement. He would often take his grand-child with him on periodic trips to the Hasidic community of Sadagora in Galicia. The profound impression which the Hasidic manifesta-tion of Jewish religion then made on the lad was a determining influence of his career in later years. As a student in the University of Vienna, young Buber came under the influences of Simmel, Dilthey and Bergson, and made a special study of the mystics of the Renais-sance and the Reformation.

During the last decade of the nineteenth century, and the first of this one, the Zionist movement gained world attention, and the Jews themselves had to take a decisive step that would insure their survival as a people. Those were the years when the Jews in Europe were confronted by a modernized Western civilization in which anti-Semitism was gaining headway. It took Theodore Herzl to foresee

---

[1] *Pointing the Way*, pp. 177–191.

[2] Friedman, *Martin Buber: The Life of Dialogue*, p. 9.

that this anti-Semitism would ultimately aim at nothing less than to render the entire European continent *judenrein*. The response which he finally succeeded in eliciting from the Jews was Zionism and the rebirth of Jewish nationalism.

Modernized Western civilization had emancipated the Jews from their political disabilities and status as aliens, with the expectation that they would become absorbed in the general population and disappear as a distinct social entity. Most Jews in Central and Western Europe, however, met that expectation half-way. In fact, the statesmen themselves, who advocated the emancipation of the Jews, had proposed a compromise: the renunciation of their nationhood and the retention of their religious beliefs and practices. That compromise was enough to make of the Jews a conspicuous minority that could serve as a scapegoat for the many economic ills to which the newly born states were subject. Thus arose the modern form of Jew-hatred known as anti-Semitism which throve in Central Europe and from there spread to the East and to the West. This new form of Jew-hatred was no longer motivated by the Christian myth, but by the rising cult of modern nationalism. The Dreyfus case was the most dramatic outburst of anti-Semitism which had been simmering for several decades, as Herzlian Zionism was the most dramatic outburst of Jewish nationalism which had been in the making during that same period, under the influence of the modern European national movements.

Young Buber, whom the university education had alienated from Judaism, was brought back to it by Zionism. At first it was the political Zionism of Herzl, but almost immediately he discerned its shortcomings as being mainly "anti-anti-Semitism." He yearned for some more profound rationale than that of escape from persecution. He looked to Zionism to transform both the inner and outer life of the Jewish People. "We must strive for nothing less," he wrote after his long experience with the movement,

than the concrete transformation of our life as a whole. The process of transforming our inner lives must be expressed in the transformation of our outer life, of the life of the individual as well as that of the community. And the effect must be reciprocal, the change in the external arrangements of our life must be reflected in, and renew, our inner life time and again. Up to now, Zionist theory has not adequately realized the importance of this mutual influence.[3]

3 "Hebrew Humanism," *Israel and the World*, p. 245.

No wonder he soon came under the spell of Ahad Ha-Am, to whom the return to Eretz Yisrael was to be a means to the renaissance of the Jewish People. But before long that spell seemed to be broken. Ahad Ha-Am's version of Judaism reborn appeared to Buber to be a synthetic product, in which Western culture had more of a share than the Judaism of tradition. He could not reconcile himself to Ahad Ha-Am's conception of Judaism, in which the belief in God played no role. Both the ineradicable influence of Hasidism and his own conviction that human life could have no worth, or meaning, without God kept him from identifying himself with Ahad Ha-Am's "cultural Zionism." A Judaism, however ethical and idealistic, which was not based on faith in God, was for Buber incapable of resuscitating the Jewish People.

Without a God-inspired zeal, Zionism was likely to be merely a quixotic attempt to imitate under next-to-impossible conditions the nationalist adventures of the awakened European peoples. The latter, had, to begin with, the most important and indispensable asset, namely, lands which they could call their own. The Jews had no such asset. They first had to recover the land from which they had been exiled many centuries before, and which the Arabs regarded as their inalienable possession. To overcome that insuperable obstacle nothing less than the resumption of the covenant relationship between the Jewish People and God would have to be the avowed aim of Zionism. Zionism could not succeed, unless it were animated by the spirit of Messianism.

For the Jews to evince such a spirit, Buber concluded, they had to be disillusioned concerning the true character of contemporary Western civilization which had held out to them the promise of universal reason, enlightenment and progress. They had to be made to realize to what extent this very civilization which was insidiously, even if not always violently, seeking to destroy them body and soul was intrinsically incapable of even understanding what man is, to say nothing of helping him to achieve salvation. Jews should rather look to their own spiritual heritage for the method of salvation of which mankind was desperately in need. Nothing less than an unprecedented spiritual awakening, as part of their effort to recover their ancient homeland, was therefore needed to recall them to their vocation of being a holy people, and an example of justice and peace to the rest of the world.

This was the final decision which Buber arrived at, after he had withdrawn for a few years from public and literary activity, in order to learn at first hand, and if possible to relive, the revelational experience recorded in the Bible and the unique mode of communal life fostered by Hasidism in its prime. What he came out with from that intellectual and spiritual hibernation is best summed up in the address on "The Demand of the Spirit and Historical Reality."

That address was delivered in the fateful year of 1938, when the world was in the grip of the demonic frenzy let loose by Hitler. It was spoken at the Hebrew University, as Buber took his place on its faculty. He then, no doubt, wished to give expression to the idea which had obsessed him during all the years in which he had been engaged in preparing the Jews for their proper role in Zion. Plato, to Buber, is the symbol of philosophic thinking, and Isaiah of Jewish religious tradition. Accordingly, the all embracing principle which he tried to set forth on that occasion was that the Jews should not look to the philosophy of the West for inspiration or guidance in their great enterprise of rebuilding their land and their People. The only dependable source of inspiration and guidance is their own religious tradition. The following is the substance of the argument advanced in that address:

Plato entertained a life-long ambition to found a republic in accordance with his concept of justice, in the hope that he would thereby influence the existing states to follow the example of that republic. Realizing how much human life depended upon the nature of the state, and noting how poorly governed all states were, he came to the conclusion that the only way to remedy that evil was to have philosophers do the governing, or to have the governors become philosophers. The problem of finding the right kind of political leaders was to be solved either by having philosophers come to power, or by educating as philosophers those who already possessed power.

The absurdity of that solution has been pointed out by Kant. Power and reason, he said in effect, do not go together. The most that can be expected is that power should at least not suppress the voice of reason. Plato, however, was convinced that his theory would work. He went so far as to train his disciple Dion to head a republic that was to be established in Sicily, and he himself journeyed thither several times to help Dion with his task, without making any headway. In the end, Dion was assassinated by a fellow-disciple of Plato's and all of Plato's expectations came to naught.

"Why did Plato fail?" asks Buber. Instead of answering that question, Buber proceeds to describe another type of failure, that of the Prophet Isaiah. Isaiah is commissioned by God to bring a message of reproof to the King Uzziah for his misrule. But Isaiah is warned that his message will not be heeded—except by a small "remnant." Isaiah is made aware that "failure is an integral part of the way he must take."

Isaiah has a different conception both of "spirit" and of "power" from that of Plato. According to Isaiah, neither the one nor the other is properly the possession of man. They have to be gifts from God. The prophet, as a man of spirit, must not expect to exercise power. The king, as a man of power, is answerable to God. In contrast with Plato who regarded his own soul as perfect, Isaiah acknowledged himself as unclean. Plato had a fully worked out plan for the structure of the just state. On the other hand, all that Isaiah did was to criticise the existing state and to demand of the people and the government that they heed the will of God who was the true King. The will of God cannot be mediated by priests who possess power, but only by prophets who lack it.

Isaiah did not address his message only to King Uzziah but also to the people. He sought to impress upon them that, if they were to be worthy of having God as their King, they would have to become a genuine people, a people free from the divisive effects of injustice and inequality. Every individual among his hearers was thus made to feel responsible for the conduct of the state to which he belonged. Moreover, Isaiah warned Israel not to engage in power politics and not to become involved in international intrigues. To survive amid the great world powers, Israel had to prove by example that it could make peace a reality in its internal life.

Isaiah also failed as did Plato later on. The fact, however, that we Jews still exist as a people proves that Isaiah's failure was different from Plato's. There were some of Isaiah's contemporaries, who not only took his admonition seriously, but who also transmitted it to their descendents. It has become the religious tradition of the Jewish People, whom it has kept alive, by giving them a purpose to live for. Plato's philosophy, on the other hand, articulated in his *Republic*, has remained a classic for classroom study. Such is the difference between philosophy and religious tradition, a difference summed up in the following statement:

The prophet's spirit does not, like Plato's, believe that he possesses an abstract and general, a timeless concept of truth. He receives one message for one situation. That is exactly why after thousands of years his words still address the changing situations in history.

Here, at last, we have the key-idea to Martin Buber's writings. It is the idea that the Jews have what to live for as a People. Western civilization has produced philosophers, but the Jews have had their prophets. Western civilization excels in the discoveries of science and the inventions of technology, but it has little to offer in the way of helping man achieve his human destiny. Judaism has not contributed to science or technology, but mankind cannot achieve unity and peace without the divine message which is embodied in the Jewish religious tradition.

Buber recalls the spiritual illumination which Pascal experienced when he suddenly discovered that the God he believed in and prayed to was the

God of Abraham, God of Isaac, God of Jacob—not of the philosophers and scholars. He turned, not from a state of being where there is no God to one where there is a God, but from the God of the philosophers to the God of Abraham.[4]

Thus Pascal, himself a great representative of Western thought, found philosophic thought inadequate as a means of helping man to live. That should suffice to prove that the Jews do not have to depend for their spiritual fulfillment upon the philosophic thinking of Western civilization. On the contrary, they have the opportunity and the responsibility to bring to mankind the only truth concerning God that can transform mankind. What mankind needs is the awareness that God is not a mere idea of the mind, but an infinite and absolute reality that exists independently of it, and that salvation depends upon man's self-commitment with his entire being in thought, feeling and action to faith in this living God. This truth has to be translated into life by the Jewish People in the land of its origin, amid conditions which would permit all of its political, economic, social and cultural activities to be permeated by the revelational spirit that prevailed during Bible days, and that was temporarily revived in the Hasidic movement.

4 "The Love of God and the Idea of Deity," *Israel and the World*, p. 53. (Included in *Eclipse of God*—Ed.)

The foregoing thesis, maintained by Buber can be best brought into sharp relief by being contrasted with its antithesis which was promulgated by Hermann Cohen, the founder in Marburg University of Neo-Kantianism. Like Buber, Hermann Cohen too, had for a time been alienated from Judaism, but unlike Buber who came back to Judaism through Zionism, Cohen came back through Kantianism. For Cohen, too, the belief in God is the heart of Judaism. But there the resemblance ends. Whereas to Cohen, the belief in God is the belief in the validity of the idea, arrived at through a process of reasoning, like that pursued by Kant in his *Critique of Practical Reason,* to Buber, such a God can have no practical significance for human life.

Buber regards Cohen as a great "system-creator," but considers his efforts wasted. "Cohen," he says, "has constructed the last home for the God of the philosophers."[5] He then proceeds to disprove Cohen's argument in defense of *idea* as reality, and as capable of being loved. Cohen asks: "How can one love anything, save an idea?" thereby implying that to be loved, God must be conceived as Idea. In reply, Buber rightly points out that while an idea can be loved, it cannot be conceived as loving. The point that Buber next makes is that Cohen, in spite of himself, really conceives God existentially. Buber accepts Rosenzweig's interpretation of Cohen, that "Cohen's idea of God should not be taken to mean that God is only an idea in Cohen's eyes"[6] and he refers to Cohen as "the philosopher who is overwhelmed by faith."

To the average person who follows that debate between Cohen and Buber, the difference may sound little more than that between tweedledum and tweedledee. As such, however, it is likely to appear only when taken out of the life context in which that debate was conducted. The life context is the situation in which the Jews found themselves in the first decade of this century vis-à-vis present-day Western civilization. Buber was convinced that the cause of authentic and vital religion demanded that the Jews become a nation once again and resume the broken continuity of its existence in Eretz Yisrael. On the other hand, Cohen as sincerely and eloquently argued that the cause of religion demanded that Jews retain their *nationality* (as distinct from "nationhood," and as the equivalent of "com-

---

[5] *Eclipse of God,* p. 74.
[6] *Ibid.,* p. 79.

munity") but otherwise become integrated into the State of which they were citizens, and there demonstrate the truth of monotheism by carrying it out to its ethical conclusions. Buber's philosophy of reality, or of religion, is as much of an apology for his "Utopian Zionism" as Cohen's is for his "Universal Judaism." Both would probably resent the notion that pragmatic considerations had anything to do with the formulation of their respective God concepts. To Buber, however, that fact should not be objectionable in the least. On the contrary, it harmonizes fully with his own principle that concreteness is the only gate to reality, and what is more concrete than the existential situation? He himself makes use of that principle in his interpretation of Kierkegaard's central category of the "Single One."[7]

II

Apart from pragmatic consequences, however, any system of thought deserves to be weighed in terms of its inner consistency. Even when, as in the case of existentialist systems, paradox is not only not deprecated, but even treated with great respect, there are limits beyond which we cannot afford to go even in paradox. Thus, although Buber himself allows considerable room for paradox in his own thinking, he refuses to go along with Kierkegaard in the latter's version of the story of Abraham's willingness to sacrifice his son Isaac at God's command, the paradox in this instance being that faith in God may on occasion demand human sacrifice. Of course, once you admit the legitimacy of paradox, there is really no point at which it can be halted. Thus even Kierkegaard's paradox is accepted as normal, when we consider dying for one's country the height of ethical behavior.

Nevertheless, Buber's entire thought pattern does reveal so much coherence that its contribution to the understanding of philosophy and tradition merits examination. Certainly his strictures of classical, or speculative, philosophy should not be disregarded. They constitute serious reasons why philosophy as such cannot get at the heart of reality:

1. In the first place, philosophy has to resort to the method of generalization. In order to generalize, it has to abstract from con-

7 "The Question to the Single One," *Between Man and Man*, p. 40.

crete objects or situations some one aspect or quality that is common
to a number of them, and study it as though it possessed independent
reality. It thus comes to treat as reality that which is only an idea
and to ignore the existential reality which is always an organic complex of aspects or qualities.

2. Secondly, philosophy seeks to discover the regularities of laws
that obtain in the processes whereby things and persons interact
with one another and with their environment. That leads to the
conclusion that all of reality is dominated by an inherent principle
of unbreakable iron necessity. Thus human freedom, without which
there can be no moral or spiritual responsibility, cannot but be
treated from a philosophical standpoint as mere illusion.

3. Thirdly, philosophy is committed to the epistemological problem of "How do we know what we know, and that what we know is
neither dream nor delusion?" Consequently the only kind of "I" or
"personality", that it deals with is the subjective one, of which the
entire content of knowledge is the object. That fact reduces even
one's personality to a subjective idea, devoid of that ontological
reality which is essential to the belief that personality itself is existentially real, existentially effective, and existentially responsible.

4. Philosophy has shown itself unable to answer satisfactorily the
question which is basic to a sense of security or at-homeness in the
world. That is because it is unable to answer the question of "What
is man, what unique quality in him enables him to be self-aware,
and to distinguish between what he is and does, on the one hand, and
what he ought to be and do, on the other?"

5. Philosophy has reduced God to an idea which is a creation, or
expression, of the human mind. In the words of Kant, which are
quoted by Buber, "God is only an idea of reason, but one possessing
the greatest practical internal and external reality."[8] This kind of
God is not a living God. If faith in God is to make a difference in
a person's life, it has to mean standing in a relationship to God as a
living entity that is independent of man.

All of the foregoing five indictments which Buber brings against
the philosophers of the Western civilizations are implied in the one
sweeping indictment which he elaborates in what is the most sustained argument in all his writings. I refer to the last chapter of his
Between Man and Man, entitled "What Is Man?" There he states

[8] *Eclipse of God,* p. 70.

in full the case against philosophy. He gives a comprehensive and penetrating, though brief analysis, of the outstanding systems of thought from Aristotle to our own day, from the standpoint of what he regards as the most basic of all questions, namely, "What is Man?" Remarkably enough, that entire section of the book is a summary of his inaugural course of lectures at the Hebrew University as Professor of Social Philosophy, delivered in 1938, after he had delivered the inaugural address on "Plato and Isaiah." We cannot but conclude that those lectures were intended to elaborate in detail what we have found to be the main thesis of the inaugural address: We Jews have nothing to learn from Western civilization as to how to rebuild our own civilization. The following is a summary of that large chapter in *"Between man and Man"*:

Buber credits Kant with having been the first to articulate the crucial question concerning the uniqueness of man, the question which was to be the subject of a new philosophical discipline, namely philosophical anthropology. Kant himself, however, did not even undertake to answer that question. According to Buber, it is inherently impossible for philosophy to deal with that question in the manner in which the philosophers since Kant, with the possible exception of Feuerbach, have dealt with it. They have all dealt with the question of what is man, as though each individual human being were an encapsulated entity. To prove his case, he passes in review one great philosopher after another only to find that each one makes the mistake of considering the person as self-contained, instead of in the light of "the wholeness of its essential relations to what is."

Buber introduces at this point a very significant observation with regard to the history of the human spirit. He distinguishes between 'epochs of habitation" (i.e., at-homeness in the world) and "epochs of homelessness." The former are the pre-Copernican epochs, and the latter are the post-Copernican epochs. Plato, Aristotle, Augustine, Aquinas, Cusa, Pico della Mirandola and Malebranche conceived man as housed in a self-enclosed universe. Though they all sensed something of the mystery of man as no less marvellous than the mystery of nature, the feeling of man's at-homeness in that universe neutralized any possible interest they might have had into probing more deeply into the mystery of man.

Post-Copernican cosmology, however, has made it impossible for man to form any tenable image of the universe. The resulting sense of human homelessness and solitude has given new poignancy to the problem of "What is man?" That is the problem of which Pascal became keenly aware. He discerned in man's capacity to reflect about life and the world a daring challenge to the universe, even though the universe crush him with its infinite might. The realization that man's daring to measure himself against the universe constituted man's uniqueness was the beginning of a new approach to the problem. More recently, Hegel attempted to recover for man the sense of security and at-homeness in the world by substituting the universe of infinite time for the universe of infinite space. Man's new house is to be time, in the form of history whose meaning can be learned and understood *(ibid.,* p. 139). Karl Marx's variation of the Hegelian dialectic, by substituting economic determinism for abstract reason, as the substance of the dialectic in time, tried to serve the same purpose of making man feel at home in the world. Buber, however, argues that the sense of security which Hegel and Karl Marx believed they had succeeded in recovering for man was deceptive. For, neither the one nor the other could *guarantee* that salvation would ensue in the future. In fact, their respective promises of salvation, Hegel's through the German State and Marx's the triumph of the proletariat, turned out to be a mirage.

The first thinker, according to Buber, who came to actual grips with the problem of "What is man?" was Nietzsche. Nietzsche's answer was that man is "the animal that is not yet established." Man is a creature in transition from the sub-human to the superman. But when Nietzsche tries to describe the transition and the goal, he goes off on a tangent. He misrepresents the actual history of man's sense of guilt, and is mistaken in his assumption that man's will to self-fulfillment is intrinsically the will to "increase in power." Since Nietzsche lacked a correct knowledge of the empirical facts concerning human life, no reliance can be placed upon his fantastic notions concerning man's place in the universe, however poetically and majestically he expressed them.

In the meantime, man's sense of insecurity has become more painful, due to what Buber characterizes as the nature of the modern crisis, namely, "man's lagging behind his works." That is the idea usually expressed in the concept of civilization as having grown into man's Frankenstein. The first genuinely satisfying answer, according to Buber, that dealt with that question in all its terrifying significance, is one that was given a century ago, but which has begun to be appreciated only in recent years. That is Kierkegaard's answer, which is based not on philosophy but upon religious tradition. Kierkegaard maintains that the only way in which man can identify his true being and achieve his destiny is through faith. But it must be faith that is lived in the wholeness of human life and not merely verbalized into a conceptional translation.

Buber has avowed his indebtedness to Kierkegaard (cf. *Eclipse of God,* p. 149) for what he himself has been pleading in all his works: the formulation of a *theological anthropology* based on a *religious tradition.* The existential nature of man is to be sought not in thought, or reason, nor in the will to power, but in "the stages and conditions of life itself, guilt, fear, despair, decision, the prospect of one's own death and the prospect of salvation." Buber next subjects to criticism the more recent philosophies of man, those of Heidegger, Husserl and Scheler. Each of these philosophies, being secular in character, renounces Kierkegaard's theological presuppositions, and consequently, according to Buber, was bound to fail in one respect or another to reckon with the totality of man's nature.

The inevitable conclusion which Buber would have us draw from the foregoing analysis of philosophic thought since Aristotle is that philosophy is inherently precluded from enabling man to translate "into the reality of his life the one characteristic element which cannot be found anywhere else in the universe." That is the point implied in Buber's contrasting Isaiah the prophet with Plato the first great philosopher whose thinking, however modified, has set once for all the pattern to all subsequent philosophizing. None of the philosophies have exerted a creative or permanent influence on human life. Isaiah's influence, on the other hand, has been creative and permanent. The existence of the Jewish People testifies to that. Isaiah is as typical of religious tradition as Plato is of philosophic thought. What then, are the intrinsic qualities of authentic religious tradition, which according to Buber, renders it indispensable to life?

III

The Jewish religious tradition, according to Buber, is the indispensable means of achieving that inner transformation of the Jewish People both individually and communally, without which the outer transformation which Zionism has been fostering is less than half the task. He quotes what Conrad Burdach, a scholar noted for his researches into the Renaissance period has to say in comment of

Dante's statement: "The greatest desire Nature has implanted in everything from its beginning is the desire to return to its origin." To which Burdach adds that it is the goal of humanism "to return to the human origin, not by way of speculative thought, but by way of a *concrete transformation* of the whole inner life."

These quotations are introduced by Buber in his essay on "Hebrew Humanism." There he states in the most lucid terms what the Jews must do, in order to "return to their origin," since only there will they find the "factor of spiritual power" which must accompany the material factor. Every word in that long statement throws light upon the place which the Jewish religious tradition has held in Buber's thinking and career. For lack of space I shall quote only the most striking passages in that essay which throw light on what Buber understood by the Jews' "return to their origin."

"It cannot be achieved," he writes,

by any spiritual power save the primordial spirit of Israel, the spirit which has made us as we are, and to which we must continually account for the extent to which our character has remained steadfast in the face of our destiny. This spirit has not vanished. The way to it is still open; it is still possible for us to encounter it. *The Book still lies before us, and the voice speaks forth from it as on the first day. But we must not dictate what it should and what it should not tell us* [italics mine]. . . . What it does have to tell us, and what no other voice in the world can teach us with such simple power, is that there is truth and that there are lies, and that human life cannot persist or have meaning save in the decision in behalf of truth and against lies; that there is right and wrong, and that the salvation of man depends on choosing what is right and rejecting what is wrong. . . . The *humanitas* which speaks from this Book today, as it has always done, is the unity of human life under one divine direction which divides right from wrong and truth from lies as unconditionally as the words of the Creator divided light from darkness. . . . What matters is that in every hour of decision we are aware of our responsibility and summon our conscience to weigh exactly how much is necessary to preserve the community, and accept just so much and no more; that we do not interpret the will-to-power as a demand made by life itself. . . . The men in the Bible are sinners like ourselves, but there is one sin they do not commit, our arch sin: they do not dare confine God to a circumscribed space or division of life, to religion. . . . He who has been reared in our Hebrew Biblical humanism resists patriotic bombast which clouds the gulf between the demand of life and the desire of the will-to-power. He resists the whispering of false popularity which is the opposite of true service to the people. . . . He knows that, in the final analysis, the only thing that can help his people is what is true and right in the light of the age-old decision. . . . That is the meaning in contemporary language of the 'return to the origins of our being.'[9]

In his essay on "National Education"[10] Buber dilates on the place of tradition in all national movements and in every kind of national education. He emphasizes the need of imbuing the minds of the rising generations with "the great spiritual values whose source is the origin of their people." There are three possible attitudes to a religious tradition, of which only one is desirable. That is the positive attitude. It expresses itself in allowing "the forces inherent in the beginnings to shape present-day life in accordance with present-day needs." Undesirable, of course, is the negative attitude, which rejects all tradition as "neither credible, nor usable, nor timely." Equally undesirable, however, is what Buber terms the "fictitious" attitude. That is characteristic of people who boast of their tradition without believing in it, even teaching it to their children, but not with the purpose of having them seriously integrate it into actual life.

Buber is convinced that the Jewish Bible has the power "to guide the life of the men of today"[11] "The Bible," says Buber,

has, in the form of a glorified remembrance, given vivid, decisive expression to an ever-recurrent happening. In the infinite language of events and situations, eternally changing but plain to the truly attentive, transcendence speaks to our hearts at the essential moments of personal life. And there is a language in which we can answer it; it is the language of our actions and attitudes, our reactions and our abstentions; the totality of these answers is what we may call our answering-for-ourselves in the most proper sense of the expression. This fundamental interpretation of our existence we owe to the Hebrew Bible; and whenever we truly read it, our self-understanding is truly deepened.[12]

Buber is very much concerned that the continuity of the Jewish religious tradition be not misinterpreted as resistance to spontaneity and change. He often keeps on reminding the reader:

Let me reiterate that such continuity does not imply the preservation of the old, but the ceaseless begetting and giving birth to the same single spirit, and its continuous integration into life.[13] Only the teachings truly rejuvenated

[9] "Hebrew Humanism," *Israel and the World*, pp. 245ff.

[10] *Ibid.*, p. 160 sg.

[11] *Ibid.*, "The Man of Today and the Jewish Bible," p. 92.

[12] *At the Turning*, pp. 49f.

[13] "Teaching and Deed," *Israel and the World*, p. 143.

can liberate us from limitations and bind us to the unconditional, so that spiritualized and spirited, united within the circle of the eternal union, we may recognize one another and ourselves, and, empowered by the fathomless laws of history, hold out against the powers moving on the surface of history.[14]

This is what religious tradition can do, when the adherents of a movement "absorb and transform what they have absorbed in response to the demands of the hour." He condemns in no uncertain terms the acceptance of tradition and law as what he calls "a once for all." Such a frozen tradition only "prevents meeting with God in the lived concrete. . . . The very symbols which man uses to address God often stand in the way of that address."[15]

The significance which Buber attaches to a functioning religious tradition is due to his regarding it as an indispensable instrument of the collective memory. "We Jews," he writes,

are a community based on memory. A common memory has kept us together and enabled us to survive. This does not mean that we based our life on any one particular past, even on the loftiest of the pasts; it simply means that one generation passed on to the next a memory which gained in scope—for new destiny and new emotional life were constantly accruing to it—and which realized itself in a way we can call organic. The expanding memory was more than a spiritual motif; it was a power which sustained, fed, and quickened Jewish existence itself. I might even say that these memories realized themselves biologically, for in their strength the Jewish substance was renewed.[16]

No wonder Buber regards nothing so ominous in contemporary Jewish life as "the disappearance of the collective memory and the passion for handing down,"[17] in other words, the failure to keep the Jewish religious tradition alive.

Buber recognizes clearly that the Jewish tradition owes its ability to function as the memory of the Jewish People, and the retention of its religious character, to the fact that *it is the product of the collective life of the Jewish People.* "In the case of some peoples," he writes,

14 *Ibid.,* p. 144.
15 *Ibid.*
16 "Why We Should Study Jewish Sources,' *Israel and the World,* p. 145.
17 *Ibid.,* p. 147.

such as the Chinese, the Jews, and the Greeks, lonely thinkers thought of the absolute as such, in its utmost metaphysical purity; but the actual life of the people was not influenced by those thoughts. Reverence for the absolute can become the life-principle of a people only when the people itself puts it into practice as a people, and not in the sphere of abstract thought, but in actual life. Reverence of the absolute does not mean metaphysical ideation, but religious event.[18]

The one truth which the Bible, as the basic religious tradition of the Jews, proclaims as its main teaching is that their ancestors had entered Eretz Yisrael with a sense of commitment to a mission from above to set up a just way of life throughout their generations. It was to be "a way of life that cannot be realized by individuals in the sphere of their private existence, but only by a nation in the establishment of its society."[19] The serious religious crisis in the throes of which the entire world finds itself has had a destructive impact on the Jews. "The true solution," Buber wrote to Gandhi,

can only issue from the life of a community which begins to carry out the will of God, often without being aware of doing so, without believing that God exists and that this is His will. . . . This is the innermost truth of the Jewish life in the land; perhaps it may be of significance for the solution of this crisis of faith not only for Jewry but for all humanity. You, Mahatma Gandhi, who know of the connection between tradition and future should not associate yourself with those who pass over our cause without understanding or sympathy.[20]

We thus have in the appeal to Gandhi evidence of how strongly Buber is convinced that a vital and functioning religious tradition is the product of the interaction of a people with its physical environment, and cannot be the outcome of lonely thinkers engaged in metaphysical speculation, however spiritual and sublime. Elsewhere in passing he states simply: "I hold that Jewry can gain an effective and more than merely stimulating share in the building of a steadfast world of peace only in its own community and not in scattered members."[21]

Hasidism had provided Buber with the main fuel, so to speak,

---

[18] "The Gods of the Nations and God," *Israel and the World,* p. 198.

[19] *Ibid.,* "The Land and Its Possession," p. 229.

[20] *Ibid.,* p. 230f.

[21] "Dialogue," *Between Man and Man,* p. 5.

for the flame of his Jewishness which was sparked by Zionism. Buber regarded Hasidism as "the one great attempt in the history of the Diaspora to make a reality of the original choice (for the true God and against Baal), and to found a true and just community based on religious principles."[22] Nevertheless he was not blind to its corruption and failure which he ascribed mainly to the fact that it did not aim

for the self-determination of the people, or to state it differently, because its connections with Palestine were only sporadic and not influenced by the desire for national liberation. . . . But, [he adds,] finally the Jewish national movement, either consciously or unconsciously took up the age-old social message, and impelled by it, set up as the goal of national education the pattern of the new type of man, of the man who can translate ideas into life, who along with the national idea will satisfy the longing for a great communal life.[23]

IV

In the light of what we have found in the foregoing discussion to be Buber's attitude toward philosophic thought and religious tradition we might be inclined to say that Buber prefers to regard himself as standing on the shoulders of the Jewish religious tradition and seeing beyond it rather than as standing on the shoulders of philosophic thought and seeing beyond it. He apparently believes that philosophic thought, no matter how deeply it may try to explore the truth about reality, can never know it, because it starts out with the wrong premise, by assuming the existence of a self-enclosed mind, on the one hand, and of a world that is completely outside it and heterogenous to it, on the other. This premise is particularly misleading when the matter of concern is the salvation of man, or the attainment of that which is uniquely and fully human in him.

An objective and fair evaluation seems to point to the fact that Buber has consistently followed his own standard of "the narrow ridge," in the new synthesis which he achieved between the two. His pattern of thought on the subject in question is far from being anything like that of the medieval theologians who sought to harmonize tradition with philosophy. It is truly a third alternative to both of them, in the sense of implying their mutual supplementation.

---

[22] "On National Education," *Israel and the World*, p. 159.
[23] *Ibid.*

But this conclusion seems to be contradicted by what he himself keeps on emphasizing. He gives the impression that he considers the Jewish religious tradition as self-sufficient, and capable of answering the needs of every new situation as it arises, without any recourse whatever to philosophic thinking.

Take for example, the following: after referring to the *halutz* (the Jewish pioneer in Eretz Yisrael) as motivated by the will to realize the ideal human community, which is "a union of persons living together, a union founded on the direct and just relations of all to all," Buber adds:

The *halutz* does not draw his will to realize this ideal out of himself, or out of his era, or out of the Western world; nor does he derive it from the occidental socialism of his country. Whether he knows it or not, whether or not he likes it, he is animated by the age-old Jewish longing to incorporate social truth in the life of individuals living with one another, the longing to translate the idea of a true community into reality. The new type of human being such as the *halutz* promised to become is a result of the development of very early traits. What we call 'Israel' is not merely the result of biological and historical development; it is the product of a decision, made long ago, the decision in favor of a God of justice and against a god of instinctive egoism, etc.[24]

This statement could not emphasize more strongly the adequacy of the Jewish religious tradition for enabling man to achieve spiritual security and fulfillment. In view of what we have shown to have prompted Buber to take this extreme position with regard to philosophic thought vs. the Jewish religious tradition, that emphasis is understandable. But in a thinker of the stature of Buber we do not like to see overstatement of a case. We should have preferred to have seen him keep to the "narrow ridge," despite the strong temptation to depart from it, even though by so doing he might have been able to display less fervor as a prophet and greater consistency as a thinker.

It would take us far afield to explore the problem of the extent to which Zionism and the entire modern Jewish renaissance would have been impossible without the impact of Western civilization of our day. No one can question the influence of modern secularist nationalism on contemporary Jewish life in all its positive and negative aspects. In the words of Salo Baron,

[24] *Ibid.*, "Learning and Education," pp. 58f.

Reflecting in many ways the ideologies shaped under the peculiar conditions of their varying environments, often helping to formulate new nationalist theories, various segments of Jewry searched for a comprehensive rationale of their own to maintain their world-wide ethnic and religious unity.[25]

Modern secularist nationalism which has exerted a revolutionizing influence on contemporary Jewish life and thought, including that of Buber himself, is the unmistakable product of contemporary Western philosophic thought.

No less true is it that in the reinterpretation of the religious tradition, on the assumption that it must not be conceived as "a once for all," and that it has to be renewed by each generation in response to the highest needs which only a genuinely spiritual community can define—in all of these qualifications of the religious tradition, we cannot help but discern the influence of philosophic thought. Karl Mannheim, as a philosopher, has arrived at exactly the same conclusion as did Buber concerning the role of religious tradition. "The complete penetration of life by religion," he writes,

will only occur, if those who represent the religious tradition are once more able to go back to the genuine sources of religious experience and do not think that the habitual and institutional forms of religion will suffice for the reconstruction of man and society.[26]

Moreover, from the side of philosophic thought itself one may question whether it could not of itself evolve a pattern of human life calculated to bring about a type of human community that would be capable of enabling its members to achieve spiritual self-fulfillment, and at the same time contribute to world peace and wellbeing. However cynical we may be about the establishment of the United States, its Declaration of Independence and its Federal Constitution do represent the deliberate commitment of a great people to the creation of a community founded on the principles of freedom, justice and peace. Even the initial policy recommended by Washington, of avoiding entangling alliances with other powers, brings to mind the ancient prophetic warnings against entering into alliances with the world empires of those days.

Who, indeed, inspired the founders of the United States to build such a nation, if not Aristotle, Locke and Rousseau? To be sure,

---

25 *Modern Nationalism and Religion*, p. 213.

26 *Diagnosis of Our Time*, p. 27.

with the vast increase of population and the growing threat from the Old World, the United States has strayed from the dream of its founders. But it has nevertheless had a Jefferson, a Lincoln and a Wilson among its political leaders, and an Emerson, a William James and a John Dewey among its philosophers, to keep it ever mindful of its spiritual mission. What is interesting about all of them is that they managed to achieve their spiritual conception of the American People without the "benefit of clergy." One has only to glance at Dewey's *A Common Faith* to discover how much in common there is between his ideas about the normal relation of religion to community life and Buber's ideas on the same subject in his *Israel and the World,* or how the two thinkers independently arrive at the same distinction between the two possible kinds of faith that make a difference in people's lives.

To cite a personal coincidence which throws light upon the problem as to the relationship between philosophic thinking and religious tradition, the writer of this essay received on the very same day two announcements: one was that *The Library of Living Philosophers* was about to publish a volume on "The Philosophy of Martin Buber;" the other was that *The Library of Living Theology* was about to publish a volume on "The Empirical Theology of Henry Nelson Wieman." On the face of it, Buber and Wieman would seem to be poles apart from each other in their respective approaches to philosophy and tradition. But, upon a careful study of what they both have to say, they will be found to agree far more than to disagree. To quote but one characteristic passage of Wieman's which expresses the result of his own empirical inquiry into religion and which deals with the subject of faith.

"I distinguish," says Wieman,

two levels in the self-giving of faith. At one level commitment is guided by an idea which one happens to have at the time concerning what transforms man creatively. But there is a deeper level of commitment. At this second level one is motivated by the intention to give himself in the wholeness of his being, so far as he is able, to what in truth does save and transform, no matter how different it may be from one's ideas about it.

Is this not virtually the key-thought of Buber's *Two Types of Faith?* And does it not take empirical philosophy to discern these two types of faith in the Judeo-Christian tradition?

The fact is that it is possible for Western thought to be inherently self-corrective and to arrive at conclusions virtually identical with those of Buber concerning the basic shortcomings it has harbored hitherto, as well as concerning the need of entering into living relation with other individuals as a means of entering into relations with Reality that is independent of us. What more striking proof of this self-corrective capacity inherent in philosophy than the phenomenon "Bergson," whose influence on Buber is no less recognizable than that of Kierkegaard? "Our thought," we read on the very first page of Bergson's *Creative Evolution,*

in its purely logical form is incapable of presenting its true nature of life, the full meaning of the evolutionary movement. Created by life, in definite circumstances, to act on definite things, how can it embrace life, of which it is only an emanation or an aspect? (Introduction, p. x)

Buber himself has occasion to refer frequently to the inherently self-corrective character of philosophic thinking. The Sophists, according to him, played such a role. "The function of the sophists, and consequently of their like in later times," writes Buber,

has been recognized as the functions of dissolving and preparing. . . . As Protagoras leads toward his contemporary Socrates, Stirner leads towards his contemporary Kierkegaard. . . . What Stirner, with his destructive power successfully attacks is the surrogate for a reality that is no longer believed.[27]

As far as philosophy's ability to realize that only through the attitude of faith and the interaction of organic community life can man achieve what is essential to his becoming fully human, it is a pity that Buber should have limited his survey of philosophic thought to continental philosophers. Apparently accepting the continental estimate of American thinkers as not being philosophers but only "pragmatists," he ignores their existence entirely.

It is a fact, however, that the very conception of ideas as "instruments" which the human mind employs in its attempts to get at reality stresses the same principle as happens to be the central truth of Buber's own philosophic thinking. "Instrumentalism" is as emphatic as Buber in deprecating the tendency of generalizations to falsify reality. American thinkers like Lewis Mumford and Baker Brownell have arrived by means of that "instrumentalism" at con-

27 "The Question to the Single One," *Between Man and Man,* pp. 44f.

clusions concerning the role and function of community that coincide entirely with those of Buber. Note for example the following typical statements by them:

"Men are individually nothing," writes Mumford,

except in relation to that greater reality Man. And Man himself is nought, except in relation to that greater reality which he calls divine. Thought, art, love, are all intimations of this divinity; flickerings of man-made filaments that connect in our imaginations, with distant flashes in the dark impenetrable sky.[28]

And Baker Brownell on the very first page of his book entitled *The Human Community: Its Philosophy for a Time of Crisis,* has this to say:

As William James suggests, we must continue to start freshly with integral situations, not with conceptual terms. Though specialism and term-creating ways of thought have their importance, they are not in themselves sufficient unto life. The inner unity and substantiation of things, which James approaches through what he calls *conjunctive relations* [ital. mine], must be recognized in any vital procedure. These are the confluences in our experience. Central in them, a creator of confluence as it were, is the community.

And here is another paragraph from a section of Brownell's book entitled *"Corrupted by Universals."*

Through the technique of the universal, whatever that may mean, our western theory, as well as that of most of India, has withdrawn the sacred essences of things from the humid contexts of living. . . . Thus the dualisms emerged. These, suggests Dewey—unlike Plato—answer no problems, take us nowhere, and leave us stalemated in the strategy of life (*Ibid.,* p. 223).

This time it is not Plato and Isaiah but Plato and Dewey, who are set off against each other, to the disadvantage of Continental philosophy.

All of which proves that the sharp distinctions which Buber draws between philosophic thought and religious tradition does not hold water. The fact is that it all depends upon the philosopher's perspective, and upon how much latitude one allows oneself in reinterpreting a religious tradition. How far Buber avails himself of such latitude may be inferred from the way he equates the tradi-

[28] *Faith for Living,* p. 210.

tional belief in creation with the modern belief in evolution, and the traditional belief in revelation with the modern increase of knowledge. It is only with regard to the traditional belief in *salvation* that he assumes we have nothing to learn from philosophy. Is that quite true? Why does he not subscribe to the traditional conception of bodily resurrection, or of reward and punishment in the hereafter? When he reinterprets the fear of God to mean something entirely different from what it has meant in tradition, namely, awareness of the incomprehensibility of God's being, does he not avail himself of ideas which emanate from philosophic thought?

If philosophic thought were as radically heterogeneous to the spiritual teachings of the religious tradition as Buber states, it could not possibly illuminate that tradition and give it that creatively adaptive capacity which Buber himself has demonstrated in his *The Prophetic Faith.* I am inclined to disagree with Buber's suggestion that the Jewish religions tradition is intrinsically capable of *indefinite unfolding.* Actually that tradition has, in the course of existence, undergone the very *metamorphosis* which Buber negates, and to which he himself as "the spokesman of Judaism before the world" has been one of the greatest contributors. That metamorphosis the religious tradition owes to philosophic thinking, and it is fortunate that Buber is highly expert in both. With a slight modification, Franz Rosenzweig's saying still holds: "Divine truth wishes to be implored with both hands," that of philosophy and that of tradition.

MORDECAI M. KAPLAN

JEWISH THEOLOGICAL SEMINARY OF AMERICA
NEW YORK, N.Y.

11

Emil L. Fackenheim

MARTIN BUBER'S CONCEPT OF REVELATION

I

THE CORE of both the Jewish and the Christian faiths is the belief that a God who is other than the world nevertheless enters into the world; that He enters into the world because He enters into the life of man. The Jewish and Christian God descends to meet man, and "a man does not pass, from the moment of supreme meeting, the same being as he entered into it."[1] Judaism and Christianity, or groups within either faith, may differ as to what, more specifically, revelation is; they may also differ as to when it has taken place, when it takes place, or when it will take place. But they agree that God *can* reveal Himself and that, in the entire history of man, He has done so at least once.

This core of religious belief persisted unimpaired until the Age of Enlightenment. But since that time it has become the object of ever more formidable criticism. There may be no conflict between modern thought and Biblical "monotheism," taken by itself, or between modern thought and Biblical "ethics," taken by itself. But there does seem to be a necessary conflict between modern thought and the Biblical belief in revelation. All claims to revelation, modern science and philosophy seem agreed, must be repudiated, as mere relics of superstitious ages. But Biblical "monotheism" is the monotheism of a self-revealing God, and Biblical "ethics" is an aspect of His revelation. Neither the monotheism nor the ethics can, without distortion, be taken by itself. The conflict between modern thought and the Biblical faith is therefore radical.

This fact did not become fully clear until the nineteenth century. Until that time, most modern thinkers were prepared to exempt spheres of reality from critical inquiry, provided they were protected by the walls of a sacred authority, and the "supernatural" was per-

---

[1] Martin Buber, *I and Thou* (Edinburgh, 1957), p. 109.

mitted to live behind such walls. But the nineteenth century—the age of critical history, Biblical criticism, and, last but not least, critical psychology—did away with all authorities, sacred or otherwise, and the moment this happened the modern assault on revelation exhibited itself as unqualified and radical.

The modern attack was directed not merely on a particular claim on behalf of an actual revelation, or even on all such claims. It was directed on the very *possibility* of revelation; and this was because it seemed radically incompatible not merely with this or that modern principle, but with the one principle basic to all modern thought, namely, the supreme principle of rational inquiry. This asserted that knowledge consisted in the discovery of uniformities, and that to hit upon the non-uniform was not to discover an exception to uniformity, but merely to become aware of one's ignorance. There were no lawless or causeless events; there were merely events whose laws or causes were not, or not yet, known.

It followed from this principle that there could be no revelations, that is, events not wholly due to natural laws or causes. There could only be a belief in revelations; and this was possible only because of partial or total ignorance of the laws or causes actually responsible for the events in question. To refute the belief in revelation, it was not necessary to discover the particular natural laws or causes of particular "revelations"; it was enough to know that all events must have such laws or causes: and to know *that* was to understand that revelation is in principle impossible.

Despite his rationalism, a mediaeval metaphysician such as Maimonides could allow miraculous interruptions of the order of nature, of which revelation was the most important instance.[2] A modern metaphysician could not allow such interruptions. To him, all miracles were only apparent miracles, and all revelations only apparent revelations. God, if admitted at all, was either a power beyond the universe or a force within it. The Biblical God—who is beyond the universe yet enters into it—was a mere myth of bygone ages.

The same conclusion was reached by those who, scorning metaphysical speculation, confined themselves to the analysis of human

[2] Cf. E. L. Fackenheim, "The Possibility of the Universe in Al-Farabi, Ibn Sina and Maimonides," *Proceedings of the American Academy for Jewish Research,* **16** (New York, 1947), 39–70.

experience. A mediaeval empiricist such as Judah Hallevi[3] could argue for revelation by pointing to the authority of the six hundred thousand Israelites who had been present at Mount Sinai. A modern empiricist would reject this argument even if the dubious appeal to authority could be eliminated, that is, if he could project himself into the past so as to be personally present at Mount Sinai. To be sure, he might, in such a situation, hear not merely the thunder but also the voice of God. But his subsequent analysis would quickly eliminate the latter. He had heard the thunder because there had been thunder to be heard. But whatever the causes of his hearing of a voice of God, among them had not been an actual voice of God. For such a voice was not, on the one hand, a physical or psychical event, nor could it, on the other, interrupt the orderly sequence of such events. Hence the hearing of the voice of God had merely been an imagined hearing, mistaken for real hearing only by the ignorant.

How could the modern Jew or Christian meet this attack on revelation? He could, of course, simply refuse to meet it at all. But this could perhaps satisfy his heart but hardly his mind. Or he could seek shelter behind ancient authorities. But these no longer provided shelter. For a time it seemed that there was only one thing that could honestly be done, and that was to give in by "modernizing" the ancient faiths. A modernized faith was a faith without revelation. God became—as in Deism past and present—a reality external to the world unable to enter into human experience; or He became—as in religious idealism past and present[4]—a force immanent in human experience which could not exist, or could exist only incompletely,

---

[3] While Judah Hallevi is hardly an empiricist in any precise sense of the term, there is some justification in applying this term to a thinker who frowned on efforts to support the Jewish religion through metaphysical speculation, pointing instead to the testimony of those who had been present at Mount Sinai.

[4] Buber recognizes with the utmost clarity that Jung's "religion of pure psychic immanence," for example, is nothing but a "translation of post-Kantian idealism into psychology," *Eclipse of God* (Harper's Torchbook Edition), pp. 78ff. We might add that the translation is rather less impressive than the original product, cf. E. L. Fackenheim, "Schelling's Philosophy of Religion," *University of Toronto Quarterly*, 22 (Toronto, 1952), 1ff.

apart from human experience.[5] All these modernized versions of the ancient faiths had this in common: God could not reveal Himself, that is, be present to man. The God of religious idealism is at most present *in* man, never present *to* man; and the God of Deism cannot be present at all.

But since the middle of the nineteenth century, it has become gradually clear that retreat was not the only way in which to meet the modern attack on revelation. It was possible to counter-attack. But this had to be done in rather a special way. One could not meet the attack on revelation by simply attacking, in turn, the principle on which the attack was based. To reject, or arbitrarily limit, the principle of modern rational inquiry was merely to fall prey, wittingly or unwittingly, to obscurantism. But it was possible that that principle, while unlimited in application, nevertheless applied only within a sphere which was itself limited, and that revelation fell outside that sphere.

This possibility first became obvious through the work of Immanuel Kant, who argued that the law- or cause-discovering kind of knowledge discloses only a phenomenal world. But Kant's argument neither sprang from a wish to defend revelation, nor did it issue, in Kant himself, in a defense of revelation. This latter task was undertaken by religious existentialism. If the law- or cause-discovering kind of knowledge is phenomenal, existentialism argues, it is because it presupposes the detachment of a knower who makes the world his object. So long as he perseveres in this standpoint he discovers laws upon laws or causes upon causes. But what he discovers in this way is, as a whole, not reality, but merely reality made into an object or objectified. Reality ceases to be an object if we cease to view it as an object; that is, if instead of viewing it in detachment we become engaged with it in personal commitment. In such a personal commitment there is knowing access to the transphenomenal, an access which consists not in the discovery of laws or causes, but in a direct encounter. And the most important fact that can be encountered is divine revelation.

This argument, first stated by Schelling and Kierkegaard in the mid-nineteenth century, has found its most profound spokesman in

---

[5] For the transcendental kind of idealism there is an idea of God but not an existing God, while for the ontological kind the existing God becomes fully real only in human experience. Kant and Hegel do not wholly fit into either of these classes.

our time in Martin Buber. To examine his argument is the task of the present essay. Such an examination must necessarily subordinate all its efforts to answering a single question: is Buber's counter-attack on the modern attack on revelation successful? Does he make it possible at the same time to accept without compromise the modern principle of rational inquiry and yet to embrace the ancient faith in a self-revealing God?

II

This question cannot even be raised, let alone be answered, by a biographical account, that is, the kind of account which explains an author's teachings in terms of his personal experience. The more perceptive of the modern critics of revelation are quite prepared to admit that there is experience-of-revelation; but they deny that there is revelation. They grant that there are those who sincerely believe themselves in dialogue with God; but they assert that all such dialogues are but disguised monologues.[6] If Buber has a reply to this criticism, it cannot consist in his personal experience; and the interpreter who looks for such a reply cannot look for it in that experience. For the question is not whether, from the standpoint of religious experience, there appears to be revelation. The question is whether there is, or at least can be, revelation; that is, whether the religious standpoint which accepts the category of revelation is justified.

The faults of the biographical approach are not remedied by an emphasis on Buber's life-long encounter with traditional sources, notably Hasidism and the Hebrew Bible. There is no doubt that Buber's historical studies are closely related to his own views, particularly as regards revelation. Indeed, his chief merit as a Bible-interpreter may well be seen in his insistence that the Bible be understood in Biblical ("dialogue between God and man") rather than in modern ("religious experience," "evolution of ideas" and the like) categories. But by itself this insistence only means that Buber has

---

[6] Buber clearly recognizes the criticism which asserts that "religion has never been anything but an intra-psychic process whose products are 'projected' on a plane in itself fictitious but vested with reality by the soul"; and that, therefore, "every alleged colloquy with the divine was only a soliloquy, or rather a conversation between various strata of the self." *Eclipse of God,* p. 13. In recognizing the criticism, he also recognizes the task confronting those who would answer it.

understood the Biblical belief in revelation; it does not mean that
he has justified his own acceptance of it.

This last point is nicely illustrated by the fact that Buber did
not always accept the belief in revelation. In 1911 he wrote:

the spiritual process of Judaism is . . . the striving for the ever more perfect
realization of three internally connected ideas: the idea of unity, the idea of
action and the idea of the future; these ideas . . . are not abstract tendencies,
but natural tendencies of folk character.[7]

Had Buber retained the standpoint indicated in this passage he could
without doubt have mustered, as a historian, the imagination necessary in order to understand the Biblical belief in revelation; but he
would have at the same time asserted, as a philosopher, that what
was to Biblical man a dialogue with God was in fact a form of human
self-realization and nothing else; that is, a disguised monologue.

The conclusion, then, is clear. Our approach to Buber's work
must be systematic, not biographic. Only a systematic account can
answer the questions which must be answered if Buber's stature as a
thinker who is modern and yet affirms revelation is to be fairly
appraised. The questions are: does Buber offer a doctrine intended
to meet the modern critique of revelation? And if so, does his doctrine
in fact meet that critique?

III

The first of these two questions can be answered at once in the
affirmative. Buber does offer a doctrine of revelation intended,
among other things, to meet the modern critique of revelation. This
is an extension of a wider doctrine which must first be considered
briefly. We refer to the celebrated doctrine of the *"I"* and the
"Thou."

There are, Buber teaches, two types of relation I may establish
with another, namely, an *I-It* and an *I-Thou* relation. I have an *I-It*
relation when I use the other, or when I know the other in an attitude of objective detachment. These relations are one-sided, for the
other is for me while I am not for the other. When I use or observe
the other, my person remains unengaged. The other cannot *do* any-

[7] *Drei Reden Ueber Das Judentum* (Frankfurt, 1920), p. 71. For a full account of
Buber's early thought, cf., Maurice S. Friedman, *Martin Buber: The Life of Dialogue*, pp. 27–53.

thi g to me; that is, even if the other happens to be a person, I am not open to him as a person but treat him as a mere object.

The *I-It* relation is abstract. Users and objective observers, on the one hand, objects of use or observation, on the other, are interchangeable. In using an object, I never intend the unique object but merely a *kind* of object; and in observing it my inevitable aim is to bring it under general laws of which it is a mere instance. The unique individuality of the other does not enter into the *I-It* relation.

Nor does the unique individuality of the *I*. *Qua* user, I am only a *kind* of user; and the supreme condition of all objective observation is that anyone who would take my place would observe the same. In the *I-It* relation anyone else *could* take my place.

The *I-It* relation contrasts in every respect with the *I-Thou* relation. This relation is, above all, mutual. The other is for me, but I am also for the other. I do something to the other, but the other also does something to me. This happens in the relation of dialogue, which is a relation of address and response-to-address. The other addresses me and responds to my address; that is, even if the other happens to be a lifeless and speechless object, it is treated as one treats a person.

It would, to be sure, be gross anthropomorphizing to assert that the lifeless object *is* a person; that a tree or a stone can be an *I* to themselves and I a *Thou* to them. But it is not anthropomorphic to assert that I can be an *I* to myself, and the tree or stone a *Thou* to me. From the standpoint of one partner at least, the human partner, *I-Thou* relations are possible, not only with other human beings, but with anything whatever. This is not to say that such relations are easy, or possible to anyone, or possible at any time. It is merely to say that there are no a priori limitations to the possible partners I may have in an *I-Thou* relationship.

While the *I-It* relationship is necessarily abstract, the *I-Thou* relationship cannot be abstract. The partners communicate not this or that, but themselves; that is, they must *be in* the communication. Further—since the relation of dialogue is mutual—they must be in a state of openness to the other, that is, to *this* other at *this* time and in *this* place. Hence both the *I* and the *Thou* of every genuine dialogue are irreplaceable. Every dialogue is unique.

All this is possible only because the *I* is not a complete, self-sufficient substance. In the *I-Thou* relation I *become* an I by virtue of the relationship to a *Thou*. My whole being enters into the meeting, to emerge from it other than it was. And what is essential between an *I* and a *Thou*—such as love and friendship—is not in the mind of either the *I* or the *Thou*, or even in the minds of both; it is *between* an *I* and a *Thou*, who would both be essentially different if the relation did not exist. To be sure, there are relations in which there is nothing between the *I* and the other, and which do not alter the substance of the *I*; but these, far from being original relations with another, are merely the kind of derivative relations in which "reflexion" or "withdrawal"[8] has corrupted the immediacy of openness: in other words, *I-It* relations. Only from the standpoint of this corrupt state—into which we all perforce often fall—does the dialogue with a *Thou* appear as an unessential act on the part of a self-complete and self-sufficient *I*. In truth it is what constitutes both the *I* and the *Thou*, to the extent to which they are constituted at all. And in the actual dialogue this is known to both.[9]

It is not necessary, for our present purpose, to describe Buber's doctrine of the *I* and *Thou* in further detail. But it is necessary to ask: is it a doctrine at all, that is, a body of metaphysical and epistemological assertions? Or is it a pure homily, that is, the kind of teaching intended solely for spiritual guidance?

This question is of crucial importance. It will be seen that Buber's teaching concerning revelation is an application of his teaching concerning the *I* and *Thou*. If the latter were a pure homily the same would necessarily be true of the former. But whatever the undoubted religious merits of a homily on revelation, it could only ignore, but not come to grips with, the modern critique of revelation. This latter, as we have seen, readily admits that there may be experience-of-revelation yet stoutly denies that there can be revelation. If this criticism is to be met rather than ignored, there is need, in addition and indeed logically prior to appeals which might make men spiritually receptive to revelation, for a doctrine which argues, against the modern critique, that the category of revelation in terms of which the religious standpoint understands itself is the category in terms of which it must be understood.

But Buber's teaching concerning the *I* and *Thou* is not a pure homily; it is a doctrine as well. Indeed, it is the latter rather than

[8] Cf. *Between Man and Man* (Boston, 1955), pp. 22ff., and *I and Thou*, pp. 115ff.

[9] It is obvious that some of the above remarks apply only in the case of relations which are *I-Thou* relations from the standpoint of both partners, such as interhuman relations.

the former that distinguishes his work   from that of many others. Literature abounds with poems which describe, and sermons which exalt, the wealth of interpersonal relationships. *Buber's distinctive teaching lies in his interpretation of the* I-Thou *relation, as such, and as contrasted with the* I-It *relation, as such.*

An illustration will serve to show, both that Buber's teaching is a doctrine, and what the doctrine is. Consider a scientific psychologist who also, it happens, has near-perfect *I-Thou* relations with his wife, his children and close friends. His professional business is to understand people as cases falling under laws; but his private life is such as to enable him to understand those close to him in living dialogue. But would such a person grant that both kinds of knowledge *are* knowledge? If his outlook were typical, he would assert that only the former kind of knowledge has any chance of getting at the truth about human nature, for it alone is objective; the latter kind of "knowledge" cannot be regarded as knowledge at all precisely because it is engaged; it is the sort of "biased" opinion which has a right to persist only because it is indispensable in life.

Now if Buber has a quarrel with this hypothetical psychologist, it is clearly neither with his psychology nor with his way of life. As for his psychology, it must be, like all science, a form of *I-It* knowledge. And as for his way of life, it is *ex hypothesi* such as to find Buber's complete approval. It follows that if Buber's teaching were a pure homily, there would be no quarrel at all. Yet a quarrel there certainly is. It concerns the epistemological status of *I-Thou* and *I-It* knowledge, and the metaphysical status of *Thou* and *It*, respectively. The hypothetical psychologist has one doctrine in this matter, and Buber can quarrel with it only because he too has a doctrine.

But Buber's doctrine is diametrically opposite. It asserts that *in the committed* I-Thou *relation there is knowing access to a reality which is inaccessible otherwise; that uncommitted "objective" knowledge which observes as an* It *what may also be encountered as a* Thou *is a lesser kind of knowledge, and that the most profound mistake in all philosophy is the epistemological reduction of* I-Thou *to* I-It *knowledge, and the metaphysical reduction of* Thou *to* It.

We must subsequently ask whether, and if so how, Buber defends this most basic of all his doctrines. For the moment it is enough to observe that, if adequately defended, it can be the basis for a counterattack on the modern attack on revelation. For, first, it implies complete acceptance of the modern principle of rational inquiry; secondly, it yet limits the sphere to which that principle applies; thirdly, it points beyond this sphere to quite another sphere in which it is at least not impossible that revelation could be found.

Buber accepts the modern principle of rational inquiry because he finds a legitimate place for *I-It* knowledge. His acceptance of the principle is complete because there is no attempt on his part to limit arbitrarily the range of *I-It* knowledge. Science has the world as its object, and this world—which includes the psychological world—displays itself to rational inquiry as a unity shattered by no irrational incursions of God. The doctrine of the *I* and *Thou* is not at war either with specific conclusions of science or with the assumptions which underlie science as a whole.

It is at war, however, with all metaphysics which regard reality as an *It* or a system of *Its*, and with all epistemologies which reduce all knowledge to *I-It* knowledge. It is also at war, therefore, with the kind of philosophy which identifies reality as understood by science with reality as it ultimately is, and scientific with metaphysical knowledge. For the doctrine of the *I* and *Thou*, every *It*, including the *It* of science, is something less than the fullness of reality, whether an "objectification," "abstraction" or "logical construct"; and all *I-It* knowledge, including scientific knowledge, falls short of being metaphysical knowledge, that is, of grasping reality in its fullness. Rational inquiry ties *It* to *It* but remains itself tied to the world of *It*. Thus Buber limits the sphere to which the principle of rational inquiry applies.

This sphere is transcended not when the *I* comes upon an *It* supposedly escaping rational inquiry, but when the *I* abandons the detachment of the *I-It* relation for the engagement of the *I-Thou* relation. If the *Thou* escapes rational inquiry, it is not because the latter is rational but because it presupposes detachment.[10] And the shortcomings of rational inquiry are epistemological and metaphysical only because the engaged *I-Thou* dialogue is itself a form of knowledge; indeed, it is the form of knowledge in which the fullness of reality is encountered.

It follows, as we have said, that the doctrine of the *I* and *Thou* can be a basis for a counter-attack on the modern attack on revelation.

10 This is why Buber can call *I-Thou* knowledge "higher than reason" (*uebervernuenftig*) rather than irrational, *I and Thou*, p. 49. The implications of Buber's term are too many to be considered here.

For while the system of laws or causes is never shattered from the standpoint of *I-It* detachment it is always shattered from the standpoint of *I-Thou* engagement. If the doctrine of the *I* and *Thou* is true, there is no need for special doctrinal provisions for the reconciliation of the category of revelation with the principle of rational inquiry.

But the doctrine of the *I* and *Thou* is no more than a mere basis for a modern doctrine of revelation. By itself, it justifies not the positive assertion of the possibility of revelation, but merely the bare empty denial of its impossibility; and it justifies even that only on the assumption that it is part of an *I-Thou* rather than of an *I-It* relation. To justify more positive assertions, it is necessary that the general doctrine of the *I* and *Thou* be extended into a doctrine of revelation. This latter must accomplish three tasks. It must show that religion is an *I-Thou* rather than an *I-It* relation; it must identify the criteria which distinguish it from all other *I-Thou* relations; and it must locate revelation within it.

IV

We may begin with Buber's critique of the widely held view that religion is feeling. For Buber, all genuine religion is an *I-Thou* relation with God, rather than merely subjective feeling.

Feelings are a mere accompaniment to the metaphysical and metapsychical fact of the relation which is fulfilled not in the soul but *between* the *I* and *Thou*.[11]

A "religion" whose essence is feeling is either the mere solitary disport of the soul with itself, cut off from God; or, if not cut off from God, not a relation; or, if a relation, not immediate. But the first—subjective feeling by itself—is not religion but merely the pseudo-religion of a degenerate age.[12] The second—God found in and identified with religious feeling—is mysticism, and mysticism is only a grandiose illusion. The third—God inferred from religious feeling —is at once pseudo-religion and bad philosophy.

Buber's argument in support of these assertions is the doctrine of the *I* and *Thou*. In every *I-Thou* relation the *I* is open to a *Thou*,

[11] *I and Thou*, p. 81, my italics. Cf. also *Eclipse of God*, pp. 3, 123.

[12] *Eclipse of God*, p. 13.

not absorbed with images of a *Thou;* the latter state is not
original, but the mere product of the corruption of "withdrawal."[13]
Absorption with God-images too is a mere corruption; and this corruption is by no means overcome by an attempt to proceed by inference
from the God-image to God Himself. For the God-image is a mere part
of the self, and the inferred God a mere *It.*[14] If there is genuine religion at all, it can only consist of the direct dialogical meeting of the
human *I* with a divine *Thou.*

This is why mysticism, too, is a form of pseudo-religion. For it
denies either the reality of all meeting, or else at least that the
supreme moment is a moment of meeting.[15] In the supreme moment
of mysticism the *I,* rather than meet a *Thou,* dissolves into the
Ineffable. But "all real living is meeting."[16] Mysticism, far from being a way into reality, is on the contrary a flight from it.

If there is such a thing as genuine religion it involves, on the
human side, the kind of committed openness which is ready to address God and to be addressed by Him. But it also involves, on the
divine side, a God who at least *can* be the partner in such a dialogical
relationship. To be sure, it is not necessary that God should always be
available for partnership, and genuine religion may consist, for long
periods of time, of the mere human address which listens in vain
for a reply. But all such addressing and listening would be wholly
vain if God could not, by His very nature, be addressed or listened
to. If religion is to be—as it must be—*between* God and man, revelation must at least be possible. Thus, the "modernized" religions
without revelation are not merely religions which Buber happens
to disagree with; they are not genuine religions at all. *Merely by
virtue of being an* I-Thou *relation,* all *genuine religion involves at
least the possibility of revelation.*

Further, merely by virtue of being part of an *I-Thou* relation,
revelation must have certain characteristics. Above all, it must be the
address of a *Thou* who *is in* what He communicates. Consequently,
revelation cannot be either a system of dogmas[17] or a system of

---

[13] Cf. *supra,* note 8.

[14] *I and Thou,* pp. 80ff.

[15] *Ibid.,* p. 84. Cf. also *Israel and the World* (New York, 1948), p. 22: "He who
imagines that He knows and holds the mystery fast can no longer face it as his
Thou."

[16] *I and Thou,* p. 11.

[17] *Eclipse of God,* p. 135; *Between Man and Man,* p. 18.

laws.[18] For both would cut the communication off from Him who communicates, thus perverting the living *I-Thou* dialogue into the fixity of the *I-It*. It will be seen, to be sure, that revelation must translate itself into human statement, and that an essential part of the statement is commandment.[19] But a genuine translation must spring from, and reflect, the pregnancy of the event of divine presence; and the commandment must give Him who commands along with the commandment. A *system* of dogmas is not the reflection of His presence, but a statement made about Him in His absence; and to obey a *system* of laws—independent in its validity of the Giver and of the hour for which He gives it—is not to respond to revelation but on the contrary to flee from it.

All this is true because the Giver who is present in the given is not a timeless Presence. The God of dialogue, like any Thou of any dialogue, speaks to a unique partner in a unique situation, disclosing Himself according to the unique exigencies of each situation. "If we name the speaker of this speech God, then it is always the God of a moment, a moment God."[20] If He has a general name at all, it is "I shall be who I shall be,"[21] that is, He who cannot be comprehended as He may be in His timeless essence, but can only be encountered in each here and now, as He may show Himself in each here and now.

These above implications for revelation may be derived from Buber's assertion that all genuine religion is an *I-Thou* relationship. But we must now ask what distinguishes religion from every other *I-Thou* relation, the divine *Thou* from every other *Thou*, and revelation from every other address. Such a quest for distinguishing criteria is clearly necessary. For in their total absence the very words "religion," "divine" and "revelation" would be meaningless to those not —or not yet—participating in a human-divine dialogue; and Buber would have to persuade them to decide to participate in such a dialogue, in total blindness not only as to whether it exists but even as to what it means. In short, Buber's doctrine of the *I* and *Thou* would turn into a pure homily at the precise point at which an

---

[18] *Moses* (Oxford and London, 1946), p. 188, and a letter to Franz Rosenzweig published in: Franz Rosenzweig, *On Jewish Learning* (New York, 1955), pp. 111ff.

[19] *Israel and the World*, p. 209. Perhaps Buber's most explicit statement on the Torah is found in *Two Types of Faith* (London, 1951), p. 93.

[20] *Between Man and Man*, p. 15.

[21] *Exodus* 3:14. Cf. Buber's commentaries, *Israel and the World*, p. 23, *Moses*, pp. 52ff., *The Prophetic Faith* (New York, 1949), pp. 28ff.

attempt is made to extend it into a doctrine of revelation. And as we have already seen, such a homily on revelation, whatever its religious merits, could not come to grips with the modern critique of revelation. Why, even if he granted that there are all sorts of *I-Thou* relationships, should anyone grant that among them is a divine-human relationship, if the very word "divine" is meaningless to all except those who stand in such a relationship?

But would that word be meaningful even to those who *do* stand in such a relationship? To be sure, Buber tells us that the self-revealing God must be a *moment*-God, that is, a God whose self-disclosure cannot be anticipated by means of universal criteria. But he also tells us that the moment-God is a *God,* and that "out of the moment-Gods there arises for us with a single identity the Lord of the voice, the One."[22] But if all criteria of identification were totally lacking, how could the moment-Gods merge into the One God? Indeed, how could the moment-Gods be, and be recognized to be, Gods at all?

It is clearly necessary, then, to seek criteria in terms of which *concepts* of God, religion and revelations may be framed. But we must not seek the wrong kind of criterion and the wrong kind of concept. A concept of revelation which contained, even only implicitly, the whole content of revelation would be a contradiction in terms. For revelation is the reception of the wholly new, but the concept would deny that it is wholly new; revelation demands committed openness which the concept would make impossible. The kind of concept required is the same that may be given of a *Thou* as such, or of a human *Thou* as such. The former may be defined as the kind of other who can be in dialogue with me, and the latter, as the kind of other who can be in human dialogue with me, that is, the kind of dialogue carried on through words and gestures. Both definitions, far from denying the uniqueness of every *Thou* and of every address, explicitly contain this element.

God, Buber asserts, is the *Thou* "that by its nature cannot become an *It*."[23] All genuine religion, therefore, is an *I-Thou* relationship with the *Thou* that cannot become an *It;* and every revelation reveals the *Thou* that cannot become an *It*. Here we have Buber's criterion of distinction.

But it is one thing to state the criterion, another to understand it.

[22] *Between Man and Man,* p. 15.
[23] *I and Thou,* pp. 75, 112.

How can revelation be tied to the moment of encounter, revealing only a God of the moment, and yet reveal a God who cannot be an *It* at *any* moment? How can the God of the moment at the same time be recognized as infinite[24] and eternal?[25] And yet if He is not so recognized, it now seems, He is not recognized as God at all. Does this not mean that expressions such as "moment God" and "divine *Thou*" *are nothing less than contradictions in terms?*

The answer to all these questions is this, that *in the moment of revelation no* It *retains its independence.*[26] In that moment, every *It* becomes either a symbol through which God speaks, or the partner to whom He speaks. But the former is not an independent *It* and the latter is not an *It* at all. In making transparent every *It*, in the moment of His presence, God discloses that no *It* can remain opaque to His presence; that there can be both an independent *It* and a present God, but not both at the same time. In revealing Himself as "I shall be who I shall be," God does not disclose when or how He will be present. But He does disclose that He will be present as an *I*, if present at all.

Thus if God is known as eternal and infinite, it is not by thought which rises above the encounter to speculate on His essence; it is known *in* the encounter. God is infinite, because in the moment of encounter there is no *It* which can limit Him; He is eternal, because it is known in the here and now that He cannot turn into an *It* in any here and now.

This, then, is the minimum content of all revelation. But why is the minimum content not also the maximum content? Why does the God who reveals Himself as God nevertheless speak differently in every situation? This is because, while in the presence of the divine *Thou* no independent *It* remains, an independent human *I* remains; indeed, it must remain if the divine *Thou* is to be a *Thou* at all. But while the divine *Thou* is infinite and eternal the human

---

[24] *Ibid.*, p. 80.

[25] *Ibid.*, p. 75.

[26] This point is most clearly brought out in Buber's comments on Biblical miracles, cf., e.g., *Moses*, p. 77: "The real miracle means that in the astonishing experience of the event the current system of cause and effect becomes, as it were, transparent and permits a glimpse of the sphere in which the sole power, not restricted by any other, is at work." Cf. also *The Prophetic Faith*, p. 46, and *Israel and Palestine* (London, 1952), p. 26: "wherever the action of nature as well as spirit is perceived as a gift, revelation takes place."

I is finite and temporal. The divine *Thou* speaks *into* the situation to a human *I* who can respond only out of the situation. But what He says into each situation transcends all conceptual anticipation.

Can there be conceptual anticipation of the human response to the divine address? Not, to be sure, of the particular response appropriate to each particular situation. But just as every revelation reveals the divine *Thou* every human response must be *to* the divine *Thou*. And this lends it a characteristic which distinguishes this response from every other kind.

Any response to any *Thou* requires, ideally, total commitment. But committed *I-Thou* relations in general can, and always do, degenerate into uncommitted *I-It* relations. Commitment, therefore, admits of degrees; and perhaps total commitment is an ideal which may be approximated but not wholly attained. But all this is impossible in the case of the human response to revelation. For revelation reveals the divine *Thou* who cannot become an *It*. The kind of *I-Thou* relation which it initiates cannot, therefore, degenerate into an *I-It* relation; and commitment cannot here admit of degrees. This relation is the absolute relation,[27] that is, the relation which exists either absolutely or not at all.

We have given an account of the divine address and of the human response. We must now turn to their relation. The central question here is this: is revelation independent of the response? Or does it not become revelation unless and until there is response? Buber would appear to lean at times toward both alternatives, but to end up rejecting both.

Revelation is an address to a *Thou*. It is not revelation unless it has its *Thou*. This implies that, if revelation is independent of human response, being-a-*Thou* is, in this case, not a matter of human response but a product of revelation.

He is the infinite *I* that *makes* every It His *Thou*.[28]

In order to speak to man, God must become a person; but in order to speak to him, He must *make him* too a person.[29]

In addressing us God forces us to listen; and having been forced to listen we give our free response.

---

27 *I and Thou*, p. 81.

28 *Between Man and Man*, p. 56, my italics.

29 *The Prophetic Faith*, pp. 164ff., my italics.

But this conclusion is difficult. For according to Buber, the essence of human response to revelation is the committed turning to God; and this committed turning is involved, not only in whatever we do subsequently to hearing, but in the hearing as well. For unless we listen in commitment we do not hear at all.

Must we conclude, then, that revelation is not revelation until we respond? That it is not, at any rate, an address to *us* until we decide to listen? This would appear to be implied in Buber's suggestion that God speaks at all times,[30] for revelation manifestly does *not* occur at all times. Our committed listening would translate, in that case, what is in itself only potential revelation into actuality.

But this alternative, too, is in the end rejected, if only because there are times in which God is silent. To be sure, an eclipse of God may be due to our failure to listen to what there is to be heard; but it may also be due to a divine silence which persists no matter how devoutly we listen.[31]

Buber's final conclusion is that the relation between divine address and human response is an antimony which thought cannot resolve.[32] In speaking to *me* the Infinite *Thou* makes me His listening *I*; yet unless I make myself His listening *I* neither shall I be His *Thou* nor He mine.

I know that 'I am given over for disposal' and know at the same time that 'It depends on myself'. . . . I am compelled to take both to myself, to be lived together, and in being lived they are one.[33]

This conclusion has important implications concerning the content of revelation. The philosophical task here is not the identification of a particular content, for this can be done only, primarily by the person who lives in the revealing situation, secondarily, by the historian who relives it in his mind. The task is to define the status of the content of revelation, namely, the extent to which it is divine and the extent to which it is human. But the attempt at definition ends in an antimony.

[30] Cf. *I and Thou,* esp. p. 119.

[31] Cf. *Two Types of Faith,* p. 168 and many other passages. But it would appear that Buber has not wholly decided his stand on this last, and in an age of manifest "eclipse of God" most troubling, question, cf., e.g., *At the Turning* (New York: 1952), pp. 61ff.

[32] *I and Thou,* p. 95.

[33] *Ibid.,* p. 96.

It was seen that the core of revelation is not the communication of content but the event of God's presence. Nevertheless, revelation must assume content. For it is an address which calls for a response; and the response called for is not some universal response, but the unique response appropriate to the situation. Speaking *into* the situation, "into my very life"[34], revelation assumes the most concrete content there can be. But does revelation assume this content independently of our response or only by virtue of our response? Both alternatives are impossible.

Revelation is "hearable" content only in relation to committed listening. If it is to be nevertheless independent of our response, revelation must force us into committed listening. But this, we have already seen, is impossible. Hence there cannot be a divinely-handed-down content, passively received; all content is the result of committed appropriation, and thus "a statement which is human in its meaning and form."[35]

I experience what God desires of me for this hour . . . not earlier than in this hour. But even then it is not given me to experience it except by answering before God for this hour as my hour.[36]

Is revelation, then, wholly without content apart from my answering? This too is impossible. Revelation would, in that case, not be an address at all, let alone an address to *me*. And the "statement which is human in its meaning and its form" would be, not a translation of revelation into human speech, but the product of self-sufficient human spontaneity. Yet it *is* a translation,[37] and the listener knows it to be a translation, that is, a human product "stimulated"[38] by God.

Once more Buber admits frankly the antimony at which he has arrived.

It is not man's own power that works here, nor is it God's pure effective passage, but it is a mixture of the divine and the human.[39]

[34] *Between Man and Man,* p. 12.

[35] *Eclipse of God,* p. 135.

[36] *Between Man and Man,* p. 68.

[37] *The Prophetic Faith,* p. 164.

[38] *Eclipse of God,* p. 135.

[39] *I and Thou,* p. 117.

In my answering I am given into the power of His grace, but I cannot measure Heaven's share in it.[40]

With this last point Buber's concept of revelation is complete. Whatever goes beyond it is concerned with the actuality of particular revelations, and this transcends the limits of the present essay.[41]

But if Buber's counter-attack on the modern attack on revelation is to be wholly successful there is one task he must still accomplish. We have suggested that if Buber's doctrine of the *I* and *Thou* is true, and if it can be extended into a doctrine of revelation, the latter constitutes an effective answer to the modern critique of revelation. The question remains *whether* the former doctrine is true, and hence whether the latter is acceptable; or—to put it more modestly— whether the grounds on which both are advanced lend them an impressive claim to truth.

V

But in a search for such grounds one fundamental point must be borne in mind with the utmost clarity. Buber's doctrine—which asserts that in the committed *I-Thou* relation there is knowing access to a reality which escapes *I-It* knowledge—cannot itself be an instance of, or be based on, *I-It* knowledge. For the latter, which either ignores the *Thou* or else treats it as an *It*—can neither understand its own limitations *as I-It* knowledge, nor can it recognize *I-Thou* knowledge *as* knowledge.

Thus a psychologist who examined *I-Thou* relations would use *I-It* knowledge, not furnish a critique of it; and he would arrive, not at the doctrine of the *I* and *Thou*, but at laws of interhuman relationships. In his studies of religion, he would not be the committed partner in a dialogue with God, but only the detached observer of other people's dialogue with God. But for this detached standpoint there could not be an address of God, but only other people's *feeling-of-being addressed-by-God*; in short, "psychic phenomena." The investigation would be carried on within a system of categories which

---

40 *Between Man and Man*, p. 69.

41 Our reasons for omitting this aspect of Buber's thought—which includes his interpretation of Judaism—are first, as indicated, that this transcends the mere abstract *concept* of revelation; secondly, the fact that it is treated by other contributors to the present volume. We by no means suggest that the aspects of Buber's thought here treated are more important than those omitted.

is merely "a temporary construction which is useful for psychological orientation."[42]

Must Buber's doctrine, then, be classified, without qualification, within *I-Thou* knowledge? This conclusion is inescapable if *I-Thou* and *I-It* knowledge constitute exhaustive alternatives, and this Buber in at least one essay[43] clearly implies. Conceivably there could be a third kind of knowledge which is unlike *I-It* knowledge in that it understands, and at least to that extent transcends, the limitations of *I-It* knowledge; but which is unlike *I-Thou* knowledge in that it is detached rather than committed. Such a knowledge would have to be classified as philosophical. But philosophy, Buber asserts in the essay referred to, is *I-It* knowledge pure and simple.[44]

But can the doctrine of the *I* and *Thou* really be classified, without qualification, within *I-Thou* knowledge? Let us begin our consideration of this question by turning once more to the hypothetical psychologist to whom we have already had recourse for illustrative purposes.[45] We have argued above that Buber would find fault with neither his science nor his way of life, but rather with a third thing, namely, his interpretation, respectively, of *I-Thou* and *I-It* knowledge. But if this interpretation is to be classified, without qualification, within *I-Thou* knowledge, how can it be a third thing? Would it not follow that the psychologist, if in possession of the knowledge of but a single *Thou*, would *ipso facto* possess knowledge also of the true nature of *I-Thou* and *I-It* knowledge? Would Buber not be driven to the unpalatable conclusion of having to cast aspersions on the way of life lived by wrong-headed philosophers?

But perhaps this conclusion need not follow. For surely even if the doctrine of the *I* and *Thou* is to be classified wholly within *I-Thou*

---

[42] *Israel and the World*, p. 98. Cf. also Buber's incisive criticism of the thought of C. G. Jung, *Eclipse of God*, pp. 78–92, 133–137.

[43] "Religion and Philosophy," *Eclipse of God*, pp. 27–46.

[44] "*I-It* finds its highest concentration and illumination in philosophical knowledge," *Eclipse of God*, p. 45. Consequently, Buber argues in this essay, philosophy deals in abstractions in which existential reality is lost. Its objects are mere "constructions" and "objectifications." Presumably philosophy is unaware of these limitations. For it either fails to discover God among its objects or else mistakes Him for a mere object. Could it look for Him among objects, or mistake Him for an object, if it *knew* that objects are only "constructions" or "objectifications"? Cf. *infra*, pp. 294ff.

[45] Cf. *supra*, pp. 281ff.

knowledge, a distinction must still be made between the immediate dialogical knowledge of a *Thou* and the knowledge of the *doctrine* of the *I* and *Thou*. The latter could not be identical with, but at most only be somehow implicit in the former. And it would be the philosopher's task to show how it is implicit, and to make the implicit explicit. It would follow that the hypothetical psychologist's mistake was, after all, not due to a lack of *I-Thou* relations, but merely to a failure to recognize their metaphysical and epistemological implications, or else to a tendency to forget them whenever he turned to his professional job.

Such a view may seem plausible enough in the case of interhuman *I-Thou* relations. After all, in the case of these even the most fanatical devotee of *I-It* knowledge must make two admissions: first, that there is an actual address by another, secondly, that this address is never *wholly* understood in terms of *I-It* knowledge. (Of these two admissions, the first is primary; for unless it is made the question of understanding the address *as* address does not arise.) In the case of these relations, therefore, it is not difficult to be persuaded that the doctrine that the *I-Thou* relation yields a unique knowledge of another should be implicit in the actual dialogical knowledge of the other. But it is not easy to be persuaded of this in the case of *I-Thou* relations in which the *Thou* is not human, whether it be a stone or a tree or God. For here one does not have to be a fanatical devotee of *I-It* knowledge in order to doubt that there is an actual—rather than merely an apparent—address by another; indeed, one should be lacking in intellectual responsibility if one did *not* doubt it, demanding an argument for the removal of the doubt. But the crucial difficulty is that, if the doctrine of the *I* and *Thou* is wholly derived from the dialogue with the *Thou,* such an argument must be in principle unavailable. The doctrine of the *I* and *Thou,* far from being able to argue that there is actual rather than merely apparent dialogue, would on the contrary wholly flow from the belief that there is the former rather than the latter. Buber could do nothing to argue that the category of revelation in terms of which the religious standpoint understands itself is the category in terms of which it must be understood; for his doctrine of revelation would, in the end, wholly spring from the religious standpoint, that is, from a dialogue with God whose actuality is accepted simply on faith.

Such a conclusion, we hasten to emphasize, would not be as irrational as it may at first sight appear. For Buber's body of doctrine, even if wholly derived from committed *I-Thou* knowledge, would still be a body of doctrine. It would contain a critique of *I-It* knowledge and an interpretation of the status of *I-Thou* knowledge; it would identify revelation as part of a kind of *I-Thou* knowledge and refute those who assert that revelation is impossible. It would, to be sure, in all its doctrinal assertions be unconvincing to those who stubbornly remain on the *I-It* standpoint; but it would at least show that the objections raised from the *I-It* standpoint have no force for those who adopt the *I-Thou* standpoint. It may be said that this is all that may be asked of a body of doctrine, particularly of a body of religious doctrine into which faith must presumably at some point enter.

But the fact would still remain—at least in the case of all but interhuman *I-Thou* relations—that Buber's entire thought would spring from, rather than be able to argue for, the reality of dialogue; that is, it would have to presuppose that there *is* a reality of dialogue. But is it possible for the modern-minded to grant this presupposition? An ancient prophet could take it for granted that the voice of God may be heard by the committed listener; a modern man can hardly take this for granted, though he may very well be led to accept it. But he will surely accept it only if he is offered some kind of argument, cogent to the *I-It* standpoint, which points to the *I-Thou* standpoint as being, in the case of divine-human as well as interhuman relationships, a standpoint of truth. But if the whole doctrine of the *I* and *Thou* derives from *I-Thou* knowledge such an argument cannot be given.

But perhaps Buber's doctrine does not derive wholly from *I-Thou* knowledge, after all. To the present writer at least it appears that while Buber characterizes philosophy as *I-It* knowledge,[46] the pure philosophizing which he himself does is a *critique* of *I-It* knowledge. It is pure philosophizing because it is detached rather than committed, but it nevertheless transcends the realm of *I-It* in that it recognizes its limitations and, in recognizing them, points beyond them to the realm of the *I and Thou*.

Consider the following very remarkable passage.

The philosopher, if he were really to wish to turn his back on that God [i.e., the *It*-God of the philosophers], would be compelled to renounce the attempt to include God in his system in any conceptual form. Instead of including

46 Cf. *supra*, note 44.

God as one theme among others, that is, as the highest theme of all, his philosophy both wholly and in part would be compelled to point toward God, without actually dealing with Him. This means that the philosopher would be compelled to recognize and admit the fact that his idea of the Absolute was dissolving at the point where the Absolute *lives;* that it was dissolving at the point where the Absolute is loved; because at that point the Absolute is no longer the 'Absolute' about which one may philosophize, but God.[47]

How is philosophy to "point toward God without actually dealing with Him"? If the division into *I-Thou* and *I-It* knowledge is exhaustive this must be impossible. For the latter knows nothing of the *Thou*-God and hence cannot point to Him, whereas the former not merely points to, but deals with Him; moreover, being committed it is not philosophy. The passage quoted clearly implies that the division into *I-Thou* and *I-It* knowledge is not exhaustive; that philosophy, at least at its profoundest point, is not *I-It* knowledge but the dialectic of *I-It* knowledge. As such it mediates between *I-It* and *I-Thou* knowledge; for, being a detached critique of detached knowledge, it points beyond detached knowledge and thus beyond itself; and what it points to is the commitment of the *I-Thou* standpoint. This is the kind of philosophizing which Buber, at least on important occasions, would appear to be doing. And it is, at least in the opinion of this writer, the only kind of philosophizing which properly belongs, not only with Buber's doctrine of the *I* and *Thou,* but with any kind of existential thought. Indeed, a study of post-Kantian and more particularly post-Hegelian thought would show that it is in connection with this kind of philosophizing that existential philosophy has emerged as a philosophy.[48]

But while there are many samples of such philosophizing to be found in Buber's writings,[49] it must be said that they do not add up

[47] *Eclipse of God,* p. 50.

[48] The philosopher most instructive on this fundamental problem is Schelling who, in his *Philosophie der Mythologie und Offenbarung, Werke* 11-14 (Stuttgart und Augsburg, 1856–61), distinguishes between a "positive" philosophy which is based on a commitment, and a "negative" philosophy which is a dialectical argument for this commitment. Cf. E. L. Fackenheim, "Schelling's Conception of Positive Philosophy," *The Review of Metaphysics,* 7, no. 4 (1954) 563–582.

[49] We confine ourselves to a single but crucially important example. Buber asserts that revelation is "the inexpressible confirmation of meaning. Meaning is assured. Nothing can any longer be meaningless. The question about the meaning of life is no longer there. But were it there, it would not have to be answered," *I and Thou,* p. 110. Buber clearly teaches that the question about the meaning of life *is* there prior to the meeting with the divine *Thou.* He also clearly teaches that it cannot be

to a systematic body of thought. Possibly this is because Buber has chosen, throughout his life, to concentrate on the kind of thinking which flows out of the reality of the dialogue, leaving it to others to supply the propaedeutic, namely, the thinking which argues for the reality of the dialogue. But it is possible that Buber's ultimate stand is that philosophy is only *I-It* knowledge, after all. This would mean that not only the critique of *I-It* knowledge but Buber's doctrine as a whole would derive from *I-Thou* knowledge and nothing else. It would also mean that it is not, strictly speaking, philosophical. Such detached criticizing of detached knowledge as Buber may be doing would have to be regarded, in that case, as a mere series of lapses, due possibly to Kantian or post-Kantian influence.

If this interpretation should be correct, Buber would emerge, in the ultimate analysis, not as a philosopher but as a Hebrew sage in modern garb. He would be in modern garb because, taking note of the modern attack on revelation, he develops a body of doctrine wholly capable of repulsing that attack; but he would be a sage rather than a philosopher because the ultimate basis of his doctrine is an unargued commitment to the dialogue with the ancient God of Israel, a commitment which the reader is called upon to share. Buber's own commitment, and the commitment he asks of his reader, would simply rest on the ancient and irrefutable faith that God can speak even though He may be silent; that He can speak at least to those who listen to His voice with all their hearts.

answered—or rather removed—by anything but the meeting with the divine *Thou*. For, every other *I-Thou* relation being incomplete (*I and Thou*, p. 99), man's "sense of *Thou* cannot be satiated till he finds the endless *Thou*," (*I and Thou*, p. 80) . All this implies that, prior to the commitment to the dialogue with God, it is possible to point to the commitment to this dialogue, indicating at least something of what it would mean should such a dialogue take place. It follows that the concepts of religion, revelation, and the divine *Thou* are at least not *wholly* derived from the actuality of the divine-human dialogue.

EMIL L. FACKENHEIM

UNIVERSITY OF TORONTO

12

Hugo Bergman

MARTIN BUBER AND MYSTICISM

I

IN AN early essay, "With a Monist," written at the beginning of 1914, Martin Buber replies to the question, "Are you a mystic?," in the following manner:

No, for I still grant to reason a claim that the mystic must deny to it. Beyond this, I lack the mystic's negation. I can negate convictions but never the slightest actual thing. The mystic manages, truly or apparently, to annihilate the entire world, or what he so names—all that his senses present to him in perception and in memory—in order, with new disembodied senses or a wholly supersensory power, to press forward to his God. But I am enormously concerned with just this world, this painful and precious fullness of all that I see, hear, taste. I cannot wish away any part of its reality. I can only wish that I might heighten this reality. . . . And the reality of the experienced world is so much the more powerful the more powerfully I experience it and realize it. Reality is no fixed condition, but a quantity which can be heightened. Its magnitude is functionally dependent upon the intensity of our experiencing. There is an ordinary reality which suffices as a common denominator for the comparison and ordering of things. But the great reality is another. And how can I give this reality to my world except by seeing the seen with all the strength of my life, hearing the heard with all the strength of my life, tasting the tasted with all the strength of my life? Except by bending over the experienced thing with fervour and power . . . until the confronting, the shaping, the bestowing side of things springs up to meet me and embraces me so that I know the world in it? The actual world is the manifest, the known world. And the world cannot be known otherwise than through response to the things by the active sense-spirit of the loving man.[1]

These words express with intensity all that Buber had to say in his early period in regard to the question of his attitude toward mysticism. We may summarize it in the following fashion:

1. Buber recognizes the perfect right of reason (*ratio*) to control and use everything. He asserts in the aforementioned essay that rationalism is his only "ism."

[1] *Pointing the Way*, p. 28.

2. But rationalism is not able to carry its task to completion. It is unable to rationalize itself notwithstanding the fact that it rationalizes the entire world. Rather the spirit is the master of rationalization and constantly slips through the meshes of the net which rationalism has devised for the conceptual control of the world. "This is the glorious paradox of our existence that all comprehensibility of the world is only a footstool of its incomprehensibility."[2]

3. Buber rejects mysticism if this be understood to mean that the mystic negates the world and believes that he will find beyond it a path to God. Buber insists that the way to God leads directly through this world.

4. There is a road to the inwardness of the world which is neither that of reason nor yet of world-negating mysticism.

What the most learned and ingenious combination of concepts denies, the humble and faithful beholding, grasping, knowing of any situation bestows. The world is not comprehensible, but it is embraceable: through the embracing of one of its beings.[3]

II

We must discuss more thoroughly this last point which shows the distinctive nature of Buber's mysticism and his positive attitude to this phenomenon at that time. This is his way to the aforementioned "Great Reality" or to the "Great Experience" as Zen Buddhism would term it. It is reached through the highest intensification of our experience of things.

We have already said that the human spirit does not submit to rationalization because, though it executes the rationalizing process, it remains outside the world of concepts it sets up. But it is not only the I that has its empirical, tangible, and its "great" unrationalizable reality; for this is indeed true of every single thing.

Each thing and being has a twofold nature: the passive, absorbable, usable, dissectible, comparable, combinable, rationalizable, and the other, the active, non-absorbable, unusable, undissectible, incomparable, noncombinable, non-rationalizable. This is the confronting, rationalization, the shaping, the bestowing in things. He who truly experiences a thing so that it springs up to meet him and embraces him of itself has in that thing known the world.[4]

[2] *Ibid.*, p. 27.

[3] *Ibid.*

[4] *Ibid.*

In this connection Buber reminds us that the Hebrew word "to know" also means "to embrace lovingly." True art is loving art and the same applies to true science and philosophy and, indeed, to every authentic action. To these there is revealed the secret form, the secret life, and the secret meaning of things.[5]

In *Daniel* (1913) Buber provides a series of illustrations of this unifying process. The hero, the poet, the sage, the prophet achieve such binding. This is not meant in any subjective sense as though these men could produce reality *for themselves*. Rather does it mean that out of the experience of this type of man reality arises, which encompasses him even as it embraces all things. The world is a vortex before there is performed within it the act making for "realization." Thereupon it comes to rest around the "direction" of fulfillment which man brings to it out of himself. The mystery of the world becomes revealed only through the realizing man. Hence the basic distinction in "existence"—we may use this modern expression here though Buber nowhere employs it—is that between realization and non-realization. Whoever does not bring about realization himself remains unrealized. Moreover the world itself is brought to fulfillment only through the person who is performing this act of realization and by doing so raising it into that higher level of being which is termed reality. It is the distinction of man to bring about such realization both for himself and for the world. "Real" is defined, however, as "relating an experience exclusively to oneself." For man God cannot become fulfilled or realized in any other way than through the innermost presence of an experience. God must be brought to realization; and there is no other reality than through man who realizes himself and all being.

This is naturally a mystical approach to the world, whether or not we desire to term it that. Out of the "agitation," there may arise the unity, the grace of which may become radiantly visible regardless of the content—be it the countenance of a man or the view of a landscape or a pile of stones. The man of the here and now perfects himself into "the *I* of the world" when he "embracing the world does not become manifold in its manifoldness; but rather, out of the strength of his world-embracing, has himself become unified, a united doer. . . . He bears the world upward to its self. He, the united one,

5 *Ibid.*, pp. 29f.

shapes the world to unity."[6] The living unity of the world is not found *behind* the manifoldness; rather it is we who have the capacity to *engender* the living unity *out* of the multiplicity.

Now certain difficult questions arise at this point. To be sure since we are dealing with an *experience* there can be no discussion as to its factuality. If a person does not have the endowment for having such experiences he has no right to discuss the matter intellectually, yet he may ask certain questions:

(A) Apart from the subjective aspect of the experience, what is the *cosmic* significance thereof? Is it that *man* effects unity in the *world?* Or has the act of unification, for the person who has fallen out of the unity of the world, a subjective significance which may restore the unity *for him?* To this question Buber gives the *first* answer. The unifying act of man has *cosmic* significance. Man has absolute value. Human unifying we read in the Introduction to *Der Grosse Maggid,*—"is not 'subjective' at all, but a subjective-objective event, an event of meeting, it is the dynamic form of the divine unity itself."[7]

The cosmic significance of this unification was recognized by *Asia.* The Orient recognized that there were impediments to the self-disclosure of the inwardness of the world, and that the world needs the human spirit to release it and to unify it. It knew that by virtue of this alone man's life upon the earth has significance and power. As Buber puts it: "Man is appointed to bring reality out of its bifurcation into unity. The world waits for man to unify it."[8]

This is the source of the activistic tendency which inheres in Buber's doctrine of unification. "True religiousness is an *activity*." In the third of his *Three Addresses on Judaism* Buber particularly emphasizes this *activistic* character. At that period Buber occasionally employed certain formulations which placed such emphasis upon man's share in the divinising of the world that they recall Feuerbach's doctrine of the creation of God by man, except that Buber's position is based on very different presuppositions. Thus he writes: "The religious act is the realization of God through man." And again "God's visage rests invisibly in the block of the world. It must be

[6] *Ibid.,* pp. 18f.

[7] "Spirit and Body of the Hasidic Movement," *The Origin and Meaning of Hasidism,* p. 133.

[8] *Vom Geist des Judentums* (1916), p. 19.

hewn out and given form . . . God is not something to be believed in but to be fulfilled."9 At a later period Buber no longer employed such a formulation.

(B) There is a second question which the person who has not achieved unification may pose to the one who has. This is the interrogation as to the nature of the *way* that needs to be followed in order to achieve such unification. All religions endeavor in their respective ways to point out such a "path". Judaism, for example, if we were to interpret it in a "mystical" fashion as the present context requires, regards the six hundred and thirteen commandments and prohibitions as the proper way. On the other hand Zen Buddhism whose experience of unity is, if I am not mistaken, closest10 to that depicted in Buber's early writings, developed a severe technique for leading a man to the "great experience." What does the Buber of the early writings answer to this question? We receive only scant help as to the direction to follow for achieving unification. He stresses repeatedly the obligation "to produce unity out of your and all other duality, and to establish unity in the world."11 But what is unity? In his second *Address* concerning Judaism, Buber listed "the unity of the individual person, unity between portions of a nation, unity among the nations; and unity between mankind and all other living things, and between God and the world." But this itemization still leaves the direction vague and ambiguous. For what is the meaning of unity between mankind and all living things if we do not bring in the doctrine of redemption and what follows from it,—the revolutionary transformation of the world order? We shall have more to say about this later. Moreover the meaning of unity among nations is not clarified, although it can scarcely refer to the kind of unity brought about by Napoleon in his fashion. What is really meant here? Clearly the person who has experienced unification cannot explain this to one who has not undergone this experience. Inasmuch as no way of discipline is given for learning the way there is a danger that misunderstandings may arise—and this actually proved to be the case.

9 *Vom Geist des Judentums.*

10 Buber discusses Zen in "The Place of Hasidism in the History of Religion," *The Origin and Meaning of Hasidism.*

11 *Daniel.*

III

The doctrine that God is brought to "fulfillment" through man's deeds became increasingly important in Buber's writing during the last years of the First World War. He was deeply moved by the misery of society and the breakdown of ideals which the war made so obvious. In those years he addressed himself to social problems and he now connected his *sociological* ideas with the religious. This synthesis found its clearest expression in the address "*Der heilige Weg. Ein Wort an die Juden und an die Voelker*", (1919). This oration was dedicated to his deceased friend, Gustav Landauer, who died a martyr's death in the cause of social revolution. He notes here that

whosoever desires to see God in things does not truly live in the sight of God. God is only germinally present in things. Our task is to realize Him between things. . . . This will take place wherever immediate and direct relationships develop among creatures, where the dungeon of the person is unbarred and men become freely open toward one another, and where in the between, in the apparently empty space, the eternal substance will arise. The true locus of realization is community and true community is that in which the divine becomes realized among men.

But the establishment of community is an ethical, indeed *the* ethical task. Now what is the significance of the fact that this ethical obligation is now conceived as a religious one? In various places Buber endeavors to clarify this problem but, as I believe, without success. In those years the social factor swallowed up the religious one.

IV

At about 1919 there took place in Buber the great shift which was first proclaimed in the address *Cheruth. Ueber Jugend und Religion.* This is the last of his eight addresses on Judaism which Buber then collected into one volume (1923). We have seen that in his earlier statements there was a danger that the divine and the human would run into one another and we even found certain expressions which recall Feuerbach's anthropocentrism. Now Buber makes a very clear and sharp distinction between God and the manifestation of God to men. The primary reality is the working of God upon man; the unconditioned is "the great confronter." Buber now warns sternly against the deviation to which many of his own disciples were exposed, of exploiting God as an "experience" as a "mood" and a "sublime hour" to be enjoyed, which ultimately may lead to the evaporation of God resulting from a psychologizing of Him. Buber would prefer the atheist to the person who is a pursuer of religious experiences or a prattler about God. For religion *imposes responsibilities*. If in earlier writings Buber had distinguished between "official" and "subterranean" Judaism and so created for himself an artificial platform outside of the tradition, he now spoke with great reverence of the "primal forces", and "of attachment to the great sequence" of earlier generations which must be generated anew in the people of our time.

The great change that had come about in Buber's thinking achieved full expression in the Introduction which he prepared for the collected edition of his *Talks on Judaism* in 1923. This brief preface is a document which has more than merely biographical significance. For here Buber clearly formulated his rediscovery of the *real* reciprocity of God and man. Practically all the philosophers of that time regarded religion as a distinctive form of *human* productivity, belonging to a particular period of culture, like the other creative activities of mankind, and hence as determined by the epoch in question. Buber's retort to this was that religious reality precedes and is primary to the morphology of the time. Its origin is the revelation of God. This revelation takes place in man and he has his share in it as God has His. God is neither a metaphysical nor an ethical idea; nor is He a projection or a creation of man but only God Himself. He is not the product of the mythopoetic imagination. At this point Buber definitely cuts off all ties between himself and the facile enthusiasts about God. The psychological excesses which are dressed up in feelings of the divine "are a psychic, indeed a cosmic perversion." What matters is not religious experience but rather religious life, i.e., the *complete* life of a person or of a people.

In his earlier period Buber had spoken, as we have seen, of the "realization" of God, and this expression was retained by those who held the position that God was not in existence but rather in the process of coming to be either in man or in mankind. Now Buber termed this interpretation "hopelessly perverted", for to "realize" God can only mean to prepare the world to be the place of God's reality and to help the world to become divine reality *(gottwirklich)*.[12] At this point Buber had in mind an important polemic with Hermann Cohen who had maintained[13] that God could have no "reali-

---

[12] Introduction ("Vorrede"), *Reden über das Judentum* (1923), p. xviii.
[13] *Religion der Vernunft*, p. 186.

ty," as the latter is based upon human perception; hence to attribute reality to God is an anthropomorphism of a grievous sort. When Christian theology argues for the reality of God it does so because it desires to render the mundane reality of Christ beyond doubt. To this Buber's reply to Cohen was that it was unthinkable that we should permit the earth to which we are moored to remain closed to the life of God. Rather, he maintained, we are upon earth in order to "unify reality." This is the vocation of our human existence; God does not will to accomplish this without us. It is the responsibility of man to reunite the world with God; the Christian language for this would be to prepare the way for the incarnation of God in the world. Buber does not use this teminology but that of "unification" which is derived from Jewish mysticism. But this unification does not refer to that of the *soul* with God but rather to the unification of God with the world and the penetration of the world by God. In the language of the Kabbalah this would be the unification of God with the *Schechinah*, i.e., with His "radiant Presence" which informs the world. The clarification in Buber's attitude towards religion was a product of his preoccupation with the religious and mystical movement of Chassidism.

Is Buber's new position mysticism? He himself has supplied the answer in the Foreword to "The Baal-Shem-Tov's Instruction in Intercourse with God."

The Baal Shem was the founder of a *realistic and activistic mysticism,* i.e., a mysticism for which the world is not an illusion from which man must turn away in order to reach true being, but the reality between God and him in which reciprocity manifests itself, the subject of the message of creation to him, the subject of his answering service of creation, destined to be redeemed through the meeting of divine and human deed. . . . A 'mysticism' that may be called such because it preserves the immediacy of the relation, guards the concreteness of the absolute, and demands the involvement of the whole being; one can, to be sure, also call it religion for the same reason.[14]

V

But at this point there arise many questions. Once again we are bound to ask a pedagogic question, as we did above in relation to Buber's early mysticism—what *way* is being recommended? Contemporary men cannot escape the necessity of demanding from their teachers that they show them the way to follow. They ask, "What

---

14 *Hasidism and Modern Man,* pp. 180f.

then shall we do?" How do we learn "to carry out actions with the whole of our being directed to God", or to endow our action "with the power of intention?"

Such a "realistic mysticism" is found today not only in Buber but also in other writers. When Sri Aurobindo calls upon us to "offer every action to the Divine and do it as the work given," the agreement with Buber is obvious. But we are entitled to expect of the teacher that he give us direction as to how we are to traverse the road for it is long and every inch of the ground must be won anew against both internal and external impediments. These include egoism, indolence, impatience, weakness of will, cowardice and distraction produced by the mad "whirl" in which we all are threatened by engulfment. Where are the weapons in this struggle for inner growth and for a gradual unfolding of the spiritual nature of man? What role does prayer play in this contest? Although Buber shows us the goal and in his dialogical writings he points out the great dangers of the de-personalization of our life and the disappearance of true dialogue, —we frequently miss his directing hand.

The second question that we must put concerns the redemption of the world, and the Messianic final goal, in the thought of Buber. Does the path of the unification of God and the world have a goal? Is there a *growth* of God in the world? Shall we await a time of final redemption? Buber's answer is as follows:

Not merely toward the goal of perfection, but in itself, too, the redemptive moment is real. Each one touches directly on the mystery of fulfillment . . . each inserted in the sequence of time . . . and there being effective, but each also sealed in its testimony . . . in the wavering fraction of time, the fullness of time announces itself. . . . It is a mistake to regard Jewish Messianism as exhausted by a belief in an event happening once at the end of time and in a single human figure created as the center of this event . . . the Messiahship of the end of time is preceded by one of all times, poured out over the ages.[15]

I must confess that I am considerably troubled by this formulation. The notion of a "Messiahship . . . of all times, poured out over the ages" suppresses, I am afraid, any real belief in the ultimate Messiahship—in the redemption of nature, in the overcoming of hostile forces and the conquest of death (Isaiah 25:8; Hosea 13:14). I understand Buber's reluctance, possibly in order to clarify his departure from his own youthful position or to set himself apart from the enthusiasts who "seek to accelerate the end", to speak of the

---

[15] "Spinoza," *The Origin and Meaning of Hasidism*, pp. 106ff.

"All-Day of redemption" (*"Alltag der Erloesung"*), for the sake of remaining faithful to the idea of the "redemption of the everyday" (*"der Erloesung des Alltags"*), and to insure that there will be no escaping the responsibilities of the here and now. But it is my belief that in spite of all such hazards it is our obligation precisely at this time to hold fast to the reality and concreteness of the ultimate goal of redemption, to strengthen the awareness of such concreteness, and to measure the progress of man by this goal. Otherwise there is the danger that in our efforts to serve reason and to remain true to the earth, we shall forget the meaning of human existence.

VI

This report concerning the role of mysticism in Buber's thinking would remain incomplete were we to omit all reference to Buber's relationship to *gnosticism*. In many of his writings Buber has spoken of this theme, and most recently in his essay "Christ, Hasidism, Gnosis."[16] The reader has the feeling that Buber's rejection of gnosticism has become ever sharper until in the aforementioned essay it reaches the point of vehemence.

It is not easy to give a simple definition of gnosticism and, anyhow, the writer of these lines by no means possesses the competence to evaluate Buber's position in regard to ancient Gnosis or the historical questions related thereto. We are not concerned with the historical aspect but with the very current question of the justification of gnosticism and its significance for the religious and scientific situation of our time. In view of the fact that the term gnosticism has so many historical connotations it might perhaps be advisable to employ another term in relation to our contemporary situation, possibly the expression "Geistesforschung" coined by Rudolf Steiner.

Buber places in opposition *devotion* and *gnosis*. Speaking of the gnostic he says, "He draws the map of the seventh heaven," even as in reference to the Kabbalah he had once said that it draws "a map of the primal mysteries." The gnostic interprets *his own self* as divine and hence he cannot serve God. "He cannot serve and does not want to be able to." The gnostic relationship "naturally involves no responsibilities." On the other hand the man of *devotion* "does not

---

[16] *The Origin and Meaning of Hasidism*, pp. 242–254.

concern himself with the mysteries of his Lord, who at one time and another shares with him what He shares with him."

I fear that I must challenge the justice of Buber's interpretation at this point. It seems to me that for polemical reasons Buber has here created for himself artificial abstractions of gnosticism and devotion and that he is tilting against an artificial construction to which he applies the term gnosticism. Actually both gnosis and devotion are ways to God and it is inadmissible to contrapose the two in this fashion and play them off against one another.

The Hindus speak of the way of devotion on love of God (*bhakti*) and the way of knowing (*jnâna*) as two equally justified and equivalent ways to God, two radii from the periphery to the same center. Thus in this religious tradition devotion is not only a spiritual discipline and a way of life but also a way to God as is gnosticism. On the other hand we are always assured by the modern gnostics that without religious devotion no progress can be made in gnosis. I would like to bring examples from two investigators of the spirit far removed from each other. Rudolf Steiner begins his book *Wie erlangt man Erkenntnisse hoeherer Welten?* by emphasizing that the first condition for the development of spiritual experience is devotion. He writes:

The researcher into the spiritual realm terms this basic attitude the path of reverence, of devotion to truth and knowledge. Only he who possesses the basic attitude can become a student of the mysteries.

Again may we quote Sri Aurobindo's counsel to anyone who would enter the path as a disciple of gnosis: "to give oneself, to surrender, and to receive with joy, whatever the Divine gives, not grieving or revolting. To turn all actions into worship." Where now is the contrast between devotion and gnosis on which Buber bases his entire argument?

Furthermore is it correct to say that the gnostic interprets *his own* self as the divine self and therefore cannot serve God? Is it not rather the case that the goal of the gnostic is to extinguish his ego completely and to serve God by the full surrender thereof? It cannot be denied of course that there are people who receive an "inflation" (Jung) and identify their ego with the Divine. But shall we then orient ourselves by reference to phenomena of decadence, which in any case also occur in the realm of the *bhakta?* Actually Frithjof

Schuon in his book[17] has differentiated between the devotional and gnostic way to God. He stresses that for the *bhakta* God is "He" and the "ego" is "I"; whereas for the *jnâna* God is the "Self" and his own ego is regarded as a "he", and "other". This is, in his relationship to God the practitioner of the method of devotion retains his ego in relationship to God whereas the gnostic endeavors to shed it completely and to regard himself as a stranger.

In one of his essays Buber asks, "What concern of ours, if they exist, are the upper worlds!"[18] This appears to me to be an inadmissible simplification. For if there were upper worlds and man could know them, that would be tantamount to the most tremendous revolution. But even if they should turn out to be nothing more than projections of our subjectivity, they would still have taught us decisive things concerning man. With respect to these "upper worlds" we have the same *obligation* to know as in regard to the world present to our senses.

There is only one way I can explain Buber's rejection of our responsibility to know in this case. Revolted by many of the degenerative aspects of the practice of gnosticism in periods of decline, which includes our own time, Buber here sought to erect a barrier against our curiosity which might lead us into peril, even as the gnostics themselves have frequently emphasized. The root of Buber's position comes to very clear expression particularly in his *For the Sake of Heaven* where the hero of the book "refuses to enter into a conversation concerning the mysteries but prays with great enthusiasm." The "primal opposition between *Gnosis* and *Devotio*" of which Buber speaks is represented here by two major figures of the story. This volume demonstrates how deeply and painfully he felt this contrast in his own experience. Nonetheless it appears to me that at this point his thought remains enmeshed in a rationalistic prejudice and that he is really paying tribute here to the world view of the nineteenth century. It is necessary to pierce through these limitations if we are to develop further Buber's own thought in the direction of that "Great Reality" of which the mystical books of his youth give evidence and to which Buber's entire life work shows us the way.

[17] *Sentiers de Gnose* (1957), p. 79.

[18] *The Origin and Meaning of Hasidism,* p. 181.

DEPARTMENT OF PHILOSOPHY   HUGO BERGMAN
THE HEBREW UNIVERSITY, JERUSALEM

13

Emil Brunner

JUDAISM AND CHRISTIANITY IN BUBER

IN A WAY I regret that it was this particular topic which was assigned to me. For, Buber's true greatness becomes apparent precisely where he does not speak as an interpreter of Judaic or Christian writings or as a scholar of comparative religion, but where, by his religious intuition, he elucidates the situation of contemporary man. Contrasting Judaism and Christianity is not suited to bring out his deepest insight. Such a comparison will make it inevitable that the object of this essay will appear as a representative of Judaism and its author as a representative of Christianity. This will make it impossible to avoid that—in spite of the mutual deep respect of the two partners for each other—what the one affirms the other must negate, at least to a certain extent. In view of this fact, I may be allowed to begin with a word of deeply felt gratitude and appreciation.

Buber's simple yet ingenious discovery of the great difference between the I-Thou relationship and that of the I-It relation constitutes indeed—as Karl Heim seems first to have put it—a 'Copernican Revolution' in the thinking not only of Europe but of the whole of mankind. In point of actual fact this qualification [by Heim] was applicable not so much to Martin Buber as to an at that time unknown Austrian thinker, Ferdinand Ebner, who, in his book, *Das Wort und die Geistigen Realitäten (The Word and the Spiritual Realities)* had published the identical discovery a year before Buber, without either one knowing of the other. However, Ferdinand Ebner, shortly after the publication of his book, was struck by tuberculosis and fell victim to it within a few years. Buber, on the other hand, had the opportunity to explain and make public his discovery in a large number of publications.

The entire philosophical traditions of the East and of the West are marked by the subject-object antithesis. According to the respective preponderance of the knowing subject or of the known object a philosophy is idealistic or materialistic or attempts mediation between the two by way of pantheism. Buber could not derive his idea from the philosophical tradition, therefore. Rather, his intuition had its source somewhere else altogether, namely, in the world of the Old Testament, with which, as a pupil of the Hasidic doctrine, he was familiar and which he revered from his early youth. But he was the first who pursued the idea reflectively and who, fully equipped with the instruments provided for him by the philosophical tradition, was able to translate it into the terms of philosophy.

It is not my task to compare this discovery with that associated with the name of Kierkegaard and which is known as existentialism. Let me here merely state this one thing: existentialism as it has developed since Kierkegaard does not by any means reach the depth of Buber's simple but profoundly revolutionary fundamental insight. If I see correctly, Buber would judge every ontological attempt as belonging to the I-It world; whereas it is his greatest passion and his sacred calling to keep the I-Thou world free from the former.

It may seem strange that a Jewish and a Roman Catholic thinker were first destined to make this discovery. Sometimes a third name is added, that of Ludwig Feuerbach, who also pointed to the significance of the Thou. Even a merely peremptory reading, however, shows that Feuerbach only *seems* to belong to this line; actually he was a descendant of German idealistic philosophy. What Martin Buber discovered—I shall speak no further of Ferdinand Ebner—is indeed something which does not touch the difference between Judaism and Christianity, but which concerns what is common to both religions. That there is such common ground appears already in the fact that both, Christians and Jews, acknowledge the same Old Testament as Holy Scripture.

That Buber identifies himself with his people and their religion is apparent from the fact that he placed himself at its disposal in its effort to build a new national existence. He accepted the call to the newly created Hebrew University in Jerusalem and even today still shares the sufferings and dangers of the newly won national life with his people. Moreover, by his writings and lectures he wrestled for the very soul of his nation, and has written many books and articles in which he gave prophetic guidance to the educators of Jewish youth. Anyone who has heard him lecture on a topic of the Old Testament or is acquainted with his Hasidic stories, knows where his spiritual home is.

At the same time, he has also taken far greater pains than most scholars of his background to understand Christianity, and has, for years, maintained a warm friendship with some Christian theologians, more particularly with a few representatives of a group characterized as 'religious socialists.' It is, therefore, nothing to be marvelled at that, in the work, *Two Types of Faith*, which most directly deals with Christianity and in which he also states his own attitude to Christianity in terms of a personal confession, he writes:

From my youth onwards I have found in Jesus my great brother. That Christianity has regarded and does regard him as God and Saviour has always appeared to me a fact of the highest importance which, for his sake and my own, I must endeavour to understand. A small part of the results of this desire to understand is recorded here. My own fraternally open relationship to him has grown even stronger and clearer, . . . I am more than ever certain that a great place belongs to him in Israel's history of faith and that this place cannot be described by any of the usual categories.[1]

One who is and wants to remain a Jew could scarcely express his communicative proximity to his Christian partner in a more tangential way than he has done it.

There is a something in Israel's history of faith which is only to be understood from Israel, just as there is a something in the Christian history of faith which is only to be understood from Christianity. The latter I have touched only with the unbiased respect of one who hears the Word.[2]

It is in this same attitude of profound respect that I would like to continue our conversation, after it has, within these latter years, often been my good fortune to meet Buber personally and to exchange views with him on some of the most far-reaching issues.

However, having been asked to write on "Judaism and Christianity in Buber"—a topic which is indubitably of the most delicate nature for a Christian theologian who not only desires to do justice to Buber but who freely acknowledges that he has received something decisive from him—I shall try to carry out my task by taking the already mentioned book as my starting point. His *Two Types of Faith* is, in any case, Buber's only work in which he discusses the relations of the two religions with each other specifically and in principle. From the very first, however, I place this critical analysis within the intent of my programmatic thesis—however daring this may appear—that, in my interpretation of Christianity, I expect to

[1] *Two Types of Faith* (London, 1951), pp. 12f. Hereafter cited as *TTF*.
[2] *Ibid.*, p. 13.

make use of Buber's discovery even at points where Buber himself no longer is able to do so. Why and in what sense this is being done can become clear only in the course of this investigation.

The relatively small book, weighty in its exegetical insight and in the author's great knowledge in the field of comparative religion, has a threefold purpose and, correspondingly, a threefold object:

(1) to clarify the religious message of Judaism from its basis in the Old Testament;

(2) to illuminate the message of the Jesus of history as a phenomenon belonging to this same Jewish world; and

(3) to demonstrate that the theology of the apostles, particularly that of Paul, is separated from the preceding two by an unbridgeable chasm.

For everything Buber has to say on the first two points the open-minded Christian reader can only be thankful. Here Buber stands on his own ground, familiar to him from his youth and endeared to him by his deeply affirmed attachment to his people. Here, too, his basic insight—his I-Thou philosophy—which derives, after all, from nothing if not from this same world, proves to be congenial to the matters at hand; and the unique view which Buber brings along from his incomparable knowledge of Hasidism proves fruitful for a grasp of the inmost meaning as well as for a number of specific problems. Here he also demonstrates his capacity as well as his readiness to acknowledge *that* in Jesus by which the latter towers above his contemporaries, yes even to concede to him a kind of—conceptually no longer definable—uniqueness, connected with the peculiarity of his *kairos*.

Jesus . . . means to summon the elect in the catastrophe of humanity to come as near to God as is made possible to it only in the catastrophe.[3]

All in all, the saying of Jesus about love for the enemy derives its light from the world of Judaism in which he stands and which he seems to contest; and he outshines it.[4]

Originating from the enthusiasm of eschatological actuality, this statement, viewed from the point of view of Israel's faith, implies at the same time a supplement to it. Somewhere, apparently quite on its own accord, the most daring arc has been described, and yet a circle has thereby been completed.[5]

---

3 *TTF*, p. 61.

4 *Ibid.*, p. 75.

5 *Ibid.*, p. 76.

These are probably the utmost conceivable approximations to faith in Christ possible to a Jew who wants to remain true to his own religion. What, beyond this, he owes to himself is a statement for the reasons which make any further approximation impossible to him and which give him the good intellectual conscience not to become a Christian, but to remain a Jew. And this, then, is the third purpose and object of his book.

And with this third aspect Buber succeeds in such a superbly impressive manner that it is just here that Buber's attempt could easily become a real temptation to an open-minded Christian reader. The picture which Buber draws of the theologies of Paul and John— by adding piece onto piece of his penetrating exegetical analysis— is, on the one hand, so much of a piece, and, on the other, so strangely gnostic-hellenistic that anyone who feels himself committed to the biblical personalistic conception of faith can only exclaim: If *this* is the Christian faith, then it is clear to me that I must, with Buber, decide against Paul and for the Judaic faith of the Old Testament. Although Buber, in the preface to his book, declares that both apologetics as well as polemics are entirely foreign to his intentions— and anyone who knows him will not question his word—his presentation of Pauline theology is so convincing that, without or even against the author's will, the book turns out to be a major attack on Christianity.

What, then, precisely is the antithesis of the "two types of faith" —on the one hand the Judaic faith of the Old Testament which is also that of Jesus and of his teachings, and, on the other, the Pauline-Johannine which constituted Christianity and on which it rests as its foundation? That it *is* an antithesis Buber declares many times and altogether unambiguously.

Here not merely the Old Testament belief and the living faith of post-Biblical Judaism are opposed to Paul, but also the Jesus of the Sermon on the Mount, although from a different motif and with a different purpose.[6]

The difference between this 'It is true' and the other 'We believe and know' is not that of two expressions of faith, but of two kinds of faith.[7]

The boundary line is drawn again in such a way that, having regard to the type of faith, Israel and the original Christian Community, in so far as we

---

[6] *TTF*, p. 55.

[7] *Ibid.*, p. 35.

know about it from the Synoptics, stand on one side, and Hellenistic Christianity on the other. . . .[8]

If we consider the Synoptic and Johannine dialogues with the disciples as two stages along one road, we immediately see what was gained and lost in the course of it. The gain was the most sublime of all theologies; it was procured at the expense of the plain, concrete and situation-bound dialogicism of the original man of the Bible, who found eternity, not in the super-temporal spirit, but in the depth of the actual moment. The Jesus of the genuine tradition still belongs to that, but the Jesus of theology does so no longer.[9]

This immediacy of the whole man is directed towards the whole God, that which is revealed in Him and that which is hidden. It is the form in which Pharisaic Judaism by its doctrine of the *middot* renewed the Old Testament Emunah, the great trust in God as He is, in God be He as He may. It excludes the two great *imagines* which the Pauline world-view set over against the immediate Emunah; the demonocracy, to which this aeon is given over, and the mediatorship of a Christ at the threshhold of that which is to come.[10]

The most pointed expression of this antithesis we find in the following interpretation of the essence of the Christian doctrine:

God suffers as the Son in order to save the world, which He as the Father created and prepared as one which needs salvation. The prophetic idea of man who suffers for God's sake has here given way to that of God Who suffers for the sake of man.[11]

What is to be said to these sharp antitheses?

1. They are the result of a penetrating exegetical analysis and of an objective scientific study in comparative religion.

2. They accord with a good part of historical Christianity as it expresses itself in the classical dogma.

3. More specifically, however, Buber's criticism strikes at the Christian doctrinal tradition which, indeed, came about by a kind of belief determined by the principle of belief "that something is true"[12] (*pistis*) in opposition to the faith-principle of the Biblical *emuna*.

4. On the other hand, Buber renders us Christians the great service of making clear that the teachings of Jesus, as thus understood by its connection with the Jewish faith, cannot ever be made

8 *TTF*, p. 33.
9 *Ibid.*, p. 34.
10 *Ibid.*, p. 154.
11 *Ibid.*, pp. 149f.
12 *Ibid.*, p. 11.

the basis of the Christian faith in contradistinction to the Jewish one. Rather, what divides us is the faith in Jesus as the Christ, the certainty of reconciliation by his death on the cross.

In his proclamation of justification by faith, Paul undeniably makes use of a number of gnostic ideas which were at least in part incorporated into the Christian dogma. This corresponds with the thesis, stated already by Harnack, concerning the Hellenizing of faith in the course of the development of the dogma in the first centuries. However, the radical understanding of the doctrine of justification by faith implies at the same time the repulsion of these hellenistic cinders and the break-through to a personalistic and existential interpretation of faith, which maintains not merely its continuity with the Old Testament conception of faith as faithful obedience, but at the same time constitutes its completion. From this process there follows a certain critique of Buber's conception of the faith of the Old Testament. Without entering into detailed controversy, let us keep this one point clearly in mind:

If it seems to Buber that Paul forsakes the Old Testament line of the faith of obedience by making an historical event, namely Jesus Christ, the object of faith, it is Buber himself who must be reproached for the fact that, in his presentation of Jewish faith, he leaves the factor of historical revelation as good as out of consideration. The faith of Israel is based upon the fact that, by way of deeds and words, still more so in events which, through the prophets, became the Word of God for Israel, Yahweh revealed his name. But this is precisely that in which, according to the testimony of the Gospel according to John, Christ sums up the meaning of his work of revelation and reconciliation: "I have manifested Thy name to them." (John 17:6) To recognize the life of Jesus, and more particularly his death on the cross, as God's self-revelation and in it to know oneself as judged and as graciously pardoned—this is faith as Paul and the other apostles who speak to us in the New Testament understand it. "To believe that . . .," which, for Buber, is a mark of the Hellenization of faith, is not, as he thinks, a pre-condition of faith (in the sense of *pistis* or *Emuna*), but an aspect of an indivisible act in which man opens himself to the self-communicating God.

True, justifiable faith can be understood only from a conception of sin which I cannot find either in Buber's exposition of the Jewish nor in the Paulinic-gnostic concept of sin. As I write this, there comes to mind the very first conversation in which three of us participated in the home of a mutual psychiatrist friend, where I met Buber personally for the first time. It must have been in the late twenties or early thirties. The subject of conversation was: the concept of sin. I do not clearly recall the course of the conversation—unfortunately, the minutes our mutual friend (who since then has passed away) took, were lost—but I remember quite clearly that we parted without having reached any agreement.

For us Christians sin is the *cor incurvatum in se,* from which, as we think, no man can absolve himself, and which, the more seriously one takes the will of God, separates us from God; which cannot be met by any moral effort or by any will to turn back, and which cannot be outmaneuvered by any "forcefulness of address,"[12b] be it ever so great.

In the event of the cross Paul recognized a new way of salvation: that in that event there occurred a self-communication of God in which God addresses man as a child of God in spite of his sin. By believing in Christ as the vicariously suffering Servant of God, there is imputed to the believer the righteousness of Christ as a free gift of God and thereby the communion with God, which had been destroyed by sin, is restored, a communion to which man had no access by his own repentance.

But this faith is of the same kind as the trust and obedience of the Old Testament believer and is not a gnostic-hellenistic "believing that . . ." For this faith is a daring to go out of one's self, out of and beyond the possibilities of what is immanent in man. It is a looking away from oneself, even from the pious believing self, and a depending solely upon the grace of God; it is a grounding oneself on the foundation which God by His own act—precisely by His self-communication on the cross—puts beneath man's feet. Whereas in the Old Testament the believer is always still gazing on himself and focussing on the rightness of this his trust, here every regard for oneself stops and the total confidence depends solely upon the gracious promise of God. This faith, therefore, exhibits in complete purity what "trusting in the Lord" in the Old Testament always intended but could never fully attain.

On the other hand, this faith is the perfect "return to God," because the I identifies itself with him who is condemned on the cross and, by so doing, turns away from its previous being, from everything

---

[12b] *Ibid.,* p. 65.

it is. By this [act of faith] the "curve" of the *cor incurvatum in se* is annulled by the reaching towards God who, in His incredible mercy, comes to meet us more than halfway in His self-communicating love. This "turning back to Him" is at the same time obedience to the will of God, recognized no longer primarily as demanding but rather as granting; because the human heart, by this granted love, is enabled to love God with all his strength and to direct this love [in turn] to his neighbor as one who is loved by God.[13]

Luther was the first to grasp this meaning of the doctrine of justification by faith. Buber was unable to gather this meaning from the Pauline formulations because he got stuck in the thick of Paul's gnostic terminology. We can, however, blame Buber all the less for this because Christian theology itself for centuries did not succeed—and has not entirely succeeded even yet—in interpreting Christian faith in such a way that it was understood primarily as an "act of obedience."[14]—or rather, to use Paul's own language, "trusting obedience." The weight of a tradition which, for centuries, had taken this faith as belief in a creed or in events was altogether too great. But I think I can assure Buber that this task is recognized by the best among us and that we are in the process of disposing of that fatal misunderstanding of faith—a misunderstanding which is at the same time the *Misunderstanding of the Church.*[15] In this endeavor we shall always welcome Buber's critical warning. On the other hand, we would most cordially ask him on his part not to meet the efforts of Christian theology with the prejudice that it is necessarily concerned, in its faith-principle, with "recognition and acceptance" in the sense of "believing something to be true," when it is actually much more concerned with the new concept of *"Truth As Meeting."*[16]

To anyone who has once grasped this, the interpretation which Buber gives of Paul's theology will appear just as strange as Paul's own thought appears to Buber. He will experience what Buber himself experienced in reading Bultmann's *Theology of the New Testa-*

---

[13] For a more detailed and precisely reasoned exposition of this interpretation of faith and of justification by faith I must refer to Part 2 of my *Dogmatik III,* which will appear shortly.

[14] *TTF,* p. 98n.

[15] The title of my book of 1952 (which originally appeared in German in 1951).

[16] This is the literal translation of the German title of my book, *The Divine Human Encounter,* which appeared in 1938 (in English in 1943).

ment, of which he says that it "has not been able to convince me."[17] Perhaps we have here reached just that point of which Buber himself declares that "there is something in the Christian history of faith which is only to be understood from [within] Christianity."[18]

In any case, Buber's major concern, which follows from his basic insight, is ours also: to differentiate the relationship with God as one of an I-Thou relation from every abstract, material It-relationship, and to understand the responsible being of man from this standpoint, viz., as the necessity of responding to God's call. This means that a task has been set for us which neither Buber nor any of the rest of us has yet solved in all its aspects. Rather, it seems to me to be a task the mastery of which will cause a number of generations to hold their breath. For all of us are impregnated with the—false—ideal of objectivity, or It-ness. To achieve a break-through from this fatal habit in the age of scientific technology without falling prey to a romantic antithesis will require not merely the application of the intellectual faculty of the very best, but above all a thinking-out-of-faith which, in our age of the "eclipse of God" (Buber), is particularly rare.

It seems to me that—among Jews as among Christians—a successful stand will above all have to be taken against the "fanaticism of inertia," that is to say, against the fundamentalist and orthodox tendencies in both traditions—tendencies which all too often go hand in hand with religious revivals and manage to form themselves into imposing theological systems. In this spiritual battle we existentialist theologians have to defend a common front with Martin Buber. I would like to close this brief essay with the wish that he who first was able in all clarity to point out this front to us may for many years to come be preserved as a leader in this battle.

17 *TTF,* p. 98n.
18 *Ibid.,* p. 13.

EMIL BRUNNER

THEOLOGICAL FACULTY
UNIVERSITY OF ZÜRICH
SWITZERLAND

14

Max Brod

JUDAISM AND CHRISTIANITY IN THE WORK OF MARTIN BUBER

"IT HAS become customary to regard the process which leads from the belief in God held during the period of the Exodus to that current at the time of the Exile, as one of growing difference," we read in Buber's decisive work *The Kingship of God*. "This differentiation is generally understood as an accession of new values of the spirit and of morality, but occasionally it is also interpreted as a loss in real content." Buber has combatted this view of an alteration of the Jewish belief in God in a powerful series of historical books which he regards not as constituting a history of a religion but rather, in the strictest sense of the word, as "the history of a faith." In the Introduction to his *Moses* he distinguishes between the two terms in the following manner: The history of religion concerns itself with religious doctrines, symbols, and institutions as such; whereas in the history of faith these are all symptomatic elements "immersed in the common life of a community." The faith seeks to become embodied, and to rule the community; it is the most significant element in the veritable life of the Jewish people. In his *The Kingship of God*, Buber began this authentically true history of Judaism with the dictum of Gideon spoken in the period of the Judges, though he refers, to be sure, to more remote antiquity—to Moses and the Covenant at Sinai. Sixteen years later (aside from *The Prophetic Faith* which he wrote in Hebrew in 1942), Buber followed *The Kingship of God* by the most penetratingly expressive of his books, *Moses*, which of all his exegetical works is most clearly illumined by the radiance of poetry. The presence of this poetic element does not, to be sure, mean a diminution in scientific accuracy but rather an increase in power transcending the most conscientious scholarly work.

Penetrating ever more deeply into the darkness of history, he has most recently scrutinized the primordial sagas concerning the life and achievement of Abraham, in his *Sehertum* (1954), to which the chapter on "Israel in Egypt" in the volume on *Moses* is thematically related, constituting a sort of prelude. In the entire series, however, which includes also the complicated structure of *The Prophetic Faith,* and in a very real sense in the entire body of tales and studies concerning Hasidism (including the chronicle novel *For the Sake of Heaven*), the basic concept remains the same: YHVH alone is King over His people which stands in a covenant with Him, and carries forward its unmitigable task of becoming a "holy people," a people made up of those "directly serving" Him; and consequently faithfully and lovingly realizing in all of their actions and abstentions the order of God, the inviolable justice.

Thus in Buber's view it is erroneous to maintain that any changes took place in the core of Judaism in the course of its historical development! For such change here means apostasy which means downfall. The faith itself, to be sure, appears in every concrete life situation in the course of history (in the life of the people as in the life of individuals) as something continually conquered anew and given fresh form through this sacred struggle. But in the deepest core, in the heart of the faith, the central concern is ever the same, just the becoming real without exception of the Kingship of God. At the most, a *tema con varia-zioni* is tolerated, but never an unfaithful abandonment of this theme of all themes.

In this monothematic symphony resounds the word of Gideon, whom, after his victory over the Mideanites, they wanted to summon to be king and who declined to become king (Judges VIII:22)—resounds like other sayings, but in full agreement with words of knowledge and will of the same nature. In Buber's paraphrase, which stresses lasting rather than the variable elements, Gideon's saying reads thus:

His refusal, born out of the situation, is valid as an unconditional one for all ages and historical configurations. For it leads to an unconditional yes, a proclamation of the king in eternity. I Gideon will not rule over you, my son will not rule over you—therein is resolved: no man shall rule over you. For it follows: it is YHVH, the God Himself and He alone who shall rule over you. This saying dares to take theocracy seriously.

Buber has labored indefatigably to clarify the distinctive aspects of this unique theocracy, the central point of the Jewish faith. It is characterized by the

exclusiveness which prevails in the relationship of faith, as it prevails in true love between man and man . . . Israel's faith in God is characterized, finally, by the fact that the relationship of faith by its very nature wants to be valid for the whole of life and to work in the whole of life. This would preclude turning from prayer to YHVH toward a mode of life in which one honors other powers or even recognizes them in one's 'Weltanschauung.' He who speaks to his King and God this fervent, singular Thou cannot at other times dwell in spheres for which he is not competent; he must subordinate them all to the One.

In another place Buber formulates the same problem in an especially precise fashion: "There are no political spheres outside of the theopolitical. All the children of Israel have immediate access to YHVH Who chooses and rejects, assigns commissions and withdraws them; all the children of Israel are Kohanim in the original sense, which is customarily translated as priests." The absolute sovereignty of God cannot be diminished and He cannot be manipulated,—for which reason magical rites are excluded and prohibited. The person endowed with grace feels that God offers Himself to him; but this divine presentation cannot be coerced in any fashion, although man does have the power to remove the impediments in its way. "It is impossible to reach after immediate contact with God, but one can keep himself free and open for it; it is impossible to produce the true dialogue with God, but one may place himself in readiness for it."[1]

Karl Jaspers[2] commenting on Biblical faith comes to similar conclusions: "The person who really becomes aware of his freedom simultaneously becomes sure of God for the two are inextricably related. I do not achieve freedom by dint of my own effort, but it is bestowed upon me: for I may miss it and I certainly cannot in any case forcefully achieve it. The highest freedom, namely that which brings liberation from the world (or earthly powers), simultaneously recognizes its deepest ties to transcendence."

The notion of God's rule remained alive, as we can see from the stories of Gideon, Samuel, Saul, and David. It continued to be effective in the Prophets who for the sake of God's kingdom dared to oppose the kings of Israel and Judah as soon as they deviated from the correct line. "The uncontrollable drive toward independence characteristic of the Semitic nomad, who will not permit anyone else to lord it over him and to coerce him, finds satisfaction in the thought that all the children of Israel may stand in the same immediacy of

---

[1] Sehertum, p. 73.

[2] In his Einführung in die Philosophie und der philosophische Glaube.

approach to YHVH. But this drive toward independence is controlled by the fact that YHVH Himself is the author and guardian of the law."[3]

From this there results the paradox, already inherent in the covenant at Sinai, of all original and direct theocracy,—that it accepts the inviolability of the human person,—the drive of a man to be independent of another, not for the sake of freedom but rather in the interest of the highest type of obligation."[4] What is required of Israel is the unlimited recognition of the actual dominion of God over the entire life of the people.[5] This implies that no segment of the national life may be excepted as constituting a "secular domain." According to the fundamental orientation of Israel's faith there can be no recognition or acceptance within its domain of the kind of sufferance of "necessary injustice" or the "harsh facts of *Realpolitik*" which are all too often served up as excuses.

Hans Kohn in his biography of Buber[6] which is particularly instructive for the earlier period of Buber's life, shows clearly what this faith meant when it was temporarily resurrected in Hasidism. For it and for Buber, who became the authentic interpreter of this brief renaissance of Israel's faith, the essential faith of Israel was the "total sanctification of all human action." Other historians, e.g., Dubnow, have represented Hasidism as not much more than a dismal confusion of diverse currents, communal struggles, denunciations to the government, and similar malpractices, with only occasional flashes of spirituality. In these very diverse depictions of Hasidism by Buber and Dubnow one has the clearest possible demonstration that in historical accounts everything depends on whoever it is that is reconstructing the past.

In his early works Buber still endeavored to grasp the distinctiveness of Judaism by means of theoretical definitions which now and then found their mark accurately but on occasion led to a certain danger zone precisely because of the sharpness of the abstract expressions or the distinctions employed. I have in mind Buber's famous

---

[3] *Moses,* pp. 158ff.

[4] *Das Königtum Gottes,* p. 143.

[5] *Ibid.,* p. 160.

[6] *Martin Buber—sein Werk und seine Zeit—ein Versuch über Religion und Politik,* pp. 75ff.

addresses[7] before the Prague circle over which he exerted so enduring an influence. Even in the book that followed, *Vom Geist des
Judentums,* (1916), there still are to be found such distinctions as
those between "an orientating attitude toward the world" *(orien-
tierende Einstellung zur Welt)* and realization *(Verwirklichung).*
These seem indeed to be precursors of the coordinates of the later
view of the world developed by Buber—viz., the I-Thou relationship;
I-It relationship; and dialogical life *(Dialogisches Leben,* 1947). But
compared to the subsequent work there is still lacking the unique
characteristic of this activistic thinker, his really vehement insistence
on the concrete and existential. In the language of 1916 he still employs rather obscure conceptualization such as, "not the content of the
deed makes it into truth but whether it occurs in the conditional
fashion characteristic of man or in the unconditional which is the
mark of the divine." This language later gave way to a luminous
clarity.

In my mind there has remained unforgettable a small remark,
actually a footnote, made by Buber in his book of 1916, *Vom Geist
des Judentums,* because *in nuce* it clearly foreshadows the significant
changes which were to come about in Buber's point of view. Indeed
it has been my experience frequently that such a tiny passage may
make an author more comprehensible to me than many chapters.
"It is through the cracks that one becomes aware of the abysses,"
is Flaubert's description of such passages which suddenly vouchsafe
deep insights. My opinion is that one may forget the entire *Iliad* but
one will never forget the moment when the infant son of Hector, who
is saying his farewell, is terrified by the plume of his father and
clings sobbingly to the breast of his nurse while his mother smiles
through her tears. This detail is unforgettable. So too is the point
where Buber endeavors to explain the plural form of *Elohim,* one
of the names of the Eternal. His point is that despite the plural
form this term conveys the unity of associated creative powers, of the
"divine clouds." Marginally he observes in small type as follows:
"Here I can merely point to the results; whoever reads the Biblical
text without prejudice and with understanding for the meaning of
the original Hebrew words will easily be able to assemble the proofs."
In this remark one senses the essence of his whole subsequent work
on the Bible, the translation which he and Rosenzweig undertook to

[7] Later published in *Drei Reden über das Judentum* (1911).

produce with the greatest faithfulness to the structure of the Hebrew language. And after the translation? "The results of many years of Biblical study," Buber writes in the Preface to the *Königtum*, "I had originally planned to assemble into a theological commentary which would treat the problems of the Hebrew Bible in the same order in which they occur in the text." Because of the tremendous scope of this enterprise he abandoned his plan and instead produced a long series of historical and critical monographs. Fortunately Buber did not leave it to each one of us to "assemble the proofs easily." He himself undertook this labor and, as was suggested at the outset of this essay, has carried it forward to such an extent that we have before us a history of what Judaism is and has meant from the pristine days of the patriarchal sagas until modern times. There is one possible gap in this almost unbroken sequence which reaches from the ancient apocalyptic literature to Hasidism, but in the volume *Israel and Palestine* (1950), he has supplied significant materials for closing this gap.

"Actually all these are manifestly attempts on the part of Scripture to point to traces that are almost erased," Buber once exclaimed poignantly,[8] as he confronted the monuments of Jewish antiquity which are so difficult to decipher and indeed yield up only hints as to their meaning. Yet he scores a surprising success in apparently the simplest fashion as he reconstructs the situation in which a particular verse of the Bible was spoken. This learned and intuitive reader of the Bible has thereby called into being a new method which does not dissect and disintegrate the traditional text into various "sources," bur rather regards every section which has a unity of content as a unit, seeking only to liberate it as far as possible from what are manifestly later additions and reworkings. For the rest he approaches the Scriptures with impressively painstaking philological erudition. He takes the Hebrew text more seriously than is normally done, giving close attention to the vocabulary and particularly to the repetitions of words, be the latter normal, infrequent or rare. The connection of related passages is disclosed by a system of cunning signals provided by the words that are repeated which point to one another; and the significance of events memorable to the Biblical narrator, viz., an unforgettable concrete meeting with God, is wondrously conveyed by the rhythm. I regard as masterful Buber's treatment of the burn-

8 *Moses*, p. 131.

ing bush, the Egyptian plague, the battle with the Amalekites, the Decalogue and the rebellion of Korah. In all cases Buber remains fundamentally closer to the tradition than all the modern exegetes who are not of orthodox persuasion. He seeks and defines in his own distinctive way,—which lies somewhere between literal acceptance of the text and vapid cleverness.

The last period of the history of Israel's faith treated by our interpreter, apart from his work on Hasidism, is that of prophecy at the point of its contact with the great apocalyptic visions which appeared alike in Judaism, Christianity and Gnosticism. It seems to me that in this matter Buber does justice to prophecy, but here and there seems to react negatively and ironically to the apocalyptic message in a way that I do not understand. In his judgment the apocalyptic literature contained something of the "literary" in the pejorative sense of the inauthentic. But for my part I hear the cry of genuine frustration and despair combined with impotence, hence the voice of the darkest desperation. On the other hand, the prophet still stands in conversation with God, proclaiming his summons to repentance and demonstrating the way of salvation which lies only in a return to God.[9] In this instance, as always, Buber teaches us with great clarity how to distinguish the two movements. Whereas the prophet is always able to permit hope to shimmer through, the apocalypticist unveils the catastrophe that has already befallen, and from which there is no escape, as becomes terrifyingly clear in the sulphurous atmosphere of that final time. But I am unable to accept Buber's evaluation of apocalypticism. Concerning John the Baptist, Buber writes in his *Sehertum:*

He charges his hearers that they must themselves undertake the desired repentance in their own behalf and thereby he places this charge as a daring self-surrender and as an inner transformation of the entire human world at that hour of history. After Jesus as well as his apostles renewed this call to repentance, the apocalyptic writers and their friends proceeded to disclose that there was no longer any possibility of repentance and consequently no possible alteration in the destiny of the world. But the depth of history which is ever at work to renew creation is on the side of the prophet and covenanted with him.

There is beauty and consolation in this remark, yet it seems not to have assigned sufficient weight to the fact that between the ap-

---

[9] Cf. *Der Glaube der Propheten—Sehertum, Anfang und Ende.*

pearance of John the Baptist and the apocalypse of Ezra something as terrible and unthinkable as the destruction of Jerusalem and the terror of the year 70 had ensued. Certainly these events must have distracted the minds of all who lived through that unbearable suffering—at least for a whole generation. Yet when the philosopher in concluding this small but weighty book turns to the modern scene and speaks of the "contemporary apocalyptic" which has "so to speak now become a permanent condition," he expresses a criticism of our time with unwonted satire, with which we must declare ourselves to be in hearty agreement. Rarely has one heard Buber crack the whip of irony so sharply as in the following remarks:

Yes, it is known precisely what in our aging world is right and what is not. Should anyone proceed to reject the impediments which have arisen in all human relationships, and that atmosphere of a false factualness or scientificism whereby people no longer regard others as partners in their life but merely as objects to be manipulated in certain concrete situations, such a critic would be accused of giving voice to an illusory romanticism. If today a person arises to protest against the paralysis of the dialogical relationships among human beings, he is answered that he has failed to recognize the fateful loneliness of modern man—as though it were not the basic lesson of every new loneliness that it must be transcended in a more comprehensive fashion than every preceding one.

As he traced the sequence of the various epochs in the development of the Jewish faith, Buber came to the threshold of early Christianity. In his book *Two Types of Faith* he crossed this threshold. Now he read the Greek text of the Gospels and the Epistles with the same critical dedication to the sound of the words and their meanings, to style, rhythms, and repetitions, and with the same contemporary and direct understanding for the particular situation involved, which has unfailingly characterized his exposition of great religious texts. In short, methodologically he read the New Testament with the same dedication of a person resolved to experience concretely the unique full meaning of the text as he had interpreted the Hebrew sentence structure of Israel's Bible. One of his major findings is that the concept "I believe" in the realm of ancient Jewish Christian writing at the time of the emergence of Christianity has two distinct meanings. The Hebrew word *emunah* means belief, confidence, steadiness, faithfulness, loyalty. In the chapter on "The Battle" in his *Moses*, Buber notes it is not the same as *pistis*, the Greek word used in the Gospels, which means belief in the sense of "recognizing that something is true—that something is one thing rather than another." Elsewhere[10] it is suggested that the concrete content of this Greek word is "that a man crucified in Jerusalem is their [i.e., of all souls] saviour." Buber believes that when the Greek word *pistis* occurs in the Synoptic Gospels it generally is still employed in the sense of *emunah,* i.e., a confidence and trust in the depth of the unique situation and the fulfillment of that which is believed, the transformation of the whole soul of man ("for the Kingdom of God approaches"); in short to employ the customary expression, this connotes the complex of ideas of the Biblical prophets. On the other hand in the Johannine Gospel and particularly in Paul's teaching, *pistis* has already taken on its distinctively Greek connotation. "What was gained was the most sublime of all theologies; but it entailed the loss of the simple, concrete, situation-bound original dialogical relationship of the man of the Bible, a position which the Jesus of the authentic tradition still occupied, who, like Biblical man, found eternity not in some super-temporal spirit but in the profundity of the real moment of time."[11] In Buber's view, faith in the sense of holding certain propositions to be true was something alien to the Hebrew Scriptures and represented an intellectualistic transformation of the concept of faith, and one that was borrowed from Greek teachers. In my view, this differentiation of the two elements is excessively sharp and rather places into the background the Platonic elements in the Greek mode of thinking. Indeed Greek thought and philosophizing, understood as a type of life (demonstrated in Plato's *Seventh Letter*), also evolved from a "community of living" (*Lebensgemeinschaft*) which may not be equated simply with other subjects of instruction. Rather does it "emerge suddenly in the soul like a light enkindled by a darting spark which subsequently nourishes itself by its own effort."

No matter how highly one may value the importance of these exceptional Platonic components in Greek culture we must nevertheless learn from Buber's exposition that in general usage the two complexes of life and modes of attitude designated by *emunah* and *pistis,* represented two very different things. Buber admits, however, that in Judaism there were strong elements comparable to *pistis* and that conversely in Christianity there were components of the personal *emunah.* The boundaries are not rigidly fixed, nor must the common elements be overlooked, as developed in Buber's very important final

[10] *Zwei Glaubensweisen,* p. 176.
[11] *Ibid.,* p. 33.

chapter which treats of the crisis in both religions and his hope of a common transcendence of this crisis, about which more will be said below.[12]

Notwithstanding the very important reservations and limitations of his thesis, which Buber himself voices, we read from the outset of his book with increasing explicitness the divergent aspects of the two types of faith. "To believe in the sense of *emunah* means 'to have faith in someone without being able adequately to prove or justify my faith in him.' On the other hand to believe in the sense of *pistis* signifies the recognition of some proposition as true without being able adequately to prove or justify the acceptance of this proposition. "In both cases we are dealing with an inability to prove the belief in question not because of any lack in my intellectual capacity but because of some fundamental uniqueness of my relationship to what I have confidence in or recognize to be true."[13]

In both cases rational factors are involved together with others but they do not play a decisive role. What is fundamental in both is that the personal wholeness of the believer is set in motion and consequently the capacity for rational thought also becomes involved with other powers of the soul, in which it finds its place. But the relationship of faith is a contact of my wholeness with the being in whom I have confidence. "On the other hand the *pistis* relationship is a recognition, avowal, or assertion that something or other is so, and specifically that Jesus Christ is the Son of God and that only through belief in him can one be saved." This complex of theses is particularly developed by Paul. "There is no salvation other than through Christ. Paul is almost completely silent in his Epistles on the subject of the turning to which Jesus, like the prophets and the Pharisees had summoned man. He recognizes only the attachment to Christ through

[12] Buber evaluates these components and the Seventh Epistle of Plato in his *Gottesfinsternis*, p. 52, but not in the same context as we have just adduced. In subsequent pages (124ff.) Buber gives one of the most magnificent expositions of Plato's system of thought known to me. The only thing I miss in it is that the reference to that which unites it with classical Judaism, the notion of "Moses-Atticus," is not developed sufficiently. The extremely important essay on "Religion und Ethik" in the same book recapitulates once again the position set forth in *Zwei Glaubensweisen* concerning the relationship of Judaism and Christianity and his objections to Pauline theology.

[13] *Zwei Glaubensweisen*, p. 5.

which alone primeval innocence, the basic relationship of mankind
before Adam's original sin, could be restored."[14]

It is apparent that Buber draws a different line of demarcation
between Judaism and Christianity than is ordinarily done. Jesus is
placed together with the prophets and the non-hypocritical wing of
the Pharisees, the true representatives of this attitude, in the camp of
classical Judaism which Buber in the long line of works mentioned
above has depicted as a living unity. Essentially Christianity begins
with the passionate and magnificent conceptual structure of Paul and
his followers, into which much Hellenistic thought had entered along
with classical Judaism. This tremendous shift is described by Buber
as the termination of "immediacy in relationship to God."[15] Henceforth the formula was to be "I am the Door" (John X:9). This did
not entail, as Jesus had meant, to knock upon whatever door was near
to where one happened to be standing: nor did this mean as the
Pharisees had thought to enter into an open gate. Access was now
limited to those who believed in "the Door."

. . . In Paul we no longer find the doctrine of Jesus concerning the immediacy of prayer. . . .It is as though since the time that Jesus had instructed
his apostles, a wall had been erected about the Deity in which only one
door had been broken open. Only to those individuals for whom it opened
would there be vouchsafed the sight of the gracious God Who has redeemed
the world; whosoever remains remote from this door is given up to the
Satanic host to whom the god of wrath has abandoned man.

Hans Joachim Schoeps has made available to us new and rich
material concerning this problem in an important and thorough investigation.[16] His general conclusion is that the surprising doctrine
of Paul met with much resistance and indeed decisive rejection in
the circle of the original disciples of Jesus. I am not certain, however,
whether such precise differentiations were possible within the passionate circle of believers. In this respect I incline, as one who has constantly learned much of importance from Buber, to a position expounded by him in another context that, in judging a complicated
historical situation, one must be wary of excessively sharp alternatives.

In order to provide maximum clarity for his differentiation
between two types of faith Buber goes back to the Book of Job.

---

[14] *Ibid.*, p. 164.

[15] "Die Unmittelbarkeit ist abgetan."

[16] *Theologie und Geschichte des Judenchristentums* (1949).

For Israel, in keeping with the essence of his faith, everything depends upon being able to realize one's faith as an experienced trust in God. One can 'believe that God exists' and yet live in the shadow of God; but whosoever has trust in Him lives in His sight. Indeed trust can exist only in the full actuality of the *vita humana*. Naturally there are different degrees of trust but none which needs for its fulfillment only the realm of the soul as contrasted with the entire domain of human life. To have trust means by its very essence to demonstrate one's faith in the fullness of life, despite all possible experience to the contrary.

In the theology of Paul and earlier in Alexandrine and Hellenistic Judaism (the faulty Septuagint translation) Buber sees a narrowing and impoverishment of that fullness of life which had blossomed forth in pristine Biblical Judaism. In place of the person characterized by a simple trust in God who endeavors by dint of this faith to transform all of life in the direction of justice without reservation, there now appears the man whose sins God does not count, who is justified, declared innocent in the trial. But according to the view of Paul man is acquitted of his guilt only through a belief in Christ (Romans III:22, Galatians II:16) through the belief in one who has come, and died on the cross, and has risen again.[17]

In the Lord's Prayer and the Sermon on the Mount Buber finds a whole string of original Jewish elements. Indeed this holds true even of those passages which are introduced by Jesus' assertion "but I say unto you." Even in these, where he manifestly appears to depart from the tradition of Judaism, he remains within it, when it is correctly understood, taken in full seriousness, and eschatologically sharpened.[18] Buber demonstrates this emphatically and, by and large, I agree with him, though with some difference in details, as is indicated by my novel *Der Meister*.[19] Buber puts it as follows:

All in all the dictum of Jesus regarding love for one's enemies derives its illuminating power from the Jewish world in which he stands and which he appears to combat,—and he irradiates it. So it is ever when one who stands under the sign of the Kairos demands something impossible like this, with the result that he compels men to desire more strongly than hitherto that which is possible. But one must not overlook the bearers of the invisible light from below, the level from which he has risen. These had required of men many things that were possible in order to prevent them from despairing of fulfillment, that they could serve God with their poor work-a-day routines.

[17] *Zwei Glaubensweisen*, p. 49.

[18] *Zwei Glaubensweisen*, pp. 68ff.

[19] Cf. also my *Heidentum, Christentum, Judentum*, 2 (1921), 171ff.

When Buber speaks of the bearers of "the invisible light" he means the Pharisees and the official leaders of the Judaism of that day, insofar as they did not belong to the "hypocrites" (i.e., those who simulated inwardness). But at that time the ruling party was that of the anti-Pharisees who enjoyed the protection of the Roman army of occupation; these were "Quislings," if one were to use a half-forgotten term of opprobrium, but recently so actual.

Jesus regarded the Torah, the traditional instruction, as capable of fulfillment. Indeed, following the Rabbinical example, he even went beyond its requirements. It is of note that Buber translates the Hebrew word Torah as "instruction" in keeping with its root meaning, even as the word moré, deriving from the same root, means "teacher." The dynamic power, love-suffused, of this instruction which continues forever and involves the teacher in ever new forms of vital relationships (cf. Plato's "sparks") becomes greatly impoverished if one, following the Greek translation and Paul, translates Torah coldly and rigidly as "law." According to Paul, the law has been given to us only to drive sin forward by virtue of the impossibility of fulfilling it. Only faith (pistis) in a Messiah who has already come can liberate us from sin. No system of thought has been able to enkindle in like fashion such illustrious spirits as Augustine, Thomas, Luther, Pascal, and Kierkegaard, finding confirmation or contradiction therein, as the paradoxes of Paul. These do not come down to us "sicklied o'er with the pale cast of doubt," but erupted volcanically, glowing with lava, and revealing a hundredfold his inner stresses.

Buber unequivocally indicates his opposition to Paul, sometimes marking off his own stand with vehemence. He points to a whole series of vital complexes, for example, of "obduracy" which has quite another meaning in the Hebrew Bible than the one assigned to it by Paul. Buber remarks that he is unable to recognize in the deity described by Paul, the God of Jesus' doctrine. "Like the prophets, Jesus regarded this epoch not as the domain of evil but as one in which the powers were struggling for supremacy. There is in the world a kingdom of Satan which resists the coming of the Kingdom of God. But the domain of evil has only invaded the Kingdom of God and is not co-extensive with it." In the last formulation Buber sums up the core of classical Judaism which in all areas of life regarded the threat of evil as real but also emphasized the possibility both of man's free decision for the good and of his voluntary action, as well as of the *return* to the good way through trust in God. Paul, on the other hand, regarded the world and "all flesh" as being in the power of the evil inclination, with the one exception, which was sharpened to the demand for belief in Christ as the saviour of the world on the basis of a divine cosmic plan operating from the very beginning of things. According to this faith only the sacrificial death of Christ and his subsequent resurrection could break the power of . evil. With regard to this position Buber remarks that for one who follows the Jewish type of faith there is required "an almost impossible act of believing." "On the other hand the way was completely open for the Hellenistic 'heathen' by virtue of his belief in dying and resurrected mystery gods."

In connection with this problem Buber devotes a chapter to the much discussed and essentially insoluble riddle of the "self-image" or "self-understanding" of Jesus, which he brings into relationship with the suffering of the "servant of God" in Deutero-Isaiah, to the traditions about Enoch and Elijah, and to the Book of Daniel. "The history of his [i.e., Jesus'] last days is so densely covered over with dogmatic certainty as to make impossible all attempts to reconstruct his actual utterances at that time." Yet one dictum of Jesus reported in the "account of the trial which in general must be regarded as unhistorical,"—namely that regarding "the son of man or the man whom one will see coming in the clouds of heaven," (a reminiscence of the vision of Daniel) Buber believes to be particularly revealing as to what Jesus thought about himself in the final period of his struggle. In Buber's judgment he regarded himself as "one to be removed in the future and subsequently sent forth to fulfill His service." This is a continuation of the Deutero-Isaiah conception of the "suffering Servant of God" who has been removed and will return and who will be transformed from his earthly condition to a heavenly being. At this point apparently "especially through Paul and subsequently through John the work of deification has begun."

As opposed to these later developments there stands the remark of Jesus rejecting deification (Mark X:17): "Why do you call me good? No one is good save God alone." Buber asserts that "no theological interpretation is able to weaken the directness of this assertion." Furthermore, noting that this dictum has been preserved in spite of the Christology which later developed, Buber stresses that its genuineness can scarcely be doubted. Concerning it he makes the following significant observation: "This dictum of Jesus concerning himself continues the great line of the Old Testament proclamation of the non-human status of God and the non-divine status of man in a unique fashion expressive of his own personal point of departure and system of reference. Moreover in opposition to the tendencies toward deification current in the post-Augustinian ecumeny and its preoccupation with becoming divine and the making of gods, it asserts the fact of continued human status. The historical depth of the moment in which the remark was uttered must be understood from the deification which the speaker expected after his death. It is as though he were resisting this development, as though he were rejecting the faith in himself in favor of an immediacy of faith in God which he felt and which he wished to help man attain. Truly, what is involved here is the Hebraic *emunah*."

On the other hand, Buber does not lose sight of the impressive historical fact that a great salvation came to the Gentiles by virtue of their belief in Christ,—the belief in Jesus elevated to the status of God,—and that by virtue of this belief (that is, through *pistis* and not *emunah*) they came by a god "who did not fail them in the hours when the world fell to pieces about them and who offered them atonement in the hours in which they found themselves fallen into guilt." Buber also adduces quotations from Dostoyevsky and from the book, *Vater, Sohn und Geist* (1909) of Söderblom which contains the paradoxical observation that "a person may feel a doubt concerning the divinity of God but not about that of Christ." In his perspicacious presentation Buber does full justice to a great faith that is not his own (and in his judgment is not the belief complex of Jesus either).

In the introduction to *Two Types of Faith*, he mentions four Christian theologians to vital and occasionally polemical contacts with whom he owed much,—Rudolf Bultmann, Albert Schweitzer, Rudolf Otto, and Leonhard Ragaz (whose loyal friendship to Israel is particularly praised.) It may well occur to the reader that the depiction of Christianity might have been even richer if reference had been made to Christian *poets* as well as to *thinkers*. Of course Dostoyevsky is mentioned; but I am rather suspicious of him because of his enthusiasm for war. I have in mind, however, such figures as the pure personality of George Bernanos from whose writings the *Sun of Satan, Deception, Diary of a Country Priest,* and *Lettres aux Anglais* so much may be learned regarding true repentance and consequently concerning the bridge between *pistis* and *emunah*.

In Buber's book, *Two Types of Faith,* the mysterious figure of the
Apostle Paul, from whose essential position our sage occasionally sets
himself apart with a vehemence that is not customary with him,
finds a positive affirmation which suddenly breaks through in almost
surprising fashion. As a result, this book is the most dramatic of the
series of works in which Buber traced the history of Jewish faith,
even as *Moses* is the most poetic and *The Prophetic Faith* the most
subtle. In Buber's account it was precisely at the moment when he
surrendered himself to the mystery of a Christ that Paul deviated
from the original Jewish religious constellation in which Jesus had
still remained. This is a view for the significant aspects of which
proofs may be found in the two major works of Klausner dealing
with Jesus and Paul. Thereupon Buber considers a particular passage in Romans (V:10ff) in which Paul referred to himself as having
been formerly an enemy of God. According to Buber this passage
does not refer to the fact that Paul had previously persecuted the
community of Christ, but rather that until then the love of God
for man had not yet been adequately demonstrated to him. "He was
the enemy of a loveless god, or one who appeared to him to be without love" (in another place Buber correctly points out that there are
roads leading from the doctrines of Paul to the thought of Marcion
who assumed an "evil Creator God"). From this erroneous belief, to
which our daily and indeed hourly experience leaves us prone,
Paul first felt himself healed when he came to believe that God
provided atonement between Himself and mankind by means of the
death of His son whom He had sacrificed for the salvation of mankind. Only when he came to realize this significance of Christ's death
upon the cross did Paul know that he had found atonement since
"God had thereby demonstrated His love for mankind." To this Buber
exclaims as if in surprise "From here on I understand His way—now
there are enough clues."

Buber's dialectical understanding of the position and path of Paul
by no means leads him to be satisfied with it despite his insight into
it, and this is highly dramatic too. For basically what appears in the
Pauline conception of history is not any "loving countenance of
God." Rather does he depict "an abyss overflowing with wrath" in
which God gives the "law" so that man may stumble over it and consequently require all the more drastically the grace of the saving
Christ. Buber shows how different is the indignation ascribed in the
Old Testament to God who smites His disobedient child, the people

of Israel, when they do not harken to Him. Paul too regards Israel
as chosen from the very beginning of its history; but he regards all the
generations between the election and the salvation by Christ to have
stood, so to speak, with their hands stretched out in thin air. For
in all that "abyss of time" evil was dominant, having been assigned
automatic control over mankind, completely cancelling out the
spontaneity of human moral effort.

Buber amplified this point in the following admirable passage:

In all this there is no longer room for that immediate relationship of God to
His creatures which is extant in the Old Testament even when God is most
indignant. In the Pauline view God does not wax wrathful but rather hands
man over into the power of fearful wrath permitting him to be tortured until
Christ arrives to rescue him. . . .There is an interlocked cog-wheel of history
which as objectified 'wrath' crushes man until God permits rescue of His
elect ones out of the mechanism at the hands of His son. . . .For Paul
there is no divine compassion in the dimension of pre-Christian history
counterposed to the demonic sovereign power of the raging 'wrath.'

In contrast to this Pauline construction of the course of history
Buber expounds clearly the Pharisaic doctrine of the attributes
and modes of action of God (the *"middot"*). Important supplementary references to the divine attributes are contained in another book
of Buber's, *Images of Good and Evil,* which, if ours were a well-
conducted world, would be found in very many homes as a sort of
domestic Bible, a noble and consoling work and indeed *the* saving
book of our time. In this work Buber presents his own view, which is
diametrically opposed to this pessimistic doctrine of Paul concerning
original sin and the existence of radical evil in us. In Buber's account,
which is based on the events in the garden of Eden and the narratives
concerning the murder of Cain and the Deluge, the primeval Biblical
view does not regard evil as the polar opposite of the good and not as
strong as the good (a view which does not come to light until the
Iranian Avesta). Rather does the Biblical view hold evil to be a sort of
inaction, indecisiveness, and loss of direction of the human soul. "Evil
cannot be perpetrated with the entire soul, only good can be so
wrought." This fundamental doctrine concerning the weakness of
evil in man has its divine counterpart in God's mode of action in
which there inheres gracious mercy as well as punitive judgment,
but God constantly passes from one of these basic modes to another.
He cannot be chained to any one formula and in His innermost
essence He remains true to the dictum enunciated at the burning

bush: "I shall be that which I shall be." "The living God always encompasses the total polarity of that which is experienced in the world of both good and evil. . . . The transition (i.e., from one *middah* to another) simply means that on one occasion one will be primary, and then again on another occasion another will be dominant, according to the purpose that God wishes to accomplish. Nevertheless, and this is of decisive importance, the attributes are not equivalent in power. The *middah* of compassion is more powerful." Buber also cites a Talmudic dictum that the measure of the good is greater than the measure of retribution. This insight into the *middot* again leads to the direct relationship of a man as a totality to God as a totality, both the self-revealing and self-concealing God.

This is the form in which Pharisaic Judaism, by means of its doctrine concerning the *middot,* renewed the Old Testament *emunah,* the great trust in God in all His possible manifestations. It excludes the two great *imagines* which the Pauline world-view set up in opposition to direct and immediate *emunah,* namely, the demonic evil to which the epoch has been abandoned, and the mediatorship of a Christ at the threshold of the next aeon.

As was suggested above, the Pauline view remained that the frenzied force of sovereign evil in the world resulted in the crushing of man and his impulses in a "machine" devoid of grace (apart from the sole avenue of escape through the grace of Christ). I believe that this basic view of Paul, as of the Apocalypse, cannot be understood apart from a comprehensive view of the history of that period and the apparently impregnable power of the Roman military force, even though its chief attribute may strike us as being timeless and appropriate to all human conditions. For there have been recurrently similar "Pauline ages" besides that period in which the Jewish state and beyond that very significant portions of the Jewish way of life and the other great cultures were struck down by the irresistible force of the Roman might. Indeed Buber interprets *our time* correctly as a Pauline age and he has devoted to this hour of human history in which there resounds through the humble cottages of literature the call of Hegel and Nietzsche that "God is dead," his most significant book, *Eclipse of God.* In it he squares accounts soberly and sternly with Sartre, Heidegger and Jung. In the final chapters of *Two Types of Faith* Buber supplements these and other effective critical analyses of so-called modern forms of thought by references to three books: Emil Brunner's *Der Mittler,* which emphasizes particularly the Pauline wrath and rage of God, and Franz Kafka's novels *The Trial* and *The Castle*. Actually the reference above to "machinery" ("of the interlocked cog-wheels of the world," which grind man down) has evoked mental associations with Kafka's *Penal Colony*. Now Buber works out a theory establishing a relationship between the Pauline world view, with a certain pessimistic modification, and the world view of Kafka. "There is a Paulinism of the unredeemed, one in which a fixed location of grace has been eliminated. In this view the world is experienced in Pauline fashion as having been surrendered into the hands of unconquerable forces. But there are significant differences, for there is lacking here the manifest divine will to redeem;—and Christ is absent." This mood exemplifies that status of "permanent apocalypticism" to which reference was made above. That such a world view could arise and could also conquer many non-Christian groups Buber attributes not to any changes in our subjective views but to objective factors deriving from changes in the world situation. We have only to look at our own period of ethical denudation, materialism and technology, culminating in the atom bomb.

This "Paulinism of the unredeemed," which in one decisive respect is even more despairing than the mood of Paul as it has lost the grace of Christ, Buber brings into relationship with Kafka in order to demonstrate the *diversity* of the two positions. Buber stresses that "Kafka remained untouched by this treatment" (i.e., this juxtaposition to Paulinism without salvation). For he is safe no matter how exposed he has become. "The Jew, to the degree that he has not become detached from his primal roots,—and this holds for the most exposed Jew and hence for Kafka—is 'safe.' To be sure he is no longer able to take refuge 'in the covert of Thy wings' (Psalms LXI:5), for God has hidden Himself from the age in which he lives and of course from him, its most exposed son. Yet he is safe because of his recognition of God's being concealed. This means that for Kafka God is not dead. He knows about God's existence, even though it has become concealed for him and He has become an unattainable being from which he is separated by hateful masks and intermediate powers" (cf. the conclusion of "A Message from the Emperor").

Kafka's security comports well and without illusion with the course of the world which constitutes the foreground of his three great novels and numerous short stories, where it is depicted in all its labyrinthine duplicities, with both realism and suggestiveness. In spite of all the

manifest contradictoriness, senselessness, vanity, and ignominy of the
occurrences represented in the buzzing chaos of events and images
depicted by Kafka, Buber hears issuing from it all an affirmation that
"no harm can come to you." A gate leading to the world of meaning
is predestined for every man, even when he does not know this and, a
prey to such ignorance, permits himself to be scared away from this
gate (cf. Kafka's legend, "Before the Law"). Buber also quotes the
following aphorism from Kafka:[20] "We were created so that we
might live in Paradise; and Paradise was designed to serve us. Now
our destiny has been altered, but it has not been declared that a similar alteration is to ensue in the purpose of Paradise."

In contrast to many others Buber does not interpret Kafka as being
merely a nihilistic writer, and he appends to the aphorism just
quoted this illuminating and most welcome remark of commentary:

> From the very heart of this Pauline depicter of the hell which is at the
> foreground of the world, his anti-Paulinism softly and shyly comes to expres-
> sion in his declaration that Paradise is still there and is serving us. It exists,
> that is; it is also present wherever the dimmed ray reaches a heart in tor-
> ment. Are the unredeemed in need of salvation? They are suffering because
> of the unredeemed status of the world. 'All the suffering round about us we
> too are destined to experience.'

Surely this is again a message from out of the very heart of Israel.
The unredeemed soul refuses to give up, for its own salvation, the
existence of the unredeemed world, for which it suffers. It can make
such a refusal because it is secure. This is the aspect of the Paulinism
without Christ and one that is indeed anti-Pauline, that has infiltrated
into Judaism in this age of the deepest concealment of God. The
course of world history is depicted more somberly than ever before
and yet there is a renewed annunciation of *emunah*—soft and shy but
unequivocal, a deepened trust "despite all." In Kafka this *emunah*
has taken the place of *pistis* at the very heart of the Pauline constellation of ideas. Despite all his reserve this latter day wanderer
in a darkened world proclaims anew to the suffering world of nations
that ancient prophecy of Deutero-Isaiah: "Verily thou art a God that

[20] I have repeatedly pointed out, and most recently in the additions to the Third
Edition of my biography of Kafka, that for any interpretation of Kafka's life the
aphorisms are at least as important as his novels. Indeed they are of primary importance, for in his narratives the immortal imagination of the poet has occasionally
overshadowed the factual observations of the author, at least for the less knowledgeable reader.

hidest Thyself, O God of Israel, Saviour!" (Isaiah XLV:15). In this fashion *emunah* must become transformed at an hour of history when God is under eclipse, if faith in God is to be preserved, yet without denying reality. In addition to the aphorism just quoted Buber might have cited many another, some which reveal even more strongly the hope of a break-through beyond the temporary concealment of God, a striving to find some suitable form to express this eventuality. Let me cite one of these passages—the metaphor of a travelling coach—which is among the strongest images in Kafka. It expresses fully the spiritual malaise of our time, the "semi-trance of speed" ("Halbschlaf der Eile"), but it also points in a positive direction; moreover it contains very clearly the implicit trust of a child in his father which Buber has described as the essence of *emunah*. Here is the metaphor:

If you keep on forever speeding ahead paddling the soft air with your hands at the side like flippers, you will see fleetingly in the semi-trance of speeding, everything you are passing by; this may even result in the coach's rolling over you. But if you remain steady and enable yourself by means of your glance to grow deep and broad roots, so to speak, nothing can swerve you from your course though the roots are only the power of your directed glance. Then you will also see that nothing can emerge from the unchanging dark distance but only the coach itself—which will approach ever nearer becoming ever larger and at the moment when it reaches you it will seem to fill the whole world; but then you will enter it and relax like a child on the padded seat of the coach which rides on through storm and night.

In the same spirit of patient trust Buber treats of the contemporary crises of both Judaism and Christianity. To be sure, the crisis is different in the two religions (p. 174ff) because *emunah*, the confidence in God's leadership, is connected with the history of a people and consequently is in danger of splitting off. Indeed, in view of the secularization which has overtaken the people there is a danger that it will lose its spiritual foundation and that on the other hand the religion will remain isolated in the Diaspora without the necessary vital base. Only a great renewal of the holy people, that is one dedicated to God as its Master, can find a remedy for this ill. "Those few who, regenerated in the present crisis, faithfully maintain themselves in their *emunah* have fulfilled their function by virtue of the fact that they have carried the living substance of the faith through the darkness."

Conversely the Christian type of faith is oriented to individuals and so, too, is its crisis. The danger arises in the measure that the autonomy of the redeemed soul and the domain of the personality are no longer able to maintain themselves against the decisive social pressures of the group.

The nub of the matter is the incongruity between the consecration of the individual and the experienced unholiness of his society—a conflict which is necessarily transmitted to the innermost operations of the human soul. The difficulty that thus arises directs attention to Israel's inherited responsibility and the complex of problems resulting therefrom. Yet we may be permitted to surmise that out of these difficulties, too, a way will be found leading from a rigid Paulinism to another structuring of *pistis* which is closer to *emunah*. The faith of Judaism and the faith of Christianity are different in essence, in accordance with their sociohistorical origins. In all likelihood these fundamental differences will continue until mankind will be gathered in from the exile of 'religions' into the Kingdom of God. But an Israel striving for a renewal of its faith through the rebirth of the person, and a Christianity aspiring for a renewal of its faith through the regeneration of nations, would have much to say to each other that has never been said, and could render such assistance to one another as is scarcely imaginable today.

MAX BROD

HABLIMAH THEATER
TEL AVIV, ISRAEL

15

Hans Urs von Balthasar

MARTIN BUBER AND CHRISTIANITY*

MARTIN BUBER is one of the great creative minds of our age. Most of those who have become acquainted with him through his remarkably rich literary work and by the fascination of his personality in lectures or personal meetings, note only one of his aspects: they see the man of wisdom, the religious philosopher, the brilliant translator of Scripture whose genius captured for the first time something of the spirit of the old Hebrew language in German, the indefatigable renewer and interpreter of Hasidism, or, finally, the theorist of contemporary Judaism. They recognize the irrefutable fact that Martin Buber has not just taken his place as one more Jewish writer in the pantheon of German literature, but that he is the only one who, since 1915, has maintained his position in the top rank of German literary figures, despite the fact (or, rather, because of it) that he has represented the reality and essence of the Jew *qua* Jew, and, cutting straight through the blind hatred of everything Jewish, has, in Germany, of all places, gained for himself an undisputed position.

One should keep in mind what this means. Until now educated Jews—from Moses Mendelssohn to Hermann Cohen—as part of their almost exclusive attempts at assimilation, have portrayed the authentic spirit of Judaism as that of humanism. Now comes this bold return to the unique, the distinctively Jewish and it is presented, of all things, with the claim to universality of the Jew of the Diaspora.

There have been others besides Buber who pursued the same end with equal depth and power, among them Leo Baeck[1] and Franz Rosenzweig;[2] but unqualified success was achieved only by Buber.

And it is precisely this success which calls our attention to the most astounding aspects of Buber: the artistry of his spiritual architectonic

---

*Translated from the original German manuscript by Paul Arthur Schilpp and Hans Uffelmann.

[1] *Das Wesen des Judentums*, 2d ed., 1922.

[2] *Der Stern der Erlösung*, completed in 1919; 3d ed., 1954.

and strategy; the integration of his feeling for the right with the appropriate and complete; the integration of the specific weight of ideas with an understanding of their spiritual relationships to each other, of the balance between them, the net of co-ordinates in which to weave the structure of thought created by his own genius. It is an ultimately very simple, monumental structure, well integrated, with no weak spot, except perhaps (and only perhaps) the one which will be our theme.

He draws firm, clear lines, leaving nothing to chance, not even the play of the developing life-process; even the new emergent must prove itself to be the unfolding of what is already given; nothing is taken back. Nor is he concerned to play intellectual games, but with what must constantly be verified in the reality of the here and now. And all rounds which an intellectual might fence with Buber will eventually end by demonstrating the Jewish position in actual history. Buber's *Reden über das Judentum,* which, in ever new variations, are expressed throughout his whole life, are fundamental documents for the Jewish case, regardless of whether or not they are recognized as such by today's Israel (as a world people and as a country).

Inasmuch, however, as Buber wants to demonstrate and formulate the Jewish Idea in today's world in and for this world, the Christian also has no choice but to concern himself with it as well; and, indeed, to do so primarily neither polemically nor apologetically, but in Buber's sense dialogically. Where could one expect, a priori, a more intensive dialogue throughout history than one between the "old" and the "new" Covenant? A glance into Hans-Joachim Schoeps' *Jüdisch-Christliches Religionsgespräch in neunzehn Jahrhunderten*[3] will show how meager this dialogue between Judaism and the Catholic Church of antiquity, of the Middle Ages, and even of modern times actually has been. The existential dialogue came to an end with the letter of Barnabas[4], and the sufferings inflicted upon Jews by Christendom have, for the latter, been nothing more than God's just retribution, not an incomprehensible supplementing of the mystery of suffering—certainly a much more nearly Christian view—, in which Christianity, after all, sees the act on which it was founded.

With the Enlightenment and in liberal Protestantism a breath of fresh spiritual air came into the Ghetto: from the point of view of the

---

[3] Published by the Vortrupp Verlag, Berlin, 1937.

[4] Cf. Karl Thieme, *Kirche und Synagoge* (Olten, Verlag Otto Walter; 1945).

liberal thesis which looked upon Jesus as the religious man who reveres, purifies, and furthers the religion of his fathers, any kind of communication and even mutual understanding became at once possible. [5] But, what was accomplished thereby? One was discussing irrelevant differences in the area of the philosophy of religion. Real dialogue, on the other hand, takes place where the issues are difficult and the results neither simple nor easy. When the issue is not one of fighting for position, but the defense of what everyone takes to be his mandate from God, it cannot be claimed that the severity of such face-to-face "severance of communication" constitutes a denial of the dialogue. And yet there is, of course, such a thing as the situation of an "ultimatum," which can come very close to such severance. The manner in which the two great dialogists of our day, Buber and Jaspers [6], are in the habit of conversing with the Catholic Church points up this situation. Stated concretely, it can only imply the reproach of the Church that, in view of the latter's insuperable dogmatic intolerance, she is actually incapable of any real dialogue. Whatever may be true of Jaspers, we are now only concerned with Buber: it can truthfully be said that, in principle, he has never denied himself to any partner who offered himself as such, although one must say that his conversations with Catholics (aside from the numerous private ones) in no sense equal either in frequency or in intensity those with Protestants.

1. The Voice of the Source

What initially gripped me in my reading of Martin Buber—and, in a dialogical situation it is perhaps permissible to speak of one's self—was the note of original source (*Ursprung*). Not his manner of expression, not even that of his thought (both of which remain caught in their own specific time), it was rather the immediacy and simple directness of being spoken to by the faith of Abraham. We had considered the Old Covenant to be the voice of the past, at most capable of reconstruction from the sacred book in its authentic tone. But, let's be honest: as Christians we did not expect to be touched in depth, questioned, moved, and simultaneously strengthened and comforted in the substance of our act of faith from this direction. Later on we must

[5] Cf. the comprehensive monograph by Gösta Lindeskog: *Die Jesusfrage im neuzeitlichen Judentum* (Uppsala, 1938).

[6] *The Perennial Scope of Philosophy* (New York, 1949).

mention how foreign to each other, for Buber, are the "two types of faith," how much he detests all encounters and short-termed reconciliations: for him with his remembrance of the fate meted out for millenia by Christians to Jews. But in this voice there sounded something of the living source, a sap oozed out from the roots, and, for the first time, I thought I understood the words in the Epistle to the Romans: that (beyond all differences between Jews and Gentiles as concerns the law, ritual, and scripture) both are rooted in the faith of Abraham, "of our common father," who, as father of the one people, was the physical ancestor of the Jews, but, as the bearer of the universal promise ("I have made thee the father of many nations"), the just as real spiritual father of all who really have put their existential faith in His attitude, of the "hope against all hope," in daring venture "giving glory to God." (*Rom.*4) This thought is made even more plain in the 11th chapter, where it becomes clear that the becoming rooted of the spiritual children in the Source does not bypass the physical Israel, but rather, because "God's gifts are irrevocable" (11:29), the Gentiles have to be grafted unto the roots of the physico-spiritual Israel, which was the bearer of the promise. St. Paul does not just mean the "holy remnant," which had saved itself into the Church of the New Covenant from the rejection of the rest of Judaism. Rather he speaks of the "holy root," which, just as it is, sanctifies the grafted wild shoots (the Gentile Christians). "Not thou bearest the root, but the root thee." (11:18) The objection: "Existing branches were broken off, in order that I might be grafted on," is turned down on two accounts: the dialectic of "rejection" and "reconciliation" (11:15) comes, so to speak, from within the Old Testament; and the acceptance of the Gentiles into this encompassing process permits their presence only if they behave as believers (in the sense of Abraham, which precludes all boasting and presumption) in the holy olive tree. St. Paul does not go beyond the insight of the exile-theology of the Old Testament, that the "being cast away," the diaspora among the Gentiles, in the final analysis aims at the universal salvation of all peoples in Israel.

It can be said that Christians have realized this experience of being permanently grafted onto the Holy People only very minimally and often not at all. For them the idea of being rooted in Christ is so central that, from out of the Old Covenant they at most sense a few "precursors" who stood in the bright light of the Promised One as their spiritual ancestors; i.e., that pious band who, throughout life, waited for the coming Messiah, of whom one thinks as being congregated in limbo and who constitute the "spiritual Israel," which, as such, already belongs more to the New Covenant than to the Old. This is the way Origen, Gregor of Nyssa, and St. Augustine interpret the Old Covenant. What remains of the Old Tribe after Christ is merely the "stumbling ones," with a "veil before their eyes and in their heart" (2 Cor. 3:13f), who at most render the Church the service of hearing the holy books in the manner of servants. But this all too narrow theology came to an unexpected end in the new, also ecclesiastical, biblical research—to this extent time is on the side of Israel, and Buber's self-conscious voice speaks at just the appropriate moment. Vital and indisputable biblical theology causes one to realize, first, a much deeper being rooted of primitive Christianity in the Jewish environment and tradition than we had supposed; and, secondly and more generally, the much deeper existential participation of the Jew in the substance of revelation itself: God reveals Himself not merely apropos of a very questionable human history, but a history of God in relation with man (even unto the personal lives of David, of the prophets, of the Psalmist and of Job) can exist only in participation (*Dabeisein*), in man's answer. Not merely isolated individuals, but the anonymous mass of praying and suffering Israelites have, in their hearts, created those words which remain the Word of God to Christians, the "People's Prayer" of the New Covenant, daily singing their psalms. In prayer the Christian soul feels what the Jewish soul has felt.

However the relationship between Judaism and Christianity may finally be precisely formulated, the following remains basic: there can be no Christianity which is not in immediate, inner, existential contact with the "sacred stock," even as is the leaf with the root. This contact cannot proceed from Judaism. Judaism can only either find itself again in Christianity or else find something alien, or a mixture of itself with something foreign. This has been Buber's position from the beginning: at first voiced rather vehemently, later more temperately, but in substance spoken with unchanging precision:

To those who only recently advised us to try to "feel" and sympathize with Christianity, we may perhaps reply that the creative element in Christianity is not Christian but Judaic, so that there is no *need* for us to "feel" with it; all we have to do is to recognize it within us and take possession of it, for we bear it irrevocably within us. And, on the other hand, everything in Christianity that is uncreative is not Judaic, but is compounded of a thousand rites and dogmas, and—speaking as Jews and as men—we have *no intention* of trying to adjust our feelings to it.[7]

The driving power of Christ's message consists in the old Jewish demand for an unconditional decision which transforms man and raises him into the Kingdom of God. This has always been the driving power of Christianity, to which it has always resorted whenever it wanted to rejuvenate itself.[8]

Because Judaism, even before Christ, walked the Path from Abraham's pure faith, the source and origin (as, historically, it becomes even more understandable in the words of Gideon and in the oldest extant songs), through the Law and cult, Kingdom and Priesthood, all the way to the demolition of these husks and forms and, finally, to the acceptance of pure suffering—Jeremiah, Job, the "Servant of God" of Deutero-Isaiah—, therefore it anticipates Christology in its racial existence from then till today. Already within the area of the old revelation, whether as a whole people or in individual representatives, Judaism has experienced itself as the by God ordained for the world's sins vicariously suffering people, has interpreted and known itself the "spectre" among the nations,[9] accepted by no one, not even Christians.[10] The understanding of itself is Israel's simple statement of what it has become in faithful intercourse with God; it is the formulation of something experienced, not that of something believed. Israel is not transcending in this claim—pointing, as it were, to a Messiah, only whose suffering would become truly redemptive for the people and for mankind—, rather it remains self-contained. Insofar as any transcendence would be demanded of her at this point (because in essence the quality of Christ's suffering and redemption would surpass that of Israel), Israel stands before something "alien," at best before a "mystery": "We are incapable of judging its significance, because we do not know it from within as we know *ourselves* from within."[11] Here the door falls shut.

2. Preliminary Scruples

There are many easier ways of coming to terms with Buber than the one we have chosen. For example, one could find fault with Bu-

[7] *Reden über das Judentum* (Gesamtausgabe, 1923), p. 54.

[8] *Ibid.*, p. 88.

[9] Cf. *Die Stunde und die Erkenntnis* (1936), p. 42.

[10] *Ibid.*, p. 161.

[11] *Ibid.*, p. 162.

ber's fundamental theses, theses concerning the essence of Judaism which are put forth with a dogmatism bordering on absoluteness, by which he wants to show that the other (in this instance Christianity) does or does not fit it, and thereby attempt to discredit the entire position.

(1) Doubtless, at the very start where Buber comes to grips with and determines the essence of the Judaic there is a storm sweeping everything before it, a reckless *reduction* cutting straight through the entire history of this ancient people all the way back to its original sources. The abolition of the cult in the year 70 has no significance for Buber, because at that time it had already been superseded: or should we today perhaps begin again to sacrifice animals and to establish an hierarchy of Aaron? But neither is the material content of the Law meaningful to him, and the restriction of Jewish piety in the faithful carrying out of external legalism is an abomination in his eyes. The concept of reward, insofar as it is not a misunderstanding of the sacred texts, is dropped as a now surpassed expression of the ethical. Scripture itself, especially in Buber's earliest period, is seen as purely the expression of the Jewish people's experience of faith. All bars which might interpose themselves materially between the unalloyed personal I-Thou relationship of the Lord of the Covenant and His people fall right and left. Pure, unmediated faith: this alone is life. Every form which presumes absoluteness for itself is already escape, betrayal, partial death, incipient dualism. But for faith unity is essential: this means that there can be no distinction between the sacred and the secular; rather, every aspect even of ordinary, every-day life: family, community, state, economy and politics, etc., must be permeated by the power of faith. There is one thing Israel may not do: divide; God is her King, and already the demand for an earthly king was a retreat from immediacy. However, with this the post-exilic turn towards apocalypticism is also exposed and abandoned: as flight from reality into a visionary Beyond; as is also the turn towards the messianic-eschatological (viewing salvation not as of today, but in an indeterminate future for which one can only wait passively) exposed as degeneration (towards Christianity!). Here and now Israel must be, labor, hope and suffer in faith. Every form of dualism is forbidden. Thus only the "Prophetic" remains as the enduring core: an ever new fidelity to ever new freedom and realization.

With this reduction Buber places himself beyond Jewish orthodoxy and Jewish liberalism, beyond Eastern and Western Judaism, and beyond the spirit of the Synagogue and the Zionist movement. Proceeding from the Source, which is neither ethical nor political but unconditionally religious, he encompasses both sides. What is impossible in Christianity, to view Catholic and Protestant or Protestant orthodoxy and Protestant liberalism from a *single* standpoint, seems here possible. And, inasmuch as this possibility is the source not only of everything Jewish but, at the same time, of *everything* Christian as well, Buber is able, like a sort of judge, to look down upon the interplay of the relativities and nuances of Christendom: Catholicism is said to be right in its emphasis on "works," i.e., in the "conversion" of man as his personal effort of faith; it is right in its emphasis on tradition as over against the letter of Scripture. Protestantism is said to be right in its dissolution of all the contrived absolutes in Catholicism (dogma, sacramental obligation, strict obedience to the Church), in its fusion of all things into pure faith. But both are said to be profoundly wrong where they have followed the heresy perpetrated on the old Law by St. Paul (as insufficient for justification, untenable by man, yes, and even as provoking to sin), thereby committing themselves to an implicit Marcionism.

To this reduction one could possibly reply that it bears the mark of its epoch all too unequivocally: the age of the philosophy of life (*Lebensphilosophie*) and of its absolutistic dynamism, where life always gives birth to form and therein threatens to harden, in order at the same time to demonstrate its life-force by the fact that its waves always keep rolling over everything newly formed. Bergson and Simmel presented such dynamism in an exceedingly restrained and cultivated form. However, this dynamism was preceded by the all-dissolving ethical dynamism of the Marburg School with its unrelenting reduction to the Idea. A dynamism which, in its turn, was to be continued and superseded by the personal dynamism of Scheler, who, proceeding from Bergson and not satisfied to remain with Husserl, penetrated to the absolute of the encounter-in-love, only to end with a tragic-heroic dualism of idea and life. The "Jewish Movement" developed in the midst of these dynamisms, and the young Buber tried to test himself in determining the essential qualities of Judaism: which, in part, in the form of a mystical vitalism, makes Israel out to be the unifying people between East and West; and, in part, exhibits in itself the most deeply wrenched tragedy and dualism, which, precisely because of this, strives after the highest type of unity and therefore achieves the ideal form of human existence. Later, around 1920, as the mystic-monistic vitalism ennobles and softens into the form of the personal, it still retains (as is similarly the case in what has become the classic theology of Karl Barth) the underlying tendency to reduction. One could say it would not be difficult to compare such a religion—synthetically produced on paper or purified and reduced to pure dynamics (a sort of species of extant philosophy) —with a Church like the Catholic, grown through millenia, and to represent the former as pure and the latter as questionable and greatly to be deprecated. True enough, Buber in no way spares the empirically Jewish; he can be cuttingly hard on it (he speaks of the "gruesome pathology of two millenia of our people"[12]). But in its inception the Jewish is pure, whereas the Christian by contrast is in its very essence impure, because it is a composite: it is Judaism with the essentially foreign Pauline-Johannine additions, especially that of the absolutizing of the prophetic in Jesus into the divine.

But, indeed, what does epoch-conditioning mean here, if these dynamisms in the main were created and carried out by Jews and for this very reason have as valid a title to be interpreted as an expression of the Jewish essence as any other derivation? Would Buber, in that case, not simply have found his way back, right through the philosophical disguises, to the primal source? And, as a Jew, does he not have the right to interpret the basic doctrine of Jesus, the Sermon on the Mount, out of its primal sources? The argument from contemporary history can here prove no more decisive than in the case of any great phenomena of history. Everyone lives in his own age; the question is, how much of the inherited situation he is able to re-fashion.

(2) The first notion by which Buber places the Judaic in the limelight and as the human standard for mankind is the highest *simplicity* gained in the reduction: man in pure faith before God. Out of this arises the second characteristic, emphasized by Buber no less strongly and ceaselessly: the perfect unity of this simple human being. The Judaic essentially is the unity of religion and civil society. Without a country Israel is nothing; in the Diaspora it can only be severely ill. In his book, *Israel und Palästina* (1950), Buber developed this ever repeated idea in all aspects. In the theocracy of the Source this unity is set down as the grace of God and a demand upon man. Only in this unity (of spirit and body) does man realize himself before God. For Buber this is the decisive doctrine of the Hasidim, by means of which they

---

[12] *Die Jüdische Bewegung* (1916) , p. 70.

overcome the demonic spiritualisms of the preceding epoch. But this too is the vocation of Israel, to work decisively on the future community of mankind. If capitalism is a degenerate form of a Judaism alienated from its religious motherland, then socialism and communism are closer to its original essence. In *Paths in Utopia* (1950), one of Buber's most exciting books, he contrasts the genuine socialism of religio-ethical realization, proceeding from man to man and federally building itself into nation and state (the ideal scheme for the new Israel) with the totalitarian misunderstanding in Marx. And here it is that Buber, in order to elucidate the complete unity between the sacred and the profane, dares to appropriate the category of the sacramental, of "sacramental existence."[13] The highest embodiment of the sacred for Israel is the land: the land at once to be won by laborious toil in truly human fashion and to be tilled, but also given by God's free grace; at once possessed and only loaned, promise and ever new mission. Moreover: did the severing of the clerically governed Church from the sod, from the politics and technics of humanity produce more redemption than Israel's earthly patience? Somehow, every dualism of sacred and profane, of Church and State, always is mere flight from the real task: here and now to make room for the Kingdom of God by the return to God. Jesus had this in mind, as Ragaz saw quite correctly:

. . . but his message reached the nations not in its genuine form, but in a dualistic form. This dualism which comes to us in its strongest form through St. Augustine—by whom the sphere of the community, of the State, the presupposition that man has to respond with the *whole* of his life, is sacrificed and cut off from the Kingdom of God—, in its ultimate consequence leads to the separation of "religion" from "politics." Again and again the thought of empire tried to overcome this dualism, but always in vain."[14]

But the beginning of this erroneous path is to be found already in the apocalyptic eschatology of later Judaism: the postponement of what is of ultimate significance from the present to a (messianic) future. If one takes the Jewish concept of unity seriously, it can point to the future only by way of the unconditional nature of the demands it makes of the present. And the Utopia which cannot be expressed by anything except a forward projection finally is found to lie nowhere except in present realization. In order to grasp Buber's position here fully, one could assert the absolute *identity of nature and super-*

---

13 See *Eranus-Jahrbuch* (1934); and *Die Chassidische Botschaft* (1952), p. 140f.
14 *Die Stunde und die Erkenntnis,* p. 160.

nature in Buber. Not, of course, any identity of God and man; but the I-Thou relationship between them which for man is at one and the same time both nature and grace. And when man no longer experiences and lives nature as grace, he has forgotten himself as well as God: he has broken the Covenant and is exiled by God.

But it is precisely at this point that the first decisive question has to be put to Buber. If the religion of Judaism is to such an extent "faithful to this earth" that it requires a particular area for its "sacramental" existence, why not also a particular part of time? Must not a genuine sense of the future (which implicitly is to be assumed for humanity in general, for otherwise its temporality would be meaningless) lie in the temporal extension of Israel and of her task for mankind? And, indeed, Buber speaks in this vein. The present form of human society is rudimentary, "unredeemed." In its commission Israel is said to hold the key to a redeemed, emancipated human society. According to the prophetic promise, an Israel which would be faithful to its divine commission could unite the totality of all nations around the radiant Holy City. But what is this [emancipated human society] supposed to be? Is it to be a humanity in which, by way of conversion from below, i.e., proceeding from the individual, the sin and coercive power of the State would be overcome in an organism of perfected community? And this [thought of] as Utopia, Idea, in eternal approximation? Attainable or unattainable? In a system which equates nature and supernature, what meaning can redemption have? Perhaps Buber will reply that this is where the insuperable limitation in the relationship of the people with God can be seen. In Judaism up to the time of the Exile there occurs no such thing as individual eschatology and (therefore!) also no "doctrine" of national perfection. Everything is reduced to momentary obedience; every look into the future is only [seen as] an "alternative." In that case, logically, we would have to return to that limited view, abandon the personal and social perspectives, and live the Truth simply in the claim of each day. But, in this case, whence comes the immense movement toward transcendence on the part of Israel and her futuristic impulse? Does she not aim to transcend herself, after all? Is she not, after all, a child wanting to be born, who is everything except a flat, shallow, socialistic, futuristic perfectionism?

3. Israel's Uniqueness

One central concern remains unchanged in the interpretations of Judaism which accompany Buber's long road: the unification of the particularity and the universality of the essence of Judaism. The Jewish people are one people, just like other peoples and races; but the Jews are not ruled by national deities, but by God Himself, and they are, for this very reason, singularly chosen for the sake of all others. In order, however, to be able to fulfill this universal mission throughout all space and times Israel's particularity must contain within itself a most profound relationship to the universal. The Jew—this is Buber's early solution—in his essential nature possesses the human essence in its broadest and most marked form: his dualism is more dualistic than that of all other races, and this also accounts for his drive towards unity, not merely in God or merely in the world, but, beyond these, between God and world. Thus seen, Judaism is original humanism and, *qua* such, is, whether openly or concealed, the form and propelling force of world history. Nothing entitles Israel more to this claim than the previously mentioned link between fidelity to God and fidelity to the world, two immediacies which no other religion is capable of uniting. This position permits Buber to seesaw between theology and philosophy of religion: everything which he asserts as unique in Israel is a clarification of religious anthropology in general and exists again for it. The Jew is openly what man in general is in disguise and oblivion. The path can simultaneously begin from either end: from the "ecstatic confessions," from the "mystique" of all religions, *and* from the absolute particularity of Israel's mission.

Yet there can be no doubt: the interpretation of this "synthesis" of the unique structure and the universal intent and mission—still maintained by Buber in his later thought—in the course of Buber's development undergoes a change: in the beginning the emphasis lies on the anthropological in Israel, that is to say, on religious philosophy; whereas at the end, it lies on the theological, on the incomparableness of Israel's mission. In the beginning on the kinship with everything human, and at the end on the great loneliness of the call.

The fact of Israel's existence is unique and cannot be fitted in anywhere. The very name, not inherited from father and mother, but given by God to the father of the race, marks out the community as a community which can not be grasped by the categories of ethnology or sociology.[15]

---

[15] *Ibid.*, p. 156.

What liberation, what decisiveness there is in this sentence! However, fundamentally this notion had already been reached in the decision against a mere political Zionism, in his demand for a bond between "Israel and Palestine" which was not relative but absolute, not grounded in mundane values, but in the true theological sense God-created and of sacramental character! A decision so absolute that basically it is scarcely still capable of being carried out by the "modern" Jew of New-Israel; and Buber, in the midst of Jerusalem, remains a solitary figure. Neither the Argentine nor Uganda, though Palestine would be preferable on purely emotional grounds, but Zion and nothing but Zion! Here is the end of all relativism, here we touch rock bottom, here is—*dogma*. Here is the same absoluteness, the same offense to the tolerant person, who, in the end, is able to transpose every religious system into every other one, the same scandal of the absolute bond of an invisible heavenly command to an earthly This and Here. All rambling of the nomad Abraham is here staked to this earth.

Buber may here talk as much as he likes about "two modes of belief," which supposedly are mutually contradictory and incapable of reconciliation. He may reject any and all dialogue between religions (as he did so brusquely with the sympathetic and wise Panwitz who did not quite agree with him at this point), because "each has its origin in an exclusive revelation and aims ultimately at the removal of all exclusiveness," each has its "adytum," which in each instance can only be entered from the inside.[16] Despite this it is still true that Judaism as Buber understands it and the Christian Church as the Catholic understands it are the last two witnesses to an absolute mandate from God to this world: absolute in the irritating sense of being bound to a visible Thus-and-not-otherwise. Everything else is anthropologically and sociologically and depth-psychologically reducible to "philosophical faith" and to the "true catholicity of reason." Buddhism, Taoism, Zoroastrianism, the wisdom of Sumeria, Egypt and Greece: each has its own particular root, but all eventually debouch into the universally human. At only two points does the religious mission resist this reductive tendency. One can become an adherent of any religion; but who is not a Jew cannot become one. And, whoever enters the Church as the Catholic understands it, through the door of inextinguishable baptism, has definitely left behind him the uncommittedness of the "invisible churches" (and even of the World Council of

16 Cf. article in *Merkur* (8, 1954), p. 923.

Churches). No matter how much Jews and Catholics may turn their
backs on each other, on the stage of world history they are bound together involuntarily in a partnership which produces great anxiety.
How they behave towards each other "practically," but also how, beyond this "practice," God handles them "factually," this one may read
in the 11th chapter of Romans.

Everything true that you possess, Buber says to us, you have from
us Jews; we recognize it again in you; and in our primeval depth you
steep yourselves again and again and bathe yourself young again when
you have again become sick and tired of your Greek and Manichaean
ways! Every time the New Testament has cut itself off from the Old,
it went astray, even from the Christian point of view. Too bad that
this tendency of cutting yourselves off is in your very blood, because
it began not merely with Marcion but already with Paul! And the
Jew knows that (the case of Paul left aside for the moment) we cannot but say "yes" to this. We have received everything from the Old
Covenant, because we have received Jesus Christ from it, who was—
and remains—a Jew, and who is inseparable from his people and its
divinely guided history. For us the Old Covenant is so great and indispensable because it is the pre-history of the incarnation of God in
Christ. This event in world history could not be true history at all without the horizontal historical dimension; but as (from the Christian
point of view) the Absolute of history, it demands in its pre-history
the "prophetic," i.e., true, but in its final demonstration, presence of
the Absolute being found in what is to come. Israel's question is so
profound that it can only be answered absolutely. It is in this sense
that the historical dialogue between the Old and the New Covenant is
the *Dialogue of History as such.* It is well known that the young Hegel
discovered here his entire dialectical method and developed it from
here. The synthesis of Christ demands the thesis and antithesis of
Israel.[17] Precisely because of this the form of Israel's Absolute transcends itself inwardly, towards the New Covenant. In its essence
Israel is indeed formal Christology, whose fulfilling content (which
even in its empty form is becoming) is Christ.

This is not the place to demonstrate these contentions; only some
indications are possible. The dialectical "contradiction," again newly developed in the almost shockingly impressive presentation of Martin Buber, lies at the very heart of Israel's divine mission. The one

---

[17] Cf. *Hegel's Theologische Jugendschriften,* ed. by Hermann Nohl, pp. 243f.

people is singled out for the sake of all others, yet not excluded from this world, but horizontally integrated into the rest of the nations: in a boundless loneliness. For, fundamentally there can be no proselytizing: no one who is not a Jew can become one. That from which the communion of all peoples is to proceed is incommunicable, carried so far, in fact, that concretely even the Jewish-Gentile mixed marriage can never lead to a "synthesis" (in the children). The "contradiction" which lies in this true mission becomes nowhere more evident than in the factual twofold pattern of Jewish existence: in the dispersion among the nations and in the reunion (assuming that it should be successful in the long run) in their own country. In the diaspora, where, according to her own theology of the Exile, Israel could be a light and leaven to the Gentiles, she fails to be true;[18] she can flourish, but, in the concrete geographical sense, she ceases to be the leaven of the world. Therefore: can she at the same time be the center of health on her own soil, and the center for the distribution of the healthy ones into the world?

Yes, but this is precisely the revelation of the boundary and of the inner contradiction. The Jew in his homeland is full of longing for the world to which he feels himself to have a mission; but the Jew in the world is sick because of his longing for his homeland. To the Jewish existent there is not granted that synthesis which was experienced by the first Christians as the miracle of a new type of being:

For Christians do not differ from other people by the country in which they live or by language or by their customs; nowhere do they live in separate cities or use a deviating language or live a conspicuous way of life . . . They live in cities of Greeks and non-Greeks, as destiny happens to ordain in each instance . . . though they are only there as visitors; they participate in everything as though they were citizens and submit to everything as though they were strangers . . . every foreign country is fatherland to them and every fatherland is foreign country . . . They love everyone and are persecuted by everyone.[19]

The same synthesis applies to the Christian sacraments which have freed themselves from the temple without the temple's destruction and yet are not in the Diaspora, but are the earthly visible but freed concretion of the God man.

But now, this impulse of the Absolute, which, in Israel, point-

18 Cp. *Die Jüdische Bewegung* (I, II, 1916, 1921) ; "Kampf um Israel," in *Reden und Schriften* 1921-1933 (1933) .

19 *Diognetbrief*, c. 5.

ing to God's becoming man, opens up thesis and antithesis like a pair of tongs, is, where it does not grasp the synthesis, without proper object. The dynamic toward the Absolute exists, but whither is it supposed to turn? Perhaps towards the temporal future of mankind? If this happens, then Israel can become only the organizer of the realm of apocalyptic animals. Her absolutisms devastate the world, just as the dreadful reduction in Sigmund Freud has become a world-wide destruction of the holy in man, raging in the Western world even more dreadfully than in the Eastern. Behind capitalism as behind communism stand Israel's absolutisms. "Man is good!," he has it in his power to convert himself and to change this world, society, the face of the earth into this genuine good. These are the paths of Utopia, and Buber cannot do otherwise than walk in them. (In the strictest, impenetrable consistency of the prophetic principle) Buber cannot offer any future other than the human, the social. And yet this "hope" contradicts Buber's profound wisdom, and his hope is, in reality, no hope at all, and I would suppose he knows this.

Already this, but even more so the final words which remain to be said lie probably no longer on the niveau of the dialogical between a human I and a human Thou, but on that of a mutual demonstration of one's own mandate from above—a mandate which man has not given to himself and which, for this very reason, he can neither prove nor justify as his own. Humanly considered these mandates can, as Buber says, appear to each other only as alien. But, when two sincerely and in humility try to obey their respective mandate, neither on the niveau of the mandate nor on that of the one who gives them are they so far removed from each other as it appears on the merely human view. What remains to be said are, just as this lastly stated one, matters which the Jew, so long as he does not become Christian, cannot possibly admit, but which the Christian thinks he can read off from what is inherently Jewish.

The two open arms of the tongs which in Judaism reach out towards the absolute future of the world, in their openness point no less to the mystery of the Absolute as such, to the mystery of God. In the beginning Buber conceived of Judaism as the exponent of the East in Europe, surpassing all the Asiatic monisms and transposing, therefore, the "Dialogue" of the absolute voice with the finite consciousness into the innermost heart of being. "It is not the word in itself that is the truth here, but life, life lived and the life to be lived;

the word is only true by virtue of life."[20] "Doctrine may assign the Divine to the sphere of the beyond . . . but the springs of life lead us on beyond that separation in that they allow unity to be born in the free act of the complete man":[21] and is this unity not itself the Absolute, God? But then Buber meets the Word in the Scriptures. With his whole being he learns to bow before it as before the objective presence of the wordless mystery—and the monistic metaphysic yields to the "original distance" (*Urdistanz*) which penetrates now from the between men sphere into that of between God and men: a *distance* which is the absolute presupposition of personality, freedom, reverence and love.[22]

Without ever falling into oversimplification by erecting the 'I-Thou' relationship into a general (univocal) category which would embrace the relation of man to man as well as of man to God, it becomes nevertheless a principle which for Buber is decisively indicative of the creature's relation to God. Wisdom was his youthful drive towards a unity beyond words; wisdom is where old age remains in the mystery of the "distance": both ciphers of the Absolute. In an ultimate respect for the unanswerable question Buber leaves the matter open. Only the Christian can here offer an answer in mystery: the Absolute itself is the identity in original distance of the three persons in one being. Nothing but this assertion can answer the question of human existence: why there should be any world at all which is not God? Otherwise the dialogical must relentlessly proceed to Job's question to God; and it is difficult to see how it could ever be saved from the final step which leads from Job to Kafka and to all Jewish complainants against God.

In order to make the absolute "Otherness" of God bearable to suffering man—without escaping into religious magic—Buber takes recourse to the cabbalistic myth which is advanced by Hasidism: the myth of God's *Schechina,* who, together with the suffering ones, wanders into exile, into alienation, into divine darkness ("*Gottesfinsternis*"). They suffer in the invisible shadow of God, their suffering is not merely safe in God, but itself the expression of an absolute, of a God who is suffering in His world as well as for it, a sympathizing God. This is the point where Buber borrows from the cross; for,

20 *Cheruth* (1921), p. 218.

21 *Ibid.,* p. 228

22 *Urdistanz und Beziehung* (1951).

the suffering "Servant of Yahweh" in the Deutero-Isaiah knows the substitution of the suffering man for the sinners, but does not know the divinity of his suffering. In order to demonstrate the mystery of this ultimate solidarity of God with His creatures and yet not interpret it in the form of the incarnation, it was only possible to express it in the concepts of cabbalistic pantheism; But this contradicts the principle of the "original distance" (*Urdistanz*). In the determination to show that no genuine Christian value is foreign to Judaism, the line of what is demonstrable from the Old Testament has here been crossed.

What has here been said could not remain unsaid if Christian and Jew are to talk seriously with each other. And the resounding hardness of the head-on collision here sounds better than an informal parlor-conversation about the contribution of Hasidism to world-piety or about the excellent applicability of the dialogical principle. Only here, where all talk seems useless, in this apparently eternally losing battle, is an ever new encounter worth while. Here in this seemingly frozen silence, in this hidden midst of the religion of mankind, here the only real dialogue takes place, of which all other religious conversations, even those of ecumenicism, are only a feeble echo. The Church which contains within itself both the Old and the New Covenant (and not just the books, but the *Existenz!*), in her essence must constantly experience the fact that this dialogue is due. As long as there is a world the dialogue remains unfinished, unless it be in the only Christ, who, however, could not finish it except by "letting the Jews stand aside" in order to go to his and to their cross.

Buber, however, is eternally right in insisting that the cross of Christ was no cut and dried program of a dramatic castastrophe which was already intended at the cradle and which unfolded itself in a mounting tension throughout Jesus' life. The cross came into view only when the opportunity of the Sermon on the Mount, the opportunity for a "reversal," the chance of Judaism, the opportunity for the Kingdom of God had been passed up. Passed by for Jesus *and* for His people. The Jews rejected the opportunity, therefore the cross; therefore the turn to God's new people; therefore also the Church as the institution on the rock of Peter: this, after all, is the meaning of Matthew's peculiarly Jewish gospel. Buber rejects whatever he finds to be "undynamic," un-Jewish in the Christian Church (what the Protestants for the most part characterize as relics from the Old Testament in the Catholic Church): hierarchy, dogmatism, sacramentalism, legalism, casuistry, etc. All of this is intimately connected with the cross. All belongs to the suffering of the kingdom of God in the world and would not have become necessary if God's people had been converted. The Sermon on the Mount knows nothing of all this. But the delivery of the keys to Peter and the prediction of the coming passion are one. And thus let the final picture, before which both of us are struck dumb with horror, remain: Jesus' tears shed over Jerusalem (Luke 19:41).

HANS URS VON BALTHASAR

THEOLOGICAL FACULTY
UNIVERSITY OF BASEL
BASEL, SWITZERLAND

16

Nahum N. Glatzer

BUBER AS AN INTERPRETER OF THE BIBLE

"Meinen wir ein Buch?
Wir meinen die Stimme."
Buber (1926).

I

FORTY-NINE years ago, in one of his memorable addresses, Buber outlined, however tentatively, an approach to the Bible. Scripture is to be studied not as a work of literature but as a basic document of the Absolute's impact upon the national spirit of Israel. Though conversant with Biblical exegesis, ancient and modern, the student must transcend such exegesis in a search for the original meaning of a passage. He should study the documentary theories of contemporary scholarship, yet penetrate to deeper separations and connections; recognize the mythical element, yet not introduce mythical interpretation if the historical is sufficient; be appreciative of the poetic forms, yet intuit what is more than poetry and form. "Knowledge as a service" (*dienendes Wissen*) is the term Buber uses when speaking of the care to be applied to the original Hebrew of the Bible.[1]

The term properly defines Buber's own work as interpreter of the Hebrew Bible. Its overt beginning falls in the Spring of 1925 when Buber and his friend, Franz Rosenzweig, undertook their epoch-marking translation of the Bible into German.[2] Out of the intensive

[1] "Cheruth, eine Rede über Jugend und Religion," *Reden über das Judentum*, Gesamtausgabe, p. 232.

[2] By 1929, ten volumes (Genesis to Isaiah) were completed. After the death of Rosenzweig in 1929, Buber continued the work alone which he completed in 1961. A four-volume second, revised edition was published by Jakob Hegner Verlag, Köln and Olten 1954, 1955, 1958, and 1962 respectively).

preoccupation with the Biblical text grew organically first a number of scholarly essays on various individual Biblical problems, then a series of books, from *Königtum Gottes* (Kingship of God, 1932), via *Torat ha-Neviim* (The Prophetic Faith, 1942), *Moses* (1946), *Zwei Glaubensweisen* (Two Types of Faith, 1950), *Right and Wrong* (1952). *Bilder von Gut und Böse* (Images of Good and Evil, 1952), to *Sehertum* (Abraham the Seer; Prophecy and Apocalypse, 1955). These books, complemented by a succession of studies and articles, form an Old Testament commentary on a great number of exegetic and linguistic problems as well as on most of the main issues of Israel's internal history and Biblical faith. Buber's tentative rules, formulated in 1918, were fully realized in the following four decades. Knowledge was turned into service.

The present essay cannot aspire to be a comprehensive treatment of the subject. The field of Biblical studies is vast and Buber's contribution to many of its aspects far-reaching and, at points, revolutionary. His studies resist classification into any of the current schools of Biblical interpretation; they resist all classification. Any serious attempt at critical analysis would have to consider the status of Buber's work on the Bible in the context of his own religious, historical, linguistic, and personal philosophy. This short essay cannot, therefore, do more than point to some of the more basic lines of his thinking.

II

In trying to understand a Biblical story, Buber takes as his clue the choice of words and images, of key phrases, the structure of the tale, the rhythm of the report. The purpose of the story is to convey a teaching, to offer instruction, an aim not achieved by an explicit reference. The teaching is unobtrusively inherent in the story itself; here "perfect attentiveness" (*vollkommene Aufmerksamkeit*) is required. This demand of perfect attentiveness—by no means self-understood—best describes Buber's approach. In the long history of Biblical exegesis this attitude was never taken; it "became the task only of this late age to point out the significance of what has so far been overlooked."[3]

Believing that the text as a whole preserves a genuine tradition

[3] *Sehertum*, p. 25.

and that occasional errors in later transmission could not distort its essential accuracy, Buber may safely question the relevance of the theory of parallel documents. The intricate composition of the central stories cannot be conceived as resulting from excerpts from older documents; only a full, rich, plastic narrative tradition can be the source for the Biblical writer's work. Preoccupied neither with problems of literary or linguistic influences on the Biblical texts, nor with historical dependencies, parallels, or relationships, Buber follows the guidance of the text itself.

Thus, Buber cannot read the Abraham cycle as a redactor's combination of stories drawn from divergent sources; a detailed analysis of the texts suggests to him a closely knit composition.[4] Its unifying aspect appears to be a sequence of seven interrelated revelations to Abraham: stations on a way from trial to trial, and progressing to an ever deeper relationship between Abraham and God. Through skillful linguistic allusions, Abraham, the first to make his way into history, is set off against Noah who, standing in nature, a "husbandman" (Genesis 9:20), represents a pre-national humanity. Unlike Noah's work, which is bound up with his time and "his generation" (Genesis 7:1), Abraham's activity marks the beginning of a historic process which is to culminate in the ultimate union of mankind (Isaiah 2:1-5). The consistent recurrence in the text of various forms of the term "seeing" leads Buber to the assumption that it is a "theme-word" (*Leitwort*) chosen by the Biblical annalists to characterize the first patriarch. This theme-word is used with special emphasis in the story of the Binding of Isaac on Moriah (Genesis 22), the last of the seven acts of the drama. Abraham sees, and sees also that he is being seen. Buber calls him the first in the long sequence of seers in Israel. Abraham, the originator of a people, is also the first recipient of the gift of prophecy and is remembered as such by the tradition of later prophets.[5]

This example demonstrates Buber's reliance on structure, style, and choice of words as guides to the intention of whoever wove into one the various tales, memoirs, and reports. The relevant leads come from within.

4 *Ibid.*, p. 33.
5 *Ibid.*, p. 45.

III

Buber's translation of the Bible has freed the ancient text of the layers upon layers of overgrowth. The most often quoted passages especially had lost their original freshness and immediacy of impact. Primeval speech forfeited its power before the mighty array of theological, historical, psychological, and literary ideas. A language of concepts abstracted from reality replaced a language of living words. Moreover, the primary intention of the world-historically important translations, the Septuagint, the Vulgate, Luther's, was not preservation of the original character of the Bible, but establishment of a valid testimonial writ for their respective communities: the Jewish Hellenist diaspora, the early Christian oikumene, the church of the Reformation.[6] In such historically determined situations, the need to accentuate certain facets of the Biblical teaching far outweighed concern for the structure of the text, the primal meaning of the word, and the correlation between content and form.

Buber's (and Rosenzweig's) Bible work is characterized by the attempt—at times it is admittedly no more than an attempt[7]—to go back to the very sources, to rediscover the original writing (*Grundschrift*); Buber himself uses the term palimpsest.[8]

Thus, *torah* is no longer rendered by the much too specific *Gesetz*, law, but by *Weisung*, or *Unterweisung*, which at least approximates one of the denotations of the root.[9] *Prophet*, the customary translation of *nabi*, suggests a prognosticator, although the meaning of the Greek term is rather closer to the Hebrew one; Buber's translation is *Künder*, announcer (of the word of God). *Malakh* has long been presented as angel, which, since it denotes a being of a special order, is misleading for many parts of the Bible. The new translation uses *Bote*, messenger, allowing for a fluid transition from the divine to the human carrier of the message. *Qorban*, the common German translation of which (*Opfer*, sacrifice) evokes associations not intended by the Hebrew (the English "offering" is much closer to the original Latin *offere*), is rendered by Buber as *Darnahung*,

---

[6] "Über die Wortwahl in einer Verdeutschung der Schrift," *Die Schrift und ihre Verdeutschung*, p. 137.

[7] *Ibid.*, p. 139.

[8] *Ibid.*, p. 135.

[9] This, the following, and other examples Buber discussed in some detail in the essay previously mentioned, pp. 144–167.

thus suggesting the meaning of the Hebrew root *qarab,* to come near, be near, and, in its causative form, to bring near. This rendition implies the existence of two personalities, one of which, in an endeavor to reduce the distance between them, comes near (*qarab*) to the other by means of a *qorban.* A careful reading of the Korah story (Numbers 16) shows how important for the understanding of the "offering" is the motif of being distant and coming near. A similar attempt to go back to the original, pre-theological, pre-conceptual, meaning of the Hebrew root, is evidenced in the translation of *kipper* and *kopher* by *decken* and *Deckung* (cover), respectively, instead of the theological *sühnen* und *Sühnung* (atone, atonement). Probably the most significant example of the Buber-Rosenzweig method of translation is the effort to render all the derivates of the root *ya'ad* by the corresponding forms of *gegenwärtig sein,* to be present. *Ohel mo'ed* was understood by the Septuagint and the Vulgate as the tabernacle of the testimony, by Luther as *Hütte des Stifts,* tabernacle of foundation. Mindful of the basic meaning of *ya'ad,* Buber renders the term in question by *Zelt der Gegenwart,*[9a] the tent in which God makes Himself present. Assuming that there is an original linguistic connection between *mo'ed* and *'edut,* the latter, used in connection with the tent, the shrine, and the tablets of law, becomes *Vergegenwärtigung,* the place or the object which will re-present, remind of an event that was once present. So, e.g., the tablets of the law which bore the record or revelation will make the event present to those who were not themselves present on Sinai.

Buber realizes that the meanings, allusions, and associations read into the text by countless Bible reading generations are part and parcel of human history.[10] Such interpretations, regardless of the degree of proximity to the actual text, were the means by which humanity could rally around this book. But Buber considers it his task to decipher the writing itself and read it anew, knowing that the result may be paradoxical and vexing to modern man. "Yet, even paradox and vexation will yield instruction."[11]

[9a] In the 2nd edition Buber changed it to 'Zelt der Begegnung.' In *Königtum Gottes* (3rd ed.), p. 64, he speaks of "das Zelt der göttlichen 'Begegnung' oder Gegenwärtigung."—Ed.

[10] The limit of the justifiable is reached, or possibly overreached, in translating *shabbat* by *Feier, Feiern;* the common rendition *Sabbath* is avoided because of its possible stiffness *(Erstarrung). Feier* is linguistically correct, but historically colorless.

[11] *Die Schrift und ihre Verdeutschung,* p. 167.

IV

The endeavor to explore Biblical faith cannot, in Buber's thinking, be separated from an attempt to discern its relevance for the present-day reader. However, the didactic aspect in no way diminishes the scholar's obligation to examine objectively the scientific evidence and to establish the historic status of a passage, or a book. On the other hand, scholarly investigation, if it concerns the Bible, cannot be an end in itself. When the scholar has done his job, the whole man is called upon to make the scholar's findings the basis for his action. The scholar's work is the necessary presupposition for all that is to come. The untrained mind will stay on the surface of the text, gloss over difficulties, and fail to notice linguistic allusions, implied references, internal connections, to which the ancient reader more readily responded. It is the scholar's task to restore the original structure of the text and to point to its underlying plan. Then, however, the text resumes its perennial function of teaching. Buber will admit that, technically speaking, the actions of the scholar and the "listener" may at times be two distinct roles. But he will point to interdependence, even to the essential unity of the process. The scholar's work would remain incomplete were he satisfied with the archivist's achievement. He would, too, betray his office, were he to deal with his texts so as to suggest a definite and ready application to problems of his day and age. But he will forever keep in mind that the heart of the text, silenced for the duration of his surgical performance, will beat again. The realization that he, the scholar, is not engaged in the analysis of documents of a dead past but confronted by a living text will only increase his vigilance. The criteria of detached scholarship are not sufficient for the achievement of even an adequate understanding of the text. The Bible, document of the dialogue between God and man, can be validly understood by that reader alone who is ready to become a partner in the dialogue, that is, by a man who expects the Biblical word to be as meaningful to him as it meaningfully addressed itself to the generations before him. Only then will he be able to evaluate the special power, the measure of concreteness, inherent in the Biblical narrative, speech, or psalm. The latter is a wholly scientific issue, yet its comprehension is made possible by something admittedly non-scientific: the personal involvement of the scholar.

As an example of how Scripture can give contemporary man a

sense of direction, Buber points to the Biblical motif of correlating, of fusing even, "spirit" and "life."[12] It is one of the errors of modern man that "spirit," in the past seen in its broadest implication, appears to him narrowed down to mean "intellect," while the realm of "life," sovereign, independent, assumes ever larger proportions. This loss of a sense of proportion is countered by the Biblical reference, repeated in colorful variations, to the *ruah*, which is both spirit and wind, dynamically moving between the two poles of the material and the immaterial, nature and spirit. Genesis 1:2 speaks of the *ruah* of God "hovering" over the face of the waters; the ancient Hebrew reader sensed the double meaning of *ruah* and knew that God cannot be restricted either to the "natural" or the "spiritual" realm, that He is neither nature, nor spirit, but the origin of both. In the cycle of the wilderness stories the *ruah* appears both as the "spirit" which God puts upon the elders (Numbers 11:17) and as the "wind" which "went forth from the Lord and brought quails from the sea" (*ibid.*, 11:31); the reader cannot fail to notice the correspondence in the divine activity between nature and spirit, spirit and life.[13]

The narrative of the desert Sanctuary, as compared with the story of Creation, is cited as another example of how Scripture may instruct modern man. As in the former instance, Buber does not discuss overt moral teachings, but issues which only a scrupulously attentive reader will discover in the text. The first of the two accounts of the Creation is distinguished by the pointed use of certain key words: here are the "days" that flow into the thrice mentioned "seventh day"; the activity of God in "speaking," "making"—recorded seven times—and doing "the work"; the sevenfold "seeing" through which God examined His work and found it "good"; the threefold "blessing" and, finally, the reference to the "completion."

The same motif-words reappear in the story of the erection of the tabernacle. The cloud covered the mountain "six days" (Exodus 24:16). The work of creation is completed above the darkness; similarly, the pattern of the tabernacle is perfected in the dark of the cloud; no witness is present at either event. On the "seventh day"

12 "Der Mensch von heute und die jüdische Bibel," *Die Schrift und ihre Verdeutschung*, pp. 31–45. The sections here discussed were not included in the English translation of the essay in *Israel and the World*.

13 The Buber-Rosenzweig Bible translation does justice to this situation; its rendition is *Braus*, or, *Geistbraus*.

(*ibid.*) Moses is called to "see" the pattern which is "shown" (i.e., "made to see"); this "see" verb, in a variety of forms, reoccurs several times in the report (Exodus 25:9, 40; 26:30; 27:8). Unlike the account in Genesis, God does not create here; only the pattern is designed in the "six days"; the tabernacle must be "made" by man. Indeed, the word "make" appears over and over again in the description of the "work"; it becomes the central phrase. The tabernacle completed, Moses, (not God, but His mediator) "sees" all the work and "blesses" it (*ibid.*, 39:43). And the motif of completion corresponds to that in the Creation story.

This parallelism is no coincidence. Buber interprets it as a Biblical device to call attention to the relationship between Creation and Revelation (a motif we shall meet later in this essay). Creation implies an original Revelation *(Uroffenbarung);* Revelation, however, fulfills the mystery of Creation: it is in the act of Revelation that God bids man to become "a partner in the work of Creation," as the Talmud expresses it. God has made the world and has offered it to man; the Tent where He will abide "in the midst of their uncleannesses" is shown to men but they themselves must make it. Man learns how to build; but no one directs his working hand. The abode of the Holy must be erected by him alone or it will not be established. The example of the Tent, like that of the *ruah,* teaches man to confront the world in faithful responsibility.

V

In *Königtum Gottes,* the first volume of a planned trilogy,[14] Buber attacked the central issue of Old Testament Messianism, its origin, meaning, historic development and its place in the faith of Israel.

The main aspect of Israel's Messianic faith is defined as "the readiness *(Ausgerichtetsein)* to realize the relationship between God and the world in a universal kingship of God."[15] While the statement *per se* could be accepted by many Biblical historians, its qualification, which constitutes Buber's main thesis, challenges the critical

[14] Three chapters of the second book *(Der Gesalbte)* appeared in the Ernst Lohmeyer volume (1951), *Tarbitz* XXII, *Zion* IV, respectively. The main thesis of the projected third book appears in the second half of *The Prophetic Faith.*

[15] *Königtum Gottes,* p. xi.

reader. Buber believes that divine kingship in Israel is not a late theological theory but a faith rooted in the memory of a historical reality. It is his understanding that early Israel actually rejected human kingship and placed itself under the kingship of the invisible God. Gideon's refusal to accept hereditary rule over Israel, for "the Lord will rule over you" (Judges 8:23), is viewed by Buber as a report of an event and a "political demonstration."[16] The early form of Israelite theocracy, he argues, is not a rule by a priesthood or princes receiving their authority from a god but "an unmediated, non-metaphorical and unlimited"[17] direct dominion of God. Not a god in " the religious sense" who leaves the reality of worldly life to the devices of man; it is on the contrary, precisely this worldly realm God wishes to control; "there is nothing which would not be God's."[18] From time to time, He may entrust a mandate to one chosen by Him; the chosen leader, however, is not to transfer his office to his son after him: hereditary kingship is the absolute contrary of un-mediated theocracy.[19] Man, then, will fulfil his mission as demanded by a particular situation (*situationsbezogen*), but beyond this he will have no power. The will of God, the King, will be made known through his constitution (which comprises not only cult and custom but as well, economic and social life) ; priests, even as members of a sacred institution, are to give answers only to queries addressed to them; in the main, the will of the God and King will become known to those seized by the freely moving Spirit. The unity of religion and politics will be maintained, the separation of the two realms, treated by human history as mutually exclusive entities, will be over-come.[20] "There is no political sphere outside the theo-political sphere."[21] The ritual office is indeed hereditary, but this office does not imply leadership; the political office is charismatic—here Buber uses Max Weber's terminology—and dependent on God, the ori-gin of the charis.[22] The wandering tribes of Israel accepted "for ever

[16] *Ibid.*, p. 3. In the context, Buber attempts to refute all Biblical criticism which considers the Gideon answer as unhistorical and an anti-monarchical theocracy not in evidence before Hosea.

[17] *Ibid.*, p. 60.

[18] *Ibid.*, pp. 106f.

[19] *Ibid.*, p. 140.

[20] *Ibid.*, p. 107.

[21] *Ibid.*, p. 140.

[22] *Ibid.*, p. 144.

and ever" (Exodus 15:18) the reign of God who bid Israel to be "a kingdom" of priestly men (*ibid.*, 19:6); "thus the Lord became King in Jeshurun" (Deuteronomy 33:5). Standing within this tradition, Gideon could not agree to replace divine kingship by a dynasty of princes.

Compared with the Near Eastern idea of divine kingship, is Israel's corresponding concept more than a doctrine and a "historizing theology?" Buber devotes a major part of *Königtum Gottes* to answering this question. He attempts to show that the reports of the proclamation of God as Israel's king, belonging to an authentic tradition, echo actual historical events, and not, as often assumed, a fiction of theologico-literary origin.[23]

He finds the ancient Israelite tribes psychologically predisposed to theocracy. Like the pre-Islamic bedouins, the independent Israelites found it inconceivable to submit to a sovereign. This anarchical drive is the negative side of Israelite theocracy and its preconditioning. It spells the wish to be free of human domination. The will to be independent, paradoxically coupled with its positive counterpart, readiness to accept the leadership of the Invisible One who led the tribes on their way and liberated them from Egyptian bondage, resulted in the theocratic covenant.[24]

The theophany on Mount Sinai is, in its ultimate aspects, a political act which confirmed the kingship of God over the people of Israel. Against Mowinckel's interpretation, Buber defends the historicity of the Biblical report. The covenant which bound the two parties, divine and earthly, in the task of establishing a kingdom was consecrated by a ritual (Exodus 24:3-8) unique in the traditions of both Israel and the Near East.[25] Through it both joined in a sacral and juridical mutual agreement: God to be the King, *melekh*, Israel to be His *mamlakhah*, His legal retinue. God the King issued His proclamation in the Ten Commandments.[26]

According to Buber, the theo-political community established on Sinai existed in its pure form until the death of Joshua. The popular assembly in Shechem (Joshua 24) reduced, in Buber's interpretation, the full scope of the initial, Mosaic, theo-political organization to a

---

23 *Ibid.*, p. 108.
24 *Ibid.*, pp. 139–143.
25 *Ibid.*, pp. 112ff.
26 *Moses*, p. 137.

"purely religious" one.[27] Charismatic leadership assumed an institutional character.[28] However, the memory of the original form of the Kingdom of God was kept alive by groups of faithful Israelites; these are the early prophetic enthusiasts and men chosen as "judges." Their anti-monarchical stand underlies the hidden polemics against the institution of an earthly king which Buber detects in the first part of the book of Judges,[29] with, finally, implied criticism turning into Gideon's open statement. Only the pressure of external political events brought about the institution of hereditary monarchy in Israel. As the anointed (mashiah) of God, the king was charged with a responsibility he was unable to carry.

VI

From among the Old Testament types of leaders—patriarch, lawgiver, judge, king, prophet, psalmist, wise man, teacher—Buber chooses the prophet as the most significant spokesman of Biblical Israel. After having occupied a secondary position in classical and medieval Judaism, the phenomenon of the Israelite prophet (rediscovered by Protestant theology) fascinated nineteenth century Jewish philosophers. A high point of acceptance was reached in the thinking of Hermann Cohen who found in Biblical prophecy the great affirmation of pure monotheism and radical ethics.

Buber's interpretation of Old Testament prophecy surpasses his nineteenth century predecessors in scope and in penetration. It succeeds in fusing into a consistent whole the manifold phenomena of inspired leadership which thus far had been treated as isolated instances and assigned to varying strata in the growth of Hebrew religion.

We have already noted Buber's analysis of the texts on Abraham in whom he detects primarily a receiver of divine revelation, a seer, remembered as such in the later prophetic tradition. In the Moses traditions, too, the nabi element predominates. Buber assumes, with Yehezkel Kaufmann, that Moses derived from an old family of seers.[30] He is the carrier of the Spirit: he had entered "into a dialogic rela-

---

[27] Königtum Gottes, p. 158.

[28] Ibid. (3rd ed.) , p. lxiii.

[29] Ibid., pp. 15–22.

[30] Moses, p. 168; Y. Kaufmann, Toledot ha-Emunah, II, 1, pp. 46, 122.

tionship with the Divinity." The seventy elders receive—as a temporary grant—a part of the *ruah* that is upon Moses; his own experience of the *ruah* is permanent. He desires the whole people to be *nebiim*, prophets in immediate contact with God.[31] Joshua and the Judges are carriers of prophetic charisma. The "bands of the prophets" preserve the original sense of the kingship of God which the people accepted in the covenant on Sinai. When permanent, hereditary, kingdom replaced charismatic judges and the kings failed to fulfil their function as vice-regents of the one true King, there were prophetic critics to confront king and people. It is the prophet who, in the breakdown of the kingdom, envisages the rise of the Messianic king. The prophetic message culminates in the concept of the Suffering Servant, a prophetic man, who, in Buber's interpretation, replaces the royal Messiah.[32] The suffering *nabi* "is the antecedent type of the acting Messiah."[33]

There emerges a presentation of a variety of *Gestalten* assumed by the prophetic spirit in response to the need of the particular historical situation. Seen in their succession, they form an internal history of Biblical Israel to which the external history is but a foil. It is the history of "the Torah sealed in the disciples" (Isaiah 8:16) and preserved for the day when the hidden Torah will be realized in the fullness of life, when the hidden God "will be King over all the earth" (Zechariah 14:9).

This being the scope and the impact of the prophetic element, Buber may well consider it the answer to what he regards as the constant threat to the spirit of Israel: the apocalyptic escape from the concreteness and the dialogical character of faith. The two types, prophet and apocalyptic, are not equally true interpreters of divine judgment, distinguished only by the respective historic situations. They are, rather, representatives of essentially different views concerning the position of man before God.[34]

The prophet teaches the freedom of choice. Israel is in the hand of God like the clay in the potter's hand. God plans the destiny of

---

[31] *Moses*, pp. 162–171.

[32] *Two Types of Faith*, p. 106. This is, to Buber, the sense of the message of Deutero-Isaiah, who "as a posthumous disciple of Isaiah renewed the main motifs of his Messianic prophecies with an altered meaning." See the interpretation of *limmud* in Isaiah 8:16 and 50:4, *The Prophetic Faith*, pp. 202f.

[33] *The Prophetic Faith*, p. 231.

[34] *Sehertum*, pp. 52f.

nations and of men. Yet, in choosing the good, man will cause God to "repent" the decree of judgment; in choosing to turn away from God, man will make Him "repent" from doing the good He had planned.[35] Because there is a covenantal relationship between God and man, man has the power of turning to the good or the evil, and thus also the power of turning the tide of events. What happens to him is, then, the divine answer to his choice. The connection between human deed and divine action is to be understood not as a mechanical relationship of cause and effect but as a dialogical correspondence between God and man. God wants man to come to Him in perfect freedom; the future, therefore, cannot be a result of pre-determination. The spirit of God assumes the attitude of "waiting" for man to fulfil the intention of Creation. Prophecy, then, considers man to be what Buber calls ein *Überraschungszentrum der Schöpfung*. Man will forever have the power to act upon Creation, positively or negatively: this prophetic faith addresses itself to all generations, to each in its language.[36]

The apocalyptic evades this responsibility of choice. In his world (Buber concentrates on *Fourth Ezra*) there is no room for man as a factor of historical and meta-historical decision. The apocalyptic visionary does not speak directly to the human person; he is a writer rather than a speaker. Man can no longer act meaningfully; the future is predestined. Adam's original fall—a concept foreign to the Old Testament—has involved all mankind. The end is inescapable, and near at hand. "The creation has grown old" (5:55), says Ezra the apocalyptic; "our time hastens to its end with might." Whatever may still happen in history has no longer historical value; man is unable to take an active part in the drama.[37]

Apocalyptic elements are at work in our own age, Buber finds. Karl Marx's view of the future is not of the prophetic kind, as some have thought, but follows the pattern of the apocalyptic. In Marx's system an immanent dialectic takes the place of the transcendent power that brings about the transition from the present period to the one to come. As in the apocalyptic, man, bound into a pattern of rigid necessity, is not fit for individual decision and free action.

[35] Cf. Jer. 18:8.

[36] *Sehertum*, pp. 53–59. Buber treats Deutero-Isaiah's view of history as an exception from the dialogic concept of classical prophecy.

[37] *Ibid.*, pp. 59–68.

Another expression of modern, secular apocalyptic is western man's feeling of futility, his notion of living in a late period of decline, when poetry indulges in self-irony and art glories in an atomization of the world around us; of the world—no longer understood as Creation—as grown old indeed; and of man as grown silent and lonely.

Such apocalyptic can be validly challenged only by renewed reference to the prophetic faith in the faculty of man to overcome the rigidity of de-personalized system, to act freely, to "turn," to decide, to dare face issues as they occur, to do his share in the rejuvenation of the world, created as a meeting ground between man and God.[38]

One may challenge Buber's prophetic thesis by arguing that if things go wrong in history and ancient, sacred, promises fail to be realized, disappointment with history and hope in a meta-historic event become a perfectly valid stand. Apocalyptic thought rests, after all, on a firm belief that if this Creation failed, there will be another aeon, which, like ours, will be a work of God. Loss of patience with history and the men who act in it is not loss of faith. The author of *Fourth Ezra,* so concerned with the implication of the Roman victory, could not have expected a "turning" in the hearts of man to affect the powerful wheels of history. Yet, even he, radical in his condemnation of the present aeon, saw a vision of a new Jerusalem rising upon the ruins of the old (10:54). True, the new city was not built by human hands, but it was a human heart that longed to behold the mighty acts of God.

Buber will not accept this argument and will sense the danger inherent in "expectations" and in the all-too-ready replacement of this world by another. Both are God's, but it is this our world which has been created for man and entrusted to his service and his care. Buber will side with the Tannaites, early rabbinic masters, who, as keenly aware of Rome's might as *Fourth Ezra,* still maintained the reality of the Kingdom of God. He will (thinking especially of the Christian partner in the Biblical faith) point to the formidable ally of apocalyptic abandonment of the world and of gnostic admission of dualism: Marcion.[39] It is in fact the extreme consequense of dual-

---

[38] *Ibid.,* pp. 68–74.

[39] "Gnosis and not atheism . . . is the real antagonist of the reality of faith." *Eclipse of God,* p. 175.

ism as reached by Marcion which motivates Buber's relentlessly sharp criticism of its milder manifestations. At stake is the issue of tearing asunder Creation and Redemption, Creator and Redeemer (and, for the Christian, the severance of the Old and New Testaments).[40] What Buber does, then, in different places of his Bible interpretation, is restore the prophetic faith in the Creator and in His creation. "That man exists at all is . . . the original mystery of the act of creation."[41] Buber speaks of the fact of Creation as implying "an unfathomable mystery which becomes evident only in the spontaneity of man."[42] Such Creation is not meant to fall, but to achieve ever greater realization in the history of man. It is the Creator Whose Kingdom was accepted on Sinai, and in Whose work all men will become partners in Redemption. God's presence with man under various forms and guises—which to Buber is the meaning of the enigmatic thorn-bush declaration, *ehye asher ehye*[43]—the element of the Personal, originate in Creation. Here the neutral, blind, cold, unconcerned universe was transformed into a place where man is addressed by the Thou and where he, as a person, may or may not give answer. At the summit of prophetic development—in Deutero-Isaiah—Creation and Redemption are analogous events, interrelated factors.[44] The redemption of the world, which is "the establishment of a unity in all the multiplicity of the world: the fulfilment of the Kingdom of God," is but the perfection of Creation.[45]

Once the "work of the beginning" snaps in the consciousness of man, and the hope for Redemption is separated from the covenant of Creation, men's own schemes, theories, constructions, assume the vain task of explaining a disjointed world. Man undermines his very existence by re-introducing the element of chaos, even if he intends to find new means to overcome it. In Creation, God had freed the world from chaos, *tohu* (Genesis 1:2); he "created it not a *tohu*," is the prophetic warning (Isaiah 45:18).

Elsewhere in his Bible work, Buber opens himself to the critical

---

[40] *Zwei Glaubensweisen*, p. 171.

[41] *Two Types of Faith*, p. 136.

[42] *Ibid.*

[43] Exodus 3:14; commonly translated "I am that I am"; for Buber's (and Rosenzweig's) interpretation see the latter's "Der Ewige" in *Die Schrift und ihre Verdeutschung*, Buber's *Moses*, pp. 46–55, and *Königtum Gottes* (3rd ed.), pp. 66–71.

[44] *The Prophetic Faith*, p. 213ff.

[45] *Die Stunde und die Erkenntnis*, p. 154.

suggestion, right or wrong, that "basically his interpretation of the Old Testament is a documentation of his own views."[46] However, in his defense of the prophetic idea of Creation, perhaps more than in the defense of any other point, Buber appears as a genuinely Jewish Bible exegete and as a link in the long series of Hebrew interpreters who struggled with the issue. And this is the ground, on which Buber, representing the faith of Israel, faces Pauline Christianity and the Marcionite impulse everywhere, an understanding critic, a brotherly helper.

Does Buber's acceptance of the world as Creation—it would be frivolous to apply here the worn-out term optimism—obscure his view from the tragic side in existence, or, Biblically speaking, from the situation of Adam, expelled from the Garden, and Job facing a hostile world and an unconcerned God?

It is intriguing to see Buber interpreting the Garden of Eden[47] story as man's—a light-minded creature's acquiring not the divine power of knowing, not "knowledge of good and evil," but "the latent paradoxicality of being"—and as God's mercy in making death a harbor for this wandering creature conscious of the paradox. The darker, more demonic motif of the story Buber considers as the residue of an old myth of the envious and avenging gods; in the Biblical context, the curse implies a blessing: "the eating of the Tree of Knowledge leads out of Paradise but into the world."[48] The exile from the Garden is set "on his way into the history of the world, a world which acquires a history and a historic goal only through him."[49]

Job perceives God as "dreadful and incomprehensible."[50] He "hides His face" and thus contradicts His revelation. There is no justice; He annihilates the honest and the wicked. Job struggles against the silent, remote, sinister power. In God's answer, as Buber interprets it in one of the most profound sections of his Biblical work,[51] Job's experience of the absurd is not argued or explained; the answer consists in God's reference—in all detail—to the Creation.

---

[46] J. Coert Rylaarsdam, "The Prophetic Faith," *Theology Today*, 7 (1950), pp. 399ff.

[47] "Der Baum der Erkenntnis," *Bilder von Gut und Böse*, pp. 15–31.

[48] *Eclipse of God*, p. 58.

[49] *Bilder von Gut und Böse*, p. 31.

[50] "Religion and Philosophy," *The Eclipse of God*, p. 51.

[51] *The Prophetic Faith*, pp. 188–197. *See also At the Turning*, pp. 61f.

In this vast panorama of heaven and earth there is not even a mention of man; to such a degree (if I understand Buber correctly) is man's experience of tragic isolation acknowledged by the deity. But it is God Who gives this answer; the absolute power, as Job has known it, becomes a speaking, answering personality for the sake of the questioning, doubting, protesting, despairing personality of man. "Creation itself" (which is the contents of the answer) means communication between Creator and creature. Job's position is extreme among those of Biblical men; it is a situation of crisis comparable to the crisis of innocent man facing the Tree of Knowledge. Here, revelation, revelationary answer to man, must take recourse to Creation. And Buber remarks rightly that in the Job dialogue "Israel's ancient belief in Creation . . . has reached its completion." In the *finale* of his analysis. Buber recognizes (exegetically not convincing!) in Job's quest "to see" God a prophetic experience and places Job "who prays for his friends" in the company of prophets.[52]

In the Paradise story and in the Job poem man and God could be interpreted as antagonists, of quite unequal strength, yet rivals nevertheless. Buber succeeds (by softly toning down the tension in the Paradise story, by sharply focusing attention on the Creation motif in the Job poem[53]) in reading both within the context of the Hebrew Bible which in its entirety is, to him, one great document of the prophetic spirit.

Here, finally, a reference to a critical point in Buber's work may be in order: the problem of Law.

Buber interpreted the event on Sinai as the theo-political act of establishing the divine kingdom, which is, from the point of view of man, the concrete acceptance of God's rule in human life. But Buber does not wish this to be reduced to a one-time occurrence in the history of Israel; he opposes an interpretation which would tend to fix in time a revelation however eternally valid.

Creation is the origin, Redemption is the goal, but Revelation is not a stationary . . . point between the two: the revelation on Sinai is not the center . . . poised between the two, but that it (*i.e.*, the revelation) can at any time be perceived (is this center).

God cannot be restricted to any one form of possible manifestation;[54]

---

[52] *The Prophetic Faith*, p. 197.

[53] However, this reader at least feels that if Buber's interpretation holds, the exclusion of man in the picture of the universe (ch. 38–40) requires more attention.

[54] *Moses*, p. 52.

it is His means of entering the dialogue with man which presupposes complete freedom. This thought, we have seen, underlies Buber's exegesis of Exodus 3:14.[55] Revelation, according to him, must preserve the character of the personal address; there is no relevant falling back upon previous revelations or upon revelations addressed to others. "The soul of the Decalogue . . . is the word Thou. . . . It is possible that only the man who wrote down the words had once had the experience of feeling himself addressed. . . ."[56] Therefore, Buber must question the immediate relationship between the recorded content of Sinaitic revelation and the fact of revelation itself. The words, once meaningful (as personally addressed to the listener) "become emptied of the spirit and in that state continue to maintain their claim of inspiration. . . . The living element dies off and what is left continues to rule over living men."[57]

It is well to remember that Buber is aware of man being "a receiver of the law" and of the importance of law for "the historical continuity of divine rule upon earth."[58] But this no longer belongs to the realm of Revelation. Man is a receiver of the law, but God is not a "giver of the law."[59] "Revelation is certainly not Law-giving."[60] Confronted by a law man must ask himself: "Is this particular law addressed to me and rightly so?"[61] And, more generally speaking: "The Torah includes laws . . . but the Torah itself is essentially not law."[62]

The arguments against Buber's stand can be reduced to one. Regardless of one's personal attitude towards the authority of Biblical law and one's historical orientation about Near Eastern parallels, it can be said with certainty that *within the context* of the Old Testament the laws do appear as an absolutum. Granted that to men or societies law may become routine, devoid of the fulness of original meaning; it can deflect the heart from man's ultimate duties to God

---

[55] *Ibid*, pp. 46–55.

[56] *Ibid.*, p. 130.

[57] *Ibid*, p. 188.

[58] *Ibid*.

[59] Letter of July 13, 1924 to Franz Rosenzweig on the problem of Law raised by the latter in *Die Bauleute*. F. Rosenzweig, *On Jewish Learning* (New York, 1955), p. 155.

[60] *Ibid.*, p. 118.

[61] *Ibid.*, p. 114.

[62] *Two Types of Faith*, p. 57.

and fellow-man: it is the law nevertheless. "Hear, O Israel, the statutes and the ordinances which I speak in your ears this day, that ye may learn them, and observe to do them" (Deuteronomy 5:2). This is the covenant, made "not with our fathers, but with us, even us . . ." (ibid., 5:3). It occurred but once in the history of Israel that God made His will known: in the law, which is, then, essentially immutable. The Voice speaking is the origin, legalism a sign of late decline; between the two is Torah, living record of the Word. Torah is more than law; but in the law is Torah.

Buber knows this. He made his position especially clear in an address (1930) when he described it as not a nomistic one though not an a-nomistic one. On that occasion he defined the teaching of Israel as "a Sinaitic one, teaching of Moses (Moseslehre) while the soul of Israel is pre-Sinaitic . . . it is Abraham's soul. . . . The soul itself is not of the Law."[63] Knowingly, therefore, Buber dissociates himself from Sinai the mount of the Law while adhering to Sinai the mount of revelation; in the context of the Bible, Sinai is, in all paradoxicality, both. Had he followed the rule which he so masterly represents, the rule of closeness to the actual text, Buber's exegesis would have had to take a different course. But the prophetic motif determined the course he had taken: he became the grand expounder of the prophetic meaning of the Voice speaking in Revelation and of the prophetic criticism of the distortion of the law in ritualism and legalism. The Torah, mastering day-to-day life between early Revelation and late decline, this Sinai, the central concern of Israel, Biblical and post-Biblical, remains outside the main province of Buber's work. "Do we mean the book? We mean the Voice!"

Yet, in a decisive moment, the Law does enter Buber's vision: in his valiant debate—this term suggests itself because of the pronounced personal, immediate nature of the controversy—with Paul's concept of the Law.[64] It is as if only Buber, who, as no Jew before him, has gained freedom from the yoke of the Law (while all the more carrying the "yoke of the Kingdom of God"), could call for an understand-

63 "Die Brennpunkte der jüdischen Seele," Kampf um Israel, p. 51.

64 Two Types of Faith, passim. See also "Pharisäertum," Kampf um Israel, pp. 115–130.

ing of Israel, free in the Law, in the presence of the Jew of Tarsus whose unfreedom under the law had such far-reaching consequences in the history of faith.

NAHUM N. GLATZER

DEPT. OF NEAR EASTERN AND JUDAIC STUDIES
BRANDEIS UNIVERSITY

17

James Muilenburg

BUBER AS AN INTERPRETER OF THE BIBLE

THE DISTINCTIVE position which Martin Buber occupies in the contemporary study of the Bible is to be explained by something more than his independence as a critical scholar or by his wide-ranging interests in fields which lie beyond the immediate biblical horizon. For more than a generation he has devoted himself to a careful scrutiny of the Biblical text and has entered into a living and interior encounter with the ancient Hebrew words as no other scholar of our time. He has a profound grasp of the Biblical way of speaking: he discerns the accents, stresses, and culminations of words, their nuances and connotations; the ways in which they stand in relation to each other and the way of their ordering; their re-occurrence in fresh contexts where they are remembered, appropriated, re-fashioned, and actualized, yet continue to stand in relation to the context in which they first appeared and then press on into the contemporaneity of the new situation, where they are again actualized into the present (*vergegenwärtigt*) and are there given new depth and dimension. Buber's extraordinary recognition of the power and vitality of words is rooted in his sense of the nature of human life in speaking and listening, in his understanding of man as a hearing-speaking being and of the *sui generis* nature of that engagement, of its implications and dynamic.

Martin Buber's independence is further shown by his approach to the Jewish Scriptures. While he has schooled himself in the methods and techniques of historical criticism and the criticism of literary types (*Gattungsforschung*) his own methodology represents a radical departure and, indeed, a protest against their adequacy as a means of arriving at the heart of the Biblical message. Not infrequently he raises the same questions as the modern critic, but his means of answering them is different. One of the most striking features of Buber's study of the Bible is the way in which he employs the ancient Near Eastern materials for an understanding, either by way of comparison or by way of contrast, of the uniqueness of Israel's faith. Arabic, Accadian, Egyptian, and Canaanite (Ugaritic) literary traditions and practices are constantly drawn upon for the elucidation of particular passages. The sociological interest is often marked, thanks in part to the influence of Max Weber, with whom he was associated in his early years at Frankfurt. In comparison with other modern Biblical scholars, his interest in historical background is relatively slight, despite his frequent emphasis upon the historical character of Biblical revelation. His primary concern is the existential appropriation by the individual of the Biblical event in the present moment. The existential encounter is for him always central and is not subject to historical conditioning.

Buber is not only the greatest Jewish thinker of our generation, not only a profoundly authentic exponent and representative of the Hebrew way of thinking, speaking, and acting, not only a celebrated teacher 'both to Jew and to Greek,' but also the foremost Jewish speaker to the Christian community. He, more than any other Jew in our time, tells the Christian what is to be heard in the Old Testament, what the Old Testament is really saying and what it certainly is not saying, what the direction is in which the words are moving on their way through history. He, more than any other Jewish writer, tells the Christian what he ought to know and what he ought to see, what the road on which he walks is like, whence the journey begins and whither it leads. Whatever else may be said of him, Buber is the great Jewish teacher of Christians. What is more, he has a deep interest in and sure grasp of much of the New Testament, a warm appreciation of the historical Jesus, and a recognition of the place where Jew and Christian go different ways. More than any other Jewish thinker of our time, he stands at the frontier which separates Christianity from Judaism.[1] He is the best contemporary corrective to the persistent Marcionism of large segments of the Christian Church. He gives Jewish answers to Christian questions, the kind of answers Christians must have if they are to understand themselves. Interestingly, the parts of the Old Testament which most engage his attention are those which are most cherished by Christians. Considering the profound influence of the theology and eschatology of Ezekiel upon the development of Judaism, it is significant that Buber has so little to say concerning him. On the contrary, Hosea and Jeremiah and, above all, Second Isaiah play a central role in his un-

[1] *Two Types of Faith; Between Man and Man,* pp. 5–6.

derstanding of the *Heilsgeschichte*. With this all Christians, but perhaps not all Jews, will heartily agree.

General Categories of Biblical Interpretation

Let us examine, first of all, several of the points of view which dominate Buber's understanding of the nature of the Old Testament. The Bible for him is essentially one book, united by several great themes and by its pervasive existential character. He is impressed by the continuity of its various parts, even when on the surface it may not be apparent to the modern Western reader. As we shall see, the presence of persistently recurring key words and key sentences provide for him a way of understanding this continuity. Everywhere man is called to meeting and encounter (*Begegnung*). Whatever the historical situation and whatever the literary guise—whether narrative, song, lament, or prophetic proclamation, Israel is called upon to meet her God, Yahweh, in encounter, a live and lived dialogue in which the eternal first person I addresses the second person Thou. Revelation, Buber is saying, comes in community, through the immediacy of word and event. Israel can address her God with the intimacy of *Thou* because He has first addressed her with His divine *I* and has accompanied His unique words with the eventful words of His activity. The Word of God is never, therefore, a generalization or abstraction, but always a living, concrete, historical *here and now* in which Yahweh and His people engage. The word of God is the symbol *kat' exochen* for the dialogical encounter. "Everything in Scripture is genuine spokenness" (*Gesprochenheit*).[2] We must not seek to distil from it a moral or a 'truth'; to do so would separate the hearer from his involvement and meeting; it would make of him a spectator rather than a hearer. Again, the Bible is unified by its constant proclamation of a message (*Botschaft*); everywhere the reality of the messenger's proclamation is present or assumed.[3]

The three central themes which control the dialogue 'between heaven and earth' are creation, revelation, and redemption. The demand with which the Bible meets the generations, says Buber, is to

[2] *Die Schrift und ihre Verdeutschung*, p. 56.

[3] *Ibid.*, pp. 55f. "Die hebräische Bibel is wesentlich durch die Sprache der Botschaft geprägt und gefügt . . . Gleichviel wie es sich mit irgendwelchen Stücken der Bibel verhielt ehe sie in die Bibel eingingen: in jedem Gliede ihres Leibes ist die Bibel Botschaft."

become recognized as the record of the authentic history of the world; namely, that the world has an origin (*Ursprung*) and a goal (*Ziel*). It demands of the individual that he surround his life with this true history, that in its origin he may find his origin and in its goal his goal. Between origin and goal is revelation, but not as something I can appropriate to myself or possess but as something which is ever moving according to concrete time and circumstance, the concrete moment in which the hearer listens to the voice speaking of origin and goal. "Creation is the origin, redemption the goal. But revelation is not a fixed, dated point poised between the two."[4] Buber is in accord with Oscar Cullmann that Judaism knows no midpoint of the *Heilsgeschichte;* even the revelation at Sinai is not such a midpoint, but rather an ever-recurring hearing and becoming aware in the present moment of its actualization (*Vergegenwärtigung*). One must admit that all of this is exceedingly interesting and suggestive and that it is an adequate statement of many great contexts of Old Testament faith. It is a question, however, whether they hold true for all of the Bible.[5]

Buber's discussion of creation, redemption, and revelation should be understood and pondered in the light of what he has to say about mythology and eschatology in the introduction to his *Königtum Gottes*. Whether or not one agrees with his definitions, the reality to which he points is one of the first importance for a grasp of many great prophetic and liturgical contexts (e.g., Second Isaiah and Psalms), and more especially for a true understanding of Biblical eschatology:[6]

The myth is the spontaneous and proper speech of the expecting as of the remembering faith. But it is not its substance. Out of mythical plasticity (*Bildsamkeit*) the figures of eschatology, though not its impetus and power, are to be understood. The true eschatological life of faith—in the great woes of historical experiences—is born out of the genuine historical life of faith; every other attempt to discern its derivation mistakes its nature.

The Biblical Text

Basic to an understanding of Buber's interpretation of the Bible is his view of the original Hebrew text and, more particularly, of the

[4] *Israel and the World*, p. 94.

[5] *Prophetic Faith*, pp. 194, 197, 213–217. For a discussion of creation, redemption, and revelation, see Maurice Friedman, *Martin Buber*, and Will Herberg, *The Writings of Martin Buber*, pp. 29–32.

[6] *Königtum Gottes* (2nd ed.), p. IX.

ways in which the ancient Semitic original may be transmitted to the
modern Western mind in modern Western speech. It is highly significant, therefore, that his first great undertaking, in cooperation with
Franz Rozenzweig, was a translation of a large part of the Old Testament into German, in which he sought to reproduce as faithfully and
closely as possible the original words into their modern equivalent.
The volume by Buber and Rozenzweig on *Die Schrift und ihre
Verdeutschung* (Berlin, 1936) gives us an excellent account of their
views concerning Hebrew literary composition, the nature of the
Hebrew language, and the methods by which the genius of one
speech may be transmitted into the genius of another.[7] All previous translations, they aver, are like a palimpsest which obscures the
underlying text, reflecting the literary modes and theological terminology of the times in which they were composed. It is the design
of Buber and Rozenzweig to remove the palimpsest, to recover the
original speech with all its manifold features, and to employ only
such words, alien as they may sometimes seem to modern ears, as will
express the Hebrew original. Not only must the symbols and images
of the Hebrew be preserved, but also the subterranean stream of ancient Hebrew sensuousness, its sentence structure and 'architecture,'
its repetition of key words and sentences in varying contexts, and
above all its rhythm and speaking quality. Such literary features as
assonance, alliteration, and rhythm provide the clue for discerning
the intent of the speaker and are an indispensable tool for sound
exegesis. Here Buber is calling attention to matters which are indeed
of the first importance for a grasp of the text, for to arrive at its
true meaning one must be able to articulate the major motifs as they
are bodied forth in form and sound. All too often scholars have
dealt cavalierly with the text and have deleted passages which are
absolutely essential to their true understanding. Yet one may question
whether Buber's attempt to preserve the rhythmical units (*Atemzüge*)
has not sometimes involved some loss, for the parallelism of lines, to
which Bishop Lowth originally called attention in 1753, is in reality
sometimes obscured. Rhythm is present, however, not only in poetry,

---

[7] This work is basic to an understanding not only of the translation but also to
the methodology involved in the interpretation of the text. Among the more relevant
discussions are "Über die Wortwahl in einer Verdeutschung der Schrift," "Zur Verdeutschung der Preisungen," "Leitwortstil in der Erzählung des Pentateuchs," "Das
Leitwort und das Formtypus der Rede," all by Buber, and "Die Schrift und das
Wort," "Das Formgeheimnis der biblischen Erzählungen," by Rozenzweig.

but, according to Buber, throughout the Old Testament, and the translation presents it effectively. Scores of illustrations might be drawn from the translation to show how the form and sound is presented. I limit myself to but one illustration taken at random:[8]

> Darum
> will ich so dir tun, Jisrael!
> Deswegen,
> dass ich dir dieses tun will,
> bereite dich,
> deinen Gott gegenüberzustehn,
> Jisrael!
> Ja denn, wohlan,
> der die Berge bildet,
> der den Geistbraus schafft,
> der dem Menschen ansagt
> was sein Sinnen ist,
> macht nun aus Morgenrot Trübnis
> und tritt einher auf den Kuppen der Erde,
> sein Name:
> ER IST DA, der Umscharte Gott.   Amos 4:13.

The form clearly demonstrates where the accents lie; the emphatic words *Darum* and *Deswegen* and the repetition of the lines which follow them, the repetition of *Israel,* the succession of participial phrases (the threefold *der*), the single word *prepare (bereite dich)*, and the superb climaxes *to meet your God* and *his name, Yahweh of hosts (sein Name:* ER IST DA, *der Umscharte Gott),* and much else aid us in entering into the interior nature of prophetic speech. This example is by no means exceptional: indeed it may be said to be characteristic of the whole Old Testament. It can be readily seen how important these formal devices are for Biblical hermeneutics. Buber has made use of these stylistic devices again and again in his interpretation; e.g. the Song of Deborah, the Tower of Babel story, the covenant narratives, and the Psalms.

Much attention is given to linguistic matters. Many cultic *termini technici,* such words as *mishpat, ṣedakhah, ḥesed, emunah, ruah, kabod,* and the divine appellations *Yahweh* and *El* are treated at considerable length.[9] It is doubtful, however, whether Buber has taken into sufficient account the diversity of their usages. For example, *ḥesed* seldom means lovingkindness or grace in the Old Testa-

---

[8] *Das Buch der Zwölf*, pp. 70–71.

[9] *Die Schrift und ihre Verdeutschung*, pp. 144–167.

ment; *covenant love* or the RSV *steadfast love* expresses the covenant connotation better. It is even more doubtful that the pronominal words ER, DU, SEIN are an adequate rendering for the divine name Yahweh. The assumption that throughout the Old Testament the original meaning of the word, *he who is present* (as Buber assumes it to be), was recognized by Israel is, to this writer, extremely unlikely. Even if Buber's interpretation of the tetragrammaton were correct, which is doubtful, the persistence of the original denotation in the minds of succeeding generations is highly questionable. For Buber to render *Yahweh* in the Amos quotation given above as ER IST DA goes against all that we know of the history of words. Moreover, this is by no means an isolated example of Buber's linguistic understanding. In his effort to preserve the primitive, dynamic connotations of words he goes too far, and sometimes allows what he conceives to be their etymology to determine their subsequent meanings.

Hermeneutical Methodology

A major issue in Buber's interpretation of the Biblical text is his methodology. We have given hearty approval to his stress upon the presence of key words, upon the interior structure of compositions, and to his appeal to the rhythm of a passage. But he would be the first to admit that this method does not answer many important critical questions, the questions with which historical and literary criticism are concerned. Yet he finds this approach to the text not only inadequate but mistaken. In the introduction to the first edition of *Königtum Gottes*, he says he can give to the symbols J and E, the strata which historical critics find in the Hexateuch, only very limited validity. Modern scholars, he says elsewhere,[10] have not proved the existence of such independent documents. He would speak rather of types of traditions, which, to be sure, have passed through a long period of transmission and have there received supplements and expansions. He is intent upon discerning the substance of the tradition in its original form and to note its tendencies and directions in the later development of the tradition. Of the Abraham stories, for example, he says that "the whole work serves a single intention: to stretch a line . . . every single point of which has its precise place and value."[11] The most thorough and detailed illustration of Bu-

10 *Prophetic Faith*, p. 4.
11 *Ibid.*, p. 88.

ber's methodology is to be found in a long article on the narrative
of Saul's election as king.[12] In sharp disagreement with prevalent
historicocritical views, such as is represented in Otto Eissfeldt's *Einleitung in das Alte Testament* (1934), he rejects the presence of two
or three major sources and finds instead four major sections of material: (a) the narrative, (b) a very slightly edited battle history,
(c) annalistic notes, and (d) insertions within the sections of the
narrative. His analysis is thorough and painstaking and one with
which scholars will have to come to terms.

Our task is to begin with "the first stage at which we find evidence,
the stage which no literary evidence can shake," and we must inquire
of the text what the faith of Israel was at that particular stage. Then
we must go back to earlier stages where the same faith is clearly
reflected and so on until we arrive at the place where it first finds expression. Having established this point we are prepared to move forward and to trace the development of the faith in the light of the
major affirmations of the original 'event.' In his *Königtum Gottes*
Buber begins with Gideon's famous rejection of the kingship (Judg.
8:23) where he finds such a stage, but in his *Prophetic Faith* he begins
more appropriately with the Song of Deborah, and then proceeds
to the Shechem assembly in Josh. 24, the Sinaitic covenant (Exod.
19-24), and the narratives of the Fathers in Genesis.

Buber's reflections on the nature of saga and legend are of considerable importance, for he properly calls attention to the historical nucleus preserved in them.[13] But once the legend has been
crystallized, there can be no additions or changes. He can appeal
here to primitive Semitic mentality in such matters. The only question here is the extent of the nucleus, and here Buber obviously
would go much farther than most scholars. He then sets himself to
separating the 'historical content' of a text, a question of the first
importance to the modern student. He mentions first of all the
social-historical background, then 'the point of view of the history
of the Spirit and especially the history of religion.' Here it is not a
matter of the authenticity of the external event, but of the religious
act or position of the period under discussion. Again, he appeals to
the *uniqueness of the fact,* which only 'the intuitively scientific meth-

---

12 *Vetus Testamentum,* 6, No. 2, pp. 113–173.

13 *Prophetic Faith,* pp. 5–6; *Moses,* pp. 13ff.

od,' which seeks for the *concreteness* at the basis of an evidence, can recover.[14]

There can be no question that Buber has raised issues of the very first importance for an understanding of the Biblical text. One can only applaud his appreciation of the creative forces that go to the making of Hebrew literary composition and his constant concern to relate critical questions to the crucial and central matter of faith. In his studies of Abraham he has rescued the patriarch from a mere figure of the *Urgeschichte,* and the traditions from a collection of more or less inchoate fragments. "His work," Buber says finely, "became the basis of a narrative system of faith." One might wish, however, that he had taken the motifs of Gen. 12:1ff. and worked them out more concretely in terms of their fulfilment in the birth of the child. What he has to say of the traditions here are, as a matter of fact, best illustrated by a recognition of the Yahwist source, against the existence of which, however, he protests.[15] Again, in his analytical treatment of the Samuel-Saul narratives (I Sam. 7-13), he argues much in the fashion of any modern historical critic. With his rejection of the usual formulation of the Wellhausen hypothesis and the minute dissections of the critics he will find widespread agreement today, not least of all among the Scandinavian scholars, who apply their own methods of traditio-historical criticism to the Biblical texts, although it must be added that Buber would diverge sharply from them in their tendency at times to subordinate the historical revelation of the Old Testament to the patterns of Near Eastern mythology.

To begin with the Song of Deborah as the starting point of investigation into the history of Israel's faith is entirely appropriate; the same is not true, of course, of the Gideon utterance, which has no such claim to historicity among many critics. In his attempt to isolate the historical content of a passage, his appeal to the social-cultural background is certainly valid, and he has employed it in several contexts, notably in the Elijah narratives, with telling effect.[16] When he calls upon the *uniqueness of the fact* (italics are Buber's), he is dealing with a much more difficult matter, however, and the

[14] *Prophetic Faith,* idem.

[15] *Prophetic Faith,* p. 87; *Moses,* p. 6: *Königtum Gottes,* pp. XIV-XV. In the last-named work, however, he makes a considerable concession to the usual critical view, and his characterization of the 'tradition' (XV) both of J and E is one with which many scholars would agree.

[16] *Ibid.,* pp. 70–80.

invocation of 'the intuitively scientific method' as a way of approach
to the text, as over against what he styles 'speculative theory,' only
makes difficult matters more difficult. Perhaps this may account for the
charge of subjectivity which is often levelled at him. The results of
this attitude may explain such categorical and unsupported expressions as 'this undoubtedly ancient verse' (I Sam. 3:1), 'which is also
unmistakably early' (3:11), 'this is not a late source' (I Sam. 8), 'the
antiquity of which cannot be doubted' (2 Sam. 23:1-7),[17] 'which
I regard as inimitably Isaianic' (Isa. 19:23-25).[18] In many of these
judgments, as a matter of fact, the writer concurs, but for very
definite reasons which he believes will stand the test of scholarly inspection. Finally, it must be said that only a detailed discussion can
deal fairly with Buber's critical views. There is one sentence, however in the *Prophetic Faith* (p. 4) which is of such importance for a
study of the Bible that it must be given in its completeness.

But even if we were allowed to speak of "sources" and if it were even
possible to fix their dates (and also the dates of the additions and redactions),
we would thereby only be able to establish layers of the *literary*, not the *religious* development, and these two need not in any way parallel one another,
as it is very possible that a primitive religious element is only found in a late
literary form.

If these wise words had been heeded in the past, the course of
Biblical criticism would have been quite different from what it has
been. Fortunately, the force of Buber's comment is today widely
recognized, above all in our understanding of the priestly traditions.

The Application of the Methodology

We turn now to several major examples of Buber's interpretations. In all of them he employs the methodology of key words to
great advantage. A wonderful example is his treatment of the Song
of Deborah (Judg. 5). This early poem of ancient Israel has received
much attention in the history of Old Testament research, but Buber's
approach illuminates the text in an entirely fresh way by his calling
attention to the literary stresses of the poem, above all upon Yahweh
and Israel. It is thus out of his recognition of recurring key words in
crucial contexts that he is able to discern the central disclosures of

17 *Ibid.*, pp. 61f., 68.
18 *Ibid.*, p. 150.

the poem and the nature of the faith which inspires it.[19] In *König-tum Gottes* Buber discusses another very early poem, the 'Song of Moses' (Exod. 15:1b-18), where he is inclined to isolate vv. 1b-11, 18 as the original poem, and vv. 12-17 as a later supplement. But if one is to employ the clue of key words, which proved so fruitful in the Song of Deborah, then it is clear that the poem is a literary unit, for here we have the same fundamental relationship of Yahweh and His people Israel. The motif of the people is clearly dominant in vv. 12-17 (cf. especially vv. 13 and 16cd); Yahweh's activity in this section (12-13) connects well with v. 10; the motif of the enemy is present in both (10-11 and 14-16). V. 18 does not follow well upon 11b but comes excellently after v. 17 as the tenses *inter alia* plainly show.[20]

In his diminutive book, *Right and Wrong*, Buber sets himself to an interpretation of five of the Psalms of the Psalter (12, 14, 82, 73, 1). In his translation of this book he speaks of all the poems as *Preisungen*, but as a matter of fact the number of laments exceeds the hymns and are, indeed, an authentic expression of Israel's life in relation to 'the God of the sufferers' (*Prophetic Faith*, pp. 155-235). All of the psalms studied are interpreted in the light of their key words. The study of Psalm 1 is especially rewarding because of the low estimate in which it is held by many commentators. The motif of *the way*, so central a motif of Biblical faith, is properly emphasized, and due recognition is given to the Law, which elsewhere in Buber's writings seems to receive less than its due. The one criticism I would have with the study is its distinction between *sinners* and *wicked*. I doubt whether a close analysis of the form and key words justifies such a conclusion.[21]

One of the best expositions of the prophets of Israel is to be found in *Prophetic Faith*, particularly the chapter on "The Great Tensions," in which Buber gives us a profound interpretation of the prophetic activity of Elijah, Amos, Hosea, and Isaiah. It is not only filled with keen insight and warm appreciation, to which few parallels can be found in contemporary treatment of the prophets, but also with a deep understanding of the fateful issues involved in the ministry of these prophets. Relatively little is said of the historical situa-

---

[19] *Prophetic Faith*, pp. 8–12.

[20] *Königtum Gottes*, pp. 129–131. See the valuable study by F. M. Cross and D. N. Freedman in *Journal of Near Eastern Studies*, 14 (1955), pp. 237–250.

[21] *Right and Wrong*, pp. 52–62. (Included in *Good and Evil: Two Interpretations* —Ed.)

tion, national and international, of their times, but what is given is penetrating and succinctly stated. For example, very little is said of the great international movements of the ninth century B.C., of the rise of Assyria under Assur-nazir-pal and Shalmanezer III, of the inner politics and mercantile interests of Phoenicia, or of the complexity of Israel's international problems during this period. These are by no means minor considerations. Yet one may agree that what Buber has to say about the nature of Baal worship is of great consequence. Nowhere, so far as the writer is aware, has anyone succeeded in portraying the inner mysteries of nature worship and of the sexual drives associated with them with such power, lucidity and interior grasp.[22] Only through such an appreciation of the hold which nature religion exerts on its devotees is one able to sense the momentousness of the conflict between Yahweh and Baal or its significance in the history of world religion.

The Origins of Israel's Faith

On more than one occasion Buber has addressed himself to the crucial questions associated with the beginnings of Israel's faith in Yahweh as her God.[23] He rejects emphatically the widely current view among scholars that Israel first came to know Yahweh at Mount Sinai and argues forcefully that the traditions which represent him as the God of the Fathers have a secure historical foundation. When it is pointed out that the prophets constantly place the origins of Israel's religion in the time of Moses, he replies that with one exception (Hos. 12:9; 13:4. cf. 11:1) this is nowhere stated, and that Hosea's words are to be understood only as referring to the adoption of Israel as the people of Yahweh (cf. Exod. 4:22). The relevant passages in Exodus make it indisputably clear that the God who revealed himself to Moses at the Burning Bush was the God of the Fathers (Exod. 3:3, 13-16). When Moses inquires about the name of the God who speaks to him (Exod. 3:13), the true meaning of his words is "what finds expression in or lies concealed behind the name." "Moses expects the people to ask the meaning and character of a name of which they have been aware since the days of their fathers."[24]

---

[22] *Prophetic Faith*, pp. 74–76, 78f.

[23] *Königtum Gottes* (2nd ed.), pp. XXIII-XLIV, 73–86; *Prophetic Faith*, pp. 13–59; *Moses*, pp. 39–55, 94–100, 100–118.

[24] *Moses*, pp. 48–9.

Again, when the Priestly historian (the designation is mine!) reports Yahweh as saying, "I am Yahweh. I appeared to Abraham, to Isaac, and to Jacob as El Shaddai, but by my name Yahweh I did not make myself known to them" (Exod. 6:2-3), the meaning is that the Fathers "did not know him in the quality characterized by his name; and that this had now been discovered."[25] Further, Buber asserts that in the period of religious laxity in Egypt "the name itself degenerated into a sound simultaneously empty and half-forgotten." In such an hour as that in which Moses proclaimed the holy event which he had experienced, the people were saying, "What is this God really like?"[26] Yahweh's reply to Moses' question is *'Ehyeh 'asher 'ehyeh,* which is explained as meaning "I shall be present as I shall be present," somewhat in the manner of Exod. 33:19: "I will be gracious to whom I will be gracious, and will show mercy on whom I will show mercy."

Now it must be admitted that there is force in much of what Buber has to say. His discussion exhibits learning as well as insight. On the other hand, his explication of the question about the name leaves this writer unpersuaded. The whole tenor of the passage seems to him to indicate that what is happening here is something really and decisively *new*; that Yahweh should say that He was the same God who had revealed Himself to the Fathers is perfectly natural and precisely what one would expect. Religious founders find support in their appeal to an antecedent past. Yahweh is saying substantially, "I am the God you have been worshipping all the time, the God of your fathers." Moreover, the very striking statement of the Priestly historian in Exod. 6:2f. can only mean what it clearly says, that He was known to the Fathers as El Shaddai and not as Yahweh.[27] The comment about Israel's failure to remember the name and its vital significance is neither persuasive nor likely. Into the vexing question of the meaning of the tetragrammaton we cannot enter here, but, again, Buber's explanation, which in this case is in some ways attractive, does not seem convincing. Surely the meaning 'to be present' is not the usual interpretation of the Hebrew verb *hayah*, as refer-

25 *Ibid.,* p. 49.

26 *Ibid.,* p. 51.

27 Observe that in Genesis Yahweh employs the same revelatory or theophanic words, "I am Yahweh" (Gen. 15:7; 28:13). Are they to be understood in the same way as in Exodus?

ence to the standard lexicons will show.[28] Rather the primary meaning *is to come to pass, to happen,* i.e., *'I cause to come to pass what I cause to come to pass.'* Yahweh is the God of event, of eventfulness, and He will bring about that which He assures Moses and his people He will bring about. This suits the context admirably and strikes at the center of the Bible's understanding of the nature of divine revelation. It was the supreme event in the life of Israel when Yahweh made Himself known in the great theophany with his *hieros logos, I am Yahweh,* and then, significantly, "who brought you out of the land of Egypt, out of the house of bondage." He had caused to come to pass what actually did come to pass; this is the demonstration that He is Lord of history and the Sovereign of Israel's historical destiny.

In the light of the foregoing discussion, it is clear that Buber rejects the Kenite theory of the origins of Israel's faith in Yahweh. Now it must be recognized that the arguments in support of this theory are by no means coercive and that there is much that is wrapped in obscurity. In the second edition of his *Königtum Gottes* he seeks to meet the objections to his view and to his rejection of the Kenite hypothesis, and in *Moses* he enters into the subject again.[29] He is surely correct in stressing the family character of the narrative, but to say that Jethro did not come to Israel as priest of Midian runs counter to the very opening words of the narrative in Exodus 18: *Jethro, the priest of Midian.* The position of the narrative in its present context is said to be the work of the Redactor, for which no explanation is offered or defence given. The fact that Sinai is specifically called 'the mountain of God' (Exod. 3:1, 4:27) is not given any weight. Buber finds it incredible that Jethro should speak such momentous words as his "Now I know that Yahweh is greater than all gods" to a community which was not his own. But this does not take into account that Moses had married into the priest's family with all that that implies, and that on the 'mountain of God' he had received his revelation of Yahweh. Later in the discussion we are informed that the true meaning of Jethro's words is as follows: "I have now come to know that your god is the greatest, but have also recognized in him the true form and the true name of my god, the

[28] Little if any support will be found in Brown-Driver-Briggs Hebrew lexicon, or in Köhler-Baumgartner, or in Gesenius-Buhl (17th ed.). *See also* Thorleif Boman, *Das hebräische Denken im Vergleich mit dem griechischen* (Göttingen, 1954), pp. 27–39.

[29] Pp. 42ff.

fiery gleam of the middle whose rays have illumined me." Entirely
aside from the unwarranted interpretation in the final phrase of
this sentence, Jethro's admission here is scarcely less astonishing than
the interpretation of the Kenite theory which Buber finds so incredible. Moreover his assertion that it was after all Moses who offered
the communal sacrifice 'without the need for making any special
mention of the fact' (!) is hard to credit in view not only of the
words of v. 12, but also of the whole movement and structure of
the passage: the *berachah* (v. 10), the solemn and momentous "Now
I know," and the culminating sacrifice. The three events follow one
another in almost inevitable sequence. Buber holds that it was Jethro
who was won over to Yahweh and was convinced by the demonstra-
tions of his power that his God and Moses' God were one and the
same. The whole movement of the narrative seems to suggest quite
the reverse.

The god of Midian is a mountain and fire god (p. 97), which is
in all probability true. Now it has often been pointed out that the
character of Yahweh in Genesis and Exodus is quite different in this
respect. With the exception of the Sodom story, which is in many
ways unique in Genesis, Yahweh nowhere reveals Himself in the
imagery of fire, whereas in the period following Moses the associations
of fire with Yahweh are characteristic and frequent. Further, it is
said that Jethro may have recognized the name *Yahweh* as the correct
one as the result of the mighty wonders of the Exodus. It is just
as likely that he came to a fresh recognition of the *new character*
which Yahweh his god had revealed in the events of the Exodus.
It is Yahweh's *mighty works* in deliverance, leading, and providing
which make all the difference. Other objections might be raised; we
shall confine ourselves, however, to the episode of the adjudication of
disputes in Exod. 18: 13-23. Such an undertaking is religious: the
people 'inquire of God' and Jethro delivers a highly significant speech
beginning with "Listen to my voice." It is Jethro, priest of Midian,
who instructs Moses, and in language which leaves little doubt as to
his expertness in such matters (cf. 18:19-23!). It must be admitted
again that the Kenite theory has not been demonstrated, but the
arguments in its favor are somewhat more impressive than is suggested by Buber's analysis of the narrative.

We must deal more briefly with another event, but one of great
importance not only for an understanding of Israel's origins, but also
of the whole Old Testament. I refer to the 'Eagle Speech' in Exod.

19:3-8. Buber rightly calls it 'the hour of the Covenant.' He calls attention to the rhythmic character of the utterance, "almost every word of which stands in the place fixed for it by sound and sense;" indeed one should say 'every word' without qualification. But then we are told to our amazement that the words "when ye hearken, hearken unto my voice and keep my Covenant" do not find a place within the firm rhythm. The truth is that the rhythm demands these words, the grammatical construction requires them,[30] without them the excellent literary structure is destroyed, and, most serious of all, the very heart of the Covenant reality is obscured. The issue here is neither speculative nor academic; it raises the question of the nature of the Covenant itself. First a word about the rhythm: the deletion of the words in question actually destroys the parallelism of lines, so marked a feature of the passage, a consideration to which Buber so often and properly appeals. The structure of the narrative is plain for all to see, and this applies more particularly to the words of the three sub-sections, each introduced by a key word ('atem, 'atah, 'atem 4, 5, 6.) More important is the weighty word *And now*; hereupon follows the great sentence, composed of a *protasis* (*If you will truly listen to my voice and heed my Covenant*) and *apodosis* (*then you shall become my precious possession,* etc.). The omission robs the utterance of the great contingency, strikes out the underlying imperative of obedience, and opens the floodgates of anti-Semitism, which misunderstands the uniqueness of Israel's election and the uniqueness of its accountability and responsibility. This protasis-apodosis construction continues in the tradition from beginning to end, and many of the most exalted passages of the Bible preserve the authentic memory of its deep-lying origins. It is highly significant that the Deuteronomists and the prophets who preserve the authentic Mosaic covenantal tradition perpetuate it, and in contexts of great importance.

That the excision of the crucial covenantal words of Exod. 19:5 is well pondered is shown by the discussion of the decalog. As usual, there is much here that is illuminating and suggestive, but there are also a number of questions of interpretation which raise doubts. The

---

[30] It is very doubtful whether Buber has done justice to the grammar and syntax of the passage. Note his unusual rendering of the particle *'im* as *when* and of the infinitive absolute of the verb to hear, and observe the awkwardness which results from the deletion of the crucial word.

most important of these is that the decalog was not the basis upon which the covenant was made.[31]

The concept of the document in the making of the Covenant appears to me secondary, and to have derived from the fact that the Covenant was misunderstood at a late time as the conclusion of a contract.[32]

That contractual relationships do not adequately express the meaning of the covenant is surely true. The great introductory words spoken in theophany (Exod. 20:2), the genuine *hieroi logoi* of the revelation, are words of grace corresponding to the New Testament *kerugma*, but the words which follow are the Torah belonging with the *kerugma* of grace, the *didache* of the early Christians. The omission of the decalog from its present context or from the theophany is not only contrary to what we know of all other Old Testament theophanies, where the theophany *always* issues into words and living speech, but also a cancellation of Israel as the people of the Torah in its covenantal origins, Torah as understood as direction, guidance, and teaching. The matter raised here is of special consequence since Buber so staunchly and rightly upholds the historicity of the event. It must be made clear that he does not reject the decalog as Mosaic; he simply detaches it from its present theophanic, covenant context, but this is precisely the issue both here and in the Eagle Speech.

The God of the Sufferers

The final chapter of *Prophetic Faith* is devoted to 'the God of the Sufferers.' Jeremiah, Job, Ezekiel, Psalm 73, and Second Isaiah are discussed in the light chiefly of the perplexing problems of theodicy. The chapter is so rich in insight that it is impossible to do justice to it; the Biblical figures are grasped in all their profundity, and their relationship to the major motifs of the *Heilsgeschichte* is clearly and vividly discerned. As we have had occasion to observe, Ezekiel does not figure large in the on-going drama of faith, and the treatment of the prophet is brief and perhaps not as illuminating or sympathetic as one might wish. The Book of Job 'in its basic kernel' cannot, according to Buber, be assigned to a time later (or earlier) than the beginning of the exile, a position which has the weighty

[31] *Moses*, p. 137.

[32] *Ibid., idem.* It is to be noted again that Buber gives no defence for this judgment.

support of R.H. Pfeiffer (*Introduction to the Old Testament,* p. 677).

Buber has a most interesting interpretation of Jeremiah's 'obituary notice' on King Josiah (Jer. 22:15-16); actually, however, the passage is part of the invective against Jehoiakim. The words referring to Josiah read as follows:

> Did not your father eat and drink
> and do justice and righteousness:
> Then it was well with him.
> He judged the poor and needy;
> then it was well.
> Is not this to know me?

The reference to 'eating and drinking' is a famous *crux interpretum* which has received many different explanations. But Buber proposes a solution which has much to commend it.

Josiah's 'eating and drinking' here belong [he says], to the *covenant making* as much as the 'eating and drinking' of the elders of Sinai (Ex. 24,11), and henceforth fulfils it by himself practicing justice and righteousness, and as regards men by vindicating the cause of the poor and needy. 'This is to know me,' YHVH says to Jeremiah—that is that knowledge which Hosea declared to be the innermost essence of the relationship of faith; whosoever helps the suffering creature, comes into close contact with the Creator, and this is here called 'knowing YHVH'.

More might have been given us concerning Jeremiah's attitude to institutions, especially in comparison with his contemporary Ezekiel.

The most detailed and perceptive discussion of *Prophetic Faith* is the treatment of Second Isaiah. Buber rightly recognizes the close relation between Isaiah of Jerusalem and Second Isaiah and also the latter's familiarity with the so-called Priestly tradition, as we have it, for example in the first chapter of Genesis. Interestingly, considering Buber's general critical conservatism, several passages are denied the prophet's authorship (e.g. chap. 47; 49:14-16; 50:1-3).[33] I should assign all these passages to the prophet, but there are scholars who would defend Buber's position here. The section on the Suffering Servant is an original contribution to a subject which has engrossed the attention of Biblical scholars perhaps more than any other in the Old Testament. Buber seems to support the view that the so-called 'songs' come "from another period in the life of the prophet than the rest of the book, and apparently a later period."[34] This view is still

[33] *Prophetic Faith,* p. 205.
[34] *Ibid.,* pp. 218–9.

championed by many scholars, though the present direction of research supports their originality. The writer is quite confident that the literary structure of the poems demands that we accept them in their present contexts.

Outside the 'songs' the Servant is clearly Israel, as is explicitly stated again and again. Buber recognizes that the reference to Israel in the heart of one of the servant songs (49:3) is original, but he interprets it as referring to an individual: "*Thou* are the Israel in whom I will glorify myself."[35] The Suffering Servant cannot cover the life span of a single man. The three stages of the Servant's activity are rather to be understood as the way of one servant.

passing through all the different likenesses and life cycles. We do not know how many of them the prophet himself saw in his vision. . . . Neither can we presume what historical figures he included in the servant's way; it was laid upon the anonymous prophet to announce the mystery, not to interpret it.[36]

There is much to be said for this view; it is more than an interesting proposal and must be reckoned with as a genuine possibility. Yet the critical foundations are questionable; *viz.* the separation of the poems from their contexts, the notorious *Irrweg* followed by many scholars since the publication of Duhm's commentary in 1892. Moreover, Buber does not do full justice to the reality of corporate personality in biblical faith. Nowhere in the Old Testament is this mentality more clearly present than in Second Isaiah, and it is through an understanding of its meaning and significance that Israel as a community and Israel as a person are joined into one. Precisely for this reason the Servant of the Lord, both the 'songs' and the rest of the prophecy, were susceptible to christological formulation.

Yahweh as Melekh

We come finally, to what is the most significant and fruitful of all of Buber's contributions to Biblical study: the kingship of God and the role he plays as Leader. While the imprint on the title page of the first edition of *Königtum Gottes* bears the date of 1932, Buber had been lecturing for some twenty years on the origins of messianism and its later development. The messianic faith of Israel

---

[35] *Ibid.,* p. 223. The Masoretic text hardly supports this rendering, and it must therefore be considered highly precarious.

[36] *Ibid.,* p. 230.

is for him its central content. From its early beginnings it presses
forward toward the fulfilment of the relation between God and the
world in the complete kingly rule of God. *Königtum Gottes* deals with
the early period of Israel's faith, and it is already there that we encounter the representation of Israel's faith in a divine kingship as
actually historical. The second stage in Buber's study is concerned
with the sacral character of the Israelite king as the Anointed of
Yahweh, while the third stage brings the two foregoing motifs together in attempting to show how both conceptions—already in the
period of the kings—move out of history into eschatology.

For the eschatological hope—in Israel the historical people in an absolute
sense (Tillich), but not in Israel alone—is first of all an historical hope; it is
'eschatologized' first through the growing disappointment of history.[37]

   This representation of Yahweh as *Melekh* is naturally shrouded
in all sorts of mythological imagery, and is influenced by the great
Near Eastern myths of the divine king. But what is unique in
Israel is its experience *in history* of a divine call to recognize Yahweh
as their only king. Nowhere is the myth central; it is merely the guise
in which historical memory is preserved in all its dimensions. We have
witnessed the important place which the Gideon utterance (Judg.
8:23) has in Buber's thought and how he finds the expression of
this same faith in earlier periods. Indeed, it goes back to the Sinaitic
covenant and before that event to the call of Abraham. We are left
in no doubt as to the central meaning of Yahweh's role as *Melekh*.
Buber traces the development of the faith through the anti-monarchical period of the 'judges' (*shophetim*), then turns, in extraordinarily
well-documented discussions, to the divine kingship in the ancient
Near East, the West Semitic tribal god, Yahweh as *Melekh*, the royal
covenant, and the theocracy. All of these chapters in *Königtum Gottes*
are of the first importance, not least of all because of the detailed
and excellent notes which accompany them.
   The divine *Melekh* is first of all and always the Leader. He is
the leading God of Abram, he is Israel's leader from Goshen to
Sinai and from Sinai to the Land of Promise, and so on throughout
Israel's history. He is the God of the way, *der Wegegott* (Eichrodt);
he leads Israel on its 'way' through history. Buber supports his
interpretation of Yahweh as Leader with ample documentation, so
that there can be little doubt of the correctness of his position. In-

[37] *Königtum Gottes*, p. X.

deed, one would have no difficulty in showing how this faith in a leading God moves throughout the whole of the Bible, from its earliest
strata and throughout the New Testament also. The theological importance of this understanding of the faith of Israel is very great.

A vast literature has gathered about the subject, both of Yahweh
as King and of the sacral kingship, in recent decades, but it is not always borne in mind that Buber has been a pioneer in this field.
The myth and ritual school in England; the Scandinavian school
of the divine kingship, especially represented in the work of Engnell
and his followers; and the American school of W. F. Albright have all
given strong support to many of Buber's views, though in different
ways. Sigmund Mowinckel's *He That Cometh* discusses at great length
the same theme of messianism to which Buber has devoted so much
attention. Aubrey Johnson has written a careful and restrained study
of the *Sacral Kingship*. To be sure, Buber would part company
with many of the views expressed in some of this literature; he
certainly would not accept Mowinckel's interpretations throughout,
nor would he go to the extremes of some of the members of the
Swedish school of Engnell or of the English myth and ritual school.
But all of these movements in modern scholarly research are in one
way or another dealing with matters to which Buber has devoted a
lifetime of painstaking study. Moreover, it is doubtful whether anyone
has presented with greater vividness and lucidity the reality of the
divine kingship and the sacral king than Martin Buber, and it is
certain that no one has discerned or set forth their theological implications with equal profundity.

Today scholars recognize that the ark was the throne upon which
Yahweh was seated as King, though invisibly. The celebrations of the
divine enthronement in the New Year's festival, which have become
generally known through Mowinckel's famous work in the second
volume of his *Psalmenstudien,* corroborate many of Buber's views,
although he is hesitant in giving assent to Mowinckel's admittedly
exaggerated position. G. Ernest Wright has demonstrated the presence of royal terminology in the accounts of the covenant relation,[38]
and George E. Mendenhall has rendered probable the influence of
Hittite covenant treaties between king and vassals upon their form

[38] "The Terminology of Old Testament Religion and Its Significance," *Journal
of Near Eastern Studies,* 1 (1942), 404–14; "The Faith of Israel," *Interpreter's Bible,*
1, 355–6.

and structure.[39] Martin Noth has called attention to the similarities between the prophetic commissions and the words of the messenger from the king in the Mari inscriptions.[40] Many passages in the Old Testament, hitherto considered late, but now recognized as early, are precipitates of the royal ideology of the court, and the Psalter bears clear testimony to the importance of the sacral king in Israelite thought.

In all these ways and, indeed, in many others, Buber's views are receiving striking confirmation. While we have not dealt in any detail with his existential interpretation of the Bible, this, too, has left a deep impression upon contemporary scholarship, not least of all in the current stress upon the actualization into the present moment (*Vergegenwärtigung*) of the *heilsgeschichtliche* events in the cultic celebrations. Even his classical treatment in *I and Thou* has influenced contemporary Biblical hermeneutics. One has only to examine the Hebrew of many psalms or of Second Isaiah to see how fruitful this category of understanding may be for the elucidation of the text. Yet it is still true that Buber's many studies on the origins and history of messianism are his most important contribution to an understanding both of the Old and New Testament. He, more than any other Jewish scholar of our time, has opened the Scriptures of the Old Covenant for the Christian community. Without an understanding and appreciation of the Old Covenant, the Scriptures of the New Covenant must remain forever closed.

[39] *Law and Covenant in Israel and the Ancient Near East* (Pittsburgh, 1955).

[40] "History and the Word of God in the Old Testament," *Bulletin of the John Rylands Library*, 32 (1950).

JAMES MUILENBURG

DEPARTMENT OF OLD TESTAMENT
UNION THEOLOGICAL SEMINARY

18

Rivkah Schatz-Uffenheimer

MAN'S RELATION TO GOD AND WORLD IN BUBER'S RENDERING OF THE HASIDIC TEACHING

I

A SPECIAL place is reserved for Buber among students of Hasidism. This is so just because he does not set out to "make a study" in the narrow sense, but aspires, rather, to grasp this phenomenon as a pattern of life complete in itself: an attempt at a life of man with God within the world. Because of this, and because Hasidism as it is presented in Buber's writings heralds the closing of the rift between matter and spirit, and between God and world, Buber has become the spokesman of Hasidic teaching in the eyes of the public. There is no doubt that Buber has done more than any other scholar to open men's hearts for a profound understanding of Hasidism. And even if portions of his teachings appear to me open to question on essential points, it remains true that these questions grew on that soil which Buber prepared and sowed.

The development of Buber's thought in his fifty years' occupation with Hasidism would undoubtedly make an interesting study; not only would it reveal to us the path of a personality full of conflicts in his relationship to the inner meaning of Hasidism; it would also show us how difficult it is to determine the nature of a phenomenon which always is greater than the sum of its elements, so that to give undue prominence to this element or that will alter the true picture of the whole.

In this essay, however, I have only one intention, in line with the purpose of this whole volume: to raise a few problems that come to mind when one reads Buber's words on Hasidism in the light of the Hasidic sources. And I refer to Buber's mature thought which crystallized in the 1940's. Let me say at once that I know very well that it is easier to criticize a conceptual synthesis than to construct one; but, while recognizing the limitations of criticism, we are not free to abstain from it.

I ought to make it clear that the severity of my criticism is not meant as a verdict on the final value of Buber's teaching; this value must be measured by another standard than that of historical criticism.

Buber asserts that he has no system in his representation of the Hasidic world; he reiterated this point in a recent conversation. It is obvious that from the historical and philological point of view there is indeed no system here, since Buber makes no use of analytic methods; but his synthetic tapestry is woven of selected strands, and it is he who determines the hue of the cloth.

One can state the essence of Buber's great vision of Hasidism as the closing of the chasm between God and world. Buber sees the failure of Western civilization in its attempt to live with a God removed from the world. In this schizophrenic life two possibilities were contained from the beginning; denial of the world and separation from it, or an acceptance of the world that will have it both ways. Buber thought to find healing for this bi-polar life in the teaching of Hasidism, understood as a philosophy of life whose basic assumption is the existence of God who is approached through creation. No longer do logical contradictions and pangs of conscience pave the way to him; but the direct and steady gaze to the heart of creation, life as it is "here" and "now"—this is the meeting-ground between man and his God.

From this basic insight Buber draws all the necessary conclusions. The affection with which Buber regards reality as such, the garlands he fashions for man's work in the secular sphere of his existence, determine not only the pattern of his general philosophy but also are the point of departure for his interpretation of Hasidism. In his stress on the affirmation of the thing as such, in his absorbed devotion to it, all "special cases" recede and there results a conception that seeks to swallow up every essential distinction between things, times, persons and actions and to create mono-valent categories for their evaluation: as though Hasidism taught that there is nothing to distinguish this time from the time of the Messiah, the Zaddik from the ordinary man, the holy from the profane.

Buber's realistic, activist approach—in contrast to Hasidism—ignores the ontic line of thought on such basic problems as God and world, and from the first confines itself to the realm of the *relation-*

ship of man to God and to the world. The Hasidic sources themselves distinguish between the ontic problem of the world and that of man's relationship to it; thus in Hasidism this problem becomes greatly complicated. The attitude to the concrete here is most problematic, and in studying the sources one senses a hidden contest between those who want to carry their ontological scheme to its logical conclusion and those whose desire it is to narrow the chasm between the everyday body of teachings, with its positive obligations, on the one hand, and the products of speculation on the other. In any case even the moderates among the Hasidic thinkers are far from espousing the realism of Buber.

Man's relationship to the concrete is a secondary problem in Hasidic teaching. The attempt to clarify this relationship grew out of the discussion of the main problem, that of devekuth—cleaving to God. This point must be stressed because it is decisive for the inner character of Hasidism and shows where the interests of its theorists truly lay. The doctrine concerning the Hasid's relation to the concrete made its appearance when it became evident how difficult it was to adhere to the exacting discipline demanded by the Hasidic doctrine of devekuth. This extended its rule over the soul of every Hasid and claimed all of his being; it came to denote a life with God without any concession to the secular world: to turn one's attention to sensory phenomena or to states of mind was considered a sin.

In a pamphlet entitled "The Testament of the Baal Shem Tov" we find a saying attributed to the founder of Hasidism that expresses in all its rigor this concept of "devekuth" to God: " 'For my thoughts are not your thoughts, neither are your ways my ways (Isaiah 55:8)': this means that when man separates himself from God he *immediately* serves false gods *and there is no middle way,* and this is what is meant by the verse (Deuteronomy 11:16): 'and ye turn aside, and serve [other gods];' and the Gemarah states (Kiddushin 39): 'When a man sits still and commits no transgression it is *considered as though* he performed a commandment,' and this is what is meant by 'neither are your ways my ways.' "[1] The Baal Shem Tov found it necessary to twist the words of the Gemarah and give them an interpretation the very reverse of their literal meaning in order to find support for his extremist position on devekuth: the Gemarah in fact recognizes the "middle way," the neutral state in which man remains inactive, and

[1] According to the text printed in Jerusalem, 1948, p. 18.

accounts this to his credit as though he had performed a positive commandment—only let him not sin. The Baal Shem Tov argues as a matter of basic principle against the existence of such a moment of neutrality: a man can either perform a commandment—for which, according to this conception, we must read: be in a state of devekuth to God; or else he can commit a transgression—i.e., be in any state other than that of devekuth. And thus we must understand the latter part of the Baal Shem Tov's saying: "and this is what is meant by 'neither are your ways my ways' ": that is to say, anyone who imagines he has performed a commandment in such a moment of neutrality is as one who has turned aside from the true way of God. From what has been said it follows that Hasidism demanded the subjugation of all realms of life to "devekuth" and saw in devekuth a way of service and not an ecstatic state.[2]

Buber is right in his perception of the weight attached to this question in Hasidic life, but he displaces the positive center of gravity onto the relationship to the concrete, whereas this is in fact the great problem of Hasidism, not its great answer. Hasidism came to consider the problem of the concrete, or, to use its own expression, of *gashmiut*, "corporality," out of necessity and not out of desire. For after all it had to find an answer to the problem that willy-nilly confronted anyone who wished to adhere to the doctrine of the Baal Shem Tov: to be in devekuth with God all day long and still to fulfill the obligations of flesh and blood on earth—how is this feasible? It must be remembered that a solution along monastic lines was completely out of the question.

I am here not raising the question of "cause and effect" in order to determine the "history" of the idea. This question does not interest Buber, and he has a right to his own approach. My sole intention is to question the enthusiasm for the concrete that Buber finds in Hasidism. In what follows, I shall attempt to examine the position taken on this problem in the speculative writings of the Hasidic movement.

Buber's boundless love for the world has impressed itself on his teaching: "Early I foresaw that . . ., no matter how I resisted, I was inescapably destined to love the world,"[3] that very "world" whose whole ontic existence is set at nought in the eyes of Hasidism.

---

[2] Scholem already dwelled on this distinction in his account of the evolution of the concept of "devekuth" in Jewish thought. "Devekuth, or communion with God." *The Review of Religion* (January, 1950).

[3] *Origin and Meaning of Hasidism*, p. 99.

The doctrine of the Maggid of Mezritch already contains within itself the tension between the two poles of man's life—the pole of the spirit and the pole of matter; this is a basic premise, and moreover its theoretical significance is an unswerving decision for the pole of being. And only one being exists: the divinity. Every other existence that we know is without autonomy. To attach an independent significance to existence and to the world means to detach it from its metaphysical source of life.[4] This point of view determines Hasidism's fundamental attitude of negation to the world as lacking ontic significance.

Hasidism in fact never for a moment divested itself of the gnostic mode of consciousness and never forgot that our world, in its present state, is the result of "the breaking of the vessels" of the divinity. It never, even on one page of the thousands on which its teaching is transmitted, forsook its yearning for the restoration of the world to its "primordial" condition. It never renounced the one essential act, the restoring of all things to "nothingness", in favor of "an equal value of all functions."[5] Hasidism did indeed introduce changes into the scale of values governing actions in traditional Halakhic Judaism; but for all that, it remained a scale. This change of values found expression first and foremost in the conception of man's role: "Man must remove himself from all corporality until he ascends through all the worlds and is united with the Holy One, blessed be He; until he is released from existence, and then he shall be called man."[6] The paradox here is that this "release from existence" does not mean the sacrifice of the world but its redemption. The ability to nullify the personality is a condition for the nullification of the world which is its redemption; in the language of the sources, "the raising of the sparks," i.e., the raising of the sparks of the divinity to their source— sparks that were imprisoned in matter at the time of the breaking of the divine vessels.

Buber accepts the Hasidic doctrine of the "raising of the sparks" only as a synonym for God's presence in the universe,[7] since he

---

[4] *Maggid devarav le-Ya'akov*, p. 9a.

[5] *Origin*, p. 50.

[6] *Maggid*, p. 4b.

[7] *Be-Pardes ha-Hasidut*, preface, p. 6. (This preface is not found in the English version.)

categorically rejects all gnostics and kabbalistic elements; he no longer has any use for the authentic meaning of this concept but only for its actuality as "locus" for the meeting between man and God.

The "raising of the sparks" no longer involves, for Buber, either "raising" or "sparks." Where Hasidism set at nought the place of the encounter between man and God, i.e., the concrete, Buber saved the concrete, and set at nought the original meaning of the concept. And I am not using a figure of speech. It seems clear to me that Hasidism not only accepted all elements of the Kabbalah as unquestioned premises but even went further in its conclusions against the concrete as soon as it turned its attention to this subject. I shall discuss Hasidism's practical solution of this problem later on in this essay.

Here I ought to mention that in discussing Buber's view I must sometimes have recourse to an *argumentum ex silentio,* which, undesirable as it is in scholarly analysis generally, yet seems legitimate to me in dealing with so selective a representation as Buber's. Buber's neglect of a realm of importance in Hasidic thinking and his concentration on the element of "the meeting" between man and God *within this world* result in a truncated image of Hasidism and blurs the problematic aspect of its thinking.

The problem of Hasidism was how man should do what is required of him in order to be redeemed and to redeem the world, not the world as it is but the world as it ought to be: and this "ought to be" refers to the state of its primordial creation, to a neutral existence living in the divine thought, to that same problematic "nothingness" of Hasidism. In the eyes of the Hasidim, the greatness of the Zaddikim lay in their knowing how to turn "being" into "nothing," to turn the divine "being" that has fallen into the world back to its "nothing," which is the true being. The world as the concrete garment of the divine being does not thereby become holy even if it has become the transparent register of God's presence. Man's contact with creation, which is an inescapable necessity, did, it is true, in Hasidism turn into an ideal and a mission, a misson that demanded of man the nullification of creation and of the concrete as such. In this, more than anything else, Hasidism demolished the locus of the "dialogical" encounter which in Buber's eyes is the central concern of Hasidism,[8] whereas in the sources its role is only that of the mystic point of transformation to "nothing."

The purpose of man's creation is that he should raise up the worlds to their roots, that is, restore them to nothingness as they were before, by means of study, prayer and good deeds, and should join them to God, but in such a manner that he himself clings fast to the rung of nothingness;[9]

or, in another place:

Man must consider himself as nothing and must forget himself absolutely and completely and all his entreaties in all his prayers must be for the Shekhinah (the indwelling of God); and thus he can reach a level above time, that is, the world of thought where all things are of equal value, life and death, sea and land, and this is what the Zohar says: 'Elai (to me): this word must be interpreted with care, thus: everything depends on the Ancient of Days'; i.e., one must surrender oneself and forget one's troubles in order to arrive at the world of thought, and there all things are of equal value; but this is not so when one is attached to the corporality of this world, then one is attached to the division between good and evil. How will one then arrive at a level above temporality where there is complete unity? And likewise, when one thinks of oneself as being and seeks the fulfillment of one's wants, the Holy One, blessed be He, cannot clothe himself in such a one, for He, blessed be He, is without end and no vessel can endure Him; and this is not so when one considers oneself as nothing, as stated above.[10]

The redemption of the world therefore means that it must be emptied of its independent significance as world. In this fundamental conception of relation to the world, I think that there are no differences among the leading Hasidic thinkers; the disciples of the Maggid understood the matter just as he did: "Be exceedingly careful, call on all your intelligence and judgment, not to perform any action in the world except what pertains to the service of the creator and the restoration of his seven attributes."[11]

In all his writings, Buber stresses the important place Hasidism accords to man in the world, and this is certainly one of the most attractive elements he found in it. The spiritual intensity of a life directed toward sanctification is indeed one of the outstanding marks of Hasidic communal life: a life of unlimited significance, that does not set apart special times for celebration, but subjects every domain

---

[8] Origin, pp. 99, 236.

[9] Maggid, p. 8a.

[10] Ibid., p. 14b.

[11] Ze'ev Wolf of Zhitomir, Or ha-me'ir (New York, 1954), p. 13b.

of human existence to the service of God. The attraction such an integrative view of life has for us is obvious, but it seems to me that here again Buber gained too much by it. Buber asserts that Hasidism overcame the dualism of God and world: "Bound to the world, receiving and acting, man stands directly before God."[12] To me it seems apparent that Hasidism never attempted to blur this basic dualism; world and God were always in its eyes two opposed sides. Hasidism did in fact attempt to overcome the division between "life in God" and "life in the world," but this is not the same thing. Life in the world was transformed into life in God not because it was itself sanctified, thanks to some intrinsic "potentiality for sanctification"; but because Hasidism developed an indifference to the concrete and raised its eyes to the *meaning* of existence and not to existence itself, to the element that establishes and maintains it and not to its outer garments.

This contact with the world as a sacrament, which seems at first sight a bridging of the chasm between the two realms, is in fact a contact that divides; and most paradoxically, this is the integrative concept of Hasidism. It was the obligation of contact with the world that led Hasidism to be so all-embracing in its view of things; there is no affirmation of the world in this.

It is very easy to misconstrue Hasidism's own understanding of its problem, for its parables are often obscure and its method is that of homiletics; but as the Jewish saying has it, the words of the Torah are scanty in one place and ample in another, and it is continually explicating itself. Let me cite one of the utterances of Jacob Joseph of Polnoe on the subject of service in corporality[13]:

By means of man's position between heaven and earth, so that he stands on earth and his head reaches to the heavens—by means of this, earth and firmament touch, etc. And I think I heard from my teacher [the Baal Shem Tov] the explanation of the sentence that earth and firmament touch: to bind together and to unite the corporeal action with the spiritual etc. Another thing that I heard from him or in his name: 'Whatsoever thy hand findeth to do, do it with thy might' (Eccl. 9:10): that when one links a corporeal action to a spiritual, by this means there takes place a unification of the Holy One blessed be He, etc.

This harmonistic conception, which seems at first sight to represent an ideal of cooperation between matter and spirit, emerges with

12 *Origin*, p. 99.
13 *Toldot Ya'akov Yosef*, p. 19a.

increasing clarity further on in Rabbi Jacob Joseph's text[14] as that same transformation to nothing, *qua* "the return of things to their root," the nullification of their actual existence which makes possible the unification of the spirit by means of the neutralization of matter. "Thy might is the thought of binding the two together," i.e., the spirit that is freed from matter and the spirit that is contained in matter.

The main question before us is in the end this: how, then, did the Hasidim actually put this teaching into practice?

They went with a light heart to the market place; the outer world no longer stood as an obstacle to the service of God, it became a means for the service of the Creator.

This doctrine of "the service of God in corporality" has become the central idea of Buber's message. What does Buber see in this concept which becomes for him almost synonymous with Hasidism itself? Buber sees in it a pansacramentalist process, a message of the hallowing of the world, which he interprets as an act in which the world is endowed with direction. The world, meaningless in itself, is brought into a holy covenant with man who directs it toward God —a covenant renewed again and again in every moment of "true" contact between man and world. A problem emerges here when one asks oneself what is the nature of this "directing" which Buber introduces into his teachings. For Buber, after all, sees in the act for its own sake the true realization of the Hasidic ideal; this is the act that transforms the "undefined" to substance, to holiness, through the meeting—the meeting in itself—between man and world. How does man bring the world to God?

According to the Hasidic sources it is possible to give an unequivocal answer to this question: the "raising of the sparks" is the restoration to their source of the lights that fell into the world. It is the building up of the full stature of God, and when a man intends this —and this alone—in his contact with the world, he is performing an act of redemption. But Buber from the first pushes aside this idea; what is more, most of his statements on the matter specifically have reference to the world "as such." Our question therefore is this: what is the relationship between this God toward whom the world must be directed, and the world itself? Perhaps they come to the same thing? Perhaps we find ourselves directing our acts only toward

14 *Ibid.*, p. 20a.

existence, while God willy-nilly answers Amen and impresses on our hearts His seal of truth? This hidden law by which God presents the "things" to man along the road of his life in order that he should redeem them—this law has a clear meaning in Hasidic teaching, where it derives its authority from the existence of the transcendent being who directs, who ordains for every man the "field of his mission" in accordance with the root of his soul. In Buber's teaching, where man is bidden to draw out all that is contained in the setting of the encounter just in itself, and where it is in this setting that he hears God's answer—an answer that itself is no more than a vague "Amen"—in Buber's teaching, the metaphysical presuppositions of the Hasidic doctrine are lacking; and Buber, in "liberating" man from these "fetters" of the Kabbalistic system, removes much of the rigor that characterizes the framework of Hasidic thought. Why must God agree to the will of man, if our turning to him is only a paraphrase of our turning to the world as it is in itself, even if we tag on the formula "directing (the things, or our acts) to God", a formula whose meaning is not always clear? When Hasidism considered the question of "service in corporeality," its answer was that this is an inescapable necessity, this is the challenge of reality which comes before us to plead for its redemption at our hands. Thus Hasidism held that God speaks to us *also* by means of this reality. Even though it is incomprehensible to us human beings why God chooses to reveal Himself in the material world too, we are bidden to accept His decree and to serve Him in all His various manifestations. Hasidism never supposed that God wishes us to serve Him in the world bcause "it is that in which He wants to receive an answer from me."[15] Certainly it did not hold that "man answers through his action in relation to just these things and beings," and that "all specific service to God has its meaning only in the ever-renewed preparation and hallowing for this communion with God in the world."[16]

Hasidism labored hard to explain to itself this necessity which was difficult to reconcile with its theoretical views. It never changed its attitude to reality; it found the remedy, the way in which reality would cease to be an obstruction. Buber ignores this problematic situation in which Hasidism saw itself, when he says:

[15] *Origin,* p. 97.
[16] *Ibid.,* p. 94.

The decisive step is thereby taken to the renewal of the relation to reality. Only on the path of true intercourse with the things and beings does man attain to true life, but only on this path can he take an active part in the redemption of the world.[17]

And is not this "true life" of Buber's a surrender to "the flowering fullness of fate of the here and now [before which] the horizon of 'the last things' visibly pales"?[18] And yet the Hasidic doctrine abhorred this "flowering fullness," for just this is enthralment to the world of the senses! This "fullness," for all that it is a fact—you may not look on it as it is in itself[19]: you may and even must use it only as a basis of inference from the lesser to the greater: if such is God's manifestation in the material world, how much greater must be his manifestation in the transcendental world of the spirit! That example of the encounter with the ensnaring woman, which is already well known from the days of the Great Maggid, obliges us to give serious attention to the problematic character of our relation to this world. These are the Maggid's words: "Man may not cling to this terrestrial beauty, but if she [the woman] came before him suddenly, he must by means of her beauty cling to the beauty of the upper world."[20]

The shift in Hasidic thought on the service of God in corporality did not entail a shift in principle in its attitude to reality. As soon as Hasidism realized the danger that its doctrine would turn into the "service of corporality" instead of the service of God, it held back from preaching these doctrines to "the ordinary man." Already in the generation of the disciples of the Great Maggid one may discern an attitude of cautious reserve in the face of the vulgarization of the idea of "service of God in corporality." Eating and drinking and other secular acts which man performs as potential vehicles for the service of God—these become problematic, not indeed in themselves, but from the point of view of man's ability to carry them out. The Hasidim were willing to give up "the service of God in corporality" as a legitimate way in the service of God as soon as it became apparent to them that it was purchased at the price of true devekuth, i.e., man's cleaving to the divine element in material things while renouncing the matter in which it is clothed. Even R. Elimelekh of

[17] *Ibid.*, p. 86.

[18] *Ibid.*, p. 130.

[19] *Maggid*, p. 11b; "You shall not have other gods: you should not and may not serve any thing that is clothed (in matter) but only God alone in his glory."

[20] *Ibid.*, p. 4b.

Lizhensk, who cannot be suspected of aristocratic leanings, said that while the service of God in corporality is, to be sure, a legitimate one, it is better to leave it to the Zaddikim, and let the rest of the people serve God in the traditional way of study and prayer, which is less perilous.[21] More extreme than R. Elimelekh was R. Meshullam Feibush of Zbarazh, who did not leave the decision to the individual; he went further, and asserted that service in corporality, i.e., the possibility of remaining in constant "devekuth" to God even in the midst of secular occupations, without the latter causing a cleavage in the state of the soul—this service is possible only for the very few, and the ordinary man is not able and not permitted to attempt it. He cites the following in the name of his teacher R. Mikhal of Zlotchov[22]:

> With reference to the sentence of the Mishnah (Shabbat): 'The sons may go with bindings and the sons of kings with little bells, and so may any one; but the sages spoke only of the present': this means that those who are called sons, who have higher levels of soul in addition to the animal soul and the spirit, and *they are bound in thought to the Creator blessed be He, they* are permitted to go out even to the market place occasionally when it is necessary for them, and because they are strongly bound to the Creator blessed be He, even the wayfarers will not disturb their devekuth: that is the meaning of 'the sons may go with bindings,' i.e., bound to the Creator in their thoughts. And 'the sons of kings': they are those who have nothing but the animal soul or even the spirit but no part yet of the higher soul; such a one *ought not to rely on his being bound* [to God] in his thoughts because he has not yet attained the levels of thought and perhaps the binding will not be strong enough and he will fall; therefore he ought not to go idle but, like a bell that rings out, thus his voice should always ring out with words of Torah and prayer and fear of God; and he should not rely on devekuth in thought, for the wayfarers will interrupt him, God forbid, seeing that his devekuth is feeble. 'And so may any one': this means that all men are equal in this and there will be found almost no one on the level of the sons who go out in bindings. '[The sages spoke] only of the present'—i.e., in terms of what *they* were; they speak about themselves, and not about others.

These words certainly do not evince "a new attitude to reality." It would be possible to argue that this "aristocratic" view of Meshullam Feibush is not representative of Hasidism; it is exceptional in its practical conclusions even if it contains no innovations in principle with respect to the doctrine of the Great Maggid.

The other trend in Hasidism, which leans to a kind of "propaganda" in favor of service of God in corporality, and which is rep-

---

21 *No'am Elimelekh* (Lemberg, 1874), end of the commentary on Korah.

22 *Derekh 'emet* (Jerusalem), p. 22.

resented with distinction by R. Ze'ev Wolf of Zhitomir—even this trend does not, for all that, teach a change of attitude in principle to reality as such. The very need for preaching service in corporality, when the preaching is addressed to "men of the spirit" who apparently considered it beneath them to put the new ideals of Hasidism into practice in the realm of worldly intercourse—this need indicates that the religious ideal was devekuth and not "the consecration of the natural relationship with the world."[23]

These are the words of R. Ze'ev Wolf of Zhitomir[24]:

And that is what is meant by the injunction 'skin carcasses (*nivlata*) in the market place (Talmud Pesachim 113b)': the word *nivlata* is equivalent to *novlot*, "fallen fruit" of wisdom; that is, those letters that fell from the supreme wisdom above to the market place. . . . 'And do not say I am a priest, I am a great man', and *it is not in accord with my honor to descend to the lower levels*, but rather to stand on his sacred height and to perform the divine service in study and prayer and the like.

Contact with the world has become the factor that liberates man from the world and his dependence on it. It is on the ground of the concrete that man must pass his hardest test: to perform the external act in an attitude of indifference, while concentrating in devekuth on the divine spark it contains and on the task of raising this to its root in the Divinity. This liberation which man obtains for himself from the world and all its gifts stands him in good stead in the hour of prayer to save him from "alien thoughts"—i.e., from thoughts of worldly occupations. And this is how R. Ze'ev Wolf of Zhitomir puts it:[25]

Also in matters of corporality of this world, let his actions be below while his thought cleaves to the Divinity, blessed be He, on high; then it will be easy for him to study and to pray without the intrusion of alien thoughts; and nothing will hinder him in his devekuth. And with God's help it will be clear to us whence come the alien thoughts that disturb man in the midst of his prayer and his occupation with the Torah: because when he is occupied with corporeal matters he does not direct his thoughts to perform everything while binding himself to God.

Hasidism was faced with the critical problem of the splitting of life into external action and inner intention; and the problem became

23 *Origin*, p. 107.
24 *Or ha-me'ir*, p. 25a.
25 *Ibid.*, p. 14a.

more acute precisely because of Hasidism's insistence on not abandoning the realm of action. At the very beginning of its way it was already conscious of this, as witness the famous homily of R.Nahman
of Kossow:

> I have heard in the name of our teacher and rabbi, R. Nahman of Kossow,
> that he reproved people who do not put into practice the verse 'I have set
> God before me' also when they are engaged in commerce and trade. And if
> you should say, how can this be done? Why, when a man is in the synagogue
> praying, he finds it possible to think about all sorts of things, about Torah
> and about business too; well, then, the reverse should also be possible. And
> the words of the wise are pleasantness.[26]

II

Buber goes too far, it seems to me, from the moment he attempts
to find in the encounter between man and world the echoes of a
Hasidic ethics. Once Buber has lost the original meaning of the
doctrine of the raising of the sparks, which knows nothing of "the
infinite ethos of the moment"[27], he seeks to anchor this doctrine
to ethical teaching.

The redemption of things to Buber means man's turning to them
in "good will and faithfulness"[28]—redemption through dialogue.

I think that Buber's excessive concentration on the element of the
encounter of man and God within the world gives rise to a dispropor-
tion in his rendering of the Hasidic world image: he purchases the
redemption of the moment at the price of that which was the declared goal of Hasidism. He wishes to see the goal in the "moment"
itself; he abhors the pretensions to greatness, the Messianic phrases
"I have come in order to . . ."; he has no love for the banners proclaiming the goal by its name. The goal must remain hidden, undefined, for otherwise it is doomed to burst apart. Buber is indeed
correct in his feeling that in this respect Hasidism was more moderate
than the movement that preceded it, Sabbatianism; but it by no
means stands for an atomistic ideology in which every moment and
every action is of equal worth and equally endowed with "sacramental possibility."

---

[26] *Toldot Ya'akov Yosef*, p. 20a.

[27] *Origin*, p. 117.

[28] *Ibid.*, p. 84.

Buber's intense desire to see in redemption the redemption of the moment, devoid of theology and of history, leads him to extreme formulations: "The Hasidic message of redemption stands in opposition to the Messianic self-differentiation of one man from other men, of one time from other times, of one act from other actions."[29] It seems to me that one must distinguish between the moderation shown by Hasidism with regard to the Messianic idea—a result of the lesson it learned from the failure of Sabbatianism—and the conception Buber tries to see as central to Hasidic thought, which he describes as though it stood for a fundamentally anti-Messianic world view, or as though it conceived of the redemption of the moment as a substitute for the glorious proclamations of the Messianic age. Buber sometimes is led to extreme formulations on these points, as when he declares that "Messianic self-disclosure is the bursting of Messiahship"[30] in the eyes of Hasidism.

Even though Buber insists that "Hasidism has no place for priests,"[31] it is impossible to ignore the basic fact of Hasidism: the existence of the zaddik, who, even though he was not privileged to live by a different "law" from the rest of the congregation, was nevertheless a charismatic personality, and this from the metaphysical as well as the sociological aspect. The zaddik "works in the upper worlds" more than the ordinary man does. This function loses its meaning in Buber's thought both theoretically and practically. The zaddik's work in the upper worlds presupposes the existence of a goal beyond the encounter with the concrete, which requires for its attainment more than "the performance of man's daily allotted tasks." Buber's characterizations do not do justice to the figure of the zaddik because they fail to take note of the mystic side of his life. After all, it was not from his pedagogical talents that he derived his authority, and even if the Hasidic ideal was not always realized, it should be emphasized that the tension between the two poles of the zaddik's work—the purely mystic pole and the social pole—does constitute a problem in Hasidism.[32] Moreover, this disparity between the zaddik and the rest of mankind is of a Messianic character. It is obvious that an extremist doctrine like that of R. Nachman of Bratzlav, which

---

[29] *Ibid.*, p. 111.

[30] *Origin*, p. 109.

[31] *Be-Pardes ha-Hasidut*, p. 67. (The English text differs somewhat; *Origin*, p. 128.)

[32] See my article on this question in *Molad*, no. 143–144.

speaks of the "perfect zaddik," focussed entirely on the Messianic figure; but Messianism lived on in the much more moderate Hasidic schools as well, a latent life associated with the figure of the zaddik who brings redemption closer.

In these comments, my intention has been only to raise some doubts about the one-sidedness of Buber's account, which blurs over, in principle, the distinctions between men. The same holds true for Buber's third assertion, that Hasidism does not distinguish "one act from other actions." I am far from wanting to assert that Buber's view is a superficial one. Buber knows well the place occupied for the Hasidim in the world of action by Torah and commandments, and he knows too that by this primary fact of its great conservatism in the observance of the commandments, Hasidism from the very start fixed the bounds of the permitted and the forbidden, the clean and the unclean. It follows that not everything is capable of being hallowed, and Buber's liberal formulation that all existence is endowed from the start with "sacramental possibility"—whose meaning for him is confined to the act of direction toward God—this formulation does not reflect Hasidism's new attitude to reality. Buber does not draw the proper inferences from this discrepancy; instead he makes it the occasion of a serious charge against Hasidism itself. He blames it for not being consistent and for stopping half-way, instead of drawing the conclusions that would logically follow from its attitude to the concrete, as Buber sees it.

He writes:[33] "The *mitzvot*, the commands, designate the realm of things that *are already explicitly given to man* for hallowing . . . The Torah indicates the circumference of revelation as it is till now." This is a very significant sentence, and Buber explains his meaning in two ways. On the one hand, he claims that that realm which is not *yet* capable of sanctification—i.e., the realm which from its very foundation is one of impurity according to the Torah, has become the subject of an eschatological dream: "In the Messianic perspective the essential distinctions of the Torah appear provisional and temporary."[34] And though such a statement decidedly mars the perfection of Buber's system, according to which Hasidism makes no distinction between this era and the Messianic era, he nevertheless takes up this idea because he thinks that perhaps it was Hasidism's secret dream to

[33] *Origin,* p. 50.
[34] *Origin,* p. 73–74.

bring about a more inclusive neutralization of existence, one not limited by the bounds of "revelation as it is till now." On the other hand, Buber is dissatisfied with Hasidism because it does not expand the realm of revelation, and in this he sees its failure: "The conserving force secretly remained superior to the moving and renewing one and finally conquered it within Hasidism itself."[35]

If Hasidism had been more universal and had dared to broaden the "horizon of revelation," instead of confining itself from the start to the revelation set down in the Torah, it would have achieved this greatness at the price of antinomianism, as Christianity did in relation to Judaism; and is it not thus that we must understand Buber's position?

It is true that Hasidism recognized an infinity of levels on which the Torah might be read—in this it added nothing new to the Kabbalah;[36] but it had in mind not the breadth of revelation but its depth. These are the Maggid's words on the subject:[37]

In the future the Messianic age the Holy One blessed be He will draw forth the sun from its sheath, i.e., men will be able to perceive it as it is without a covering, whereas now they would not be able to endure its brightness as it is in itself; for not every mind can endure this; but only the zaddikim who have freed themselves from corporality can attain to this, each one according to the degree to which he is free of corporality. . . . The more he clings in devekuth to a higher world, the more will the reach of his perception and understanding be enlarged and he will no longer be so restricted; and the more he removes himself from his root [in the divinity], the more restricted the Torah becomes, until he reaches this world where everything is restricted so completely that you have hardly a commandment that does not involve quantities and measures. Thus the Holy One blessed be He restricts (metsamtsem) himself and is present in this world through the Torah and commandments which exist here in restriction and according to measured quantities. And he who is worthy and sees higher worlds while he is performing the commandments—that is, he who frees himself from corporality—has greater joy since whatever is higher is wider . . . and there he knows a joy from it [the commandment] that he cannot know here since it is restricted and veiled.

And further on:

When the Torah was given at Sinai, it was given through the medium of speech; and when we consider this, then certainly there must have been

35 *Ibid.*, p. 127.

36 *See* G. Scholem, "La signification de la loi dans la mystique juive," *Diogène,* no. 14, April 1956; and the beginning of the second part of this article in no. 15, July 1956.

37 *Maggid,* p. 19b.

thought there also, since speech follows from thought. Thus we find that the Torah was given in speech and in thought, but the action is in our own hands.

The generation of the Maggid knew that the last word on the essence of the Torah will never be said, but this spiritualistic tendency or the "Torah of thought and speech" does not cancel out the concrete demands of the "Torah of action," and this is the essential difference between Hasidic and Sabbatian spiritualism. The unclean as such will never be transformed to holiness at the hands of man. That is a realm that can be redeemed solely by God, if he wills it.

Hasidism does not strive to eradicate the duality of holiness and *Sitra Ahera* ("the other side"—i.e., evil). On the contrary, it rejects this possibility and recognizes that the *kelipah* (the unclean shell) has a legitimate right to existence; only it wants this existence to be a passive one. The Hasid's problem begins when the unclean attempts to set itself against the holy in a contest for supremacy over the life of the individual and of the community. Hasidism itself is not free of ambivalence in its attitude to this question; and from this ambivalence spring also the two ways it indicates as solutions to the problem: the way of keeping the alien thought at a distance and the way of "transforming it to holiness"; but it is clear that with respect to the realm defined from the start as unclean (such as unclean fowl whose consumption is forbidden, and the like)—no one would be so bold as to approach this realm from the ideological standpoint that it should be "hallowed."

Buber certainly perceived the prior limitations placed on the extension of the holy over the profane realm by the claims of the Torah. And since he himself came to Hasidism without these prior "shackles," he was able to keep his neo-Hasidic doctrine clear of that conflict which, in original Hasidism, sets bounds from the first on a conception of conquest of the profane realm by the holy.

III

In connection with the sanctification of the profane realm, I should like to deal with one more point that does not seem very clear to me in Buber's teaching: I refer to the doctrine of the *"mahshavot zarot,"* the alien thoughts. I want to raise two questions which are essentially one: the first, as to Buber's distinction in principle between the nature of the "alien thoughts" and the "corporeal," or concrete

(I do not mean a simple distinction between the corporeal and the spiritual); and the second, as to his attempt to find a distinct approach and a distinct significance for each one of these realms.

Buber does not attach sufficient importance to the doctrine of the alien thoughts in Hasidism, and he dismisses it in a few sentences which introduce complications into his own system. Hasidism preached constant service of God. "Service" was no longer identical with prayer but with "devekuth"—for which prayer itself now became a means, one among others. The means here became very many, and embraced all spheres of life, as Buber rightly notes; but even now it was possible to speak of two kinds of service of God: service in spirituality, i.e., in study and prayer, and service in corporality, i.e., in all everyday activity.

We have seen already how Hasidism struggled with the problem of putting in practice the service of God in corporality; it struggled because it did not always believe man capable of overcoming corporality itself. The battle against "alien thoughts" during prayer is only one facet of this problem, which assumes greater acuteness because this is the last station in the retreat from the encounter with corporality. In the profane realm this encounter does not depend on man's free will. "Alien thoughts" are defined in Hasidism as essentially the appearance in man's mind, at the time of prayer, of any thought whatsoever that by its very nature is extraneous to the prayer. This "thought" deflects man from his devekuth to God, and as such it is "alien." In other words: the *world* persists in rising up before the person in prayer when he is seeking God.

All the thoughts and associations with which he busied himself when he went out to his work and his business . . . and talked and bargained with the uncircumcised: now at the time of study and prayer they rise before his eyes, and these are the very 'alien thoughts' that come to man at the time of study and prayer.[38]

And Buber defines the situation well: The appearance of the alien thoughts

signifies an appearance of God in the things that are seemingly farthest from Him, as it is written (Jeremiah 31,2): 'The Lord has appeared to me from afar.' We should receive this appearance willingly and do what it demands of us: in the sphere of our fantasy to liberate the pure passion from its object which limits it and direct it to the limitless.[39]

38 *Or ha-me'ir,* p. 30a.

39 *Origin,* p. 54–55.

"What matters is not to surrender to the images of fantasy that appear, but to separate the kernel from the shell and to redeem those elements themselves."[40]

Buber states this matter accurately. According to him, the "alien thoughts" are characterized by a sort of "transparence" that cancels out their concrete significance when man applies himself to them with the intention of raising them to their root, somewhat as though he stripped off the shell and concentrated on the inside. Is not this exactly Hasidism's view on service in corporality, of which "alien thoughts" are only one facet? Is it not precisely thus that it seeks, in its encounter with the concrete, to strip off the shells of all existence? But Buber cannot be consistent and conceive of the "alien thoughts" as he conceives of "service in corporality," since in following this line he would arrive at a positive valuation of the alien thoughts, as such—something far from his heart. For Hasidism this is not a problem at all, since it rejects the realm of the concrete in itself, just as it rejects the "alien thoughts" in themselves.

Buber sees in Hasidism the tidings of a new confrontation of man with God and world, or, more precisely: the secret of the ever-recurring encounter with the inwardness of existence, it being in *this* that you hear the voice of God. It is not my intention here to analyze the place of this thesis in the catalog of religious and philosophical phenomena, and I do not wish to call it by a name which generally does more to obscure than to clarify the thing it names; in order to understand Hasidism one must realize that it did not ask itself how it might obtain an "answer" from God, but how to serve God. It seems to me that this matter is of the greatest importance for understanding the consciousness of the Hasidic believer.

"The service of God" is not, in Buber's doctrine, a strictly-defined and exacting concept, such as it emerges from the Hasidic sources. This "service" is a discipline that subjugates the periphery to the center whose radiation is constantly streaming down on it; it works steadily for the absorption of the profane realm in the holy, but its activity is strictly delimited and so is its mandate. The breadth of the spectrum of activity, including for instance the possibility of serving God by dancing and by eating, is not meant to mitigate the severity of this discipline, but to claim this realm too for "the service of God." In other words: nothing any longer exists for its own sake.

40 *Origin*, p. 79.

How shallow is the happiness man feels in his existence if it is not bent toward the service of God: if it is bent toward happiness as such. Such happiness is construed by Hasidism as happiness having *"peniot"*—a "bent"—its face bent toward something that is not "service of God". It was this same spiritual position that gave rise to the concept of *"shivyon"*—equanimity—the quality of seeing all circumstances as equal, the equanimity of man with regard to his personal fate; and that quality of irrational "trust" (*"bitahon"*) in which Hasidism gloried. This is a trust that from the start forgoes even a theodicy.

The true reason for the Hasidim's reservations about service to God through self-mortification also is not emphasized in Buber's writings. Merely to note the fact is likely to give the reader the impression that here is a turn toward affirmation of life of the body and of temporal life as such, even if not necessarily with a materialistic intention. Not only this, but it is possible to argue that the opposite of self-mortification is joy: this pair of concepts creates the sought-for illusion. On the nature of true joy it is said in "The Testament of the Baal Shem Tov"[41]:

And let him not be dejected when he lacks the desires of this world; on the contrary, *let him rejoice in having attained to the subjugation of his desire for the glory of the Creator, blessed be He,* as our sages of blessed memory say: 'and rejoice in suffering'—in this, that he is not drawn after his desire even in thought, but humbles it and vanquishes the kelipot.

The opposite of joy is dejection, and the negation of this does not arise from love of life but from love of God and from the appreciation of the place which "the service of God" occupies in Hasidism. In other words: dejection deflects man from his chief aim and turns him back to occupation with himself; and you will find no evil urge greater than this occupation with oneself: indeed it is an egregious case of service of God with a "bent", "peniot." Self-mortification too is prohibited for this same reason: one must beware lest he become self-conceited; and the Hasid prays: "May He aid me that men shall not know of my deeds."[42] In these doctrines with their extreme conclusions there echoes a little of that paradoxical idea, so pregnant with danger: "He must perform his deeds in secrecy so that it will appear to men as though he were no Hasid."[43]

[41] *Zawwaath ha-Rivasch* (Jerusalem, 1948), p. 4.

[42] *Ibid.,* p. 11.

[43] *Ibid.,* p. 15.

Thus Hasidism understands "service of God" for His sake alone. It seems to me that these concepts of "equanimity," "trust," joy and self-mortification do not find full expression in Buber's teaching. Moreover, a detailed examination of them, which is not possible within this framework, would probably lead us to a less homogeneous view of the problems of Hasidism than that which Buber presents us with.

It is difficult to find in Buber's teaching the daring of man's upward climb to God as it emerges in Hasidic doctrine: that burning desire to cleave (*devekuth*) to the upper world, which was recognized already by the first *Mitnagdim*, opponents of Hasidism: that encounter which transcends the "encounter through the concrete." And equally difficult is it to find in Buber Hasidism's basis for that encounter in the lower world: the code of obligations which it imposes.

IV

Buber does not draw his conclusions about Hasidism's "healthy" view of life ("healthy" without any shade of vulgarity) out of thin air. He succumbed to the plenitude of the Hasidic world of aphorism: this plenitude sharpened to a point, in which you can find everything in the most brilliant and exaggerated form, in which every saying embodies a revolution. Here there is no leisure to explain and to clarify "problems," here Hasidic society seizes the sinner by the forelock and cries, "You are a zaddik—a righteous man!"—not because, God forbid, it has mistaken a sinner for a zaddik, but because it is too short of breath to express itself at length, and so it flings forth a proclamation.

In *For the Sake of Heaven* we read that the disciples of the "Seer" call his attention to the fact that he is cultivating the society of a sinner. To this his answer is:

I know all that you know about him. But what can I do? I love joy and hate dismalness of soul. Now this man is a very great sinner. Even immediately after the accomplishment of sin when nearly all men are wont to repent, though it be but for a moment, though it be only to plunge back into folly soon enough, even in that hour this man resists heaviness of heart and does not repent. And it is joy that attracts me.[44]

This formulation "it is joy that attracts me" is not at all the same

[44] *For the Sake of Heaven*, p. 6.

as those admonitions against "black bile" which the "Seer" gave to R. Menachem Mendel of Kotzk, who was known to be under the influence of "black bile"; for the demand that one free oneself from "black bile" on the grounds of religious principle[45]—because it is an obstacle in the service of God—is far from the expression of a personal opinion on the anecdotal plane. Since the anecdote, as I have said, makes no effort—and by its very nature makes no effort—to define itself in terms of the categories of a theoretical framework, we easily risk distorting its meaning if we take it and breathe into it the breath of life along the lines that we desire. And one who reads the words of the "Seer" thinks erroneously that joy as such became the highest religious value in Hasidism.

In a similar way Buber presents the legend about the Baal Shem Tov, who refused comfort after the death of his wife and said: "I had hoped to journey to heaven in a thunderstorm like Elijah, but now it has been taken from me, for I am now only half of a body." And from this Buber comes to conclusions on the attitude of Hasidic ethics to woman.[46] Yet in this anecdote Hasidism teaches nothing new, and certainly it has nothing to do with ethics. The halachic perfection of the Jew requires that he be married; on his status depend the requirements of purification, which has a religious, not an ethical significance. About the attitude to woman in Hasidism we read in the name of R. Menahem Mendel of Mezritch:

Let him love his wife only as he loves the tefilin (the phylacteries), only because they are God's command; and let him not muse on her, for he is only like one who travels to the fair, and he cannot travel without a horse, but should he therefore love the horse? Is there a greater foolishness than that? Thus in this world man needs a wife for the service of God, *in order to merit the world to come.*

This should not be understood as implying any disparagement of woman; everything is a *means* for the service of God, and so is woman. Altogether, ethical arguments very seldom serve as motivation in Hasidism—surprisingly enough. One could go on giving examples to show the many possibilities of inauthentic interpretation inherent in the anecdotal form, but my intention was not to analyze this subject for its own sake but only to express my doubts as to the

[45] This demand is indeed found in the writings of the "Seer" (see *Or ha-Torah,* Warsaw, 1911, to the Bible portion "Va-yeshev"), but it does not differ in this from the general conception found in Hasidism.

[46] *Origin,* p. 126.

possibility of using anecdote as the sole source for understanding any of the phenomena of life and especially a religious phenomenon. Buber argues that it is precisely through the anecdote that teachings were transmitted, and precisely here that it becomes possible to feel the pulse of life.

Buber's struggle to clarify the nature of the Hasidic doctrine of man finds its expression, more than in any of his other works, in the novel *For the Sake of Heaven.* Here Buber contends with the problem before our eyes, as he presents a confrontation between two versions of Hasidism: "Pshysha," with which he identifies himself, and "Lublin."

True, the main theme of the book is the question of how to bring about redemption, but this subject is only one of the facets of a fundamental problem: man's path to God and to the creation. The position of each of the two schools on the question of redemption is the outgrowth of its attitude on the more fundamental question. Because of this, it may be appropriate to undertake to clarify a few points in this novel.

The coming of the "holy Yehudi" to the "Seer" of Lublin partakes from the first of the ideological struggle over the way of Hasidism. This is also hinted at in the Hasidic sources.[47] The ecstatic mystic, who secludes himself in a garret and there occupies himself with the secret teaching in order thus to attain "the highest rungs in the service of the Creator"—this mystic, the Yehudi, is seized by doubts. A question stirs in his mind: perhaps this extreme individualism and the mystic attainment of "rungs" are not the essence; perhaps we are wrong in asking God to take us from this world as the price of attaining high "rungs" which can no longer be attained in a garment of flesh and blood. On which side will the scales tip—on the side of life with God, through renunciation of the world and flight from it: or on the side of action within the world, action that does not trouble itself about questions that are not meant for it?[48]

---

[47] *Nifla'ot ha-Yehudi,* p. 8b of the Yiddish version.

[48] I am dealing here only with Buber's presentation of the question, since the sources give no indication as to the nature of the basic difference between the system of "Pshysha" and that of "Lublin." The pupils of the two academies also admitted that they never understood the inner motivation of the rift. The compiler of *Nifla'ot ha-Rabbi* (Warsaw, 1811) writes on p. 58b: "I heard a certain great man say that whoever understands the rift between King Saul and King David in the Bible will understand the depth of the matter of the rift that occurred in the end between our

And Buber presents the principal problem already in the first meetings between the "Seer" and his disciple the "Yehudi," who comes to find in this brotherhood gathered around his teacher the path he should go, and finds it only in part. He does indeed find the brotherhood, but it is not engaged in bringing about "the rebirth of hearts," or, as the Yehudi calls it, in "teshuvah"—turning back to God. The doctrine of the "teshuvah" evolves in the heart of the Yehudi during his stay at the court of Lublin, and it transparently bears an existentialist stamp. The conversation between the "Seer" and the "Yehudi" about the existence of evil represents the two different points of departure:[49]

" 'But do you not see, Jacob Yitzchak,' the *Zaddik* asked, 'that God Himself uses evil?'

'God may, Rabbi. God can use all things, seeing that nothing can prevail against Him. But the good . . . I do not mean God's good . . . I mean the good that exists on earth, mortal good—if it seeks to make use of evil, it drowns in that evil; unnoticeably and without noticing it itself, it is dissolved in the evil and exists no longer.'

'Yet the ultimate principle is God alone!'[49a]

'Assuredly it is. And I hear His words: "My thoughts are not as your thoughts." But I hear also, that He demands something of us, concerning which His desire is that it proceed from us. And if I cannot endure the evil, which He endures, then it becomes clear to me that here, in this impatience of mine, there is manifest that which He demands of me.' "

God's revelation to man is a revelation that takes place in human existence. "If I cannot endure . . ." The meaning of this is that this is not the right way; the meaning is that I am required to act from out of the facts of my own situation and to look on things out of my own eyes, and not from a metaphysical point of view.

The words of the "Seer", that "the ultimate principle is God alone," are reasonable and lucid ones for Hasidism, whose struggle with the forces of evil did not take place on the existential plane. The existential problem received only an incidental answer: how can you complain that it is ill with you when you do not know in the least

rabbi of Lublin and his disciple the holy Yehudi; 'and the secret things belong unto the Lord our God.' "

49 *Nifla'ot ha-Yehudi*, p. 58.

49a Lewisohn, following the German version, translates: "Yet ultimately it depends on God alone!" I have here made use of the Hebrew version. (The translator.)

what is good and what is ill, and perhaps your sense of ill is only your failure to understand God's good, since "all that the Merciful One does, He does for good"! It seems doubtful to me that Hasidism indeed taught the ethics of "impatience" which is here put in the mouth of the "Yehudi."

What did the "Yehudi" learn in Lublin? He came half of the way he had to go: the "Seer" taught him that one must free oneself from the "compulsion" of the world as world, the world as temptation to sin. He taught him the way of Hasidism, of liberation from the world even while one is observing it and in contact with it. He taught him the doctrine of the Maggid of Mezritch. In the same conversation in which the "Yehudi" makes his confession about the great temptation he had to withstand when the woman appeared naked in his room, and he was forced to jump through the window in order not to fall into sin, the "Seer" recounts his own version of a temptation in a similar matter: the "Seer" found the way by which one need not flee but instead transforms everything to "the road that leads straight to Lisensk," to his rabbi R. Elimelech.[50] And indeed it was thus that Hasidism taught the doctrine of man's freedom, his liberation from his dependence on the world, for in truth "the ultimate principle is God alone." It is doubtful whether Buber too subscribes to the words which he puts in the mouth of the "Seer" in the full force of their meaning. I lean more to the impression that the way of "Lublin" signifies for the "Yehudi" no more than the beginning, the turning-point: he learns there primarily what not to do, namely, not to flee any longer from reality. This marks the beginning of his independent path which takes him far from the position expressed by the rabbi. From here onward his way is in the sign of rebellion against all that constitutes the core of Hasidism. Thus this matter is understood also by R. Meir and R. Mordecai of Stevanitz, who see in the "Yehudi"

an alien element which had penetrated the sanctuary and was boldly in revolt against the whole realm of mystery: against the sacred majesty of that high man who stands in the middle of the world, against his covenant with the higher powers, against his influence upon the blendings of the spheres of heaven, against his combat with the demonic forces.[51]

The activism of "Lublin" is directed toward the redemption of

50 *For the Sake of Heaven*, pp. 58-60.
51 *For the Sake of Heaven*, p. 214.

the world on the basis of gnostic and theocentric suppositions. The activism of "Pshysha," as it is conceived by Buber, is agnostic and anthropocentric. Pshysha's opposition to the "forcing of the end" does not stem from a despair that says "Israel has no Messiah because they have already devoured him," nor does it take the position, "sit still and do not act" since the Messiah will come "when one is not looking for him." On the contrary—according to Buber—it demands a life that is all preparation for the days of the Messiah. This preparation lies in the special activity man displays in his inner life with the creation, an activity that does not know "calculations of the end" and does not seek them. Here Messianism stands stripped of its historic garments and emptied of its historic content. The "Yehudi" abhors the Messianic apocalyptic of Menahem Mendel of Rymanov and the kabbalistic "doctrine of the *kavanot*" (spiritual intentions) of the "Seer" of Lublin. The historic Messianic doctrine becomes on the lips of the "Yehudi" a doctrine of man's life with the creation.

This to Buber is in the nature of "a revelation of the Shekhinah" (God's indwelling) and indeed the Shekhinah appears to the Yehudi in a vision and tells him: [52]

Dost thou mind how thou meantest to follow me and estrangedst thyself from me the more? One cannot love me and abandon the created being. I am in truth with you. Dream not that my forehead radiates heavenly beams. The glory has remained above. My face is that of the created being.

The message of Hasidism in Buber's view is its great faith that we can act and are bidden to act; even if "the paths of heaven" are not clear to us, the paths of earth are clear to the Holy One; even if "His thoughts are not our thoughts," our thoughts nevertheless are His thoughts. Messianism will be that "Amen" of God to mankind.

This is the tenor of the marvelous conversation between the "Yehudi" and R. Yeshaya who represents the anti-activism of despair: [53]

Yeshaya: 'Effectiveness is made a conscious goal here.'
'That is it.'
'But shall one not strive to be effectual, Yeshaya?'
'Ah, you do understand me. Assuredly, so long as God lets us crawl in this mortal dust, it is well that we improve each other's lives a little and even, if you will, each other's souls. And there are some here who have a hidden as

[52] *Ibid.*, p. 229.
[53] *Ibid.*, p. 100f.

well as a manifest power to do this. But it is too much when the little worm rises and with mighty gestures adjures the Heavens, precisely as though the world's redemption depended upon it . . ."

'Perhaps the redemption of the world really depends on us, Yeshaya?'

'On us?'

'Not on our incantations. They probably have power only upon our own being. Not on anything wherewith we may strive to bring about redemption. Our very striving is the proof of our failure. But when we seek to effect nothing, then and then only we may not be wholly without power.'

This is Messianism without eschatology.

Buber wishes to see in the "Yehudi's" doctrine a religious, non-orthodox version of Ahad ha-Am's idea of the "rebirth of hearts," seasoned with the tiniest pinch of religious anarchism which finds concrete expression in the "Yehudi's" disregard for the appointed times of prayer.

The problem of deferring prayers beyond their appointed time arose already at the beginning of Hasidism's history. And it appears that even then there were conflicting ideas on this subject in the Hasidic camp.

In the pamphlet "The Testament of the Baal Shem Tov"[54] we find an opinion that the Baal Shem Tov himself was punctilious about observing the time of prayer, like the first Hasidim (of the Mishnaic period).[55]

At the very least let him take care that the prayer, whether in winter or in summer, be before sunrise, that is, the greater part of the prayer, nearly up to the prayer 'Shema', should be completed before sunrise, and the difference between saying it before sunrise and after sunrise is as the distance between east and west. . . . Let not this matter seem trivial in your eyes, for it is of great import, and the Baal Shem Tov of blessed memory was very punctilious about this; and sometimes when it was time, and he did not have a prayer quorum, he would pray alone.

On the other hand, the prevailing opinion in this pamphlet is that man ought to pray with fervor at any price (and this of course must be understood to mean: also at the price of deferring the time of prayer.) It is not my intention here to enter into a textual discussion as to the various possible sources from which this pamphlet was compiled: what is important is only to know that the difference of opinions is an old one, and to know its significance.

In the same pamphlet, p.21, it is said:

---

54 "The Testament of the Baal Shem Tov," p. 6.

55 According to Talmud Berakhof 9b.

Let a man not say, if I can pray with fervor, I will pray, and if not, I will force myself to pray; but on the contrary, let him strengthen himself all the more, for does not this [the obstructions to his praying] mean that the king is in that very place and they [the alien thoughts] are concealing the king from him [i.e., their resistance becomes stronger the closer he is to his goal].

Forced prayer is the antithesis of fervent prayer, and if fervor cannot always be attained at the hour appointed for prayer by the Halachah, one must wait for it to come. It is obvious that in such a case one can let the time of prayer go by. The tendency of the "Yehudi" to delay his prayers regularly is only a more extreme expression of those same anarchic elements that revealed themselves in Hasidism already at the start and that were curbed by the movement itself. The strict halachic framework was weakened when the new religious content forced its way in, when the scale of values was revised and "devekuth" occupied the highest rung. But Buber transposed this problem to another sphere. The "Yehudi" answers R. Yeshaya's remonstrations over his delay in the time of prayer[56]:

The word, that it may be a living word, needs *us*. True, it has appointed times and seasons. But those who neglect them and wait do not do so in order to have an easier time. They tarry till they can enter wholly into the spirit of the praying and thus prepare in their aloneness the rebirth of the congregation. When I stand alone before the Lord, I stand there, not as a single soul before its Maker, but as the community of Israel before its God.

The Yehudi's motive is not convincing and the connection between "the rebirth of hearts" in the congregation and the delay in the appointed time of prayers is not as clear as it should be, not to mention that this motive is not in the least Hasidic. I do not know what R. Yeshaya means when he says, "This particular meaning of yours is not communicable, nor can it be handed on;" but from the historical point of view we know that it was indeed not handed on, and that the Hasidim of Gur abolished the custom of deferring the time of prayer.

In spite of all, it seems to me that Buber lets himself be ruled by the account of the Yehudi's life in the sources more than his own personal leanings would have permitted. The "Yehudi" does not renounce the path of ecstasy, according to Buber's account, and this path becomes the symbol not only of his life, but even of his death.

---

[56] *For the Sake of Heaven*, p. 102.

In the struggle between heaven and earth, heaven prevails, and the secret of the losing struggle is set down in these words:[57]

How is it, if one is conscious of a plane which one cannot reach so long as one lives in this world and is imprisoned in this body? Ought one not to beseech God to take one hence? And yet it is assuredly true, as Rabbi Moshe Loeb told me: It is here below, that we are stationed. . . . It is here that we are to combat evil—here!

But the secret of the Yehudi's death lies in the mystic "unification" which he performs, and which is not to be performed except in the land of Israel.[58] He seeks truth in heaven, and joins himself to those who are "forcing the end." To be sure, according to Buber's version, there is in this more a submission to the "Seer" of Lublin who asks him to perform this "unification" in order to bring him true tidings from heaven: "Do you really not know, Benjamin, what it means to be a hasid? Will a hasid refuse to give his life?"[59] the "Yehudi" says to R. Benjamin who begs him not to submit to the "Seer." But in the sources there appears more prominently the personal tragedy of one who wanted to "work"—and to "work" is a technical term reserved for one who strives with the upper world.

A marvelous tale about a vision that came to R. Meir Hayyim of Mogielnice, in which he meets the "Yehudi" in the temple of the Messiah, will show us how the "Yehudi's" disciples understood their teacher.

As I was walking along, I came to the temple of the Messiah and knocked for them to open the door to me; and they did so. And there I found the holy Yehudi of blessed memory. And when he saw me (he thought I had already died), he said, 'Listen: they made fools of all of us, and it's all over and done with. I'm a stubborn fellow to be sure, but not such a terribly stubborn one; but you, Meir'l, they've made a fool of you too, and yet you're a terribly stubborn fellow. So don't pay any attention to what they'll promise you.' Then I told him that I had not yet died. Said he to me: 'Meir'l, there's still one chance for you. Go to the land of Israel, and there you'll be able to effect what I could not effect.' And he said to me: 'Meir'l, don't stand idle, go down, do something.' And his intention in this was to counsel me to go to the land of Israel in order there to undertake the same 'unification' which he undertook; and whoever undertakes it outside the land of Israel must needs die at once, as we know happened to the holy Yehudi.[60]

[57] *Ibid.*, p. 62.

[58] *Sihot Hayyim*, Pietrikov 1914, p. 10a; also *For the Sake of Heaven*, p. 285–86.

[59] *For the Sake of Heaven*, p. 280.

[60] *Sihot Hayyim*, p. 10.

Did "Pshysha" then not submit to "Lublin"! And is not this the "truth" which the Yehudi was sent to impart to those below: that the way is the way of *"yihudim"* and *"kavanot"*, of mystic "unifications" and "intentions"? Buber, to be sure, does not refer to this tale, but he gives a hint of its authentic interpretation;[61] nevertheless he comes, for some reason, to the strange conclusion that at the very heart of "Lublin" there was traced the way of "Pshysha," to which "Lublin" itself unconsciously inclined.[62]

The Hasidic tradition does not stress the substantive difference between the path of the "Seer" and that of the "Yehudi" as sharply as Buber does; it tends to give prominence to the personal difference between them and the personal tension at the court of Lublin, but of course one cannot object to the development of the novel along the lines that the author thought right. On the other hand, there is more anecdotal and biographic material in the sources than Buber was interested in using.

This is material to shake one to the depths. The most extravagant elements, elements of the abyss, found a place in this personality who was called "the holy Jew": beginning with his act of indifferently handing the rabbi's shirt to a drunken pauper—an act which Buber turns into an instance of rational ethical conduct—and with the hints in the sources that he sold his "gertel" (the symbolic waistband worn by the pious Jew) for a glass of brandy, and ending with the figure that emerges from the accounts of his admirer Simha Bunam of Pshysha, in which the Yehudi is likened to

'a drunkard and good-for-nothing' whom everyone drives away, but in the end they realize that salvation depends only on him . . . His attitude to his family, too, and especially to his wife, is not marked by that dignity one would associate with a man who cannot care for his household because 'he is in the hands of God.'

On this last point, one finds in the sources a franker approach and less tendency to take the part of the "Yehudi" and to justify him than one finds in Buber. The Hasidim of Pshysha were concerned for their rabbi's honor and struck out printed passages that touch on this matter, but it is quite possible to read through the cancellations, and they did not cancel out the passages in all the editions.

---

[61] *For the Sake of Heaven*, p. 285—6.
[62] Preface to the new English edition *For the Sake of Heaven,* 1953, p. X.

It has not been my intention to argue against Buber's understanding of this subject; I was trying only to clarify for myself in general terms this tangled episode in the story of the Lublin court.
The book deserves detailed criticism, and there is much to say
about a number of basic questions regarding Buber's method of
adapting the material, but these matters have no direct bearing on
the topic I set myself in the present essay. It seems to me that in
spite of the overdrawing that is unavoidable in the medium of the
novel, we have here the advantage of a less naked account than is
possible in any work of systematic thought.[63] Here we stand solidly on
the ground of the Hasidic world: the court of Lublin is flesh and
blood; every conversation in *For the Sake of Heaven* is a chapter
of life in the spiritual world of Hasidism, a chapter sifted free of
all banality and sentimentality, all of it polished by the masterful
use of adumbration, so that if you have not read it several times, you
have not read it at all. Here we are taught by Buber how man should
face the world and God.

[63] E. Simon already pointed out the importance of this in his essay in the special
issue of *Iyyun* in honor of Buber's 80th birthday (v. 9, no. 1, January 1958, p. 38).

RIVKAH SCHATZ-UFFENHEIMER

THE HEBREW UNIVERSITY
JERUSALEM

19

Robert Weltsch

BUBER'S POLITICAL PHILOSOPHY

TO MANY it may appear that Martin Buber is not a political scientist. He is regarded as a religious thinker and as a social philosopher, not as a man of politics. Such a classification, however, would be a fallacy. Buber's concern is with life in its totality and with man in his confrontation with the manifold world. Moreover, any interpretation of the word of God covers the entire human life and activity. From this totality political life cannot be excluded.

The actual world is full of politics, in our time more than ever. It is a demonic force which directs man from the truth and leads him into confusion. In the age of democracy, politics is not simply a struggle for power within the State, but is linked with ideologies like socialism, nationalism and their counterpart. Imbued with such rationalized emotional forces men genuinely believe that the pursuit of their political goal is the fulfilment of the highest human duty for which they are ready to sacrifice everything, even their traditional scale of values. That is one of the dangerous pitfalls of mankind, perhaps the most dangerous of all. Nobody who cares for the human destiny can ignore it. Within the orbit of politics itself men appear helpless. They seem to have lost their way in darkness. Nobody has given such forceful expression to this anguish as Buber. He knows what is wanted, and sees the political bustle of our time with all its shortcomings:

We live at a juncture in which the problem of a common human destiny has become so obstinate that the experienced administrators of the political principle are, for the most part, only able to go through the motions of matching its demands. They offer counsel but know none. They struggle against one another, and every soul struggles against itself. They need a language to understand one another, and have no language except the current political jargon fit only for declamations. For sheer power they are impotent, for sheer tricks they are incapable of acting decisively. Perhaps in the hour when the catastrophe sends in advance its final warning, those who stand on the cross-front will have to come to the rescue. They who have in common the language of human truth must then unite to attempt in common to give at last to God what is God's, or, what here means the same thing, since when mankind has lost its way it stands before God, to give to man what is man's in order to rescue him from being devoured by the political principle.[1]

To prevent man from "being devoured by the political principle" is a task that can be achieved only if we do not regard politics as a separate and secluded realm where the ordinary values of humanity are not valid. As a matter of fact one cannot distinguish precisely between closed compartments of human interest. Man is not a bundle of separate autonomous provinces of the soul. He is a living entity and his actions are determined by his character and by his views, by his principles and by the situation in which he is placed. In this respect, religious and social concepts are bound to influence political thinking unless political passion induces man to betray all this and to subordinate everything to one principle, the lust for power. This is the temptation that always lies in ambush for him who has sold his soul exclusively to politics. Only clear thinking and the appeal to the conscience can rescue man from this abyss.

The job of the philosopher is to point the right way to deal with those problems with which the political man deals in the wrong way. The first question is to enquire what kind of political aim should be striven for. The second question is what means should be employed in the pursuit of the goal.

The challenge of politics begins with the association of men. The fundamental human problem of the relationship between man and his neighbour is the starting point of what Buber calls the Dialogue; the basic relation of "I and Thou" involves a social principle which has also political consequences. When society is organized, even in its primitive stages, the struggle for power is bound to ensue. Someone has to dominate the community. This becomes necessary when the natural conflicts and rivalries between people start and the internal troubles of society have to be checked. It is essential to draw the line between co-ordination and subordination, between co-operation and domination, between society and the state. In human terms the social principle is the more natural and more creative one as it springs from the immediate interdependence of men. Social spontaneity engenders the vitality and cultural unity of the nation. This spontaneity is continuously diminished by the predominance of the political over the social principle, resulting in what Buber calls the "political

[1] "The Validity and Limitation of the Political Principle," *Pointing the Way* (1953), p. 219.

surplus." The political principle, embodied in the state, is the regulating force because of the internal and external dangers which threaten the existence of society:

Society cannot . . . quell the conflicts between the different groups; it is powerless to unite the divergent and clashing groups; it can develop what they have in common, but cannot force it upon them. The State alone can do that. The means which it employs for this purpose, are not social, but definitely political. But all the facilities at the disposal of the State, whether punitive or propagandistic, would not enable even a State not dominated by a single social group (that is to say, by one relatively independent of social divarications) to control the areas of conflict if it were not for the fundamental political fact of general instability. The fact that every people feels itself threatened by the others gives the State its definitive unifying power; it depends upon the instinct of self-preservation of society itself; the latent external crisis enables it when necessary to get the upper hand in internal crises. A permanent state of true, positive, and creative peace between the peoples would greatly diminish the supremacy of the political principle over the social.[2]

This permanent peace, however desirable, is, alas, far away from our reality. It will be reached in Messianic times when the prophesies of the Prophet will be fulfilled. In the meantime, with peace unsecured, the might of the State is still paramount. The political principle is not extinguished. To hold it in check we must turn to the social reality; we must ask what kind of association of men conforms to true human values. True political action should create the conditions for the realisation of justice and individual freedom, preservation of human dignity and fulfilment of the commandments of human ethics.

In his early writings at the beginning of the century, Buber based his social philosophy on the distinction, originally made by Ferdinand Toennies, between Society (Gesellschaft) and Community (Gemeinschaft). It is the distinction between a mechanical and an organical formation. "Society" is an artificial order of people who have to live together in a collective of many common interests and purposes but without a feeling of inner human relation, everyone possessed by his own private business and often with mutual hostility. "Community" is a natural group of people bound together by bonds of blood and family, living close together in genuine neighbourliness, developing ties of personal friendship and brotherhood from which arises a common spirit. From the very definition it becomes clear which form of collective life is considered superior. It is the organical

[2] *Ibid.,* "Society and the State," p. 173.

form, the community with immediate bonds between man and man, not only for practical purposes but because of their close belonging-together, their emotional congeniality, their deep mutual understanding. Mechanised and rationalized "Society" in our age—it was at the beginning of this century—is of the bourgeois-capitalist type. But Marxism clings to the same concept; its social ideal remains within the orbit of the mechanical structure. Although Marx himself in his Communist Manifesto proclaimed the goal of a state-less, free society, somewhat similar to the concept of what was here called community, we know now that the practical effect of Marxist policy was a stronger centralization and a strengthening of the state machinery to the extent of extinction of individual freedom.

Community as a natural creation according to Toennies was originally founded on blood and instinct, but it also became an ideal to be established through the free will of men. It is difficult not to think of the religious communities frequently established in the course of history, of which the original Christians are perhaps the best known example. The recently discovered so-called Dead Sea Scrolls bear the message of a similar group. To bring about such a community, even to transform the whole human society into a "Community of communities" of true human relationship, should be the aim of true Socialism: that was the essence of Gustav Landauer's "Call to Socialism" (Aufruf zum Sozialismus). Buber associated himself wholeheartedly with this doctrine. Socialism cannot be born out of mechanical acts like change of institutions or transfer of the means of production; what is required is the spirit of love which creates the natural forms of living-together, family, herd, nation, and explodes the petrified forms created by hatred and injustice[3]. This social ideal appears unpolitical; but it would have to wait until the transformation of all men and the opening of all hearts to love, unless it is achieved by political means. Theoretically, Landauer conceived his communities as existing outside the state. They have to be built according to the social, not to the political principle; decentralized and not centralized. Buber makes a special point of the strict

---

[3] "Darum braucht es, wie die Welten durch die Brücken des Lichtes verbunden sind, zwischen den Menschen des Geistes, der die Liebe ist, der die Formen des Mitlebens schafft, die Familie, die Herde, die Nation (Sprache, Sitte, Kunst), und der die starrgewordenen Formen, die Hass, Geistlosigkeit und Unbill erzeugt haben, in neuer Gemeinsamkeit sprengt." Gustav Landauer, *Die Revolution*, ed. Martin Buber (Frankfurt, 1907).

differentiation between the two principles which, he says, were confused by most of the thinkers of ancient times, Plato and Aristotle included. What "community" demands is not its inclusion in a political proclamation or programme, but immediate realization by direct action of human beings who transform their life according to this ideal, and do it here and now. The concept of "realization" plays a decisive part in all these ideas which were based on Buber's thought. It was the antithesis of mechanical and organical, of word and deed, of intellectual approach and actual living, of "orientation" and realization, it was the difference between ideologies and ideas, between subscribing to a party programme and opening one's heart to the love of the neighbour. It may be added here in parenthesis that this influence of Buber was strongly felt in the Zionist movement which at the turn of the century was the place of Buber's "political" activity. The same ideas contributed to the rise of the Halutz movement during and after the first World War and in the beginnings of what is now called Labour Zionism. It was the demand to transfer the ideas into one's own life, to realize them on the soil of the Holy Land, instead of making them a political programme on which to vote. Buber found a close affinity between the ideas of Landauer and those of the Jewish Labour philosopher A.D. Gordon.

In spite of the stress laid on the separation of the two principles Buber agrees with Tarde's statement that there is no form of social activity which cannot, on some side or at some moment, become political. This seems to me obvious as there is no social movement of fundamental importance to which the State could be indifferent. The true community which was in the mind of Landauer (or his predecessors like Proudhon, Kropotkin, and others) has never been realized except to a very small extent and for a short time, preferably on virgin land. The title given by Buber to his book devoted to these ideas, "Paths to Utopia," could be interpreted as a sign of resignation. The only exception he makes, the communal settlements in Palestine (now Israel), were born under such special political, military and economic conditions that they require a separate enquiry; it would also have to be examined whether the human principles on which they were established forty years or so ago have survived and remained effective in the second generation.

Owing to his friendship with Gustav Landauer, Buber was a close observer of the Socialist revolution in Bavaria in 1919. At that time many literati—among them a considerable number of idealistic

Jews—believed that the opportunity had come to fulfil the hopes of justice and love. Gustav Landauer was one of those serving on the revolutionary committee which acted as Government. He believed that the community imbued with the spirit of true humanity, which he had advocated in his books, had a chance of coming true. He suffered profound disappointment. The "political principle" was victorious. Landauer himself became a victim of his error. He had to learn that what he saw and heard in the revolutionary committee was the very opposite of what he had sought. In his obituary speech on Landauer at the Prague Conference of the Jewish Labour movement Ha-Poel Ha-Tzair in April 1920 Buber told a story how Landauer had sent him a note from the government meeting containing only the words: "What a torture, what a pain!" The true community did not arise.

It cannot be created by political terror, but only grow from within ("Von innen!"). The first demand is the transformation of men themselves. Socialism had to be religious. The movement of religious socialism with which Buber co-operated knew that only transformed men were able to live together in a true community. But men of this kind had soon to face the choice whether to follow God or Caesar. Something like a test case for the relation of religion and politics arose when one of the few men of this era, who undertook to introduce moral and religious principles into politics, Mahatma Gandhi, started his campaign for Indian independence. Buber was fascinated by this new phenomenon of political approach but he warned Gandhi of self-deception. Was it really possible to use religion as a means for political success? Gandhi had become a political leader, but he preached religion and he could easily be misunderstood to recommend to his followers religion for the sake of politics, even though he himself regarded politics as a means for creating the conditions for religious life. Buber was skeptical:

Does religion allow itself to be introduced into politics in such a way that, nonetheless, a political success can be obtained? Religion means goal and way, politics implies end and means. The political end is recognizable by the fact that it may be attained—in success—and its attainment is historically recorded. The religious goal remains, even in man's highest experiences of the mortal way, that which simply provides direction; it never enters into historical consummation. The history of the created world, as the religions believing in history acknowledge it, and the history of the human person, as all religion, even those that do not believe in history, acknowledge it, is what takes place on the journey from origin to perfection, and this is registered by other signs than that of success.[4]

Politics and religion cannot be reconciled so easily. They exist in quite different spheres. They have a different approach. The unconditionality of the spirit cannot be equated to the conditionality of a situation. Gandhi, says Buber,

refuses to exploit human passions, but he is chained as political actor to the political, to *untransformed* men. The serpent is, indeed, not only powerful outside, but also within, in the souls of those who long for political success. The way in which Gandhi again and again exercises self-criticism, going into heavy mortification and purification when the inner serpent shows itself too powerful in the movement, is worthy of the purest admiration. But we do not follow him in this; we know that if we consider the *tragic* character of his greatness, that it is not the tragedy of an inner contradiction, but that of the contradiction between the *unconditionality of a spirit and the conditionality of a situation,* to which situation, precisely, the masses of his followers, even of the youth belong. [My italics—R. W.] This is the tragedy that resists all superficial optimistic attempts to bring about a settlement; the situation will certainly be mastered, but only in the way in which at the close of a Greek tragedy, a theophany (the so called deus ex machina, in truth ex gratia) resolves the insoluble fate. But that is the very soft, very slow, very roundabout, not at all successful step of the deity through history.[5]

Buber and Gandhi agree that the genuine immediate relationship between man and man is the ultimate object of collective life. Though this may be achieved by unpolitical means, by the renunciation of power, even this negation of politics is a kind of political domain. It is to be dissociated from religion because it falls under a different category. This difference has to be kept in mind. On the other hand,

One should, I believe, neither seek politics nor avoid it, one should be neither political nor non-political on principle. Public life is a sphere of life; in its laws and forms, it is, in our time, just as deformed as our civilization in general; today one calls that deformity politics as one calls the deformity of working-life technique. But neither is not deformed in its essence; public life, like work, is redeemable.[6]

Public life is redeemable! It is redemption man is called upon to attain. Politics is so interwoven with life in general and with all the functions of man, so dependent on his general outlook on questions

---

[4] "Gandhi, Politics, and Us," *Pointing the Way.*

[5] *Ibid.,* pp. 129–3C.

[6] *Ibid.,* p. 136.

of morals, of religion, of social behaviour, that the standard and the norm of politics cannot be separated from other considerations. If that happens, politics became a "deformity." Kant said that "true politics cannot make a step without having paid homage to morality." But there can be no rigid laws of political moral and no dogmatic approach in this matter. Politics is not concerned with deciding abstract principles in a philosophical manner; it is a task of decision for a living man confronted with a situation. Situations are variable, endless, complicated, they compel man to consider all factors and the realities of power, and to give his answer. This answer cannot be detached from moral judgment. It cannot be inspired simply by the necessities of power or by the *raison d'état*. It is also inadmissible to regard the political sphere, as Karl Schmitt has suggested, as amoral and solely defined by the criterion "friend-enemy." On the other hand, the obligation towards one's own group cannot be dismissed or neglected. If this were so, the moral norm in political matters would be easy to define, but it would remain an abstraction, ignoring the complex reality of life. Against such temptation of sermonizing Buber is guarded by his own humanity. He draws the logical conclusions from the basic concepts with the utmost intellectual acumen; on the other hand he sees man in his distress when confronted with the collision of duties arising out of an existential situation. A human being cannot live up to the abstract extreme demand, but he has to do his best to reach what Buber calls the "line of demarcation." No man can transgress the limits of the ideal without perverting it, like Ibsen's Brand, when he ignores the essentials of the human world. One cannot do more than to make the honest effort of "quantum satis," as far as it can go in a given situation. "Situation" is the operative word. No dogmatic principle is valid beyond the power of human beings to realize it. This is perhaps the most important insight of Buber's political philosophy. He says:

I have no warrant whatever to declare that under all circumstances the interest of the group is to be sacrificed to the moral demand, more particularly as the cruel conflicts of duties and their unreserved decision on the basis of the situation seem to me to belong to the essential existence of a genuine personal ethos. But the evident absence of this inner conflict, the lack of its wounds and scars, is to me uncanny. I am not undertaking to set material limits to the validity of the political principle. That, rather, is just what must take place in reality time after time, soul after soul, situation after situation, I mean only to say that this occurrence has obviously become an exceptional one.[7]

What then can man do to try to pave the way for the good within the deformity of public life where the group interests demand his loyalty? What can he do? The answer is: "as much as he can". Beyond this, individual responsibility does not extend:

That one cannot serve God and Mammon is an entirely true saying, for Mammon embraces the soul and leaves nothing of it free. On the other hand, I believe that it is possible to serve God and the group to which one belongs if one is courageously intent on serving God in the sphere of the group as much as one can. As much as one can at the time; *'quantum satis' means in the language of lived truth not 'either-or,' but 'as-much-as-one-can.'* [My italics —R. W.] If the political organization of existence does not infringe on my wholeness and immediacy, it may demand of me that I do justice to it at any particular time as far as in a given inner conflict, I believe I am able to answer for. At any particular time; for here there is no once-for-all: *in each situation that demands decision the demarcation line between service and service must be drawn anew* [My italics—R. W.]—not necessarily with fear, but necessarily with that trembling of the soul that precedes every genuine decision . . .[8]

Modern politics and especially the political party does not know this true conflict of conscience (it is an "exceptional occurrence"). Party politics simplifies the moral problem availing itself of the comfortable principle of dividing the world into friend and enemy. It is startling what effect can be produced by this device:

Among the members of the political party are people of the most scrupulous integrity in their private lives. Yet when their party has specified who the (in this case internal) 'enemy' is, these same people will day after day, with peaceful and untroubled conscience, lie, slander, betray, steal, torment, torture, murder. In the factories of party doctrine good conscience is being dependably fashioned and refashioned.[9]

In political struggle this uncritical or intentional distortion of the moral issue leads to an insoluble conflict which constitutes a grave danger to mankind and to the peace of the world, apart from its moral absurdity:

In such a situation man is more than ever inclined to see his own principle in its original purity and the opposing one in its present deterioration, especially if the forces of propaganda confirm his instincts in order to make better use

[7] *Ibid.*, "Validity and Limitation of the Political Principle," p. 217.

[8] *Ibid.*

[9] *Ibid.*

of them. Man is no longer, as in earlier epochs, content to take his own principle for the single true one and that which opposes it as false through and
through. He is convinced that his side is in order, the other side fundamentally out of order, that he is concerned with the recognition and realization of
the right, his opponent with the masking of his selfish interest. Expressed in
modern terminology, he believes that he has ideas, his opponent only ideologies. This obsession feeds the mistrust that incites the two camps.[10]

The claim that moral is always on one's own side only, is at least
an implied admission of the validity of moral in politics. Often this is
cynically denied. Whether politics has anything to do with morals
has always been controversial. True, for Aristotle and his followers
there is no doubt. But those who practise politics often argue that a
state cannot be based on moral principles: it has to fight for its interests, right or wrong, and the sole aim is the survival of the nation,
which inevitably involves quest for power. If Lord Acton was right in
saying that nothing corrupts like power, politics would necessarily
have to be corrupt from the point of view of morals. We all could
observe that politicians who pretend to follow higher moral principles—apart from the well-being of their own nation, often described
as an ethical ideal in itself—incline towards a simple self-righteousness.
By claiming to defend certain well-sounding objects like freedom,
peace, justice, etc. politicians have an easy way of appearing morally
superior while actually pursuing their own interests. Most of the contemporary political phraseology is based on this approach. It is difficult
to say what is worse, this hypocrisy or the overt profession of Machi-
avellian *Realpolitik*.

Buber's admission of a specific political problem does not imply
disregard of moral which imposes limitations on collective actions.
Nationalism can only be justified if it is conscious of its human and
social responsibility. This applies especially to the Jewish people
which has been called upon to bring about the Kingdom of God. If it
used means which contradict the ends, it would sin against its own
meaning. But the drawing of the demarcation line is by no means
simple, and here is one of the pitfalls of the intermingling of religion
and politics. Some have invoked the Bible to show that the nation's
task, willed by God, has sometimes to be carried out at the expense
and to the detriment of others. The idea of the chosen people exempt from moral objections when its own destiny is at stake, is inherent in all nationalism, but has its origin in Judaism. It justifies

---

[10] *Ibid.*, "Hope for this Hour," p. 221.

Yaakob's fraud in obtaining his father Isac's blessing. The man Isac with his limited understanding cannot be allowed to determine the course of history. This overruling of human moral judgment is one of the mysterious paradoxes of religious faith, as Kierkegaard has shown. In modern literature Richard Beer-Hofmann has tried to explain the metaphysical and meta-ethical necessity of Jacob's succession and Edom's deprivation. It is, however, not compatible with the human conception of ethics. These religious aspects have great political implications. Jacob-Israel's selection as recipient of the blessing is of far-reaching consequences for the interpretation of history. It involves the temptation to find an excuse for any means and ways which help towards the realization of the will as expressed in these words. In modern times it has become topical in a new sense. Is it to be assumed that when they conduct politics again in the literal sense the people of Israel, or the state of Israel, are always right in relation to other peoples, to Edom? That would remind us dangerously of the famous dictum on which fascism was based, namely, "The Duce is always right," or, still worse, the demonic—or cynical—formula of Goebbels "Right is what benefits the German people." Moral justification would then only be a question of believing in one's own mission. Nationalism would always be right, at least in its own eyes, as every action could be construed as a necessary stage on the way to the fulfilment of the mission. Against such deviations Buber raises his voice with all his passion. His political conception is determined by social motives and moral ideas. The formation of the true Community of Men—Die wahre Menschengemeinschaft—cannot be achieved by a series of crimes. The political aim does not sanctify the means.

Beware of secularized Messianism! It is not permitted to confound the Messianic vision with the temporary objects of politics. Nothing is more objectionable than to use pseudo-Messianic promises in order to stir up nationalism and ferociousness. In modern Zionism, and especially since the establishment of the State of Israel, this temptation is obvious. To identify nationalism with the will of God is an error. The Jewish position has always been twofold. Side by side with the self-righteous nationalism of the people, the Prophets interpreted Israel's sufferings as God's punishment for His people. Defeat was not, as with paganism, a humiliation for the god of the defeated people; on the contrary, God Himself had engineered the defeat in order to teach His people a lesson. Prophetic politics is politics of the materially powerless, fighting against the hybris of rulers. To invoke Messianism in support of temporal powers would be the opposite of the Prophetic message. At the so-called Ideological Congress in Jerusalem in summer 1957, Buber strongly opposed such misuse of Messianism.

It would appear that to the religious man politics must be utterly repugnant; that the best thing to do would be to abstain completely and to preserve one's own purity by standing aloof and condemning the whirl of Gog and Magog. But that would be easy escapism masquerading as superior morality. It would not conform to the views expressed by Buber already in 1912 in "Daniel," of the necessity of living "on the brink of the abyss," in perpetual danger, "jeopardizing one's soul ever anew, pledged to the holy uncertainty." When Buber was asked in 1919 "what is to be done"—i.e., what political or un-political action or unaction was to be recommended in the confusion of post-war Europe—his answer was: "You shall not withhold your-self." He rejects retirement from the world into the relative safety of monastic life. A division of the world into two separate spheres contradicts the vocation of the human being. Man cannot avoid confronting the oddities of life, and his task is to overcome them. Nor can he avoid being involved in political action unless he inten-tionally blinds himself against reality. Even if he is not able to exert his influence and to form life according to his ideas, he must try to take as many steps in the right direction as is humanly possible in a given situation. It is a meliorist approach which refuses to use loyalty to the "pure" ideal as an excuse for doing nothing and leav-ing the field to evil forces.

An example may be quoted from the orbit of the political com-plex that engaged Buber all his life and confronted him many times with the critical decision whether to "withhold himself" (and live the life of an honoured and successful writer) or to take part in the struggle as far as he could. In Zionism, he fought from the very beginning of his active participation in the movement as a student; he fought against formal nationalism and stressed the necessity of humanism and cultural education as against the concentration on politics. In a letter to Stefan Zweig, written on February 4, 1928 (apparently a misprint for 1918) Buber rejected Zweig's doubts about the concept of a Jewish state as—so Buber thought in 1918—Zweig misrepresented it. He wrote:

Heute nur dies, dass mir von einem'Judenstaat mit Kanonen, Flaggen, Orden' nichts bekannt ist, auch nicht in der Form eines Traums. Was werden wird, hängt von denen ab, die es schaffen, und gerade deshalb müssen die wie ich menschlich und menschheitlich Gesinnten bestimmend mittun, hier, wo es wieder einmal in den Zeiten in die Hand von Menschen gelegt ist, eine Gemeinschaft aufzubauen. Ich kann Ihre geschichtlichen Schlussfolgerungen für das neue Volk, das hier aus altem Blut geschaffen werden soll, nicht gelten lassen. . . . Ich ziehe es jedenfalls vor, das ungeheurliche Wagnis eines Neuen mitzumachen, in dem ich nicht viel von 'Wohlergehen,' wohl aber eine Reihe grosser Opfer sehe, als länger eine Diaspora zu ertragen . . .[11]

Buber himself lived up to his philosophy. Only by taking part in politics could one assure that the ideas for which one stood, could exert their full weight. Zionism was the only field of his extended political activity, as he went all the way from the first beginning of a vague idea until the tenth anniversary of the State of Israel, coinciding with Buber's 80th birthday. It was not an easy way—perhaps one could say it was a sequence of failures and disappointments, if one takes into account only the actual visible results. Buber's life-long effort to give the Jewish renaissance a more than political meaning (which naturally would also have to be reflected in its politics), to make the humanist and religious content of the new community the touchstone of the enterprise, was drowned in the events of wars, revolutions and cruelties. All his pronouncements on Zionist problems during almost sixty years are strongly critical of the prevailing tendency to conceive Zionism as an ordinary political nationalism, seeking for the Jewish people "free development of its potentialities in its own land," so that the Jews could be "a nation like all the nations, a country like all countries, a national movement like all national movements; this is being proclaimed as a demand of commonsense against all 'mysticism'."[12] Against this view, Buber appeals to the testimony of generations of Israel: that this is not enough. Deeper and higher is the idea of Zion. "National forms without the eternal meaning from which they have arisen, would be tantamount to the end of Israel's specific creativeness." It would not be re-birth, but self-deception which conceals the death of the soul.

Buber's practical steps in Zionist politics were in harmony with this conviction. His faith in the national mission of the Jewish people has always been combined with humanity and with the belief in the

[11] Quoted in Hans Kohn, *Martin Buber, Sein Werk und seine Zeit* (1930), p. 170.
[12] *Israel und Palästina.*

priority of the Spirit. He refused to put such abstractions as "nation" above the concrete human beings on whom all depends. From the very beginning he stressed the necessity of transforming man by education and culture instead of using him for political purposes only. He favoured constructive work, cooperation and collective settlements as instruments of the great transformation required. He opposed inhumanity and injustice committed against the inhabitants of the Promised Land. The situation required peaceful co-existence with the Arab people in Palestine. Buber's leadership in "Ihud," the Organisation established by Dr. J. L. Magnes with the aim of finding a just settlement for both peoples of Palestine was a logical consequence of political thinking based on human and religious premises.

In Judaism, religion has a special relation to politics because it addresses itself to the nation. The prophet rises against an erring people and its political leaders; his criticism and demand are pronounced on behalf of the Kingdom of God that is Israel's ultimate task to bring about. The man of the spirit is without political power. "None but the powerless can speak the true King's will with regard to the State and remind both the people and the government of their common responsibility towards this will." In history, the prophet fails and cannot prevent catastrophe. But his warning has not been in vain. Over thousands of years, it has been the pattern of politics rooted in Judaism. From this message derives fundamentally Buber's political philosophy. It has a practical lesson for a small people, which indicates the relation between religious admonition and political reality:

There has been much talk . . . of 'utopian' politics which would relate Isaiah's failure to that of Plato, who wrote the utopian Republic. What Isaiah said to Ahaz is accepted as sublimely 'religious' but a politically valueless utterance, implying one which lends itself to solemn quotation but one inapplicable to reality. Yet the only political chance for a small people hemmed in between world powers is the metapolitical chance Isaiah pointed to. He proclaimed a truth which could not, indeed, be tested by history up to that time, but only because no one ever thought of testing it. Nations can be led to peace only by a people which has made peace a reality within itself. The realization of the spirit has a magnetic effect on mankind which despairs of the spirit. That is the meaning Isaiah's teachings have for us. When the mountain of the Lord's house is 'established' on the reality of true community life, then, and only then, the nations will 'flow' towards it (Is. 2.2), there to learn peace in place of war. . . . The Hebrew prophet invariably receives only a message for a particular situation. But for this very reason his word still speaks after thousands of years to manifold situations in the history of peoples.[13]

13 "The Demand of the Spirit and Historical Reality," *Pointing the Way*, pp. 189f.

ROBERT WELTSCH

LONDON, ENGLAND

20

Jacob Taubes

BUBER AND PHILOSOPHY OF HISTORY

I

INTERPRETERS of history since Hegel tend to regard the arena of world history as the high court of justice against which there is no further appeal. In the succession of ruling empires the eye of the Hegelian philosopher discerns a meaningful pattern and brings order into the criss-cross of events. But at what price is this pattern of meaning, this order in the succession of events achieved? By what criterion is order and meaning established in the course of history? The suspicion arises that Hegelian philosophy of history proceeds by a mystification, turning the *post hoc* into a *propter hoc*. The succession of events is explained and justified by the success of the stronger who through his victory closes the alternatives of a specific historical situation and forces the course of history into one direction.

Is the eye of the philosopher or historian who reads meaning into history not dazzled by the success of the victor? Since the rulers of any time are the legitimate heirs of all those who have ever conquered before, the chain of succession of the periods of history reads as an apology of the successive successes throughout the ages. The booty carried along in the triumphal procession of the ages settles down as the heritage or tradition of man. History is written by the verdict of the victor, so that the silent suffering of the conquered does not enter into its annals.

The success of the successive powers in the course of history becomes all the more the last judgment when the principalities of the world claim to draw the legitimacy of their power from divine authority. Then, indeed, every soul becomes subject to the higher powers of the magistrate. For there is no authority but of God. If the powers that be are said to be ordained by God, then whoever resists the powers resists divine ordinances. And therefore, the first great Christian interpreter of history warns those who resist the authorities that they call upon themselves divine judgment and damnation. It is against such an apotheosis of history that Martin Buber feels called upon to protest. The dilemma, but also the crux of his historical thinking is prescribed by the apparently contradictory task of taking the course of history seriously and yet brushing history against its grain.

II

Hegel's philosophy of history by elevating the course of history to the high court of justice destroys, according to Buber, the dialogical meaning of history. It liquidates both the question that a particular situation has in store for man and the answer he has in all freedom to give to the questions posed by the situation. All human decisions are turned by Hegel into sham struggles. Buber traces the root of Hegel's monological concept of history to the Christian, especially to Paul's concept of history as a history of salvation. In short: in order to oppose Hegel's philosophy of history Buber has first to strike at Paul's theology of history.

Since Paul nowhere in his epistles summarizes his theocentric conception of history Buber must piece together Paul's theology of history from scattered statements. Paul considers the drama of history as the "mystery" predetermined by God, kept hidden before the aeons and generations. But with the coming of the risen Messiah the mystery has "now" become manifest and should be disclosed and proclaimed by the apostle as the "good news" to the nations. This mystery was hidden in particular from those who were assigned the principal roles in the drama of history. For had they known this mystery then the princes of this world, whose leader Paul calls on occasion the god of this aeon, would not have fallen into the trap of crucifying the "Lord of Glory." The crucifixion of the Messiah by the powers and principalities (represented by the authorities of the Synhedrion and Pontius Pilate) is a ruse of divine providence whereby the powers help to promote their own overthrow and thus accomplish, surely against their will, the end of history.

But not only in the last stage of the drama of history does the ruse of God work through the principalities and powers toward the redemption of man. Even the gift of the Law to Israel, which occupies a significant and indeed central position in Paul's mind, the purpose of which is the redemption of man and the world—even this Law serves to multiply transgression so that grace can hereafter abound.

The Messiah is "delivered up" to the rulers of this aeon in the concealing "form of a slave" and is delivered unto death according to the Law, thus cancelling the bond which stood in the Law against man. The Messiah sets aside the claim of the Law "nailing it to the Cross." In his death on the cross the Messiah disarms the principalities and powers and makes a public example of them.

This divine Law, Paul intimates, has not been ordained by God Himself but was mediated, through angelic powers. They employ the Law which is in itself holy to make men self-righteous so that he may become completely subject to them. The Law, contrary to the original designation which was announced to Israel, is no longer something which gives life and no longer effects, as was intended, the justification of man, but brings about sin and wrath. "God, whom Paul speaks of as the God of Israel, gave them the law in order to cause them to be frustrated by the fact of it being incapable of fulfilment."[1] The Law was not given in order to be fulfilled but rather to call forth sin—and thus prepare the way for man's redemption. Everything is predetermined in this drama of redemption. Paul's process of history "no longer cares about the men and the generations of men which it affects, but uses them and uses them up for higher ends."[2] In the modern period, Buber remarks at the conclusion of his analysis of Paul's theology of history, the philosopher Hegel has torn up the Pauline conception of history from its root in the actuality of faith and transplanted it into a dialectic in which "Reason" by its "ruse" forces the historical process unwittingly toward its perfection.

III

Paul's theology of history develops in the context of the apocalyptic messianic experience. This experience as we know it from "the apocalyptic writings of Jewish and Jewish-Christian coinage in the age of late Hellenism and its decline"[3] grows however out of Hebrew prophetism. Therefore Buber feels compelled to stress the difference between the apocalyptic and prophetic experience of history. Buber's

[1] Martin Buber, *Two Types of Faith* (1951), p. 88.

[2] *Ibid.*, p. 86.

[3] Martin Buber, "Prophecy, Apocalyptic, and the Historical Hour," *Pointing the Way* (1957), pp. 192ff.

typology, concerning the prophetic and apocalyptic spirit is fundamental for his understanding of history.

Common to both is faith in the one Lord of the past, present and future
history of all existing beings; both views are certain of His will to grant salvation to His creation. But how this will manifest itself in the pregnant
moment in which the speaker speaks, what relation this moment bears to
coming events, what share in this relation falls to men . . . at these points the
prophetic and the apocalyptic messages essentially diverge.[4]

The prophet announces "what God is working" in two different
ways. The one speaks in terms of an open alternative. But even if
those to whom the prophet appeals persistently resist the call and he
no longer proclaims the alternative, but announces the approaching
catastrophe as inevitable—even in this threat the undertone of an
alternative is still audible. The divine call and man's response are
related in the Hebrew text by a correspondence of the key term of
prophetic language: *teshuva,* the turn. Man's turning as well as the
divine response

are often designated by the same verb, a verb that can signify to turn back as
well as to turn away, but also to return and to turn towards someone, and this
fullness of meaning was taken advantage of in the texts.[5]

The prophetic message preserves, according to Buber, the dialogical intercourse between the divine and the human from all temptation to encyst the mystery of history in a dogmatic fashion as in the
Pauline message of the crucified Messiah. The mystery of history rests
for the prophets in man's power of actually choosing between the
ways. Only a being who has the power to choose between alternatives

is suited to be God's partner in the dialogue of history. The future is not
fixed, for God wants man to come to Him with full freedom to return to Him
even out of a plight of extreme hopelessness, and then to be really with Him.[6]

Man is created to be a center of surprise in creation and therefore
factual change of direction can take place towards salvation as well
as towards disaster, starting in each hour, no matter how late.

The apocalyptic message stands in direct antithesis to the prophetic experience of history. Nowhere in the text of the apocalyp-

4 *Ibid.*
5 *Ibid.*
6 *Ibid.*

tic writers does Buber discern the experience of history actually open to alternatives.

Everything here is predetermined, all human decisions only sham struggles. The future does not come to pass. The future is already present in heaven, as it were, present from the beginning.[7]

This future can therefore also be "disclosed" *(apo-kalypsis)* to the ecstatic visionary and he, in turn, can "disclose" it to others in letters or pamphlets. The apocalyptic

though he knows, of course, of the struggle in the soul of man, accords to this struggle no elemental significance. There exists for him no possibility of a change in the direction of historical destiny that could proceed from man.[8]

In short: The apocalyptic no longer knows an historical future in the real sense. The present aeon hurries to an end, and ultimately the proper (and paradoxical) subject of the apocalyptic is a future that is no longer in time. The consummation of history that the apocalyptic expects has no longer an historical character. "Man cannot achieve this future, but he also has nothing more to achieve."[9]

IV

Buber's analysis of the historical categories of prophecy and apocalyptic is heavily charged with language rooted in the existentialist protest against Hegel's philosophy of history. In order to understand some of the presuppositions of this protest it is imperative that we turn to the perplexities of modern philosophy of history. Philosophy of history was born in a time of crisis, in response to the birthpangs of modern society in the time of the French revolution. A new consciousness of time broke through in the revolutionary age. Time became an urgent concern of philosophy, more urgent than ever before in its history.

The problem of history came first into focus in the romantic nostalgia for passed possibilities. Since the traditions were rapidly exhausted, this nostalgia had to feed on a progressive erosion of past traditions. But soon it became obvious that philosophy of history could also be used as an algebra of revolution: The passed possibili-

---

7 *Ibid.*

8 *Ibid.*

9 *Ibid.*

ties of history had to be surpassed in the future. The loss of tradition made a search for a new basis of human existence imperative. Hegel's philosophy of history is still midway between the romantic and the revolutionary version of modern philosophy of history. His philosophy of history is no longer philosophy as a theory or contemplation of eternal ideas in the Platonic sense, but as philosophy a theory of action. Nevertheless, Hegel's philosophy of history is still philosophy in the classic sense and therefore, necessarily, theory of *past* action: i.e., the understanding of the essence, beginning, middle, and end of history. The course of history as a whole could, according to Hegel, only be object of philosophic analysis if history does not extend into an unknown future. Therefore Hegel had to "close" history with the advent of the French revolution and the empire of Napoleon (or later with the Prussian state).

The students of Hegel, however, considered "the spirit of time" no longer as a measure of insight into past history only, but also as a guide for *future* action. Philosophy of history thus became for Hegel's disciples a theory of action: past, present *and* future. Philosophy of history becomes messianic prophecy in the historic futurism of the Young-Hegelians as the latent messianic element of Hegel's philosophy of history broke through and gained currency in two major versions: in the social-universal gospel and in the national-universal gospel of redemption. A social class or an ethnic-national group was singled out to be the carrier of the universal message of redemption. This messianic carrier was destined to "realize" the Heavenly City on earth.

Marxism is only the best known version of the historic futurism current in the nineteenth century. In the Marxist drama of redemption the class of the proletariat functions as the redeemer of society. The proletarian class being actually deprived of all human dignity is summoned in this hour to act as the servant of humanity. But the messianic role in the drama of history could also be assigned to other groups: Kirejewski, Bakunin, Belinsky, Dostoyevski, and Count Cieszkowski interpreted the role of the Slavic nations in messianic terms. Like Marx they are rebellious disciples of Hegel. Hegel, they argued with Marx, still belonged to the philosophers of the old dispensation who "interpreted" but did not "change" the world. The key terms that express this new sense of history and philosophy: the charged use of terms like "realization" or "action" (versus idle, irresponsible contemplation or theory), of the adjective "concrete" (versus "abstract" which was the damning accusation against the entire thought and life experience of the West since Descartes or since Plato and Thales), of symbols like "I and Thou" or "the relation between men" (versus the neutral or neutralizing concept of spirit in Hegel's philosophy)—these and other peculiar uses were current in the language of the left-wing disciples of Hegel who stood in open revolt but also (and perhaps therefore) in total dependence to the master.

In this context of social and national messianic ideologies current in the circles of the left wing Hegelians we find also Moses Hess who couches the experience of the dispersed Jewry awakening to its national destiny in the language of historical messianism. Buber himself points to Moses Hess as one of his forerunners. And this hint is more than merely a bibliographic footnote. In 1904 already, in a survey on the origins of Zionism, Buber draws attention to Moses Hess, who (as Buber sees it) anticipated the coming generation of Zionists. Hess grasped that the living seed of the future of Jewish life rests exclusively in the Jewish masses of the East; he perceived the regeneration of the heart as the first task of the coming revolutions, he also recognized the significance of Hasidism as a paradigm for the Jewish historic movement of the future.[10]

In this early note, sketching the role of Moses Hess in the development of Zionism, Buber, indeed, anticipates in outline his own life-work: a theory of Jewish national humanism out of the sources of the messianic experience latent in Jewish life and religion. The relation between Moses Hess and Buber is not simply a matter of filiation of ideas, but points to a structural kinship: Hess anticipates Buber in his strictures against the Marxian chiliasm (and was therefore "liquidated" by Marx and Engels in the last version of the *Communist Manifesto*); in his stress on the individual, (which Hess develops in a short brochure on the *Philosophy of Action*, influenced by Feuerbach and Bruno Bauer); in his theory of nationalism that assigns to different nations and peoples different modes of experience and tasks for historical realization; in his critique of Christianity that seeks the salvation of the individual in a realm not of this world; in his stress on the messianism of the prophets and the rabbis that seeks the perfection of man in the actual life of the social community.

[10] Martin Buber, "Herzl und die Historie" (1904), *Die Jüdische Bewegung* (1916), pp. 156f.

This congruence in structure between Moses Hess and Martin Buber goes beyond a general tendency in sketching the historical development of mankind. The parallelism touches the very core of their symbolic language and shows that the symbols and criteria of contemporary existentialism in general and of Martin Buber's dialogical philosophy of history in particular have been forged in the generation after Hegel. What was controversial in the small circle of intellectuals on the margin of bourgeois society and of the academic institutions in the thirties, forties and fifties of the last century has become in our century the general temper of continental thought and experience. The generation of the Young-Hegelians forged in their controversies the symbols that became the signals for the revolutionary, socialist and nationalist movements of the twentieth century.

If, therefore, Buber aims his arrows against the apotheosis of history current in Marxism and in the German variety of existentialism, he only continues the argument of Moses Hess. Marxist theory of history, Buber contends, has erroneously been related to the messianism of the prophets. In the Marxist

announcement of an obligatory leap of the human world out of the aeon of necessity into that of freedom the apocalyptic principle alone holds sway. Here in place of the power superior to the world that effects transition, an immanent dialectic has appeared. Yet in a mysterious manner *its* goal, too, is the perfection, even the salvation of the world. In its modern shape, too, apocalyptic knows nothing of an inner transformation of man that preceeds the transformation of the world.[11]

Apocalyptic, old or new, by linking the events of history in a scheme of necessity passes over and obliterates the efficacy of individual resolutions and actions.

The shadow of Hegel, according to Buber, also looms over German existentialism. As

for Hegel world history is the absolute process in which the spirit attains the consciousness of itself; so for Heidegger historical existence is the illumination of being itself; in neither is there room for a suprahistorical reality that sees history and judges it.[12]

In the ontological affirmation of history, inaugurated by Hegel and unfolded by Heidegger, historical time is absolutized. Then it can happen, Buber remarks (in view of Heidegger's inaugural address

[11] *Pointing the Way, loc. cit.*

[12] Martin Buber, "The Validity and Limitation of the Political Principle," *Pointing the Way* (1957), p. 25.

as rector of the University of Freiburg in the fateful year 1933), that in the midst of current historical events the time-bound thinker ascribes to the powers that be the character of an absolute. Thus the goblin called success may occupy for a while the divine seat of judgment.

V

Martin Buber's critique of philosophy of history remains, however, entangled in the realm of history. He cannot take an Archimedean point outside of the process of history and, like Indian sages or Greek philosophers, declare history as an illusion or dismiss it as a tale told by an idiot surely not worthy of the attention of philosophers. His protest against the judgment of history does not lead him to an escape from history, but to dissent in the midst of history against the actual course Western history has taken. His protest against the judgment of history is itself philosophy of history, or perhaps formulated more sharply: in Buber's critique of Paul's history of salvation and of Hegel's dialectic of reason in history messianism is pitched against eschatology, one version of messianic hope is put over and against another version of messianic consummation.

Futurism is, according to Buber, rooted sociologically and psychologically in the Jewish experience, and therefore the early Buber can call messianism—in a totally mythic-immanent fashion—"the most deeply original idea of Judaism."[13] In the later writings of Buber (after the first World War) the mystic-immanent interpretation of messianism gives way to a more religious-transcendent view. God is no longer chained to the social and psychic set-up of Jewish experience, but He forges the recalcitrant clans into a unit in the encounter at Sinai. And in response to this encounter the tribes recognize YWHW as King over Israel and dare the expectation that He will be king over all the nations.

The origins of messianism are now traced by Buber back to the primitive charismatic theocracy in early Israel. But even in this later period (which comprises Buber's monumental works on *Moses,* on the *Kingship of God,* and on *The Prophetic Faith*) the basic symbols of the early period are carried over and overshadow the free and utterly sovereign will of God in His calling of Israel. Ezekiel in his

---

[13] Martin Buber, *Drei Reden über das Judentum* (1920-23), p. 91.

great review of Israel's history (ch. 16) surely did not find much of a natural context for the divine action in and through Israel. Buber's statement about the prophetic theologem on history (even as late as in "Prophecy, Apocalyptic, and the Historical Hour" [1954]) still stresses man's action as an agent of redemption so as to recall the revolutionary activities interpretation of messianism of the early days. In the prophetic message I hear, however, first and foremost overwhelmingly announced that God is God and not man and that His ways are not to be measured with the yardstick of man. Even the experience of the covenant does not erase for the prophets the inscrutable and hidden God as the prime agent in history.

In this perspective the difference between prophecy and apocalyptic loses much of its weight. Perhaps it is characteristic that when speaking of prophecy Buber speaks of "the prophets in the ages of the kings of Judah and Israel"[14]) while I pointed to Ezekiel—and Buber himself has to admit that the other great prophet of the Babylonian Exile is an exception to his concept of prophecy. But what crucial exception does Deutero-Isaiah present! What use is a typology concerning the prophetic and apocalyptic experience of history if Deutero-Isaiah, whom Buber rightly calls "the originator of a theology of world-history"[15]) has to be exempt from the rule?

Among the prophets he was the man who had to announce world history and to herald it as divinely predestined. In place of the dialogue between God and people he brings the comfort of the One preparing redemption to those He wants to redeem; God speaks here as not only having foreknown but also having foretold what now takes place in history—the revolutionary changes in the life of the nations and the liberation of Israel consummated in it. There is no longer room here for our alternative: the future is spoken of as being established from the beginning.[16]

This transformation of the prophetic perspective has been made possible, according to Buber, by the unheard-of new character of the historical situation:

Here for the first time a prophet had to proclaim an atonement fulfilled through the suffering of the people. The guilt is atoned for, a new day begins. During this time in which history holds its breath, the alternative is silent.[17]

14 *Pointing the Way, loc. cit.*

15 Martin Buber, *The Prophetic Faith* (1949), p. 209.

16 *Pointing the Way, loc. cit.*

17 *Ibid.*

and remains outside it.[172] There is no world of appearance; there is only the world which appears to us in two ways, according to our twofold attitude.[173] For there is a separative power. I-It is the word of separation.[174] We come upon a melancholy destiny which is a fundamental melancholy.[175] We are then beneath the fundamental word.

For there is a mysterious *Zwiefalt* of the I. This *Zwiefalt*, this duality, this bifurcation of the self is not merely a duplicity of the I: there is a metacosmic force before which Buber places us in as mysterious a fashion as Heidegger. It is a primitive form, and the duality of the attitudes of the fundamental words ("I-Thou," "I-It") and of human visions of the world is but a particular form.[176] This notion is further developed in *Eclipse of God*. There is a *Zwiefalt* in which man stands and sustains himself; there is a dual structure to the human being, such that on the one side there is a totality (the I-Thou in its lived togetherness) and on the other side there is a multiplicity of separations (the I-Its in their diversity). There is a separation of non-separation and of separation, explicable only because there is intervention.[177] Are we not confronted with an almost gnostic ground common to Buber and Heidegger? Let us note in passing the battle waged in common by Buber and Heidegger against the invasion of the religious (though Heidegger does not so label it) by the non-religious: by metaphysics, gnosis, magic;[178] and also the battle against the predominance of the sense of sight, which Buber terms the *Optisierung des Denkens,* so marked in Plato and Plotinus.

When we dwell in the sacred, we are in a region of sacrifice and risk.[179] We must realize that the resting forces of the face of the earth also manifest themselves.[180] The silence of which we spoke abides with the I in an abiding in which the spirit is not revealed,

[172] I.D., p. 43.
[173] I.D., p. 78.
[174] I.D., p. 27.
[175] *Ibid.*
[176] I.D., p. 102.
[177] Gf., p. 56.
[178] Gf., p. 43.
[179] I.D., p. 14.
[180] I.D., p. 59.

but is.181 Can we return to the original world, undifferentiated, prestructural, to the burning obscurity of chaos, to unlighted space?182 Buber notes that Heidegger promises, even if only as a possibility, a transformation of thought by which daylight will come again, and in which the appearance of God or the gods will begin again. It will be necessary to move existentially toward a new transformation of being, toward a new annunciation of the Word between heaven and earth.183 For his part, Buber writes: "The I-Thou relation has gone into the catacombs—who can say with how much greater power it will step forth!" For Buber as for Heidegger, we are in the darkness of those who wait.

Thus, participation in the world, importance given to the word, a reversal by which man is in the word and within love, the birth of objects and the abstract I from a separative power, and the fantasy [*Wunschlehre*] of a thousand year empire, are some of the aspects common to the thought of Buber and the recent thought of Heidegger.

But let us turn to the disagreements. Agreements teach us about the general character of the underlying attitudes of contemporary philosophy. Disagreements at the very least tell us something of each philosopher.

Let us note first some points on which, it seems to us, Buber corrects with some justification certain conceptions of Heidegger. It is a mistake to link together closely, as both Nietzsche and Heidegger seem to have done, the affirmation of God and the affirmation of rational principles. He who speaks to us in the storm surpasses also the sphere of ideality.184 "The living God who approaches and addresses an individual in the situations of real life is not a component part of such a suprasensual world; His place is no more there than it is in the sensible world."185 (And we may recognize here the cult of the here and now, which for brevity may be termed the Hasidism of Buber.)

Shall we pause a little longer over the criticisms of the Heideggerian interpretation of Kant, since they occupy more space? For Kant, there is knowledge, and what is important is that I can know some-

181 I.D., p. 42.
182 I.D., pp. 29, 30, 32.
183 *Eclipse of God*, pp. 91, 167.
184 Gf., p. 71.
185 *Eclipse of God*, p. 32.

thing (not, I would say, that Buber wishes to deny the importance in Kant that I can only know certain things). It is not a matter of my finiteness, but of my participation in knowledge. Similarly, there is action, and there is hope. And Kant's question is this one: what is this being who can know, who must act, and who dares to hope? Through this question we see not only the finiteness of man, as Heidegger says, but man's participation in infinity. And these are not two properties alongside each other.[186]

But let us consider the study of *Sein und Zeit*. Is it true, says Buber, that in the *Dasein* of "everyday," things reveal themselves only as instruments? Do they not reveal themselves equally in their totality, in their independence, in their lack of any precise goal? The man who fixes upon a tree, without a goal, is no less an everyday man, writes Buber, than he who views it in order to place it in a species. Technique is not necessarily prior, and what in its later form is termed the esthetic is not necessarily posterior.[187] Let us acknowledge that on this point it is difficult to say who is right; and it is apparent that "the everyday man" is a limiting concept, itself utilized for certain ends—legitimate ones—by Heidegger.

Let us go still further: is it true, as Buber alleges, that Heidegger has dissociated the *Dasein* from real human life, that he presents a *Dasein* in separation,[188] reduced to its attitude regarding its own being,[189] that he has contrived an essence, a metaphysical composite?

It does not appear that one can say of Heidegger, who like Buber assigns such importance to the word, that he treats social relationships as the great obstacle which prevents the human being from coming to himself.[190] Heidegger would not deny the fact of the meeting, nor that "that being is other than myself, often frighteningly other, and other than I expected."[191] The determinative, writes Buber, is less myself than the presence of being, in so far as it alters its very aspect and its very appearance.[192] If the Heidegger of

186 P.M., pp. 13, 14, 15.

187 P.M., pp. 120, 21.

188 P.M., p. 95.

189 P.M., p. 127.

190 P.M., pp. 88, 96, 97, 99.

191 *Ibid.*

192 *Ibid.*

Sein und Zeit seemed to deny this (but in truth he did not seem to), the Heidegger of the latest writings would never deny it. Nor would Heidegger deny that remaining with oneself is the original sin.[193] And one would think one heard the Heidegger of the most recent writings when one reads:

If a form and appearance of present being move past me, and I was not really there, then out of the distance, out of its disappearance, comes a second cry, as soft and secret as though it came from myself: 'Where were you?' . . . It is not my existence *(Dasein)* which calls me, but the being *(Sein)* which is not I.[194]

For anyone who has read *Holzwege* and *Vorträge und Aufsätze,* Heidegger is in agreement with Buber.

It seems untrue to say that in being-with-the-world the limits of the self cannot be broken, nor that the *Dasein* fulfills himself in *Selbstsein.* And Heidegger saw as clearly as Feuerbach that the individual man does not carry in himself the essence of man. The self of the resolute decision is not necessarily—and even is necessarily not— a separate self. And we do not believe, I do not believe, that Heidegger substitutes for the Kierkegaardian saying, "Everyone should essentially speak only with himself," the dictum, "Everyone can essentially speak only with himself."[195] We may also ask whether the Heideggerian *Fürsorge* has been correctly interpreted.[196] Is it nothing but a practical aid? Must it be presented as something accidental that extends itself into the nonessential?[197] Need it be opposed to a real relationship? Must we say that in pure *Fürsorge* man remains with himself, that "the limits of his being are not broken through"? But is it not Heidegger who with others, along with others, and following others, has taught us that the self is not limited to itself, is ceaselessly outside itself? It is indeed a pity that the second volume of *Sein und Zeit* is not ours any more than the second volume of *L'Être et le Néant.* But some of Heidegger's assertions, and some of the social and political articles of Sartre can complete these incomplete works. Does not Buber interpret the *Mitsein* rather narrowly?

193 *Between Man and Man,* p. 166.

194 *Ibid.*

195 *Ibid.,* p. 171f.

196 P.M., pp. 105, 110.

197 P.M., pp. 106, 120, 123.

And is it quite accurate to say that for Heidegger the *Selbstsein* is an ultimate datum? The Heideggerian *Selbst* open to the world has nothing of the isolated self of classical philosophies, and one cannot claim that it is a closed system.[198] Buber would grant this, no doubt, since he writes[199] that Heidegger does not see the highest stage of the self as an isolation but as consent through resolute decision to the *Mitsein,* along with others; and he sees perfectly that the Heideggerian man does not sever himself from the world, but arrives by a resolute decision at a *Dasein* which is with the world.

We would agree, and it is important, that there is lacking in Heidegger any indication of a relation with the impersonal multiplicity of men.[200] "The authentic self strikes the spark of being-oneself when it encounters the crowd. It enables the self to link up with the self, it grounds opposition to the anonymous 'One,' it makes possible the union of Unique Ones, it constitutes the structure in the stuff of social life."[201] We may fear that here Heidegger is only too much in agreement with Buber. Frightened, we see a grim specter rising. It comes from afar, to end where it does. In Heidegger, it is not isolation that is the most terrible thing, far from it; it is "the gregarious under the mask of nobility." Buber spoke in 1936 of the crowd as conceived by Kierkegaard, the crowd which is unworthy of respect, which is negative, which approaches transcendence, but in the form of a diabolical concentration[202] through that actualizing of the masses by which the person is tossed into the movement of a public reality. There arises, he said, a surging instinct of identification. Then one is really plunged into One (*das Man*), meaning what it means, wanting what it wants. Hegel touched upon history twice; Heidegger, once, in an unhappy hour. Let us recognize with face averted that at the moment at which history encountered Heidegger, more perhaps than he encountered history, he was carried away, as Buber says, by historicizing history, *die Geschehende Geschichte.* It was in November of 1933 that Heidegger saw in "the sinister leading personality" of the historical process, as Buber says, " 'the present and future German reality and its law.' " "Heidegger, the philosopher for whom history rarely shows itself, made a serious error in the hour during

---

198 P.M., p. 108

199 P.M., p. 113.

200 *Ibid.*

201 P.M., p. 121.

202 F.E., pp. 222–223.

which it showed itself for him, all around him." "He bound his thought to his hour, affirmed as historical, more closely than has any other philosopher, even Hegel."[203]

Let us turn to being-for-death. The two thinkers seem to be in agreement that man may receive life without underwriting death. The difference turns on the distinction between the existing being and the living being, which is affirmed by Heidegger and denied by Buber. Buber would have us separate the matter of the subjective attitude of man toward death regarded as a terminal point, from the objective being of man in which the power of death and the power of life are present at every moment. He requires that we distinguish man considered as a being who has a recognition of death and man objectively considered as he who begins to die when he begins to live.[204] The question would then be whether this objective consideration of the presence of a power of death at every moment, contemporaneous with the power of life, is a real objection to the Heideggerian theory of being-for-death.

We have seen that according to Buber the situation of man cannot be separated either from the world of things or from the world of other men, or from community, or, for that matter, from the mystery which surpasses both the world of things and the community, as well as man himself. But we see no real opposition between Buber and Heidegger on any of these points. Let us examine the third point. In terms of the recent books of Heidegger, it is difficult to place him in complete opposition to St. Augustine, to Pascal, and to Kierkegaard.[205] He, too, seeks a divine aspect of being with which to converse and toward which he holds out his hands. He, too, extends his hands toward that form which is not integral to this world. Yes, Heidegger would assert, human life has its absolute meaning in the fact that it transcends its own character; yes, man can enter into relationship with other beings who are no less real to him than himself.[206] No doubt it is true that for the early Heidegger man in his solitude could not extend his hands toward a divine form. Yet even then one could not say that for Heidegger the sole question was that

203 Gf., pp. 93–94; *Eclipse of God*, pp. 102f.

204 P.M., p. 96.

205 P.M., p. 100.

206 P.M., p. 102.

of the relationship of the *Dasein* to its own being.[207] Today one can no longer say that for Heidegger there is no link between the self and the absolute, between the self and the secret of being. And Buber willingly grants that Heidegger experienced deeply this secret of being; that poetry, particularly Hölderlin, is for him a relation to being, a relation of the soul to a being which is not itself, which visits it, assails it, enchants it. Do we not see, then, that the self is not for Heidegger that closed system which, according to Buber, Heidegger presents? Heidegger and Buber agree in seeking an open system.

In *Gottesfinsternis (Eclipse of God)* Buber finds in Heidegger's hesitation between God and gods the sign that he has not experienced the divine.[208] But ought not the possibility of a search be admitted at this point? Many a passage in Buber speaks of the value of an anxious search for divinity. Buber is doubtful about calling "divine" or "God" that whose appearance or possible reappearance Heidegger guesses at.[209] Regarding Heidegger's statement that "neither men nor gods can ever of themselves bring about the direct relation to the holy," Buber tells us that God cannot be conjured, nor does God wish to compel. "Always, again and again, men are accosted by One who of Himself disconcerts and enraptures them, and, although overcome, the worshipper prays, of himself, to Him." This someone is in His own right, and He lets the existent [*l'étant*] be in his own right. These two characteristics distinguish divine forces from demonic ones.[210] We are carried here into a realm in which it is difficult to make a judgment, especially as Heidegger has asserted almost nothing. It seems at least that Buber has exaggerated Heidegger's involvement in what Buber calls "modern magic." One cannot believe to be God Him whom one can conjure, says Buber. Almost certainly they would be in agreement on this point. Perhaps—surely, indeed—Heidegger has emphasized what is to distinguish the divine of the future from the divine of the past.[211] This does not mean that a being which manifests itself in different forms cannot be for Heidegger the same being.

---

207 P.M., pp. 122–124.

208 Gf., p. 30.

209 Gf., p. 89.

210 *Eclipse of God*, p. 100.

211 Gf., pp. 92–93.

Thus there would remain two fundamental differences, at least
at first sight. Being certainly does not have the same place in Buber
as in Heidegger. The concept of being which would signify anything
but the fact inherent in every being that it is, is doomed to remain
vacuous, writes Buber.[212] And on the following page: "I am, my
corporeal person is; if by that phrase 'Being is' I wish to say something different and more intimate than that, the concept of being
has lost for me every trace of a legitimate conception." The question
would then be to know what are the relations in Heidegger between
the being [*l'être*] which he affirms and that highest being [*Étant*]
which is the god, and which he sometimes glimpses, at the end of
an ascension still unrealized and passing through the sacred and then
the divine. In the second place, Buber notes that after having cited
in his commentaries on Hölderlin, "Since we exist as talk, and can
hear from one another . . .," Heidegger never returned to this notion
which shows the dialogical relationship between human reality and
divine reality. But let us note that Heidegger often speaks of man
being questioned by things and by being. A man who is put to a
question must reply.

Buber would readily agree with Sartre, and moreover with philosophers as different as Karl Jaspers and Ernest Bloch, in seeing the
essential trait of man in his problematic nature, in his connection
with the idea of the possible. Man is potentiality, the plenitude of
possibility of the *Dasein*. Man is the center of all surprise in the
world, says Buber, in a phrase which may remind us of Bloch. And to
invoke another philosopher of possibility, Victor Jankelevitch, let us
recall that for him, as for Buber, man is a midway creature, a creature
of the mixed.

From Nietzsche to Sartre, such is the road of modern philosophy.
In the one as in the other, values are posited without having any
foundation. Above all the old cry, "God is dead!" which was uttered
by Nietzsche, is still heard in the mouth of Sartre, but no longer as a
cry. Now it is nothing but an expression of a state of affairs. There is
nothing specifically existential about it, says Buber.[213] No doubt
there is such a thing as an atheism which expresses the unnamed
from the night and out of nostalgia, and which is not an atheism

212 Gf., p. 88.
213 Gf., p. 77.

without God.[214] And perhaps there is a critical atheism which is but
the prayer of the philosopher to the God who has become unknown
to him.[215] But such is not the atheism of Sartre.

Nevertheless, it is legitimate and necessary, according to Buber,
to give a theological and theocentric interpretation of Sartre's non-
existential affirmation of the death of God. For the living God is not
only a God who reveals Himself, but also, as Isaiah said, a God who
conceals Himself. This is not to say that we have had no part in this
silence of God. "Sartre began with the silence of God without asking
himself what part in this silence is played by the fact that we have
closed and have been closing our ears."[216]

Sartre thinks that man has attributed to God the freedom which
he himself possessed. Is it legitimate to believe, with Sartre, that man
must be restored his creative freedom? Is that not demagogic talk?
Did Descartes really begin with a desire to give to man an infinite
freedom only to ascribe this infinite freedom to God? In fact, moreover, is not our freedom always inserted in the totality of creation?[217]

In his study of man Sartre always begins with the subject-object
relation. "It is well known that many existentialists believe the fundamental fact among men to be that one is an object for another. But
that is to eliminate to a very large extent the reality of the interhuman, the mystery of contact." The important thing, if one considers
the relationship between two human beings, is not to see that the
one makes an object of the other, but to see why that never completely succeeds. Such is the privilege of man.[218] Sartre fails to see
the relation between the I and the Thou, which is the most fundamental relation of which the other is but a subsequent elaboration.
Hence the sort of solipsism that Buber attributes to Sartre. For him
there would be insurmountable barriers between men. Each has to do
only with himself; there is no immediate relation with another.[219]

We have noted that the theory of the creation of values is the
same in Sartre as in Nietzsche; and, says Buber, "it is no more true in
Sartre than in Nietzsche." "One cannot believe in, espouse, a meaning

214 I.D., p. 109.
215 Gf., p. 57.
216 Gf., p. 82.
217 *Ibid.*
218 E.Z., pp. 260–261.
219 E.Z., p. 268.

or a value unless one has discovered it rather than invented it. The value must have come to me in my meeting with being." (And we know that for Buber "being" is either an empty word, or it signifies God, the absolute Thou.)[220] Existence is not decision without foundation, but a destiny and a task. This is doubtless not the place to engage in a discussion of the creation of values. There is a certain grandeur, Buber would undoubtedly recognize, in the theory of Nietzsche and Sartre. Is it not one of the miracles of man to accept and take back what he creates, to make the eternal out of time, to transcend time in time?

As for the Sartrean theory of communication, no doubt we have in *Being and Nothingness* but a portion of what it should be in its totality; to be exact, the portion consecrated to bad faith and to man as an object.

The final judgment of Buber on Sartre is quite severe. He is a psychologist of penetrating observation, a gifted man for whom ontological considerations are always mingled with different considerations.[221] Sartre pushed the Nietzschean theory to absurdity. To which we would promptly reply that one can scarcely push the absurd further than Nietzsche tried to push it and did push it. We would be more readily in agreement with Buber's judgment on the ontologies of the philosophers of existence. They speak willingly of the whole and of nothingness. "I do not know," says Buber, "either what the whole is, or what nothingness is. The one seems to me as inhuman and as fictitious as the other, and what I aim at is the simple *quantum satis* of what this man can accomplish and take unto himself in this hour of his life."[222]

There are many points in common between Buber and the two philosophers of existence of whom we have yet to speak. When Buber affirms the non-unity of being,[223] when he presents the religious situation of man as characterized by an essential and insoluble antimony,[224] when he asserts that every real relation to a being or to an essence is exclusive,[225] when he defines the relation to God as at

220 E.Z., p. 83.
221 E.Z., p. 94.
222 Zs., p. 178.
223 I.D., p. 90.
224 I.D., p. 97.
225 I.D., p. 79.

once exclusion and unconditioned inclusion (thus coming to the notion of *das Umgreifende*,[226] or rather anticipating it, adumbrating it), and when he criticizes the scientific *Weltorientierung*,[227] it is impossible not to draw Buber and Jaspers together. Buber grants and admires in large part the Jaspersian theory of communication and cipher.

Regarding Jaspers' theory concerning the I-Thou as an approach to transcendence, Buber makes several fundamental objections. Buber terms it a "reductive" view, and explains this term and this approach as follows:

This theory treats the link between transcendence and the concrete as a matter of arbitrary volition and thus cancels out its abrupt approach toward the unlimitedness of the Thou; it is no longer rooted in anything productive of a real belief.[228]

In the second place, the invocation to a divinity as to a Thou becomes illegitimate, whereas the Biblical union of the love of God and the love of man, while directing our eyes toward the transparency of the human Thou, also directed them toward the grace which comes from the absolute Thou, let Him appear where He will. No doubt, Buber adds, the philosopher has the inalienable right to explain that "philosophical existence" can afford not to approach the hidden God; but he has no right to characterize prayer as a dubious matter merely because it is foreign to his own experience. Probably, adds Buber, Jaspers arrives at these views because for him contemplation is the highest form of prayer.[229]

In the third place, is it not a bizarre transcendence whose ciphers inevitably intermingle inextricably? What is signified may then as well be the devil as God; and what is visible is the one no less than the other. If the notion of a cipher-script involves a unique meaning, nevertheless there must be some case which allows me to decipher accurately this script which is destined to guide my life, some case which makes deciphering possible, however surrounded by difficulties. In the last analysis transcendence in Jaspers refuses to be a Thou. God cannot be a person for Jaspers, says Buber, because by definition personality is a manner of being oneself which essentially cannot be

226 I.D., p. 80.
227 I.D., p. 111.
228 Nw., p. 299.
229 Nw., p. 300.

solitary.[230] "As if," he says, "such a definition would remain tenable when it is a matter of the paradox of the absolute person; the absolute, in so far as it can be thought, having to appear to thought solely as a *complexio oppositorum.*"

Finally, Buber contrasts to his own view the passage in which Jaspers says that if man speaks directly to God he thereby degrades and stultifies his communication with other men.[231]

We shall not enter into this dialogue as a third party. We may well concede that there is a sort of Jaspersian dogmatism, explicable by a distrust, perhaps legitimate, of certain overly "theological" theories of communication, and that he does not take into account the possibility of a double communication, with God and with man, the one in the light of the other, and vice versa. Doubtless at a certain point in his exposition Jaspers speaks too much like a champion of logic—and that he is not. Also it is appropriate to ask whether the idea of the creation of man by God *for* communication is satisfactory, and whether the notion of *for,* even the notion of creation, do not need to be transcended. And on this point the thought of Jaspers re-establishes its validity. As for the first objection mentioned above, is there really *Willkür* in the relationship between immanence and transcendence? Is there an absolute loss of the reality of belief? The reality of prayer as a cipher is beyond question for Jaspers. Only prayer to a God too determinate is questionable. And it is not claimed that this overly determinate God has no value as a cipher. In the end one must certainly admit that, as Jaspers has said, there is an ambiguity about the cipher-script.

"He who maintains himself in a relationship participates in a reality, that is to say, in a being which is not simply outside him and is not simply in him."[232] Like Gabriel Marcel, Buber is a philosopher of participation; not the Platonic participation or communication of the soul and the Ideas, but participation, communication of the I and the Thou.[233] "Such facts as the fundamental proposition of *Ich und Du,* that the eternal Thou can never in its essence become an It, confirmed for me," writes Buber, "the universality of spiritual process." Interestingly enough, what Buber found in Stirner (that

230 *Ibid.*

231 Nw., p. 302.

232 I.D., p. 65.

233 Nw., p. 97.

was to surprise Marcel at first, though to be sure he would come to accept it) was that Stirner undertook to dissolve "had-truth," truth which is possessed, which is capable of being the property of a multitude of persons, which is the general good accessible to the person and independent of the person.[234] For true truth, if one may so speak, is that which cannot be had.[235] For Buber true truth cannot be possessed, even if it is in a sense dependent upon the person.[236] And the same notion may be applied to man himself. "As long as man 'has' himself, possesses himself, 'has' himself like an object, he experiences himself as a thing among things." The true truth is reached when man does not "have" himself but is himself.[237] We are very near to the thought of Gabriel Marcel.

Ought we not to mention Karl Barth as well? In *Gottesfinsternis* there are passages which cannot fail to recall Barth. There are the dialectical character of his theology ("Every religious expression is a futile attempt to fulfill the desired meaning"[238]—which, moreover, endorses the teaching of Kierkegaard), the vacillation of all certainties under the relieving weight of the mystery,[239] and his affirmation of contemporaneity in faith.[240] But, on the other hand, Buber criticizes Barth for the purely Christological foundation of his thought. After having recognized the fact of the meeting of the I and the Thou, Barth wishes to base it solely on Christ.[241]

When Buber tells us that it is a matter of advancing before the face of God, before the face of the Thou, of living before this visage,[242] in the mirror of the divine visage,[243] what comes to mind is that which the thought of Buber has in common with the thought of Emmanuel Levinas.

If now we glance at the sources which constitute the thought of Buber without ever explaining it completely, sources at once diverse

[234] F.E., pp. 194–195.
[235] F.E., p. 195.
[236] F.E., p. 253.
[237] P.M., p. 21.
[238] Gf., p. 44.
[239] Gf., p. 45.
[240] Gf., p. 88.
[241] Nw., pp. 303–394.
[242] I.D., pp. 44, 54, 55, 110.
[243] Zs., pp. 128, 130; Gf., p. 42.

and one like the ocean, we are led to the religious sources of existential thought: the idea of the freedom of the children of God in Saint Paul, then in certain mystics, and even in certain heretical mystics of the Middle Ages;[244] the spark of Eckhart, that surrender which appears to Eckhart[245] as to Novalis essential to any veritable decision;[246] or the negative theology which appears most clearly in *Gottesfinsternis*.[247] This negative theology enables him to join Heidegger in the idea of the concealment of God,[248] and Kierkegaard in his idea of the paradox and the denial of every proposition concerning God.

If we were to seek here the origins of Buber's theory of the I and the Thou, we would need to follow the indications given by the philosopher in *Nachwort*, and thus we would be led to name several great—and some very great—precursors of the philosophies of existence. We would have to name not only Humboldt, Jacobi, and Hamann, but also Fichte; Novalis, whom he is fond of citing; not only Stirner, but also and most especially Feuerbach.[249] Finally, Hasidism often shows through, a natural and living flower in the thought of Buber ever since the passage in *Ich und Du* in which he wrote: "We wish to preserve and cultivate in sanctity the sacred good of our reality which is paid to us as a gift for this life, and perhaps not for any other life which could come nearer to the real."[250]

Naturally, one would need to make precise, to try to make more and more precise, the notion of a person who is spirit. The spirit is between the I and the Thou. It is the reply of the man to his Thou, a reply which appears in mystery,[251] which is heart[252] and vital understanding,[253] which is not only kernel and substance,[254] but a

---

[244] I.D., p. 58; F.E., p. 238.

[245] I.D., p. 56.

[246] F.E., p. 232; I.D., p. 78, on "non-doing."

[247] Gf., p. 71.

[248] Gf., p. 72.

[249] Nw., pp. 287-291, 297-299.

[250] Nw., pp. 90, 110, 112, 113; F.E., pp. 227, 293, 304, 305; Zs., pp. 130, 132, 144, 145, 148, 162, 177; Gf., pp. 42, 44.

[251] I.D., p. 41.

[252] Gf., p. 71.

[253] P.M., p. 65.

[254] I.D., p. 34.

depth which is a foundation, an abyss,[255] and finally, body. "Man dwells in his love," says Buber;[256] but he dwells also in his body. "He must judge with all the pores of his body."[257] There is a corporeal fact of otherness,[258] and beneath the corporeal thought there is a corporeal non-thought *(leibhaftiges Nichtdenken).*[259] "And Eros Pandemos has but to move its wings for the original fire to reveal itself in the play of the bodily."[260] For what takes place takes place in corporeality itself.[261] The dialogue arises between person and person. To each real person, his Thou;[262] the sun is the sun of our being;[263] God is the God of all beings.

As for the other fundamental word, that is to say, the I-It, let us not suppose that the It is to be neglected. "Every reply ties the Thou to the world of the It. Such is the sorrow and such is the greatness of man." "Thus is knowledge achieved, thus is the work accomplished, thus are the image and the pre-image, or the symbol, generated full in the midst of the living."[264]

Perhaps this is the place, before concluding, to ask about the notion of the reply, and even about the ontological value of the Thou. In several passages it very much seems as if for Buber there is no definitive reply. Moreover, we have cited the passage in which he tells us that the reply implies the It. It remains no less true that the dialogue is as he says a real responding *(un répondre réel].* We respond to the moment. Thence, the notion of responsibility.[265] The spirit, we saw, is response,[266] the response of man to *his* Thou.[267] The dialogue is a combination of questions and responses.[268] One

255 F.E., p. 233.

256 I.D., p. 18.

257 Zs., p. 127.

258 Zs., p. 165.

259 Zs., p. 166.

260 Zs., p. 166.

261 Zs., p. 77.

262 I.D., p. 69; F.E., p. 211.

263 F.E., p. 208.

264 I.D., p. 42.

265 Zs., pp. 147, 149, 150.

266 I.D., p. 55.

267 I.D., p. 41.

268 Gf., p. 43.

can indeed see how the It can be inserted into the dialogue and transmuted in the light of the Thou. As for the objection which would consist in saying that there is no definitive response, we should no doubt distinguish purely intellectual responses which are endless from the divine response which puts a final and original term to everything. And the word of God, at least the first, is not a reply. And in the dialogue between man and God, as we see it in the Book of Job, it is God who replies. But how does He reply? Again, by a question. Such is the dialogue.

In *Zwiesprache* Buber puts the following question: Is it true that here, where, as the philosophers put it, the pure subject frees itself from the concrete person to found a world, a citadel, towering above the dialogue of life, unattainable, there is a station where man, the Unique One, suffers and triumphs alone, gloriously? Buber answers first by evoking the idea of Plato: Thought is a silent dialogue of the soul with itself; and he tells us that every man who has really thought knows that within this remarkable process there is a stage in which an internal readiness is questioned and answers. But, he says, that is not the origin of thought; it is only its first examination and its first trial. The origin of thought is not achieved in a dialogue with oneself. According to Buber, at this very origin one will find a dialogue. It is not the thinker who is talking to himself, it is the fundamental relation which is speaking to him.269 We sense once more that we are close to a Heideggerian notion, and we see clearly that if there is a fundamental dialogue, it is that of the soul, not with itself, but with the primordial event, whatever one may call it.

The philosophies of existence are philosophies of the break-through, of the rupture, and such is indeed the expression which Buber uses at times to designate the action by which man must go beyond his ordinary life.270 At the same time, all of them want to set up an ontology. Buber, like the philosophers of existence, wishes to establish an ontic philosophy; and sometimes he says, an ontology, an ontology of the "between."271 True dialogue is an ontological sphere. "When Nietzsche says, 'Then oneness came to two,' and when Eckhart says, 'One is united in one,' they say what can never be

---

269 Zs., p. 163.
270 Zs., p. 177; E.Z., p. 268.
271 E.Z., p. 276.

ontically true."[272] It is from the ontic point of view that Buber criticizes the mystic. There is even an ontic alienation of the I and the
Thou, to which neither Eckhart nor Stirner, to cite extremes, were
faithful.[273] There is an ontic relation with the absolute.[274] *Dasein*
goes ontically beyond *Selbstsein.* Thus we may say that the philosophy
of Buber might be characterized at once as a philosophy of existence
and as an ontology.

The philosopher of existence, the partisan of the ideas of Kierkegaard, Heidegger, Jaspers, and Sartre, in so far as these are criticized
by Buber, may perhaps speak up again: Is it true that in contrast to
any other utterance the Thou does not limit? Is it true that when I
say "it is," "it" remains a metaphor, whereas "thou" does not?[275]
Is it true that if we say "Thou" to God, the ineluctable truth of the
world is endowed with a human meaning? In the second place,
how can love testify to the *Dasein* of one's partner?[276] That the
terminus of love surpasses all philosophical thought does not prove
once and for all its existence. These are the two ultimate questions
before which we find ourselves.

That to which Buber testifies is that "creation happens to us,
burns itself into us, recasts us in burning—we tremble and are faint,
we submit."[277] "O lonely Face like a star in the night, O living
Finger laid on an unheeding brow, O fainter echoing footstep!"[278]
Without being closer to a deciphering, to an unveiling of being, we
have come near to God.[279]

For there must be an infinite dialectic between the idea of God
and God, a process which always comes back to the same point until,
abruptly, it is interrupted.[280] We cannot speak dialectically of God
because He is not subject to the principle of non-contradiction. But
there is a limit to dialectic, at which nothing more is expressed, but
where an understanding occurs.[281] There we find action which is

[272] F.E., p. 202.
[273] F.E., p. 291.
[274] P.M., p. 92.
[275] I.D., p. 8.
[276] Gf., p. 75.
[277] *I and Thou*, p. 82.
[278] *Ibid.,* p. 42f.
[279] *Ibid.,* p. 111.
[280] Gf., p. 73.
[281] F.E., p. 207.

pure silence before the Thou.[282] Let us not be surprised, therefore, to hear Buber speak of a response, and of the spirit which replies, and yet say as well that there is no reply.

For Buber, as for Heraclitus and the Psalmist, we are before the appearance of the absolute that never disappears.[283] Pointing to the reply and the non-reply, such is Buber, so do we find him again and again, before the term which questions him and which he questions. "To be old is a wonderful thing when a man has not yet forgotten what it means to begin."[284]

[282] I.D., pp. 42, 44.
[283] Gf., p. 144.
[284] Gf., p. 12.

JEAN WAHL

THE SORBONNE

23

Paul E. Pfuetze

MARTIN BUBER AND AMERICAN PRAGMATISM

I

FOR some years now *Existenz-philosophie* has been ruffling the intellectual waters of two continents, and the historians of thought have been busy tracing its meanings and sources. Existentialism is not a familiar part of the American tradition, or even of our classical inheritance. Consequently, when existentialism first became known to American thought, it was treated with either curiosity or contempt—at best a bleak philosophy of pessimism and despair; at worst, a symptom of intellectual collapse, an abdication of philosophy's task to construct logical foundations for understanding our world. But perceptive thinkers soon recognized it as a distinctive way of philosophizing which sprang from the tensions of the continental, and perhaps chiefly the German, intellectual and spiritual situation of the nineteenth and twentieth centuries, strongly influenced by the political and moral catastrophes of our generation and by the mood of despair, hopelessness, and confusion of Europe during and after World War II. It was further recognized that the main concerns and contentions of *Existenz-philosophie* had been earlier formulated by thinkers like Schelling, Kierkegaard, Feuerbach, Marx, Nietzsche, Dilthey, and Bergson in their criticisms of the reigning "rationalism" of Hegelian Idealism, Cartesian dualism, mechanism, scientism, and all of those intellectual and social forces which seemed to be destroying human freedom and dignity.

Some discerning American thinkers also observed that Pragmatism had been saying some of the same things that European *Existenz*-thinkers were emphasizing. But though this notion doubtlessly occurred to several American philosophers, no one seemed to make any use of it in philosophy, psychology, or theology. Whether the connection is logical or only historical, or both, to me the idea held great promise for illuminating many obscure places in our understanding of ourselves in our world. Pragmatism and Existentialism *seem* to live in such different worlds and speak such different languages. But I believe that they should be brought together, placed at least on speaking terms with each other. This I have tried to do.

Now that the bizarre phase of existentialism is passing, the first morbid shock is turning into a real interest in what the serious existentialists have to say. The full import of Heidegger, Jaspers, and Sartre, of Berdyaev, Marcel, Buber, and of Kierkegaard, the master of them all, is being worked out by responsible philosophers. We now realize that existential philosophies are symptomatic of and parts of a more general and powerful movement which counts its representatives in many lands and in many of the arts, as well as in philosophy. These thinkers have set in motion the thinking of our time, have opened up new possibilities of hearing and understanding. These thinkers are appealing from the conclusions of "rationalistic" thinking, which equates Reality with the object of thought, to Reality as men experience it immediately in the actual lived-life of personal existence,—a Reality which includes time, change, finitude, unfathomable risk, and death. Their most searching questions arise from a recognition, expressed by Max Scheler, that we live in an epoch in which man and his tortured existence have again become fully "problematic" to himself, "in which he no longer knows what he essentially is, but at the same time *knows* that he does not know."

Actually, *existenz*-thinking is neither new or peculiar to modern thought; it is new only in its sudden vogue. It did not spring full-blown from Jean-Paul Sartre. Like pragmatism, it is "a new name for an old way of thinking." The roots and motives of existentialism are subtle and diverse, and they have a long history. It is, if I mistake not, essentially a form of Romanticism deeply embedded in the pre-Cartesian and German tradition of supra-rationalism and *Innerlich-keit* represented by the German mystics. It can trace its line back to the terms and tones of the Hebrew prophets, its philosophical analyses through Kierkegaard, Kant, and Pascal to St. Augustine.[1]

In America, traveling by a different route, and feeling little of the urgency and despair born of cultural crisis and disaster, the pragmatists arrived at some strikingly similar conclusions respecting the need for re-examining the theory and practice of modern man. They called for a sharp break with the traditional canons of philosophical

[1] Van Meter Ames finds striking if, to him, strange and disturbing kinship between Zen Buddhism, pragmatism, and existentialism. See his article, "America, Existentialism, and Zen," *Philosophy East and West*, 1 (1951), 35–47.

respectability; they opposed granting any privileged status in the universe to the human mind (with its penchant for precise analysis and stifling abstractions); they boldly swept away many of the notions and distinctions which had held for centuries and began to search for new values and methods in a dynamic new world.

It would not be far off the mark, I think, to call Pragmatism the American version of this general movement of protest and reconstruction within philosophy, and to count James, Dewey, and Mead as the chief American spokesmen of this movement. Accordingly, it has seemed to me worthwhile to attempt to trace out the possible parallels and relationships between American Pragmatism and Continental Existentialism, and to show, on the basis of the internal evidence, whether or to what extent this initial assumption of similarities and parallelisms is valid and verifiable as alleged.[2]

To make this essay manageable, within the limits of allotted space, and appropriate within the context of the present volume, I will confine myself largely to the Pragmatism of George Herbert Mead and the distinctive *Existenz-philosophie* of Martin Buber.[3] Indeed, the thing which first attracted my attention to Mead and Buber was the fact—or so it appeared to me—that in spite of almost complete divergence in their background, methodology, and philosophical tradition, they came close to each other in numerous and remarkable respects—particularly in their anthropology and in their social philosophy. One is reminded of Kierkegaard's comment on Schopenhauer: "I am astonished to find an author who, in spite of complete disagreement touches me at so many points."

---

[2] A first serious difficulty is that of defining our terms. Pragmatism and Existentialism include so many elements and have been refined into such very complex developments and varied linguistic jargons that it is difficult to define them with precision and inclusiveness. Actually, both terms cover a great number of philosophical and psychological views not completely in agreement with one another. Since there is not space here to make the kinds of distinctions one should make, we must risk the attendant dangers of over-simplification.

[3] Professor Buber might repudiate the "existentialist movement"—just as Heidegger and Jaspers have done. He would probably decline to accept any label of the movement. His highly personal philosophy is uniquely his own and bears its own unmistakable hall-mark. Yet there is no denying that he and his writings bear the stamp of *existenz*-thinking, one requirement of which is that each thinker must "think Existence" and what it means on the basis of his own personal experience.

II

Martin Buber is one of the pioneers who helped develop what Franz Rosenzweig called *das neue Denken,* the heart of which is the idea of *making true* (Bewährung) by decision, venture, and commitment, into its place of great influence in Europe. It is similar to what Emil Brunner means when he speaks of the "knowledge of faith" or "existential" knowledge. And Mead, in America, was one of the four outstanding pragmatists who developed the pragmatic "new thinking," the others being Peirce, James, and Dewey. Mead had turned his back upon Europe, thinking that the "furniture" of the Old World was incongruous in the new home. Even Royce's warm and luminous idealizing was, for Mead, "part of the escape from the crudity of American life, not an interpretation of it." It was out of his attempt to formulate a philosophy indigenous to the spirit and practice of America that Mead's social idealism arose. In most important respects Mead's general position is the same as Dewey's. Mead learned much from James and Dewey, and most that is sound in Mead is also in James and Dewey.[4]

---

[4] There is in Dewey the same notion of mind and morality as social and functional; the same emphasis upon the instrumental and experimental functioning of thought in the service of conduct; the same conviction that mind is the symbolic functioning of events; the same position that symbols are social in nature, and that language is the matrix of mind and meaning: Nature in man is simply nature grown intelligent.

Of the many things in James's thought which appealed to Mead, there are two major elements which need to be underlined: (1) James's idea of consciousness or mind as selective, functional, and relational; and (2) his idea about the nature and criterion of knowledge wherein thinking is a part of action, and action finds its fulfillment and test in consequences. The organism operates interestedly and selectively within the total environment, and "carves out" its own world from the stream of experience. In the process and flow of experience, the active unity of consciousness is teleological, willful.

James's theory of meaning and truth was dominated by three main points: (1) it emphasized the categories of will, interest, selective attention, venture; (2) it appealed to satisfactory working as the test of any idea or hypothesis; and (3) it reduced relations, substances, activities and other alleged transcendent elements to the continuities of experience. Of these three notions the first led to James's *voluntarism,* the second to his *pragmatism,* the third to his *radical empiricism.* Mead had his roots in the same soil, and, if my thesis is sound, so do the existentialists.

It is interesting and relevant to recall in this connection that Peirce was a careful and sympathetic reader of Schelling's writings. And there is a remarkable similarity between Peirce's theory and Kant's doctrines. For example, the distinction between

By existential thinking, Buber means that participation is the essence of truth; he means that truth must be discovered and confirmed by the whole being and with one's very life in pledge. It is this which sets him in unalterable opposition to all philosophies which seek for the essence of things in abstraction from the concrete reality of our personal existence in the lived-life. This is a way of thinking that hopes to win some truth and certainty and freedom through decision, involvement, the venture and risk of faith. It is subjective, autobiographical, experiential, marked by an inwardness and a need to transcend personal limitations and to solve personal problems, especially in those predicaments of men where discursive thought only builds up paradoxes. When the meaning of life is at stake, when one is seeking what he can live and die for, he places his whole self at the disposal of what he has faith in.

According to Franz Rosenzweig, this "new thinking" came into use, largely independently, by such thinkers as Martin Buber, Hermann Cohen, Eugen Rosenstock-Huessy, and Ferdinand Ebner.[5] The fundamental belief of *das neue Denken* is that truth ceases to be merely what "is" true (i.e., the adequacy of ideas to things known) and becomes a truth that must be confirmed in the active life. The grasp

the terms *pragmatic* (based on experience) and *practical* (as a priori was suggested to Peirce by his reading of Kant.

It has often been noted that there is a latent pragmatism in the various forms of American idealism and a tendency of pragmatism to slip into idealism.

Royce adhered only with serious reservations to Hegelian idealism. There was ever something of the empiricist and pragmatist in Royce, although his solutions to the problems of philosophy took him beyond pragmatism and voluntarism. He was a pupil of Peirce and James, and for a while agreed with James; especially they agreed on the importance of volition in thought.

Thought is not representative but purposive. Reality is something postulated, not given; it is for us because we will it to be. Human activity is an expression of basic interests; the final basis of our thought is practical, ethical, religious. Man's freedom is essentially a moral postulate about the universe with man in it.

Royce, too, was deeply interested in the "I" and "Thou" and in the individual within the beloved community.

Because of these elements in his thought, Royce's philosophy marked "a kind of transition between absolute idealism and existentialist thought," and contributed to certain phases of contemporary existentialism. (See Gabriel Marcel, *Royce's Metaphysics*, p. xii.) In a similar way, Mead and Dewey mark the transition from absolute idealism to pragmatism.

5 See Franz Rosenzweig's essay, "Das neue Denken," *Kleinere Schriften* (Berlin, 1937); also his *Briefe* (Berlin: Schocken Verlag, 1935) and *Der Stern der Erlösung* (Frankfurt, 1921).

of truth and untruth is not simply a matter of logic; it is a mode of human existence in the present moment. Man must collect his scattered, distracted life, and as a whole man answer the call of God. History is not something to be contemplated as a neat logical proposition, but something to be acted upon and transformed. The monologues of the idealistic philosophers must give way to the dialogues of human beings, beings of speech, beings of will and passion, beings of personal approach and living encounter.

Concerning this theory and method of knowledge, Rosenzweig wrote vividly:

From those unimportant truths of the type 'twice two equals four' in which men lightly agree, without any other expenditure than a trifle of brain-fat, a little less with the ordinary multiplication table, a little more with the theory of relativity—the road leads through the truths for which a man is willing to pay something, on to those which he cannot prove true except at the cost of his life, and finally to those principles, the truth of which can be proved only by the staking of the lives of all the generations.[6]

Truth is a matter between man and something else. Mathematical propositions are true, of course, but they rank low in the hierarchy of truth. It is the degree of earnestness and sincerity with which a belief is avowed that constitutes its truth and ultimate value. How, then, shall one distinguish true from false? There is no absolute way, surely not in reason alone. Man can never claim finality, because he can never escape his finitude, which includes the finitude of reason. It is impossible, therefore, to eliminate the element of trust from truth, a trust that rests on a trust in the whole man, of whom reason is only a part.

Existentialism (whatever else it is) is in part the cry of men who move on the narrow edge of chaos and tragedy, groping for some value and meaning where none seems to be. This is not to deny objective empirical knowledge arrived at through science and logic. It is only to insist that in ultimate issues it is impossible to find decisive living truth through the intellect alone. The whole person must be involved: the hopes and fears, the passions and commitments of the thinker must be involved, if one is to find and clarify and test his relationship with reality. The human situation, like man himself, is ambiguous, filled with uncertainties and contradictions; yet it is potential, full of possibilities which one may grasp and shape

6 See "Das neue Denken," *Kleinere Schriften*, p. 396.

to one's free creative will. There are no rigid or complete determinations, no rehearsed outcomes, no infallible guidance, no final answers as to how man shall use his freedom. But use his responsible freedom, he must. There is no escape from the torment of moral conflict and decision. And it is through the exercise of this capacity and need and risk that he exists as a man.

So pragmatism too would hand over to will and faith and action the deep questions about human destiny in the hope of reaching some conclusion in vital matters of belief. Pragmatism also asserts the right of the free active self to reach out for a positive plan of life, taking belief in its total sense as something to live by. We cannot permit our doubts to paralyze our actions. Whatever our doubts or insecurity, we must still make momentous choices and *act* upon those choices. A belief is a proposition upon which we are prepared to act. Beliefs which stand the test of personal and social experience may be regarded as "true." Pragmatism is thus seen to be a way of thinking which defines "reality" and "truth" in terms of the values that inhere in action successfully performed,—although there is some difference of opinion as to the criteria by which success shall be judged. Pragmatists and existentialists have in their various ways endeavored to weave this conviction in with others so as to make out a theory of meaning and of truth.

III

"The catastrophe of historical realities are often at the same time crises in the human relation to reality," wrote Buber in 1930, a year after Rosenzweig's tragic death. "For the special way in which our time has experienced this, I know of no greater and clearer example than that of Franz Rosenzweig."

A somewhat similar observation could be made of George Herbert Mead. Mead died in 1931, but without any grave realization of impending catastrophe. Living in America, on the frontier, Mead felt all the beneficent promises of the twentieth century, but few of its evil fulfillments. He believed that the creative forces of life were on the side of the men of science and intelligent good will; and furthermore, the means for building the good society exist naturally and in the present. Therefore, Mead's interpretation of historical realities and his response to the changes in thought and culture, and the resulting answers to the issues and discontents of our era, are very different in some respects from those of Martin Buber, the European Jew, as he wrestled with the Jewish problem and the larger spiritual problems of all humankind. The significant thing for our present purposes is that a new understanding of man has been developing in which Mead and Buber play major roles.

If our thesis is sound, these two thinkers of such divergent backgrounds, experience, and method succeeded in calling attention to a simple and familiar truth to which we had been unaccountably blind: namely, the fact and significance of *relations between persons* and of the "social" nature of reality.

A fundamental problem of all men and all eras, and therefore of all philosophers, is the relation of the individual to the whole of things. It is also to the solution of this problem that Mead and Buber devoted the earnest endeavors of their seminal minds. As Mead writes:

Stating it in as broad a form as I can, this is the philosophical problem that faces the community at the present time. How are we to get the universality involved, the general statement which must go with any interpretation of the world, and still make use of the differences which belong to the individual as an individual?[7]

Martin Buber, the man of faith, would add: "We may come nearer the answer to the question what is man when we come to see him as the eternal meeting of the One with the Other."[8]

George Herbert Mead was an American philosopher and social psychologist, a pragmatist of the so-called "Chicago School." He studied at Harvard with Royce and James and Palmer. Simmel and Tarde and Wundt contributed to his thinking. He knew well the work of Bergson, of Adam Smith, of James Mark Baldwin. He taught with Charles H. Cooley at Michigan and with Dewey at Chicago. Dewey, Bergson, and Whitehead held the places of highest honor in his esteem, for these three he regarded as the vanguard of modern thought.

Mead responded to the optimistic moral challenge of the scientific age and the American frontier. In meeting that challenge he made much of scientific method and its uses for philosophy. His social psychology was an outgrowth of his interest in evolutionary biology and relativity physics. And in his psychology of social behaviorism he

[7] *Movements of Thought in the Nineteenth Century* (Chicago: University of Chicago Press, 1936), p. 417.

[8] *Between Man and Man,* p. 205.

thought he had a device to free both his theory of knowledge and his theory of value from the dualisms of earlier thinkers. His belated, and not too successful, attempt to develop a metaphysics grew out of his effort to firm up and round out his philosophy so as to make it consistent with modern physical theory and evolution.

Trained in the Hegelian tradition, he soon transformed that idealism into a pragmatic "social idealism" which included reliance upon experimental science, the moral values of democracy, empirical naturalism, historical and psychological relativism, the primacy of experience, and the employment of biological and sociological categories in the consideration of philosophical and psychological problems. Mead is what an idealist becomes when he turns pragmatist and denies the problems of essence and transcendental reality,—with thinkers like Dewey, Bergson, Whitehead, and Alexander for intellectual neighbors. Arthur Murphy has described Mead's variety of pragmatism as a "biological romanticism." Mead therefore rejected, on the one hand, the idealistic, mentalistic, dualistic psychologies (and the theories of the self based upon them in which the atomistic, individual-minded, antecedent substantive self is taken for granted). On the other hand, he discarded the sociological realism of European, especially German, psychology with its monistic, organismic part-whole concept of selves in society which gives a "soul" to the State and tends to lose the individual in the Absolute and to deny the individuality of persons. Mead also opposed the extreme Watsonian behaviorism with its radical mechanicalism in which the complexities of thought and inner experience are really denied, since they are dealt with exclusively in terms of conditioned reflexes and the mechanisms of the lower animals. Mead's objection to the former theories was that they made the genesis, functioning and growth of mind and self a super-natural mystery. His objection to the latter was that it explained mind by explaining it away. But still he held to a "social behaviorism" and to rigorous conceptions of objectivity, for, on his view, only as we interpret reflective intelligence as a distinctive kind of behavior and in terms of human interaction and communication can we develop a natural and empirical account of mind and self. His basic criticism of all his predecessors and contemporaries was that they did not go the whole way in explaining how minds and selves arise within conduct.

The ultimate unit of existence is, for Mead, the *act*—the self-caused, self-sustaining, ongoing behavior of the organism, initiated by want or problem, and directed to the end of satisfying the want or solving the problem. Not only in biology but also in ethics, Mead exemplifies the instrumentalist emphasis upon the ongoing life-process and inter-action, defined in terms of time rather than in terms of space and structure. Doing is more fundamental than being or knowing. Knowing is for the sake of action. Knowing begins in doing and has doing as its end. What is known must be true in the sense that it conforms to our experience and that means are pertinent to ends in an integral whole. An idea is verified as true when it unblocks in-hibited acts and processes.

Mead was therefore concerned to trace out the natural history of thought, of mind, and of the self, starting with the observable activity of organisms. His major preoccupation was to show that man, the responsible rational animal, develops in the process of conduct from a biological form into a mind and self. Beyond that, Mead, as a moralist and sociologist, was interested in elaborating techniques and social strategies which would harmonize the individ-ual interest with the community welfare. He thought that he could solve that problem and provide the basis for the socially necessary virtue of sympathy, if he could show that psychologically the indi-vidual self is really a "socius" and that creative intelligence is not simply a means for expanding human knowledge but is part and parcel of the nature of the universe.

Perhaps the most distinctive product of Pragmatism has been its theory of mind and intelligence—the instrumental viewpoint that "mind" has the biological function to serve the organism and further-more, that "mind" or "thought" is itself a specific kind of relational functioning of natural forms when confronted by organisms and engaged in a conversation of gestures. Mead's own major contribu-tions to pragmatic philosophy are his analysis of mind and self as functional emergents out of a bio-social context, his analysis of the origin and working of gestures, meanings and significant symbols, and his detailed description of the *mechanisms* of role-taking and language (in the form of vocal gesture) as basic to the correlative rise of the self and cognitive meanings.[9] Mead's basic postulates, therefore, can be summarized as follows: We think to guide action. Mind, so-called, is an organization of responses and a reacting to the

---

[9] Mead's clearest and most systematic statement of these matters is to be found in *Mind, Self and Society* (Chicago: University of Chicago Press, 1934).

phases of a social act. All action is part of a social process. And self-consciousness arises only in the presence of others, in a social medium, in symbolic interaction. In other words, mind is not an antecedently existing substance or entity; it is the *functioning* of significant symbols. And such symbols arise only in a social process, in a situation of reciprocal and meaningful gesture.

To *use* a symbol is to *be* a mind, and the "self" emerges when a mind is *self*-conscious, that is, conscious of itself as an object, indicating to itself its own role in a gesture situation. Symbols, in general, are linguistic and have the special virtue of affecting the individual who speaks in the same way in which they affect the one addressed. Therefore, there is "mind" where there is speech, and a "self" wherever self-communing occurs. The social group consists of those who attach the same meaning to the same gestures and objects. In such generalized agreement as to meaning and response of recognition, Mead believed he had provided for a behavioristic account of universals.

The active, impulsive nature of the organism furnishes the basis for this achievement, and the *mechanism* is seen in the capacity of the human organism to take the roles or play the parts of others (inadequately designated by Baldwin and others as "imitation"). This is possible for human organisms because they are able to devise and employ vocal gestures or language. In playing the parts of others, the human animal reacts to his own playing as well. And, when the organism comes to respond to its own role assumptions as it responds to others, it has become a "self" and an object to itself, i.e., a "socius."

From the many roles assumed successively, there gradually arises a sort of "generalized other" whose role may also be assumed. It is this attitude of the generalized other or the organized community that gives to the individual his unity of selfhood and exercises control over him.

It is at this point that Mead distinguishes between the "me," which is this organized set of attitudes which I assume and which I introject into my own self, and the "I," which is the organism's response to the attitudes of others. It is the private self of memory and awareness, of freedom, impulse, initiative. Taken together, the "I" and the "me" constitute a personality. The potential psycho-physical organism is the *given*, the "I"; the "me" is the introjected "other"; the "self" is the *given as socialized* through the experiences and interplay of living in a group.

It now becomes clear, on Mead's view, that self-realization of this social individual is accompanied by at least a partial reconstruction of the environment and of the social patterns, so that the socially nurtured self is not wholly at the mercy of the existing mores, societal stimuli, and institutional pressures. Self and Society are twin-born, mutually conditioned and causally interdependent. The self thus assimilates reality to its own pattern, creates, as it were, its own environment. Mead found in the democratic, socially-minded community the finest example of and the fullest opportunity for this correlative and full development of self and society, permitting individual expression while maintaining social order. Thus, teleology and mechanism, freedom and necessity are reconciled. Novelty and reconstruction are built into the social structure.

In sum, there are three conditions necessary to the rise and existence of selves: (1) There must be a mechanism for self-stimulation. This is found in the unique capacity of human beings for vocal gesture or language, and the vocal-auditory relations of human beings. (2) Another obvious condition essential to the rise of the self is life in cooperative, reciprocal association and communication with others. (3) One other factor is required: the ability to *get over into* the experience of the other, to experience "from the other side." The human being, alone among the animals, can fulfill this condition; and it is done, says Mead, by "taking the role of the other," that is, by becoming an object to himself, by acting toward himself as he acts toward another. In so doing he gets the sense of himself as a self, and therein he reaches the stage where he can carry on the conversation of attitudes within himself. Thinking is simply the internalized conversation of the individual with himself, in which the person is both subject and object, self and other, at the same time.

Mead's attempted reconciliation of determinism with emergence grew out of his notion of perspectives in nature and in time, and resulted in his groping toward the outlines of a metaphysics in which sociality appears as a trait of emergent evolution and of nature, since nature is in evolution.[10] "I have wished," said Mead, "to pre-

---

[10] See the essays and fragments collected in *The Philosophy of the Act* (Chicago: University of Chicago Press, 1938); also his Carus Lectures, *The Philosophy of the Present* (LaSalle, Ill.: Open Court Publ. Co., 1932) in which Mead made a belated

sent mind as an evolution in nature, in which culminates that sociality which is the principle and the form of emergence."[11]

In Mead's thinking, the relation between objects, events, and
organisms in nature is not only *spatial* but, and more significantly,
temporal. That is to say that the processes within nature are conditioned by the past, take place in the present, and are directed to
and controlled by the future.[12] This means that the teleological
act has a temporal character: (1) it has continuity or duration; (2)
it has direction; and (3) it has uniqueness or perspectivity. An act
stretches over a period of time, "beyond the stimulus to the response."[13] The existence within the present of both the past as
condition and the future as control is what gives the character of
continuity to the present. An act, then, is a single whole of concrete
time within which are distinct phases of duration, direction, and
discreteness.

For Mead, "reality is always in a present,"[14] since it is the ongoing
act which is the unity of existence. The present is always becoming
and disappearing; it is the occurrence or emergence of something
new.[15] "Presents" are continually sliding into each other, marking
themselves off from previous presents as qualitatively different, then
disappearing to give way to future presents emerging as novel
events.[16] Each "present" reconstructs a "past" peculiar to itself and
also a "future" peculiar to the present-and-its-peculiar-past. Every
individual and every generation re-writes its own history. Novelty
stretches out in both directions from each present perspective.[17]
This view commits Mead to a pluralism and a qualified relativism.[18]
This pluralism and objectivity of perspectives, plus his stress on
the primacy of experience, adds up to what we have called his "social
idealism." The individual is ultimate; but his reality is not complete
if isolated. It must be achieved in part through being related to a

thrust in the direction of a systematic presentation of his ideas which would include
the hint of an emerging metaphysics.

11 *The Philosophy of the Present*, p. 82.

12 *The Philosophy of the Act*, p. 351.

13 *Ibid.*, p. 65.

14 This is the theme of Mead's Carus Lectures.

15 *The Philosophy of the Present*, pp. 1, 23.

16 *Ibid.*, p. 33.

17 *Movements of Thought in the Nineteenth Century*, p. 291.

18 *Ibid.*, pp. 290f, 408–412; *The Philosophy of the Present*, pp. 1–31.

wider process. Belonging to more than one system contemporaneously, or the capacity for being several things or in several systems at the same time, is precisely what Mead means by "sociality."

The nature of the past is that of conditioning the present; the form of the past is that of a cognitive structure in the present; and the function of the past is that of a remembered chronicle which is seen to lead up to, and thus explain, the present. Only a past which has its origin in a present can have meaning for that present, and only a present which has evoked its own past is one which can properly serve to determine its future. Each individual or event "slices" the world from the standpoint of a different time system.[19] There is a relativity of the individual and its environment.[20]

If all this sounds strange as well as novel, it must be remembered that Mead is reacting against all those systems—particularly the naive materialism and the absolute idealism of the nineteenth century— which minimize the individual. He is trying to maintain a place of dignity and uniqueness for the concrete individual. His philosophy of experience which denies the rigidity of all forms and structures enables Mead to reject the presuppositions and propositions of both mechanistic materialism and objective idealism; namely, that reality including man is, on the one hand, only an aggregation of abstract parts, or, on the other hand, a simple, all-inclusive rational whole. It is Mead's strong conviction that both mechanism and idealism fail to do justice to the individual's unique reality as an experienced and experiencing perspective in the present. In the case of mechanism, the present is conceived as completely determined by the past. In the case of absolute idealism, the present is completely determined by the future. In other words, the world is defined and limited either by its beginning or its end; and either limitation implies a closed system. Mead is rather pleading for an open, dynamic, emergent system; and he hopes to accomplish this by setting up the present as the locus of reality. Each present is in some respect discontinuous with its past. In it there is always the emergence of something novel, something not completely determined by its past.

It is clear that Mead was trying to present a picture of nature or reality as an organization of perspectives or free percipient events, each of which would be characterized by persistence *and* discreteness,

---

[19] *Philosophy of the Present,* p. 176.
[20] *Idem.*

within a spatio-temporal process. Mead exploited the concepts of "emergence" and "relativity" and "interdependence" to enable him to accomplish this feat within a thorough-going naturalism. Any object or event in nature is dependent upon a percipient individual, and what is seen from the perspective of one individual is not necessarily what is seen from the standpoint of another.

The significance of Mead's doctrine of time, with its stress on the emergence and relativity of discrete and persistent events, is made clear by pointing out the corollaries of this doctrine:

(1) Individuals are thus given exclusive identity as well as continuity—both of which are essential to individuality.

(2) Society is thus conceived as an organization of all the individuals in it.[21]

(3) The social and psychological processes are but instances of what takes place in nature, if nature is an evolution.[22] The "present" is emergent and it is social.

(4) Mead is thus committed to a relativism and a "standpoint" philosophy which approaches the existential view which he might be expected to reject as romantic and subjective nonsense.[23]

Each perspective as an individual act has an independent identity and autonomy. Each one has its own value, its own standpoint, something precious and peculiar to itself. But, concludes Mead, this does not mean "solipsism" and the defeat of a universal philosophy. For to retain its identity, each individual (act, event, perspective, or person) must carry on a continuous and changing relationship to the rest of nature. Mead's monads are not without windows; they are not isolated from nor indifferent to their environment. Indeed, they imply and require the environment as a condition of their own existence. All of nature is in a process of continual flux and emergent development; therefore each individual or perspective must change along with its environment as the price of its own existence.

Let us pause long enough to point out the implications of Mead's

---

[21] *Movements of Thought in the Nineteenth Century,* pp. 413, 415.

[22] *The Philosophy of the Present,* pp. 173-74.

[23] On second thought, I rather suspect that Mead could have read Buber, as he read Bergson, for inspiration and insight, precisely because pragmatism (with its attack on all absolutes, the "block universe," and traditional logic and metaphysics) has stated some of the same themes for which Buber and other existentialists argue—but without leaving what the pragmatists regard as the firmer ground of empirical analysis.

interpretation of the psychical process; for if Mead is correct, certain things follow:

(1) Psychical or mental behavior *precedes* the object, and is not to be identified with it.

(2) Gesture and communication come before mind or self.

(3) The process is one in which objects are in continual process of disintegration and reformation. There are no fixed objects, no absolutes, no final entities, no complete conditioning from either the past or the future. Change is as ultimate as structure, and they mutually implicate one another.

(4) The process is in the form of social interaction carried on within the individual. Thought is only internalized conversation, the dialogue of a thinker with himself. Mental activity is *social,* and the individual, though ultimate, is really a miniature society.

(5) Out of the process arise the attitudes of the individual and the perceptual objects of his world.

(6) Only human beings can have "selfhood" and, consequently, objects and meanings.

Mead believed that these same principles of social and behavioristic psychology provided a fruitful basis for aesthetic experience, ethics, social reform, value theory, economic practice, democratic political theory, and international relations. All of these areas of human activity involve a similar integration of impulses at the level of interacting selves. As social, the self has become the other, and the values of the other are his own. Thus the self escapes the egocentric predicament, both epistemologically and ethically. A social self has "social" impulses and values that demand fulfillment as imperatively as any other impulses. Moral ends are social ends. Moral action is intelligent, socially directed action, guided by consequences and experiment and by all the knowledge that science can give, and in which the interests of others are considered equal, indeed identical with, one's own. It is in a society of such selves that Mead finds the social ideal. The implications for democracy and socialism are that each person should realize himself through moral participation in a cooperative commonwealth.

Mead was a humanist; he had no use for religion, especially organized religion. He did not find help or comfort in the idea of a Life or Self greater than man himself. Science and Social Reform supplied for Mead what most men find in religion: an object of worship, a motive for useful service, an outlet for personal devotion, and a creed which was intellectually satisfying. Edward Scribner Ames, colleague and friend of Mead for many years, differs with him chiefly in his unwillingness to use the "Generalized Other" as an interpretation of and psychological equivalent of the historical concept of God. Religious experience Mead interpreted as the extension of social attitudes to the universe at large, but he never suggests a possible connection between the theistic conceptions of God and his concept of the "Generalized Other".

IV

We are now ready for a more detailed comparison of Mead and Buber in our attempt to show what we trust is already becoming clear; namely, that Buber's existentialism has notable points of contact with Mead's pragmatism: its anti-intellectualism; its stress on freedom; its functional active theory of knowledge and meaning; its stress upon the act or deed; its accent on social or inter-personal relations; its emphasis upon the reality and integrity of the "other"; its taking of time and telic process seriously; its insistence upon the unity of theory and practice; the element of faith, venture, and immediate experience; its philosophy of speech; and, most notably, its social philosophy, with its central concept of what I have called the "social self", which sees the self as a self-other, I-Thou system, rather than as a mind.[24]

Lest we claim too much for this alleged kinship, let us enter some reservations. Remarkable and significant affinities and agreements there surely are. This much is clear. But since philosophies are, in a sense, expressions of deep emotional visions, of basic insights and of cosmic allegiances, we need to remind ourselves that Mead and Buber work in two quite different *Weltanschauungen* and with very different intellectual tools. Some will conclude that their differences are as important as, if not more important than, their likenesses.

The first and basic disparity to be noted is that Mead employs a strictly genetic and naturalistic method, whereas Buber carries on his reflections within the intuitive, romantic, and religious tradition. Mead

[24] The "social self" is my term (not Buber's nor Mead's) and is employed simply as a convenient and adequately accurate term to mean that the self is a product of social or inter-personal relations involving symbolic communication. Some readers may feel that my term "the social self" is too general a linguistic form to cover precisely both Mead's self-other dialectic and Buber's I-Thou dialogic relation.

accords what Buber would call a quite unwarranted significance to the techniques and conclusions of natural science. Mead worked within the frame of secular behaviorism, concerned as a social psychologist with the empirical study of mind, self, and society in their social evolution. He was in open hostility against anything that smacked of the super-natural or the transcendental. Buber's writings, on the other hand, are shot through with the sheen of the transcendent. Buber voices and brings into sharp focus the basic struggle between religious faith and secularism. He speaks the language of faith and revelation, of Jewish Hasidic mysticism, attempting to assimilate social meeting with theonomous meeting. Mead stresses a single horizontal dimension and man's involvement in human society only; Buber conceives of man as living in a three-fold relation with nature, fellowman and God, thus providing a ground for a moral imperative beyond the community which begets the self. This fact also makes for important distinctions between the "social" as a general category and Buber's concrete I-Thou dialogue. Again, Mead equates the moral with the social, and thereby fails, in my judgment, to show how the self is more ethical than the social group which molds the self; whereas Buber holds to certain eternal values grounded in God or in the relation with God. Finally, Mead's analysis is confused, as I read it, because of a residue of Hegelian social idealism which includes part-whole identical, as well as self-other responsive relationships.[25] Buber's view seems to me to be more adequate because his I-Thou relation is also set in a finite-infinite system.

It is not my aim, nor is it possible, to present here a complete or exhaustive comparison and critique of Mead and Buber.[26] It is intended only to identify some of the central motifs in their thought and thus to show how two quite different but first-rate minds have tried to formulate the human problem in relational terms. I am

[25] In spite of Mead's heroic efforts to free his thought from the fetters which nineteenth century idealism put upon it, I doubt that he ever completely lost his early idealism, and his subjectivism remained as rigid as his naturalism. All of the pragmatists, like Kierkegaard, learned much from Hegel, yet came to regard him as their special adversary.

[26] In a volume entitled *The Social Self* (New York: Bookman Associates, 1954), I have attempted a full-scale exploration of the concept of the social self, comparing and criticizing both Mead and Buber respecting their views, and venturing an appraisal as to the value and validity of the inter-personal notion of the self. See also *Self, Society, Existence* (New York: Harper Torchbooks, 1961).

especially interested in their social philosophy, their common view of the self and the basis of its formation involving the symbolic mechanisms of speech or dialogue.

If my thesis has merit, it should be clear by now that both Buber and Mead establish a philosophical anthropology which conceives of man as a self-other system, comprising a duality of an *alter* in the *ego* in which the self in the dialectic is both subject and object at the same time, knower and known, transcendent and empirical. It must and does regard itself with the eyes of an other—neighbor, society, impartial spectator, God, etc. In thus emphasizing this *ego-alter* dialogue or living encounter, Mead and Buber appear to have directed attention to a more fundamental factor than the idealists have done with their interest in the rational-empirical self-dualism. So Mead writes: "We are in possession of selves just in so far as we can and do take the attitudes of others toward ourselves and respond to those attitudes."[27]

Similarly, the central idea of Buber's philosophy is given in his now celebrated distinction between the two primary attitudes, the two fundamental types of relation, of which man is capable: the *Ich-Du* (I-Thou, person-to-person relation) and the *Ich-Es* (I-It, person-to-thing connection). Through the I-Thou meeting the primary reality of the spiritual life emerges; neither the *I* nor the *Thou* is ultimately real, but the *I-Thou meeting,* the "between man and man."[28] The person, the "single one" (*der Einzelne*) is born of the I-Thou encounter. "I become through my relation to the Thou: as I become I, I say Thou."[29] "The real self appears only when it enters into relation with the Other. Where this relation is rejected, the real self withers away."[30] "Its essential life, whether it admits it or not, consists of real meetings with other realities, be they other real souls or whatever else. Otherwise, one would be obliged to conceive of souls as Leibnizian monads."[31] There can be no I without a Thou.

The fundamental fact in both accounts is *man with man.* What is uniquely characteristic and constitutive of the human world is something that takes place *between* one person and another in community. Man's essential nature is not grasped from what unfolds in the indi-

[27] *The Philosophy of the Present,* pp. 189f, *passim.*

[28] See *I and Thou* and *Between Man and Man, passim.*

[29] *I and Thou,* p. 11.

[30] *Eclipse of God,* p. 128.

[31] *Ibid.,* p. 110.

vidual's inner life, but from the distinctiveness of his relations to things, to other living beings, and (Buber would add) to God. It appears to be a paradox of human existence that man needs others in order to be himself. For human existence is essentially dialogue, address and response, claim and counter-claim, pledge and promise. Man is the only being who can address another, who can make promises, who is united with other men in bonds of covenant. Community is the common acknowledgment of selves and of bonds. The true self is the loyal self, the bound self, accepting responsibility.[32] This whole self is a unity of tension, an embracing of polarity—a tension and a polarity which should not be abrogated, but encircled, embraced, reconciled.

We know ourselves, then, only in the presence of another. We become or acquire selves when we know ourselves to be known, when we are apprehended and valued by a self-disclosing other. It is social inter-play, contrast-effect, resistance, reflected appraisal, a life of dialogue that turn the human organism into full selfhood. The finite individual self is mutually dependent upon and mutually determinative of other selves in a network of mutually supporting, dynamic, inter-personal relations.

Man, on this view, is a "socius"—a "social self" grounded in essential otherness. Man is not a self-sufficient atom, not "an intradermal self," nor a mode or function of some Absolute. Man is rather a *Mitmensch* living in a *Mit-welt*. This is the key-note in both Mead and Buber.

What we have been saying is as revelatory of the nature of reality as of the self. Not only man, but all existence has a social structure, is constituted of and mutually determined by social relations. It seems to be characteristic of both existentialism and pragmatism that they develop their ontologies (such as they have) in psychological, biological, or sociological terms. And in this respect Mead and Buber are no exceptions. There is an ontological quality to Mead's "experience" and to Buber's "between." In every being is laid the All-being, but it cannot develop save in relation with all else. The universe also

[32] The meaning and significance of the concept of responsibility is a central theme of *Zwiesprache, Die Frage an den Einzelnen,* and *Was ist der Mensch.* As the translator rightly remarks, the meaning is brought out more vividly in the German, with the use of such words as *Wort, Antwort, antworten, verantworten,* etc., which are all closely interwoven in a play of meaning in which speech and response, answering to and for the person or the moment are intimately related.

acts in ways which are characteristic of social selves; human experience accords with a reality beyond itself.[33] From cells upward in the
ascending scale of emergence—and up to God, if Buber is correct—
the social-relational aspects of reality assume a more prominent
role. Nature, self, and society are alike "fields of forces," organizations
of perspectives, occasions of mutually determining lines of influence.
And if "person" means being related to other persons in a world of
persons, then God may be considered the supreme case of personality,
and is related to all otherness by sympathetic concern. If God is love,
then He must be personal and social—for love is meaningless apart
from persons in gracious personal relations.

Buber speaks of the *"a priori* of relation," of the instinct to make
contact, to create.[34] In one sense, relation does not exist until we have
entered it, but in another sense it has been there already, potentially,
waiting to be realized,[35]—like the *Shekinah* of God's "world-in-
dwelling glory" ever waiting for release and unification. Some feature
of reality, perhaps dimly seen, stands over against us; we stare and
grope and wrestle with it; we try to grasp it, speak to it, while it invites
and evades us. The environment says variously: Stand and meet me;
I am here, come! The beginning of meeting and relatedness is in the
natural and animal world. The Thou-relation is there potentially.
Buber is intensely conscious of the subjective integrity of objects in
nature. The very existence in actuality of Beauty, Love and Truth is
evidence of the latent Thou-quality and Thou-relationship coming to
awareness, becoming actualized.[36]

Even if we exclude God, we can still assert with Mead that "social
psychological process is but an instance of what takes place in nature,
if nature is an evolution."[37] Sociality and relativity are to be understood as special cases of a process that takes all nature as its province.
Appeal can be made in this connection to some of the greatest
philosophers from Plato to Whitehead who have held, with varying
degrees of explicitness and consistency, that "social structure" is the

---

[33] See, e.g., Charles Hartshorne, *The Divine Relativity* (New Haven: Yale University Press, 1948), where he argues with acute logical analysis for a personal God who
"has social relations, really has them, and thus is constituted by relationships and
hence is relative . . ."

[34] *I and Thou,* pp. 9–10, 14–16, 27–28, *passim.*

[35] *Ibid.,* p. 8.

[36] *Ibid.,* pp. 27, 65–66.

[37] *The Philosophy of the Present,* pp. 173–4.

structure of all existence. Fechner and Whitehead, even Peirce, not to mention many recent thinkers like Charles Hartshorne, have held that deity is the supreme case of the social category, rather than an exception to it.[38] It appears that in both Mead and Buber we have a philosophy which affirms that man and reality are "social" or relational in essentially the same way. Furthermore, it appears (especially in Mead) that the universe, as real, is a generalization from this conception of persons in relation.

The individual grows to selfhood in an intensely social process. Man, the individual, is incomplete; therefore, he is set in families and communities as the condition of his being. Independent selfhood is never absolute nor a priori with respect to others; it is reciprocal and potential to relation. This means that self and society are correlative terms; self and society are twin-born. Neither self nor society is the fundamental fact of human existence; the individual and the community are equally primordial and correlative entities. The more fundamental fact is *man with man* in a self-other dialogic and communal relation. The self is a being-in-community.

And in the community, language is the mark of man. It is speech, the Word, which unlocks person to person. In the thought of both Mead and Buber, *speech* is central to the origin and development of human selfhood. We are literally talked into selfhood. The human fish swims in a sea of signs and symbols, as Charles W. Morris has it. Or to change the figure, through language the self becomes "dressed in social clothes," looks at itself in a social mirror, approves or disapproves of itself through social eyes.[39] We are human because we can talk.

Franz Rosenzweig has pointed out in his famous essay on "The New Thinking" that the "old thinking" is timeless and monological, often for no one else but the isolated thinker. The "new thinking" is grammatical or dialogical. It uses the method of speech which is bound to and nourished by time. Because it takes the *other* seriously and happens *between* oneself and the other, it cannot anticipate what the other will say, nor rehearse what oneself will say, nor know where it will end. One simply has to be ready to enter the dialogue. The

---

[38] Precisely this point, and this whole point of view, is the subject of rigorous treatment in Hartshorne's Terry Lectures, *The Divine Relativity*. One need not share Hartshorne's idealistic theory of knowledge in order to find his treatment of deity trenchant, suggestive, and reverent.

[39] *The Open Self* (New York: Prentice-Hall, 1948), p. 48f.

Sprachphilosophie always means that one is speaking to someone else, someone who has not only ears but a mouth, someone who can talk back. This is why real dialogue is the way to existential truth, since it places us in the concrete reality of our personal existence, compels us to see what is unique and real in the person or situation.

Speech and deed, language and active engagement with the neighbor—these are the essential media in human relations. Both Mead and Buber stress the "histrionic tendency" which seems to run through all human experience and illustrates aptly the dramatic capacity and tendency to take the role of others (*personae*), to speak to and for another, to project oneself over to the other and play his part. Incidentally, this is also the psychological basis of justice.

But more than this, speech and role-taking are somehow creative, constitutive. In the process of symbolic communication, in the invention and use of language, in the effort of speech—and Buber would add, in the agony and leap of prayer—man becomes or acquires a "self." Speech is the bridge between two poles, the act by which the potential between the two poles becomes actualized in a self. *Being* is not just *being known* (in Berkeley's terms), but being addressed, answering, *knowing that one is known.* Only as a person can one speak to others as well as to oneself. Man is peculiarly a fellowman, living in a world of relatedness; and the symbolic process, principally vocal gesture or language, is the chief mode of communication. This capacity of man for speech, for symbolic interaction, is the basis of man's selfhood. Man's being, in the deepest sense, is *respon*-sible.[40] *Respondeo ergo sum.*

If this be true, there follows another corollary in which both Mead and Buber agree: Selfhood is not simply a birthright, but an achievement; and there appear to be levels or stages of achievement up to full true selfhood. And, if we may include Buber's religious dimension, man is not truly and fully a self or person in all the rich meaning of those terms unless and until he knows himself before God.

There is an ancillary problem of human selfhood: How to remain oneself in the very process of being related? Can the autonomy and

---

40 The German language which Buber uses so beautifully enables him to employ several very expressive compound words to denote this peculiar characteristic of human selfhood. So Buber (as well as Ebner, Brunner, and Barth) speaks variously of the *Ansprechbarkeit* and *Wortmächtigkeit* of man, and asserts that the true man is *angesprochene Mensch* and *wortempfängliches Wesen.*

integrity of the "social individual" be protected against every tendency either to make of the individual a function of some Absolute Socius, or to assimilate the other to the subject? Both Mead and Buber *intend* and attempt to preserve the reality, freedom, and integrity of their finite social individual. Both reject atomistic individualism as well as organic monism, but Mead is less convincing than Buber at this point because of his radical empiricism and the residue in his thought of Hegelian social idealism. There is considerable evidence that Buber succeeds in this attempt somewhat better than Mead because of his consistent Biblical personalism and because of his more avowed Kantian view of the knowing and acting self.[41] While the self develops as a reflection of the personal and communal relations, the social group has no existence apart from the selves which reflect it.

It appears to me, however, that Mead's excessive stress upon the social and cultural factors led him to minimize, though he certainly did not neglect, the factors of uniqueness, singularity, and autonomy which Buber (and such American psychologists as Gordon Allport) would underscore. There is more than a hint that Mead, being so much a "social Hegelian" (if such a term may be aptly employed), is open to the charge that he loses his social self in the Socius. Mead seems to be trying to hold a middle course. He was ever trying to find a formula for assuring individual expression and functional differentiation while guaranteeing social order. He wanted freedom consistent with order in the community. His own answer of the "social individual" suggests that self and society are laid down together: correlative aspects of the same natural experience. Selves develop only in a social matrix, and society exists only in and through and for individuals. Self and society are mutually interdependent and reciprocally conditioned. The universal is nothing if the particular is nothing; but the particular comes to self-awareness and effective freedom only within a complex and responsive universal. Thus the universal and the particular are harmonized.

The same basic question for Buber, as for Mead, is that of the person within the community. The person, while real and free and responsible, is mutually related to society. The strange and wonderful fact about the mutual relations which obtain in Buber's I-Thou

---

[41] Buber's "self" is not, of course, to be equated with the Kantian "subject". Buber's self is the whole person, both transcendent and empirical, conditioned and free, the result of I-Thou relations.

world is that the activity of one self-conscious, self-directing, unique person is conditioned by that of another in such a way that both remain free, autonomous, responsible. "Each life is a life in itself, but as such it forms the community."[42] Buber writes in the memory of those Hasidic communities which he knew as a youth: men of many-sided individuality and strong differences, yet each surrounded by a community which lived a brotherly life.

Neither Buber nor Mead are sociological realists. The form-urge in the inner life of each individual is the ultimate fact. Selves make society and are made by society; yet each self is a unique, unrepeatable person. Man is bound up in relation, but he is still free with respect to both society and nature. Neither sociological nominalism nor sociological realism does justice to the data of experience—on this Buber and Mead agree. Not the private life versus the public life, but *man with man* in the uncurtailed measure of the dialogic life. Man's way lies through overcoming his isolation without forfeiting the responsibility of his real aloneness. "Only men who are capable of truly saying *Thou* to one another can truly say *We* with one another."[43] To be free, to be responsible, to be a real person, and to be in mutual relation with all otherness—all these mean the same thing.

The self, then, is essentially a self-other system rather than a mind. Mead's view is somewhat qualified in that it includes part-whole relations as well. Buber's view is less ambiguous because his I-Thou system is also a finite-infinite system.

The social and political philosophy of both Mead and Buber lends support to an essentially democratic or moderately socialistic view of society and the state. Mead tends more than Buber to an organic interpretation of society, but he avoids any extreme statism by insisting that the generalized other to be complete must include the perspectives of all the individual acts.

Their effort clearly is an attempt to provide an adequate basis for moral obligation and moral dissent from the social patterns, which may become rigid and vicious, while also preserving social order, nay more, genuine community. Again, on my reading of the record, Buber seems to present sounder and more adequate grounds for a moral imperative beyond the society which begets the self, and

[42] *Hasidism*, p. 3.

[43] *Between Man and Man*, p. 176.

thus accounts more adequately for moral reformation and progress. He is able to do this because he brings God into the community as a third and higher and more inclusive loyalty.

There is little doubt that in both Mead and Buber the social and ethical interests are predominant,—yes, and in James and Dewey. All of these thinkers have a sensitive and knowledgeable interest in many of the same value problems of men and societies—a tendency characteristic of both pragmatism and romanticism. Mead and Buber hold the view that human conduct in its true functioning contains the resources and tools for ethical action and social progress; they were therefore concerned to elaborate a theory and a strategy which would harmonize the individual interest with the common good. Mead, more explicitly than Buber, holds that he can achieve this harmony of interests if he can show that psychologically the individual is a "social self." Mead thus equates the "moral" with the "social"; they are relative and relevant only to human life, and have no cosmic rootage. Buber, on the other hand, finds a place for an objective and transcendent reference for the moral sanction. He believes that there are certain eternal values, and that man stands responsible to a Being or Reality superior to man and society. Mead holds only that men arrive at "objective" standards or universals which approximate practical absolutes. Buber's self stands in a threefold relation to nature, other men, and God. He seems, in this way, to provide a moral authority and transcendent judgment of more urgency and radicality than is to be found in Mead's merely human and societal "other." Mead's self, it seems to me, is not more ethical than the social group which molds the self. And Mead fails to show how to get an harmonious integrated self from a discordant and pluralistic society, especially if there is no nuclear permanent Center. His behavioristic treatment seems hardly adequate to protect the individual person against the societal pressures of such modern idolatries as Nationalism, Fascism, Naziism, and Russian Communism—all social pseudo-religions, all deifying the Tribe, the Folk, the State. Buber, by contrast, seems to be on firmer ground to protest all forms of tyranny over personality, whether of reactionary individualism, religious orthodoxy, or of revolutionary political movements. We are forced to conclude that Mead's social theory of the self has not wholly succeeded in explaining the origin and development of the higher moral values that go beyond particular group interests.

I have thought that Mead and Buber were too optimistic, even utopian, concerning human nature and the ability and strategy of human action to build the great community of good on earth. They foresaw a liberated, humane, and united humanity, living in fulfillment and peace. I have the feeling that they were beguiled by their own generous natures, as well as by their social philosophy, into regarding an acknowledged noble ideal as an operative social force. Mead recognized hardly any limits beyond which science, and particularly scientific sociology, might not go in its cure for the ills of life. And of peculiar interest here is Buber's utopian socialism and his support of the Jewish cooperative settlements in Palestine, the *kibbutzim*. Buber, it must be added at once, grounded as he is in the Biblical faith, has a much firmer and realistic view of the stubborn difficulties involved in achieving a harmonious common welfare in a very complex social order. Actually, Buber has an acute comprehension of Hebrew prophecy and a deep feeling for man's tragic finitude, indecision and turmoil. He is aware of the sin of human self-postulation. In his *Good and Evil* he considers the radical stages of evil resulting from absolute self-affirmation and man's presumptuous usurpation of the moral and creative role of God. In this respect he would surely be critical of Mead's humanism. He has not yet, however, answered in satisfactory manner the following kind of questions: If "sociality," if *man with man,* is the real way of things, why is it so hard to "socialize" people? Why is it so difficult to live in the World-of-Thou, so easy to slip into the World-of-It and treat persons as things? Why is it that men, even at their best, feel an inordinate tug of self-interest? If man as "social individual" is actually in harmony with the law of life, how shall we account for the constant rupturing of the human community by egoistic men? Why is moral evil, sin, human self-will and egoism so powerful? Here is the unsolved problem of human relations.

Truth is related to doing and being. In both Mead's pragmatism and in Buber's philosophy their metalogical anti-rationalism and their functional activistic theory of truth and meaning involve a stress upon the act or deed over thought and lead to an insistence upon the unity of theory and practice, of inner idea and outer deed. These themes, and the related attempt to overcome all dualisms, are apparent in Mead's pragmatism and in Buber's interpretation of Judaism as the prophetic call to over-bridge the tensions of life through action, to reconcile the duality of the ideal and the actual, of being and becoming, of spirit and matter, of time and eternity. Buber's hope for the rebirth and redemption of Israel lies in a recovery or fresh breaking through of that eternal inexhaustible spirit which finds expression in the three principles of Unity, Deed, and the Future (*Einheit, Tat, und Zukunft*). There is this instinct, almost as though in the blood of Israel, that demands an inner unity, the expression of faith in action, and the striving for the messianic Kingdom of love and justice upon the earth. "Unity is the inner state, action its result, the future its aim."

Accordingly, there can be no divorce between ethics and religion, between the sacred and the secular, between self and other, between ends and means, faith and practice. The perception of truth and a responsible acting upon it are inseparable. The test of your belief or knowledge is that you act upon it. The believer *knows* out of his own life. In a sense, you *know* only after the deed. It is the doing, in the lived-life, which brings the proof. This is Buber; but since Bain and James, pragmatism's general definition of belief is "that upon which a man is prepared to act." Pragmatism and Existentialism, if I mistake not, appear to be divergent statements and corollaries of this definition of truth and meaning which finds final confirmation in the consensus of the community.

I have, on my reading on the accounts, felt that both Buber and Mead are vague, unsystematic, and ambiguous in their metaphysics. Until late in life, Mead eschewed formal metaphysics completely, and Buber, in rejecting metaphysics, has described his standpoint as being on the "narrow ridge" to indicate that there is no sureness of expressible knowledge about the absolute, but only the certainty of meeting what remains undisclosed. The I-Thou relation as such does not procure objective criteria. Uncertainty and insecurity are inherent in human existence. Hence the necessity for faith, venture, risk. For this reason, Buber also uses his "narrow ridge" to refer to his stance between the abyss of irrational subjecticity and the abyss of abstract objectivity. There on the ridge is the concrete meeting with the particular Thou, human and divine, in which there is awareness and response with the whole being. Buber regards "metaphysics" as necessarily putting the absolute idea in some form or other in place of God—just what he refuses to do. He believes it is presumptuous of man to think he can have an adequate idea of God or to submit God to the laws of human logic. Accordingly, he has only the choice between silence and saying just so much as he does say.

For this general position I have respect. But there is something equivocal and inconclusive about the whole account. It simply will not do to dismiss metaphysics, since it deals with the structure and substance of the ultimately real. There are, if you like, *kinds* of metaphysics, but they all deal with the fundamental questions, with first principles. Furthermore, I believe that both Mead and Buber have metaphysical assumptions throughout: in Mead, they are naturalistic, temporalistic, and allegedly realistic—derived eventually from his view of human nature as "social;" in Buber, they are certainly theistic, and probably realistic, personalistic, and holistic. Both of our thinkers take time seriously, stressing the reality, creativity, dynamic quality and flow of time, one result of which is to give metaphysical support to their human hope for a better world. Mead's social positivism prevented him from achieving a clear philosophical realism.[44] Mead, it would seem, came late in life to heed the warning of his fellow-pragmatist Peirce, who remarked: "Find a scientific man who proposes to get along without any metaphysics . . . and you have found one whose doctrines are thoroughly vitiated by the crude and uncritical metaphysics with which they are packed."[45] After having delivered the Carus Lectures, in which he was groping toward a metaphysical formulation of his thought, Mead was busily reading Bergson, up until the time of his death.

A metaphysics is involved whenever one attempts to characterize the ultimate ground and content in which natural and human events take place. Buber denies that he has a metaphysics. If he has a metaphysics, it lacks any clear, closely-knit, and complete statement. Perhaps the difficulty is partly a verbal one, since he seems to make a distinction between metaphysics and ontology, which I consider a part of metaphysics. And he certainly has a primary conception of the universe in which he can place his understanding of human personality: a theistic conception rooted in the faith of the Hebrew people about the reality of God, His unity with His world, and the concrete polar conditions under which God and man can speak to one another. Strongly anchored in the Jewish tradition, the most concrete, matter-of-fact, "pragmatic" tradition in our Western heritage, Buber affirms against all naturalisms that, first and last, man stands

44 See Charles W. Morris, "Peirce, Mead and Pragmatism," *Philosophical Review*, 47 (1938), 109–27.

45 *Collected Papers of Charles Sanders Peirce*, 1 (Cambridge: Harvard University Press, 1931), 129.

in personal relation to God. The Eternal Thou is also the world purpose and power which is the basis of world unity and of the appearance on the world stage of "a being who knows the universe as a universe, its space as space, its time as time, and knows himself in it as knowing it."[46] While giving up any dogmatic knowledge about the ground of being, Buber stands squarely within the theistic faith of Israel. He makes no apologies for conceiving of man's relationship to God in "personal" terms as the only appropriate way to speak of God's ways with men. God meets man "as a Person," asserts Buber, but God is not only a person. He is not thus limited. God is Person—and how much more! No one knows. But Buber has claimed a good deal.

On the basis of such reflections, I have believed that Mead and Buber would gain by a more clearly developed metaphysics. And I have, in another place,[47] ventured the tentative but hazardous suggestion that both systems appear to be capable of finding metaphysical support or means of formulation in a metaphysics of process or of holism, in contrast to one of ideal static being. Surely one need not identify metaphysics with idealism or with neo-Thomistic hylomorphism. Some able interpreters of Whitehead and Hartshorne, for example, find their speculative cosmologies not irreconcilable with the personalism and theism of the Hebrew-Christian tradition. I am not inclined to press the point; having raised it in passing, I am content to leave the issue to the metaphysicians.[48]

VI

In any case, it should be obvious to any attentive reader that this self-other, I-Thou motif, with its effort to do justice to the factors of duality and polarity in human nature, becomes germane to the problems in which contemporary ethics, education, social and political theory, psychotherapy, and theology are interested. If the considerations by which Mead and Buber establish the "social self" as a valid doctrine have been well founded in their thought and in this exposition, the concept will be seen to apply fruitfully in many directions. Even a cursory inspection of contemporary literature in

[46] *Between Man and Man*, p. 155.

[47] See my book, *The Social Self*, pp. 273–87; 346–47.

[48] See the essay by Charles Hartshorne and others in this present volume.

many fields will display the productive and illuminating employment of this concept of the social self in helping us to understand the human situation. It may, indeed, be fairly argued that the definition of the self as "social" gains force from the fact that it can be expressed in two such divergent forms as the ego-alter dialectic of Mead's radically empirical philosophy and Martin Buber's religiously oriented I-Thou dialogue.

We have now identified the two movements of pragmatism and existentialism, with their central concerns for the nature and relations of the self. In the writings of George Herbert Mead and Martin Buber we have two foci in which these themes find explicit and persuasive, if not always clear and consistent, expression. We have further noted the remarkable parallels between Mead's pragmatism and Buber's religious existentialism. And lest we claim too much, we have indicated the real differences between Mead and Buber, from which some readers may conclude that the difference in method, spirit, and doctrine are more significant than the similarities.

In my own judgment, a reconstruction or amendment of Mead in the direction of Buber's personalistic and religious philosophy is permissible, if indeed not necessary, if we are to do full justice to their theories and to the concrete facts of the human situation.

Mead's preoccupation with the social and cultural factors led him to minimize the factors of uniqueness and autonomy which Buber underlines. Mead's biological romanticism and evolutionism induced in him a false optimism about human nature and social progress not justified by the stern facts of life. Buber's theocentric personalism provides a firmer ground for an ultimate optimism concerning the end of human destiny. In the absence of a firmer metaphysics, Mead's naturalism never accounts for the *capacity* of the human animal to develop language, take the role of others, and envisage values. He therefore assumes a self in order to get a self. Metaphysically and epistemologically, Mead appears to me to be guilty of begging the question. In denying the existence of God Mead again, in my judgment, oversimplifies the total situation. Buber's notion that the "other" might be God, the Eternal Thou, provides the basis for a doctrine of creation and redemption, grace and forgiveness, not found in a purely secular and social morality. Man can thus know the blessedness of forgiveness while responding to the lure of the infinite moral demands of the Infinite Other.

We have tried to show how pragmatism and existentialism—as

expressed respectively in the thought of Mead and Buber—have forged the intellectual tools and symbols for the philosophical and cultural revolution which was prepared in the nineteenth century and is being carried forward today on many fronts. There are, as I have attempted to show, remarkable similarities and other points of contact which supplement each other and with certain amendments might be even more closely integrated. There is, I believe, truth on both sides. And now that we have brought these two movements together in dialectical encounter, I trust that the "dialogue" will continue.

PAUL E. PFUETZE

DEPARTMENT OF RELIGION
VASSAR COLLEGE

24

Ernst Simon

MARTIN BUBER, THE EDUCATOR

I. *The Task*

ABOUT twenty-eight years ago, shortly before Buber's sixtieth birthday, negotiations between him and the Hebrew University of
Jerusalem took place, which resulted in his being called to the newly
created chair of Social Philosophy. At first, however, the administra-
tion of the university had offered him the chair of Pedagogy. He had
declined it on the grounds that the field always interested him
practically rather than theoretically. This surprising, and even then
not quite justified assertion, which in the meantime has been vastly
contradicted, becomes more comprehensible when we consider it in
the light of his characterization of a Hasidic master, Rabbi Dov Baer,
the Great Maggid, who was, according to Buber, a teacher, though
evidently not "by profession." "Only in times of a decline of a spiritual
world is being a teacher, in its highest sense, a profession . . . , in
times of flowering the disciples live with their master, just like the
journeymen happened to do with theirs, and learn all kinds of useful
and practical things in his presence, through his will or without it."[1]

What is said here of practical teaching is even more valid about
theoretical pedagogy. It, too, appears only when a pattern of life has
become old.[2]

According to Buber's opinion, in the present pattern of life among
mankind as well as among Jewry had indeed become old. Nonetheless
it appears to Buber meaningful to present anew to an estranged generation the archetypal figure of the old "master," and to urge us to
follow him, under altered circumstances, without Buber himself being
able or willing to do so.

Buber has formulated this problematic situation. In his lifelong
discussion with Theodore Herzl (1860-1904), the founder of political

---

[1] *Die Erzählungen der Chassidim*, p. 37.

[2] Hegel, *Introduction to the Philosophy of Right*.

Zionism, Buber once refers to him as a "basically active man" (*Elementaraktiver*), calling himself a "problematician" (*Problematiker*). In contrast to his earlier—and later—much more negative judgments, he here says that the "basically active man" serves as a model to the "problematician." "The highest form of education is this: existential unity."[3] Buber, who denies the quality of existential unity for our times,[4] does not claim it for himself. His yearning is for a "master," but his insight into the essence of the epoch and of his own nature drives him to teaching, and even beyond that, to an almost unwillingly adopted pedagogical theory.

Buber is nonetheless not a systematizer, not even of a theory of education. "God has one truth, the Truth, but He has no system."[5] Thus Buber practices the *Imitatio Dei,* just in being without a system. A philosophic system either reconstructs the world according to a lost and regained blueprint, or tries to draw one for its improvement. The faithful thinker of a certain type[6] grasps the creation as he receives it and reacts to it with his reflections. This is what determines the form of Pascal's *Pensées,* the aphorisms of the late great Rabbi of Jerusalem, Abraham Isaac Kuk, the stammering of Pestalozzi, and the eloquence of Buber.

Exactly because of this Buber's doctrine of education is to be presented, if at all, only in the context of his whole work. Naturally the writings which deal directly with pedagogic themes are indispensable to the task. They are not, however, to be detached from the totality of Buber's deeds and reflections, lest one be led into a false perspective.

II. *Educational Ideals*

Buber has referred to a concept of Hasidic man repeatedly, and in several ways; anecdotal-synthetically, epic-narratively, and analytic-interpretively. It would involve a special task to extract from Buber's Hasidic writings their pedagogic value.[7] The main gist of it is the

[3] *Die Jüdische Bewegung, Gesammelte Aufsätze und Ansprachen,* Erste Folge (1900–1914), pp. 199ff.

[4] This basic conviction permeates throughout Buber's work, from the earliest to his most recent utterances. Cf. *ibid.,* p. 252; and *Sehertum, Anfang und Ende,* p. 61.

[5] *Hinweise* (Zürich, 1953), p. 168. Cf. Maurice Friedman, *Martin Buber, The Life of Dialogue,* pp. 3ff.

[6] Franz Rosenzweig belonged to another, more violent type of thinker.

[7] Cf. M. A. Sainio, *Pädagogisches Denken bei Martin Buber* (Jyväskylä, Finland, 1950), pp. 9ff.

denial of every religion which is isolated from life, and the propensity to make precisely the totality of life into a religion. In this sense did Rabbi Pinchas of Korez say: "I prefer piety to prudence, but I prefer goodness to both prudence and piety." The same was said more radically in the school of Karlin: "Prudence without heart is nothing at all; piety without it is false.[8] Rabbi Bunam, Buber's favorite,[9] put it this way: "If someone is merely good, he is a beggar; if he is merely pious, he is a thief; and if he is merely prudent, he is an unbeliever." Only with all three of these qualities combined can one serve God.[10] The path leads "from the world to God," and not the other way around; it leads, ever renewed, from the love of man to the love of God. "The educational directive is the way from 'below' to 'above'."[11] The sphere between man and man is also the religious sphere. "The genuine moral act is done to God."[12] It occurs in the deep identification with the sufferer, or even the apostate or the adversary.[13] Such a love of the nearest and farthest is unfulfillable without self-affirmation; nay more, self-love. Whoever wishes to love his neighbour, "who is like you," should not hate himself.[14]

This new archetype of a Jew shows the chief characteristics of "naiveté, vitality, simplicity and directness." In differentiation from the rationalistic standards of the old-style Rabbi, his values have altered, opposing the former.

The exemplary man is no longer the sagacious and the learned in religious scholarship, nor the isolated ascetic, given to contemplation; he is the pure and unified man, who wanders in the midst of the world with God, who participates in the life of his people, and elevates it to God.[15]

8 *Die chassidische Botschaft,* p. 179.

9 *Gog und Magog,* p. 404.

10 *Die chassidische Botschaft,* p. 180. Cf. Pestalozzi's contemporaneous synthesis of heart, hand and head, which, in a pedagogical sense, discards all severance. Also Buber: "Everything that is isolated leads to error." *Ibid.,* p. 181. Goethe: "Alles Vereinzelte ist verwerflich," "All things isolated are reprehensible."

11 *Ibid.,* pp. 182f.

12 *Ibid.,* p. 185.

13 *Ibid.,* pp. 186, 196. Cf. Pestalozzi's *Lienhard und Gertrud,* wherein Pastor Ernst finishes his sermon about the criminal bailiff Hummel with the words: "He is a man, like you!"

14 Cf. Rousseau's distinction between "amour de soi" and "amour propre," and more recently, Erich Fromm's *Man for Himself.* For Buber's influence on Fromm, cf. Friedman, *op. cit.,* pp. 184ff. Fromm considers it feasible. [Oral communication.]

15 *Die chassidische Botschaft,* pp. 72–75.

Buber depicted "the world of the Haluz"[16] with less prolixity than that of the Hasid, but with no less love. Here also he speaks expressly of an "archetype of man". His characteristics are again, quite as those of the Hasid, a synthesis, but this time of national and social impulses. Without both of these mutually complementary motivations, the building of Jewish Palestine is unthinkable, at least "in the foreseeable future."[17]

This limitation is important. It indicates that here one deals not with an absolute ideal, but a relative one, which is imitable and which could materialize through educational endeavour. Of the two elements—the national and the social—which is for Buber dominant and which is relatively recessive? The answer becomes evident from his supplementary statement, that the isolation of the national components from the complex in favour of the social ones, would be "irremediable romanticism."[18] In other words, today the transition of a revolutionary colonization of a "nation without a homeland"[19] cannot succeed without nationalism; later, however, as a permanent result, there should remain a socialistic man, with a natural national belonging, which needs no further emphasizing; a man who becomes, as it were, after the end of the actually dynamic national pioneering, the true social Haluz.

But whence will the second and all the subsequent generations of the Jewish farmer from the communal settlements of Palestine or Israel, who grew up under socialistic forms of life and who no longer needs to struggle for their founding, get the necessary impetus not only to maintain his specific way of communal life, but also to penetrate it anew persistently, and to make it more deeply rooted? Primarily, of course, from inner impulses, but also from a high public opinion for "the self-employed labourer . . . who is and remains the most highly valued and respected in the nation." Otherwise, surely, the sons of the Haluzim would be no longer Haluzim, and would certainly not permeate their surroundings with their spirit, as a radiating centrum does. In this sense, at least, the "building of Palestine must be socialistic." The people of the Kibbutzim are themselves a "living

[16] The Israeli agricultural pioneer. Cf. Buber's essay of the same title.

[17] *Kampf um Israel, Reden und Aufsätze* (1921–1932), p. 417. Cf. *Reden über das Judentum*, p. 149.

[18] *Ibid.*

[19] *Ibid.* (1928), pp. 285–288.

experiment."[20] Not only the economics experts, however well-qualified, but the whole nation participates in its success, and is co-responsible for it. Buber, however, deals not only with Zionism, nor even with Jewry as such, but through their media shows a concern for all mankind just as well. Accordingly, he asks in the same connection: is there still an authentic human countenance maintaining its dignity between the fascistic deification of brute facts on one side and the communistic deification of ideology on the other? Does a first true self-realization develop in the era of pseudo-realization?[21] In other words, ones actually used by him, is there between "Rome" and "Moscow" an eternal, and at the same time temporal "Jerusalem," which stands for the image of man realizing himself in a working and righteous community, imperfect as she may be; herself unable to "preserve her purity at all costs," yet while struggling within the concrete situation, still attempting to live up to the idea?[22]

Since Zion concerns itself with this, and nothing less, it is to be understood not merely as a territorial concept, just as Judaism not merely as a national one.[23] In this respect, however, the question presents itself with exceptional acuteness; to what extent has this experiment with this new Jewish archetype of man, the Haluz, actually succeeded? In a later evaluation Buber does not give a clearly affirmative answer, though he is even farther from a negative one. Despite some sad experiences, the saddest of which he does not mention, namely that many kibbutzim could not withstand the temptation to enrich themselves in and after the Jewish-Arab war with Arab lands, he calls the experiment "a test which did not miscarry,"[24] and so he ventures to designate it with the great name "Jerusalem."[25] Assuredly, full success cannot be recorded but, thanks to "ever renewed striving, self-dedication, becoming critical, and re-attempting" a "nonsurrender," yea an "exemplary non-surrender."[26]

How are these two Jewish ideals of education, which were fully moulded by Buber, interrelated; the Hasidic one, which, in his opin-

20 *Ibid.*
21 *Ibid.*, p. 295.
22 *Ibid.*, p. 301.
23 *Die Stunde und die Erkenntnis, Reden und Aufsätze* (1933–1935), p. 162.
24 *Pfade in Utopia*, p. 233.
25 *Ibid.*
26 *Ibid.*, pp. 221f.

ion, has miscarried because of the religious decline of the orthodoxy,[27] and because of the false reactionary and opportunistic poli-
ticking of its later leaders,[28] and the Haluz, which has not miscarried,
and thus still stands as a living example? As far as I can see, Buber
never refers to the religiously traditional Haluz, who represents a
small, but nevertheless visible and considered minority within the
total movement. This attempted synthesis between the Hasid and
the Haluz never really comes in view because of reasons which are
related to Buber's negative attitude with respect to religious legalism.
Nevertheless it remains unquestionable that Buber sees and loves[29]
in the Haluz the true follower and the contemporary actualization
of the Hasid. This is the meaning of his religious-socialistic credo:
"The true community is the Sinai of the future."[30] What he has said
about the Hasidim is also valid for him about the Haluzim. Neither
is an "order of isolated men, nor a brotherhood of the elect, but a
community with all its diversity."[31]

No elite, then! Nevertheless Buber has, just when speaking of
pedagogical ideal types also something significant to say about the
elite. He censures the Kibbutzim, especially the big ones, for their
unsatisfactory considerations of individual talents.[32] He also relates
the development of a Hasidic elite by Rabbi Mendel of Kozk and Rabbi Aaron of Karlin, without censuring them.[33] Nor does he approve
the use of the honorific "Hebrew Man," for every man who speaks
Hebrew, but only for those who are characterized by the "normative primal strength," of "Hebraic Humanism," which is striven
after by Buber. Even they become no "Biblical men," but only
"Bible-worthy men."[34] A non-Hebrew also can be a "Bible-worthy
man," but on him who speaks and understands Hebrew, this requirement is repeatedly imposed. Indeed only single ones can comply to
become forerunners of a new society. They acquire the capacity to "let
themselves be addressed by the Bible," which, though it is not literally
"God's voice," guides one to it, so to speak, like an acoustic palimpsest.

---

[27] *Reden über das Judentum*, p. 54.

[28] *Ibid.*, p. 176.

[29] *Ibid.*, p. 96.

[30] *Ibid.*, p. 185.

[31] *Hinweise*, p. 187.

[32] *Kampf um Israel, Reden und Aufsätze* (1921-1932), p. 416.

[33] *Die Stunde und die Erkenntnis, Reden und Aufsätze* (1933-1935), pp. 96f.

[34] *Ibid.*

Biblical-Hebraic humanism stems from the secret of the Hebrew language, and leads to the secret of the Hebrew man. It leads to his primal ground, which he finds where he "hears, resounding in Hebrew, the voice of the Unconditioned." It teaches him to distinguish between right and wrong, and true and false. This formulation corresponds exactly to the precept of ends in the pedagogic address on "Education and World-View." "That man alone is qualified to teach, who knows how to distinguish between appearance and reality, . . . no matter what world-view he chooses."[35]

In another pedagogic essay, "On Character Education," the elite man is called "the great character." Of him it is repeatedly stressed that he cannot serve as the ideal for the whole school class. Every class is composed of a variety of characters and talents, tempers and abilities, and each meets the teacher-educator as a part of the reality of the world. In the first stage of the educational process the teacher has to accept this heterogeneous segment of reality. First of all, it is fitting to teach discipline and order "to this given, unselected group."[36]

At the beginning, this is done even from without, heteronomously, in the hope that they become "gradually ever more inward, more autonomous." However, the ultimate goal which must influence all of his particular actions, is "the great character," who is to be conceived of neither with Kant and Kerschensteiner as a "system of maxims," nor with Dewey, as "a system of habits." Certainly under no circumstances does the "great character" stand "beyond norms,"[37] but the commandment to him never turns into eternally fixed maxims, and its fulfilment never into mere habit. Every living situation like a newborn child, like one who has not yet existed, each one unexemplified and atypical, demands from him a uniquely present decision. Buber defines the great character as "one, who from a deep readiness for responsibility with his whole life satisfies the claims of the situation by his actions and attitudes. . . . This he does in such a way as also to indicate through the sum of his actions and attitudes the unity of his essence, his willingness to accept responsibility." Here something noteworthy occurs; each individual reaction is unpredictable, seemingly singular; but together all these activities constitute a unity of re-

[35] *Reden über Erziehung,* p. 61. (Included in *Pointing the Way*—Ed.)

[36] *Dialogisches Leben,* p. 309; *Reden über Erziehung,* p. 81.

[37] *Dialogisches Leben,* p. 309; *Reden über Erziehung,* p. 82.

sponsibility. "Yea, one might perhaps say that for him there rises a unity out of situations he has responded to responsibly; the undefinable unity of moral destiny." That is, not only what the great character does, and how he does it, but what approaches him, what occurs to him, that to which he reacts, has an inner unity. In complete independence from the great Jewish-Hungarian psychologist, Szondi, Buber here constructs that choice of destiny which was made known by Szondi's archetype-psychological studies.

Szondi tries to correlate the active strivings of a human being with his seemingly most passive fate, and relate both of them to the inherited and acquired focus of his personality. He believes to have detected laws which can be experimentally proven, biologically and psychologically analyzed, and statistically presented. Here Buber would part company from him. According to Buber, the unity of destiny cannot be exactly demonstrated; it is a metaphysical postulate, or better still, a religious hope. Buber puts it at the outermost horizon of his pedagogical thought; as a possible perspective, not for all, including the criminal, as by Szondi, but for the great character, "who always remains the exception."[38]

The few bearers of such a unity of being between their acts and their destiny are clearly not "ready born," and must "first ripen,"[39] but something like grace lies above them. Are they "religious geniuses"?

Buber denies this possibility, in full agreement with Franz Rosenzweig.[40] The way to God stands open for everyone. In the final seriousness there is no elite, but, if one may put it this way, a "mythical democracy." It can be stated this way: God requires independent men; but evidently each one of us can and should become such a one, even though he is not a "great character."

Thus Buber seems to entangle himself in a hardly soluble contradiction by his dichotomous position with respect to the problem of the elite. Further considerations for and against a development of an elite can be demonstrated by his total work, from almost every one of his creative periods. In his polemic with Hermann Cohen he speaks with pride of those Zionist "Gideonites"[41] who have been educated

---

[38] *Dialogisches Leben*, pp. 309f.; *Reden über Erziehung*, p. 84.

[39] *Dialogisches Leben*, p. 312; *Reden über Erziehung*, p. 86.

[40] *Dialogisches Leben*, p. 215.

[41] *Voelker, Staaten, Zion* (Berlin-Wien, 1917), pp. 23f. Cf. also the strong Biblical relationships.

by him and his friends, and have been "tried and sifted" to take up
the fight of youth for a realizing and against a fictive Jewry. Incidentally, the young Buber relates himself somehow to Constantin Brunner's elite concept of "the Creatives" versus "common people" ("*Die
Schaffenden und das Volk*"), but in a considerably weakened form
because he defines "cultural work" ("*Kulturarbeit*") as an education of "the creative ones" as well as of the people.[42] Buber turns
against every detachment of the intellectual from life, and with particular acuteness, against every "bourgeois privilege of education,"
which threatens culture with collapse everywhere, but which would be
of special danger to a developing nation and country like that of the
Jews.[43]

Buber finds the solution to this seeming contradiction, the ethico-
religious as well as the sociological, in the realm of education.
Though the "great character" is exceptional, the insight into his
structure can help many who have fallen to the "collective Moloch,"
to reach the degree where they learn to suffer themselves, so as to
free and save from collectivization their given bit of individuality,
their "self," which is their part of God.

"The teacher should establish and strengthen in his disciples the
yearning for personal unity, from which the unity of mankind should
be born." The messianic tone of this sentence cannot be disregarded.
In fact, the solution of the contradiction between the exemplary lives
of the few, and the dull vegetation of the many, between the "elite"
and the "masses," lies primarily in the future. But this is a future
which one can anticipate and for which one must prepare now, lest
one spoil it. Today the "great characters" are "enemies of the
people." These, however, love their society, and exactly because of
that love, they try not only to maintain but to elevate it. "Tomorrow
they will be the builders of a new unity of mankind."[44] Or, with a
word of Proudhon, which Buber evokes, evidently in thorough agreement: "We shall not see the workings of the new era; we shall fight
in the night. One has to adjust oneself to bear this life without too
much sorrow, while doing one's duty."[45] The educator who does

---

[42] *Die Jüdische Bewegung, gesammelte Aufsätze und Ansprachen*, Erste Folge
(1900–1914), p. 80.

[43] *Kampf um Israel, Reden und Aufsätze* (1921–1932), pp. 404ff. *Zion als Ziel und
als Aufgabe, Gedanken aus drei Jahrzehnten*, p. 50.

[44] *Dialogisches Leben*, p. 312; *Reden über Erziehung*, p. 86.

[45] *Pfade in Utopia*, p. 62.

this, "helps to redirect man to his proper unity, and thereby helps to put him again in the sight of God."[46] The consistency of Buber's work in general, despite some contradictions, becomes again clear from a Hasidic parallel to this passage; a saying of his favourite, Simcha Bunam of Pzycha: "If man has established peace within himself, he is capable of establishing it in the world."[47]

That this is meant active-pedagogically and not quietistically, at least in Buber's understanding, can be seen from his sociological comments on the problem of the elite.

It is not the aim that there should be only leaders and no followers any more; that would be more utopian than any utopia. The aim is that the leaders should remain leaders and not become dominating rulers. More precisely stated, they should assume only those elements of domination which are necessarily demanded by the circumstances.[48]

Herewith the problem of the social elite appears to be theoretically solved. Buber himself refers to the fact that it is not practically solved in the added parentheses: "The decision concerning the issue (namely the selection of the absolutely necessary rulers) naturally cannot be left to the ruling ones themselves."[49] Of course, in the political life it occurs this way, and Buber knows it very well: each prolonged control of decisive functions in every society, even the democratic, and so much more so in the totalitarian, works toward class-formation. Therewith the maintenance of status becomes an end in itself rather than a means. This process estranges the leaders from their original legitimate task and makes them to be mere representatives of vested or even imperialistically expanding interests.

From the viewpoint of pedagogy, which evidently cannot solve this problem alone, everything depends on tying the rights of the established elite or of the elite in the making, to certain duties. Privileges and duties should be held in such a strong equipollence that instead of a rigid elite of birth, money, social status, or political office, a "serving elite" would develop. It should remain flexible in its personnel, without becoming totalitarian, or centralistically chan-

---

[46] *Dialogisches Leben*, p. 314; *Reden über Erziehung*, p. 88. This is the final sentence in the essay on Charactereducation, as well as of the *Reden über Erziehung*.

[47] *Die Erzählungen der Chassidim*, p. 759.

[48] *Pfade in Utopia*, pp. 177f.

[49] *Ibid.*, p. 178.

neled. This, again, is its specific danger.[50] The above terms do not actually occur in Buber, but he intends them, or ones very similar to them, when he next affirms that historically the situation of crisis among the Jewish people had driven into the forefront an "élite," that of the chaluzim, the pioneers, who were gathered together "from all classes of the people," and who stand "beyond classes."[51] The same is also expressed when he sums up the problem systematically as follows:

In the life of nations, and particularly . . . during an historical crisis . . . it is of decisive significance whether or not élites arise in them, which are genuine, that is, nonusurpatory, and competent to carry out their central functions. Also, whether they remain faithful to their task toward society, and do not replace their concern for it with self-concern. [In my terminology, that they do not establish themselves into a ruling class from a serving élite. E.S.] Finally, it is decisive whether they can suitably complement and renew their tasks.

This third condition is directly a pedagogic one, and Buber says so. Its realization depends on "whether the elites can influence their natural progeny so that they may properly continue the work, . . . and whether they can through right choice and correct education bring up spiritual descendants," who would contain all the possibly suitable individuals, but no unsuitable ones; at any rate, none who cannot be reached "through proper education influence."[52]

Thus, Buber's final opinion with regards to the problem of the elite, is in short this: a legitimate elite serves the aim, instead of serving its own end: domination. It is born in and by the historical crisis, but it can maintain and continue itself only through education. (It might be added restrictively, that with education alone, which also has its limits, we cannot perpetuate the elite.)

Here again decisive assignments fall to the educators—parents and teachers—and again a vicious circle is generated, which Buber does not discuss in this form.[53] Namely, to select and educate the elite, the educator himself should belong to it. This is not and cannot be the case, since they, as teachers, constitute a mass-profession.

[50] Cf. my Hebrew address to a conference of Israeli secondary schools on this theme, published in Jerusalem, 1953.

[51] *Pfade in Utopia*, p. 223.

[52] *Ibid.*, p. 225.

[53] This constituted J. G. Fichte's chief pedagogic problem in his *Closed Commercial State* and his *Addresses to the German Nation*.

Buber has not so far tackled sociologically, but only historico-phenomenologically and systematic-anthropologically, the problem of the teacher, his archetype, and his ideal. It is not accidental that in the historico-phenomenological treatment patterns from the Hasidic or the zionistic-haluz world encounter him ever recurringly, which he utilizes as examples. The Baal-Shem-Tov is characterized by Buber as "simultaneously a leader and teacher," who lived for a "yet unformulated doctrine."[54] For him there was no dichotomy between leadership and teaching which so characterizes our time.[55]

The "Great Maggid" is also a teacher, but he is less of a conscious "leader" to "new aims" and to a new "mode of life"[56] than any of those masters who are influential through their total being.[57] With his own teacher, the Baal-Shem, he stands in a relation of reciprocity; he not only receives the blessing from the older one, but he is allowed to return the same.[58] This efficaciousness from individual to individual characterizes the full bloom of Hasidism; its lack, the beginning of decline. The Rabbi of Riscin already prefers to the regular disciples, who gather themselves around the true teacher for a lasting reciprocal effect, new "listening guests."[59] The "happening between teachers and pupils" is the "highest object" of the legitimate Hasidic legends,[60] manifesting their eminently pedagogic character. In contrast with Zen Buddhism, which otherwise bears some related traits, the act of transmitting a doctrine stands in the center of Hasidic activity.[61] Both, Zen Buddhism and Hasidism serve to "move the truth" from one generation to another, but Zen does it through "stimulation," while Hasidism, through "transmission." This is a difference which primarily affects the educator.[62]

[54] *Die chassidische Botschaft*, p. 33.

[55] *Hinweise*, pp. 294f. *Kampf um Israel, Reden und Aufsätze* (1921–1932), p. 153. Cf. *Die chassidische Botschaft*, p. 49; *Hinweise*, p. 183.

[56] *Die chassidische Botschaft*, p. 44.

[57] *Die Erzählungen der Chassidim*, p. 37.

[58] *Ibid.*, p. 196.

[59] *Ibid.*, p. 71.

[60] *Die chassidische Botschaft*, p. 200.

[61] *Ibid.*, p. 212. Cf. *Dialogisches Leben*, pp. 95f. on Buddha, who, like all "genuine teachers," wants to teach "the way" rather than "a point of view," but also knows how to say "Thou" to men, as it arises from his considered but immediate intercourse with his students. However, he does not teach this.

[62] *Ibid.*

Characteristically, Buber finds again in his Zionistic patterns of ideals each basic trait of Hasidic pedagogy. However, he does not make the comparison explicitly. Ahad-Ha-Am, the zionistic cultural philosopher and opponent of the political Zionism of Theodore Herzl, who originally came from Hasidic circles, belongs, just like the Baal-Shem-Tov, to those men who stand in the service of truth, and are "leaders while they are teaching."[63] They do not desire, and do not compel a "belief" in themselves. This is a terminological difference to which Buber will return later, in his argumentation with Christianity.[64] For the time being, however, it is employed politically, not theologically, when Buber continues: "We call that man a teacher of a people who recognizes both eternal truths and present reality; that man who measures one through the other."[65] Thus the teacher-leader stands in a remarkable cleavage, but one which characterizes the human situation as such. He is not a naive doctrinaire, who prefers the untested and untempted "purity" of the idea to its actualization, with its hazards; but he is even less an opportunistic "politico," who loses from sight and mind the idea on the way to its pseudo-actualization. "Our age wants to get rid of the teacher in every aspect. Today one believes to be able to manage himself with the leader alone." Buber adds ironically: "Leadership without teaching has success. One achieves something." Yet a people without a leader are unfortunate, but thrice unfortunate is the nation whose leaders no longer have teachers.[66]

A. D. Gordon, who at the age of fifty went from Russia to Palestine in order to till the soil in a communal settlement, was for Buber, probably even more directly than Ahad-Ha-Am, the model of a "true" teacher, partly because of his theories, which are related to those of the Russian communitarians and Tolstoy, but primarily because of the uncompromising involvement of his own person into silent existence.[67]

From these patterns of ideals it is but a short step to Buber's theory of the exemplary teacher. He once defines him, again in a hasidic connection, "as a man who acts, and acts adequately. The

[63] *Kampf um Israel, Reden und Aufsätze* (1921–1932), p. 146.

[64] *Zwei Glaubensweisen, passim.*

[65] *Kampf um Israel, Reden und Aufsätze* (1921–1932), p. 152.

[66] *Hinweise*, p. 254.

[67] *Kampf um Israel, Reden und Aufsätze* (1921–1932), p. 165.

core of his teaching is this: he lets his students participate in his life, and so he lets them grasp the secret of action."[68]

So the true teacher's ideal approaches again that of the old master, though Buber knows very well that the latter is lost for us today. Buber expresses the same in a systematic relationship in his "Address on the Educational": "Intentional education has irrevocably won the day; we can no more retrogress regarding the reality of the school than we can regarding the reality of technology." We ought, on the contrary, to progress into the "transhumanification" of the new harder reality.[69] But even in this new reality "the master remains the model for the teacher";[70] though only that existential master remains the example for the modern teacher, called to conscious activities, who has merely to be there and who needs not even to be active. How can this become possible? How is the bridge from "being" to "doing" to be built? Through an "as if." When the educator of our era wants to act, and act consciously, he must do it "as if he were not doing it." Each lifting of a finger, each questioning glance is his genuine act."[71] But if such a radical opponent of every fictionalism as Buber can solve an immanent contradiction only through an ever so subdued "as-if," it indicates an aporia in his thoughts, which will occupy us later, in a critical way.

However that may be, a meaningful fiction of action, "as if one were not doing it," ought never be so coarse as to shatter the confidence of the pupils once they have penetrated it. Everything depends on that. "Trust"—this term from the characterization of Ahad-Ha-Am and the argumentation with Christianity is here again, and now in a systematic-pedagogical core-position.

Trust the world because there is such a man [as the teacher], this is the innermost work of educational relationship. While there is such a man, the chaotic cannot be the true truth. Surely there is a light in the darkness, and redemption in terror. Great love is hidden in the dullness of coexistents.[72]

In order that the educator should be able to achieve this, he needs not the sum-total of all the virtues. All he needs is to be really there.

[68] *Die chassidische Botschaft*, p. 206.
[69] *Dialogisches Leben*, p. 269.
[70] *Ibid.; Reden über Erziehung*, p. 24.
[71] *Ibid.*
[72] *Dialogisches Leben*, p. 282; *Reden über Erziehung*, p. 39.

III. *The Subjects of Education*

"The human race begins in every hour,"[73] with every newborn child, but the world is, nonetheless, already there. How those new living beings, "determined yet still determinable," encounter the already existent creation, and what they make of the world, is decided by the countenance of each historical hour. Each choice of the world which the consciously willing educator, primarily the teacher, offers to the rather malleable child, will have an important part in such a decision. It is the teacher who knows the environment and is a selective sieve through which the majority of creation must pass when it again would encounter a new soul. But even the newborn child is a "fact of creation." Thus understood, education, both conscious and subconscious, occurs in every minute through the encounter between the "old" and the recurrently "young" creature. If this encounter is brought about and guided consciously, we speak of an actual educational procedure. Today the teacher is the most important, though not by any means the sole executor of it.

The child itself, then, is not "creative," and possesses no "creative powers," the "liberation" of which modern pedagogy likes to equate with education.[74] Buber grasps more deeply. The child is a part of creation, and not the creator. But he conceives creation not merely passively as it is, but as a human child he participates in its transformation. The tool which is given him for this task Buber calls the "primeval urge." Spontaneously, and not derivable from other urges, such as those for love and satiety, it evolves in his essence of a becoming member of the human race, who wants to make things rather than be active purposelessly. He is this way even if he appears to be thinking only of destruction.[75] Buber's acknowledgement of this "primeval urge" in the child to transform the world is not identical with the pedagogical credo of radical progressive education that the "liberation of the creative powers" is the sum total of education. It is necessary to liberate the "educative powers" of the teacher himself. Only when the child's "primeval urge" is harnessed by the "educative powers" of the teacher does it become possible that the urge transcends the isolation of an individual work, which may pos-

[73] *Dialogisches Leben,* p. 259; *Reden über Erziehung,* p. 12.

[74] *Ibid.*

[75] *Dialogisches Leben,* pp. 262ff.; *Reden über Erziehung,* p. 14ff.

sibly succeed, and becomes a partner in a common task, founded on the interrelation between man and man.[76]

Therewith an important limitation is carried out, contrasting to a merely aesthetic education which could be based on that isolated primeval urge. At the same time, the total problem of aesthetic education is posited.

This has fascinated the young Buber, and occupied him ever since. His earliest statements concerning the subject call on the Jewish youth to learn again to "look,"[77] to free themselves from "pure spirituality," and to carry out the specific "resurrection" of the modern Jews, from a half-life state to a fully live one. He calls on them to become again an "organism with new, unbroken feeling for life." With a pseudo-religious and aestheticising imagery, the like of which never recurs in his later writings, he calls this appearance "the fiery pillar of resurrection."[78]

There were two active motivations in these overemphases; one permanent, and one that has been totally overcome. The former is the historically explicable Jewish deficiency of a fulness of life in the abnormal existence of a diaspora people, which is expressed particularly clearly in the realm of art and its relation to Jewish education. In order that decay of the whole man should not encroach, or set in, balancing and complementation are required here. Buber says this even today.

On the other hand, Buber has completely rid himself of the second motivation, which is related to something non-Jewish, namely the modern movement of art education, which originated in England (John Ruskin), and later, at the turn of the century, had a brief flowering in Germany, with many well-attended congresses (Alfred Lichtwark et al.). For these men, as for Herbert Read even today, the only aim of education is "to create," or to develop "creative" understanding. Buber was for a certain time the representative of this attitude in the Jewish-Zionistic quarters.

The purpose of the "Address on the Educational" is the final settlement with this view, and so Buber takes there his own former views to account.

[76] *Ibid.*, pp. 264ff.; *ibid.*, pp. 17ff.

[77] *Die Jüdische Bewegung, gesammelte Aufsätze und Ansprachen,* Erste Folge (1900–1914), pp. 132f.

[78] *Ibid.*, pp. 9–15.

The mature Buber defines "art as work and testimony of the relationship between *substantia humana* and *substantia rerum*; the materialized 'between'."[79] Thus art also has entered into the realm of "dialogical life." The pedagogical meaning of art can be traced back to it. While from the point of view of the technician, the technology of objects demands merely an "I-It" relation (to which the circumspect engineer, who evidently materializes his plans, or the mechanic who loves his machines may object), art has an essential relation to objects. At any rate, it never comes to a full "I-Thou" relation. "Pygmalion is an ironic figure in the legend already."[80]

Thus the anthropological intention of art is to be grasped neither as the "object" of the "I-It" relation, nor as the actuality of the "I-Thou" relation. Its image lies between the two.[81] The image is hidden in the raw stuff of the material, and is liberated from it. This procedure becomes significantly visible in some statues of Michelangelo's and most of Rodin's. They leave the texture and form of the primal stone untouched beside the figures, as if they had emerged from it.

Though the spoken language fashions more strongly the artistic structure than the more amorphous medium of the sculptor, it too requires the redeeming touch of the artist in order to assume a permanent form. The artist is not the one who objectifies things, but one who shapes forms, thus making evident a part of our human world which from now on will be necessary, but up to now was a hidden surplus of nature.[82] The tool of which the artist makes use for this purpose is his imagination. It discovers that which up to now was unseen, and existed only potentially. It is actualized through "shaping."[83]

Not every man, but only the artist is "full of shapes," but in a certain sense each young human child is potentially an artist. This much Buber has, after all, retained from the teachings of the "movement of art education." Both the child and the artist try to actively conquer the world which encounters their senses with the power of their minds, by making images, sounds and words.[84]

[79] *Urdistanz und Beziehung*, p. 28.

[80] *Dialogisches Leben*, p. 265; *Reden über Erziehung*, p. 18.

[81] *Der Mensch und sein Gebild, passim.*

[82] *Ibid.*

[83] *Der Mensch und sein Gebild*, p. 41.

[84] *Dialogisches Leben*, p. 445.

This fact, which is both developmental-historical and individual-psychological, permits the translation of anthropological cognitions into pedagogical ones. Buber lets himself be guided primarily by an aphorism of Albrecht Dürer's: "In truth, art is contained in nature; whoever can extract it, has it."[85] With this statement the German master becomes the model of all painter-teachers, "who possess and communicate the knowledge of the process of extraction from nature."[86]

Even Goethe and his followers had this confidence which was presupposed by Dürer, that nature is proper for perception. In view of the new world-image of atomic physics, which is no longer an image, and in the light of the "heroic resignation" of many modern research scientists, who have renounced the unification of their self-contradictory "complementarity" theorems, the confidence in the rationality of independent "objects" of nature went to pieces in our generation. Only as a partner, only as "my Thou," can the other person and perhaps even a thing—be again grasped in his total independence, without his rationality being decreased.[87] Through these considerations previously thought to be final, the "image" of art shifts even farther away from the "It," the "object" of science that disintegrated into process, and approaches more closely than ever the actual "presence" of "I-Thou" relations, which, though they too are not constant, are, nevertheless, always re-established. And yet these two, "image" and "presence," never become identical, and so the contrast between them that is made in the "Address on the Educational" remains valid as against an exclusively aesthetic pedagogy. In that essay the authoritarian instruction of drawing was contrasted to a libertarian one. The former had compelled the pupils to stick to a valid regulation or model, while the latter encouraged them to transform the actual or remembered impression into an expression of individual reaction. The new element that is superadded to these two in Buber's position is called a special form of "criticism and guidance" on the part of the teacher. Teachers orient themselves according to an unacademic but fixed value-scale, which, though it is individualizing, has a clear knowledge of "good and bad."[88]

[85] *Der Mensch und sein Gebild*, p. 16.
[86] *Ibid.*, pp. 19–29.
[87] *Ibid.*, pp. 19–29.
[88] *Dialogisches Leben*, p. 267; *Reden über Erziehung*, p. 21.

The choice of words, as is always the case with Buber, is of utmost importance. We might expect: the authoritarian instruction of drawing evaluates in terms of "correct and incorrect"; the libertarian, in terms of "beautiful and ugly," or, in its highest degree, of "genuine and specious"; the issue, however, is about the "good and bad."

Does Buber then arrive at an identification of aesthetics and ethics as asserted by Read? That this is not here the case can be shown from those very examples, where aesthetics becomes important for ethics and vice versa.

The youthful impetuosity of the imagination holds in itself the "utmost danger and the highest chance."[89] Only the constrained power of imagination which has been tamed to the production of an image has an ethical meaning. Thus aesthetics has only a relative independence. Only after its legitimate and necessary placing in the context of the total system of sciences are we allowed to recognize again our insight, that "only that artist's lot is the internal development of mastery and decision who is worthy of his work."[90] In other words, no genuine masterpiece succeeds to a spurious man; no superior achievement, to an inferior one. An artist may not meet the moral standards of his time and society in one or another aspect of his private life, and, as a "sinner," not even his own standards. However, where his performance requires "mastery and decision," he must be "whole"; that is, he must have negated the twilight of temptation and sin. While the artist is at work, he acts morally. If he is not moral, then regardless of the technical brilliance of his work, its defect will show at an unexpected place, however well it may be hidden.

The artist is moral, but he is also solitary. "There is a power inside a person which emanates from him and penetrates into the material. Thereby the work is considerably elevated, and the act is at its end."[91]

Education, however, is not being in solitude, but becoming in encounter. It is not an act of the isolated "primeval urge," ending in the object of creation, but the act of the total man, which ends only in death; his working toward his own perfection which, how-

---

[89] *Bilder von Gut und Boese*, p. 48.

[90] *Hinweise*, p. 17.

[91] *Dialogisches Leben*, p. 265; *Reden über Erziehung*, p. 18.

ever, can be approached only through the togetherness with other
people.

This contradiction between the essential solitude of the artist in
the act of the "creative deed," and the essential sociality of all education, even the aesthetic, leads to the paradoxical result that the artist
cannot be the art-educator. Often a personal union may and does
take place between the two, but in the zenith of creation the artist
has not a moment's leave for the pedagogic intercourse. While he is
doing this latter, in relationship with other men, his work has to
rest not only factually, but spiritually. Now he has turned his self
not to a thing, not even to his own, but to another self. The characteristic which is unavoidably necessary to the educator, be he an artist
or not, is a type of imagination which is related to an artistic one,
but is not identical with it. Buber has created a new word for it:
"realistic imagination" (Realphantasie). Its significance for the limits of aesthetic education and its integration into the total pedagogy results from its relation to "empathy," the term which was first
formulated for aesthetics by Theodore Lipps, and which is frequently
applied today psychologically and pedagogically. "Realistic imagination . . . is the capacity of putting before the soul a reality which
exists in the present moment but which cannot be perceived through
the senses."[92] This is particularly valid about the reality of other
people. The person who is educated to a realistic imagination will
observe the other as he is. This contrasts to the artistic vision of the
raw material, which can be fashioned by him relatively freely. Such
a perception of the other as the other, even if he is an opponent, is
the presupposition of genuine communication, which in turn is that
of the future understanding in the realm of the interpersonal. "I say
'yes' to the person whom I oppose."[93] I grasp the other man, that is, I
perceive his totality as a person who is directed by the spirit, and his
"dynamic core which stamps all his expressions, actions and attitudes with the comprehensible sign of uniqueness." This succeeds
only on the way to "personal actualization." This, and its most important tool, the realistic imagination, is differentiated from empathy
by the fact that in the former the individuality of each of the partners
is fully maintained, while in empathy, because of the attempted
participation in the internal experiences of the other, temporarily

92 *Urdistanz und Beziehung,* p. 40.

93 *Die Schriften über das dialogische Prinzip,* p. 269.

one partner becomes identical with the other, or, at least, tries to do so. In the act of the realistic imagination something of the essence of an act of will is added to the act of will of the other, that is, each "full realization" is not merely spectator-like and passive, but participating and active. What remains nonetheless decisive is that the "self-realization-for-myself" of the other becomes rather a "self-realization-with-me."[94] The reciprocal character of the two individual persons, which cannot be reached in the aesthetic relation between men and their images nor in the aestheticising, aimless pedagogy of evolution, is maintained in this fashion.[95]

The realistic imagination influences also the realm of politics. Buber's central example is Zion. It can be erected only in Palestine. "It is the image which is hidden in the substance of this land."[96] One can continue that the pioneer who is to redeem it is aware of a similar expectation as the creative artist is of his material. The limit of these aesthetic parallels, and also of a purely aesthetic education, becomes again immediately visible if it is demanded from those who endeavor the establishment of Palestine and Zion to use their realistic imagination in determining their relationship with the Arabs through a lasting pact. Such a pact could only become established if it were preceded by a Jewish realization of the innermost feelings of the indigenous Arabs who now share their country with newcomers. That feeling would place the Jews in the psychic situation of "the original inhabitants."[97] This is no longer a purely aesthetic act, but one of the educated character.[98]

The "education of character" is one of the few special subjects of pedagogy which was treated by Buber monographically. The address dedicated to this topic was originally given in Hebrew at a teacher's convention in Tel-Aviv in 1939. It starts with the programmatic words: "Education which deserves the name is essentially education of character." It has to do not only with the single functions of the pupils, but also with the pupil as a total human being, with his "present actuality" as well as with the fullness of his possibilities.[99]

[94] *Urdistanz und Beziehung*, pp. 40–42.

[95] *Ibid.*

[96] *Israel und Palestina, Zur Geschichte einer Idee*, p. 180.

[97] *Kampf um Israel, Reden und Aufsätze* (1921–1932), p. 439; *Zion als Ziel und als Aufgabe, Gedanken aus drei Jahrzehnten*, p. 69.

[98] *Ibid.*

[99] *Dialogisches Leben*, p. 293; *Reden über Erziehung*, p. 63.

Such a unity of a human sum-total of "actuality and potentiality" has a double meaning. Firstly it designates the "unique spiritual-somatic figure" which is how Buber defines "personality." It is essentially a given, or develops only as a by-product, like a community,[100] and is thus hardly to be influenced by pedagogy, except through care for and furtherance of its self-fulfillment. Secondly, however, this "unity" of essence can be called "character," defined as the connection between the particular individual personality and the consequence of its actions and attitudes. Here, in character development, lies the specific, though self-limited task of the educator.[101]

Neither the comparison between Buber's definitions with those of others nor the complementation of the concept of "personality" with those of "individuum," "temperament," and "person" will be here attempted. The pedagogic conclusions as drawn by Buber are of significance even for those who hold other pedagogical and terminological presuppositions.

Character education is not instruction of ethics. Algebra can be taught directly, ethics only indirectly.[102]

Buber has used direct language and made direct propositions in the realm of the religious (although even he does not dare talk of directly commanded "acting for God's sake").[103] So he contradicts Kierkegaard's thesis that in the present situation of faith only indirect propositions "are possible and legitimate." Once he was confronted with this latter attitude in a discussion with one of the most important German philosophers and ethico-religious thinkers, who had asked Buber: "How can you bring yourself to using frequently the word 'God' . . . what other word is so misused?" Though Buber had admitted the possible and real misuses of it, he had replied: "Where would I find another word that would designate the Highest like it does?"[104]

[100] *Kampf um Israel, Reden und Aufsätze* (1921-1932), p. 260.

[101] *Reden über Erziehung,* pp. 63f.

[102] *Dialogisches Leben,* p. 294.

[103] *Die chassidische Botschaft,* p. 31.

[104] *Gottesfinsternis,* pp. 13f. The unnamed partner in this discussion was Paul Natorp. [Oral communication by Prof. Buber.] Cf. Albert Schweitzer's letter on his Sunday sermons in Lambarene; "I do not talk much about piety—it should make itself be noticed through its mere existence," from *Von Mensch zu Mensch;* a selection from the letters of Albert Schweitzer and his co-workers, ed. R. Kitz (Freiburg, 1956), p. 30.

In the realm of character education Buber's distinctions fall in the reverse. Here he knows that the direct method challenges the resistance of the best and the most independent. This is not only because they themselves seek their way, but also because they would oppose someone dictating to them what is its goal, namely the possibility to differentiate between "good and evil . . . as if these had been determined forever."[105] The educator has to reckon with this not only psychological but also metaphysical situation. Therefore he must carry out the education of character, though indirectly, never surreptitiously. "Education bears no politics,"[106] not even that which is successfully cloaked; even if the pupil does not detect it, it falsifies the teacher. "Only the totality of the teacher, with his whole involuntary existence, affects the totality of the pupil."[107] Here again an aporia seems to be generated, similar to the "as-if" which had occupied us above: the existence of the "willing" teacher is not quite as involuntary as all that.[108] Using the words of Heinrich Schuenemann, the school-reformer of Bremen, exactly the will to participate in the forming of character[109] differentiates the conscious educator from all the "secret co-educators." Buber says that "everything shapes: nature, and the social environment; the house, the street, the language, and the mores . . ." and yet, without will, consciousness, or selection. The educator, however, shapes the character, intentionally, consciously, and selectively. From the abundant reality he chooses the "right," which ought to be, humbly sensing the partiality of his task, and yet fully aware of the responsibility for its uniqueness.[110] The seeming self-contradiction of this "involuntary" and yet "willing" existence of the character-educator is probably solved in the following way: the teacher feels himself sufficiently sure of his natural and unwilled being that he is able to set it willingly and consciously into the educational process.[111] His assurance, on the other hand, awakens such a trust that it possibilitates the relation of the pupil to

---

[105] *Dialogisches Leben,* p. 295; *Reden über Erziehung,* pp. 65f.

[106] *Dialogisches Leben,* p. 295; *Reden über Erziehung,* p. 66.

[107] *Loc. cit.*

[108] *Dialogisches Leben,* p. 296; *Reden über Erziehung,* p. 67.

[109] *Ibid.*

[110] *Ibid.*

[111] Cf. the similar conception of Buber *re* the genuine deed of atonement, "which is done not in premeditation, but in the involuntary acting of my existence which had been won by effort," *Schuld und Schuldgefühle* (Heidelberg, 1958), p. 67.

him.[112] This trust has to be sufficiently strong to permit the maintenance of a direct relationship—even in the case where there is no agreement, or conflict arises—even conflicts educate! The educator has to exercise pedagogic precaution, and yet with an objective devotion wage the fight for truth, with magnanimity in victory, and with loving-kindness in defeat.[113] His true victory will be manifested by the fact that the trusting pupil will ask for his advice in his moral dilemmas.[114]

Hugo Gaudig had once defined the school ironically as that remarkable institution in which questions are asked by those who know, while the answers are attempted by the ignorant. Thus has this great German school reformer unmasked most of the questions of teachers as open and undisguised examinations, and he had wished to replace them from centrality by the genuine unrhetorical questions of students who really wish to learn.[115] In character education Buber seeks a similar switch from the teaching of morals, which is catechized or is illustrated with external examples, to the spontaneous questions of pupils, who in their need undertake to examine their own conscience as well as that of the teacher.

In both cases the teacher must have the know-how, and be able to answer, if not immediately. However, he must be able to intimate the way to it. In the old method, he had the initiative, and inquired only about things which he factually knew, or about problems in which he believed himself capable of making an ethical decision. But now, he might suddenly be faced with an intellectual or ethical difficulty for which he could not prepare himself. This moment of surprise, which becomes always important in the scope of the questions of pupils, is, however, not of the same importance for Gaudig as for Buber. In mere instruction an unanswered question can only lead to a transitory embarrassment, and not even that, if the teacher had not assumed the false nimbus of omniscience. Should it occur, he ought to have the courage to say: "I don't know it at this moment, and I shall give you the answer tomorrow," or, better still, "We could find that out together in the following way: . . ." Therefore, here the delay of an answer is only of an accidental nature. But it is

---

112 *Dialogisches Leben*, p. 297; *Reden über Erziehung*, p. 68.

113 *Dialogisches Leben*, pp. 298f.

114 *Dialogisches Leben*, p. 297; *Reden über Erziehung*, p. 68.

115 Cf. primarily "Didaktische Ketzereien" (Leipzig, 1919).

different in character education. The inability to answer is there existential and belongs to the substance of the value-crisis of our time.

Buber believes in "eternal values," which he has envisaged. He had listened to the address of the "eternal norm," though in the sense of an uncodifiable and inexpressible secret, which nevertheless is capable of being addressed and which one can and must learn to revere.[116] At the same time he knows that "it is an idle beginning to call to a mankind which has become blind to eternity: 'Look! Here are eternal values!' "[117] The only way out is to refer the individual to his disturbed relation with his own self. There where one is quite alone with himself he may sense "with sudden pains" the "ailing" of his person and of mankind.[118] The inescapable first step toward recovery is the feeling and consciousness of illness, carefully awakened and never drugged by the understanding educator who knows of the secret remedy.

Buber evidently speaks here in the language of modern psychiatry, and due to these assertions, his argumentation with its different schools arose subsequently. For the problem of character education his most essential writings are the preface to Hans Trueb's book, *Healing through Meeting*,[119] a book which turns away from Jung and towards Buber, and his lecture to the School of Psychiatry in Washington in April 1957 on "Guilt and Guilt-feelings." Complementary to the methodically absolutely necessary self-limitation of the psychiatrist as to the treatment of subjective guilt-feelings, Buber says of ontic, existential guilt, that even the psychiatrist lacks adequate knowledge of it. It does not derive from, nor is it explicable by either primitive or childish frustrations, nor by taboos, as the Freudian school would have it, nor by a disturbance in the relation of men to their own "selves," their "individuality," not even in the highest sense of the term, as taught by Jung.[120] The exact opposite is the case. Taboos

116 *Dialogisches Leben*, p. 313; *Reden über Erziehung*, p. 87.

117 *Dialogisches Leben*, p. 313; *Reden über Erziehung*, p. 75.

118 *Dialogisches Leben*, p. 313; *Reden über Erziehung*, p. 87.

119 H. Trueb, *Heilung aus der Begegnung* (Stuttgart: Ernst Klett Verlag, 1952), cf. *Schuld und Schuldgefühle*.

120 *Schuld und Schuldgefühle*, p. 147, but cf. p. 27 about "the great moments of existence," when a man determines over and over again to become what he is . . ." and pp. 29, 41, 49, and 66 *re* the perseverance of the said person. Is therewith the

and guilt feelings are possible because "men can become guilty, and know it."[121]

"Existential guilt occurs if someone offends an order of the human world whose foundations he knows and recognizes in essence as those of all common human existence."[121a]

These "foundations" are mostly not identical with those of the presently existing society. Their offence is thus qualitatively differentiated from a socio-psychological taboo.[122] One's conscience plagues one exactly when one has not lived up to a personal situation which is without precedent, and lacks an accepted behavioral norm. It pricks him again and again every time he recalls his default, which may be such as "a betrayal of a friend, or of his cause."[123] Buber defines conscience as the "capacity and inclination of men to differentiate radically between what they can assent to or dissent from within their past and future attitudes."[124] The "common conscience" may not penetrate the "ground and abyss" of its guilt, and may like to be acquiesced by neurosis.[125] The "great conscience"[126] or the "high conscience,"[127] on the other hand, is characterized by its relation to existential guilt.[128] The realization of existential guilt is the privilege of a "strongly personified character,"[129] while the Christian-theological concept of "radical evil" refers to the whole human race.[130] No fear of celestial or terrestrial punishment serves as a motivation to a "great conscience"; it functions without these. It knows that each occurring event is unique within its temporal limits, and has irrevocable consequences. The great conscience also knows that the time granted to man and used up by

Jungian position not relatively recognized though only as a part but as a necessary part for the total requirement for the conversion of the guilty?

[121] *Ibid.*, p. 18.

[121a] *Ibid.*, p. 19.

[122] *Ibid.*, pp. 37f.

[123] *Ibid.*, p. 21.

[124] *Ibid.*, p. 36.

[125] *Ibid.*, pp. 38f.

[126] *Ibid.*, p. 39.

[127] *Ibid.*, p. 39.

[128] *Ibid.*, p. 38.

[129] *Ibid.*, p. 39.

[130] *Ibid.*, Cf. p. 7.

him is neither repeatable nor reversible. "From no aspect other than guilt is time to be felt as a downfall."[131]

In the tumble of life toward death conscience feels the prick of guilt unless it is blunted by a psychotherapeutic device, which, if functioning flawlessly, can take the place of "the aching, warning heart." The destruction of the thorn of conscience is too highly paid for by the destruction of the opportunity to become the being to which one is destined by one's highest abilities.[132] If, however, a man does not let his conscience be blunted, he may experience great moments of entry and return into "the realm that reveals his essence, and ever again rediscovers it on a higher plane," the realm which grants him a genuine relation to the world as one who becomes.[133] The ascendancy of a man by virtue of his conscience leads through three stages; they almost correspond to the rungs established by the Talmud and Maimonides.[134] The first is "Self-enlightenment" (i.e., insight into the depths of guilt); the second, "Continuity" (i.e., the acceptance of "responsibility," as a person who became guilty and is now in the process of purification);[135] and thirdly, "Atonement" (i.e., compensation for the damage afflicted on another), "to the extent I can reach him on earth,"[136] and in any case, wherever I am and act, "because the wounds of the order of reality are capable of being healed in infinitely many other places than the ones where they were inflicted."[137]

However, the remarkable fact of the "great conscience" is that it is not reserved exclusively for "higher" human beings[138] which is certainly the case with the "great character."[139] This latter educates only through his example, which addresses us mutely.

It is a great and not yet sufficiently recognized task of education to elevate to a higher outlook and spirit the lower common form of conscience. For, the ability to elevate itself is inborn in the conscience of man.[140]

---

[131] Ibid., p. 17.

[132] Ibid., pp. 25f.

[133] Ibid., pp. 26f.

[134] Mischneh Torah, Hilchot Teschuwa.

[135] Schuld und Schuldgefühle, pp. 35, 66f.

[136] Ibid., p. 67.

[137] Ibid., p. 41.

[138] Ibid., p. 39.

[139] Dialogisches Leben, pp. 310f.; Reden über Erziehung, pp. 84–86.

[140] Schuld und Schuldgefühle, p. 39.

How so? Each one can and should become by education a bearer
of a "great conscience," while the "great character will still remain
the exception."[141] As Buber has hardly intended here a democratiz-
ing self-correction—at any rate, he has never indicated such an intention—we must either state a further aporia, or attempt a solution. This
solution could lie in the difference between the conceptions which
were here applied by Buber. Though a "great character" without a
"great conscience" is unthinkable, someone with a "great conscience"
needs not be a "great character." The grace of finding is endowed
to the "great character." He maintains the mastery in every situation,
even if it seems from without that he has succumbed. But "he does
not owe an answer to life and the world."[142] On the other hand, the
man with the "great conscience" continues in his serious search for
an answer, even if he does not find it. He defends heroically his
discovery (of his own innermost essence) and his determination ("to
becomes what he is")[143] against his every-day-consciousness and against
that subconscious which keeps on leading him to the temptation of
"assuming his shadow."[144]

Another difficulty presents itself. A theory of character education
must lean on a certain basic ethical view. But how is Buber's to be
determined? It surely is not a pragmatic or utilitarian one, nor a
psychologically or sociologically relativizing one. Nor is it a formalism
in the Kantian sense, because it does not recognize a law-giving categorical imperative, which stands rigorously in every situation. It is not
a material theory in Max Scheler's sense, because it does not construct
a hierarchy of personal bearers of values, nor in Nicolai Hartmann's
sense, because it does not have a scale of value-perceptors. It most
resembles a believer's occasionalism, if this term is not limited as in
the anti-Cartesian metaphysics of Geulincx and Malebranche, as to the
relation between matter and reason. Rather, it refers to the "occasions," or, in Buber's language, to the situations, which are sent by
God to man, so that he may live up to their demands. Surely the
contents of the Ten Commandments are also essential, and Buber
thrice draws his examples from them, certainly not accidentally, in

---

[141] *Dialogisches Leben*, p. 310; *Reden über Erziehung*, p. 84.

[142] *Dialogisches Leben*, p. 311; *Reden über Erziehung*, p. 85.

[143] *Schuld und Schuldgefühle*, p. 27.

[144] Cf. the writings of the late Erich Neumann, who was one of the most important
Jung-scholars, *Tiefenpsychologie und neue Ethik* (Zürich, 1949).

an ethically decisive relationship. These express Buber's negation of the possibility of a "moratorium of the Decalogue," as if "killing would become a good deed if it is done in the interest of one's own society"[145] and false witness, on behalf of one's own nation. Once Buber tells us of a man, "whose heart was pierced by the thunderbolt of the 'Thou shalt not steal!' at an hour when he was occupied in something altogether different from a wish to appropriate a property. This has penetrated his heart to the extent that he not only forsook what he was doing, but he began to do its exact opposite, with all the power of his passion."[146] Despite these and other places, however, the most important aspect of the **Ten Commandments** is not their content, but their power to address. "In such hours it speaks to one in the form of the second personal address, but the Thou in it is no one other in the world than one's self."[147]

IV. *The Line of Demarcation*

The elements of decision are provided by the individual, who is co-responsible for his community, and the situation wherein one finds oneself time and again and in which the educated character has to stand his ground. One may ask, however, how one can be prepared for and educated to these situations, which arise from the course of the world, in every case new and unforeseeable, and to which every reaction is freshly drawn from the deepest well-springs of the personality. Buber's reply to this question is his doctrine of "The Line of Demarcation," one of his most original contributions to pedagogical theory.

His other especially genuine contribution to educational insights and terminology is his doctrine of "Inclusion." Buber characterizes the educational relationship as an "I-Thou" without full mutuality. The teacher has to understand both himself and the student, but for the student it is enough to understand himself. Moreover, though the student may and should understand the teacher's words, he can never be expected to understand the teacher's being in its full dimensions. The true teacher will understand this not-being-understood by

[145] *Dialogisches Leben,* p. 301; *Reden über Erziehung,* p. 72.

[146] *Dialogisches Leben,* p. 309.

[147] 'Thanks to its 'Thou', the Decalogue means the preservation of the Divine Voice,' *Moses* (Harper & Bros., 1958), p. 130. Cf. the whole chapter, "The Words on the Tablets."

his pupil, and will never be offended or disappointed by this, but rather, he will "embrace" the whole situation with its two poles; his own, and that of the pupil. The latter is concerned only with himself.

The basic position of Buber affirms that "true purity is not the same as being untouched."[148] In other words, the moral man should not seek to maintain himself aloof from the troubling fight of life. He should dare to engage in it, dedicate himself to it, to the certain danger of dirtying his hands. This purity is not to be "preserved" statically, it is to be maintained in a state of continual motion, in ever new situations. The "possibility of man's fall" means the "ability of man to rise."[149] Thus, though the good man does not exist on earth, the good does,[150] which can be striven for unceasingly, but cannot be achieved in the premessianic situation of the unredeemed world.

This idea is not to be expressed in the idealistic symbol of mathematical asymptotes of an unending convergence,[151] because someday, "on the day," the miracle of a perfect salvation and fulfillment may take place. Buber does not speak of it, but here and there his tone divulges his faith in it, or rather, the legitimate possibility of such a faith.

In the meanwhile the rule of the "Line of Demarcation" is valid. It is to be drawn anew daily between the absolute commandment and its temporarily relative fulfillability. One can say that two false ways seemingly and one true way genuinely lead out from this dilemma between the objective meaning of the commandment and the possibility of its realization on the personal level. The first pseudo-solution leads from the relativity of the fulfillable to the relativization of that which is to be fulfilled. This degrades the commandment itself to relativity and deflates the ethical tension between the "Is" and the "Ought." The second aberrant way forks into two paths, one heavenly, in which the Absolute rules untouched and untouchable, and one terrestrial, in which the most cynical personal or collective opportunism thrives, polarizing dialectically the ethical tension be-

---

[148] *Kampf um Israel,* p. 301.

[149] *Die chassidische Botschaft,* p. 23.

[150] *Recht und Unrecht, Deutung einiger Psalmen,* p. 60.

[151] Cf. Hermann Cohen, *Logik der reinen Erkenntnis* (Berlin, 1922), pp. 123ff. and *Ethik des reinen Willens* (Berlin, 1907), pp. 408-411.

tween the "Is" and the "Ought," often producing a daemonic self-enjoyment of its unbridgeability.[152] The truth of the third way lies, though not in the middle, but between the two extremes.

The Aristotelian and Maimonidean doctrine of the golden mean is not a bourgeois compromise; nor is it the average between all existing quantities; nor an aesthetic device for dividing a certain line, not into equal parts, but once and for all. It is much more a problem which is yet to be solved in new ways, according to the extreme values concerned between which the right point of view is always to be found.[153] Maimonides, in his introduction to his *Chapters of the Fathers*—of early Talmud period, has individualized the Aristotelian position. The self-education of man should be accomplished in such a way as to compensate for the negative characteristics by the occasional overemphasis of the opposite. For example, the miser should exaggerate generosity.[154] Buber's conception of the "Line of Demarcation" belongs to this philosophical tradition, but instead of the Aristotelian doctrine of objective goods of various ethical value, or its Maimonidean psychologization, the emphasis is given to the situation in which a certain man is posited at a certain time and place, with predetermined, though not foreseeable possibilities and limitations of realization of certain value-commandments. This situation is sent by God and happens to man. He should accept it not passively, but actively, just by finding his "Line of Demarcation."

There is no recipe[155] for the adequacy of this line, because it presents itself differently every time. Consider an example from politics: revolutions cannot be brought about without violence. Buber does not disapprove of them under any circumstances, but demands from those who think them inevitably necessary that they make a prior resolution "to go so far and no farther."[156] Under no circumstances should they allow themselves to be swept over this "Line of Demarcation" by the mere force of the events. States and people have a right of self-preservation, but they should include in their calcula-

---

[152] Cf. my Hebrew essay, "Philosophy of History and Philosophy of Culture as Basic Disciplines of Pedagogy," in a volume published in honour of S. H. Bergmann's 60th birthday (Jerusalem, 1944), pp. 106–120.

[153] *Nicomachean Ethics* Book II, 267, V, 9.

[154] The eighth chapter, IV.

[155] *Zion als Ziel und als Aufgabe*, pp. 76f.

[156] Cf. *Hinweise*, pp. 280, 285–289.

tions the right of others—not only their might, but also their right.[157]
The internal power struggles of states are also not to be disregarded.
In democracies they manifest themselves essentially as party struggles.
Sometimes a "moral moratorium" is demanded of the parties, and
approved "without spiritual conflict." This is bad. If one can draw
the line of demarcation at the right time and place, one simultaneously serves both God, the Absolute, and one's own group, the ter-
restrially conditioned.[158] See how far Buber, who is often labeled
a doctrinaire ideologist, goes in order to be loyal to reality!

Marx and Lenin failed to draw the demarcation-line between the
requirements of centralistic action and the possible workings of decentralized social development, which would not jeopardize the
first.[159] But Buber knows that assumedly

there necessarily never will be freedom so long as man is such as he is, and
for that time there will always be a state, which means, compulsion. What is
demanded is this: from day to day there should be no more state than is indispensable, and not less freedom than is admissible.[160]

We see that Lenin talks about an *eschaton* in which the states
will wither away, but up to that time the dictatorship of the proletariat will rule unconditionally. Buber is silent about the *eschaton*,
but he seeks to prepare for it, and to make its coming possible
through the self-limitation of the coercive states.

In all this Buber labours toward the solution of a problem which
he has not formulated precisely, and which the present writer has
not encountered in any other pedagogical theory. Kant approaches
it most closely in one of his small polemic dissertations, "On the
Sentence: 'This may be Right in Theory, But it is Impracticable.' "
His rigorous solution, however, is unacceptable. The problem is,
how a modicum of coordination between ethical and civic education
can be reached in the unredeemed world.[161] Are we not teaching

---

157 *Zion als Ziel und als Aufgabe*, pp. 76f.

158 *Hinweise*, pp. 343f. Buber's formulation is open to critical question whether
a partial moral moratorium, under circumstances, arrived at *after* a "spiritual conflict," may be admissible.

159 *Paths in Utopia* (In Beacon ed. of English trans. p. 100.)

160 *Ibid.*, p. 104.

161 Cf. Ernst Simon, *Das Werturteil im Geschichtsunterricht* (Leipzig, 1931), pp.
46ff.; and my more recent essay, "Military Education and the Vindication of the
Good," in *Scripta Hierosolymitica*, 13, *Studies in Education* (Jerusalem, 1963), pp.
3-31.

the children and young people just the contrary to what they will later be forced by the state and its rulers to practice, and indeed often be willingly compelled to do it? We direct them not to injure life and property, and they will kill and burn; we teach them truth, and they will lie. Are we absolutistic hypocrites, educating relativistic cynics? Does what we teach hold for children, but not for grown-ups? Is it valid only for one's own people and one's own clan, but not for all humanity?

Buber's answer, which is true both to his ideas and to reality, is that a moral teaching is valid for every stage of life, for every part of the human race, in any of man's conditions. It should always be in our minds, animate our consciences. We must never let a Stoic *ataraxia* prevent its maximum possible realization. Know that you cannot remain guiltless, but be resolved "never to do *more* wrong than you must, in order to live."[162]

The consequence of this ethical theory for the education of character is not without its problems. Its shortest, almost crude formula would be that the good is a compromise between absolute law and concrete reality. On the other side, a phrase frequently employed by Buber in this connection is that the good can "be done only with the whole soul."[163] What is objectively a balance between highest aim and achievable reality, being something synthetized, and therefore divisible, should be subjectively grasped and done as a whole. The education to "compromise," which was attributed to the adult citizen of a mature democracy by Matthew Arnold, forms for Buber not only the aim but also the basis for the formation of character.

The problem becomes more acute if we first consider the literal and doubtless intentional analogy between Buber's two assertions: like one can do the good "only with the whole soul," and evil never with the whole soul, so the basic word "I-Thou" can be spoken only "with the whole being," while the basic word "I-It" can never be spoken with the whole being.[164] Thus, the ethical good belongs to the relation of totality, "I-Thou," while evil, to the broken relation, "I-It." The foregoing sentence is in no way reversible. Not

---

162 *Kampf um Israel,* p. 438.

163 *Schuld und Schuldgefühle,* p. 42.

164 *Dialogisches Leben,* p. 15.

all "I-Its" indicate some non-good, although no non-good can be done with the totality of the "I-Thou."

Nevertheless, that doubt which Franz Rosenzweig expressed personally to me in the following words after Buber's lecture on the "I-Thou" rises again: "Buber gives more recognition to the 'Thou' than anyone ever before, but he wrongs the 'It'." One could formulate this in reverse, in an ethico-pedagogical connection. Buber demands too much from the "Thou," asking of men and youths to search for the good even and just at the "line of demarcation," and to do it even and just in the brokenness of compromise, but with "the whole soul," with the "whole being" of the "I-Thou" relationship. Exactly this is the pedagogical consequence of his Believing Occasionalism, however difficult its fulfillment may be.

ERNST SIMON

HEBREW UNIVERSITY
JERUSALEM

25

Leslie H. Farber

MARTIN BUBER AND PSYCHOTHERAPY

I. *Psychiatry and the Fully Human*

In relation to their systems, most systematizers are like a man who builds an enormous castle and lives in a shack beside it; they do not live in their own enormous buildings. But spiritually that is a decisive objection. Spiritually speaking, a man's thought must be the building in which he lives—otherwise everything is topsy-turvy.

Kierkegaard

MOST psychoanalysts have probably asked themselves, at one time or another, whether they most aspired to be the 'genital character' with 'object relations,' or the 'syntactic interperson' whose interrelationships are 'consensually validated.' In either case, these may be only aspirations. Perhaps many psychoanalysts, like myself, have settled for a modest shanty existence beside one of these splendid constructs, hoping to share in some reflected glory by living so close to the castle. And perhaps some of them have even begun to wonder if the castle itself—though elegant enough from an esthetic stand-point—may not, like Kafka's castle, have a strangely crippling effect on those who try to live in it.

Although the young science of psychiatry has already built several rival castles, or competing systems, so far none of them—to my present way of thinking—is fit for human habitation. Nor, for that matter, have many of their architects claimed that these systems are a way of life. Certainly Freud went to some occasional pains to dissociate his theories from those of metaphysics or religion. And yet, for lack of any other definitions of the fully human, it is virtually impossible nowadays for the psychiatrist not to derive his norms and standards from his own theories—thus creating definitions of man out of his fragments of psychopathology. For example:

The final stage of [genital] character-formation . . . borrows from [the pre-ceding stages] whatever conduces to a favorable relation between the individ-ual and his objects. From the early oral stage it takes over enterprise and energy; from the anal stage, endurance, perseverance . . . from sadistic sources, the necessary power to carry on the struggle for existence.[1]

[Mature dependence] is characterized neither by a one-sided attitude of in-corporation nor by an attitude of primary emotional identification. On the contrary, it is characterized by a capacity on the part of a differentiated indi-vidual for cooperative relationships with differentiated objects.[2]

The self-dynamism is "the relatively enduring organization of processes which manifests itself in situations related to former experiences of anxiety . . ."[3]

A person is a psychic system which, when it affects another person, enters into reciprocal reaction with another psychic system.[4]

Without examining these normative statements in detail, the reader can see why psychiatry is so often charged with being reductive. For while the creatures described above may bear some resemblance to animals, or to steam engines or robots or electronic brains, they do not sound like people. They are in fact constructs of theory, more humanoid than human; and whether they are based on the libido theory or on one of the new inter-personal theories of relationships, it is just those qualities most distinctively human which seem to have been omitted. It is a matter of some irony, if one turns from psychology to one of Dostoevski's novels, to find that no matter how wretched, how puerile, or how dilapidated his characters may be, they all possess more humanity than the ideal man who lives in the pages of psychiatry.

Like Pascal, I believe that it is perilous to remind man of his resemblance to the animals, without at the same time reminding him of his greatness. If the psychiatrist cannot look to his own theory to find man's superiority to 'other' natural objects, and if common sense is too unreliable a guide, where can he turn?

[1] Karl Abraham, "Genital Character Formation," *Selected Papers of Karl Abraham* (London: Hogarth Press, 1942), p. 415.

[2] W. Ronald D. Fairbairn, *An Object-Relations Theory of the Personality* (New York: Basic Books, 1954), p. 145.

[3] Harry Stack Sullivan, as quoted in Patrick Mullahy, "The Theories of H. S. Sullivan," *The Contributions of Harry Stack Sullivan,* ed. Patrick Mullahy (New York: Hermitage House, 1952), p. 39.

[4] C. G. Jung, "Principles of Practical Psychotherapy," *Collected Works,* 16, 3–20 (New York: Pantheon Books, 1954), 3.

For certainly the practice of psychiatry requires some steady conception of the fully human. To find an answer to this question, I propose that we turn now to the philosophical anthropology developed by Martin Buber.

Unlike the medical and social sciences which take as their province some partial aspect of the human, Buber's anthropology considers man as subject rather than object, and asks specifically, What is man in his wholeness? In other words: Who am I, in my unique and essential being?

Since this is the question which every man has to ask himself, one can see that it ought to be a central question for psychology as well. And yet, expressed in this way, it becomes quite different from the question *What is man?* as this was asked by the nineteenth-century sciences and, following the sciences, by nineteenth-century philosophy in general.

The medical and biological sciences were asking, What is man in his relation to nature—to natural history, the evolution of organisms, and the physical forces regulating his body? They were asking, What is man as a natural object, a physical or biological organism? And it was upon this naturalist basis that all the other sciences of man—anthropology, sociology, political science, and finally the new Freudian science of psychoanalysis—asked their question, What is man? What is the natural man, what is the primitive man, as opposed to the man created by sociopolitical, cultural, and economic forces? What is man in his natural inheritance, in his prehistory as the human animal or primate or primitive, as opposed to his more recent history as a civilized or social being? Thus, none of the sciences was asking the *whole* question, What is man? Nor were they asking the unique question, Who am I, in my uniquely human essence? They were asking two partial questions—What is the natural man—man as natural object or organism—and what is the sociopolitical man—man as sociopolitical organism?

Against this background of nineteenth-century philosophy, as we inherit it in the sciences today, we can see that the question, What is man in his wholeness?—or Who am I in my uniqueness?—has not been answered. These are not smaller, or more personal questions; they are larger and more comprehensive than the ones which science has been asking. They include a larger view of man, as well as a larger view of history. They include man's personal being—*my* personal experience and knowledge of myself—as well as my philosophical and scientific knowledge of what "man is." And they include more history: They include our more ancient history as religious beings, as well as our quite recent history of being only socio-political, only natural organisms—in the peculiarly modern definition of history.

The relation between philosophical anthropology and psychotherapy may be looked at more concretely if we compare two dissimilar passages of writing, each dealing with a very similar experience in the lives of Martin Buber and Harry Stack Sullivan, the psychiatrist. As Buber describes his experience:

What happened was no more than that one forenoon, after a morning of 're-ligious' enthusiasm, I had a visit from an unknown young man, without being there in spirit. I certainly did not fail to let the meeting be friendly, I did not treat him any more remissly than all his contemporaries who were in the habit of seeking me out about this time of day as an oracle that is ready to listen to reason. I conversed attentively and openly with him—only I omitted to guess the questions which he did not put. Later, not long after, I learned from one of his friends—he himself was no longer alive—the essential content of these questions: I learned that he had come to me not casually, but born by destiny, not for a chat but for a decision. He had come to me, he had come in this hour. What do we expect when we are in despair and yet go to a man? Surely a presence by means of which we are told that nevertheless there is a meaning.

Since then I have given up the 'religious' which is nothing but the exception, extraction, exaltation, ecstasy; or it has given me up. I possess nothing but the everyday out of which I am never taken. The mystery is no longer disclosed, it has escaped or it has made its dwelling here where everything happens as it happens. I know no fulness but each mortal hour's fulness of claim and responsibility. Though far from being equal to it, yet I know that in the claim I am claimed and may respond in responsibility, and know who speaks and demands a response.

I do not know much more. If that is religion then it is just *everything*, simply all that is lived in its possibility of dialogue . . .[5]

And as Sullivan describes his experience:

I worked at one time with a youth of 17 who manifested a severe and ominous schizophrenic state. We had some hour-long conferences, the first few of which amounted to very little, so far as communication was concerned. There came finally an hour in which the patient, as the end of the hour approached, mentioned the sexual performances in which he had been engaged by a boarder who had subsequently married the patient's mother, shortly be-

5 *Between Man and Man*, pp. 13f.

fore the psychosis occurred. I was then working in the room in which clinical conferences of the hospital staff were held. As the patient ended his communication, and I was attempting in haste to convey reassurance to him, the first group of the staff came in. I had to interrupt, continuing my remarks as I walked with the patient to the entrance of the hospital wards. On his way from that door to the door of his ward, he eluded the attendant who had joined him as we parted, rushed into a sun room, whipped off his belt, tightened it around his throat, and fought off an attendant and a nurse until he collapsed from asphyxiation. The subsequent course of his mental disorder was uninterruptedly unfortunate and he has resided for years in a State hospital. I have not since then permitted a patient to enter upon the communication of a gravely disturbing experience unless I have plenty of time in which to validate his reassurance as to the effect of the communication on our further relations.[6]

Each instance, touching in its confession of failure, speaks of "conversion:" Buber is converted from the private, the rhapsodic, the mystical, into the world; Sullivan, on the other hand, shakes the claims and interruptions of the hospital world to move into a more private attention to his patient's existence which would allow for relation. While Buber convicts himself for his fragmentary response to his friend's despair, he resists arrogating to himself prideful responsibility for the other's fate: he could not necessarily save this young man; he could only have been "present in spirit" when his visitor sought confirmation and meaning from him.

If we turn now to the instruction Sullivan derived from his tragedy, we find him perhaps more faithful to his science than to his humanity. On the one hand, psychiatry is indebted to him for his ideal, still unachieved, that the psychiatric hospital should exist primarily for the psychiatric patient. On the other hand, unlike Buber, Sullivan's devotion to the techniques of his science leads him to the immoderate claim that such desperate moments may be postponed until there is time to "validate" the "reassurance." Leaving aside the question whether "reassurance" can or should be "validated," I believe that with more modesty or less devotion, he might not have taken on the sole responsibility for his patient's fate. Underlying this almost mystical devotion to the techniques of knowledge, one feels that mystery has disappeared; the truth is all disclosed. If so, a paradox emerges here. Is it the scientist, in his presumption, who is the true mystic of our time? And is it the philosophical anthro-

[6] Harry Stack Sullivan, "Conceptions of Modern Psychiatry," *Psychiatry*, **3**, 1 (1940), 90.

pologist, as ex-mystic, who can with true scientific propriety protect psychiatry from the idols of a false devotion? But these questions may be excessive. More accurately, it could be that philosophical anthropology and psychiatry, as Will Herberg has written, "stand in a dialectic tension, significantly questioning, though not necessarily denying, each other's underlying presuppositions."[7]

When Buber speaks of the I-Thou as it may occur either in the young infant or among primitive races, it is clear that he is relying upon his own imagination to give him knowledge of these unknowable states of subjectivity. He is thus able to avoid the genetic fallacy which is common to all nineteenth-century psychology. This fallacy springs, like behaviorism, from a natural-science view of objects which is then applied to such invisible phenomena as human subjectivity or experience. For example, when the nineteenth-century psychologist 'looked at' an imaginary child or primitive, he was not imagining their experience but quite literally visualizing an object: a bodily object, in its bodily behavior.

Seen through the spectacles of natural-science theory, this bodily object would appear as a 'natural object': a 'human animal' or 'organism.' And since he supposed the origins of man's experience to lie in his bodily behavior, the psychologist could then suppose that the behavior of children, of primitives, and even of animals, would give him the 'real' origins—and thence the 'real truth'—about the whole of human experience. But the most striking fact about human experience is, of course, that so much of it is invisible.

As an example of the twin fallacies arising from this natural-science view of objects, Freud's view of the young child or primitive can be adduced. When he looked at the child's behavior, Freud saw megalomania, narcissism—libidinal drives operating in isolation, abstracted from the human experience. With this behaviorist view of motives, he sees "parental love," too, as something which is "touching" but is "at bottom . . . childish." Indeed Freud defines "parental love" as *"nothing but* parental narcissism born again."[8]

Here is an example of the genetic fallacy, according to which the supposed origins of parental love are somehow more real or important than the known experience of love, so that love becomes *nothing*

[7] Will Herberg, "Depth Psychology and Religion: Encounter and Dialogue," *Catalogue of The Washington School of Psychiatry* (1957–58), p. 15.

[8] Sigmund Freud, "On Narcissism: An Introduction," *Collected Papers*, 4, 30–59 (London: Hogarth Press, 1934), 49. Italics mine.

but the narcissism of the child. This springs from the behaviorist fallacy, which claims that what cannot be seen or observed in a man's behavior cannot be known to man. As a further example of these two fallacies—which are, of course, equally reductive—I would like to quote Sullivan's definition of "tenderness" between a mother and her child:

My theorem is this:
The observed activity of the infant arising from the tension of needs induces tension in the mothering one, which tension is experienced as tenderness and as an impulsion to activities toward the relief of the infant's needs.[9]

This is a way of defining love as *nothing but* anxiety. And an anxiety which needs to be relieved is not very different from an instinctual or libidinal drive which needs to be discharged. Thus through these reductive views of man current philosophy has arrived at both a biological and a steam-engine psychology of motives. Love is nothing but a physiological drive which needs outlet—nothing but an emotional tension which needs relief.

When Buber describes those early or primitive experiences of the *Thou,* he is not looking at the behavior of the infant or its mother. Nor is he imagining any abstract relation which may exist between the two. He is rather imagining the experience of the mother toward her child, and of the child toward his mother. And he is imagining this to be a mutual experience of reciprocity—of shared relation. Buber therefore believes that human experience begins, both in the race and in the child, with *relation.* And, as I have already suggested, what he means by relation may be quite the opposite of what a psychiatrist means by the same word. For a relation imagined from the inside, as a mutual experience, is not the same thing as an abstract concept of relationship. The latter is 'seen' or imagined from the outside, as an event occurring between two human objects.

II.   *I-Thou and I-It*

The I of I-It has no present, only the past—and by projection or prediction, the future. But *"the present* arises in virtue of the fact that the *Thou* becomes present."[10] Of all the qualities of the I-Thou

[9] Harry Stack Sullivan, *The Interpersonal Theory of Psychiatry,* ed. Helen Swick Perry and Mary Ladd Gawel (New York: Norton, 1953), p. 39.
[10] *I and Thou,* pp. 3–4.

relation, presentness—the suspension of chronological time, the falling away of time past and time future—is the quality we all seek to invoke, in the absence of mutuality and directness, as a symbol of the I-Thou or as a first step toward relation. With boredom as the other side of presentness, all manner of distraction will suggest itself for "killing time," as we say—whereby, to quote Eliot, we are distracted from distraction by distraction. In lieu of relation, much of life can be exploited for the experience of presentness: laughter, tears, physical pain, anger, outrage, sleep, sex. And perhaps the chemist's contributions ought to be included too—alcohol, benzedrine, marijuana, morphine—and, to stretch a point, the offerings of neurosurgery, lobotomy, and shock. The pursuit of presentness as an end in itself, without necessarily relinquishing hope of the Thou, would be described in current psychiatric theory under the heading of anxiety and defenses against anxiety—a formulation which, when hypostatized, can mistake the measure for the goal, or the means for the end.

By relegating feelings to the world of It, Buber not only avoids the usual romantic overevaluation of 'feeling' but also cuts through the usual dichotomy between thought and feeling.

In psychiatry especially there is an illusory opposition between so-called fact and so-called feeling. The therapists of a psychiatric hospital—more by virtue of temperament than theory—are apt to split into two seemingly opposing sides as they argue the quality or skill most conducive to recovery in their patients: the Oracles of Feeling apply to themselves such evocative terms from the age of romanticism as "warmth," "love," "intuition," "inspiration," and "empathy," while they indict their adversaries as "cold," "unfeeling," "intellectual," and "compulsive." From the other side, the High Priests of Fact pride themselves on their "objectivity," "judiciousness," "sobriety," and "scientific approach," while they accuse their opponents of being "mushy," "sentimental," "mindless" and "unscientific."

For Buber, this war between Sense and Sensibility belongs to the world of I-It—a particular circumstance in which the I is held off from the It, the former inside and the latter outside, dividing the world conveniently into feelings and facts. If the argument is transposed figuratively from therapy and soap opera to the diagnostic categories of psychiatry, the dialogue now would be between the hysteric and the obsessional. For the hysteric, with his overblown sensibilities, a necessary step in treatment would be the acquisition of some logical capacity to deal with facts. And for the obsessional, the compulsion to free-associate might in itself furnish the beginnings of sensibility. Of these two extremes, Buber writes:

But the separated It . . . is an animated clod without a soul, and the separated I of feelings an uneasily fluttering . . . bird. . . . Neither of them knows man . . . or mutual life. . . . That feelings yield no personal life is understood only by a few. . . . If, like the modern man, you have learned to concern yourself wholly with your own feelings, despair at their unreality will not easily instruct you in a better way—for despair is also an interesting feeling.[11]

Thus Buber avoids the romantic attitude toward feeling which is peculiar to current philosophy. The romantic regards feeling as a spontaneous impulse arising either from above or from below: either as divine or poetic inspiration, or else as some daemonic force or instinct—as represented, for example, by the id. Buber rejects this kind of mysticism, with its Manichaean division between the forces of Light and Dark.

III. *Buber and Sullivan*

The dimming of the inborn Thou, following the separation of the I, and the emergence of the world of I-It, is not intended as a psychological description of the development of the child or the race. But more detailed theories of psychopathology, whether they emphasize disturbances in libidinal development or the anxious relationship between parent and child, suggest the special morbid pathology which may disturb the ordinary course of development, as described by Buber, and which may cripple the child for later I-Thou relation. Whether the defect would consist of premature dispersion of the early Thou or later retardation of I-It experience, or both, cannot be said without miscroscopic examination of the particulars, insofar as this is possible.

By now it must be clear that Buber's theory of the two primary words bears some resemblance to Sullivan's interpersonal theory. Both appear to be social in nature—at least insofar as they regard the self as a series of dialogues. Both place a primary importance on the concept of relation, in some sense. But here the resemblance ends—not between the two men in their approach toward people, but between their two theories, as revealed by their very different termi-

[11] *I and Thou*, p. 44.

nologies. The view expressed—or, I would rather say, enforced—by Sullivan's language is often a physical-science view of objects, which is certainly not representative of his actual experience with people. No such split occurs, however, in Buber's language, which is always appropriate to man in his relations with the world. Sullivan's domain, of course, was psychopathology, or what is not-man, while Buber's domain is precisely what *is* man.

Yet even here the differences may be less great than the terminology would suggest. Sullivan worked devotedly to revive the smallest flickers of relationship, the faintest murmurs of the human, in that extreme situation known as schizophrenia. Buber's concept of relation between man and man came, of course, from the community life of Hasidic Jewry. But Sullivan, in his own way, strove equally to dispel that rabbinical aloofness—that distance placed between the omniscient 'observer' and the lowly 'subject'—which had afflicted psychiatrists in both their theory and their practice, reminding them that since involvement is inescapable they had best admit it for scrutiny. Both men, in fact, abhorred the kind of analytical detachment which places the letter of the law above its spirit.

To describe those distortions in dialogue which are occasioned by the past, Sullivan used the word *parataxic*. Insisting that the psychiatrist could be no mere observer, since he was inevitably and inextricably involved with his patient, Sullivan coined the expression *participant observation* to describe the shift between involvement and scrutiny of the manner of involvement. Here he was hoping to break through, in his own way, the usual subject-object formulations of the past. At this point, however, unlike Buber, he saw his larger framework in the operational field theories of the physical sciences. Early in his career he adopted another term, *consensual validation,* to indicate agreement on the terms of dialogue by the participants. Underlying his theory, then, is a norm or goal having to do with the capacity for communication, whether verbal or nonverbal. Thus it is no accident that many communications engineers or cyberneticists should, like many of the sociologists, find support in Sullivan's theories.

But of this type of social communication or sociality, Maurice S. Friedman writes:

It is important . . . not to lose sight of the fact that though the world of the *It* is a social world which is derived from the world of the *Thou,* it often sets itself up as the *final reality*. Its sociality, as a result, becomes largely "technical dialogue" . . . the mere communication and interaction between human beings who may in fact largely relate to each other as Its.[12]

For Buber the goal of all dialogue is the Thou relation, toward which "consensually validated" communication must of course assist. The difference between the two men lies as much in their approach to language as in their approach to subjectivity. For while Sullivan felt that subjective relations could be studied from the objective viewpoints of a scientist—moreover, of a physical scientist—and that experience could be adequately described in the terminology of the sciences, Buber knows that language may not only determine our concepts but radically change our experiences as well.

IV. *The Thou, the It and Schizophrenia*

Buber's thought can help us as psychiatrists, I believe, not only in providing a general framework against which to measure the special virtues and limitations of our special craft, but also in revising some of the most technical or specific details of our craft. The mistake is often made, especially with the schizophrenic, of overvaluing his lonely gropings toward the Thou and of underestimating his actual incompetence in the world of It, so that he becomes a tragic saint or poet of the Thou, martyred by the world of It.

Once it is realized, however, that the Thou relation depends upon the world of It for its conceptual forms or meanings, then psychosis can be seen as not only a failure of the Thou—of so-called personal relations. It is an equal failure of knowledge, judgment, and experience in the world of It. Whatever class the disorder falls into— whether it is marked by a recoil from relation, as in schizophrenia, or by a grasping at relation, as in hysteria or mania—underlying its manifestations one can always find much ignorance of the world, much ineptitude with people, much early failure to acquire the elementary tools of knowledge.

If schizophrenia can be thought of as an extreme withering of the Thou capacity, with corresponding impairment in the world of It, it is not surprising that it should be accompanied by a crippling of the intellect. I mean intellect not in the narrow sense, of a measurable reason or intelligence, but in a larger sense—experience informed

---

[12] Maurice S. Friedman, "Martin Buber's Theory of Knowledge," *Review of Metaphysics*, 8 (December, 1954), 264–280.

with imagination, and imagination ordered by knowledge and judgment.

Without sufficient knowledge, memory, or judgment, every Thou invoked is apt to be a perilously shy and fleeting one. It recedes very quickly into its impoverished world of It, where there is little promise of return. And with each loss of the Thou, the schizophrenic is in special danger of retreating more permanently or deeply toward his far pole of alienation: into that loneliness of which both Sullivan and Fromm-Reichmann have written.

Psychiatry owes them both a debt for adding so untechnical a term as loneliness to our technical vocabulary. Such loneliness might, in Buber's language, be called hopeless longing for the Thou, and so might be seen as the despair which afflicts all of us at moments, and overwhelms the more desperate ones we call psychotic. Even that mad chattering by which we detain an unwelcome guest at his moment of departure—even that madder chattering by which the 'manic' patient detains all humanity as his parting guest—is this not a desperate or guilty recognition that the whole social enterprise, the whole wedding of minds, has been a total failure? We strive wildly on the doorstep for one departing Thou.

To speak only of the schizophrenic, he feels, of course, that having lost all hope or chance of intimacy, any further efforts will only carry him further out of paradise. He fears, in other words, that should his loneliness be entered momentarily by a Thou, the ensuing loss—the return, empty-handed, to his vacant world of It—would be more than he could endure. Since he can neither take it with him, nor find it there on his arrival, the schizophrenic exiles himself from both earth and heaven and, with a surprising dignity, takes up his residence in limbo.

V. *Meeting and Therapy*

Were we to look only at the theories presently sustaining psychotherapy, we could scarcely say what the contradictory views of Freud and Jung, Adler and Reich, Sullivan and Klein have in common—apart from an abiding interest in the patient's improvement. For if few of these systems can agree on what "improvement" means exactly, they share a common interest in effecting it.

What lies beyond the various schools of theory and of training, however, is something we all recognize when we are obliged to refer a close friend or relative for treatment. When our relationship with the patient is casual, we make our referral on the basis of training— or even schools of training. But as our concern for his fate increases, we abandon our technological rules and ask instead, What manner of human being will deal with our friend's distress? To what extent will he be able to know that friend, without relinquishing his own actuality or identity in the knowing?

In other words, to what extent will there be the possibility of meeting between these two beings—the mutual encounter which Buber calls the I-Thou relation? It is here that our prescriptive powers fail us and we must fall back on an older wisdom as we imagine the kind of relationship we hope for. Although often invoked, extrapolations from psychopathology will be of little assistance here. The fact that therapist and patient share, say, "obsessional" or "schizoid" or "hysterical" traits asserts only that the two have in common a disability which prevents meeting. Extrapolations from psychopathology, by definition, will say nothing of those more fully human qualities which we call "imagination" (intelligence in the large sense) or "taste"—humor or kindness or "common sense"—which are all that can make meeting possible despite pathology. Experience with schizophrenia tells us that such meeting will not guarantee the successful outcome of treatment. On the other hand, I am convinced there has been no successful treatment without it.

What is the relation of this meeting to what we call "transference"? Compared to any ideal of relationship, a transference situation must be called not only illusory but idolatrous—whether the therapist is cast as hero or as villain. Indeed it is precisely this overblown situation, with all its romantic distortions which is, so to speak, the disorder itself. It is thus at the opposite pole from the mutual encounter which I have called "meeting." When we examine the words used to define such meetings—words ranging from empathy, spontaneity, "warmth" or "contact" on the one hand to "consensual validation" on the other—we find that the qualities generally invoked are twofold. Something like mutuality or trust must be accompanied by something like truthfulness or appropriateness. The truthful quality of relationship would preclude the kind of idolatry or self-seeking by which various delusions, called "wishful thinking," projection and so on, become substitutes for truth. Similarly, mutuality precludes the kind of distrust or fear which leads equally to falsification.

Because of his habit of thinking in medical terms, the psychiatrist often conceives of transference as a malignant obstruction which needs to be removed or unpeeled, layer by layer, in order that the capacity for relationship may eventually be uncovered. This concept of therapy as a kind of psychic surgery is not unlike the original concept of depth psychology, in which the Freudian surgeon performed rather as an archaeologist digging for buried truth. (And for the buried truth of Nature, I might add, undistinguished from the human truth.) It is not only that these metaphors may prevent our recognizing such hopes or efforts toward real meeting as do take place. What is more dangerous, I think, is the general habit of translating all end-goals and positive values of therapy into the same terms of pathology which describe the disease. A good example of this is the term "emotional maturity." Deduced negatively from the fact that most patients are emotionally immature, this has become a norm which often defines the goal of treatment, and is even thought sufficient to define the fully human.

In view of the general inadequacy of present terminology, it would not be surprising if the effectiveness of therapy were found to lie in precisely those areas which have been least acknowledged or defined: let us say those which have most successfully resisted scientific theory. Obviously, if meeting is to occur in psychotherapy, it will occur *despite* "transference": despite inequalities in position, status, background, education or awareness. Within the therapeutic dialogue, the initiative, hopefully, is the therapist's. It is up to him whether he can forsake the academy in order to address his patient not as an object of knowledge, but as a being engaged in the task [as Kierkegaard puts it] of becoming "what he is already: namely a human being." But let us remember that every psychiatric disorder represents not merely an emotional failure in relationship, but also a larger failure in meaning or intelligence, in judgment or imagination. To breach this failure, even momentarily, requires a knowing of the other in his singularity with no surrender of one's own identity.

Closely connected with transference is the problem of identity, which often becomes a needless hazard. Since a crucial goal of treatment is the development or, in some cases, the acquisition of an identity, it is inevitable that the patient will at some stage begin to borrow his identity from the therapist. Indeed the recovering patient will often appear to the outsider to be more artifice than person: a rag-bag of oddly assorted scraps of theory, manner and language, filched mainly from the therapist. Now it would be manifestly unfair to conclude from this that the therapist was using some hypnotic method, or that the cure is even more inauthentic than the disease. But without denying that authoritarian methods do exist, most of us have gone to the opposite extreme—especially if we have succumbed to that belief, usually acquired during our student days, that a good scientist would never inflict any of his own values on his patient or student.

If we therefore accuse ourselves of inflicting a pseudo-identity on the patient, this becomes another needless burden, as pointless as for parents to accuse themselves of setting an example for their children. With schizophrenics, of course, we count ourselves lucky if they consent to borrow anything at all from their surroundings. But in many other cases where identity is shadowy—in much so-called hysteria, for example—we are less apt to inflict a pseudo-identity on the patient than to have one inflicted on us. In fact, the therapist is so often forced, against his better judgment, to play the role of oracle or all-knowing authority that I wonder to what extent we have developed our vocabulary of transference and countertransference, of father-surrogates and mother-surrogates, in order to accout for this phenomenon.

Once we recover from the delusion that psychology is an exact science, or that scientists do not have values, then it is easier to help the patient through these supposedly inauthentic stages of his recovery. For one thing, we are more willing to admit that what has to be recovered from is not only the disease, but also the treatment. And while we generally leave it up to the patient to recover from us, so to speak, as best he can, there is no reason why we should not try to help him through this period of recovery, during which he tries to decide just which of our values should be kept and which discarded. For it is upon this critical process of selection that the final phase of recovery will depend, whether it occurs during or after treatment.

Here I would emphasize the twofold nature of the therapeutic process, which reflects the dual nature of experience. In setting up an opposition between Thou and It, it would be extremely dangerous to regard one as inferior to the other. True meeting cannot occur under a false theory of meeting. And no amount of warmth or spontaneity can provide a substitute for meaning: i.e., for concept, judgment and the critical discrimination of values. Under present theories, which ironically contain an often romantic devaluation of "theory" itself, the therapist is always in danger of making two kinds of error. First the patient's feeble or misguided efforts toward meeting will either be ignored or else interpreted as their opposite: as positive efforts toward the false ideal we call transference. And conversely, for lack of more precise definitions, the therapist is often deluded into accepting the false or idolatrous attitudes of transference as though they represented that "empathy" or "contact" of the ideal relationship. Though I believe meeting does occur, even at the beginning of therapy, more often than present theory will allow, it is clear that many of the distortions seen as "transference" could more usefully be seen either as gropings toward, or as recoils from, the hope of mutual relationship.

At present, mutuality between patient and doctor is too often regarded as a distant goal, perhaps signalling the end of treatment. Meanwhile such meeting as does occur will be translated, not only as transference, but in false terms of "insight": "insight" often meaning no more than some passive reaction, or abreaction, on the part of the organism. Clearly it makes a difference what we call such experiences. Insight can mean that critical and creative act, by which meaning is achieved; or it can be reduced to mere self-expression, by which feelings merely find an outlet. It is through such verbal reductions, of course, that man himself is reduced to an organism: part animal and part machine. Indeed we can find in the history of neurophysiology how literally the "outlet" theory of emotion was based on the analogy of the steam engine.

Here it is not the danger of merely knowing *about* a person in terms of theory which must be emphasized, but the far more destructive fact that we have actually come to know him rather intimately in the most inept terms of knowledge: terms suitable not only for natural but for man-made objects. It is fatuous, of course, to strive for warmth or spontaneity with a man defined as "it"; whether as a "psychic system" or a "configuration of energies" or as the "human organism" itself.

When a man is known in human terms—whether of literature or of everyday existence—I do not find any great danger in merely knowing about him as a person. Such knowledge is an integral part of knowing him. Still we may distinguish those occasions when we are trying to unravel the puzzle of his personality from other moments, when we may be simply standing in his presence as before an irreducible fact: the irreducible mystery of his singularity. Although such moments occur every day, it is perhaps only in certain more exalted contexts, having to do with love or poetry or religion, that we become aware of their essential quality.

Here the two preconditions of meeting, which may be analyzed as mutuality and truthfulness, are blended into one whole immediacy: meeting becomes truth. But perhaps what chiefly distinguishes such moments is their non-utilitarian character; their utter lack of usefulness for any ordinary purposes of knowledge. Instead of confronting the world as something to be changed or studied, we stand in a kind of respectful silence before the tremendous fact of its mere existence. And since such transcendent moments have nothing to do with love or even liking, they may occur in our most casual encounters with a person, conferring upon him a mystery usually associated only with poetry or religion.

VI.   *Confirmation and the Therapeutic Despair*

The temptations of omniscience in the treatment of schizophrenia have been frequently remarked on in the psychoanalytic literature. It has been said, for example, that since it takes a thief to catch a thief, psychotherapists must begin with a bit of the disease they would treat. Or that the disorder is so resistant to treatment and therefore so wounding to the therapist's ambitions that it is difficult for him not to respond with grandiosity. Perhaps the most common theory—and one that smacks of black magic—is that it is dangerous to expose oneself to the unconscious of the schizophrenic, since the resultant anxiety might be severe enough to cause disorder in the therapist.

There may be a measure of truth to all the explanations cited, yet I believe that Buber's theory of confirmation can shed particular light upon these hazards by helping to distinguish between therapeutic dialogue and what he calls "genuine dialogue." As a quotidian affair stretching painfully through the years, the psychotherapy of schizophrenia has simply not been truthfully described. Reports not only give it an order and meaning which it does not possess; they also deprive it of the brutal tedium, exasperation, emptiness, futility—in short, the agony of existence in which dialogue is so fleeting as to be virtually nonexistent. Unfortunately, our case reports of such psychotherapy tend to be chivalric legends, replete with knights and dragons and soothsayers. In view of the difficulties, it is no wonder that they concern themselves with romantic accounts of those rare moments which do seem both lively and comprehensible. And no wonder these moments so often become, in retrospect, a prescriptive exercise in apologetics, taking on the quality of the full-gospel mission: as repentant sinners we announce the miraculous illumination which has possessed us, while the patient, as congregation, shouts "Amen." The conventional scientific prose in which these annunciations are made disguises, but cannot really conceal, the pathos of two maddened human beings clutching at each other, whatever the pretext.

But what of the weeks, months, years, when these two sit together for an hour a day, immersed in a silence broken only by obscure mouthings or posturings conveying no secure meaning; or by earnest professional adjurations which draw no response? How much easier it would be during these desolate periods to abandon what must often seem a bitter mockery of relationship. But the patient has no choice, being captive to his illness and to the explicit rules of the institution. Nor does the therapist have much choice, at least if he is conscientious. Although he is more captive to his conscience than to the institution, conscience obliges him to agree with the unwritten assumption that his mere physical presence each day is necessarily preferable to his absence. Thus does it happen that two people "do time" together under circumstances which, could they be manufactured, would provide the police state with a frightening new torture.

With another kind of patient, the therapist might take refuge in his own thoughts. His silence might pass for that mirrorlike impassivity which is still considered a virtue in the treatment of neurosis. But with a schizophrenic, he has no such refuge. To deprive the patient of ordinary social responsiveness might drive him further from his fragmentary gestures toward his fellows. And silence faced with silence would be arbitrary, if not cruel. Because he knows this, the therapist finds his own silence a heavy burden. He is continually on guard against the double danger of silence and the fear of silence, which he knows can easily sour into a clotted self-consciousness to be relieved at any cost.

At the same moment, perhaps, he is treading another tightrope between two other dangers. If he fails to grasp the patient's meaning, should he say so frankly or should he temporize? He knows that frankness here, although it will avoid the dangers of empty reassurance, may actually serve his scientific ideal more than his patient—his vanity more than his therapy. And regardless of the solace to be found in scientific caution, he is unhappily aware that a mere affirmation of his own incomprehension is no confirmation of the patient, unless one can be said to confirm another in his estrangement from humanity.

But the therapist cannot afford to hang in indecision: he knows that even the wrong approach is better than none. And so, carefully disclaiming the relevance of what he is about to say, he may now muse or soliloquize aloud to his silent partner in a manner which approaches free association. Or, if he has exhausted his capacity for monologue, he may try reading to the patient. Here he wisely selects some reading matter which, if it does not provoke any response from the patient, will be least be stimulating enough to dull his own self-consciousness. And if all these substitutes for conversation fail, then he may suggest some shared activity such as a walk about the hospital grounds—which may indeed offer a kind of companionship which goes beyond the limited motives contained in therapy.

Considering the grueling nature of this experience and the kind of constancy and courage it demands, it is not surprising if he is driven awkwardly and sometimes blindly by the emptiness of which he is a part. When faced with the inevitable despair, which I am suggesting must sooner or later overtake the conscientious therapist, it will not matter how indomitable or inventive may be his efforts to keep going: he cannot hope that his despair will be entirely unnoticed by his patient. Although perceptiveness may be severely impaired in the schizophrenic, the therapist knows that it can never be extinguished—a knowledge which may, in fact, add the final straw to his desolation. What I would suggest here is a possibility which, since it has been overlooked, may offer some truth as well as solace. To the extent that the therapist becomes "present" for his patient, that patient is capable of pity for his friend's distress.

If nothing has been said about the role of pity in treatment, it is because the word is associated partly with thoughts of condescension and partly with those uncomfortable sensations we call "anxiety." It is true that another's misfortune may arouse fear, as well as self-congratulation; but it may also arouse pity. I do not mean sympathy; I mean an actual sensation of pain or grief awakened by another. Thus everything would depend on the name we give to these sensations. If we call them anxiety, then the thought of arousing further anxiety in the patient can only drive us deeper into our own despair. Add to that the fear of condescension—or worse yet, of arousing condescension in our patients—and we can see that the word "pity" has formidable barriers surrounding it. Nevertheless, *pietas* is an irreplaceable and noble word which, like *caritas* or charity, has been spoiled for us by corruption and abuse. Certainly we cannot replace it with "anxiety," while "sympathy" denotes a mild and vague benevolence which is far removed from love or pity. Once we get past these verbal barriers, then we can consider two possibilities: first, that some pity is unavoidable, even in the therapeutic session, and, second, that it may have some unique value.

I believe it quite possible that a patient who has long refused some medical treatment offered to him for his health, because it is good for him, may finally consent to it out of pity. To forestall an obvious objection, I mean unsolicited pity, caused by another's real despair. I do not mean devices reminiscent of Mother's "Take your medicine, dear, for my sake." On the contrary, if pity is achieved it will be in spite of all solicitations. Pity is a rare and fleeting virtue whose essence is freedom: to be freely given, it must remain unsought or accidental, even fought against.

With this understood, let me examine the suggestion: that a patient may, out of pity, undertake therapeutic efforts which, although clearly beneficial to himself, have as their primary motive the assuaging of another's pain. In response to the therapist's despair, in other words, the patient will often try to confirm the therapist's image of himself as therapist. And insofar as the therapist is sincerely dedicated to his work—paradoxically, just because he is so dedicated—this will also have the effect of confirming him as a fellow human being. (Once again there is an awesome split between the "human" and the "scientific.")

As I said above, what is done out of pity must be sharply distinguished from the spurious recoveries which are often attempted either out of flattery or submissiveness, in response to the therapist's vanity or ambition. Pity demands an imagining of the other's particular pain to the degree that the pain is experienced as one's own. In therapy the paradox is inescapable that the man who is incapable of arousing pity will find it hard to help another.

All this means is that the therapist must be capable of feeling real despair, on another's behalf as well as—and I would stress the fact that we are not supermen—on his own. In addition to the more strenuous virtues of courage and dedication, then, the therapist must be highly endowed with imagination and perceptiveness: capable of imagining his own distress as well as the other's. If we think of the most effective therapists we have known, we can see that when all these qualities are combined to a high degree they may give rise to a further quality which is perhaps the final secret of the therapeutic success. It is a quality which may take the form of pride, but also of heroism: It is what makes the therapist fight against his own despair and take valiant measures to conceal his weakness. Since these struggles reveal a quality of courage which is universally admired, I think we must assume that it can arouse sympathy and admiration in the patient, just as it does in others. By authenticating the despair, it makes pity possible. And if we imagine such a powerful emotion as pity being aroused in the patient, we can see that for that moment, at least, he has ceased to be schizophrenic.

If such moments occur more frequently in the treatment of psychosis than of neurosis, it is not, I believe, because schizophrenics are more capable of pity. On the contrary, while the neurotic is far more capable of feeling pity, he is also capable, like the therapist himself, of more intellectual control and criticism. Those emotions which seem to him irrelevant will either be aborted or they will receive some more acceptable name than pity. But the chief reason is that therapeutic sessions with the relatively controlled and civilized people called neurotic simply do not give rise to such overwhelming despair as may evoke pity. There is ample room for both to confirm and be confirmed. And here we can no longer blink the fact that, human nature being what it is, the man who pours out his spiritual energy in confirming others will need more, and not less, confirmation of himself.

The ideal of a teacher or healer who confirms others without needing confirmation for himself: this inheritance from both the Jewish and the Christian prophets is still implicit in the Western culture. But since we lack the religious sustenance which might once have made it possible, the ideal of moral perfection operates now in a chiefly deleterious or unacknowledged form, giving rise to a too-ready cry of *mea culpa* whenever one's own fallibility or imperfection is discovered. Here it is not the imperfection of man, set against perfection, which arouses moral guilt. Guilt may be welcomed simply as a meaning, one of the handiest of familiar meanings, to get us out of chaos. Since anything is preferable to meaninglessness, the therapist longs to find some point at which he may accuse himself of moral guilt or of a failure of imagination. For with psychosis, not only are meanings elusive and discouragements ten times multiplied. A dimension of terror is added to our existence as we learn to live with the insane possibility—which is, after all, one of the facts of madness—that meaning itself can be the mirage. To avoid this insanity, we grasp at every possibility of meaning as though it were the staunchest fact.

Without minimizing the awful predicament of the schizophrenic, his illness does operate mercifully to spare him the full realization of his misery. And since those who befriend him lack such protection, I have tried to suggest how irrelevant the *mea culpa* may become: how impotent to describe a plight which must approach uniqueness. Certainly no man has been more guiltless than one who kneels at the very edge of nothingness, hoping to save a fallen stranger. To remain in this posture for days and weeks and even years, calling oneself guilty in order to stave off hopelessness—surely this is no easy brand of fellowship.

But when the despairing therapist turns to his colleagues for confirmation, he finds them all bent in the same posture. If they do have a helping hand to spare each other, they will not have time to applaud themselves as heroes. Like any rescue crew, they are more apt to snap irritably at each other "Get a grip on yourself, man—that rope is slipping."

This may explain a phenomenon puzzling and often shocking to the uninitiated. I mean the irritable and occasionally savage criticism of his technique which one member of a rescue team may turn upon another. It is for a common good, after all, that self-criticism should be brutally frank and also limited to technique. For it is on the strength and dexterity of each hand that the whole enterprise is literally hanging. And it would be neither possible nor helpful for the team to support a failing member by confirming his despair. In fact, the closer he comes to hopelessness, and the more he succeeds in conveying this to his fellows, the faster they will turn on him with the full resources of their technical vocabulary. And the psychoanalytic vocabulary is probably unique, as we know, for the ease with which it can be exploited for character assassination.

Thus if, to avoid despair, the therapist must either attack himself or be attacked for moral failure, then a circle is created by which even the confirmation from his colleagues can only drive him further to despair. Their confirmation can only reaffirm his dedication or his calling; it can only confirm the meanings and reinforce the existing theories by which his efforts are supported. And even were they willing to listen to a long confessional, or to provide absolution at the end, what is he able to confess? Not the real despair, caused by the real absence of meaning and response; not his real situation, of being too long immersed in this void of meaning. He can only confess whatever shape or order can be fashioned out of chaos—whatever moral guilt or failure his imagination can contrive. And if his imagination fails to show him any guilt, then his colleagues will gently point some out to him. For they are bound, of course, to look for hope—that is to say, for meaning—in the schizophrenic situation. Since anything is preferable, as I said, to chaos, they are driven to conclude that every situation is both meaningful and manageable—had one but the "psychological freedom" to control it.

Here is a strange paradox. For while the psychiatrist would be the first to tell you that no despair was ever cured by denying its existence, here we find him trying to climb out of his own circle by heroic feats of sacrifice and self-denial. Clearly the way out lies not in moral heroism, but in a no less arduous examination of words and meanings. The fault, I should say, is not in our characters but in our definitions. If some despair is inevitable, I have tried to show what hope may lie in it both for our patients and ourselves. And if much despair is needless, we can try to find what needless burdens have been inflicted on us by a failure of logic: by the failure of a scientific logic to define either ourselves or our calling.

If such intellectual processes are generally regarded as the province of pedagogy rather than of therapy, this may be partly because they do admittedly have less to do with interpersonal relations than with some solitary exercise of reasoning and judgment—less to do with dialogue, in other words, than with monologue. And this brings me to the last point I want to make. It has to do with monologue—not at the expense of dialogue or relationship, but as one of the necessary movements in dialogue. There is a growing tendency in modern times—not only among psychotherapists—to let our concern with the interpersonal overshadow certain other values which are personal or solitary in character.

In Buber's dialogic philosophy, as in the usual psychology of interpersonal relations, the concept of monologue carries a pejorative meaning, signifying a failure in discourse. Yet in a deeper sense, there are crucial moments for man, when his utterance must be monologic —moments when the actuality of other men must recede from his awareness. It might be argued that Buber, unlike Kierkegaard, almost out of an excess of virtue often appears too consummatory in his view of human relations. But on the other hand, he has written —in a context which has little to do with imagining the other: "The origin of all conflict between me and my fellowmen is that I do not say what I mean, and that I do not do what I say."[13] And in words reminiscent of Kierkegaard: "Every single man is a new thing in the world, and is called upon to fulfill his particularity in this world . . . Mankind's great chance lies precisely in the unlikeness of men, in the unlikeness of their qualities and inclinations."[14]

In saying what he means, what he alone means, man seeks to express his own being or the being he would become. Such expressions in no way confirm the other in his particularity. If confirmation can be said to exist at all, it is of general nature: In affirming my own unlikeness, I may be confirming yours, or asserting the particularity of all men. Dialogue must, in short, include general statements about dialogue, just as it must include our most desolate or solitary monologues.

Though I have spoken of the patient's need to recover from his treatment, there is a deeper sense in which the cure may be implicit in the disease. As Freud taught long ago, there is some health in every symptom; and this holds true, not only for the patient, but for that therapeutic despair which is, after all, a collaboration between two people. If there are moments when it seems that our only health is the disease, these are not inauthentic moments. On the contrary, it is when we stand stripped of every artifice and prop, that we are closest to reality. And if it is only then, in the moment of extremity, that we approach genuine dialogue, genuine confirmation —the lack of which has driven us to this despair—so we may find the remedy concealed in the disease. It may be that only in such moments do we approach reality at all. It may be that at such moments the patient too is obeying such deep and elementary needs that it would be gratuitous to speak of pity and despair. But however that may be, it is only when the therapist has exhausted every conceivable device for reaching his patient that he may, from the very heart of his despair, cry out with his entire being, as if to his Maker. Such a cry is as far from dialogue or confirmation as it is from love or sym-

[13] *The Way of Man*, p. 32.
[14] Reference footnote 12, p. 17.

pathy; any response awakened by it will be a response to pain and loneliness. In Kierkegaard's words:

One must really have suffered very much in the world, and have been very unfortunate before there can be any talk of beginning to love one's neighbor. It is only in dying to the joys and happiness of the world in self-denial that the neighbor comes into existence. One cannot therefore accuse the immediate person of not loving his neighbor, because he is too happy for the 'neighbor' to exist for him. No one who clings to earthly life loves his neighbor, that is to say his neighbor does not exist for him.[15]

Although such "dying to the world" is not readily or often chosen, especially nowadays, there is no denying that much loneliness and suffering can still be imposed through one's chosen profession. And unless this is to be a useless form of suffering, a total waste of spirit, we must learn how to name and accept our own despair.

[15] Søren Kierkegaard, *The Journals of Kierkegaard*, edited and translated by Alexander Dru (London: Oxford Univ. Press, 1938), p. 219.

LESLIE H. FARBER, M.D.

26

Carl F. von Weizsäcker

I-THOU AND I-IT IN THE CONTEMPORARY NATURAL SCIENCES[1]

WHAT matters most in the relationship between an I and a Thou is that we do not talk about it but that we live in it. When I had my first opportunity to engage in a personal conversation with Martin Buber—this was provided by the occasion of his address at Hanover in the summer of 1956—I requested him to give me his opinion concerning a question relating to the atom bomb. I described the following situation to him. For many years now, very distinguished scientists have again and again declared publicly that atom bombs constitute a danger for mankind. During the period following the end of the war I was, as a German, remote from any personal participation in the production of these bombs. But I did take part in various discussions concerning what public declarations should and might be made concerning this danger. In these discussions I had the strong if unarticulated feeling that all the declarations that had hitherto been made lacked something essential. On the one hand I found that they were partly unrealistic in what they proposed. By virtue of the fact that they seemed to go too far they always gave me the impression of being vitiated by a certain weakness to boot. I was not at all surprised that they remained without any practical influence upon world politics; and I confess that I was by no means sorry that my name was not associated with any of these pronouncements. On the other hand I could not approve this situation because I was thoroughly convinced that the atom bomb constituted a peril for us all.

I described this entire situation to Buber and then said to him: "The failure of all these appeals is not to be explained only by the fact that the world is unwilling to listen. Blame must also be assigned to a certain lack in all these appeals. Can you tell me what is missing in them?" He started a bit as I put the question to him

[1] Translated by Ephraim Fischoff.

in this manner but his surprise seemed to express agreement. He replied, "Yes, something is missing, but what is it?" He thought a while and then added, "What is probably lacking is involvement *(engagement)*."

The additional details of our conversation I do not remember precisely but I would like to expatiate somewhat on his remark in accordance with my understanding of it.

Nobody can deny that when the scientists issued public warnings against the atom bomb they did so with utter seriousness. It was not Buber's intention to cast aspersions on their involvement in this sense. But when an I confronts a Thou, what convinces the other person are not my words nor yet my feelings. For words and feelings are not yet the true being of a person, or what today one would term existence, to use an over-worked expression *(Existenz)*. Only when I am in a position where my words and feelings are not supplementary to my being but where they necessarily and hence convincingly follow from this being, can I reach another at the point where he himself is real. Otherwise while he may receive my words and even think something similar as a result, and while he may even be moved by my feelings and react correspondingly, he will be unlikely to act with the commitment of his person as I might have done.

The production of atomic weapons took place in part in authentic *engagement*. At the time men were convinced that they had to make an extraordinary effort in order to save the freedom of the world. They made great sacrifices in their personal lives and for many of them possibly the greatest sacrifice was the willingness to participate in so terrible a thing, for the sake of hindering something even more horrible. If now when there is a new situation in the world, these weapons appear as one of the greatest dangers threatening us, we must not expect to overcome this peril with a lesser involvement *(engagement)* than characterized the original situation out of which it arose.

After that conversation with Martin Buber it became clear to me that if I ever participated in any public utterance concerning atomic weapons such a statement ought not to be directed to an unspecified addressee—the entire world which is no Thou but just an abstract It. It was clear to me that any such statement must address somebody who knew that he was being meant and who therefore could not escape it. It would have to address a particular Thou who would be confronted by an I whose involvement would be unmistakable.

I do not wish to say more regarding the politics connected with atomic weapons. It would be an error to derive illustrations for general theses which one might wish to set forth, from campaigns in which one has participated himself and which are still ongoing. Nevertheless I would like to set at the head of my consideration this account of a personal experience. In the aforementioned conversation with Buber I learnt in a concrete case what the differentiation of Thou and It signifies. Indeed it is necessary in this context to relate specific instances even as Buber is wont to relate anecdotes, in his writings concerning Chassidism. For the abstract form of general thought is already appropriate to the It and imperceptibly transforms every general remark about the Thou into a manner of speaking in which the Thou does not occur at all.

Now has contemporary natural science an actual relationship to Buber's problem? Is it not essentially its nature as science to be concerned with the It?

I would like to turn to some abstract ideas of contemporary physics and ostensibly depart somewhat from our problem. In classical physics not only does the Thou not appear but fundamentally even the I is lacking. Indeed it treats only of the It. To be sure, I see that this tulip is red but the perception of "red" is only subjective, as we have been taught since the seventeenth century. In nature there are certain chemical substances termed colors which are constructed of atoms ordered into particular molecules. The atoms occupy space and are sufficient for the purposes of mechanics. Their geometric and mechanical properties are termed the primary qualities of things. They are what is really real. To the world of this same reality belong also the waves of light, which are emitted by the color materials, and which bring about certain chemical reactions in our retina. For several centuries there was controversy whether light was composed of particles or waves, but both are realities of the same type. The color red on the other hand is a secondary quality, that is, it is "only" an experience that I have. If I attribute it to things themselves, I fall into the error of subjectivity. But in science the subject has nothing to look for, for science is objective and knows objects only.

The inadequacies of this intellectual position were already revealed before the development of twentieth century physics. In a very profound way and in a more popular fashion both Hume and Mach pointed out that objects, insofar as we can speak of them intelligibly, are always objects for a certain subject. Also it constituted a very important step forward when the physics of our century, especially the quantum theory, used this idea in order to express rationally its data of knowledge. For us particles and waves are modes of description which relate to possible experiments, i.e., hence to possible acts of perception voluntarily produced. They describe phenomena and not things in themselves. To contemporary physics all qualities concerning which it speaks are of the same category as the color red. Accordingly it would be silly to term them secondary. The geometric and mechanical qualities are now placed on a plane which is not essentially different from the quality of color.

In any phenomenon something appears to somebody. That is, the very concept of a phenomenon introduces the relationship I-It. An important contemporary logician, Gotthard Günther, has pointed out that contemporary theoretical physics knows the I in two ways. Classical physics spoke of the It. Classical philosophy for which Hume and Kant would stand at the same level as crown witnesses, reflected on the fact that this It is the It of a particular I. That is, they also knew the polarity of the I and the It. Contemporary physics describes in every concept which is related to an experiment and indeed in its objective thinking, the relationship of the It to the I who is performing the experiment. But insofar as the physicist is himself the philosopher (which it is difficult to avoid today), who reflects upon that which he is doing as a physicist, the I of the theoretical physicist who is describing the experiment as a process between the object and the experimenter, enters into the light of analysis too. Thus according to Günther we have in physics a double I, the experimenter and the theoretician. The latter occupies a position which may be compared with the Kantian I, but the experimenter has also taken over a portion of his functions. At this point the relationship of I and Thou announces itself in very rudimentary fashion.

It suggests itself in the following consideration. Bohr is never tired of emphasizing that the concepts of classical physics are indispensable even today because we know atoms only through experiments and because we describe our apparatuses with the concepts of classical physics. Thus far this thought only places in a new light the situation described above. If one goes on to inquire, however, whether these concepts of classical physics may not be eliminated subsequently, the answer is that one still has to be able to describe to the mechanic in understandable language the apparatus he will be called upon to construct. Thus the language of classical physics remains in this view a technical language in which there is retained all that is generally understandable and necessary for comprehension. The mention of the mechanic recalls the fact that physics is a social phenomenon. During the last century it still was possible to imagine a solitary scientist. Today team work is the prerequisite for success. This is one of the facts which the many neglected geniuses did not understand whose letters are known to every physicist and whom it is virtually impossible to persuade of their errors.

Physics thus presupposes in a very abstract fashion, even in its fundamental concepts and in a very massive way in its practical applications, the relationship of human beings to one another. But insofar as it once developed and entertained the wish to look away from the I and to behold only the It, for historical reasons which it would be valuable to investigate further, so it now inclines to regard the I, which it can no longer fail to consider, in the simplest possible fashion and consequently in an unreal manner. In the technical operation of a research institute the relationship of I and Thou comes into play only in the supplementation of legerdemain and the exchange of ideas. Everything else is a purely "private matter." It is possible that the atom bomb will serve the purpose of making it clear to our entire civilization that in this manner we have seen too little of the Thou.

It will not be the task of physics to see the Thou in its fullness. But it will certainly be its task to make clear to itself that its methodological procedure excludes this fullness, and that it is not a truism that what it does not see does not exist.

This series devoted to living philosophers is intended to evoke a critical colloquy with the thinkers in question. The various contributors are invited to express their critical judgments. In this regard I must remain somewhat delinquent. As a physicist I have registered my gratitude to Martin Buber, but I have no criticism to contribute regarding the primary problem of our discussion.

CARL F. VON WEIZSÄCKER

PHILOSOPHISCHES SEMINAR
UNIVERSITÄT HAMBURG

27

Louis Z. Hammer

THE RELEVANCE OF BUBER'S THOUGHT TO AESTHETICS[1]

MODERN aesthetics is becoming increasingly more content to deal only with those questions faced by a philosophy of criticism. Its main interest lies in answering the theoretical questions posed by the descriptive, interpretative, and evaluative statements made by critics of the various arts.[2]

Although the influence of analytic philosophy has not done away completely with a speculative approach to philosophic problems in the arts, relatively little attention has been given recently to understanding art within the framework of a philosophy of man. It seems doubtful that the philosophy of criticism can succeed in its limited task without raising the question, what kind of a being is man that he should paint, sculpt, compose music, write poetry, and so forth? But even if one thinks that philosophy of criticism can succeed without asking such a fundamental question, one might allow that such a question deserves consideration somewhere within philosophy. And aesthetics, conceived more broadly than the philosophy of criticism, seems the likely place in which to undertake this inquiry.

The thought of Martin Buber is especially relevant to an inquiry of this sort, and thus of special significance for aesthetics understood as the philosophy of art and beauty. The fact that some men are artists is to be grasped, within the framework of Buber's thought, not as a mere accident, but rather as an outcome of what man essentially is. At the same time, the notion of what man is essentially is modified by familiarity with the work of artists and with the human conditions surrounding such works.

---

[1] Throughout this essay I am stating views suggested to me by Buber's writings. Except in the early part, the essay is interpretation rather than exposition of his thought.

[2] Cf. Monroe C. Beardsley, *Aesthetics: Problems in the Philosophy of Criticism* (New York: Harcourt, Brace and Co., 1958), esp. pp. 1–12.

In the essay "Der Mensch und Sein Gebild,"[3] Buber raises the question "concerning the connection between the being of men and the being of art." The question is an anthropological one, but not in the sense of a scientific empirical anthropology, rather of a philosophical anthropology. It is concerned with the relationship between the essential attributes of man and the essential attributes of art. Buber sees the artist as one who refuses to reduce what meets him through the senses to a mere object, but rather pursues the possibilities of form within sensed objects or linguistic utterance, and brings these to the fullness of a completed creation or image. The painter or sculptor compresses the entire world into the visual or spatial sphere, the composer of music draws the entire range of human presence in the world into the acoustic and temporal sphere. The poet attends not to a sense sphere, but to language, which is the presupposition of all the experience of the senses.

In this essay Buber links sense-awareness to the I-Thou relation—something he had not done so explicitly in previous writings—and in the process provides a reason for the being of art. The artist is one who will not let what is in being fall away from the sense world. He endeavors to make the real stand fast within a sense sphere. The natural world, with which we are in daily contact, meets us only as part of the sense world. The sense world itself arises out of the movement of one being toward other being; every sensible feature has its origin in a fundamental movement of one being to another. Sense perception is to be understood as rooted in a desire for the reality of the other. When we treat as a mere object that which meets us originally through the senses, we lose its sensible qualities, and can represent it to ourselves only as an "x" about which we can say only that it is, and nothing more. But when we turn toward the other as that which meets us in the world, and not as merely something surviving in a natural order of "x's," we restore to it its full complement of sensed qualities. The sense world is the arena in which one being participates with another. Only when some sensible feature comes to us from other being, and out of this some special form is clarified for us, do we commune with the other. The senses give us not "mere appearance," but a means of achieving faithfulness to that which is in being. When we reduce to a mere object what is in

---

[3] Heidelberg: Verlag Lambert Schneider, 1955.

the course of being, we have only the bare "x." But even this bare "x" approaches us.

The artist is that man who has a peculiar way of remaining faithful to what meets him in the world. He seeks its "form" and realizes this "form" in a creation or image. He answers the demand which this form makes on him to be made into a work.[4] The work of art is a sanctuary for the form which has arisen within a sphere of the sense world or within language. The artist, *qua* artist, perceives the world as figuration, as determinate form that can be brought to the fullness of a completed work. The artist elicits the work of art from the spheres of the senses or of language. He helps bring to completeness what is prefigured in the sense world. His task is to build the world of art within the range of a particular sense or of language, and by so doing to realize fullness of relation to the reality that underlies the sense world. The demand placed on him is to realize the full possibilities of form within a given sphere. By doing this he helps bring man into genuine relation with what exists alongside him and over against him in the world.

Buber's view of the activity of the artist is inseparable from his view of man's twofold relation—of an I to an It and an I to a Thou. But clearly, the artist cannot be simply allocated the I-Thou relation.[5] Nor is the artist the "Person," i.e., one who is distinguished by the consistent genuineness of his relations with other persons. It is not within the social sphere that he is faithful to other being, but within the spheres of the sense world and of language. It cannot be assumed that the artist possesses a higher moral value than other men, yet the life of the artist is filled by a kind of wholeness and genuineness. Within the sphere that he has made his special province he lives in the peculiar tension of the life of dialogue. That tension arises out of the recognition of a special demand made by form seeking to be fulfilled. It is a demand to bring what is in the course of being into communion with man. By refusing to allow what meets him in the world to be reduced to merely an object of handling and use, the artist continually leaves the world of It for the world of Thou. By giving his attention to figuration he allows what is there in the sense world to come to completeness, and so to reveal what is present in

---

[4] Cf. *I and Thou*, trans. Ronald Gregor Smith (2nd ed., New York: Charles Scribner's Sons, 1958), p. 9.

[5] Cf. *Ibid.*, translator's Preface, p. ix.

being. Certainly he "objectifies," he scrutinizes at times coolly and dispassionately, he concentrates his attention on objects, and he labors at the technical side of his art. But for all this he is not submerged in the world of It. His objectifying is for the sake of free-ing a form to be built up and completed, and so for the sake of al-lowing men to take part in the world with other men and things, that is to stand genuinely in relation with other being. Even the artist, like Valéry or Stravinsky, who would like to call himself an "inven-tor"[6] cannot escape involvement with the other as Thou.

Earlier Buber called the artist an "onlooker."[7] In looking on, the artist allows himself to see freely what appears, to perceive a concrete and whole existence; he does not merely observe a sum of traits. But the "onlooker," along with the observer, is distinguished from one who has "become aware," who addresses another being to being, who has to do with another. This is the "Person," the man who says Thou. The view of the artist in "Der Mensch und Sein Gebild" is, it seems to me, a stage beyond the onlooker. Now the artist is depicted as someone peculiarly involved with what meets him in the world. Looking on may be considered a moment in the activity of the artist, but it is a moment within a larger process that culminates in the actualization of sensible possibilities, bringing for-ward that which is in being.

I should like to point out what I think Buber has achieved in this view of art that other thinkers have not achieved. First of all, he has joined art to the fundamental relations between one being and other being. Art is shown to be implicit in the fact that all of man's relations are made possible through sensible qualities. These qualities disclose the world that must necessarily be set at a distance in order to be experienced. The movement in which art has a part is that of overcoming the primary and inescapable distance. Art is one of four human powers that bring man into relation with his world—the others being knowledge, love and faith. Art, it should be noted, is not regarded as a kind of knowledge or a kind of love, but as a distinct potency in man. We are related to the world by art through the encounter with created form.

[6] Igor Stravinsky, *Poetics of Music*, trans. Arthur Knodel and Ingolf Dahl (New York: Vintage Books, 1956), p. 54.

[7] *Between Man and Man*, trans. Ronald Gregor Smith (London: Kegan Paul, 1947), p. 9.

This is a second important point. In Buber's view, art has a role to play which is distinctly its own. Buber's view permits us to steer clear of the controversy over the cognitive import of art. Art is not labelled cognitive, yet it is not relegated to "mere emotion" or the production of "valuable attitudes." Art, no less than love or faith, involves emotion, but is not reducible to the expression of emotion. It is other than, but on a par with, knowledge. It is a way of communing with the other, that attends to a special feature of the other, namely its capacity to disclose itself in sensible form.

It is instructive, I think, to compare Buber's view with some important contemporary theories of art. The influential theory of Susanne Langer[8] labels the work of art a "presentational symbol" or "expressive form" and sees it as a "virtual image" of the "life of feeling." The work of art, according to Mrs. Langer, presents feeling to our cognition.[9] The work of art as "expressive form" has "import," and it achieves import by combining elements of the dynamic life of feeling in the imaginative mode.

Mrs. Langer takes art very seriously and writes subtly about it. But her theory rests on an inadequate foundation. She wants to explain art by the fact that men have the capacity to symbolize and that they can produce a special kind of symbol, one that does not stand for something beyond itself. The presentational symbol presents itself; it does not stand for a referent beyond. It is an ordered whole in which the parts cannot be understood except through their participation in the whole. Art is an outcome of the symbolic function used in such a way that the symbol constitutes the thing symbolized.

Mrs. Langer does not push the inquiry into the nature of art beyond the theory of the symbol. She seems to accept Cassirer's definition of man as the symbolic animal,[10] and to regard the symbol-making capacity as of the essence of man. Leaving aside the question whether the term "symbol" ought to be applied to a work of art as an aesthetic whole—and I think it should not—one can ask what it is in man's condition that causes him to produce such an aesthetic whole. And Mrs. Langer's theory has no answer beyond

[8] See esp. *Feeling and Form* (New York: Charles Scribner's Sons, 1953).

[9] Cf. Susanne K. Langer, *Problems of Art* (New York: Charles Scribner's Sons, 1957), p. 134.

[10] Ernst Cassirer, *An Essay on Man* (New Haven: Yale University Press, 1944), Chap. II.

pointing to the capacity to do so. It is precisely here, at the level of a fundamental anthropological question, that Buber has a great deal to say.

According to Buber, the work of art is form worked on and realized in a created whole. The artist brings to fulfillment the sensible possibilities of what exists and meets him in the world. He deals with the world, though in a reflective, not a practical, mode. The real in its sensible manifestation is the very substance of the work of art. The work of art is not, as Mrs. Langer would have it, a virtual image reflecting a pattern of feeling. It is figuration, encountered and discovered in the world, and brought to full actualization. In art we are brought face to face, through the mediation of form, with that side of the real that can be given to one of the senses or uttered in language. Mrs. Langer's theory cannot escape the difficulty involved in any theory that regards art as the virtual image of some real pattern: how do you identify the supposed real pattern to which the alleged virtual pattern is said to be connected? By taking the work of art as real instead of virtual, Buber's view avoids this difficulty.

Art, in Buber's view, rather than being a matter merely of the symbolic function, is a basic capacity for meeting the world. In this confrontation the whole person is involved, not only cognition, just as in knowledge, love or faith, the whole person is committed to what meets him. To have created or enjoyed a work of art is to have reached out and encountered other being by giving oneself over to form within the spheres of sight or sound or human speech. The world is not represented in art—it is allowed to take on concrete form within the range of one of the senses or of language. Strictly speaking, art is never representational. Painting, for example, realizes the possibilities of what is over against man to unfold itself in color, line, mass, texture, on a two-dimensional surface. These possibilities extend over a wide range—from forms with a close likeness to common-sense objects to highly detached abstract forms. It is not the likeness to common-sense objects or the lack of such likeness which makes a painting good or bad. It is faithfulness to emergent form, the development given to visual figuration, that makes the difference.

There can be derived from Buber's view, if not a clear criterion or set of criteria for excellence, at least some guide lines for judging certain tendencies within art. Taking again painting as an example, the modern non-objectivist movement regards painting as a process of exploring space rather than form.[11] According to the practice of the chief figures in the movement, the painter, it would seem, must allow paint to unfold the properties of the two-dimensional space of a canvas, rather than use the space of the canvas to explore visual form. Buber's view of art would repudiate this conception. Painting has to do with the visual world; it should serve that sphere to its fullest capacity, making use of all the attributes of the medium, which includes the space of the canvas, but also transcending the medium. Painting as an art has to play its role as part of a fundamental human capacity to stand in relation to what is in the world by forming what is met in the world into a created whole.

Buber's view of art clearly calls the artist back to his ancient task of encountering and remaking what is in the world. The symbolic view fails to do this. It sees art as the giving of form to feeling, as the ordering of the emotional life. But it does not stress the relation between the person and the world. Consequently it leaves the way open for the abandonment of the world that characterizes contemporary painting. It has no word to say, for example, to the abstract expressionist painter that will dissuade him from retreating into a private realm in which the spatially "interesting" or "impressive" or "shocking" holds full sway. Most abstract expressionist canvases contain a form of some sort which is said to be expressive of a feeling. They would then satisfy Mrs. Langer's definition: "Art is the creation of forms symbolic of human feeling."[12] Yet the feeling in an abstract expressionist canvas is private, vague, and general. It lacks the individuality of what steps forward from the sense world and meets us in its particularity.

These remarks do not intend any repudiation of the unconscious in the creative process. Communal symbols, working in the unconscious, and personalized, may enter the work of art with great human relevance, as, for example, in the art of Chagall. It is the anonymity of the so-called symbols of abstract expressionism that is repudiated.[13]

[11] Cf. James K. Feibleman, "Concreteness in Painting," *The Personalist*, 42, No. 1, 70–83.

[12] *Feeling and Form*, p. 40.

[13] Cf. Herbert Schade, "Abstrakte Malerei," *Stimmen Der Zeit*, 86 Jahrgang (1960–61), Heft 2, pp. 81–99. Selected translation in *Philosophy Today*, 5, No. 4/4, 290–299.

If, as has been suggested,[14] the tendency toward abstraction in art begins in anxiety before the external world, in "a great interior unrest caused by the phenomena of the world,"[15] then it may be that the genuine center of art is found where some reconciliation occurs, where some measure of trust is established, so that the artist does not run away from the world, but stands his ground. Here the "medium" springs into action to allow a portion of the world that can be drawn into the sphere of the visual to unfold itself by visual means. The artistic imagination leads the person to the world that has been set at a distance and enables him to retrieve that world. The artist necessarily distorts or abstracts from common-sense objects in their everyday appearance. But, in his genuine moments, he does so to win back the world in its relevance to man. He celebrates the range and variety of forms accessible to man within the sense world. To do this, the painter must allow the exploration of the space of a canvas to subserve the act of encounter with visual form.

If we examine for a moment another influential modern view, the "expression" theory of R. G. Collingwood,[16] the importance of the anthropological framework which Buber provides aesthetics will become even more apparent.

According to Collingwood, art is expression, and expression is the clarification and individualization of emotion. The artist creates in order to discover and explore his own emotion; he makes a vague and uncertain emotion concrete and individual. The genuine artist does not stimulate emotion in his audience; he can make use of no technique. Rather he permits his audience to perceive the expressed emotion, now freed of its oppressive quality by its having been concretized and clarified.

Collingwood, like Croce, puts strong emphasis on what goes on in the mind of the artist. And what goes on is a struggle to make a clear intuition out of something vaguely and oppressively felt. The artist, unlike the craftsman, has no end in view. He is not guided by some idea of an object which he then attempts to realize. Instead, he tries to follow a vague feeling to clarity, without a prior idea of what the finished product will be like.

[14] See Wilhelm Wörringer, *Abstraktion und Einfühlung* (München, 1959), p. 49. Quoted by Schade, *loc. cit.*, pp. 296–297.

[15] *Ibid.*

[16] See his *The Principles of Art* (Oxford: Clarendon Press, 1938), pp. 109–115.

The limitation of this view becomes apparent if we set it along-side Buber's thought about relation. The artist's struggle, on Colling-wood's view, is with the hiddeness of feeling within his own psyche. The outcome he is hoping for is a clear individual presentation of emotional experience. But Collingwood's theory fails to make the most crucial connection—that between expressed emotion and the being of the Other. If we think within Buber's anthropological framework, it seems to me, we must regard the emotion of any one individual as inseparable from the lineaments of the Other rendered accessible through sensible qualities. All that meets us dwells within a structure of emotion as it stands in relation to us. Emotion is a felt pattern in our awareness of ourselves in relation to what surrounds us. In preserving and bringing forward what is in the world through the qualities of a sense sphere or of language, the artist necessarily makes emotion definite and clear, because he elaborates "figuration."

To seek the sensible form of the Other is necessarily to clarify emotion. If a genuine artist were deliberately to seek only knowledge of his own emotion, he would be likely to find that he is encountering the Other in spite of himself. He would find that he is giving his attention to the sensible qualities of what meets him in the world, and to the inner being of the Other that grounds the sense qualities. Jacques Maritain puts the matter well when he says:

While endeavoring to disclose and manifest the artist's Self, the poetic perception which animates art catches and manifests at the same time what matters most in Things, the transapparent reality and secret significance on which they live.[17]

The work of art, seen within the framework of Buber's thinking, transcends the physical, the phenomenal, and the symbolic. While these dimensions are necessary, they are not sufficient. In order to comprehend its nature we must see the work of art within the dimension of relation between the person and the Other. The artist as such does not answer what is usually regarded as an ethical or religious demand, yet his work is not irrelevant to ethical and religious categories. Art takes place in "wholeness." It is not an alternative to the ethical or religious life nor is it necessarily in conflict with these spheres. Genuine art does not fall under the Kierkegaardian "aesthetic" category, which is characterized by preoccupation with the

[17] *Creative Intuition in Art and Poetry* (New York: Meridian Books, 1955), p. 29.

"interesting" and the escape from boredom. While the creation and enjoyment of art can easily descend to this level, at the center of art, in the variety of its manifestations and through diverse historical epochs, is the person who in wholeness says Thou to what meets him in the sense world. The genuine artist, at the center—and we must continually return to the center in order to nail down the true meaning of art—lives in the tension found everywhere within the life of dialogue. He must live and move within the limited, finite, appearing human world, and through his inner faithfulness endeavor to participate in the redemption of that world, creating as he can a work that "interests" and "moves" because it speaks with the power of what is in being.

Buber's view of the "religious"—" . . . it is just *everything*, simply all that is lived in its possibility of dialogue,"—18 is broad enough to embrace the work of the artist. But this, of course, has nothing to do with making a religion of art. That is a perversion which involves substituting worship of the creative process and self-expression for dialogue with the genuine God or Eternal Thou, in whom the believer trusts. Art is embraced by religion when artistic vigor, originality and skill create works in which the inner being of what is manifest in the sense world lives again and in a new way. Such works are directed beyond themselves toward the Absolute Thou of faith, who hovers over all genuine relation between human being and all that is in Creation outside it.

What matters most is, in the phrase of Gabriel Marcel, the artist's "creative fidelity." The artist is faithful to the Creator by his faithfulness to "creation" in a double sense. His "creative act" reflects concern for the process in which he actively responds to what meets him demanding to be made into a work. Besides the labor and the effort at perfecting the skills which make up his technique, he may be required to make many practical sacrifices, and even to adopt a way of life which sets him apart from the fellowship of a community. His willingness to give himself over to his work, to the point even of sacrificing good standing within society, comprises his faithfulness to the creative act. But this faithfulness is also the condition of his self-transcendence. He becomes loyal to the whole of Creation through his own work because this work is essentially an act of preserving Creation as present being. And, what is remarkable,

18 *Between Man and Man*, p. 14.

this loyal preserving of the presentness of Creation increases Creation, becomes an instrument of the Creator.

Since within the framework of Buber's thought the ethical totally interpenetrates the religious, the relation between the artist and the world of present being must affect the sphere of "between," the relation between man and man. The artist risks exposing subjectivity in its nakedness. While he never provides in his work an exact replica of his inner life, he does bare himself to view unmistakably, and through his work throws himself on the community for acceptance. This nakedness can be enough to set him apart, even to make him suspect. His naked condition can easily unsettle the community which encounters his work. For in exposing himself he can expose all men to themselves, by showing them subjectivity in all its profundity. They may curse him long before they praise him, and they may turn their backs on him abruptly. His creative loyalty demands that he take these risks.

The creative tension between the artist and the life of the community often comes to the fore when he deviates from conventional codes of conduct. The standards adhered to by most of the community, especially with regard to sexual experience, and the achievement of heightened forms of consciousness through alcohol and drugs, often appear confining to the artist. He may believe that the common range of experience is too restrictive. This tendency to see conventional moral codes as restrictive and to come into conflict with them can perhaps be explained by the artist's need to remain faithful to individual vision, and by his close involvement with the sense world. The artist who fulfills his calling to its depths experiences the full questioning power of solitude. His separation and even estrangement from accepted standards of conduct, when this does not descend to mere rebelliousness or self-indulgent frivolity, may constitute an important contribution to communal life. If in departing from the common standards, he remains dialogically related to the community, and in moving toward the extremes of human conduct, he seeks revealing self-knowledge, what he achieves may have profound consequences for the life of man with man.

What is most important is that the artist's experience of morbidity, of eroticism, of despair and alienation, inform his work, become fused into an artistic whole in which the life of man in the world and of man with man appears with genuine power and presence. Everything depends on the strength of his commitment to his task.

Whether from his position of isolation he can speak genuinely and movingly to other men, or whether he will have only the limited and temporary power to awaken curiosity, to excite interest, depends on whether he grasps his work as a calling and labors in responsibility.

The close link between art and the sense world may affect the person of the artist. One can, of course, give too much attention to the factor of the sensuous in the life of the artist. Many artists have been coldly rational, some even ascetics. It should be said, however, that by the very nature of his work the artist is made susceptible to sensuality. Weakness here may seriously diminish his creative powers, yet those powers have so much to do with the sense world. Sensuality is closely related to the task through which the artist shows his "creative fidelity." If he is sinful and guilty as a person, he has made himself answerable through his work. On this matter Jacques Maritain has made a beautiful remark: "God will work it out with him, somehow or other."[19]

I have gone into these issues in order to show how the person and the work of the artist can be seen within the context of Buber's view of individuality and community and the interdependence of the ethical and religious. The same view of human wholeness which denies Kierkegaard's distinction between ethical and religious categories also must refuse to accept a separated aesthetic category. The matter is complicated by terminology. The aesthetic for Kierkegaard does not designate the realm of art. Rather it designates the pursuit of the interesting, the flight from boredom, living without commitment. Yet the Kierkegaardian aesthetic category is closely connected with a certain conception of the nature of art. If the enjoyment of art is regarded primarily as satisfaction of the mind, or "disinterested contemplation," then the achievement of a work of art lies in its engaging the mind. Its power is the power to be absorbing. But where, as in Buber's thinking, art is regarded as a power for coming into relation with a world that has been set at a distance, clearly we are significantly beyond the Kierkegaardian category, and art can no longer be relegated to some essentially isolated and distinct mental sphere. Whatever may be the validity of Kierkegaard's aesthetic category, with its emphasis on the escape from boredom of a life without a center of gravity, that category does not essentially comprehend either the creation or the enjoyment of art.

[19] Maritain, *op cit.*, p. 38.

Buber's philosophy of dialogue suggests a clear direction in understanding the nature of beauty. Traditional accounts have tended to consider beauty a quality which an object possesses, whether through the supervenience of a transcendental form or as the result of a complex of natural qualities.[20] Those who have opposed the objectivist view have talked about an experience in the beholder—Santayana's "pleasure objectified"[21]—to explain what is usually referred to as beauty. Broadly speaking, the dispute has gone on between objectivists who consider beauty to be a quality which objects possess, and subjectivists who deny that there is such a quality. Buber's thought suggests that beauty be referred to the sphere of "between."

While some objectivist theories have provided formal conditions for the emergence of beauty, psychological subjectivists attempt to explain away beauty. They contend that no supervenient or emergent quality of beauty exists in objects which are called "beautiful." The term "beauty" properly refers to an affective state of the beholder. Pleasure-making features must exist in the object, but beauty is not some further feature of the object, a certain quality. It is the pleasurable state centered about the enjoyment of the object.

From the point of view of Buber's thought, this division into objectivist and subjectivist views results from a failure to comprehend the sphere of "between" where the person meets what is in the world. The dialogical relationship, it seems to me, applies to the problem of beauty. There is no distinguishable quality of beauty in objects, nor is the response merely a matter of an affective state. Beauty is a mode of being of things in dialogue with the senses of man. Things that are called beautiful present themselves from their fullness of being, and they require the person open to encounter. Beauty is the meeting between man and the sensuous presence of something in the world. It is the encounter with something in being in which the meeting place is the sense world and in which the conditions of sensuous presence are referred to. The terms "meeting" and "encounter" have here the full significance which they have throughout Buber's writing.

The "striking," the "arresting," the "absorbing," are not the "beautiful." They do not step towards the person and speak to him as an integral presence. Rather they suck him in, they shock or

---

[20] See Beardsley, *op. cit.*, pp. 505–512.

[21] George Santayana, *The Sense of Beauty* (New York: Charles Scribner's Sons, 1896), Part I.

overwhelm him. Their being is force, not presence. They do not meet the person in the quiet action of dialogue; they pounce on him and unsettle him. Beautiful things, on the other hand, address the person without overwhelming or unsettling him. They step out to him in wholeness from the course of being, as the Thou steps out to meet the I, but in this case with attention drawn to their sensuous presence. Thus the judgment, "This is beautiful," testifies to dialogue with the sense world, whether housed in Nature or in the work of art. Beauty is not some emergent quality of objects nor an affective state, but the overarching of dialogue between sensible, present being and the wholeness of a personal existence.

I should now like to show how I think two of the arts—music and poetry—might be approached within the framework of Buber's thought.

In the field of musical aesthetics much discussion has centered on the question whether non-vocal and non-program music has a meaning, or an "extra-musical reference." More precisely, a connection has been sought between the qualities of human emotional experience and "pure" musical works through the notion of meaning. Music, it has been said, "expresses" emotion, i.e., the composer has embodied or objectified certain emotional qualities. These, it is argued, can be called qualities which the music itself possesses, and furthermore the music can evoke similar feelings in a listener.

An alternative theory, to which Mrs. Langer among others subscribes,[22] considers the "expression" theory inexact, and prefers to say that music "signifies" or "symbolizes" a pattern of feeling outside the music. The music is regarded as an "iconic sign" of the inner life of feeling. Its patterns are similar to psychological processes, and the music constitutes a sign or symbol of these processes.

The "expression" theory and the "symbolic" theory claim for music a meaning, i.e., a referential relationship to something outside it, and this is taken to be human emotion. On the opposing side are those who flatly deny that music properly so called has a meaning. Music consists of organized sound and embodies only musical ideas. We may attach emotional significance to certain musical passages, but this is our own doing entirely. The music itself does not "represent" or "symbolize" our emotions. The most a proponent of this

---

[22] See *Feeling and Form*, Chaps. 7 and 8.

view, such as Hanslick,[23] and in our own time, Stravinsky,[24] is likely to admit, is an analogy between the dynamic properties of our emotions and musical passages. But, according to this view, the music in no case embodies the feeling itself, only the motion involved in the feeling.

Still another position, held for example by Monroe Beardsley,[25] recognizes "human regional qualities" in music, qualities that are said to be "phenomenally objective." Instead of referring to or representing feelings, music, according to this view, *has* such qualities as sadness or gaiety.

The view suggested by Buber's thought is that music does not refer to or represent emotions, yet does have to do with personal existence. Music is throughout organized sound, and cannot as such embody or symbolize feelings, nor may it be said to have "human regional qualities." What happens in music is that sound in its fullness of structure is brought into relation with man. In each "pure" musical work some part of the order realizable in the sphere of sound is disclosed. Every variety of structure, dynamic, shading, coloration found in encounter with the world is relevant to the encounter with the musical work. Yet nothing is given but sound itself; nothing is intended or referred to outside the work. The work does not express or symbolize any specific emotional qualities. But in its ordering of sound it can echo any phase of the world's presence to man. Each musical work calls to man as something present to him; it is a complex event from the sphere of sound which demands a response. In responding to the authentic musical work, human feeling, cognition and will are together in the wholeness of the person.

The musical work is an ordered whole which steps forward from the acoustic sphere and meets the person in dialogue. Though a phenomenal object, a pattern of sound, it has been given structure and texture by a human agent. Its musical life derives from, and speaks to, personal existence. The achievement of musical composition is to order sound in structure and texture in such a way that the total person, with feeling, cognition and will, is demanded in the response to the work. The sound does not evoke, embody, represent, or signify a feeling. Rather it has the power to address human beings as

[23] Eduard Hanslick, *The Beautiful in Music,* Chaps. II and III.

[24] Stravinsky, *op. cit.*

[25] Beardsley, *op. cit.,* Chap. VII.

an independent other, the other of sound ordered through a human act.

The response to the work involves man in his wholeness. No specific passage of music can be said to evoke a specific emotion, such as sadness or gaiety, although such emotions may dominate the response to certain passages. The response to music, like the response to any work of art, is that of the whole person; emotion is only one strand of this response. Something peculiarly whole from the sense world, specifically from the acoustic sphere, but unmistakably disclosing human ordering, confronts the listener, impinges on him, and addresses all that he is. A relation can spring up between the listener and the musical work which involves him to his depths. In such a relation sound has come to the fullness of present being. The music cannot be grasped as a symbol or an expressive form. It is tonal presence, deeply relevant to man's presence in the world. To connect music only with feeling is to suppose without warrant that feeling or emotion is somehow a separable element in man. The importance of music would seem to lie rather in its capacity to involve the listener, to interact with him, and to touch depths of the self which are not likely to be reached in any other way.

Those theories of musical aesthetics which claim that music evokes, expresses, symbolizes or has definite emotional qualities fail to see music as present sound addressing the listener and demanding a response. They attempt to connect music with human existence by speaking of a link with emotional qualities. But they have great difficulty in making clear the nature of such a connection. The connection that does seem to exist between music and human existence consists of the dialogical relationship between the musical work—sound ordered by a human agent—and the listener who makes himself present.

Buber's philosophy of dialogue suggests a certain view of poetry that may help illuminate the current situation in that art. Today, especially in America, the poem is frequently regarded as a kind of puzzle, a "structure of meanings" to be broken down, analyzed, deciphered, and miraculously reconstructed. Such features as paradox, irony, and wit are highly prized.[26] Poetry is to be studied, "under-

---

[26] Cf. Cleanth Brooks, *The Well Wrought Urn* (New York: Reynal and Hitchcock, 1947), esp. Chap. 1.

stood";[27] the poem is an intellectual treasure of complex meanings. It is something hard and opaque, formal and imposing.

This view has influenced not only the reading of poetry but the writing of it as well. Many contemporary poets in England and America, influenced by Eliot and Pound, have placed their poetic hopes on affiliating with the "institution" of poetry linked to the Tradition by formal elegance, sophisticated feeling for permanence and order, the appropriation of established symbols. They write a poetry of "technique" associated with cultivated middle-class experience.[28] Inwardness is seldom revealed in the poem; if it should break through, the poet seems to want to apologize for it. Such poetry supports Robert Penn Warren's disturbing definition: ". . . a poem is a *structure of experience* which can give us the *experience of structure.*"[29]

To offset the poetry of structured experience and technique, we have the poetry of the "beats" which often resembles a man agitating in public. Its content as well as its form feeds on rebellion, on angry and loud posturing before a society judged guilty and corrupt. The "beat" poet sees himself as a victim and his poems become weapons of resistance. The poet tries to "succeed" through the poem because society will allow him no other achievement. Unhappily however, the "beat" poet usually mistrusts genuine inwardness as much as he mistrusts "square" society. His poems are loud but empty.

In contrast to these American conceptions of the poem the words of the Rumanian-born German poet Paul Celan are strikingly suggestive: "The poem, when it is a genuine manifestation of the language and thus in the nature of a talk . . . is like a bottle ready to come to shore. . . . It is the efforts of him who . . . is without protection in a sense not known about till recently, who takes his very life into speech."[30] Directly influenced by Buber, Celan conceives the genuine poet as one who is faithful to the dialogical possibilities of language, speaking in the poem as the I who addresses the

[27] Cf. Cleanth Brooks and Robert Penn Warren, *Understanding Poetry* (rev. ed., New York: Holt, 1950), used extensively in college courses.

[28] This point has been made in several critical articles in the magazine, *The Sixties* (formerly *The Fifties*).

[29] In *Newsweek* magazine, quoted on back cover, *The Sixties*, fourth issue (Fall, 1960).

[30] *Die Neue Rundschau*, First Issue (1958). Selected translation, *The Fifties*, Third Issue (1959) , p. 58.

world as Thou. The poet is exposed, one "who takes his very life into speech." The poem is a talk, an act of the poet in which the world and other men are addressed. The poem reveals the poet in the act of encounter. The poem is not a "structure of experience" or "structure of meanings" but a living speech charged with the intensity of dialogue and dominated by a movement towards wholeness. Ordinary language takes on "form" as the poet's talk becomes encounter, a meeting of the One with the Other, mediated by language.

Such a view of poetry places "content" ahead of "technique," or formal features. It is the view to which Boris Pasternak subscribed when he said in an interview shortly before his death: "I have never understood those dreams of a new language, of a completely original form of expression. . . . The most extraordinary discoveries are made when the artist is overwhelmed by what he has to say. Then he uses the old language in his urgency and the old language is transformed from within."[31] The genuine poet preserves what is in the world in its dialogical presence through responsive and responsible speech.

I should like now to say something about criticism. The view I have suggested does not propose a kind of value premise, a normative principle from which specific critical rules can be derived. It does not offer a definition of good art in terms of observable features or of the response of an audience. Nor does it purport to offer a canon for criticism which constitutes a prediction as to what sorts of works are most likely to produce "aesthetic experience,"[32] although it takes seriously the interaction between the work and the audience.

What this view does attempt to do is to connect art with an account of what man is, an account which is in the nature of personal testimony or witness. It suggests to me that the main thing in the encounter with works of art is not a judgment of good or bad, but the creation of a dialogical relationship. One who encounters works of art may meet a world in the richness of its presence. The fulfillment of this opportunity rather than the development of "taste" would seem to be of first importance.

One would think that this point need hardly be made, except for

---

[31] "Three Visits with Boris Pasternak" (The Art of Fiction XXV), *The Paris Review*, No. 24, p. 59.

[32] See Beardsley, *op. cit.*, pp. 524–556 for an account of an "instrumentalist theory" of aesthetic value.

the attempt of analytical aesthetics to justify canons for critical evaluation.[33] This attempt raises the question of what criticism ought to try to do. The answer suggested to me by Buber's thought is that the critic ought to do little in the way of evaluation. His task ought to be primarily that of a matchmaker. He ought to try to create conditions favorable to a meeting between the work of art and its potential audience. This is not the place to go into the problem of justifying standards for objective criticism. The difficulties do seem to me to be insuperable, and I am rather happy that this should be the case. Why should anyone desire objective criticism in the first place? One who encounters works of art should claim responsibility for the exposed position he must take in responding to these works.

A critic will undoubtedly prefer some works over others. He should be encouraged to announce his preferences and certainly he should be urged to give his reasons. But for many the critic's reasons will not be persuasive because they do not value those features in works which the critic values. At this point there is nothing to justify a critic's insistence that he is right, in spite of those who hold a "best equipped observer" theory. I would also suggest that the critic should exercise care and restraint in interpretation. He must cause the work to step forward, not obstruct it by his own interpretative constructions.

I would qualify these remarks to this extent: where there is clarity with regard to value premises, as to how "good" is to be defined, critical evaluation of works of art may be carried on profitably as a kind of heuristic method to help initiate the uninitiated. But the mature person who has had a fair amount of experience of works of art should in no way feel himself bound by the valuations of any critic. He is likely to have become attached more or less deeply to certain works which for him are at the center of the world of art. These works suggest to him what art might be; they bring close to him a world which is transfigured, which has become present being. No external critical evaluations should be allowed to intervene between him and these works.

Finally it should be noted that most artists would very likely not express their own view of art in terms of dialogue. Some, such as Paul Celan, may work consciously with a view of art as dialogical involvement. Others may seem to work in the same way without a

33 Cf. *ibid.*, Chap. X.

conscious idea. Still others may explicitly or implicitly oppose such a notion, especially those who see art as play or who, like André Malraux,[34] see it as a challenge to destiny offered in an imaginative world in which alone the human spirit can be free. One who accepts the dialogical view can only attest to it and try to suggest to his opponent the unnoticed dialogical relation in his own involvement. He might also suggest that "art" embraces many ventures, that it is a seeking after its own possibilities, a constant attempt to reach its own center; that the artist, in answering the demand of a form to be made into a work, brings into being an independent Other which remains in perpetual tension with the individual existence of its maker, with the complex realm of human culture, including all the art of the past, and with the concrete existences of its potential audience.

[34] Cf. his *The Voices of Silence,* trans. Stuart Gilbert (Garden City: Doubleday and Co., Inc., 1953), esp. pp. 312–334.

LOUIS Z. HAMMER

DEPARTMENT OF PHILOSOPHY
WELLESLEY COLLEGE

28

Carl Kerényi

MARTIN BUBER AS CLASSICAL AUTHOR

THIS pointing to Martin Buber—a pointing which he did not need, but which is probably needed by those who know him only as historian of religion, philosopher, teacher, interpreter and translater of the highest competence and artistry of speech—imposes on itself a limitation since it renounces everything else and only wants to show in him that through which he already belongs in the ranks of our classical authors.

One takes in hand a youthful work of Buber's: the German selection from the Talks and Parables of Chuang-tzu (republished in the *Manesse-Bibliothek der Weltliteratur,* 1951). The translation—from English works with the help of a Chinese coworker—still hardly has the competence of Buber's translations of Hebrew literature. One reads, however, the study that follows as epilogue. It attempts to determine the three basic forces out of which the indicating spirit of the East builds itself and of which the Occident only possesses two creatively—science and law:

'Science' includes all information about the 'is,' whether earthly or heavenly, these two being never and nowhere separated, but uniting into the sphere of being which is the subject of science.
'Law' includes all the commands of an 'ought,' human and divine, these two being never and nowhere separated from one another, but uniting into the sphere of ought which is the subject of law. . . .
To science and law there belongs, as the third basic force of the Eastern spirit, the teaching.
The teaching includes no subjects, it has only *one* subject—itself: the one thing needful. It stands beyond 'is' and 'ought,' information and command; it knows how to say only one thing, the needful that must be realized in genuine life.[1]

From the moment when Buber begins to define the "teaching" (". . . it has only one subject, itself . . ."), the reader holds his

[1] "The Teaching of the Tao," *Pointing the Way,* p. 32f.

breath, even when as an Occidental he is not especially inclined toward just this "basic force": then it strikes, like lightning, then it *hits*—in content and in language. Thus speaks a classical author, not an author of the Orient, not even a biblical or a later author of the Hebrew tongue, but one of "ours," in the line that leads from the Greeks and the Romans to us, and a classical author of the German language, from whom it would be easy to produce exemplary pages—*pages choisies*—as is customary from French authors. At the same time it also lies close to that special sphere to attain which our classical authors have always striven, proceeding from Buber's definition of the "teaching," distinguishing it from it to designate and to show how he himself participates in that striving characteristic of the Occident.

The essential difference of the teaching from science and law, according to Buber, is also documented by history: "The teaching forms itself independently of science and law until it finds its pure fulfillment in a central human life." Its way, accordingly, is not that of the development of knowledge but just this: that of fulfillment in a central human life. "To fulfill" means in Palestine as in China: "To raise something that has been handed down out of the conditioned into the unconditioned." The teaching does not develop. "It cannot develop after it has found its fulfillment in the central human life; rather it becomes rule, like the teaching of the Buddha." Buber also characterizes the "central man." It is not Lao-tzu or the Buddha but Jesus who comes before him in this connection, although he does not describe this particular one but the fulfilling man in general and even him only in order to teach what teaching is:

For him, in incomparably higher measure than for the great ruler, the great artist, and the great philosopher, all that is scattered, fleeting, and fragmentary grows together into unity; this unity is his life. The ruler has his organization of peoples, the artist has his work, the philosopher has his system of ideas; the fulfilling man has only his life. His words are elements of this life, each an executor and originator, each inspired by destiny and caught up by destiny, the multitude of voices transformed through this human body into a conclusive harmony, the weak movement of many dead joined in him into might, he who is the crossroads of the teaching, of fulfillment and dissolution, salvation and degeneration. There are, therefore, logia [words of Christ] that no doubt can touch, and that, striding through the generations without being written down, preserve themselves unmixed, by the strength of their stamp of destiny and the elementary uniqueness of their fulfilling speech. For the fulfilling man . . . is the most unique of men. Though all seeking desires him and all self-communion foresees him, he is recognized by few when he appears, and these few are probably not at all those who foresaw and desired him: so great is his uniqueness—so unoriginal, so unpretentious, so wholly the final genuineness of mankind.[2]

If one regards Christ thus, or even *only* thus—that he is regarded by Christendom as God and Saviour is for Buber a fact of the greatest seriousness, indeed, "the true seriousness of Western history" that he seeks to comprehend[3]—then it becomes clear that the Occident, in so far as it became and remained Christian, could produce no "teaching," after the Greeks and Romans had failed to do so. (The Cynic-Stoic attempt led to special individuals, when need arose, to martyrs and to a more spiritual ruling figure, but not to a "central man.") Instead of it, in the West since Homer another "basic force"—next to the Greek spiritual knowledge and the law founded by the Romans—has been at work: an art of evocation whose fulfillment takes the form of works of literature, its object and subject not the "central man," but man. It was no unauthorized simplification when Goethe wanted, as the foundation of the "world literature" whose approach he greeted, to place Greek literature as the model with the justification that in the works of the Greeks *man* was always represented—with the addition of an adjective corresponding to his ideal: "the beautiful man." It is undoubtedly one of the basic forces of the West, this spiritual force that we have had *before* the "teaching" and then also *with* the "teaching," in the most fruitful, ever of itself increasing unification with it, and—for this Buber too is an example—today still have: a striving for man fulfilling itself in the working of the evocative word. The peoples of the Occident have taken over this striving from the Greeks and have ever again heightened it to a mastery that we owe to our non-Greek classical authors and that has in fact led to a world literature in Goethe's sense of the term.

We do not have a name for this spiritual force, as already the Greeks had no names for it. It is certainly an art, but no mere formation, and is not even limited to poetry. One can at the most circumscribe it or talk of it in similes. One could call it an animating or reanimating force, as were those that, through the sacrificial action of Odysseus on the rim of Hades, made the shades into beings full of life and spirit. The poet or writer betakes himself with that force into

2 *Ibid.*, p. 39f.

3 *The Origin and Meaning of Hasidism*, p. 109.

a realm of shadows that are imprisoned in yellowed and forgotten books and reanimates them and causes them to ascend spiritualized, or he seeks for a landscape of the soul, a deep level of himself, or he does both, where a level of the soul meets a level of human history, a landscape of the soul recognizes itself in one outside the soul. He animates the shadowy, causes the dumb to sound forth in words, makes man and world transparent to the spirit. The bearers of such spiritual force, our classical authors, are all discoverers and conquerors, re-conquerors of the apparently lost, and with every discovery, which seemingly takes them beyond man, rediscoverers of man.

Something powerful in man himself went down into a shadow existence in the West through the Christian teaching—in so far as it did not enter into its framework—just that powerful realm of the soul that had brought forth the great religious creations in the history of mankind. In more recent times it had no longer been entered, feared, shunned by the greatest bearers of the Western spiritual force of which we speak—until Hölderlin. He was the first of the writers of the new era who as poet and seer broke through to there where Buber, as scholar and interpreter, but finally as evocative writer, also wanders—through other historical and geographical landscapes, yet in the same realm of the human. Greek poets of the classical age—and still more so Dante—no matter how much their creation proves itself in religious material, stood within "religion," whereas there, where Hölderlin penetrates, intercourse with gods takes place—outside of the existing "religion." The religion that could take its origin from this intercourse, is best comprehended in its rise. One lingers there in the original situation of the religions, which then—in the course of history—cease to be characterized by such a state of immediacy. Thereby, however, the place is also given, to find which, to delimit it—to separate it from "religion"—to clarify it, to point to it has always been Martin Buber's passionate striving. There is hardly another scholar of religion, religious and conscious of his religiousness, who has made such severe judgments about religion as he. "Only in its decline that begins soon after this fulfilment does the teaching mingle"—so Buber sees its fate—"with elements of science and law. Out of such intermixture there arises a religion: a product of the contamination in which information, command, and the necessary are welded into a contradictory and effective whole."[4] In *The*

---

[4] "The Teaching of the Tao," *op. cit.,* p. 33f.

Origin and Meaning of Hasidism, where Buber expresses the most important findings that his research in the history of religion has ascertained, it says right out: "The primal danger of man is 'religion'." And why? Because on the human side of the intercourse with God (or with the gods) something easily detaches itself and becomes independent: the forms of the intercourse, the psychological accompanying circumstances, the devotion, the absorption, the ecstacy, in a religion rich in images—we add—the image itself. This detached realm that makes itself independent—religion—easily steps between God and man and finally replaces the irreplaceable, the immediacy of a state open, receptive and fruitful for God and the divine; whereby what is in question is not a development that proceeds from the "teaching," but from the "intercourse."

Whatever the presuppositions of such a state are, there is here a realm of the universally human. In *Ekstatische Konfessionen* (1909) Martin Buber puts together an anthology approaching this realm out of the confessions of the mystics. But his great find lies in a still more hidden sphere that must first be received into our consciousness of the history of the spirit.

One can properly speak of a discovery from the viewpoint of the world literature, into which we already saw enter as classical authors in their lifetime two contemporaries of Buber and compatriots of his youth—the four years' older Hofmannsthal and the three years' older Rilke. He who wants to assess the place of Buber in German literature must seek it in part in the vicinity of these two, in a common atmosphere of style and spirit, but at the same time also in another sphere, which extends to the East and the North, far beyond the boundaries of the cultural world defined by Vienna: in the special world of Polish-Ukrainian Judaism. Nevertheless, it would be mistaken to reckon him among the literary discoverers, that is, describers of East European Judaism. He is a dis-coverer, that is uncoverer in the basic meaning of the word, one who found what was covered over in that East-European Jewish environment no less than in himself. He hardly exaggerates when in his *Origin and Meaning of Hasidism* he observes that next to the Vedic doctrine of sacrifices the ritual formulations of Judaism are the most gigantic structure of spiritual commands. What that must mean by way of a more dangerous, more oppressive "religion" in Buber's sense of the term, is not easy to express. How deeply he had to penetrate then into a "religious" literature until he made his findings! "At first ever again repelled by the brittle, ungainly, unshapely material, gradually overcoming the strangeness, discovering the characteristic, beholding the essential with growing devotion"—so recounts his "Way to Hasidism" (1918)

Until one day I opened a little book entitled the *Zevaat Ribesh*—that is, the testament of Rabbi Israel Baal-Shem—and the words flashed toward me, 'He takes unto himself the quality of fervor. He arises from sleep with fervor, for he is hallowed and become another man and is worthy to create and is become like the Holy One, blessed be He, when He created His world.' It was then that, overpowered in an instant, I experienced the Hasidic soul. The primally Jewish opened to me, flowering to newly conscious expression in the darkness of exile: man's being created in the image of God I grasped as deed, as becoming, as task. And this primally Jewish reality was a primal human reality, the content of human religiousness. Judaism as religiousness, as 'piety,' as *Hasidut* opened to me there. The image out of my childhood, the memory of the zaddik and his community, rose upward and illuminated me: I recognized the idea of the perfected man. At the same time I became aware of the summons to proclaim it to the world.[5]

We disregard here the personal report of Buber's and keep to the objective state of facts which Buber again, now as historian of religion, describes: to that phenomenon of Jewish spiritual history that supersedes and puts aside that phenomenon in part contemporaneous with it, the also humanly instructive (although otherwise than the movement of the Hasidim, the "Pious," and their masters, the zaddikim, the "proved ones"), but unfortunately all too little known tragicomedy of the "Messiahs" Sabbatai Zvi and Jakob Frank. Five successive generations of zaddikim form together—so Buber describes this extraordinary manifestation—

a group of religious personalities of a vitality, a spiritual powerfulness, and a manifold originality such as, to my knowledge, have nowhere in the history of religions been concentrated in so short a span of time. But the most important fact about them is that each of them was surrounded by a community that lived a brotherly life and was able to live it through the fact that a leader was there who brought them all closer together by bringing them closer to that in which they believed. In an otherwise not very productive century— even in Eastern Europe—the 'unenlightened' Polish and Ukrainian Jewry brought forth the greatest phenomenon in the history of the spirit, greater than any individual genius in art and in thought: a society that lives by its faith.[6]

In addition this was a faith of so concrete a this-worldliness and of immediacy in relation to God as is possible only in the beginning—

5 *Hasidism and Modern Man*, p. 58f.

6 "The Beginnings," *The Origin and Meaning of Hasidism*, p. 27.

and at the end of religion, in the case where this end does not at
the same time mean the dying away of the creative-religious but where
everything points to the necessity of "now again reaching a beginning, a beginning of a real life for the real God in the real world."
And then the description of this state, which almost bears the marks
of Greek religiosity:

One may and should live genuinely with all, but one should live with it in
consecration, one should hallow all that one does in his natural life. No renunciation is commanded. One eats in consecration, one savors one's taste of
food in consecration, and the table becomes an altar. One works in consecration and lifts the sparks that are hidden in all tools. One walks over the fields
in consecration, and the silent songs of all creatures, those they speak to God,
enter into the song of one's own soul. One drinks to one's companions in consecration, each to the other, and it is as if one studied together with them in
the Torah. One dances in consecration, and a splendor radiates over the
community.[7]

So it is written in *The Origin and Meaning of Hasidism*, and even
such a description of a historical set of facts itself always works as a
proclamation. It is, as it were, two-dimensional, the exemplary front
side but not yet the illumination of a human phenomenon, such as
our "world literature" demands. Buber has advanced further, he has
been carried forward to an evocation which takes our breath away
in a wholly other manner than the stylistic perfection of his insights
into the phenomena of the spirit. In this case the formation of the
German language is even secondary. This work, which in addition
to the dimensions of plasticity and fullness of life also possesses those
of the soul and the spirit and reveals depths of vision beyond the
intentions of the master—to be sure, by means of this mastery—, the
work whereby Buber in a primary manner belongs to the ranks of
classical authors who form for us world literature, was first written
by him in Hebrew and only after that also in German. It bears the
title *For the Sake of Heaven*—first printed in Hebrew in 1941—but
it does not need to have a title, it could also simply be called "The
Chronicle," since, corresponding to its designation it actually is "a
chronicle," yet one that may stand in its simpler way on the heights
of prose epic next to masterworks that earlier would have been
called "historical novels"—thus next to Thomas Mann's *Erwählten*
(*The Chosen*) or Pär Lagerkvist's *Barrabbas*.

[7] *Ibid., p.* 55f.

What is the nature of this "chronicle" Buber tells us in the Foreword to the second edition. His translation of the Hasidic literature
began with retelling it in the form of legends: *The Tales of Rabbi
Nachman* (1906), *The Legend of the Baal-Shem* (1908). Then he
turned to the genus whose material fills the Hasidic writings: the
"holy" anecdote, not wholly without parallels in the philosophic and
devotional literature of other cultures, but only here a literary task.
Buber discharged it in several works that today are united in *The
Tales of the Hasidim (Manesse Bibliothek der Weltliteratur)*. It is a
matter almost throughout of the blending of an event with a saying,
since the Hasidic intention, which aims at the oneness of outer and
inner experience, in fact expresses just this blending. The event must
be narrated with extreme concentration in order that the saying
may arise from it. But the epic content of the Hasidic traditions was
not exhausted thereby. "I have been accustomed"—so Buber reports
further in the "Foreword"

to renounce material which neither was told anecdotally nor could be reduced to this utmost terseness of form. I have not been concerned merely to
narrate but to narrate something specific, something that seemed to me of the
utmost import, so that it cried out for narration, something which had not
yet been properly narrated and to which to give its right form seemed my
duty. In this process I came upon an enormous coil of stories of interrelated
content. They unquestionably formed a great cycle, even though they had
obviously been narrated according to two different and, indeed, contradictory
traditions and tendencies. This group of stories could not be eliminated,
especially because the happenings that stood at their center were of the highest significance. The material had generally been treated from a legendary
perspective, but the kernel of reality was unmistakable. It is a fact that several
zaddikim actually attempted by means of theurgic or magic activities (the so-
called Practical Kabbala) to make of Napoleon that 'God of the Land of
Magog,' mentioned by Ezekiel, whose wars, as is proclaimed by several eschatological texts, were to precede the coming of the Messiah. Other *zaddikim*
opposed these attempts with the monition that no outer gestures or events
but only the inner return of the entire human being to God could prepare
the approach of redemption. And what is so extraordinary and remarkable
is the fact that all these men, both magicians and monitors, actually died
within the space of a single year. Thus there can be little doubt that the
spiritual sphere in which they were involved, although from different sides,
consumed their mortal being. Hence it is not a legendary symbol but a simple fact of experience that in this conflict both sides were annihilated. . . .
The 'epic mood' became a duty in this case. But I could no longer, as in my

youth, use a free creative activity. I was forced to obey the law of these inner connections, to supply lacks according to the meaning of what preceded and what followed, of the events and characters themselves.[8]

The great achievement that Buber has accomplished with this work of narration is not only the successful "supplementations": the great achievement is the evocation of fighters of the spirit who are without comparison in the whole of epic world literature in the ardor and exclusiveness of the unfolding of their religious powers and of just those fiery spheres that they themselves have brought forth and in which they have consumed their lives. There is nothing more shattering in the history of the spirit than the overbearing not merely on the part of the thinker, but also on that of the seer. Greek tragedy, in which Tiresias is victorious over Oedipus, the man blinded by power, does not yet know it and neither does the Old Testament. This "height" of humanity had been reserved for later ages, and no work of our time speaks of it so unambiguously and clearly as the "Chronicle": since Buber wanted to communicate this shattering to us as no one else has. Does the seer and man of religious "deed" still correspond for him to the "idea of the perfected man," after he had succeeded in *this* evocation of the "Seer" of Lublin—or only to an image of man, to whom such genius also belongs, but which can also become tragic in its turn? The men of fire also have to do with great darknesses. In the "Chronicle" the disciple asks the Seer:

. . . 'Rabbi,' he said in an almost failing voice, 'what is the nature of this Gog? He can exist in the outer world only because he exists within us.' He pointed to his own breast. 'The darkness out of which he was hewn needed to be taken from nowhere else . . .'[9]

Buber quotes this passage in one of his wisest books—*Images of Good and Evil*—and adds: "For a full understanding of the passage one must bear in mind the time in which I wrote the narrative." It must have been the time immediately before 1941. His heart is with that questioning disciple who with powerful religious love-energy willed the turning, not the strengthening of the evil as a preparation for the good, and near whom the one loving wife died of neglect, the other became a scolding adversary. Martin Buber has also accomplished this great achievement: he has allowed the good *and*

[8] *For the Sake of Heaven* (2nd ed.) , p. viii f.

[9] *Ibid.*, p. 54.

the evil, the holy *and* the dangerous to appear in his own and his most beloved sphere. His Chronicle rises above conditions of time and people as does every work which is a "classic."

C. KERÉNYI

ASCONA
SWITZERLAND

29

Helmut Kuhn

DIALOGUE IN EXPECTATION

MARTIN BUBER is a religious author. This fact no one may disregard who wishes to communicate with him. All religious life and reflection is carried on in a state of expectancy, since it is, in its very nature, directed toward the yet withheld presence of God. Thus, in order to enter the sphere of the discussions to which Buber has given rise, we shall attempt to prepare the way for a dialogue with him "in expectation."

But that is only one—and not the most important—meaning of that term. The dialogue to which Buber himself invites his readers is concerned with truth, and nothing but truth. It is designed as a philosophical dialogue in Plato's sense. A question is posed and an answer is expected that accords with the persons, the problem, and the demands of the situation. In this sense, every philosophical conversation is a dialogue "in expectation."

This philosophic intent alone must determine the manner in which we will approach Buber's thought. We are—as he is—concerned with philosophic truth. Even the aura of religious expectation in which the dialogue begins must submit to being questioned about its philosophical significance. Since, however, the principle of dialogue in Buber's thought implies a religious position, the question as to its relationship to Christianity cannot be entirely eschewed. To make it explicit and to answer it, however, must be left to others more qualified to do so.

There is still a narrower and more specific philosophic meaning which the term expectation, in addition to its religious and its general philosophic import, can assume. It refers to one of Buber's central concepts, that of meeting, or encounter. The question has often been asked: what caused Buber's friend and contemporary, Max Scheler, to surrender his theistic metaphysic in favor of a dualism of powerful life versus an originally powerless spirit? At the risk of oversimplifying the answer, one may recall the revealing fact that Scheler found the criterion of reality in the experience of resistance. For Buber, however, the criterion of reality in all its forms, or rather, the human approach to reality, consists in an encounter—in meeting a partner. And this answer to the question concerning reality is the better answer and more in accord with the nature of metaphysics. Meeting—in contradistinction to the experience of resistance—engages the *entire* human being as a person—'be-souled' body and embodied soul—and for that reason it may disclose a perspective of the entire stratified order of reality. It knows of no absolute differentiation between intellectual intuition and sensory experience. Buber himself recognized that in meeting it is not only the human partner but the universe in its entirety that is opened up, humanity as well as nature. Thus the idea of a universal order imposes itself. Meetings require to be taken out of their isolation as events in space and time and to be integrated, through the *Logos* of Being, into the unity of human experience. The philosophy of meeting promises a liberation from the desperately self-enclosed egology of existential philosophy.

But how else can I meet the other but by our being placed over against each other within the total *societas entium* which metaphysics explores? This is the question we ask. It arouses an expectation which is to guide and pervade all other questions engendered by our interpretation. The meaning of 'Meeting', so it seems to us, needs to be counterbalanced by the conception of an all-embracing order.

I

Luther and Calvin believe that the Word of God has so descended among men that it can be clearly known and must therefore be exclusively advocated. I do not believe that; the Word of God crosses my vision like a falling star to whose fire the meteorite will bear witness without making it light up for me, and I myself can only bear witness to the light but not produce the stone and say 'This is it.'

Thus wrote Martin Buber in his essay *Zwiesprache*, first published in 1930.[1] He had then already crossed the half-century mark, and he had long made a great name for himself in the cultural life of Germany.

Much has happened since those days. We have experienced the moral bankruptcy of Nazi despotism and the military and political debacle of the Second World War. Today, we come to find ourselves

---

[1] Published in English as "Dialogue," *Between Man and Man*, p. 7.

again as in a different world. The Word of God has descended upon us as a Word of Judgment, and we, singed though not burnt by the falling meteorite, marvel at having been spared.

In this transformed world, Buber no longer lives in our midst. The "helper"—as Albrecht Goes characterized him a few years ago at the Paulskirche in Frankfurt[2]—has remained kind as he was, to be sure, and we in turn were able to show him when he visited us that there is a home for him in Germany, not only among the surviving elders but also among the young who grew up meanwhile and are affectionately devoted to him. To locate him, however, we must turn to Jerusalem instead of calling on him, as we formerly did, in Heppenheim. But in order to find him, we must, first and foremost, look at his message, which is not tied to any particular spot on this earth.

More than a quarter of a century ago he set down those lines quoted above, in years previous to the recent catastrophes, but already overshadowed by the approaching disaster. Yet those words strike our ear with undiminished force when we read them again today. Perhaps we must admit that the initial impact of this message causes in us some sort of consternation, the very effect these lines had on us before. We may remember St. Paul's "For the letter killeth, but the spirit giveth life" (2 Cor. 3:6), and find no difficulty in making this truth our own. But Buber does not intend, in the above passage, to summon the Apostle Paul against Luther and Calvin, since he regards Paul's and John's interpretation of the figure of Jesus a Hellenizing alienation and a deviation from the straight line of Jewish Messianism, from the mandate given by the King-God to His kingly people. The messianic faith of Israel, which Buber has held ever since he began to write, is "in its essence, the tendency to fulfill the God-man relationship under the aegis of the perfected Kingship of God."[3] And no redemptive act of the past, according to Buber, is needed to establish this relationship.

Yet the passage about the falling star is disturbing. This is the case not because the freedom from the "worded word" which is proclaimed therein differs fundamentally from the freedom through

2 "Martin Buber der Beistand," *Ruf und Echo* (Frankfurt a.M.: S. Fischer, 1956).

3 *Königtum Gottes* (3rd ed.; Heidelberg: Lambert Schneider, 1956), [my translation, no authorized translation available]. The book is one continuous attempt to prove the validity of the sentence quoted from the Old Testament.

grace, vouchsafed by Christ's death and resurrection, which Paul proclaimed. This, at most, is disturbing only insofar as the continued existence of Judaism as such presents Christians with a thought-provoking challenge. But has there not opened up, one may anxiously ask, between *verbum* and *verba,* between the unutterable Word and the spoken words, a gulf so wide that neither a religion, holding to dogmas and articles of faith, nor a metaphysics expressing itself through propositions, can hope to bridge it? The objection raised against Luther and Calvin may, in a somewhat different form, hold likewise against the Catholic Church and certainly against the legalistic religion of the Synagogue. All established rituals and dogmatic positions bid fair to be devoured by the flames of an inwardness which insists on an immediate manifestation of the spirit in the lived instant, the here and now.

Stirred by such doubt, we begin to scrutinize the simile employed by Buber. His metaphors and imagery can hardly ever be taken seriously enough. Buber does not invent them for the purpose of effective illustration—they rather come to him simultaneously with his thoughts. It is precisely this consanguinity of the pictorial-dramatic and the human *mise en scène* on the one hand and the ideas on the other—an inheritance from the Hasidic tradition—which, together with the rhythmic and restrained cadence of his periods, lends a quiet and dignified beauty to his German prose (though one may add that he achieved supreme mastery of style not as a narrator or philosopher, but as the creator of a Bible translation, jointly undertaken with Franz Rosenzweig, a truly epoch-making work). The simile of our text speaks of the incandescent fluid mass of the meteorite which cools after the impact and petrifies. Now, it would be misleading to search for the origin of the image in, say, the Kabbalah; and by no means, generally speaking, can all questions of origin raised by Buber's ideas be answered by pointing to the Hasidic tradition, which he so ardently loved and from which he drew so much rich nourishment. He was fond of calling himself a Polish Jew. Yet he was least of all a son of the Ghetto. The Galician home of his grandfather, the scholarly farmer, under whose care he was brought up until the age of fourteen, was pervaded by the spirit of the Haskalah, the Jewish enlightenment. From here he went back to his birthplace, Vienna, to study.[4] In Vienna and Berlin, the centers of Austrian

---

[4] Cf. Maurice S. Friedman, *Martin Buber, the Life of Dialogue* (Chicago: The University of Chicago Press, 1955), a work rich in valuable information.

and German cultural life, his mind was formed. Among the formative elements were, according to his own testimony, German mysticism from Meister Eckhart to Angelus Silesius.5 Wide awake and susceptible to the problems that engaged the thinkers around the turn
of the century, he let himself be influenced by the three great representatives of *Lebensphilosophie* (philosophy of life), Nietzsche,
Bergson, and Dilthey. It also was a type of *Lebensphilosophie* to
which he became exposed through Georg Simmel. This influence of
the "philosophy of life," a powerful and predominant influence in
the pre-war years, he has since assimilated and mastered through
critical examination. But recognizable traces have remained. The
simile of the fiery liquid and the cooled-down stone is such a trace
and, as all traces, it has a story to relate.

That modern verson of Heraclitean thought issuing in melodious
cadence from the mouth of Georg Simmel, who was teaching in
Berlin, has by now become almost a saga of bygone days. This was
essentially a picture-philosophy, the spirited paraphrase of only one
melancholic vision. The inner eye beholds life as a stream in in-
cessant flux, always identical with itself and yet changing from instant to instant. As a fog which magically thickens into shapes, clearly
delineated figures for a while rise out of this stream of life: human
institutions, social structures, forms of art, systems of science and
philosophy, doctrines, forms of belief, cultures. All these configurations display structural principles at work. In what they have in
common as well as in their special characteristics, they obey certain
stylistic laws. "Hard and strong is weak, weak and tender is strong,"
as a Chinese proverb has it. The solidity of structure conceals a fatal
petrification and an alienation from life. Structured life is the tomb
of life brought to a standstill—as in Buber's simile: the meteorite
cannot rekindle the extinguished fire.

It is difficult for us today to do justice to this kind of philosophy.
The volatile subtlety of its definitions, the open view it had for the
historical panorama with its multifarious, stylistically-determined
forms, all this, in our estimation, recedes behind the fact that here
metaphysical truth was turned upside down. That which Hegel had
termed idea or spirit has here, in the succession to Schopenhauer,
been replaced by an irrational force. The "life" of these philosophers
of life is a descendant of the blind, irrational will of Schopenhauer's

5 "What is Man?" *Between Man and Man.*

metaphysics. Through this substitution, metaphysics suffers what theology would suffer if someone were to assert: "Heaven and hell are essentially one and the same. So let us, with William Blake, celebrate the marriage of the two." And indeed, this disastrous theologoumenon lurks behind the metaphysical confusion. Its immediate consequence, however, is that the difference between supra-rational and infra-rational is canceled by the idea of an irrational absolute. The time has come for the music of Leverkühn, in which the angelic choir blends with the choir of infernal spirits.

We have approached the root of our uneasiness and now can lay it bare. The contact is there, to be sure, with the philosophy of life and its Absolute which negates all affirmations as so many petrifactions of creative life. But Buber, the author of *Dialogue,* overcame long ago this perilous affinity to a negative metaphysics. His being able to do so had been the fruit of an inner struggle which had been resolved, if not engendered, by the experience of the First World War. For Buber, as well as for many of his contemporaries, the philosophy of life had been the giddy path on which one had to grope one's way toward metaphysical truth. Now what the perversion of metaphysical truth through the philosophy of life actually amounted to was an elimination of the difference between the 'above' and the 'below.' In Buber's line about the Word of God, however, which descends before our eyes like a meteorite, nothing could be clearer, firmer, and more definite than this difference of symbolic direction. The Word comes from above, from God. The dimension in which alone one can find metaphysical and religious truth—nay, in which alone one can meaningfully look for it—this dimension is secured beyond all questionableness. Residual vestiges of the philosophy of life undeniably remain. Yet they cannot make us overlook the fact that a dam is erected here against the Heraclitean flood. A solid divide emerges that makes the waters part as in the story of creation.

Dixit quoque Deus: Fiat firmamentum in medio aquarum, et divisit aquas ab aquis.—Et fecit Deus firmamentum, divisitique aquas, quae erant sub firmamento, ab his, quae erant super firmamentum. Et factum est ita.

In Buber's translation:

> Gott sprach:
> Gewölb werde inmitten der Wasser
> und sei Scheide von Wasser und Wasser!

Gott machte das **Gewölb**
und schied zwischen dem Wasser, das unterhalb des Gewölbs
war und dem Wasser, das oberhalb des Gewölbs war.
Es war so.[6]

Buber was not the only one who endeavored to secure the threatened "divide between waters and waters." Likeminded friends gathered around him. The journal *Die Kreatur* (1926-1930) which he, the Jew, published together with the Catholic Joseph Wittig and the Protestant Viktor von Weizsäcker, did not seek a rapprochement of the three different faiths through compromise, but it sought to redefine, in an hour of deadly peril, the above and the below, thus keeping open the common dimension of faith and man's turning to God. Wherever Buber perceived that this cause was betrayed, he insisted on a strict parting of the ways. This, for instance, happened a few years after the First World War in his relation to Max Scheler. It was Scheler who, after deserting the theism of his Catholic period, had reapproached the position of the philosophy of life by means of his doctrine of the "becoming of God out of the primal ground within us and through us."[7] Even as an apostate, Scheler, to be sure, had maintained a strict differentiation between "spirit" and "life." But the shocks of the war had convinced him of the essential powerlessness of the spirit. Buber knew nothing of this change of heart and was greatly surprised at Scheler's announcing one day: "I have come very near your narrow ridge." Buber reports (in 1938):

In the first moment I was nonplussed, for if there was anything I did not expect from Scheler it was the giving up the supposed knowledge about the ground of being. But in the next moment I answered, 'But it is not where you think it is.' For in the meantime I had understood that Scheler did not really mean that standpoint which I had then, and have had since then; he confused it with a point of view which I had cherished and upheld for a long time, and which indeed was not far from his new philosophy of the becoming God.[8]

Buber had been affected differently by the war from the manner in which Scheler was. It took him away from a theosophic philosophy of life, which had been nourished by the Kabbalah and German mysticism, and placed him on the "narrow ridge." The meaning of

---

[6] *Die fünf Bücher der Weisheit.*

[7] *Die Stellung des Menschen im Kosmos* (Munich: Nymphenburger Verlagshandlung, 1947).

[8] *Between Man and Man,* p. 184.

his ridge road, which he commends us to take, will become clear when we pick up the text at the point where our quotation ended.

II

Buber continues:

But this difference of faith is by no means to be understood merely as a subjective one. It is not based on the fact that we who live today are weak in faith, and it will remain even if our faith is ever so much strengthened. The situation of the world itself, in the most serious sense, more precisely the relation between God and man, has changed. And this change is certainly not comprehended in its essence by our thinking only of the darkening, so familiar to us, of the supreme light, only of the night of our being, empty of revelation. It is the night of an expectation—not of a vague hope, but of an expectation. We expect a theophany of which we know nothing but the place, and the place is called community. In the public catacombs of this expectation there is no single Word of God which can be clearly known and advocated, but the words delivered are clarified for us in our human situation of being turned to one another.

Again we are startled first by the harsh boldness of the formulation. How is this? No Word of God is to have validity for us any more? We are to throw away the bread that is handed us in our churches and, on orders from a "world situation," take to the desert of believing unbelief? Lest we break off the dialogue in haste and heat, however, let us once more pay heed to what was said.

Two things are clear at once. We are sent on a road—"our road," as Buber calls it—the path of spiritual renunciation. We are furthermore given to understand that this renunciation is asked of us not absolutely, as an act to be performed by all men at all times, but by us, living as we do in this particular time. It is the demand of the hour. After the way is pointed out there follows an explanation, though only in the form of a suggestion, in terms of a philosophy of history or of a redemptive history ("Heilsgeschichte").

"Our road"—that is the "narrow ridge" frequently cited. Buber has often spoken about it, usually in very personal terms. "I wanted by this to express," he explained later (1938),

that I did not dwell on the broad upland of a system that includes a series of sure statements about the absolute, but on a narrow rocky ridge between the gulfs where there is no sureness of expressible knowledge but the certainty of meeting what remains undisclosed.[9]

9 *Ibid.*

That Buber remained faithful to the thought which had been formed under oppressive wartime experiences (1914-1918) is shown by his foreword to the new edition of *For the Sake of Heaven (Gog und Magog)* written after the Second World War. In it, he turns against the misunderstandings occasioned by the English edition of this book. There he speaks of the reality which alone matters, the reality of the suffering Servant of the Lord. Then he continues:

I have no 'doctrine.' My function is merely to point out realities of this order. He who expects of me a teaching other than a pointing out of this character, will always be disappointed. And it would seem to me, indeed, that in this hour of history the crucial thing is not to posses a fixed doctrine, but rather to recognize eternal reality and through it to be able to face the reality of the present. No way can be pointed to in this desert night. We can only help others to stand fast in readiness, until the dawn breaks and a path becomes visible where none suspected it.[10]

Compared with earlier utterances, this most recent confession has gained in affirmative content even though the form of its negation has grown sterner than it used to be. Recognition of eternal reality—but then: not even a way can be pointed to.

The "narrow ridge" doubtless belongs in the tradition which points back to Kierkegaard's "abyss," and the revealing watchword assigns Buber a place within the intellectual current of the Kierkegaard Renaissance of the years between the wars and identifies him as a member of, or at least akin to, the group of thinkers called existentialists. How much such labeling means is, of course, another question. The abyss which is spanned by the narrow ridge on dizzy heights is the abyss we know from Kierkegaard. It was likewise appropriated in our days by Karl Jaspers, Martin Heidegger, and Jean-Paul Sartre—by each in his own manner. It symbolizes Nothingness—the absence of all sure assertion, authoritative doctrine, or dependable disclosure. That walk on the narrow ridge, to which the simile invites us demands courage as prime virtue, the kind of courage which Nietzsche praised in Schopenhauer and found represented in Dürer's copperplate "Knight, Death and Devil." The "Courage to Be," as the title of a book by Paul Tillich significantly reads, qualifies for endurance rather than for courageous venture. It lends strength to stand firm against the "reality of the present" and against the Nothing which looms behind it.

---

[10] *For the Sake of Heaven* (2nd ed.; 1953), p. xiii. The translation has been somewhat modified by Professor Kuhn.—Ed.

Well known is the dialectic of despair which for Kierkegaard results from experiencing the abyss and from which modern existentialist philosophy derives its pathos. The reverse of the courage demanded is dread. About it, Kierkegaard writes:

One may liken dread to dizziness. He whose eye chances to look down into the yawning abyss becomes dizzy. . . . Thus dread is the dizziness of freedom which occurs when . . . freedom gazes down into its own possibility, grasping the finiteness to sustain itself.[11]

How one is to go on from here, that is the difficult question which no dialectic can answer. The continuity, in any event, is broken, and only something like a leap can overcome the paralysis of the spirit. Kierkegaard himself finds salvation in the paradox of faith. Jaspers appeals to an inner movement which he calls "Aufschwung" (elevation, soaring). For Heidegger, "in the clear night of dread's Nothingness, what-is as such stands revealed in its original overtness,"[12] and becomes the basis of his eschatology of Being; Sartre finds the transition from the same starting-point to another form of futuristic thinking, that of revolutionary Marxism.

All such dialectic is alien to Buber. He turns against Kierkegaard and, even more pointedly, against Heidegger because the thinking of both leads into a closed system; in the case of Kierkegaard it leads to the relationship of the individual to God in an exclusive sense and, in the case of Heidegger, to the self that is doomed to intimate intercourse with itself. Heidegger's conception of man is thus "a great and decisive step out from Kierkegaard in the direction of the edge where *nothingness* begins."[13] Equally determined is Buber's rejection of the Marxist dialectic as a "secularized messianism"; it stultifies decision by identifying it with the process of historical and social evolution.[14] The difference of imagery is significant. With Kierkegaard and his modern followers, man reaches the edge and stares into the abyss. In Buber's thinking, man is called upon to walk along the rocky ridge between the gulfs. Yet the disruption of con-

[11] *The Concept of Dread,* trans. Walter Lowrie (Princeton: Princeton University Press, 1946), p. 55.

[12] *Was ist Metaphysik?* (Frankfurt: Klostermann, 1949), p. 31; cf. *Existence and Being* (Chicago: Regnery, 1949), 369.

[13] *Between Man and Man,* p. 181.

[14] Cf. *Paths in Utopia.*

tinuity which is characteristic of Kierkegaard's dialectic is also found in Buber. Its precise meaning must now be examined.

The break in the continuity is marked by an act called decision or choice. Three different ways of interpreting this act suggest themselves. Two or more alternatives may be given which, with a view to attaining an anticipated end, the good-as-such, are judged as good or not good. Choice follows judgment. This, by and large, is the Aristotelian concept of preferential choice (προαίρεσις). Rationalization, in this view, preserves continuity: the act is merely the execution of the judgment of practical reason. In sharp opposition to this stands Kierkegaard insisting as he does on the radical break in the continuity and on the exclusion of reason as a guide. For him there is no anticipated grasp of the end as either good or evil. In the "qualitative leap" of decision, good and evil are first constituted, and then everything depends on whether freedom, in the crisis of despair, goes down in dread (this is the moment of sin) and cleaves to finiteness, or whether the choice of the self succeeds. Kierkegaard's either-or thus means choice or non-choice, but choice loses the meaning of choosing between alternatives. Finally there remains a third, mediating, interpretation which can be called the "classic" interpretation even though this interpretation has not received a definitive philosophic formulation anywhere. Plato and Aristotle suggested it, the Judeo-Christian consciousness deepened it, and philosophers and theologians representing the Augustinian tradition have been its main advocates. Here, in agreement with Greek metaphysics, intellectual grasp of the good in contradistinction to evil is acknowledged as the basis for decision. The cognitive act, however, has in turn for its indispensible basis the volitional act of the mind "turning toward" and "assenting to" the good, so that cognition and volition, intellection and action become one in the indivisible spear-head of decision. Continuity and discontinuity, ascent (in the sense of the Augustinian *ascensus*) and crisis, are here reconciled with each other as complementary aspects of one single movement of the mind.

Modern existential philosophers tend to radicalize the second concept of decision, Kierkegaard's, by eliminating its religious import. That applies primarily to Sartre. According to him, the individual, in triumph over despair, chooses himself in that he, as it were creates himself by freely positing a value system which by his own fiat becomes a law unto himself. Such Titanism is alien to Buber. However critical he is of Kierkegaard, he is still closer to him than

most of those who swear by his name. That gathering of inward intensity which finds release in the act of choice he compares with the
rising of the flood. There the chaos of possibilities of being becomes
the chaos of possibilities of action. The soul, seized by the dizzy
whirl of undirected all-embracing passion, strives to escape and finds
but two exits. "It can clutch at any object past which the vortex
happens to carry it, and cast its passion upon it," which is a paraphrase of the passage quoted above from the *The Concept of Dread*
where Kierkegaard says that the spirit "grasps the finiteness to sustain
itself." Or the soul can, Buber continues, "in response to a prompting
that is still incomprehensible to itself, set about the audacious work
of self-unification."15 It follows evil in the one case, in the other it
comes into the service of good. The evil is lack of direction realized
(the decision for evil is therefore actually indecision) , and only the
daring venture of self-unification is truly a way—the *one* way open
to man.

This last thought points beyond Kierkegaard and, in a certain
sense, even beyond Buber's own position. Becoming One, self unification, is by origin a Platonic thought deepened by Augustine. One
might call it the pivotal idea of Humanism. Plato knew well enough
that there also is a false self-unification: a faculty of the mind, not
meant to rule, may well enforce unity by usurping power. Buber
does not overlook this objection. "Evil cannot be done," he writes,
"with the whole soul; good can only be done with the whole soul."16
This formulation still betrays an affinity to Kierkegaard's "subjective
truth," to the idea that the truth of a belief does not lie in the apprehension of self-subsisting truth but in the intensity of the act of belief. Actually, however, Buber has gone beyond Kierkegaard's subjectivity. This is revealed by his discussion of "self-choice." The
task of unifying the self must be directed by the presentiment implanted in each person of what he and only he is destined to become. The affirmation of this archetype is the genuine self-choice,
which naturally goes hand in hand with a critical rejection of that
being which the choosing one actually happens to be. But man, that
living creature "in whom the category of possibility is so to speak
embodied," (p. 76) needs a confirmation of his personality which in
the end he can only derive from himself by means of his immediate

---

15 *Images of Good and Evil*, pp. 67f. (Included in *Good and Evil*—Ed.)
16 *Ibid.*, p. 71.

self-knowledge. In other words, he has a conscience. Now, in order to escape the unbearable self-rejection, he can seek to save himself through an act of violence. He can extinguish the archetype in his soul and choose himself as the one he actually is, here and now. But in order to be able to affirm himself thus, "he must deny and reverse the order; the yes-position, which 'good' has occupied, he must assign to the principle of his own self-affirmation, nothing else must remain worthy of affirmation than just that which is affirmed by him; his Yes to himself determines the reason and right of affirmation." (pp. 78-79) Thus we are confronted with the notion of satanic choice, and we understand that here the idea of evil as indecision has lost its validity.

Reading the third part of *Images of Good and Evil* is a breathtaking experience. Buber leads us to his goal over a detour: as a point of departure he interprets the Persian myth of Yima's defection without fully clarifying this mythical symbol. It is a steep climbing road which he bids us ascend, and the clamor of existentialist melodramatics (the pseudo-Kierkegaardian verbiage of modern nihilism which has spoiled for our ears even so forceful an expression as that of the "narrow ridge") is soon left far below us. Instead, called forth by the exigencies of the question under examination, the contours of a *philosophia perennis* begin to dawn around us. There is the order of creation, which alone furnishes the frame of reference within which alone the individual can discover the particular personal archetype that fits him and no one else. There is Being which the titanic rebel endeavors to ignore and, above all, there is God whom I acknowledge as the creator of my own uniqueness, inexplicable as it is in terms of mundane reality. Whatever the student of Iranian theology may say about this interpretation of Yima's defection, it doubtless is based on the Augustinian concept of *superbia,* of that Luciferic aberration which consists in the perverted human imitation of God's omnipotence.

We now can understand why Buber makes his way like a quiet guest through the nimble groups of existentialists. Even where the suitable expression is not or is not yet available to him, he has something different and something better to say. (And is it not the lot of anyone who philosophizes nowadays to be wrestling with the problems of language?) He again prepares the way for a meeting with Being, which existentialism has missed and positivism has forgotten. His unspectacular self-assurance stems from the deeply-rooted religious nature of his thought. The decisive act, he tells us, with which a person begins the effort of self-unification, is, "in the amazingly apposite language of religion," (p. 76) called conversion. "In the depth of suffering the return to good is born and this return it is which evokes redemption," says, in Buber's rendition, the Maggid of Koswits to Prince Adam Czartoryski, coming to seek his advice.[17] But the word of the Seer of Lublin has still more to disclose:

What is this good which God creates? It is man's turning to Him. When man turns away from evil with all that might with which he is able to rebel against God, then he has truly turned to God. For this reason the world exists by virtue of the 'turning'.[18]

And there is a similar word from Rabbi Nachman: "The world was created solely for the sake of choice and the chooser."[19] We are reminded of the platonic "conversion" ($\pi\epsilon\rho\alpha\gamma o\gamma\acute{\eta}$) of the soul toward Being, but also, and mainly, of the worthy "fruit of repentance" (Matthew, 3:8) which Christ asked for.

III

"It is this hour of history," the present desert night, which imposes upon the wanderer over the ridge the command of spiritual renunciation. By thus placing his message within a framework defined in terms of a philosophical interpretation of history, Buber shows once more his affinity to existentialism. The existentialist philosophizes as one who is confronted with the abyss of Nothingness. Coming thus face to face with Nothingness, however, does not appear to him merely as a personal destiny but as the meaningful result of historical necessity. He never ceases to be a Hegelian after his own fashion. Like Hegel, he sees history as a dialectical process—not construing it as directed toward the attainment of a perfect freedom, but as a destructive process leading toward the Nothingness of unbelief; not as progression toward future fulfillment, but as regression to a point that resembles the beginning. That is the "spiritual situation of our times" as Jaspers envisaged it in 1931.[20]

---

[17] *For the Sake of Heaven*, p. 202.

[18] *Ibid.*, p. 44.

[19] *Tales of the Hasidim.*

[20] *Die geistige Situation der Zeit* (Berlin, 1931), published in English under the title *Man in the Modern Age*, trans. Eden and Cedar Paul (London: Routledge and Sons, 1933).

It is the fate of existential philosophy that it must pretend to know too little and again too much. Too little—less than what a man needs to live, for without certainty there can be neither physical nor spiritual health. Therefore, existential philosophy is not fit for giving a basis to existence. Too much—more than anyone can know. For no one knows his own place in history. Buber does not succumb to this dilemma, despite all the resemblance between his language and that of the existential philosophers. When he speaks of the hour of history and the situation of the world, he does base his thought in a particular historical moment, but this moment cannot be interpreted in terms of the history of the occidental mind. Did the "night of waiting" begin with the French Revolution? To assume that would be naive. No, this long night is the very night which had already given rise to the voice of the anonymous writer to whom we refer as Deutero-Isaiah. Waiting is not expectation confronted with a vacuum (a vacuum which, according to existentialist thought, echoes with the appeal to spiritual awakening), but a specific and sure expectation, expectation of the salvation which the Messiah will bring, a message not identical with the Christian hope and yet intimately akin to it. "This our situation in face of Nothingness we shall call faithlessness," writes Jaspers. Waiting, however, does not mean perseverance in faithlessness, but faith in the condition of expectancy. It does not mean uncertainty but firm reliance on that which is certain to come. The hour of its coming is uncertain, the coming itself is assured.

This difference is of immense importance. It was once made clear to the writer by Buber himself, more by the manner in which he spoke than by what he said. If a personal reminiscence may be permitted,—it was in Berlin, in the ill-boding year of 1933. Public discourse had been silenced, but small groups had gathered in various quarters to foster joint reflection and consultation. Of the many things that were discussed in those days I remember only three utterances, and in retrospect it appears to me as if my memory had been much wiser in selecting what was memorable than my judgment and conscious knowledge. For I knew very little of the three divine virtues of which I became aware then, not under their own names, to be sure, and not as subject of inquiry, but through the reality of dialogue in example and illustration.

The first utterance came from Romano Guardini. He spoke of the "tragic finitism" advocated by Nietzsche—the philosopher who passionately and despairingly longed to raise a finite world to the status of an Absolute—and then of that other finite world which, beheld in faith, is not lost in Nothingness but, like a ball in a human hand, is enfolded by God. The second of the unforgettable utterances occurred on the way home from one of those meetings, late at night under a Charlottenburg street light. The speaker was a young friend, more gifted in music and philosophy than anyone else I knew—he was to become one of the earliest victims of the war—and our conversation concerned the problem of redemption. With a moving earnestness of concern, he, a person of a practical rather than a speculative turn of mind, expressed his anxious doubts about the fate of those who had died without ever knowing of Christ, and then as, in the ensuing dialogue, perplexity had deepened, he smilingly concluded: "After all, love reaches farther than doubt." The third utterance stems from Martin Buber, already bearded, but not white-bearded as he is today. The conversation had turned to theology and, while despair lurked in the four corners of our contracting world, he spoke about the miracle: how the expectation of and the belief in the possibility of the world-transforming miracle (perhaps it is near, tomorrow already it may come to pass) transforms the soul into a vessel of readiness. All this was said quite cheerfully, simply, and unemphatically. Yet I have not been tempted since to confuse waiting (*Harren*) with any historic-philosophical phantasmagoria of Hegelian origin. How, waiting is not real? Could it then become form, feature, and spoken word?

Here again we have occasion to remember Buber's Hasidic sources. In the years following the beginning of the Second World War, Buber wrote his Hasidic "chronicle" *For the Sake of Heaven,* based on data and legends he had collected for decades, a prose epic which is likely to hold an enduring place within German literature. From the first to the last line, this is a book on man in the state of faithful waiting. The dramatic subject-matter, the deadly struggle between two schools of Hasidism, between the Seer of Lublin and the "Holy Yehudi" of Pshysha, is again concerned with the right kind of messianic expectancy. On the one side stands the Seer of Lublin, the religious superman personified. A contemporary of the French Revolution and of the Empire, he considers Napoleon the prophesied "Gog of the Land of Magog"; and when the Emperor prepares his Russian campaign, the Seer believes that the final battle is drawing near. True to the maxim "Thou shalt push that which is about to fall" he takes it upon himself to intervene in the titanic battle by means of daring thaumaturgy in order thereby to hasten the approaching end and the new beginning. Buber succeeds in dealing fairly with the miracle-performing rabbi, the acknowledged leader of his generation: he shows him great in spite of his blunders. But the author's heart is with the other side, with Pshysha. When the struggle approaches its tragic climax, the "Holy Yehudi" also begins to teach that "redemption is at hand." This is ambiguous, in view of his impending submissive and sacrificial death. Nor did he ever omit to preface or to conclude his teaching with the cry *"turn* to God" or "it depends merely on our turning." He made no claim to know the circumstances or the appropriateness of time. Rather, he illumined his fellows by the message of love which says that nothing matters but man's readiness to grasp the coming redemption, "the entire turning of the human being from the way of man to the way of God, which we call *teshuvah.*" (p. 246)

One other point needs to be noted. The Rabbi of Pshysha, while preparing himself for suffering and death, manages to speak of how close redemption has come only after the Shekinah (the "indwelling" of God in the world) had appeared to him in a dream. A dusty and bleeding figure, it had said to the rabbi: "I am in truth with you . . . My face is that of the created being." (p. 229) Not only man suffers in his role as the "Servant of God," God also, in the form of His Shekinah, takes vicarious suffering upon Himself.

IV

"We expect a theophany of which we know nothing but the place, and the place is called community."[21] More than all other elements of his thought, it is this definition of the locus of epiphany which has made Buber a moving force in contemporary philosophy. "Community" here has the precise meaning which Ferdinand Tönnies gave to it as an antonym of "society." It means not only a composite whole made up of individuals but the actuality of a common life which, as an integral whole, animates and fashions its members as it is also fashioned by them. Buber lends content to the term which far transcends the meaning conferred upon it by Tönnies.

---

[21] *Between Man and Man,* p. 184.

The contemplative Saints, such as St. Catherine of Genoa, have time and again impressed on themselves and on others a simple maxim: No religious ecstacy must render the visionary deaf or indolent to the call that urges him to be ready for active charity. Buber, well versed in the tradition of mysticism, owes his turning toward community, as he has confessed himself, to a painful experience which impressed that truth upon him with dreadful cogency. Once after a morning of religious enthusiasm, he was visited by a youth who, as he later learned, had not come casually but borne by destiny with all the expectation of a person in despair, hoping to find the meaning that was eluding his grasp restored to him by the presence of a man he admired. But the man who was sought with such expectancy failed. Not that he failed to meet his visitor in a spirit of friendly responsiveness. But not being really present in spirit, he did not sense the unavowed questions. From this experience Buber drew conclusions grave enough to amount to a renunciation of contemplation. He gave up religiousness in the form of exaltation or rapture. "I possess nothing but the everyday out of which I am never taken . . . I know no fullness but each mortal hour's fullness of claim and responsibility."[22]

The commitment toward fellow-creatures, in a deeper sense even than the "hour of history," becomes the reason for spiritual renunciation. This religious pragmatism is the very essence of the spirit of Pshysha. Jubilantly the deciples of the "Holy Yehudi" listen to the tale of the man who was so deeply engrossed in thought that he did not notice how the horse, which he was posted to watch, was stolen from the bolted stables.[23] The Shekinah in the dream vision of the "Yehudi" says the same thing: "The glory has remained above. My face is that of the created being."[24] When practical responsibility becomes the basis for theoretic renunciation, it may act as a restraint, but it may also be a regulative principle of cognition. Buber's progress in thought means, *inter alia*, that his practical responsibility exercises less and less restraint without ever diminishing its usefulness as a guide for reason. In tracing this progress we must remember that community for him means: "to be present for one's fellow creatures."

An ethical definition like this still remains within the subjective

[22] *Ibid.*, pp. 13f.
[23] *For the Sake of Heaven*, p. 267.
[24] *Ibid.*, p. 229.

sphere. The essential aspect of Buber's concept of community, however, is that it pushes beyond this sphere. *Ich und Du* is the title of the
work which, conceived during the First World War, and published
in 1923, first puts forward the ideas that distinguish Buber to this
day.[25] "In the beginning is relation," (p. 18) he writes, and relation
is mutuality. The "inborn Thou" is in the I "as category of being,
readiness, grasping form." (p. 27) Still this phrase could be mistaken as a sort of co-ordination of monads that are in tune with one
another. Actually, relation—or rather its actualization through meeting—has assumed the function that had been assigned to "life" in the
preceding phase of Buber's thought. "We live our lives inscrutably
included within the streaming mutual life of the universe." (p. 16)
The I-Thou relation expresses this "Urchance des Seins" (primal
potential of being), as Buber formulated it later, "in a natural, as
it were, pre-figurative manner."[26] This primary word "can be resolved, certainly, into I and Thou, but it did not arise from their
being set together; by its nature it precedes I." (p. 22) Spirit, as
the author of *I and Thou* ventures to put it, "is not in the I, but
between I and Thou." (p. 39) To disclose the realm of the "in-
between," that is the purpose and intent of the message, rhapsodical-
ly recited rather than conceptually presented. For the theophany
which the author holds to be approaching and which he announces
does not approach the single being but it approaches the "sphere that
lies between beings." (p. 120)

Two traditional lines of thought merge in the philosophy of the
I-Thou relation. Buber himself traced them historically, but he did
not conceptually differentiate between them in delivering his exult-
ant message. First he is here laying the foundation of his phenomenology, or rather his onotology, of *Mitsein* (the condition of mutual
presence). "Without Thou, the I is impossible," as Friedrich Heinrich Jacobi had formulated it in 1785, and in the 19th century,
Ludwig Feuerbach returned to the idea that an I becomes real
only through an opposite Thou.[27] By now this idea has become
common philosophic property through Martin Buber. But although

---

[25] *I and Thou*. For the interpretation of this work, cf. Paul E. Pfuetze, *The Social
Self* (New York: Bookman Associates, 1954).

[26] *Die Schriften über das dialogische Prinzip*, p. 287.

[27] *Ibid.*, cf. Karl Löwith, *Das Individuum in der Rolle des Mitmenschen* (Munich:
Drei Masken Verlag, 1928).

the analyses of the "intentional community" (Husserl),[28] of communication (Jaspers), of the "Mitdasein" (Heidegger),[29] or of l'être-autrui (Sartre) [30] all point back to Buber, however much all those authors may have learned from the author of *I and Thou*, in all of them is missing the characteristic element of Buber's thesis: the idea of I and Thou as interdependent entities, coeval and of equal ontological status. It is necessarily missing because of the subjective starting point of their philosophies which, as transcendental egologies or analyses of existence, are committed to the idea of the primacy of the I. They cannot put the I and Thou on equal footing, because they are projected from a subjective position; their world is always "geweltet."[31] In Buber's essay the framework of a world which comprises the I and Thou equally, is not systematically developed but implied and suggested by the term "world-order." (p. 31)

The second traditional line of ideas, in which Buber's "primal relation" belongs, runs from Kierkegaard to contemporary existentialism. But a peculiar deflection interrupts this line. The existential dialectic presupposes Kierkegaard's concept of the Single One. Two cannot walk side by side on the "narrow ridge." Probably in view of this difficulty Buber later recoined his own motto and applied it to the Way of Dying.[32] But in *I and Thou,* the crisis of decision, which leads either to the choice of self or to the loss of self, is boldly "socialized," i.e., transferred from the I in the loneliness of despair to the sphere of the in-between. "Only he who knows relation and knows about the presence of the Thou is capable of decision. He who decides is free, for he has approached the Face." (p. 51) This transfer attacks Kierkegaard on his own ground and brings about a strange rewording and reinterpretation of the existential dialectic. This dialectic, as is well known, oscillates between the poles of authenticity and inauthenticity, of genuine existence and effacement in the anonymous mass. Buber, while still subscribing to a philosophy of life interpreted in the spirit of mysticism, had formulated his own dialectic in a sense that was reminiscent of Bergson, pitting fluid life against rigid form, the "realizing" against the

---

[28] "Cartesianische Meditationen," *Husserliana, I* (Haag: Nijhoff, 1950).

[29] *Sein und Zeit,* 1, Hälfte, p. 117f.

[30] *L'Être et le Néant,* p. 275ff.

[31] Martin Heidegger, "Vom Wesen des Grundes," *Festschrift zu Husserls 70. Geburtstag* (Halle: Niemeyer, 1929), p. 101.

[32] *For the Sake of Heaven.*

"orienting" attitude.[33] Now he blends these two forms of dialectic, the one included in his early philosophy of life and the existential one, so as to make them serviceable to the newly discovered principle of dialogue. Thus he can introduce the proclamation of his superior insight by a resounding either-or:

To man the world is twofold, in accordance with his twofold attitude.—The attitude of man is twofold, in accordance with the twofold nature of the primary words which he speaks. . . . The one primary word is the combination I-Thou.—The other primary word is the combination I-It . . . (p. 3)

The It, which "one of the words He or She can replace," does not by any means designate a thing or creature in contradistinction from the Thou that designates a person. Rather, two dialectically related manners of being—or "worlds"—are confronted with each other, and the It, compared with the Thou, signifies the primitive form of the Thou as well as its form of decline.

The particular Thou, after the relational event has run its course, is bound to become an It.—The particular It, by entering the relational event, may become a Thou. (p. 33) The It is the eternal chrysalis, the Thou the eternal butterfly. (p. 17)

The Thou is met in a lived and living relation. This in turn is related to the structured universe, to the rational and visible space-time continuum of the It-world as, for Bergson, intuition is related to discursive thought with its causal explanation and, for Kierkegaard, existence to truth apprehended by speculative contemplation. It is a trans-rational relation, a negative absolute as set over against the conceptual marks and entities by means of which we orient ourselves in the world. The renunciation imposed in the name of the historical situation here affects the philosophy of primary relation: in the age of ideologies, thought appears as that which separates, as the medium which deforms the Thou into an It. The world of Thou, Buber writes, "is not set in the context of space and time." (p. 33) This world lives from moments of grace in which the *ineffabile* manifests itself. At the same time, Buber secures himself against an emotionalistic interpretation of the act that creates the immediacy of relation. Feelings only accompany the metaphysical and the metapsychic act of love. "Feelings dwell in man; but man dwells in his love." (p. 14)

---

[33] In *Daniel; Gespräche von der Verwirklichung* (1913).

The consummation of the I-Thou relation, thus singled out as the point where the negative absolute strikes reality like lightning, can hardly be presented by any but emotionally-tinged illustrations. Thus Buber once describes a passionate disagreement he had with a Christian about the relation and co-operation between Jews and Christians. It ended by Buber and his opponent looking into the "heart of one another's eyes" and giving one another the kiss of brotherhood. "Opinions were gone, the factual took place."[34] The factual however, that covenant between Christians and Jews, cannot take place without fastening the covenant in an intermediate third factor, i.e., in a truth disclosed by faith or reason. For a covenant calls for joint action that is based on something which is jointly held to be right. Not that we should wish to cast disparagement on the genuineness of the reconciliation here described. But we are entitled to ask whether it is not perhaps a specially prepared Thou, the Thou belonging within the community of the faithful, which is inadvertently taken for the human Thou as such—the Thou which can also stand over against us in tragic alienation, hidden behind an iron wall which nothing can melt but the ardor of saints ready for the supreme sacrifice.

The dialogue relation must not be taken as an absolute. It is limited by two elements which also are the ones that first make dialogue possible. One has to do with the truth discerned, the other one with the authority of the divine word. The first of the two was established by the original discoverer of the art of dialogue, Plato. Even though I may not be capable of making another see the truth I have discerned, I still must hold on to it firmly. It is this stipulation which originates dialogue as a joint search for truth, as a contest in which never a person but always truth only can win. The defeated partner is actually the one who derives the chief benefit from the dialogue: he is delivered from error, transformed into a new person and opened up for his fellow-man. The second element is of similar significance. The word of revelation put in the mouth of the prophet or apostle establishes the foundation for the community from a point which is outside all human community. Here, too, the limiting principle is a constituitive one: in God, from whom the Word issues, all human conflicts are forever resolved. The pro and

34 *Between Man and Man*, pp. 5f.

con of discourse requires for its own limit and foundation that which excludes all opposition.

Buber is familiar with these limiting and supporting elements of the dialogue. In his early work, however, the *logos* in the Platonic sense is still concealed by his personal mission: he must find an approach to man lost in the anarchy of ideologies. Yet he is not blind to the truth that there is no *Zwischenmenschlichkeit* (interhuman relation) without a third reality entering between and uniting the partners; and this third factor must be more than a "sphere." True enough, one armed with opinions, encased, as it were, in a dogma, cannot step out to meet another; for such a one, there is no Thou. If we disarm him and smash his shelter and he stands before us naked and helpless in his perplexity—have we then really improved his lot? He may not be better off than he was before. Now he has no inwardness into which he could bid a partner step; he still has no Thou. Unlike his former dogmatic self, he will no longer keep his fellow-man coldly at a distance. Instead, he may be willing to submit to another's superior self-assertiveness. He may even yearn for such a deliverance from his unwieldy selfhood. But that is merely another apostasy, worse than the first. The atomization of society resulting in isolated, locked-up individuals has for its counterpart the total surrender of the self to a leader, styled 'charismatic' by his victims. In order to dwell in love—to use Buber's beautiful phrase—one needs a third reality, a creative one, and no one knows this better than Buber himself, though at times, bracketing the implications of this knowledge, he speaks of an I-Thou that is prior to the I (p. 22).

Also scarcely hidden, in Buber's early publications, merely veiled is the other element, the word of authority, the "myth" (in the original sense of the word which has become unusual today) as distinguished from *logos,* and this partial obfuscation is due to the fact that he locates the theophany exclusively within the everyday of the actualized I-Thou relation. Where the veil lifts, however, and the "Eternal Thou" as such steps forth, the divinely created order also emerges, the mundane incarnation of the initially neglected *logos.* In the third part of *I and Thou,* the saving word is spoken. The human Thou is, to be sure, a terminus within a life-creating relationship, but at the same time it is a mediating reality: every particular Thou provides a glimpse of the "Eternal Thou." Thereafter comes the decisive statement on the totality of all human I-Thou relations: "The inborn Thou is realized in each relation and consummated in none. It is consummated only in the direct relation with the Thou that by its nature cannot become It." (p. 75) All genuine love among men is love of God, and all perfect human love among men has for its source and model God's love for His creatures.

Every real relation in the world is exclusive; the Other breaks in on it and avenges its exclusion. Only in the relation with God are unconditioned exclusiveness and unconditioned inclusiveness one and the same, in which the whole universe is implied. (p. 99)

The twofoldness is and remains Buber's starting point. Still in an essay as late as 1951 he speaks of the twofold principle of human life, built up in a twofold movement, distance and relation, with distance being prerequisite, even if not causative, to relation.[35] While an animal remains functionally restricted in its environment (which actually is only a sphere of action and no world), man is the creature "through whose being (Sein) 'what is' (das Seiende) becomes detached from him, and recognized for itself." (p. 98) But then it takes the "act and the work of entering into relation with the world as such," (p. 99) so that the world as such which has thus been disclosed—the world of It in Buber's earlier terminology—may truly gain wholeness and unity. This act, which Buber terms "synthesizing apperception," culminates in the "making present" of our fellow-man as a person. I and Thou: In the mutuality of the making present and confirmation there is formed the "sphere of the between" in which the "inmost growth of the self" is accomplished: "It is from one man to another that the heavenly bread of self-being is passed." (p. 104) But in continuing further beyond this point of departure, the dual image changes into a triadic one. By its very nature the dialogue between two requires a third, invisible partner in whom are reconciled statement and reply. As Buber says in *Dialogue*: "The word of him who wishes to speak with men without speaking with God is not fulfilled; but the word of him who wishes to speak with God without speaking with men goes astray." (p. 15)

The *logos* seems to be neglected in Buber's *Dialogue*, to be sure, yet it is not ignored. Hidden within the nature of God, it does step forth occasionally, in suggestions rather than in a fully developed argument. The same holds true of the world. It, too, is there, resting in itself, true world and true creation and not—as in the case of so many of our contemporaries—subjectivated, histori-

---

[35] "Distance and Relation," pp. 105–113.

cized, or split up into innumerable non-worlds which call themselves, illegitimately, "Islamic World," "the World of the Baroque," or the "World of Schizophrenia," and the like. The "transcendental intuition" is as little restricted to the sphere of human-personal existence as is the I-Thou relation.[36] There is a life with intelligible forms, there is one with men but also one with nature.[37] The lime-tree of which Buber speaks in *Der Mensch und sein Gebild*[38] is a real tree which sinks its roots into real soil—even though a residue of Kantian phenomenalism enters here and disturbs the analysis. How real also is the dapple-grey horse on his grandfather's estate whose neck the boy would caress![39] As truly as the Thou stands for a real being, body and spirit, so also is the World, in which it belongs and which it yet transcends, a genuine World. And the idea which unlocks the World—an idea of inexhaustible fruitfulness—is called meeting. It occupies the middle ground between the idealistic and the empirical concepts of experience. The idealist knows that personal consciousness is involved in all cognition. But by interpreting the in-itself of beings as constituted by an unconscious act of creation, he annihilates it. The empiricist rescues the in-itself and existence but thereby sacrifices the spiritual nature—i.e., the intelligibility— of cognition. The idea of meeting places the fundamental fact of spiritual apprehension in the center of the discussion. Finiteness and receptiveness, instead of being relegated to sensuous experience, are conceived as defining the very essence of the human mind. We must understand Buber's philosophy as a philosophy of meeting.

At a time when mutual understanding and the intimacy of communion are threatened, Buber has with earnest insistence appealed to those healing powers which may be awakened by man meeting his fellow-man. Whoever admires Buber for this service, noble to be sure but still confined to a specific period, certainly admires him for a good reason, though somewhat mistakenly. Buber is more than a high-minded ideologist or a religious author of great eloquence. He sought to serve, effectively and directly, by persuasion and exhortation. But

36 Cf. the essay by Fritz Kaufmann, "Karl Jaspers and a Philosophy of Communication," *Karl Jaspers*, ed. P. A. Schilpp (New York: Tudor, 1957 [now published by Open Court, LaSalle, Ill.]), pp. 210-295.

37 *I and Thou*, p. 6.

38 (Heidelberg: Lambert Schneider) , pp. 30—34.

39 *Between Man and Man*, pp. 22f.

the basis of his exhortatory and educational activity was to be nothing less than truth. Thus his zealously religious oratory has ripened into the ethos of a philosophy which submits to answers but also poses questions. While presenting what he has found with the mature wisdom of his advanced years, the philosopher has never ceased to seek. The dialogue with him has not been concluded. It has to be carried on in the spirit of grateful admiration and in a state of expectancy.

HELMUT KUHN

PHILOSOPHICAL FACULTY
UNIVERSITY OF MUNICH

30

Walter Kaufmann

BUBER'S RELIGIOUS SIGNIFICANCE

I

A Personal Approach. Most serious authors we encounter after our basic attitudes have taken shape; but there are a few whom we meet earlier—writers who neither become grist for our mill nor evoke a sense of congeniality, but who do something to us. For me, Martin Buber is one of this small number.

It might be inappropriate to even mention this; writing about a philosopher, we generally try to be impartial, putting out of mind all personal involvement. Yet Buber differs from other philosophers. His major contribution to philosophy is *I and Thou,* in which the two relationships I-It and I-Thou are contrasted. There is something problematic in writing "about" the author of this work, treating him as an object for reflection, carving up his works into such fields as ethics and epistemology, philosophy of history and social thought, or even philosophy in general as separate from Buber's other interests. In this manner one stands to lose what is most distinctive about him. To perceive his significance, we must try to listen to his voice.

It is sometimes said that Buber is an existentialist, and the term is so vague that this statement is not false. Some of the differences between Buber and other so-called existentialists will be considered below. What Buber clearly has in common with some others influenced by Kierkegaard and, above all, with Kierkegaard himself, is his impassioned protest against the kind of philosophy to which he and the others are being reduced today by some of their admirers. Neo-Thomists write books on Kierkegaard and Jaspers, Heidegger and Sartre, forcing their rebellions against all traditional philosophy into an almost scholastic mold. When one writes on Kierkegaard today, one must begin by breaking down the systematic walls in which a growing literature is trying to confine him, to set free the individual.

The present volume on Buber, which I myself strongly urged years ago, in 1951, presents a similar danger. To bring together many different views of Buber's work within the framework of a single volume, one simply has to carve up Buber's thought more or less systematically to avoid egregious repetition, and one must proceed as if he had a system which can be considered branch by branch. I am not objecting to this method. Neither do I feel apologetic for my own attempt to seek a different approach. Both procedures may be complementary, and my own, though of necessity it will involve some overlapping with the thoughts of others, may yet fill a crucial gap.

II

Buber's Central Question. Buber, like Kierkegaard, is at heart a religious thinker rather more than a philosopher. His primary concern is not with the elaboration of a system, with the quest for certainty or the solution of some problems in epistemology or ethics, but, if it is not too bold to formulate it in a single question: what does the religion of my fathers mean to me today?

What distinguishes Buber is not this question which is on many lips today. His significance lies in the fact that few, if any, others have said so much of such importance in answer to this question. Not only *I and Thou, Dialogue,* and *Two Types of Faith* are relevant to his central question, but also Buber's studies of the Bible and of Hasidism, his translation of the Hebrew Scripture, and his collection of the lore of the Hasidim. Almost everything else he has written also has some bearing on this question. More than any other writer of our time, specifically including those theologians whose wide popularity is such a distinctive feature of our age, Buber has shown in great detail what religion can mean at its best.

Buber is certainly not an authoritative spokesman for Judaism. It is one of the blessings of Judaism that it does not have any authoritative spokesmen. Millions of Jews disagree with Buber about their Scriptures, about Hasidism, about Judaism, and about whatever else is interesting. But he has shown a possible meaning of religion today—which sounds like faint praise until one looks around and finds how exceedingly difficult it has become for those who are loath to part with their critical spirit to find a worthwhile meaning for religion here and now.

III

Buber versus Jaspers and Heidegger. Buber's faults are not hard to find but relatively unimportant. It has been charged against him that as a teacher of social philosophy he did not give some of his students what a less subjective teacher would have given them, and that, when he retired, they still had to acquire some fundamentals of sociology. Whether this is true or not, Buber's stature certainly does not rest on his ability to coach his students for examinations.

In a similar vein, his discussions of the thought of Nietzsche, Heidegger, and Sartre—to give only three examples—are open to objections. At important points he seems to be mistaken in his views of their views. But again this is unimportant. If he had never written about these men, his stature would be unimpaired.

Buber is not a model of impartial reading. Nietzsche once spoke of "what a man has written with his blood." Buber might be said to *read* with his blood. Or, to use a more conventional term, with his heart. He involves himself in what he reads to the point where he finds what other readers would not find. As a result, his readings are often controversial.

This is true also of Buber's Biblical interpretations and of the picture he has given us of the Hasidim. There is something intuitive, personal, partial about his readings. And this may seem to be a crucial criticism.

A comparison with Jaspers and, even more, with Heidegger seems obvious at this point. They, too, have devoted a large part of their own writings to interpretations; and their exegeses too, are open to a vast array of critical objections.

In the case of Jaspers I have tried to show in detail in another volume in this series that his two books and his several essays on Nietzsche are founded on an unsound method and his long reply to my critique confirmed my thesis that he is at least occasionally quite unable to read even a plain text. Instead of replying to the specific criticisms which I summarized in less than two pages toward the end of my essay, Jaspers devoted five pages to a piqued attempt to saddle me with views which I had not expressed and with a philosophic outlook quite at variance with the one I do profess. Whether he deals with Schelling, Kierkegaard, or Freud, the procedure is always essentially the same: nobody is accepted as he is; everybody is remodeled to play a part assigned to him. Schelling's protean development is dismissed; Kierkegaard's "forced Christianity" and Nietzsche's "forced anti-Christianity" do not really matter; and Freud becomes, next to Marx, *the* representative of "anti-reason in our age." What matters most to a man does not necessarily matter to Jaspers: Jaspers' interpretations depend on what matters to *him*.

Jaspers himself stresses communication, which he defines as a "loving struggle," but he never really exposes himself to another point of view. He is always the judge, not a combatant—or as an admirer once put it: Jaspers has remained true to his training; he has never abandoned the psychiatrist's condescension.

Nothing of the sort could be alleged of Buber. Can anyone who has ever asked him a question imagine him replying, as Jaspers occasionally answers serious questions, "I shall deal with this point in one of my books"? Buber may occasionally seem highhanded in interpretation, but as soon as he confronts a question from another human being he insists on the achievement of communication or, as he says, dialogue. Emphatically, he is not the judge nor a psychiatrist but a fellow human being, a fellow seeker, eager to speak man to man.

Buber's dialogue is not Socratic: it quite lacks the mordant sarcasm, the frank delight in the opponent's weakness, and the air of a contest. With Buber, question and answer have a religious dimension: it is not a match of intellects he seeks but an approach between two human beings which seems connected with the Biblical injunction, "love thy fellow as thyself." There is a feeling of fellowship and a vivid sense that the other human being is as myself. Listening with the heart, and not merely the intellect, means the total involvement of both participants in the dialogue: it allows heart to speak to heart and illuminates the idea of neighbor-love.

One experiences nothing like this with the other so-called existentialists. Though they begin with a protest against the academic and insist, in different ways, on staying with human existence, they soon become involved in curious modes of speech, in a conceptual machinery quite as forbidding as that of avowed academicians, and, alas, in more or less impressive monologues. Questions become scarcely possible: asked in the philosopher's own language, they answer themselves; asked in a less pretentious idiom, they are rarely answered. At best, one is offered an oral footnote to a published text.

A contrast with Heidegger proves especially illuminating. If you associate Buber above all with Judaism, and Heidegger with Hitler, the idea of comparing both will seem far-fetched. Yet there is a striking similarity between Heidegger's later writings and Buber's earlier work. The following sentences from *I and Thou* (1923) might have been written by Heidegger thirty years later: *"Man sagt, der Mensch erfahre seine Welt. Was heisst das? Der Mensch befährt die Fläche der Dinge und erfährt sie."* (11) The preoccupation with the roots of words which is so startling in Heidegger's interpretations, the attempt to penetrate the too familiar readings which allegedly impede a genuine perception of the text, and the bold departure from ordinary language are all encountered much earlier in Buber's and Rosenzweig's German translation of the Hebrew Bible.

Nevertheless, Buber and Heidegger differ decisively. Buber and Rosenzweig dealt with texts which really had been obscured by familiarity. By recovering some degree of strangeness, they created the conditions under which it became possible to hear again. Heidegger, picking out some all but unknown hymns of the late Hölderlin and a relatively little known poem by Rilke, could hardly explain his eccentric essays on these poems in parallel fashion. Indeed, the striking charges against his interpretations entered by Walter Muschg in the essay on "Zerschwatzte Dichtung" in his book, *Die Zerstörung der deutschen Literatur,* must be sustained for the most part. Heidegger does not always use the best available text; he disregards the author's intentions; he shows extraordinarily little feeling for poetry and for the personalities of the poets with whom he deals; and he regularly reads his own ideas into the poems he interprets. In his Rilke interpretation he actually finds the crucial message in a passage he interpolates where the poet left three dots. Quite generally, he concentrates on obscure poems or on fragments which facilitate his highly arbitrary procedure.

Heidegger's interpretations of some of the fragments of the pre-Socratics resemble Buber's translations of the Hebrew Scriptures in the resolve to strip away facile misinterpretations and to penetrate to the roots. But in the first place the pre-Socratics had never been as much obscured by familiarity as the Bible; they had never ceased to be mysterious. Secondly, Buber has not concentrated, like Heidegger, on a few obscure passages, to point up the inadequacy of previous translations and to remind us of their overwhelming difficulty: Buber has succeeded in giving us a really new translation of the Hebrew Bible. Finally, as a stylist Buber is above comparison with Heidegger whose prose—not to speak of his thin volume of poetry—is

gradually becoming more and more indistinguishable from the paro-
dies published here and there.

IV

Buber as a Translator. Buber's principles of translation differ
widely from those generally accepted in the English-speaking world.
He developed his ideas about translation in the course of his collaboration with Rosenzweig; and in 1936 he published a volume of
essays, replies to reviewers, notes, and letters—some written by
Rosenzweig, some by Buber, and some jointly: *Die Schrift und ihre
Verdeutschung*. This book derives its unique vitality not only from
its enthusiastic concern with the Bible, which comes to life for us,
too, but also from the rare intensity of Buber, Rosenzweig, and their
relationship. The book, though little known, is a major contribution
to our understanding of the Bible and to the fine art of translation.
And Rosenzweig's ready wit, at its acid best when he rebuts the strictures of reviewers, makes one forget temporarily that he was fatally
ill and long unable to speak when he resolved to join with Buber
to make a really new translation of the Hebrew Bible: "on some
tortuous machinery he would indicate, with unsteady finger, one, two,
three letters of each word; and his wife would guess it." (319)

The importance of the Buber-Rosenzweig translation and its principles is twofold. First, it represents an achievement sadly lacking
in the English-speaking world: a really new translation of the Bible.
Both the Revised Standard Version of the Old Testament and the
Bible of the Jewish Publication Society of America represent mere
revisions of the King James Bible and do not at all breathe the
spirit of the original Hebrew books. Neither do they strip away the
familiar veils of an idiom designed "to be read in churches"—an
idiom not altogether different, in spite of its magnificence, from
the holy tone by which one instantly recognizes preachers on the radio. Of the unaffected immediacy and stark power of much of the
Hebrew Scriptures, few English readers have an inkling, nor is there
any translation to which one can refer them. In German there are
two: that of Buber and Rosenzweig and that of Harry Torczyner
(now Tur-Sinai) which was begun at about the same time, but
completed rapidly, owing to the collaboration of fouteen scholars, and
reprinted in a single volume, revised once more by Torczyner, in
1937.

Secondly, Buber and Rosenzweig revolutionized the art of translation. This art is much more highly developed in Germany than in the English-speaking world. Voss' translation of the Iliad and the Odyssey into German dactylic hexameters comes to mind immediately as an achievement without parallel in English. Before that, Luther's translation of the Old Testament came incomparably closer to the style and sensibility of the original than the King James Bible. After Voss, there are the incredibly successful **Shakespeare translations of** August Wilhelm Schlegel, there are Hölderlin's versions of two of Sophocles' plays, Goethe's efforts at translation, Rückert's virtuosity, and, more recently, the translations of Buddhist scriptures by Karl Eugen Neumann and the several volumes of frequently inspired translations by Stefan George and Rilke.

In English there is no comparable tradition of responsibility and faithfulness to the original texts. There is no adequate translation yet of either Homer or the Greek tragedies.[1] The last few years have seen a rash of new translations of Greek classics; but as soon as they approach poetry they arrogate liberties which seem irresponsible compared to the best German efforts. In English it is considered a truism that every age must make its own translation, and it is considered perfectly all right for the contemporary translator of— never mind what, to recast it in the idiom of T. S. Eliot or W. H. Auden. Would those who hold these principles condone translations of Shakespeare into Rilke's idiom or Brecht's?

Another almost undoubted maxim of most English translators— and especially publishers—is that the translation must read as if the work had been written in idiomatic English. The idiom may be colloquial or it may be that of Eliot, but it must not be unprece-

---

[1] This essay was contributed in 1957, before Robert Fitzgerald's version of the Odyssey and the Chicago edition of The Complete Greek Tragedies appeared. But the translations of the tragedies are uneven, and that of *Antigone* (first published in 1954) exemplifies, like other English versions of this play, the pitfalls of not accepting Buber's methods of translation. Line 332, the beginning of the famous Chorus is rendered: "Many the wonders but nothing walks stranger than man." Although completely different words are employed to translate the Greek *deina* and *deinoteron,* this version comes closer to Sophocles' meaning than the popular translation that finds nothing "more wonderful than man." But what has been quite generally overlooked is that the same word occurs a third time, only nine lines earlier, where the Chicago translation renders it as "terrible." Quite especially in a line as often quoted as that of the Chorus, a translator should find a word that will serve in all three places; e.g., uncanny.

dented; it must avoid neologisms, coinages, and anything that is strange or baffling—even if the original is notable for its striking departure from the idiom of its time, even if it abounds in unusual words, even if in places it is profoundly difficult to understand or clearly ambiguous. Where the best German translators would not rest content until they had found a way of preserving every ambiguity of the original, most English-speaking publishers will expect their translators to resolve every ambiguity, to venture an interpretation which will make things easy for the reader, and, by all means, to produce a text which is smoother than the original.

Buber and Rosenzweig went much further than any previous translators of comparable stature in flouting these hallowed maxims and in going to the opposite extreme. "With the pedantry of a genius" (323), Rosenzweig insisted on Buber's faithfulness to the original in the minutest detail; and Buber brought off this feat and created a style which is equally far from ordinary German and from the holy tone of the English Bible.

A few of the Buber-Rosenzweig principles may be enumerated explicitly. The first, which is of the utmost importance, is that every word must always be translated, as far as at all possible, by the same word—not by one word here and another one there, and a third word elsewhere. This strikes many people as strange; some even think that this amounts to renouncing true translation in favor of creating a mere "crib." It does indeed amount to that, or worse, if you simply take the first "equivalent" that comes to mind and then stick by that. Obviously, this principle obliges you to try to find a truly equivalent word, one which reproduces as many of the shades of the original word as possible. If you succeed, you enrich every single sentence containing that word by animating it with all the overtones and ambiguities, allusions, echoes, and suggestions lost by translators who make it easy for themselves.

If you translate an author who has little feeling for his language and a text that lacks style and all but the barest meaning, there is no need for all this trouble. If you deal with the Bible, on the other hand, the price you pay for taking less pains than this is that your text cannot be used as the basis of any serious discussion. Any study of the love of God, or the justice of God, on the basis of the King James Bible, which translates the same word now as love and then as justice, is bound to be irrelevant to the Hebrew Scriptures.

The second principle, closely related to the first, is that you must go back to the root of the word, seeing that, especially in Hebrew, the same root may connect—quite obviously to the reader of the original—two nouns, or, even more frequently, a noun and a verb or an adjective. And this leads to a search for the, generally sensuous, basic meaning of this root which, once found, revitalizes its derivatives and enriches the meaning of the text with scores of new associations and connections. One becomes aware—and the excitement of the volume of essays on *Die Schrift* is partly due to the fact that we see Buber and Rosenzweig becoming aware—of all sorts of things which had escaped the notice of previous translators.

The third principle—another corollary of the first—is that a rare word must be rendered by a rare word. This is connected with a characteristic device of Biblical narration which Buber and Rosenzweig, varying Wagner's word, leitmotif, called *Leitwort-Stil*. A single illustration may explain it better than any attempt at definition.

After Jacob has taken advantage of Isaac's inability to see and has obtained the blessing intended for his older brother, Isaac says that he came "with guile." Later, when Laban has taken advantage of Jacob's inability to see in the dark and brought to his bed Leah to receive the love intended for her younger sister, Jacob reproaches him: "Why have you beguiled me?" As Buber points out in *Die Schrift und ihre Verdeutschung* (p. 224), this word root "occurs only in one other place in the Pentateuch: Genesis 34.13, where it refers to Jacob's sons."

Another similar device, common in the Bible, is the repetition of the same root for purposes of emphasis. And then there is the frequent use of alliteration. Buber and Rosenzweig, trying to recreate the Bible for the ear, too, felt a responsibility to the sound and rhythm which brings to life the Hebrew Scriptures, liberating them from the majestic monotony of the Authorized Version.

As an example, consider a sentence from Genesis 37. Joseph has been sold into slavery by his brothers, and they have dipped his coat in the blood of a goat and brought it to their father, saying: "This have we found: know now whether it be thy son's coat or no." The Authorized Version goes on: "And he knew it, and said, It is my son's coat; an evil beast hath devoured him; Joseph is without doubt rent in pieces." The words "It is" are scrupulously italicized to indicate their absence from the original Hebrew text; and, as often in such cases, their omission constitutes a vast improvement. The words "without doubt" do not disfigure the original either; but the passage in the King James Bible has a sublime rhythm of its own which is eminently suitable "to be read in Churches," as the title page proclaims.

The Revised Standard Version does not aspire to recapture the poetry of the original; it merely tries to correct outright errors—by changing "the coat of many colors" into "a long robe with sleeves," for example—and it tries to bring the King James Bible up to date by changing "knew it" to "recognized it," "coat" to "robe," "hath" to "has," and "rent" to "torn." But "It is" and "without doubt" are both retained. All this is better than the Moffat translation which shows no feeling for the situation whatever: "Jacob recognized it. 'It is my son's tunic,' he said; 'some evil beast has devoured him. Joseph must have been torn to pieces.'" One feels like adding: "Elementary, my dear Watson."

Buber, in the latest edition of his version (1954) *translates* the text, instead of trying to improve on it. "He saw it and said: My son's coat! an evil beast has devoured him; torn, torn is Joseph!" This may show what it means to let the Hebrew original speak to us.

In the first edition, Buber still had the disturbing "it is"; and Torczyner preceded him in rendering Jacob's outcry faithfully. What matters is that those who know the Bible only from English translations have little idea of its elementary power: they do not know how the text cries out to communicate the immediacy of experiences.

One further example may show how much is at stake. Take a verse from Hosea—14.1 in the Hebrew Bible, 13.16 in the English:

King James

Samaria shall become desolate;
for she hath rebelled against her
God: they shall fall by the sword:
their infants shall be dashed in
pieces, and their women with child
shall be ripped up.

Revised Standard

Samaria shall bear her guilt,
   because she has rebelled against her God;
they shall fall by the sword,
   their little ones shall be dashed in pieces,
   and their pregnant women ripped open.

after Buber

Atone must Samaria the guilt
that it was obstinate to its God,

by the sword they must fall,
their toddlers are smashed,
their pregnant women slashed.

after Torczyner
Damned is Shomron
for defying her God.
They fall by the sword,
smashed are their infants,
their pregnant women slashed.

Buber's translation is not definitive, and he deserves our admiration precisely for his innumerable changes in the second edition. (My English translation of his German version does not do full justice to him.)

The Authorized Version has sacrificed the sensibility of the Hebrew Bible with its unique poetry and power to its own profoundly different conception of rhetoric. In the process the translators produced the most sumptuous monument of English prose. It has its own stylistic unity, even to the extent of boldly assimilating the books of the New Testament, too, to the same style. In the end, Jacob beholding the bloody garment of Joseph, Hosea envisaging the destruction of his people, Luke telling stories, and Paul writing a letter to the Galatians all sound like early 17th Century English divines with a flair for oratory.

The Epistle to the Galatians has at last come to life in the Revised Standard Version, so we can hear Paul; but the Old Testament suffers from a half-hearted compromise between Elizabethan rhetoric and a more modern idiom. The English here does not at all approach the sublime economy of the Hebrew. In many ways, it is much easier to translate into German than it is to translate into English; but precisely the succinctness, the terse, laconic quality of much of the Hebrew text is more readily rendered in English. In the Hosea verse, the original consists of 11 words—30 syllables in all. The King James Bible requires 33 words, 43 syllables, and the Revised Standard Version one less of each. Buber, in German, uses 23 words, 44 syllables; Torczyner, respectively, 20 and 34; and my English version of Torczyner, 20 words and 26 syllables.

This method of counting may seem pedantic, but it fixes in figures the striking difference between the resplendent rhetoric of the

"Authorized" prophet who speaks "to be read in Churches" and the austere immediacy of the Hebrew prophet who cries out over what he sees—even as Jacob in Genesis cries out. In English we hear a great orator who prides himself on his imposing cadences and his rich imagery. In Hebrew we hear a voice without aesthetic ambitions; a voice that cries out because it cannot contain itself, a voice that addresses us and by the sheer force of its uninhibited directness tears the heart out of its sloth.

It is easy to hear the English Bible without listening, to be edified by it without understanding. The Hebrew Bible does not speak in some special holy tone, appropriate on the Sabbath but rather out of place on weekdays—and irrelevant and almost blasphemous after Belsen and Auschwitz. There is nothing unctuous about it. It speaks to us with a singular lack of manner. The primary significance of Buber's translation is that he has let the text speak to us again.

One of the most important things one can teach any student is to read—to read not merely after the fashion of the world but with mind, heart, and soul. Torczyner's Bible has been available in a single volume since 1937, while Buber's Bible was first published book by book, volume by volume, and then, still incomplete, collected in three imposing tomes. Only in the 1950s these were replaced by three pleasant thin-paper volumes, and the fourth and last volume appeared in 1962. So far, Torczyner's edition is far handier; and it is debatable which is preferable. But it was Buber's epic struggle with the text and with the public, first jointly with Franz Rosenzweig, and later alone, that has taught thousands of young men to read—first, the Bible, and then other books, too.

My own translations are unthinkable without Buber and Rosenzweig. When I translated four of Nietzsche's books—*Zarathustra, Twilight of the Idols, Antichrist,* and *Nietzsche contra Wagner*—as well as selections from his other works, his letters, and his notes, for a one-volume edition in The Viking Portable Library, I referred to Buber and Rosenzweig and tried to explain why it was essential to be faithful to Nietzsche's stylistic peculiarities, why his terms must be rendered consistently by the same words, and how full his works are of allusions both to his own previous works and to various classics, above all the Bible. Any failure to capture a pun, however indifferent, in translation, creates the false presumption that the author said in all seriousness what but for the pun he might never have said that way. (pp. 3-6, 107-110)

Translating several of Leo Baeck's essays at the same time, I must not let Baeck sound like Nietzsche, or Nietzsche like Baeck, or either of them like myself. Baeck's peculiar and difficult style had to be re-created. And the same was true a few years later when I published *Existentialism from Dostoevsky to Sartre* and translated Nietzsche, Rilke, and Heidegger. Heidegger must not sound like Nietzsche or Rilke, or, worse, Rilke like Heidegger.

Heidegger has the ambition to teach people how to read, but in many younger men he has encouraged a lack of respect for philological correctness, a penchant for an almost comic jargon, and a flair for the obscure—even an outright contempt for the whole plane of correctness. From Buber, on the other hand, one *can* learn how to read.

Heidegger—even more than Jaspers—disregards the context and prefers pliant fragments and notes. Interpretation becomes a device for having his own say, and the text a mere means. In Heidegger's readings there is no Thou.

Buber is always alive to the context—not only the immediate context: when he considers a Biblical sentence, the whole of the Hebrew Bible is the context. He is always struggling to hear the voice of the Thou. And he teaches a deep reverence for the voice that addresses us, and the patient resolve to listen and to let oneself be addressed. Few men could possibly teach anything of equal significance.

V

Buber and Hasidism. Buber's work on the Hasidim, including his collection of their lore, is probably more impressive for those of us who have no first-hand knowledge of Hasidism than it is either for the specialist scholar or for those who know it from their childhood. Here more than anywhere else the question arises to what extent Buber has projected himself into his subject matter: is he allowing Hasidism to speak to us, or is it he himself that is speaking?

Clearly, it is not a case in which the author makes the men about whom he writes mouthpieces of his own ideas. His own ideas were changed in the course of his concern with the Hasidim, and what we hear as we read is what Buber heard. Others, before him, did not hear it just like that. But he himself had not heard it just like that either until he came to listen to the Hasidim. He tells us what he heard, not what he had to say all along.

If you compare Buber's *Die Erzählungen der Chassidim* with Chagall's *Illustrations for the Bible*, you find two different worlds. Chagall's etchings and lithographs mirror a world of fantasy, magic, and ecstasy—closer to the Greek Orthodox church than to the Protestant, almost Puritan, simplicity and moral emphasis of Buber's tales of the Hasidim.

> Soon after the death of Rabbi Mosheh of Kobryn, one of his students was asked by the 'old Kozker,' Rabbi Mendel: 'What did your teacher consider most important?' He reflected and gave his answer: 'Whatever he was doing at the moment.' (647)
>
> Rabbi Mosheh Loeb related: How one should love men I have learned from a peasant. He sat in an inn with some other peasants, drinking. A long time he was silent like the rest, but when his heart was moved by the wine, he spoke to his neighbor: 'Tell me: do you love me or don't you?' And he replied: 'I love you very much.' But the first peasant answered: 'You say: I love you; and yet you do not know what hurts me. If you loved me in truth, you would know.' The other man could not say a word, and the peasant who had asked the question relapsed into silence, too. But I understood: that is love of men, to sense their wants and to bear their grief.(533)

Stories like these are definitive in their simplicity. That Buber did not make them up is clear. Similar ideas can be found elsewhere in the religious literature of the world. But it is the form that makes these stories, and hundreds like them, definitive. It was Buber who cut these diamonds. The fact that he did not add anything does not mean that he gave us what he found: he achieved perfection by cutting.

Rabbi Bunam once said: "Yes, I can bring all sinners to the point of return—except liars." (751)

There is courage in setting down a dictum like that, letting it stand alone. Surely, Buber was influenced, whether consciously or not, by Nietzsche's aphoristic style. He abandoned the non-functional opulence of the Victorian era and dared to end a story at the right point. Such courage is rare, not only among our contemporaries but even in the sacred books of the world. Luke, for example, generally makes up stories to frame sayings which in Matthew lack any such setting.

Consider the story of the anointing at Bethany which is found in all four Gospels. The four evangelists understand it very differently, and David Daube has discussed their diverse treatments in a very illuminating section of his book on *The New Testament and Rabbinic Judaism.*

Both Mark and John take care to point out that the burial rite of anointing was performed. For Mark, it was performed at Bethany—by virtue of a fiction —and nothing was done after Jesus' death. For John, Jesus' body was actually anointed after his death, and the action at Bethany is not represented as performance of the rite. (314)

Daube shows how Matthew follows Mark and is demonstrably much more comfortable with this solution than Mark was. But what concerns me here is a dictum for which Luke finds a place in this story— a dictum which Daube does not discuss: "her sins, which are many, are forgiven, for she loved much." (7.47)

These striking words are found nowhere else in the New Testament. If we assume that Jesus actually spoke them on this occasion, that amounts to a serious indictment of the other three evangelists who have put into their master's mouth so many unlovely sayings while suppressing words like these. If we assume that Luke invented these words or—as is much more likely—that they formed part of an oral tradition but lacked any context, and that he worked these words into the present story, then we must go on to ask how effectively he did this. Unless, in other words, we assume that he told the story as it actually happened while the other three distorted the story seriously, we must admit that Luke's story represents his own particular way of blending and shaping various traditions. Among these is a gem: what does he do with it?

Looked at critically in this perspective, Luke's story will satisfy few readers. The immediately preceding reproof which is not found in the other three Gospels and the immediately following words— "but he who is forgiven little, loves little"—greatly weaken the central dictum. And the two following verses detract still further from the weight of the word of love.

This approach may seem excessively subjective; but it is a historic fact that the words "her sins, which are many, are forgiven, for she loved much," and a few others like them, have long shaken off the shackles of their context and have gone far toward creating an image of Jesus and Christianity which is quite at variance with the full text of each of the four Gospels. In *Die Erzählungen der Chassidim* Buber presents gem upon gem without mounting each in a setting of inferior quality. Buber's stories cannot be improved by cutting. That is more than one can say of the art of any of the four evangelists.

The obvious objection to Buber is that he gives us too glowing a picture of Hasidism. The opponents of the movement, the Mitnaggdim, had some reasons on their side: miracles and magic, superstitions and authoritarianism were present in Hasidism from the start. As a historian, Buber is by no means above criticism.

The reply to such criticisms is implicit in the comparison with the Gospels which, no doubt, will strike some readers as blasphemous. What saves Buber's work is its perfection. He has given us one of the great religious books of all time, a work that invites comparison with the great Scriptures of mankind. This estimate must seem fantastic to those who have not read *The Tales of the Hasidim*. But if it should be justified, then the criticism that Buber is not an impartial historian can be accepted cheerfully without being considered very damning.

We can read the Book of Genesis and the discourses of the Buddha as reports of "how it actually happened," to cite Ranke's words, or we can read them as religious literature. The question of historical accuracy is always worth raising, and a detailed answer is both interesting and important. But the rank of these works does not depend on their positivistic accuracy but on their profundity. And that is true also of *The Tales of the Hasidim*.

Buber's collection resembles the great religious Scriptures in drawing on a living religious tradition, in selecting, in giving form. Sacred Scriptures are not so much written as they grow. Buber's collection has grown out of his own long dialogue with a tradition, and it loses none of its initial impressiveness after one has lived with it for a generation. Here the adolescent can find voices that speak to him, answer him, and help him to form his notions of the meaning of religion. A growing skepticism does not mute these voices or destroy this meaning. Here is religion that stands up to philosophic questions as the sophisticated discourses of theologians don't.

There are whole books on prayer which make less sense than these few lines:

Rabbi Shneur Zalman once asked his son: 'With what do you pray?' The son understood the meaning of the question: on what he concentrated, on what he based his prayer. He replied: 'The verse: May every height bow down before thee.' Then he asked his father: 'And with what do you pray?' He said: 'With the floor and with the bench.'(418)

The Kozker shouted at some of his Hasidim: 'What is this chatter about praying seriously? What do they mean: praying seriously?' They did not understand him. So he said: 'Is there anything that one should do without seriousness?'(791)

One may safely agree with Hermann Hesse that Buber, "like no other living author, has enriched world literature with a genuine treasure." (*Briefe*, January 1950) Although Hesse has won the Nobel Prize, his great novels are hardly known in the English-speaking world —partly for the same reasons which account for the comparative neglect of Buber's great collection of Hasidic lore: the lack of translations which equal the perfection of the originals and above all the present lack in the English-speaking world of any wide-spread sense for the kind of religion which has found expression in Buber's stories or in Hesse's *Siddhartha*.

In the United States, *intense* religion tends to be either revivalist or theological. The pseudo-religion of the bestsellers and the most popular magazines, which finds its place between stories of wise animals and miracle drugs, reports on the latest gadgets and cosmetics, and whatever is of human interest and wholesome for the family, need not detain us here. Serious religion that produces crises in men's lives, converts men, and profoundly influences them is best represented in America by Reinhold Niebuhr and by Billy Graham: Graham is the poor man's Niebuhr and speaks to the hearts of those who cannot afford ten-dollar words. Niebuhr, in spite of his years as a preacher in Detroit, speaks mainly to the intellectuals and offers them a Christian version of Marx, Nietzsche, Freud, and all the latest intellectual developments.

There is no revivalism and no theology in Buber's Hasidic lore. And for the still small voice of this religion which speaks to the emotions without rhetoric and to the mind without any imposing jargon, there are few ears in the English-speaking world.

That there will ever be a very large audience to hear Buber's Hasidim with an open heart is unlikely; but, before long, these stories will, no doubt, become part of the repertoire of educated people who have now begun to read selections from the Buddha's speeches and the Upanishads, and a free version of the Bhagavadgita, in huge popular editions. And these stories will surely be remembered widely when the theologians of our time have gone the way of Harnack and Schleiermacher, not to mention lesser names that have long been forgotten by all but specialists.

VI

I and Thou. In the United States, Buber is best known for a small book that has profoundly influenced Protestant theology. In German it was *Ich und Du,* and one could read quite far without being aware that Buber was concerned with religion: indeed, the point of the book was partly to break down the division between the everyday world and religion. Eventually, God is found *in* the everyday world, in the *Du,* in a primary relation paralleled in the relation *Between Man and Man,* to cite the English title of the sequel.

Buber himself considers the English title *I and Thou* inevitable. Partly, this is surely due to the fact that men with a German background feel more at home with Thou and Thee and Thy than Americans. By now the Revised Standard Version has all but purged the Bible of these words. It is also relevant that the child says You and not Thou. But what matters here is not a positive suggestion about a point of translation; rather, two serious pitfalls due to the translation *I and Thou.*

The first is that the phrase suggests the holy tone which just Buber has done so much to eliminate from religion. We are immediately put on our guard.

The second pitfall is exactly paralleled by the reception in the English-speaking world of a book that appeared in the same year, 1923: *Das Ich und das Es* by Sigmund Freud. Surely, this should have been translated as *The I and the It;* but the translator chose *The Ego and the Id.* And *das Über-ich* became the super-ego. A jargon developed and obscured the work of Freud. And a jargon developed and obscured the thought of Buber.

People began to talk of "the I-Thou relationship" and "the I-Thou" as they talk of "original sin" and the "natural man"—as if Buber's achievement had not been in part that he had managed to bring religion to life without the dubious benefit of an abstract terminology about whose meaning one is not completely sure. Buber had taken his stand not on concepts like "revelation" and "redemption" or even "God" but had started from an elementary experience about which no skeptic need have any qualms.

Most important, Buber had not just talked *about* it. Even as Freud had developed the major body of his work with its profound originality without the benefit of any Id or Ego, and then, more or less in retrospect, inquired whether one could summarize and systematize his results in terms of a few simple vivid concepts with which his findings neither stand nor fall, so Buber, mid-way in his work on the Hasidim, tried to state a central theme in *Ich und Du*. What he meant is not only developed in his later writings on the dialogical principle, but also in his work on the Hasidim and his translation of the Hebrew Bible.

How Buber has taught us to read can be summarized by saying that he impressed on us that the text must not be treated as a mere It; the text must become a Thou. But any jargon tends to falsify. We must learn to listen and let the text speak to us, instead of resting content with manipulating it or carving it up as the Higher Critics did.

If one approaches *I and Thou* as a philosophic essay, trying to reconstruct an argument and testing that, it is not hard to criticize the book. But if instead of examining the book as an object, an It, we open our hearts to it to hear what it has to say to us, we are confronted with a crucial question: if God is to mean something to us, can it be anything but what Buber suggests in this little book, namely *das ewige Du* (the eternal Thou)? All superstitions *about* God, all talk about him, all theology is sacrificed to the voice that speaks to us, the *Du* to which some cry out "when," as Goethe says, "man in his agony grows mute." And not only in agony.

Any formulation is disturbing; but has there ever been a better one than "the eternal Thou" (or You)? How meaningless compared to it are the "being-itself" and even "the ground of being" of Paul Tillich! The God of Abraham, Isaac, and Israel was not "being-itself"; nor was it "the ground of being" that told Abraham to leave his father's house or that commanded men "You shall be holy; for I, the Lord your God am holy" or to whom the Psalmist and, according to two of the evangelists, Jesus, cried out, "My God, my God, why have you forsaken me?" If we do not take such a phrase as "the eternal Thou" for a concept, but rather understand what it tries to say plainly, it is probably the most illuminating suggestion about the meaning of "God" ever ventured.

VII

Summary. Buber's current success in the United States is deceptive. One is conscious of his stature, one pays tribute to him, but few have ears for what Buber is saying. One attributes to him an anthropology and a theology, an ethic and epistemology, seeks "principles" of Biblical faith from him, and is a little irritated by the lack of systematic content, of clearly formulated principles, and by his excessively personal interpretations.

The Jews are proud of him and do not give full vent to their irritation, and the Christians, almost hungry for a venerable Jewish figure to whom they can show their respect, their freedom from prejudice, and their horror of the wrongs done to his people, also suppress their exasperation. Moreover, it is not fashionable to criticize religious figures. But Buber's judgments about New Testament questions are annoying to most Jews and Christians: some Jews find him not Jewish enough, while many young Jewish intellectuals are sufficiently under the influence of modern Protestant theology to question him from a curiously Christian point of view.

Buber stands in an essentially Jewish tradition, and his religion, which is opposed alike to rationalism, mysticism, and theology, is clearly continuous with central elements in the thought of the prophets, of Akiba and Maimonides, of the Hasidim, Hermann Cohen, and Leo Baeck. He speaks for himself, but he is by no means a marginal phenomenon of Judaism.

Even during World War I, at a time when baptism was no longer rare among German Jews and assimilation accepted as a goal by most of the unbaptized, too, Buber published a periodical he called *Der Jude.* Who has the right to say of him today, as some Protestants do, that he is really not a Jew? On the other hand, if some Christians consider him "the" representative spokesman for Judaism, one can only say that his present lack of rivals is not his fault.

Any such over-all estimate of a man's significance is necessarily controversial. Others are bound to see him differently—but the present attempt may help them to arrive at their own estimate. Alas, Buber may well see himself differently in many ways. If so, it may be of some interest to readers of this volume to find out not only how Buber answers specific criticisms by the other contributors to this volume but also where precisely he is displeased with this attempt at an integrated picture. Corrections of specific errors are always worthwhile—but it would also be interesting to have Buber's response to the way in which I have placed accents, light, and shade.

Buber tells of the Hasid who, asked what impressed him most about some Zaddik, said: how he tied his shoes. One gathers that this Zaddik, like another one I have mentioned, considered most important whatever he happened to be doing. Another Hasid might have been most impressed with the way the Zaddik did some other little or big thing.

What impresses me most about Buber is the way he answers questions, the way he goes about translating the Bible, the way he has opened up to us the world of the Hasidim, fashioning one of the great religious books of all time out of their lore, and the pervasive concern not with theories but with the living *Du*.

Little is gained by calling Buber an existentialist and by lumping him with men with whom he disagrees as much as he does with Kierkegaard, Jaspers, Heidegger, and Sartre. But if we find the heart of existentialism in the protest against systems, concepts, and abstractions, coupled with a resolve to remain faithful to concrete experience and above all to the challenge of human existence—should we not find in that case that Kierkegaard and Jaspers, Heidegger and Sartre had all betrayed their own central resolve? That they had all become enmeshed in sticky webs of dialectic that impede communication? that the high abstractness of their idiom and their strange addiction to outlandish concepts far surpassed the same faults in Descartes or Plato? that not one of them was able any more to listen to the challenge of another human reality as it has found expression in a text? and that their writings have, without exception, become monologues?

One might well conclude that in reality there is only one existentialist, and he is no existentialist but Martin Buber.

WALTER KAUFMANN

DEPARTMENT OF PHILOSOPHY
PRINCETON UNIVERSITY

THE PHILOSOPHER REPLIES

Martin Buber

REPLIES TO MY CRITICS

I. *Philosophical Accounting. Personal Determination*

IN THIS book the problem is discussed many times whether I am a philosopher or a theologian or something else. The question is rightly raised; for, depending on the circumstances, I am to be confronted with the rules and laws of one or the other of these realms. I cannot, however, make any of the proposed answers my own.

In so far as my self-knowledge extends, I might call myself an atypical man. My aversion to the usual excessive typology probably stems ultimately from this fact.

Since I have matured to a life from my own experience[1]—a process that began shortly before the "First World War" and was completed shortly after it—I have stood under the duty to insert the framework of the decisive experiences that I had at that time into the human inheritance of thought, but not as "my" experiences, rather as an insight valid and important for others and even for other kinds of men. Since, however, I have received no message which might be passed on in such a manner, but have only had the experiences and attained the insights, my communication had to be a philosophical one. It had to relate the unique and particular to the "general," to what is discoverable by everyman in his own existence. It had to express what is by its nature incomprehensible in concepts that could be used and communicated (even if at times with difficulties). More precisely, I had to make an It out of that which was experienced in I-Thou and as I-Thou.

I am convinced that it happened not otherwise with all the philosophers loved and honored by me. Only that after they had completed the transformation, they devoted themselves to the philosophy more deeply and fully than I was able or it was granted to me to do.

What happened to me was that all the experiences of being that I had during the years 1912-1919 became present to me in growing measure as *one* great experience of faith. By this is meant an experience that transports a person in all his component parts, his capac-

---

[1] I do not use the concept of experience critically here, as in the beginning of the book *I and Thou*, but positively. I mean by it simply what happened to me.

ity for thought certainly included, so that, all the doors springing
open, the storm blows through all the chambers.

Reason is included in this kind of experience, only not in its detached, autocratic form, but as one of the bearers. When it is as now a
matter of communication, reason, therefore, can function as a trust-
worthy elaborator. Elaboration is of necessity a philosophical, and
that means a logicizing, task. What is important, however, is that the
indispensable capacity for thought not misjudge its office and act as if
it were the authoritative recipient. It is incumbent upon it to logicize
the superlogical, for which the law of contradiction does not hold
valid; it is incumbent upon it to hold aloof from the inner contradiction; but it may not sacrifice to consistency anything of that reality
itself which the experience that has happened commands it to point to.
If the thought remains true to its task, a system will not come out of
it, but certainly a connected body of thought more resolved in itself,
more transmittible.

One might now protest somewhat as follows: if that connection
of experiences is to be understood as an experience of faith, then its
communication is certainly to be called preferably a theological one.
But that is not so. For by theology is understood, certainly, a teaching
about God, even if it is only a "negative" one which then perhaps
appears instead of a teaching of the nature of God, a teaching of
the word of God, the Logos. But I am absolutely not capable nor
even disposed to teach this or that about God. Certainly, when I
seek to explain the fact of man, I cannot leave out of consideration
that he, man, lives over against God. But I cannot include God himself
at any point in my explanation, any more than I could detach from
history the, to me indubitable, working of God in it, and make of it
an object of my contemplation. As I know no theological world
history, so I know no theological anthropology in this sense; I know
only a philosophical one.

The theological element has indeed influenced a large part of
my scholarship and reporting. It is the foundation of my thinking,
but not as a derivative of anything traditional, as important as that
also may be to me. It has, therefore, not been to "theology," but
rather to the experience of faith that I owe the independence of
my thought. I am not merely bound to philosophical language, I
am bound to the philosophical method, indeed to a dialectic that
has become unavoidable with the beginning of philosophical thinking. But I also know nothing of a "double truth." My philosophy

serves, yes, it serves, but it does not serve a series of revealed propositions. It serves an experienced, a perceived attitude that it has been established to make communicable.

This philosophy has, of course, incorporated a *theologoumenon*, if it is not to be regarded rather as a *religiosum*; the name of God is not here in general (except for inevitable combinations) replaced by a concept. I do not, to be sure, disagree with Heraclitus who, clearly from the standpoint of the subject itself, holds it to be inadmissible to say only "Zeus." But I have, indeed, no doctrine of a primal ground (*Urgrund*) to offer. I must only witness for that meeting in which all meetings with others are grounded, and you cannot meet the absolute.

II. *Philosophical Accounting. Against Simplifications*

It is necessary, first of all, to elucidate in several essential points what I mean and what I do not mean. For this purpose I must oppose many simplifications that my questioners and critics have undertaken in connection with what I have said.

Fackenheim's question whether my concept lies entirely "within the I-Thou knowledge"[2] is based on the notion that I, at least once, at least in the case of philosophy, designated this and the I-It knowledge as "exhaustive alternatives." But that is not so. I by no means hold human "inner life" in general, and within it human thinking in particular, to be exclusively composed of occurrences of the one and the other kinds. What I mean is that when man presents himself to the "world" or in general to others, when he takes up an "attitude," when he "speaks a primal word," it is either the one or the other—and that he then actualizes either the one I or the other. But I do not mean at all that the life of man or even only his "inner life" represents a continuity of such attitudes, such "speakings," such actualizations. In the one moment he is over against another as such, sees him as present and relates to him thus. In the other moment he sees everything else collected round him and from time to time singles out, observes, explores, applies, uses. Both these moments are included in the dynamic of lived life. But thinking is not properly stretched into an exclusive duality. To be sure, as I have stressed,[3]

---

[2] Fackenheim, p. 291.

[3] Martin Buber, *Between Man and Man*, "Dialogue," Section 'On Thinking,' trans. R. G. Smith (New York: Macmillan Paperbacks, 1965).

it may not be understood as a conversation of the soul with itself; it has genuine dialogical moments, alongside of monological ones. In the real stream of thinking, nonetheless, a large constituent part cannot be subsumed under either of the two spheres; it is a noetic movement from a personal meeting to a factual knowledge-structure, a movement in which the two primal words cooperate, as it were. Authentic philosophizing originates ever anew from the fulgurations of the Thou relationship that still affords no "objective" knowledge. Now the transposition into the structured order of It takes place, and, if a real workman is at work, there may stand at the end the freestone structure of a system. Indeed, "I-It finds its highest concentration and clarification in philosophical knowledge": but that in no way means that this knowledge contains nothing other than I-It, is nothing other than I-It. The fiery track of the original fulgurations is inextinguishable, even though it may remain unnoticed by the eye accustomed to an objectified image of being. To the penetrating genesis-glance each bold metaphysical setting manifests its origin in a meeting of the knowing person with an element of being that announces itself in the shape of that which meets him in a living way.

Therefore, it is incorrect to ask whether the doctrine of the I and Thou is to be "classified" without qualifications within the "I-Thou knowledge."[4] An I-Thou knowledge that can be held fast, preserved, factually transmitted does not really exist. That which discloses itself to me from time to time in the I-Thou relationship can only become such a knowledge through transmission into the I-It sphere. Carefully as in our insight we must contrast the I-Thou relationship and the I-It relationship with each other, still it would be misleading to pursue the distinction into the consideration of philosophical thinking and its events. Every essential knowledge is in its origin contact with an existing being and in its completion possession of an enduring concept.

Still something else, something particular must be added. The theme that was dictated to the thinker experiencing here, was not suited to being developed into a comprehensive system. It was, in fact, concerned about the great presupposition for the beginning of philosophizing and its continuation, about the duality of the primal words. It was important to indicate this duality. Although it is the basic relationship in the life of each man with all existing being, it

4 Cf. Fackenheim, p. 292.

was barely paid attention to. It had to be pointed out; it had to be shown forth in the foundations of existence. A neglected, obscured, primal reality was to be made visible. The thinking, the teaching had to be determined by the task of pointing. Only what was connected with the pointing to what was to be pointed to was admissible. Being was not to to be treated, but solely the human twofold relationship to being. The philosophizing had to be essentially an anthropological one; at its center, from time to time elucidating itself, had to stand the question how man is possible, just that question to which the reality of the twofold relationship under the presupposition of the primal distance peculiar to man provides the answer. Outlooks into that which transcends man were afforded where the relationship to this was to be clarified; but the tendency to a system encompassing the situation of man could gain no entrance here.

No system was suitable for what I had to say. Structure was suitable for it, a compact structure but not one that joined everything together. I was not permitted to reach out beyond my experience, and I never wished to do so. I witnessed for experience and appealed to experience. The experience for which I witnessed is, naturally, a limited one. But it is not to be understood as a "subjective" one. I have tested it through my appeal and test it ever anew. I say to him who listens to me: "It is your experience. Recollect it, and what you cannot recollect, dare to attain it as experience." But he who seriously declines to do it, I take him seriously. His declining is my problem.

I must say it once again: I have no teaching.[5] I only point to something. I point to reality, I point to something in reality that had not or had too little been seen. I take him who listens to me by the hand and lead him to the window. I open the window and point to what is outside.

I have no teaching, but I carry on a conversation.

III. *Misunderstandings*

Out of the misjudgment of the intention and character of my work of thought, and out of the overstressing of one thing and another in that said by me, but apparently also out of the not yet sufficient clarity of some points, misunderstandings have come to pass that

---

[5] Cf. the last paragraph of my preface to *For the Sake of Heaven*, 2nd ed. with New Foreword; trans. Ludwig Lewisohn (New York: Meridian Books Jewish Publication Society, 1958).

I wish to clear up beforehand. It will then be easier to come to an understanding concerning this and that question of a general nature.

1. Rotenstreich[6] writes: "Buber is eager to maintain the metaphysical presupposition of the concrete man's bond with the absolute, as he himself puts it, and it is experientially realized in the mutuality of 'Between.' " From this, far reaching consequences are drawn in relation to alleged oscillations, in particular with regard to the relation between the relationship of man to God and his relationship to his fellowman. But I have not been at all concerned about a metaphysical thesis. Rather, I have been concerned about establishing the simple fact that I do not mean by "God" the highest idea but that which can be fit into no pyramid as its apex, and that, accordingly, the link between God and man does not go by way of the universals, but by way of concrete life. And with regard to the relation between the human way to God and that to the fellowman, I was and am simply concerned that both relationships are essentially similar, because both signify the direct turning to a Thou and both find their fulfillment in actual reciprocity. The "ontological problem," which of the two meetings is "the primary one," is, from the standpoint of my basic insight, not to be posed. The human person is quite probably conceivable without the possibility of meeting with other men, but without that with God I cannot conceive of it. On the plane of personal life-experience, the meeting with men is naturally the first; nevertheless, one only has to take seriously the insight that the genetically underivable uniqueness of every man presupposes the share of a creative act, and the original nature of the contact between God and man is evident.

2. Far-reaching consequences are also drawn by him from the concept of primal distancing used by me in "Distance and Relation" (1950).[7] In so doing, it is also mentioned, but not sufficiently taken into consideration, that I understand the primal distance as the elementary *presupposition* of all human relations. It has been for me simply a question concerning the anthropological foundation of the duality of I-Thou and I-It. Man, so I have indicated, is the only living being that by its nature perceives what surrounds it not as something connected with it, as it were, with its vital acts, but as

---

[6] Rotenstreich, pp. 106f.

[7] Buber, *The Knowledge of Man*, with an Introductory Essay by Maurice Friedman, trans. by Maurice Friedman and Ronald Gregor Smith (New York: Harper & Row, 1966), Chap. II; Rotenstreich, p. 116.

something detached, existing for itself. This "first movement," which once constituted man as such, is in no way a "reflective attitude"; it is the primal act, the primal attitude of man that makes him man. It is also the presupposition for man's entering into relation. More exactly, both belong ever again to man in his primal distance. It belongs to man to leave at a distance what surrounds him, together also with what lives around him, as belonging to him as his object, as It. And it belongs to him, again and again, time after time, to turn to an existing being as his partner, really meaning this existing being, to communicate with him as his Thou. I cannot bring this primal constitution of man, without which there would be neither speech nor tools, into connection with a reflective attitude. Man, I say, "is the creature through whose being the existing being is set at a distance from him." Not through reflections, but through human being.

Therefore, it is also incorrect to see in the fact of primal distance a reflecting position of a spectator. Man does not become a "spectator" through the fact that he no longer sees his environment, as does the animal, as in the sphere of his own corporeality, but as an other, existing in and out of itself. The other also concerns him, but it is no longer his young one or his enemy; it is also what it is itself; it does not merely affect him, it also *is*, it is "outside." Once again, that is not reflection, but the manner of perception that distinguishes man from animal.

3. The clarification is made difficult through the fact that another time Rotenstreich directly equates reflection and awareness.[8] But when I say that out of the I-Thou relationship another I emerges than out of the I-It relationship, that there and here a different I actualizes itself, then it is, to be sure, correct, to understand this as the "self-realization of the I through his awareness." But it is inadmissible to continue by saying that the I is also a self because of the inner center of his existence rooted in his reflection. The I that emerges is aware of itself, but without reflecting on itself so as to become an object; the exact distinction between the first "lightning flash" of self-consciousness and the second "elaborated" one is, in fact, of fundamental importance. But also I cannot regard the first emerging of the I as the center of existence. It is only an aura about the center, not the center itself. Reflection, however, I might compare to the play of a searchlight that shines upon the aura. Without it

8 Rotenstreich, pp. 124f.

the human being known to us would not exist, yet it does not belong
to its primal phenomena.

His assertion[9] of an "oscillation" between the primacy of relation and that of the I is connected with this misunderstanding. Naturally the presence of persons is necessary in order that a personal meeting
can take place; but the degree of the development of the I-consciousness
or even the degree of its reflective elaboration is of no essential moment
for the personal nature of these persons. I see that Socrates reflects, I do
not see that Francis does so; the relation of both men to their disciples
are genuinely personal.

4. Here an only apparently episodic contribution to the psychology of misunderstanding shall be interpolated. I say that where a
situation accosts one, then that is not the time to consult a dictionary.
The image should certainly thus be clear to everyone: in the fact of
the situation that now appears—for the sake of clarification let us take
an unforeseen and unforeseeable situation—I do not have to consider
under what general concept to subsume this situation and what principle thereby to apply to it. Rather, it is incumbent upon me to
take my stand before this "new" situation, it goes without saying to
take my stand before it with all that I am and that I know, and to
master it to the measure of my ability, to do that which is in keeping
with it, to encounter it. My use of the figure of a dictionary is now
understood by my critic[10] in the following manner: "It is not by
chance that Buber stresses the overcoming of the linguistic expression because in a linguistic expression there is something that
refers to a reservoir of contents which is actually conveyed." The
opinion which is ascribed to me is directly opposed to my own. On
the one hand, there is nothing that lies so far from me as wanting "to
overcome the linguistic expression"; nothing helps me so much to
understand man and his existence as does speech, and even beyond
the human its most sensuous concreteness mediates to me daily new
and surprising insights. On the other hand, however, it is for me of
the highest importance that the dialogue have a content. Only this
content is so much the more important, the more concrete, the more
concretizing it is, the more it does justice to the unique, the coming
to be, the formed, and is also able to incorporate in it the most spiritual, not metaphorically but in reality, because the spirit seeks the

9 Rotenstreich, p. 128.

10 Rotenstreich, p. 129.

body and lets speech help find it. This great concreteness, however, does not belong to the isolated word in the dictionary, where speech only shows us its general side, its applicability, but to the word in its living context, in the context of genuine conversation, of genuine poetry, of genuine prayer, of genuine philosophy; there first does it disclose to us the unique. Therefore, I have compared it to consulting a dictionary when one, instead of withstanding the situation, turns aside into the general, into principles.

Out of this misunderstanding quite far-reaching consequences are now drawn by him.[11] It is inferred that in the dialogue that I have in mind there are, to be sure, a giver and a receiver, but nothing which is given or received as a realm of content, for such a content would erect a screen through which the immediacy between the two partners would be suspended. But I absolutely do not mean that, and the citations adduced in support of this thesis signify something else. What I mean is not that nothing is given and received, but that in the dialogue between man and man given and received contents are so manifold that he who treats the nature of dialogue as a basic relationship of human existence cannot keep them in mind. Naturally, the contents in general allow generally valid and generally binding propositions to be transmitted; but in so doing the peculiar, that which by its nature is unique, is lost. These contents are not codifiable. Of the dialogue of God with man, however, it must be said that even the most universal commands attain, in the dialogue of God with the individual persons, unforeseen interpretations: the situation furnishes the interpretation. Interpretations are needed, however, because history is real and God is the God of history.

5. Very different from this is another misunderstanding. Levinas[12] cites my statement that through Thou I become I, and infers: hence I owe my place to my partner. No; rather the relation to him. Only in the relation is he my Thou; outside of the relation between us this Thou does not exist. It is, consequently, false to say that the meeting is reversible. Neither is my Thou identical with the I of the other nor his Thou with my I. To the person of the other I owe the fact that I have this Thou; but my I—by which here the I of the I-Thou relationship is to be understood—I owe to saying Thou, not to the person to whom I say Thou.

11 Rotenstreich, pp. 129f.
12 Levinas, p. 147.

6. Another misunderstanding is of a singular nature. I have described the responsibility that is practiced toward reason, toward an idea, etc., as fictitious. From this Rotenstreich[13] concludes that thus "the realm of reason, ideas, etc. is considered to be fictitious" by me. The conclusion is false. The responsibility to an idea is fictitious because the idea cannot call me to account, because it cannot determine whether my responsibility rightly or wrongly exists. I demand of a concept like responsibility its original concrete meaning; I do not concede that it should be enabled to dissolve into inwardness under the protection of a philosophy. But through the fact that the responsibility to an idea proves itself to be fictitious, the idea itself does not become fiction. Only the idea is no living personal court that demands and judges; nothing is in any way said thereby about its reality or unreality. I do not hold the idea of eternal peace to be fictitious, but he who says to me that he is responsible to it, is an enthusiast or a phrasemonger.

It certainly makes some sense to say that one is responsible toward one's own conscience, for in the soul of the human person a real tribunal can again and again open, and there is then, clothed with mysterious might, a judging and sentencing reality that at times is able to determine the whole future course of life of the person. Although everything happens "inwardly," what takes place here is real in the highest sense. But to a discussion between a person and "reason" I cannot ascribe this character of reality.

7. The misunderstanding becomes more seriously misleading when it touches on the theological realm; at times this leads, among other things, to radical distortions of my view.

I have many times pointed out that I cannot understand the events of divine revelation in which I believe as a divine content that pours into an empty human vessel. The actual revelation signifies to me the breaking of the eternal divine light into the human manifoldness, i.e., the breaking of the unity into contradiction. I know no other revelation than that of the *meeting* of the divine and the human in which the human takes part just as well as the divine. The divine appears to me like a fire that melts the human ore, but what results is not in the nature of fire. Anything that proceeds directly or indirectly (i.e., through the oral or written tradition) out of the actual revelation, be it word or custom or institution, I cannot, therefore,

13 Rotenstreich, p. 131.

understand simply, in the form in which we possess it, as spoken by God or instituted by God. In other words, I possess no security against the necessity to live in fear and trembling; I have nothing but the certainty that we share in the revelation.

From this view of mine, that I have expressed ever again in all clarity, Fox[14] deduces the legitimacy of asking, first, why a man's own modification of revelation should be binding for him, and second, whether this modification is not then our own invention.

One sees that my critic no longer speaks of the man of whom I have spoken, namely of the bearer of a great historical revelation, but of one of us, without in any way justifying this leap. It cannot be justified.

The first of the two questions rests on a gross misunderstanding. Where the original sphere of receiving revelation was in question, I have never thought of a "modification" through human action. Moses does not modify; he speaks out what he is conscious of as received in revelation. How could he think of distinguishing between heavenly and earthly in that which here filled him as a received mission! He had been seized as he was, and what had filled him at that time as a striving was laid hold of and transformed with it; he does not recognize it again. And this process is now, flatly transferred to each of us, treated by my critic as a "modification."

In the second question, the modification has already become an "invention." How can revelation bend us, it is asked, if it is "the result of our own invention?" However, as has been said, nothing is here invention. Revelation, historical revelation, can bind us because the divine has a share in it. But what does this binding signify? An unhampered believer in revelation may trustfully follow, without reservation, a traditional codex that appeals to God's word, because the share of heaven and of earth are not objectively to be measured. But another man believes in revelation, yet is tormented by the all-too-human character of the human share in it, and resists obeying human prescriptions as divine commands. Such a man may find no other way than holding his own soul open to the whole traditional shall and shall not, in order, in the absence of objective criteria, to examine honestly in his own subjectivity what he can acknowledge as

14 Fox, p. 156.

bidden and forbidden by God and what not. That is the lot of the "beggar."[15]

8. Connected with this is another strange misunderstanding. "No act can be right, Buber teaches us," so Fox declares,[16] "unless it arises from our bond with God." Where do I teach that? If I taught that, I would, indeed, have to be of the opinion that a man who does not believe in God (or imagines that he does not believe in Him) could not act morally. But I am by no means of this opinion. As the single evidence of this from my writings my critic cites a talk on "Teaching and Deed"[17] that I gave in 1934 at the school for Jewish adult education, at that time directed by me, the *Freies jüdisches Lehrhaus* in Frankfurt am Main, Germany. But this talk does not deal at all with the relationship between religion and morality; its subject is by no means so general a one: it deals, in connection with a famous Talmudic controversy, exclusively with the relationship between teaching and deed *within believing Judaism*. The life-relation of Israel to God is here simply presupposed, and from that standpoint it is said that true life is grounded in the covenant with God. Torn out of its organic context, misunderstood as a general thesis about the relationship between religion and morality, the statement must produce further misunderstanding, with the exception of those readers who remember it in its original context, and those who read it again.

IV. *Some General Matters*

My questioners and critics have fastened on me some labels. Regardless of whether they are meant in criticism or in praise, I should like to contribute to their being torn off. Therefore, I give here, in so far as I have not already implicitly dealt with them above, a selection of them with my attempts at elucidation.

1. I begin with a question that is concerned with my language. Diamond[18] states that where my language touches on the transcendent it is full of paradoxical formulations, and that is explained through the fact that it points to the lived and not the conceived meeting with

---

15 Cf. my talk "Der heilige Weg" (1918) (in *Reden über das Judentum*).

16 Fox, p. 159.

17 Martin Buber, *Israel and the World: Essays in a Time of Crisis* (New York: Schocken Books, 1963).

18 Diamond, pp. 236ff.

God; it must, therefore, remain as close as possible to the biblical language. The latter part of this statement does not at all accord with the case. If I had had to choose my language, I should least of all have chosen one imitating the biblical; for whoever has dared in our age to take on lease the style of the prophets—as Nietzsche's "Zarathustra" announces most clearly to the present-day reader—has transformed it into an effective but basically inauthentic pathos. Now, happily I did not need to choose my language; that which was to be said formed it as the tree its bark. That which there has been to say was, as I have already stated in these responses, a pointing, an indication of reality. When a man's speech wishes to show, to show forth reality, obscured reality, it will not be able to avoid the paradoxical expression insofar as it touches on the reality between us and God. The lived reality of meeting is not subject to the logic forged in three millennia; where the *complexio oppositorum* rules, the law of contradiction is silent.

Why, it is asked, does Buber insist that paradoxical expressions, which are also of human construction, limit God less than ontological concepts? God is limited through *every* word that has Him as its object and not as its receiver; it is not of God, but of the meeting that we speak. But with the meeting it is the case that the "paradoxical" expressions respect its incomparable, unsubsumable uniqueness where the thoroughly logicized ones do not.

2. Rotenstreich has reproached me[19] with some justification that, among others, I have borrowed from psychological terminology, just as from that of epistemology. I do not hesitate to acknowledge that I have done so out of need. Without bringing forth a new terminology which would make concrete understanding necessarily more difficult, I wanted just to bring to unambiguous expression the fact that the meeting happens, to be sure, "from grace," but that it is not done to the human person, but is pre-formed in him, that man is not merely ready for meeting but also capable of meeting—and that just the measure of his preparation to enter the meeting with his whole being very often is not equal to this latent willingness and capability.

I have had at times to be my own interpreter; hence, the encroachment of borrowed terms.

3. It is stressed once again that in all my writing it is more the exigencies of the service than a free intention that has prevailed. I

19 Rotenstreich, p. 102.

cannot accept without qualification von Balthasar's praise[20] of a "security of the leading in line that leaves nothing to chance, not even life's play of becoming:" I have not, indeed, let myself be led by "chance" in this work, but certainly again and again by the task that has overcome me in the midst of life and will no longer let me go. The "security" stands in the command of the task alone.

4. Rotenstreich mistakes my attitude toward my subject when he sees in it a "cosmic optimism,"[21] by which is meant my views of the origin and future of the cosmos and within it of man. I have simply no philosophical view of either, however, and I have never sought to philosophize about beginning or end or the like. I have in these matters nothing other to establish than my faith, and my faith in the meaningfulness of creation and in its completion as a goal seems to me to exist beyond optimism and pessimism. Once again: I do not philosophize more than I must.

5. My "skepticism" or "reserve" in the face of philosophical systems is ascribed by Rotenstreich to the aftereffect of *"Lebensphilosophie"* ("philosophy of life"),[22] to which in general I am held to adhere more than I suspect. About this question of the system I have already dared in my youth to contradict my teacher, Wilhelm Dilthey, in his seminar. He wished to present to his pupils the history of philosophy precisely as a way to ever clearer knowledge, whereas I, naturally in a youthfully immature expression, understood it only as a plurality of aspects of being. Each one of these aspects, to be sure—I must add today—presupposes those that have appeared before it so that a way can still become visible here, only just a complex and at times quite unclear one. My view was connected at that time not merely with *Lebens*-philosophical but also with aesthetic inclinations. The latter were already expelled from me by 1915; three years later, on a self-examination which, according to my memory, reached deeper than the investigation of this point by my critic. I also found almost nothing more of the *Lebensphilosophie* in existence. Today that conception called "life" appears to me a questionable abstraction, all the more questionable since it pretended to remain especially close to the concrete.

My criticism of the abstract attitude is connected by Roten-

---

20 H. U. von Balthasar, p. 342.

21 Rotenstreich, p. 121.

22 Rotenstreich, pp. 114f.

streich[23] with intuitionism, with which I am presumably very strongly connected. That astonishes me. In my Bergson essay (1943) [24] I expressed with all desired clarity the fact that I cannot accord to intuition any adequate knowledge: its vision is a limited one, like all our perceptions.

But of the I-Thou relationship too I also in no way mean that it offers adequate knowledge. It can help us to a genuine contact with the being of the other, but not to an objectively valid knowledge of his being. We can reach the being of the other in the meeting, and then we do not communicate with an appearance, but with him himself. But insofar as we also seek even then a knowledge of what is concealed, it denies itself to us.

6. I would take much more seriously than all this the reproach by Urs von Balthasar of a "see-sawing between theology and philosophy of religion"[25] if I were able to acknowledge theology's claim for exclusiveness, if I were able to acknowledge the strict division between these categories. But this I cannot do. The categories themselves have before my eyes fallen into see-sawing, and they are not to be halted. Honor to those who can still today bind them with all their strength to the strong bough of a revelation; I have not been able to go their way. I pursue no theology as theology and no philosophy of religion as philosophy of religion. Where I may draw out of primal depths that have opened to me as he who I am, I must acknowledge it: where I am referred to constellations outside my own, it is not incumbent upon me to act as though I had intercourse with them from within. In particular, the plurality of religions must be dealt with in all its reality (therefore not merely historically, psychologically, etc.) and yet not like the singular of faith. Is it still called philosophy of religion when I allow God's own relationship to the religions to address me in all its dreadful seriousness? Is it still called theology when I find it necessary to distinguish within my religion, familiar to me as no other, between that in it which I believe in the responsibility of faith and that which I just do not believe? When I have to interpret a text which is sacred to me, my method is that of

23 Rotenstreich, p. 114.

24 Martin Buber, *Pointing the Way: Collected Essays,* "Bergson's Concept of Intuition," trans. Maurice Friedman (New York: Harper Torchbooks, 1963), pp. 81-86.

25 H. U. von Balthasar, p. 352.

the high philology and no other; I know no "pneumatic" exegesis. I have once announced myself as atypical in my work, and in just such a manner I practise it according to my forces.

7. Compared with this charge, the criticism that reproaches my philosophy with the postulative element that is to be found in it does not weigh heavily.[26] What Rotenstreich names this in me has nothing in common with the "postulates" that I have remarked on in the philosophy of Feuerbach.[27] I find Feuerbach "postulative" in the critical sense in that he would make out of I and Thou God, as after him Nietzsche would make God out of the heralded future man. That is a postulative mysticism that does not acknowledge itself as such. My "postulizing," which I in no way contest, is essentially of another kind; it is one corresponding to the situation and actual. In a time in which the I-Thou relationship is so obscured, so disdained as it is today, I postulate its new dawn.

Connected with this is what Franz Rosenzweig, whom Ernst Simon quotes,[28] noted about the book *I and Thou*: that it does not do justice to the It. Indeed, it does not justice to it: because I am born in the midst of this situation of man and see what I see and must point out what I have seen. In another hour it would perhaps have been granted to me to sound the praises of the It; today not: because without a turning of man to his Thou no turn in his destiny can come.

8. Rotenstreich's accusation of a "metaphysical impressionism"[29] I will suffer without reply although the one example of it that is offered, the linking of the present (*Gegenwart*) with presence (*Gegenwärtigkeit*), does not mean that there is no continuity in human life but only that there is no "fulfilled" present without Thou. Since I have never succeeded in grasping a metaphysical totality and accordingly in building a metaphysical system, I must be content with impressions.

On the other hand, I must decline the praise of the dogmatist for being a dogmatist.[30] I have not, God be thanked, had to experience in any insight of my faith the stiffening into a proposition of faith. Zion, which is cited as an example, is at once a promise and

---

26 Rotenstreich, p. 128.

27 Buber, "The History of the Dialogical Principle," *Between Man and Man*, trans. Maurice Friedman (New York: Macmillan Paperbacks, 1965), p. 223.

28 Simon, p. 576.

29 Rotenstreich, p. 132.

30 H. U. von Balthasar, p. 353.

a demand, demand not without promise, but also promise not without demand; it has never become a dogma for me. I believe, despite all, in Zion, yet Zion signifies to me no divine security but a God-given chance.

V. *I and Thou*

For what I mean by the I-Thou relation and what I do not mean by it some clarification is still desired—beyond that which has been said in the preceding sections.

1. Marcel asks,[31] whether the German term *"Beziehung"* (which is in some measure to be rendered through the English "relationship"), and particularly the French *"relation,"* corresponds to what I mean, a reality to the nature of which discontinuity eminently belongs. The question is rightly asked, and it is certainly understandable that the term *"Begegnung"* might be held to be more suitable. But *"Begegnung"* signifies only something actual. He who remains with a person whom he has just met when this event is past, now meets him no more. The concept of relationship *(Beziehung)*, in contrast, opens the possibility—only the possibility, but this really—of the latency. Two friends, two lovers must, to be sure, experience ever again how the I-Thou is succeeded by an I-He or I-She; but is it not often as though the little bird whose wings are crippled in this moment secretly seeks its soaring? And does not an incomprehensible, an as it were vibrating, connection manifest itself at times between the moments of Thou? Moreover, in the relationship to God of the man who genuinely believes, the latent Thou is unmistakable; even when he is not able to turn to God with collected soul, God's presence, the presence of his eternal Thou, is primally real.

One can only try to overcome the lack of an adequate designation through using the "skeleton word" relationship *(Beziehung)*, always according to the context, next to other, at once more concrete and more limited terms, such as meeting *(Begegnung)*, contact, communication; none of them can be replaced by any of them.

I must, however oppose Marcel's opinion[32] that language itself transforms the Thou into an It. "Quand je parle de toi," says Gabriel Marcel, "même lorsque je déclare expressément que tu n'es pas une chose, que *tu* es le contraire d'une chose, je te réduis malgré moi

[31] Marcel, p. 44.
[32] *Ibid.*

à la condition de chose." I do not see that this is so. If one uses the expression "*the* Thou," which is alien to natural speech, one does not at all mean the real man to whom I say Thou, but the word which is used in saying it; it is not otherwise when one uses the expression "the I." But if I really say "Thou," then I as little mean by it a thing as when I say "I" to myself.

2. Marcel objects to my sentence "In the beginning was relation."[33] In the beginning, it is said, there stands rather "une certaine unité sentie" which afterwards disperses into an "ensemble comportant des termes reliés entre eux." In the section of my book *I and Thou* that begins with the sentence about "the beginning" I have spoken in a quite definitely phylogenetic sense: I have pointed there to how the linguistic designation of individual persons, separated from one another, so-called holophrases, sentence-words, comes first. In these holophrases relations between persons are expressed—naturally highly primitive relations, not such as those between an I known as such and a Thou known as such—and only through their analysis have the designations for the person come forth. I have indicated that the idea of a relation between man and moon precedes the idea of the moon as existing in itself, etc. I have presented such primal relations as a forestage of our I-Thou relations, which could only arise out of the going apart of the "vital primary words." This view does not seem to me to have been refuted.

Today the use of the expression "in the beginning" does not seem to me exact enough; it is too rich in associations. At that time I wrote what I wrote in an overpowering inspiration. And what such inspiration delivers to one, one may no longer change, not even for the sake of exactness. For one can only measure what one might acquire, not what is lost.

3. The category of "the between," introduced by me in a later phase of my work, is variously called into question.[34] That I have foreseen, but I could not avoid introducing it. It now stands wholly within the unaccustomed and will undoubtedly have to remain for a good while in the unaccustomed; but I do not believe that the human spirit can do without it in the long run.

I proceed from a simple real situation: two men are engrossed in a genuine dialogue. I want to appraise the facts of this situation.

[33] Marcel, p. 45.
[34] Wheelwright, pp. 93f.; Marcel, p. 45.

It turns out that the customary categories do not suffice for it. I mark: first the "physical" phenomena of the two speaking and gesturing men, second the "psychic" phenomena of it, what goes on "in them." But the meaningful dialogue itself that proceeds between the two men and into which the acoustic and optical events fit, the dialogue that arises out of the souls and is reflected in them, this remains unregistered. What is its nature, what is its place? My appraisal of the facts of the case cannot be managed without the category that I call "the between." Marcel is right: I cannot define it in an "arithmetical or geometric" language. It seems mysterious (*mystérieux*), as he says, so it seems to me, only because one has not up till now been concerned about it. It has seemed to me for a long time no more mysterious than the duality of psychic and physical or the inaccessible, no longer phenomenal unity that stands behind that duality.

4. And now I am placed by my questioners before the great problem of mutuality.[35]

Since I have received many questions about just this problem in the thirty-five years since the book *I and Thou* first appeared, I have sought to clarify some points in a Postscript to the new edition of this book[36] and reproduce these following sections.

The first question may be formulated with some precision as follows: If—as the book says—we can stand in *I-Thou* relationship not merely with other men, but also with beings and things which come to meet us in nature, what is it that makes the real difference between the two relationships? Or, more closely, if the *I-Thou* relationship requires a mutual action which in fact embraces both the *I* and the *Thou*, how may the relation to something in nature be understood as such a relationship? More precisely still, if we are to assume that we are granted a kind of mutuality by beings, and things in nature as well, which we meet as our *Thou*, what is then the character of this reciprocity and what justification have we for using this fundamental concept in order to describe it?

Clearly there is no unified answer to this question. Instead of grasping nature as a whole, in our customary fashion, we must here consider its different fields separately.

Man once 'tamed' animals, and he is still capable of this singular achievement. He draws animals into his atmosphere and moves them to accept him, the stranger, in an elemental way, and to respond to him. He wins from them an often astonishing active response to his approach, to his addressing them, and moreover a response which in general is stronger and directer in

35 Fackenheim, pp. 292f.; Rotenstreich, pp. 105ff., and elsewhere.

36 Martin Buber, *I and Thou*, 2nd ed. Postscript, trans. R. G. Smith (New York: Charles Scribner's Sons, 1958), Sec. 2–4, pp. 124–131.

proportion as his attitude is a genuine saying of *Thou*. Animals, like children, are not seldom able to see through any hypocritical tenderness. But even outside the sphere of taming a similar contact between men and animals sometimes takes place—with men who have in the depth of their being a potential partnership with animals, not predominantly persons of 'animal' nature, but rather those whose very nature is spiritual.

An animal is not, like man, twofold: the twofold nature of the primary words *I-Thou* and *I-It* is strange to it, even though it can turn to another being as well as consider objects. Nevertheless we should like to say that there is here a latent twofoldness. This is why we may call this sphere, in respect of our saying of *Thou* out towards the creature, the threshold of mutuality.

It is quite different with those spheres of nature where the spontaneity we share with the animals is lacking. It is part of our concept of a plant that it cannot react to our action towards it: it cannot "respond." Yet this does not mean that here we are given simply no reciprocity at all. The deed or attitude of an individual being is certainly not to be found here, but there is a reciprocity of the being itself, a reciprocity which is nothing but being in its course (*seiend*). That living wholeness and unity of the tree, which denies itself to the sharpest glance of the mere investigator and discloses itself to the glance of one who says *Thou*, is there when he, the sayer of *Thou*, is there: it is he who vouchsafes to the tree that it manifest this unity and wholeness; and now the tree which is in being manifests them. Our habits of thought make it difficult for us to see that here, awakened by our attitude, something lights up and approaches us from the course of being. In the sphere we are talking of we have to do justice, in complete candour, to the reality which discloses itself to us. I should like to describe this large sphere, stretching from stones to stars, as that of the prethreshold or preliminal, i.e. the stage before the threshold.

Now the question arises concerning the sphere which in the same imagery may be termed the sphere above the threshold, the superliminal, i.e. the sphere of the lintel which is over the door: the sphere of the spirit.

Here too a division must be made between two fields, which goes deeper, however, than the division in nature. It is the division between on the one hand what of spirit has already entered the world and can be perceived in it by means of our senses, and on the other hand what of spirit has not yet entered the world but is ready to do so, and becomes present to us. This division is based on the fact that I can as it were point out to you, my reader, the structure of the spirit which has already entered the world; but I cannot point out the other. I can refer you to the structures of the spirit which are "to hand," in the world that is common to something accessible to you in reality or in potentiality. But I cannot refer to that which has not yet entered the world. If I am asked where then the mutuality is to be found here, in this boundary region, then all I can do is indicate indirectly certain events in man's life, which can scarcely be described, which experience spirit as meeting; and in the end, when indirect indication is not enough, there is nothing for me but to appeal, my reader, to the witness of your own mysteries—buried, perhaps, but still attainable.

Let us return, then, to the first realm, that of what is 'to hand.' Here we can adduce examples.

Let the questioner make present to himself one of the traditional sayings of a master who died thousands of years ago; and let him attempt, as well as he can, to take and receive the saying with his ears, that is, as though spoken by the speaker in his presence, even spoken to him. To do this he must turn with his whole being to the speaker (who is not to hand) of the saying (which is to hand). This means that he must adopt towards him who is both dead and living the attitude which I call the saying of *Thou*. If he succeeds (and of course his will and his effort are not adequate for this, but he can undertake it again and again), he will hear a voice, perhaps only indistinctly at first, which is identical with the voice he hears coming to him from other genuine sayings of the same master. Now he will no longer be able to do what he could do so long as he treated the saying as an object—that is, he will not be able to separate out of the saying any content or rhythm; but he receives only the indivisible wholeness of something spoken.

But this is still bound to a person, to what a person may have at any time to say in his words. What I mean is not limited to the continued influence of any personal life in words. Therefore I must complete my description with another example to which no personal quality clings. I choose, as always, an example which has powerful memories for some people: this time the Doric pillar, wherever it appears to a man who is ready and able to turn to it. Out of a church wall in Syracuse, in which it had once been immured, it first came to encounter me: mysterious primal mass represented in such simple form that there was nothing individual to look at, nothing individual to enjoy. All that could be done was what I did: I took my stand, stood fast, in face of this structure of spirit, this mass penetrated and given body by the mind and hand of man. Does the concept of mutuality vanish here? It only plunges back into the dark, or it is transformed into a concrete content which coldly declines to assume conceptual form, but is bright and reliable.

From this point we may look over into that other realm, the realm of what is 'not to hand,' of contact with 'spiritual being,' of the *arising* of word and form.

Spirit become word, spirit become form—in some degree or other everyone who has been touched by the Spirit and did not shut himself to it. knows about the basic fact of the situation—that this does not germinate and grow in man's world without being sown, but arises from this world's meetings with the other. Not meetings with Platonic ideas—of which I have no direct knowledge at all and which I am not in a position to understand as what is in course of being (*Seiendes*); but meetings with the Spirit which blow around us and in us. Again and again I am reminded of the strange confession of Nietzsche when he described the event of 'inspiration' as taking but not asking who gives. Even if we do not ask we should 'thank.'

He who knows the breath of the Spirit trespasses if he desires to get power over the Spirit or to ascertain its nature and qualities. But he is also disloyal when he ascribes the gift to himself.

Let us look afresh at what is said here of meetings with what is of nature and what is of spirit, and let us look at them together.

May we then—it may now be asked—speak of 'response' or 'address,' which come from outside everything to which, in our consideration of the orders of being, we adjudge spontaneity and consciousness, as of something that happens in the world of man in which we live, just in this way—as a response or an address? Has what is here described any other validity than that of a 'personifying' metaphor? It there not a danger here of a problematic 'mysticism,' blurring the boundaries which are drawn, and which must be drawn, by all rational knowledge?

The clear and firm structure of the *I-Thou* relationship, familiar to everyone with a candid heart and the courage to pledge it, has not a mystical nature. From time to time we must come out of our habits of thought in order to understand it; but we do not have to leave the primal norms which determine human thinking about reality. As in the realm of nature, so in the realm of spirit—the spirit which lives on in word and work, and the spirit which wishes to become word and work: what is effected upon us may be understood as something effected by the ongoing course of being *(Seiendes)*.

The question concerning mutuality in the relation to God remains undiscussed here; I have spoken of it elsewhere as clearly as I can. The difference regarding this question, however, is by no means that between the "rational" and the "irrational," but that between the reason that detaches itself from the other forces of the human person and declares itself to be sovereign and the reason that forms a part of the wholeness and unity of the human person and works, serves, and expresses itself within this wholeness and unity.

It is, nonetheless, indispensable to say one thing here, too, once more in unmistakable clarity, if also only in all brevity. I read with some surprise Wheelwright's statement,[37] "Buber holds that it is only in and through relationships with other finite selves that the relationship with God can be truly realized." In contrast to that one must set what, for example, was actually said in the books "Dialogue" and "The Question to the Single One."[38] The direct relation to God is here in no way contested; its actuality, indeed, is recognized in all that befalls us, hence addresses us, and in all with which we react, hence answer. It is only added that the essential relation to God must find its complement in the essential relation to man.

5. Friedman has raised the question[39] of whether relation to the Eternal Thou includes moments when our relation to any human Thou is only past and potential and not present and actual. All the

[37] Wheelwright, p. 78.

[38] The first and second sections of *Between Man and Man* (Editor's note).

[39] Friedman, p. 192.

biographical situations to which I respond are included in the life-long dialogue. The existence of "the unbroken world" by virtue of pure relation does not mean that this relation "includes" the I-It relations *as such*: it may include everything, but not in its separatedness.

6. Fritz Kaufmann understands me to the effect[40] that I dissolve the relationship to the Thou, that to God as well as that to the fellowman, in "a sort of salvo of acts of relating, so that the pure relation coincides with the present meeting." As argument for this view he refers to a passage in my essay, "Elements of the Interhuman,"[41] in which I say, "By the sphere of the interhuman I mean solely actual happenings between men." It is clearly necessary to make what is involved here more precise.

As the sphere of the interhuman I do not designate the relationship of the human person to his fellowman in general, but the actualization of this relationship. The interhuman is something that takes place from time to time between two men; but in order that it may take place again and again, in order that genuine meetings may occur and ever again occur, the Thou in relation to his fellowman must be inherent in man.

And also for the relationship of man to God it holds steadfastly that the moments in which the I, present in its wholeness, speaks into the distance of all distances the Thou of the greatest nearness and just from there knows himself as Thou, those moments flash up out of the darkness of a latency in which we perceive nothing and in which we nonetheless trust as the ground and meaning of our existence. In no way is there here, as Kaufmann thinks, an "antithesis to the Jewish *emunah*": rather our *emunah* manifests and authenticates itself just therein, in what occurs again and again between us and our Thou.

What Kaufmann says, however, of the "derivation of the concept of meeting from the concept of temporally limited experience" is not at all the case. The word "derivation" refers to a supposed process in my intellectual biography: the concept of meeting originating in the development of my ideas out of that of *Erlebnis*.* In reality it

40 Fritz Kaufmann, p. 216.

41 Martin Buber, *Essays in the Knowledge of Man*, "Elements of the Interhuman," ed. with an Introductory Essay by Maurice Friedman (New York: Harper & Row, 1966) .

*Lived or inner experience in contrast to *Erfahrung*, practical knowledge (Editor's note).

arose, on the road of my thinking, out of the criticism of the concept of *Erlebnis,* to which I adhered in my youth, hence, out of a radical self-correction. "*Erlebnis*" belongs to the exclusive, individualized psychic sphere; "meeting," or rather, as I mostly prefer to say, precisely in order to avoid the temporal limitation, "relationship" transcends this sphere from its origins on. The psychological reduction of being, its psychologizing, had a destructive effect on me in my youth because it removed from me the foundation of human reality, the "to-one-another." Only much later, in the revolution of my thinking that taught me to fight and to gain ground did I win reality that cannot be lost.

VI. *Theology, Mysticism, Metaphysics*

1. While I am reproached by Pfuetze[42] because my writings are "shot through" with the supernatural, Urs von Balthasar[43] asserts that my position is "the absolute identity of nature and supernature." In equal contrast to the one as to the other, it must be pointed out that I hold the concept of a "supernature" to be a false and misleading one. Above nature is no supernature, which must, in order to be so named, offer, so-to-speak, a structural analogy to nature, represent a "kingdom" above that of nature. Above nature is only God. He is above nature, and bears it and permeates it, as He is above the spirit and bears it and permeates it. Both are grounded in Him, and He is as little bound to them as to all the other realities, unknown and unknowable to us, that are grounded in Him. He pours out His grace right through all chains of causation, but that is He alone and no supernature.

2. Among the presuppositions of my view Rotenstreich counts[44] that God is the absoluteness of the other. With that I cannot agree. I have always guarded myself against the simplification practised by the "dialectical theology" that God is Wholly Other. One may only so name Him when in the same breath one knows and confesses that He is the not-other, the here, the now, the mine. This and not that—believe that who may; this and that in one, that is the faith that has enabled me still to sense in the namable torment the nameless grace.

42 Pfuetze, p. 528.

43 H. U. von Balthasar, pp. 350f.

44 Rotenstreich, p. 108.

3. Without Christianity, so Urs von Balthasar says to me,[45] the dialogical leads inevitably to Job's question to God. Yes, that it does, and God praises "His servant" (Job 42:7). My God will not allow to become silent in the mouth of His creature the complaint about the great injustice in the world, and when in an unchanged world His creature yet finds peace, only because God has again granted him His nearness, he confirms Him. Peace, I say; but that is a peace compatible with the fight for justice in the world.

4. In one of the contributions[46] I was surprised by the apodictic sentence: "God belongs in and to religion; why look for Him elsewhere?", which Schneider advances thus, thinking thereby also to express my conception. He errs basically. Not merely in my discussion with Jung, but in a series of writings I have turned against the popular reduction of God to a *psychologicum*.

5. I have once spoken of a love[47] that witnesses to the existence of the beloved. One asks me[48] how this is possible. I confess that I cannot answer this question in an objectively valid manner. I know only, from direct and indirect experience, that the great love for an actually existing being is differently constituted, qualitatively different from the love—even if it be poetically compelling—for a fantasy image. The first I call total acceptance: one accepts the other as he is, one accepts him wholly, just as he is. Of this kind of love I can say that it witnesses to existence. The other, the illusionary, can neither accept this nor can it make such a witness.

6. I have once said that a "He" spoken of God is a metaphor, a "Thou" spoken to God is not one. That is called into question by Wahl.[49] I will explain exactly what I mean. If one speaks of God, one makes Him into an existing being among other existing beings, into an existing being at hand and constituted so and not otherwise. But to speak to God means nothing other than to turn to Him Himself. How is that possible since He is not to be sought more in one direction than in another? Just nothing other is needed than the total turning. This says in general nothing more than that the one who has

45 H. U. von Balthasar, pp. 357f.

46 Schneider, p. 470.

47 Martin Buber, *Eclipse of God*, "The Love of God and the Idea of Deity," trans. M. S. Friedman, *et al.* (New York: Harper Torchbooks, 1957), p. 84.

48 Wahl, p. 509.

49 *Ibid.*

turned in no way limits his Thou to a being constituted so and not otherwise. The metaphor no longer has a place here.

7. Fritz Kaufmann thinks[50] that I have occasionally esteemed the significance of monotheism for Judaism less than "seems compatible with . . . the *Shema*, the constantly repeated confession of the One God." The subject deserves a further clarification.

It is repugnant to me personally to wish to find the life substance of a community of faith like Judaism in a concept like "monotheism" that smacks so of an unbinding *"Weltanschauung."* But the belief in the *Ehad* I too hold to be the living center of Judaism. The confession of it expresses, indeed, two certainties in one: that of His uniqueness— "no other beside Him!"—and that of His unity—a being, a person, an eternal Thou. That the Jews living at any one time, those who really are Jews, thus confess themselves unreservedly to the Unique and One, knowing with their whole soul what they are saying and answering for it with their whole lives, and that just these Jews from one time to another even so, with their whole souls and their whole lives, address Him, the unique and One, as their eternal Thou, in a community—"Our Father, our King!"—and each alone—nothing else than Thou—that is the life-substance of Judaism.

8. Since a presentation that I once gave of the Hasidic conception of a "messianism at all times," i.e., of an ever-recurring event of redemption preceding the messianic fulfillment in the ages, can evidently[51] be misunderstood as a weakening of the messianic belief, let it be made clear here that I by no means understand this Hasidic teaching, which I have interpreted and accepted, as something that injures the devotion to the *eschaton*. Just as I believe not merely in the creative act in the beginning, but also in the creation at all times, in which man has a share as "God's comrade in the work of creation," and just as I believe not merely in the great acts of revelation in the incomprehensible hours in which one "sees the voices," but also in the secret and yet revelatory coming into contact of above and below, so I believe in the redeeming act poured forth over the ages, in which man again has a share. These events do not add themselves to one another, but all together they cooperate secretly in preparing the coming redemption of the world.

[50] Fritz Kaufmann, p. 219.
[51] Cf. Bergman, pp. 305f.

9. On the other side[52] my religious socialism is censured by Urs von Balthasar as offering man only a social future; this hope—which lies "in following to its consequences the prophetic principle"—is "in reality none," and I must really know that. I by no means know that; what I know is something wholly different.

A prophetic "principle" is to me, of course, unknown, but I hold with the prophets of Israel. They certainly did not mean that if we introduced justice into the relations of men to one another, we could make the earth into the kingdom of God. But they understood that to the human share in the preparation of the divine kingdom belongs just this, that we succeed in living *with one another*. And they may have even agreed, these old messengers, that true institutions belong to true relations as the skeleton to the flesh.

There once existed in Berlin a union of religious socialists (Paul Tillich also belonged to it). Its leader, Carl Mennicke, wrote a programmatic paper in which he said something like this: he believed in a future perfection of society, but in a future transformation of the world he could not believe. I believe in both in one. Only in the building of the foundation of the former I myself may take a hand, but the latter may already be there in all stillness when I awake some morning, or its storm may tear me from sleep. And both belong together, the "turning" and the "salvation," both belong together, God knows how, I do not need to know it. That I call hope.

In a comparison with Jesus of the "holy Yehudi," of whom I have told in a chronicle or novel (*For the Sake of Heaven*), Taubes holds[53] that the Yehudi's relation to the world has been "entirely passive." I am inclined to take the opposite view. There is no higher activity than the call to the turning.

10. I have written a book that I call *Eclipse of God* because it discusses the obscuring of the divine light through something that has stepped between it and us. One has misunderstood that as thereby introducing an "almost gnostic" conception of a strange and hindering element.[54] Nothing of the sort is meant. I thought that I had made what was meant clear enough when I wrote in the conclusion of the book: "The I-It relation, gigantically swollen, has usurped the mastery and the rule . . . It steps in between and shuts off from us the light of

[52] H. U. von Balthasar, p. 356.

[53] Taubes, p. 464.

[54] Wahl, p. 483.

heaven." Note well, not the I-It relationship itself, without which no earthly persistence of human existence is conceivable, but its hybris overstriding all measure is meant. And thus we ourselves are meant. No demonic power works here that we have not reared ourselves.

That is the side of the event known to us. The other, the divine side, is called in the holy books of Israel the hiding of God, the veiling of the divine countenance. Nothing more than such an anthropomorphic image seems to be granted us.

One may also call what is meant here a silence of God's or rather, since I cannot conceive of any interruption of the divine revelation, a condition that works on us as a silence of God. One is right to see here a "most troubling question."[55] These last years in a great searching and questioning, seized ever anew by the shudder of the now, I have arrived no further than that I now distinguish a revelation through the hiding of the face, a speaking through the silence. The eclipse of God can be seen with one's eyes, it will be seen.

He, however, who today knows nothing other to say than, "See there, it grows lighter!" he leads into error.

11. My old friend, Hugo Bergman, is dissatisfied with my rejection of gnosis. He will forgive the fact, that, instead of with a treatment suitable to the topic, I answer with a few brief indications.

I am against gnosis because and insofar as it alleges that it can report events and processes within the divinity. I am against it because and insofar as it makes God into an object in whose nature and history one knows one's way about. I am against it because in the place of the personal relation of the human person to God it sets a communion-rich wandering through an upper world, through a multiplicity of more or less divine spheres.

In opposition to this, Bergman quotes the statement of Rudolf Steiner's, that the "investigator of the spirit," as he is called by him, practices devotion "toward the truth and knowledge." With this citation, however, Bergman misunderstands the matter about which I am concerned. When I have talked of devotion, I mean by that exclusively life as personal service of God. The reverence that a man pays to the "truth," his faithfulness toward "knowledge" I respect completely. But they have something to do with that devoted immediacy to God, that I mean, only if they proceed from it and are determined by it.

55 Fackenheim, p. 289.

I do not hold it to be a trait common to all gnostics that they presume to find the absolute in the depths of their own soul; but from Simon Magus, who identified himself with the "Great Power of God," to certain modern manifestations, characteristic expressions of this sort have not been lacking. Bergman points, in opposition, to the turning away from one's I also postulated by some gnostics. What this demand is founded upon, however, is precisely the distinction between the I, as that which is to be stripped away, and the self, as that in whose depths the Godhead is to be discovered.

12. At the conclusion of this chapter I must reply to Hartshorne. The metaphysics that he presents me as my own I cannot acknowledge, as he himself suspects, indeed. Because I say of God, that He enters into a relationship to the human person, God shall be not absolute but relative! That is proved by the sentence: the relative depends for being what it is upon some relation to another. As if an absolute being had to be without relationship!

I confess that I do not know what to do with the concept of a relative perfection; it affects me on each new examination as equally unacceptable. And when I hear, besides, the divine essence is nothing else than God's idea of his individuality," I mark once again how difficult it is for me to find a common language with a modern metaphysician.

You begin, dear Hartshorne, with the sentence, I am no metaphysician and I am one of the greatest metaphysicians. After attentive reading of your essay, I am far more strongly yet convinced than at the beginning of the reading, that we can make only the first half of your sentence the basis for an understanding.

VII. *Ethics*

1. Friends and opponents reproach me because I neither acknowledge a traditional framework of laws and prescriptions nor offer a system of ethics of my own. In fact, the deficiency exists; and it is so closely tied up with the totality of my knowledge, that filling it is unthinkable. If I sought to do so, I would injure thereby the core of my view.

"Of a teacher," says Bergman,[56] "we expect that he will give indications as to how we should walk the way." I oppose just this expectation. One shall receive the direction from the teacher, but not the

---

[56] Bergman, p. 304.

manner in which one must strive for this direction: that each must discover and acquire for himself in a work that demands of him the best possibilities of his soul but also presents him with a treasure that suffices for his existence. Shall this great work be taken away from him? Or do I perhaps expect too much of the individual? How then except through such expectation could we learn how much the individual is capable of?

But the direction—now certainly I have in the second, the essential half, of a long life again and again, directly and indirectly pointed to it. My indication of the two primary words and of their true relation to each other has always contained this pointing hidden in it.

Certainly, to one who accepts my hint I give no book of principles in hand into which he could at times look for how he is to decide in a given situation. That is not for me: the man with the outstretched index finger has only one thing to show, not many.

No, I do not, indeed, offer a system of ethics; also I know none universally valid that I need only adduce. Still I hold it to be not merely natural, but also legitimate that everyone should accept moral prescriptions, whatever helps him to go the way.

2. And now I give an opponent the word.

Fox ascribes to me the view[57] that every genuine moral decision is an event "of great struggle and searching." That is not my view. Certainly, there is at times, perhaps in one of the situations that overturn man and appear to him full of contradiction, a difficult wrestling of the soul until it can grasp what is right here and now, and if it receives help in do doing from the traditional and from the current, then that is right and fitting. But it certainly does not have to happen thus. One can also catch the situation in an instant, as the good tennis player catches the ball, and as he in the same instant makes the right counter-movement. I know and love many such men in whom all, as it were, has already been decided, and the original decision transforms itself as from beyond the dimension of time into the current and wholly special.

The same opponent ascribes to me[58] the teaching that no action is "morally significant" if it is not "linked to God." Nothing lies further from me than to teach that; I have always had a downright naïve sympathy for the good deeds of the godless or those who act

57 Fox, p. 157.

58 Fox, p. 159.

like they are godless, and I find it glorious when the pious man does the good with his whole soul "without thinking of God."

When I say of an age that along with real faith it also loses the reality of values, it is not to be inferred from this as my view that he who confesses no belief knows no values. What in general I think about the relationship between religion and ethics, however, is expressed with full clarity in the "Religion and Ethics" chapter of my book *Eclipse of God*—from which my critic also cites a passage: "Only out of the personal relation to the Absolute does the absoluteness of the ethical coordinates arise." That means: the ethical deed is also accessible to the autonomy understood to be godless; but in an ethical "system of coordinates" of absolute character and absolute validity only that deed can be enregistered that originates in the relation to the Absolute and is done in this relation.

My critic also asserts[59] that I violate my teaching of the absoluteness of the moral demand "by making each individual man the sole but uncertain judge of what he ought to do," for I set "the privacy of the individual decision" in the place of the absolute value. But that I have never taught, and I do not teach it. I have never made a secret of the fact that I cannot hold the decision of a man (not in the full security of any tradition) as to what is right and wrong in a certain situation to be a decision valid *in itself*. In my view, rather, he must understand himself as standing every moment under the judgment of God. Of the pertinent passages in my writings I shall quote here only the most recently published: "Both, the human faith not less than the human conscience, can err and err ever again. And knowing about this their erring, both—conscience not less than faith—must place themselves in the hands of grace."[60] Because I recognize, thus, that in a given situation full of contradiction a decision as to what it means here practically to follow the truth is at times not possible without earnest examination of the circumstances and of one's own soul, therefore I am accused of placing in question the absolute difference between truth and lies!

Because I declare that each situation is a special one and demands a special solution, Fox understands[61] that according to my view

59 Fox, p. 161.

60 Buber, *The Knowledge of Man*, "Guilt and Guilt-Feelings," trans. Maurice Friedman, p. 148.

61 Fox, p. 161.

there are no universally valid moral rules. I may assure my critic that I have never doubted the absolute validity of the command, "Honor thy father and thy mother," but he who says to me that one, in fact, knows always and under all circumstances, what "to honor" means and what it does not, of him I say that he does not know what he is talking about. Man must expound the eternal values, and, to be sure, with his own life.

My opponent is alarmed that if this were true, then one could "make no moral judgments of men or societies, and, perhaps, not even of ourselves."[62] Oh, myself, out of the intimate knowledge of my guilt,[63] I can competently and sufficiently judge—but against the moral judgment of others Jewish and Christian tradition warns with highest right while summoning those desirous of judging to self-examination; and how may I flatly condemn a society, naturally composed of the most variegated elements!

Now, however, Fox strides to the decisive blow. But what then shall we do, he asks,[64] with the criminal who—I must cite it literally —"may be acting in accordance with what he is convinced is the voice of God?" Must I explicitly state that this hypothetical instance is absurd, for then it would be a madman that one was talking of, who indeed might hold himself to be God? A man who is not mad can only believe that he is following the voice of God if he acts with his whole soul, i.e., if out of its corners no demonic whisper penetrates to his open ears. As I say ever again, however, one cannot do evil with the whole soul, i.e., one can only do it through holding down forcibly the forces striving against it—they are not to be stifled.

That has been many times confirmed for me in the course of my life by men who have confided in me that they have done something evil. I shall here cite only *one* example, one of a high spiritual rung. An important poet had allowed himself to accept an honorary office from the leading perpetrators of a communal guilt. Afterwards he grieved over it for a series of years until his death. When we had been together, some time before his death, and were taking leave of each other, he seized my arm and, obviously referring to a sentence in my book, *Images of Good and Evil*, said in an unforgettable tone of voice, "Is it not true that one cannot do evil with the whole soul?" And

62 *Ibid.*

63 Cf. my "Guilt and Guilt-Feelings" (1957) (*The Knowledge of Man*) .

64 Fox, pp. 162f.

I confirmed it and him by saying as answer and as farewell, "Yes."

My opponent, who is clearly an attentive reader, but one whose attentiveness stands under the dictates of his opposition, now thinks that he can make clear in a sentence the roots of my ethical anarchism. "In substance," Fox says[65] "moving in the direction of self-fulfillment is thought by Buber to be the same as moving in the direction of God." That is an interesting new notion for my old age: until now no one has ascribed to me extreme individualism—and who could do so who has read, with an attentiveness free of dictates, my criticism of individualism and collectivism in the concluding part of the book "What Is Man?" (*Between Man and Man*), where in the place of both I set the genuine, living, immediate relationship between man and man?

But where has my attentive reader found in my writings the material for his thesis that, in substance, moving in the direction of self-fulfillment is the same for me as moving in the direction of God? I have once[66] spoken of the man who with the name "God" does not name a projection of his self, but his creator, that is, the originator of his uniqueness, which is underivable within the world. Of this man I have said that he understands the good either as the direction to God or also as the direction to the realization of what God in creating him has meant for him, to the execution of the divine "design" (by which it is certainly said clearly enough that this man stakes his inner strength to know "wherefore" precisely he, just as he is, was created). Out of this my adversary has made what he has made.

3. Taubes expresses a directly contrary criticism of the man whom I have in mind.[67] He finds himself in a "transparent state of purity" and runs the risk of passing his life as a "beautiful soul." The call to "realization" and "deed," which, as it is further said, fills the pages of my writings—one should have said: my early writings—remains a gesture "so long as it is not admitted that in the process of realization and action man's original purity of intention must be transformed and sullied by the complexity of the recalcitrant reality." The writer has apparently overlooked or forgotten what I myself, although in another province, have advanced against "keeping clean" the soul.[68] "That is, in fact, just the worst of all," it says there, "this clean soul you do not

[65] Fox, p. 167.

[66] *Good and Evil*, "Images of Good and Evil," p. 141 ff.

[67] Taubes, p. 466.

[68] *Pointing the Way*, p. 119.

allow any splashes of blood to fall on! It is not a question of 'souls'
but of responsibility." That is a basic theme of my work in general.
Therefore, I still oppose "situations" to "principles," the "unclean"
reality to the "pure" abstraction. The wholeness of the soul is to
be authenticated just in the brokenness of the human situations, and
that means: not through one's floating above the situations, but
entering into them, that one enters into the fray with them, that
one wins from them from time to time as much of truth and justice
as one can here, on its ground, in the measure of the reality.

The situations have a word to speak! And the real, the biographi-
cally or historically real, situations are not simple and plain, like principles; they bear the contradiction in themselves, they lift it to our
faces, and we may not ignore it, for the reality stands in contradiction.
"All or nothing!" is of no value; what is of value is to realize as much of
our truth as the unprejudiced, penetrating insight into all the contradictions of the situation affords. And that is not a "becoming dirty"
that just happens to us: our hands, ready to mold, reach deep into the
mud.

The position connected with this, that of the "demarcation line,"
Simon has exactly understood and presented,[69] and I could content
myself here with referring to it if he did not join to it a thoroughly
appropriate and even necessary question to which an answer is
due if to any of the questions of this book. He asks: Can one perform
with the whole soul the compromise between absolute law and concrete reality that proceeds out of the wrestling of which you speak,
as one does the good according to your teaching? In theory I know no
answer, and that does not surprise me, for this is one of the points
in which the theory finds its limits. But in the realm of experience an
answer is given to us.

You stand before a political decision, more exactly: before your
share in a political decision, and for the man whom I mean, a political decision is also a moral one. You are driven by the command of
justice and, your heart stirred by it, you look into the depths of a situation, there from where the contradiction looks back at you. You
make present to yourself, as strongly as you possibly can, all: once
again and from the ground up, what you have already known and the
new, what now presents itself to be known. You do not spare yourself,
you let the cruel reality of both sides inflict itself on you without re-

69 Simon, p. 371.

ducing it. You, theater of war and judge, let the battle be fought out unchecked. And now, in the midst of the struggle, rather, in the moment of an unforeseen standstill, something happens. I may not say: always, I say truly: again and again. It happens that you perceive with surprise, at times positively overpoweringly, what of truth and justice can be realized in this situation. You perceive, you have perceived how much must be given to life in order that life accept the justice. And in just this moment—not always, but again and again (that is your chance!)—the forces of your soul, which even now were striving against one another, concentrate, they concentrate as into a crystal.

This is no universally valid answer, no guarantee lies therein, only just a chance, only just a risk. Faith in God is a risk, the begetting of children is a risk, perhaps there is still a risk in death. Even when one wants to do the right, one must risk.

4. Levinas errs in a strange way when he supposes[70] that I see in the *amitié toute spirituelle* the peak of the I-Thou relation. On the contrary, this relationship seems to me to win its true greatness and powerfulness precisely there where two men without a strong spiritual ground in common, even of very different kinds of spirit, yes of opposite dispositions, still stand over against each other so that each of the two knows and means, recognizes and acknowledges, accepts and confirms the other, even in the severest conflict, as this particular person. In the common situation, even in the common situation of fighting with each other, he holds present to himself the experience-side of the other, his living through this situation. This is no friendship, this is only the comradeship of the human creature, a comradeship that has reached fulfillment. No "ether," as Levinas thinks, but the hard human earth, the common in the uncommon.

Levinas, in opposition to me, praises solicitude as the access to the otherness of the other. The truth of experience seems to me to be that he who has this access apart from solicitude will also find it in the solicitude practised by him—but he who does not have it without this, he may clothe the naked and feed the hungry all day and it will remain difficult for him to say a true Thou.

If all were well clothed and well nourished, then the real ethical problem would become wholly visible for the first time.

5. The question has been raised in various ways (by Ernst Simon

70 Levinas, p. 148.

and others) whether what one calls my ethics is not intended and fit for the "higher men," for a "spiritual élite." So far as it is a question to me, I say explicitly "no" to it. I do, to be sure, hold élites, genuine, serving, organizationless élites, to be necessary in order that the spirit may find a foothold on earth; but the advancing of special norms for élites contradicts all my sense of the truth of the ought. I believe in no God who proclaims special norms for élites. What he announces to man as his will must, of course, be received by the human person as penetrating from the unconditional Above-being into his innermost being. But when in his spontaneous believing he is able righteously to equate the instruction transmitted by the mothers and fathers with the divine command, then I know nothing else to say to him than "Happy you!" One thing only I object to: that a man should hold fast as a command to a command traditionally held divine, without really and truthfully "being concerned about God."

In my youth Hasidism taught me to prize the "simple man" who is turned toward the divine with his whole soul without himself being able to grasp conceptually this turning. I have saved for him my love. Of him I will not, of course, demand that he make his soul whole in order genuinely to say Thou or in order to take the true direction. But must not just this, this becoming whole of the soul, time and again, be regarded as the ever-renewed task of that very different kind of man to whom from earliest times the manifoldness of the spiritual life has been delivered?

The distinction to be made here is not between norm and norm, but between way and way.

On the heights where the unreserved devotion of man to God rules, the task as such seems to disappear. But even to those "loving" him (Isaiah 41:8) the Scriptures (Genesis 17:1) have God say: "Be whole!"

6. To Friedman's observation[71] on "two stages in the transition from I-Thou to I-It" it must be said that there are, to be sure, different stages of the I-It state, according to how far it is alienated from the I-Thou relation and gives up the pointing back to it. But I am not inclined to understand these stages as two types different in nature from each other. On the one hand, there exists no abstraction so ethereal that a man who lives greatly could not conjure it with its secret primal name and draw it down to the earth of bodily meetings.

[71] Friedman, p. 194.

On the other hand, however, just in our time the gross absence of relationship has begun to find a consistent "empty" expression in novel and in drama. It may be more difficult to confront *it* with the genuine might of human relationship than the behaviorist defective description.

7. Friedman writes[72] "If I trust in a person . . . this means that despite what may and will happen, I trust that I shall find a new moment of presentness, I shall enter relationship again . . . " I cannot agree. If I "trust in a person," I do not primarily mean by it that I "shall find," that I "shall enter, etc.," but rather that, whatever this person may do, he will remain for me the person in whom I have put my trust, the person I have "accepted." This is, of course, a paradox, but all great trust is. Trust means neither the present nor the future Thou, as Friedman goes on to suggest, but just the person. What he says after that on "trust in existence itself," however, corresponds exactly to my opinion.

8. Friedman further advances[73] as my view: "One's antagonist may, indeed, be the devil or Hitler, but even such a one must be faithfully answered, contended with!" That is a subject that needs careful clarification. On the one side,[74] I hold no one to be "absolutely" unredeemable, and if a devil existed, then I would believe that God could redeem him, and even that God would do so. And not that alone, but I could also conceive that God might expect and trust in man for a share in this work of redemption. But as soon as we reflect on it with wholly concrete seriousness, a limit becomes evident that is no longer restricted to the symbolic, like the traditional image of the devil, but bears a wholly empirical character. Here it is no longer for me to speak of God, but solely of myself and this man.

Hitler is not my antagonist in the sense of a partner "whom I can confirm in opposing him," as Friedman says, for he is incapable of really addressing one and incapable of really listening to one. That I once experienced personally when, if only through the technical medium of the radio, I heard him speak. I knew that this voice was in the position to annihilate me together with countless of my brothers; but I perceived that despite such might it was not in the position to

72 Friedman, p. 195.

73 Friedman, p. 198.

74 Cf. my answer to William Ernest Hocking in *Philosophical Interrogations,* ed. Sydney and Beatrice Rome (New York: Holt, Rinehart & Winston, 1964), pp. 110-112.

set the spoken and heard word into the world. And already less than an hour afterward I sensed in "Satan" the "poor devil," the poor devil in power, and at the same time I understood my dialogical power-lessness. I had to answer, but not to him who had spoken. As far as a person is a part of a situation, I have to respond, but not just to the person.

VIII. *On the Interpretation of the Bible*

Questions have been raised concerning my interpretation of bib-lical texts and teachings, the clarification of which seems to be req-uisite. Here, too, much has been understood otherwise than meant and I must attend to a more exact understanding.

1. Muilenburg ascribes to me the view[75] that revelation "comes in community." That is not my view at all. Even when the commu-nity as such, whether merely passive, whether also with an active movement, seems to take part in an event of revelation transmitted in historical form, even when the report includes a divine address directed to a "You" (plural), I can understand as the core of the happening discernible by me only a central human person's coming into contact with transcendence.

2. It is in some measure inexact to say, as he does[76] that I am in accord with the Protestant theologian Oscar Cullmann "that Judaism knows no midpoint of the *Heilsgeschichte.*" That I have pointed long before Cullmann to "absence of caesuras" of the Jewish view of history would not be worth mentioning if what were involved therein were simply a question of individual priority; but what is involved is that the insight that for the Jew there is no fixed center of history was expressed from out of Judaism itself.

3. Muilenburg doubts[77] that I have taken sufficiently into ac-count the different usages of words. The word *hesed* is adduced as an example, in regard to which it is said that it signifies only seldom loving kindness or grace: "covenant love" better expresses "the cove-nant connotation." Muilenburg, however, has not at all taken into consideration what I myself at one time have written on this subject in the essay, "On the Translation of the 'Psalms' " attached to the Psalm volume of my translation of the Bible. I quote myself:

[75] Muilenburg, p. 383.

[76] *Ibid.*, pp. 384f.

[77] *Ibid.*, p. 386.

Hesed is a trustworthiness between the beings, *and, to be sure, essentially that of the covenant relationship* between the liege lord and his vassals, nearly always the faithfulness to the covenant of the Lord, who preserves and protects his vassals, but also that of the subjects, who devote themselves faithfully to their lord. The German word stem corresponding to this concept of reciprocity is *'hold'* (gracious, pleasing, gentle) . . . *'Holde'* means in middle high German the vassal . . . In the psalms God's 'Hasidim' are his vassals, his 'faithful followers.'

I have many times pointed to the fact that the etymology, often even the etymology within the people, of a word recurring in the Bible must be important for the translator because the repetition in the Biblical text frequently serves to allow one passage to be illuminated by another. Thus in the translation the significant transformation of words was borne in mind as much as possible.

4. Muilenburg's placing together[78] of Exodus 15:12-17 with the Song of Deborah seems to me not to withstand a more exact examination. The specific *"Leitwortstil"* (the clue of the key words) which in the Song of Deborah has taken the character of a primitive refrain is only rudimentarily still to be found in these verses.

5. Muilenberg asks why I have rendered *tehillim* by "praisings" instead of by "Psalms." Now, simply because *tehilla* signifies just praise; that is: because the redactor responsible for the title of the book evidently wanted to make clear through the choice of this word that all these songs, even the complaining one and the begging for salvation, are ultimately to be understood as songs of praise, as praisings, and thereby as the poetic expression of a great *trust*.

6. Neither in the original nor in my translation of Psalm 1 does "the Law" appear.[79] *Torah* is spoken of, the "instruction," namely the instruction of the right "way" by God. In distinction to "the Law" (*nomos*) Torah is first of all a *dynamic* concept, i.e., the verbal origin and character cleaves to the name and is repeatedly emphasized ("the Instruction that one will instruct you," Deuteronomy 17:11), and second, the tie between the divine instructor, the *"moreh"* (Isaiah 30-20), and his instruction is given in the word itself. Thus the objectification of the concept contradicts its essence.

7. My conjecture concerning Exodus 19:5 cannot be refuted through a reference to the *Leitwortstil*,[80] for a personal pronoun is in

---

[78] Muilenburg, pp. 388f.

[79] Cf. *ibid.*, p. 391.

[80] *Ibid.*, pp. 396f.

general, even when it is emphatically used, not important enough to be understood as a key-word; even so little can one derive a counter-proof from "and now" since this too, indeed, was for a reworker the word bidden here. (Parenthetically: I have only spoken of a "re-working": the words "or an interpolation" stem from a misunder-standing of the translator of which I have only now become aware.) Since I hold the reworking of the original course of words to be Deu-teronomic, the reference of my critic to "the Deuteronomists" does not prove anything. What is meant, by the way, by Muilenburg's com-ment[81] about our translation of the particle *im* in this passage being "unusual," is incomprehensible to me; the particle has not been translated differently by us here than elsewhere.

8. To refute the criticisms advanced against my interpretation of the Tetragrammaton (and against my attitude toward the "Ken-ite hypothesis" that is linked up with it) would require a special chapter; but I believe that I have already answered them in the es-sentials in my books on the subject, namely in *The Kingship of God* (*Königtum Gottes*) and in *Moses*.

9. In the question of the Decalogue the difference in opinions does not seem to me to be so great as Muilenburg[82] assumes. I do not, to be sure, hold it to be a *document* on which the conclusion of the Covenant is established, but I hold it to be the text of a proclamation whose origin is to be traced back to a revelation. I do not hold it to be an objectifiable "law," but I recognize myself in the Thou that is addressed by the commanding of this command, and I recognize my fellowmen whom I meet on the roads of my life in this same Thou.

10. Glatzer has[83] contrasted with my interpretation of the Bib-lical "law" my exegetical attitude: if I had followed this, he says, then I would have had to recognize and acknowledge that "*within the context* of the Old Testament the laws do appear as an absolutum." That they appear so in the context, however, is indeed incontestable; what concerns me is the question whether taken altogether they *right-ly* appear so, in other words: whether, for example, the details of the sacrifice stand in the same relationship to happening revelation as the Decalogue. We do not know which "Torah"—texts Jeremiah had in mind when he says (8:8), "the lying pen of the scribes" has been

81 *Ibid.*, p. 396, note 30.
82 *Ibid.*, pp. 397f.
83 Glatzer, pp. 378f.

active in it. They may be texts which afterward were not taken into the canon; it could also be otherwise. But in any case the prophet can here hardly mean anything else by "lies" than that within the "Torah," which the people call their own, to an apparently not insignificant extent human will was passed off for the divine. Thereby "laws" appeared as an absolutum that were none. I, to be sure, am not allowed to speak in the bold language of the prophets; but when as a believing thinker, a believing-thinking servant of the truth, I read and study in the Bible, I must agree in this matter. I recognize and know that revelation has taken place; I understand it when the man seized by the voice also then does not cease after he has said that which he had been bidden to say. I can understand how also in later moments something still unsaid, but awakened in him by those earlier hours and since then growing, would have been spoken by him to the heirs of his spirit with the very introductory words of the revelation, and would have remained in those spirits. Beyond this, however, it is clear and understandable to me how after him the introductory words of the proclaimed revelation that reports the "speaking" of God, has been made use of also by mere heirs of office, by "scribes." Out of all this the great context has arisen in which the laws do appear as an absolutum. I investigate, as well as I can, the legitimacy of this claim. That I cannot do, of course, if I treat the text as a mere object of my research: I must, whenever and however I read it, always myself be ready anew for meeting.

11. To my interpretation of prophetic texts Taubes has opposed some arguments[84] that I will examine briefly.

Taubes reproaches me because I "stress man's action as an agent of redemption"; to this it is rejoined that for the prophet "the inscrutable and hidden God was the prime agent in history." As if the two were not compatible with each other in the reality of prophetic faith as I have sought to present it! It goes without saying that —not merely for the prophetic, but for all biblical religiousness—the decisions are in God's hands. But in the prophetic proclamation future actions of God are time after time bound with an "if," the contents of which are the actions of man: if the people turn to him, he will turn to them. It goes without saying that the will of God is not thereby ascribed a dependence on the human will: it is God who wills to enter ever again into the dialogical relationship to man. Here

84 Taubes, pp. 455ff.

no dialectic rules, but the not-to-be-dialectized mystery of the primal
relation between God and man, forever announcing itself in moments
of factual happening in biography and history.

And in connection with this there exists no Old Testament text
on the basis of which it could be said that God is, for the prophets
or for anyone else, "a hidden God." He is no hidden, but rather a
hiding God as Deutero-Isaiah in a passage of basic importance (45:15),
has the peoples of the world liberated by God address Him: He had
hidden Himself and they were enslaved, but then He had revealed
Himself as "the liberator" and had led them into freedom. But when
does God hide Himself? That Isaiah had already clearly expressed once
(8:8, 17, 20): if a people "scorns" the "slow water" of the true historical happening, then God hides His face from before it until it
turns "to instruction and to witness."

The post-exilic prophets, like the pre-exilic ones, have spoken
this historical-dialogical If as men empowered by God. In the great
Biblical repetition style we hear from Hosea (14:2,5) to Malachi
(3:7) the divine action answers the human in a correspondence of
verb and verb at first resounding wholly freely, finally becoming formal. Only in the end-swell of the Babylonian exile, in the hour when the
liberation of Israel and the peoples of the world was taking place, did
the language of the alternative become silent, suppressed by the Deu-
tero-Isaianic double message, that of the completed historical mission
of Cyrus and that of the mission of the "servant" to be accomplished
over present and future generations. Taubes objects[85] that Deutero-Isaiah is thereby, according to my own distinction, to be counted
not among the prophets, but among the apocalyptics who no longer
know the mystery of the dialogical happening between God and
man. But that is by no means the case: the nameless speaker of history does not belong among the apocalyptics. The language of the
alternative is silent here only because in the songs of the "servant,"
in which the message is centered, the historical-superhistorical dialogic between God and man reaches its height. But it is also not the case
as Taubes says, that here and in the apocalyptic writers the prophetic
alternative is replaced by a "new" one, namely that of whether
one perceives the coming transformation or not. Such an alternative,
in fact, hence a choice before which an individual or a community
is placed, does not appear in Deutero-Isaiah. If (42:18 f.), under

85 *Ibid.*, p. 460.

emphatic fourfold repetition of the word "blind," it says of the "servant" that he was blind, no alternative whatsoever is concealed therein: God has made him see, and even awakens ever anew his hearing (50:4) in order that he might be able to fulfill the mission. And as to the image of the sons of the light and the sons of the darkness[86] that the apocalyptics have taken over from the language of Iranian dualism, it is entirely alien to Deutero-Isaiah whose God "forms the light and creates the darkness."

IX. *On Hasidism*

The essay in this book on my presentation of Hasidism gives me a welcome occasion to clarify this subject, so far as I can, with definitive precision.

It has been pointed out that my presentation is no historical work, for it does not discuss the Hasidic teaching in its entirety and it does not take into consideration the oppositions that have prevailed between the different streams of the Hasidic movement. The tapestry, which my work is seen as, "is woven of elective strands."

I agree with this view, even if, of course, not with the conclusions that are drawn from it.

Since the time in my preoccupation with this subject when I reached a basic study of the sources, i.e., since about 1910 (the early works were not sufficiently based), I have not aimed at presenting a historically or hermeneutically comprehensive presentation of Hasidism. Already at that time there grew in me the consciousness that my task by its nature was a selective one. But at the same time there grew in me an ever firmer certainty that the principle of selection that ruled here did not originate in a subjective preference. In this respect this task of mine is essentially of the same nature as my work on Judaism in general. I have dealt with that in the life and teaching of Judaism which, according to my insight, is its proper truth and is decisive for its function in the previous and future history of the human spirit. This attitude of mine includes valuation, of course, from its base up; but this valuation is one—on this point no doubt has touched me during the whole time—which has its origin in the immovable central exstence of values. Since I have attained to the maturity of this insight, I have not made use of a filter; I became a filter.

---

[86] *Ibid.,* p. 461.

But if this is so, then the nature of this filtering activity must be capable of being objectively characterized, i.e., it must be possible to explain in this case why that which was taken up was rightly taken up and why that which was left to one side was rightly left to one side. It is not difficult to explain this and thereby to make clear the objective criterion of selection.

Gershom Scholem has rightly pointed to the fact that Hasidism produced no new mystical doctrine extending in any essential points beyond the Kabbalistic tradition.[87] "Personality takes the place of doctrine."[88] Regarded from the standpoint of its theories, Hasidism is, in fact, pure epigone. But regarded from the standpoint of the personal lives of its leaders, as we are able to reconstruct them out of the unexampled fullness of the notes of their disciples, after separating out the purely legendary, it means the bursting forth of a mighty originality of the life of faith alongside which only a very little in the history of religions could be placed. Scholem has described the Hasidic movement as a "revivalist movement." But where in all the world has there ever existed a revival of such powerfulness of individual conduct of life and communal enthusiasm, stretching over seven generations? A comparison may be made, so far as I can see, between that part of the Hasidic literature that tells of the lives of the masters and that of Zen Buddhism, the Sufis, and the Franciscans; but in none of these movements do we find such an enduring power of vitality and an embracing of the human everyday as here. To this must be added, however, that here and only here it is not the life of monks that is reported but the life of spiritual leaders who are married and produce children and who stand at the head of communities composed of families. Here, as there, prevails devotion to the divine and the hallowing of lived life through this devotion; but there it is borne by an ascetic limitation of existence even where a helping and teaching contact with the people is preserved, while in Hasidism the hallowing extends fundamentally to the natural and social life. Here alone the whole man, as God has created him, enters into the hallowing.

Scholem has rightly designated *devekut*, the "cleaving" of the souls to God, as the central tendency of the Hasidic teaching. Only one must

[87] Gershom Scholem, *Major Trends in Jewish Mysticism*, Revised ed. (New York: Schocken Books, 1941), p. 338 ff.

[88] *Ibid.*, p. 344.

add that this concept of the Jewish tradition attained a twofold development here. Among the zaddikim who sought—even if, as said, unsuccessfully—to elaborate the Kabbalistic doctrine, there predominated the view, already familiar to us from Gnosis, that one must lift oneself out of the "corporeal" reality of human life into the "nothing" of pure spirit in order to attain contact with God, who is indeed already in the Bible "named the Lord of spirit in all flesh." But opposed to them—without a contest between the two taking place —is the view that this "constant being with God," as Scholem calls it in connection with Psalm 73, is rather reached through man's dedicating to God all that is lived by him. The Talmud (b. Ket. III) already answered the question of how it is possible for man to cleave to the Shekina "through good days," and that means, in the sense of the Talmudic teaching of the two urges, how shall one serve God with both urges, the good and the evil urge united: by doing what one does with the right kavana, with dedication to God, and thus hallowing it.

The first of these two views, that of spiritualization, we first find in Hasidism in its great thinker, the Maggid of Mezritch, the second, that of the hallowing of all life, we find first in his teacher, the Baal-Shem-Tov.

The Baal-Shem likes to present this teaching of his in connection with two biblical sayings: "In all thy ways know him" (Proverbs 3:6) and "do all that your hand finds to do with all your strength" (Ecclesiastes 9:10). He interprets the first saying: "Even in every bodily thing that you do it is necessary that it be a service of a higher need . . . all for the sake of heaven." And the second: "That he does what he does with all his limbs, according to the knowledge and thereby the knowledge is spread to all his limbs." Of course, only "the completed man" can wholly fulfill this command. "The completed man," says the Baal-Shem, "may accomplish high unifications" (i.e., unite God with his Shekina, dwelling in the exile of the world) "even with his bodily actions, such as eating, drinking, sexual intercourse, and transactions with his fellows over bodily things . . . as it says: And Adam knew his wife Eve."

Among the zaddikim closely connected with the Baal-Shem, it is above all Rabbi Yehiel Mikhal of Zlotchov who has developed this teaching, although after the death of the Master he attached himself to the great Maggid. The word of the Bible, "Be fruitful and multiply," he expounded thus: "Be fruitful, but not like the animals, be more than they, grow upright *and cleave to God as the sprig clings to the root,* and dedicate your copulation to him."

What I have cited is certainly proof enough that the inner dialectic of spiritualization and hallowing to which I have pointed does not belong to a later development of the Hasidic movement but already makes its appearance with its founding, and in such a way indeed that the teaching of the hallowing is the original thesis and that of the spiritualization that which follows it, clearly stemming from the ever stronger taking over of the Kabbalistic tradition.

A direct working of the hallowed human life on the divine sphere was, to be sure, already reserved in this thesis for the zaddik. But ever again, in sayings, parables, and tales the Baal-Shem and many of his disciples know how to praise the simple ignorant man whose life-forces are united in an original unity and who serves God with just this unity. Even in this lower, wholly unspiritual form, the undivided existence of man works on the higher happening.

Only later, however, did a real polemic against the Kabbalistic doctrine of spiritualization arise, and also only incidentally; a new systematic doctrine from which one could frontally attack the doctrine of spiritualization did not, indeed, arise, only a new mode of life which must ever again come to an understandig with the received life.

This polemic utterance, which is known to us from the mouth of a zaddik of the fifth generation, is concerned with the restitution of the original meaning of prayer as the speaking of man to God.

In place of the biblical immediacy of the purely personal being of the praying man to the being of God, which is not purely personal but which stands personally over against the praying man, the Kabbala set a meditation depending on the form of the prayer, whose subject was the inner structure of the divinity, the configurations of the "Sefirot" and the dynamic prevailing between them. According to the text of the prayer God is still the partner of dialogue between heaven and earth, but according to the theosophy which has been added to it, He is that no longer, He has become the object of an ecstatic contemplation and action. Corresponding to this change was the fact that the traditional liturgy, while preserving the text, was covered by a net of *kavanot,* or "intentions," that lead the praying man to absorption in the words and letters and, in closest connection with them, to the fulfillment of prescribed mutations, especially ever new approximate vocalizations of the Tetragrammaton.

The Hasidic movement has taken over uncritically the Kabbalistic prayer book formed in this manner; the Baal-Shem himself has sanctioned it. This state of affairs made unavoidable the division of those who prayed into the simple folk who in their words stilled the need of their hearts, and the "higher men" on whom there devolved the meditational or theurgical task. This division soon threatened to injure the fundamental feeling of community between the zaddik and his Hasidim.

Of the great praying men of the third generation one, R. Shmelke of Nikolsburg, seeks to cement the crack through elevating the community to praying for the return home of the Shekina out of its exile and to sacrificial devotion, evidently while in the hour of common prayer he himself acts with the others or rather steps forth; but another, R. Levi Yitzhak of Berditshev, in praying even enters wholly into the popular basic deportment of free dialogue; the third, however, R. Shlomo of Karlin, regards his own praying, manifestly only just the praying of the zaddik, as a theurgical venture to be accomplished only by him ("perhaps this time too I shall still not die").

It is understandable that it is a disciple of a disciple of this zaddik, R. Moshe of Kobryn, who utters that warning to which I point. Asked by the author of Kabbalistic writings about the secret kavanot of prayer, he answers:

You must keep in mind that the word Kabbala is derived from *kabbel:* to accept; and the word kavana from *kavven:* to direct. For the final meaning of all the wisdom of the Kabbala is to take on oneself the yoke of God's will, and the final meaning of all the art of kavanot is to direct one's heart to God.

The life meant by the primal faith of Israel, the original life in cleaving devotion to the Lord of life, opposes itself to the hypertrophy of mystical-magical doctrine. What is in question is: to accept whatever happens to me from the hands of God and to do whatever I do as directed to God. The insight of the Baal-Shem into the reciprocal immediacy of the relation to God that is attainable by man and that is able to encompass his whole life had here in a disciple of a disciple attained a semantic expression through his grasping at the simple basic meaning behind the later, specializing change in meaning.

That what is in question here, however, is not at all an affair of the spirit, affecting life, to be sure, but still floating above it, but altogether an affair of life itself, is conclusively proved by the answer that

a disciple of just that zaddik imparted to the question of what had
been most important to his teacher; it goes: "Whatever he happened
to be doing at the moment." Intercourse with God in the lived everyday, the accepting and dedicating of what is happening here and now,
is ever again the most important. Of the two elements the active is
especially stressed. "You shall," it is said, "become an altar for God."
On this altar *everything* shall be offered, according to the elaboration
made by the Baal-Shem of the Kabbalistic teaching of the holy sparks
present in all things and awaiting redemption.

It is not true, what is objected against me[89], that my "vision of
Hasidism" can be summed up in the words that here "the rift between God and the world is closed." It is not closed but bridged
over, and certainly with the paradoxical instruction to man that
he ever again set foot on the invisible bridge and thereby make it
real. For this purpose is man created and for this purpose the things
of this world that belong to each individual and, as the Baal-Shem
says, "with all their might entreat him to draw near in order that the
sparks of holiness that are in them may be raised," that is: be brought
to God through him. Therefore one shall, as it says in another saying
of the Baal-Shem, "have mercy on his tools and all his possessions." Each
action shall take place "to heaven." We know from utterances of the
Baal-Shem conveyed in the I-form, that he included everything corporeal without exception in the sphere of intention. Therefore in the
Polnaer tradition, which is undoubtedly true to the teaching of the
master, the relationship between body and soul is compared to that between husband and wife, by which each is only the half of a being
and is directed to the other half to attain the fulfillment of life.

Is that not "realism" enough? And of a "nullification" of the concrete there is in *this* line of Hasidism—which begins with its beginning
—nothing to be found. The beings and things for whom we perform
this service shall, in fact, continue to exist undiminished; the
"holy sparks" that "will be raised" must not thereby be withdrawn from them. Certainly there is also, according to the teaching of the Baal-Shem, such an art of "liberating" them that they are delivered from the wandering "from stone to plant, from plant to animal, from animal to speaking being." But when he says, "All that
man has, his servant, his animals, his tools, all conceal sparks that belong to the roots of his soul and wish to be raised by him," and

---

[89] Schatz-Uffenheimer, p. 403.

therefore "they entreat him with all their might to draw near them," then it is certainly clear that here no kind of annihilation but rather dedication, hallowing, transformation—transformation without suspension of concreteness—is meant. Therefore, the Baal-Shem can also include sin in this teaching of his (to be sure, in a meaning diametrically opposed to that of Sabbatian theology). "And what sort of sparks," he asks, "are those that dwell in sin?" And he answers: "It is the turning. In the hour when on account of sin you carry out the turning, you raise the sparks that were in it into the upper world." That is no nullification; it is a bridge-building.

What is essential has been expressed still more clearly perhaps by a great zaddik who is rather to be named a comrade than a disciple of the Baal-Shem, R. Pinhas of Koretz, when he says, there exist neither words nor actions that are idle in themselves, one only makes them into idle words and actions when one talks idly and acts idly.

What is asserted in opposition to me, that "the critical problem with which Hasidism was faced" consisted in the fact "that life split apart for it into external action on the one side and inner intention on the other," is not true. It is not "Hasidism" that is faced with this critical problem but its spiritualistic coinage, which, to be sure, won the upper hand in the school of the Maggid of Mezritch and thereby in the doctrine that was built out of it.

Only here is it possible to speak of "sensory appearance." But wherever the new mode of life became stronger than the doctrine that grew out of the Kabbalistic tradition, there the acceptance of the concrete for the sake of its hallowing manifested itself as "decision" and not as "problem." The inner dialectic of the Hasidic movement is that between an unoriginal Kabbalism remaining in the realm of "spiritual" men and a life with the world of unheard-of originality in the way it seized generation after generation of the people.

That is the basis of my selection. I have chosen what I have chosen; rather, I have let it go through my heart as through a filter because here is a way, one only to be sensed, but a way. I have stated this time after time with what seemed to me sufficient clarity whenever I had to talk of myself in this connection.[90]

90 Most recently in the conclusion of the Foreword to the new edition (1953) of *For the Sake of Heaven* and in *Hasidism and Modern Man,* the title essay (1958).

That I could have been misunderstood therein[91] as being ultimately concerned, as say Fichte, "about an act for its own sake," I
did not, of course, foresee. It seemed to me clear enough that it was an
act for the restoration of the immediacy between God and man for
the sake of overcoming the eclipse of God.

Therefore the selection has necessarily directed itself to the un-
justly despised "anecdotes"—stories of lived life—and "aphorisms"—
sayings in which lived life documents itself.

The "anecdotes" tell of the life of the zaddikim, and the "aphorisms," which are learned from the mouth of the zaddikim, express this
life of theirs with great pregnancy.

The central significance of the zaddik is no object of the inner
dialectic; it is the common and sustaining element from the beginning
of the movement, not as theory, certainly, but as fact that is interpreted by the teaching.

It is otherwise in life. Among the great zaddikim there are clearly two kinds to be distinguished: the zaddik who is essentially a teacher and whose decisive effect is on his disciples and the zaddik who is
essentially a helper and whose decisive effect is on the broad circle
of his Hasidim. That is no secondary distinction but one in which the
inner dialectic finds expression: the first kind belongs more to the
side of the spiritualizing, the second more to the other, that of realizing. In the person of the Baal-Shem both are still united, after him
they go apart. For the history of the movement the great teachers
and heads of schools, like the Maggid of Mezritch, R. Elimelekh of
Lishensk, the "Seer" of Lublin, are decisive; the popular life of the
movement concentrates itself in figures such as the Berditchever, R.
Zusya, R. Moshe Loeb of Sasov. They are the simply unique in Hasidism. The relationship to the disciples has also perhaps taken exemplary shape in the writings of Zen Buddhism, that to ignorant
people, to the street, nowhere in the world as here. An especially
characteristic trait of the zaddikim of the second kind, but one that is
common to them and to the Baal-Shem, I see in that particular
feeling of essential relatedness that here draws the high man, who
has found the unity, to the simple man who on a lower spiritual rung
truly devotes himself to God. What the Baal-Shem said to his Hasidim about the faithful stocking weaver—"Today I have seen the foundation stone that bears the holiness until the redeemer comes"—is

[91] Schatz-Uffenheimer, p. 410.

preserved, if not in the teaching yet in the legends, as a statement of primal importance. Not for nothing is a whole garland of related stories of the Baal-Shem handed down. The legendary among them supplement the unmistakably authentic.

It is entirely incomprehensible to me how one[92] can interpret my statement that the Hasidic message of redemption opposes the messianic *self*-distinction of one man from another man as if I saw in Hasidism the "representative of an atomistic ideology." In my writings I have ever again pointed to what it means when a man steps forth arbitrarily out of the hiddenness of the "quiver" in which God has sunk him as a "polished arrow" (Isaiah 49:2) and accords to himself and his actions the redeeming function. Hasidism is a movement directed against automessianism. One need only set the word "distinction" in place of the word "self-distinction," however, and already it follows that I hold Hasidism to be a "basically anti-messianic world view."[93]

What I have in fact recognized as the great Hasidic contribution to the belief in the redemption of the world is this, that each man can work on its redemption but none can effect it. This is an insight common to all Hasidism. In the inner dialectic of the movement, however, two basic views stand opposed to each other. The one asserts that man can work on the redemption of the world through exerting a magical influence on the divine configurations, the other declares in contrast that man can only work on the redemption of the world through moving with his whole being to God, "turning" to him and doing everything that he does from now on to God. He thereby enhances, in a measure corresponding to the strength of his movement, the capacity of the world to be redeemed: he "brings it nearer" to the heavenly influence.

That is the basic theme of my book *For the Sake of Heaven*, the one full-scale narrative that I have written. I had to write it because I had to try to make the inner dialectic that was visible and traceable to me visible and traceable to the man of today.

Since my critic enters into this book in some detail, I shall also contribute something here to the clarification of its subject-matter.

First a word on the story of the "Seer's" joy in the self-confident sinner who withstands all temptation to melancholy. Here my

92 Schatz-Uffenheimer, p. 416.
93 Schatz-Uffenheimer, p. 417.

critic, evidently under the influence of her polemic enthusiasm, has not noticed that I was not at all concerned with a characterization of Hasidism (within which I know of no similar utterance) but of a highly personal quality of the Seer of Lublin who as I indicate, himself ever again seized by melancholy, admires freedom from melancholy.

In opposition to the "metaphysics" of the Seer of Lublin, or rather his magical undertakings flowing out of it—the attempt to intensify to the highest the demonia active in the Napoleonic battle of peoples until it shook the gate of heaven and God come forth to redeem the world, the "holy Yehudi," without giving up the basic Kabbalistic teaching, essentially set a simple human "existence." He had nothing to do with the world-historical Gog— out of whose wars, which transform the human world into chaos, redemption shall proceed and which must therefore be intensified to the utmost—but with the dark Gog in our own breast. To transform this latter Gog, through the "turning," hence through the changing of the direction of the indispensable passion, into a light force working directly on redemption is that for which he called. One may not attempt to depreciate this message through identifying it with this or that modern pattern of thought. To call it "anthropocentric" does not make sense to me; it is rather bipolar. The "holy Yehudi" thereby reaches back to the cry that one can already hear in the prophets of Israel, that we must first "turn" before God "turns" from the "flaming of his wrath," and to the teaching perceivable in the inner dialectic of the Talmudic age that all eschatological combinations have gone by and it now depends alone on the human turning. In the teaching of the Baal-Shem it has found its mystical expression in the mysterious saying: "The beginning is up to you. For if the power of procreation first stirs in the woman, a male child is born."[94]

That the "Yehudi" in the active phase of his life was concerned about just this movement toward God is clearly shown by the saying, reliably transmitted by R. Shlomo of Radomsk: "Turn, turn, turn quickly in the turning, for the time is short and there is no longer any leisure for further wanderings of the soul, for redemption is

[94] I have intentionally placed this sentence at the end of my selection published under the title, "The Baal-Shem's Instruction in Intercourse with God" (in *Hasidism and Modern Man*).

near." That this was in fact the kernel of the sermon that he time after time repeated on his "great journey" through the Galician villages, even if in seemingly different settings, was still maintained there in my youth in oral tales. The meaning of the call is clearly this, that man must accomplish the decisive movement *now*, without depending on the idea that his soul still has time to ascend forward to higher life forms; for now the sphere of redemption has drawn close to our world and from now on the important thing is to draw it forthwith to us.

As far as the mystery of the death of the "holy Yehudi" is concerned, I have considered the different reports about it but have favored that in which one can perceive an influence of the "Seer"; I have done this because here the ambivalence, connected with his theurgy, in the relationship of the Lubliner rabbi to his disciple as well as his disciple's personal obedience, undiminished despite all essential opposition, find unsurpassable expression. Moreover, the Mogielnica Rabbi, who is cited in this connection[95], stood near the Yehudi, to be sure, but never called himself his disciple and remained essentially faithful to the tradition of his grandfather, the Maggid of Kosnitz. The question tied to one of his famous tales, "Has not Pshysha thus been joined to Lublin?"[96] is therefore misleading. Besides this, for me the most important difference between the two schools is not to be seen in a difference of doctrines but in one of "existence": in Lublin the teacher imposed himself on his disciples, in Pshysha he helped them to become themselves.

He who in the highest and most dispassionate seriousness dares to carry over that controversy between "metaphysics" and "existence" into the problematic of our own world-hour will recognize that all magicizing gnosis means an attempt to flee before the command of our human reality into the darkness above the abyss.

Conclusion

Among the contributions to this book there is one—that of Walter Kaufmann—in which it is stated with all clarity that all my mature works, no matter what field they may be in, ultimately belong to a single sphere because their theme in the final analysis is a single one. Walter Kaufmann circumscribes this unity with the concept of re-

95 Schatz-Uffenheimer, p. 432.

96 Schatz-Uffenheimer, p. 433.

ligious thought. To that I can certainly agree; only it must not be
misunderstood to indicate that what is meant is a thought that starts
from a religion. In the early stages of my way I encountered several
great thinkers whose thought started from a religion—Pascal, Ham-
aan, Kierkegaard—and I have learned from them, teaching that I can
never forget. But my way was fundamentally different from theirs,
and it has remained so: it could not be parallel to theirs.

In order to make this clearer I shall cite a few sentences that
I wrote in 1923; I also select these quotations because the essay
from which they were taken[97] has never been reprinted in any of my
books.[98] It says there:

> As often as religion has appeared once again in history, there was also in it
> a force that—not in a doubtful manner like the profane forces, but with
> the appearance of the highest legitimacy—diverted man from God. That it
> thereby enjoyed a great success was caused for the most part by the fact that
> it is far more comfortable to have to do with religion than to have to do with
> God who sends one out of home and fatherland into restless wandering. In
> addition, religion has all kinds of aesthetic refreshments to offer its adherents.
> whereas God transforms for man even formation and vision in a sacrifice that
> is offered, to be sure, by a joyful but not by an enjoying heart. For this
> reason, at all times the awake spirits have been vigilant and have warned of
> the diverting force hidden in religion—which is, indeed, only the highest sub-
> limation of the force that manifests itself in all life-spheres in this cruder
> autonomisation. . . .But either religion is a reality, rather *the* reality, namely
> the *whole* existence of the real man in the real world of God, an existence
> that unites all that is partial; or it is a phantom of the covetous human soul,
> and then it would be right promptly and completely to replace its rituals
> by art, its commands by ethics, its revelations by science.

If religion is to be understood in the former sense, then I myself
might dare to call my thought a religious one: it intends the whole
existence of man. But just for this reason it must reject every conception of a complete knowledge ("gnosis" in the most comprehensive
sense of the term). In the above chapter "Theology, Mysticism, Metaphysics" and elsewhere I have already said something about this subject, but I shall try once again to clarify it in a concentrated form.

The "complete," the legitimately religious existence of man, does
not stand in a continuity but in the genuine acceptance and mastery
of a discontinuity. It is the discontinuity of essentiality and inessen-

---

[97] "Religion und Gottesherrschaft" (a review of the book by that name by
Leonhard Ragaz, published in the *Frankfurter Zeitung* of April 27, 1923.

[98] Until the publication, after Martin Buber's death, of Martin Buber, *Nachlese*
(Heidelberg: Verlag Lambert Schneider, 1965), pp. 102–106 (Editor's note).

tiality that I understand as that of the I-Thou relation and the I-It relation to all being. To deny this discontinuity means to deny the decisive character of existing as man, which means incontestably: being able to stand in the face of Being without subsisting—and that means persevering—in the face of it. This discontinuity cannot be abrogated. But this "not" is a dual one. That a continuity of the I-Thou relation is not attainable in this our life, that it is impossible, indeed, even *to attempt* to attain it, this everyone knows who knows from his own experience what is in question here. In contrast, it is ever again possible to undertake to establish a continuity of the I-It relation: by erecting on the base of this relation a structure of knowledge, a supposedly adequate structure of what can be expressed, and now, so to speak, transmuting this structure into the being within which and with which one has to live. As long as one limits oneself thereby to the "world," one suffers only the injury to the essentiality of existence that necessarily results: that within which and with which one has to live necessarily becomes objectified in the same measure as the transmutation succeeds. Something entirely different takes place when one undertakes to include God in the structure of knowledge erected on the base of the I-It relation. Gnosis does just this. In so far as it originates in genuine personal ecstasies, it betrays its origin in which it has to do with no object at all, with nothing that could be legitimately made into the object of an assertion. Thereby it not only offends the transcendent but also human existence because it constructs a structure of knowledge which passes from now on as complete, which claims the absolute legitimacy of the transmutation in an allegedly finally valid appeal to the "known" mysterium. That the being into which this structure is here transmuted ultimately signifies the annihilation of lived concreteness, and that means: the abrogation of creation, is conclusive.

In contrast to this, religious thought in the sense in which I have indicated it means the acceptance of human existence in its factual discontinuity;—only we must give the leadership to the I-Thou relation. The I-Thou relation, the grace that appears ever anew in earthly material, does not even grant the appearance of security, and precepts that one merely needs to remember are not to be drawn from it. And yet it can lead: if only, after it has at any time been replaced by the I-It relation, we do not shun its influence: if we remain open to it. This remaining open is the basic presupposition of the "religious" life in the legitimate sense of the term, i.e., of the existence of man which has become whole. Here too the discontinuity is not overcome; we take it upon us and master it through the realized primacy of the dialogical.

This is, in fact, the theme to which, since I laid hold of it, or rather since it laid hold of me, my work in all spheres has been dedicated. Some of the forms in which it has manifested itself are "postulative"; but its core is an ontological one.

Thus understood, this thought, as I have said, is rightly called religious. But it may not—this too must be reiterated here—be treated as a thought which starts from a religion.

Mordecai Kaplan wrongly ascribes to me the view that "the religious tradition of Judaism is self-sufficient,"[99] from which it then naturally follows that I am concerned with "a theological anthropology that is grounded on a religious tradition."[100] I have in various places in these Replies as well,[101] pointed out that this is not so. As far as the tradition of Judaism is concerned: a few of its great expressions, beginning with the biblical and ending with the Hasidic, together constitute the strongest witness for the primacy of the dialogical that is known to me. Certainly this witness has been the divining-rod that has led me to water; but the water itself could not have been anything other than the experience of faith that fell to my share. Therefore, I have not been able to accept either the Bible or Hasidism as a whole; in one and in the other I had to and I have to distinguish between that which had become evident to me out of my experience as truth and that which had not become evident to me in this manner. Many of my readers, both of "the right" and of "the left," will protest against such a "subjectivism." Those with whom I am in dialogue and whose experience confirms mine know otherwise.*

[99] Mordecai Kaplan, p. 267.
[100] Ibid., pp. 267ff.
[101] Ibid., pp. 690ff.
* Translation by Maurice Friedman

BIBLIOGRAPHY OF THE WRITINGS OF MARTIN BUBER

Compiled by

MAURICE FRIEDMAN

THE LIBRARY OF LIVING PHILOSOPHERS
THE PHILOSOPHY OF MARTIN BUBER
BIBLIOGRAPHY*

COMPILED BY MAURICE FRIEDMAN

1897

"Essays on Viennese Authors": Albenberg, Hofmannsthal, Schnitzler. (Polish) in *Przeglad tygodniowy*.

1899

Referat auf dem III. Zionistenkongress. St. Basel, August 15-18, 1899. Vienna: Verlag des Vereins "Erez Israel," p. 191ff.

1900

"Ein Wort über Nietzsche und die Lebenswerte," *Kunst und Leben*, Berlin (December).

1901

"Kultur und Zivilisation," *Kunstwart*, Vol. 14, No. 15, 1. Maiheft.

Referat auf dem V. Zionisten-Kongress. Basel, December 26-30, 1901. Vienna: Verlag des Vereins "Erez Israel," pp. 151-170.

"Ueber Jakob Boehme," *Wiener Rundschau*, Vol. 5, No. 12 (June 15), pp. 251-253.

"Zwei nordische Frauen. (Ellen Key und Selma Lagerlöf)." *Neue Freie Presse* (Vienna) No. 13263 (July 20).

---

*For the most part I have not listed separately articles collected in books such as *Die jüdische Bewegung, Kampf um Israel, Die Stunde und die Erkenntnis*, and *Hinweise*. For a nearly complete bibliography of 852 items of works published by Martin Buber in various languages, see "A bibliography of Martin Buber's works (1895–1957)" compiled by Moshe Catanne on the occasion of Buber's Eightieth Birthday (Jerusalem, Israel: Mosad Bialik, (1961). For a bibliography of important books, sections of books, and articles about Martin Buber, see Maurice Friedman, *Martin Buber: The Life of Dialogue* (New York: Harper's Torchbooks, 1960). Cf. also the bibliography of works by and about Martin Buber covering the period 1897–1929 in Hans Kohn, *Martin Buber, sein Werk und Seine Zeit. Ein Beitrag zur Geistesgeschichte Mitteleuropas* (1880-1930), Köln: Joseph Melzer Verlag, 1961, pp. 381-403.

1903

(editor) *Der Jude; Revue der jüdischen Moderne.* Edited by Dr. Chaim Weizmann, Martin Buber, and Berthold Feiwel. Berlin: Jüdischer Verlag.

(editor) *Jüdische Künstler.* Berlin: Jüdischer Verlag.

"Lesser Ury," *Jüdische Künstler.* Ed. Martin Buber. Berlin: Jüdischer Verlag.

1904

"Gustav Landauer," *Die Zeit* (Vienna), Vol. 39, No. 506 (June 11).

"Zur Aufklärung," *Jüdische Rundschau,* Vol. 9, No. 48 (December 2).

1905

"Die Duse in Florenz," *Die Schaubühne,* Vol. 1, No. 15 (December 14).

"Über jüdische Märchen," *Generalanzeiger für die gesamten Interessen des Judentums,* Berlin (August).

1906

"Drei Rollen Novellis," *Die Schaubühne,* Vol. 2, No. 2 (January 11).

"Einführung" (Introduction) to *Die Gesellschaft. Sammlung sozial-psychologischer Monographien,* ed. Martin Buber. In Volume 1, Werner Sombart, *Das Proletariat.* Frankfurt am Main: Rütten & Loening.

Die Geschichten des Rabbi Nachman. Frankfurt am Main: Rütten & Loening.

"Die Geschichte von der Kräutertruhe und dem Kaiser zu Rom," *Die Welt,* Vienna, Vol. 10.

"Die Legende der Chassidim." No. 2, "Der Zukunfstbrief," *Die Welt* (August 17).

"Die Neidgeborenen. Eine chassidische Legende," *Der Zeitgeist,* Beiblatt zum *Berliner Tageblatt* (December 17).

1907

"Das Haus der Dämonen. Ein jüdisches Märchen," *Die Sonntagszeit,* Beilage zu No. 1547 der Wiener Tageszeitung *Die Zeit* (January 13).

1908

Die Legende des Baalschem, Frankfurt am Main: Rütten & Loening.

1909

Ekstatische Konfessionen. Jena: Eugen Diedrichs Verlag.

"Das hohe Lied," *Die Welt,* Vol. 13, No. 14-15.

1910

"Lebte Jesus? Ein Brief an den Herausgeber," *Diskussion,* Kulturparlament, Vol. 1, No. 1.

1911

Chinesische Geister- und Liebesgeschichten. Frankfurt am Main: Rütten & Loening.

Drei Reden über das Judentum. Frankfurt am Main: Rütten & Loening.

"Mystik als religiöser Solipsismus. Bemerkungen zu einem Vortrag Ernst Troeltschs," *Verhandlungen des ersten deutschen Soziologentages 1910.* Tübingen: I. C. B. Mohr Verlag. Pp. 206ff.

1912

(editor) *Die Gesellschaft. Sammlung sozialpsychologischer Monographien.* 40 vols. Frankfurt am Main: Rütten & Loening, 1906-1912.

1913

Buberheft. Vol. 3, No. ½ of *Neue Blätter.* Hellerau/Berlin: Verlag der Neuen Blätter. (Includes "Das Reden des Ekstatikers," "Von der Lehre," "Das verborgene Leben," "Das Judentum und die Menschheit," "Der Sinn der chassidischen Lehre," "Kultur und Religiosität," "Buddha," "Drei Legenden vom Baalschem," and Gustav Landauer, "Martin Buber.")

Daniel. Gespräche von der Verwirklichung. Leipzig: Insel Verlag.

1914

"Bücher die jetzt und immer zu lesen sind." (Antwort auf eine Rundfrage), *Wiener Kunst- und Buchschau,* Vienna (December).

"Der Engel und die Weltherrschaft. Ein altjüdisches Märchen," *Jüdische Rundschau,* Berlin (November 26).

Kalewala. (The national epic of Finland). Translated by Anton Schiefner. Revised and supplemented with notes and introduction by Buber. Munich: Georg Müller.

Reden und Gleichnisse des Tschuang-Tse. Leipzig: Insel-Verlag.

(editor) *Die vier Zweige des Mabinogi.* Leipzig: Insel-Verlag.

1915

"Bewegung. Aus einem Brief an einen Holländer" (Frederik van Eeden), *Der Neue Merkur,* Munich (January-February).

"J. L. Perez," *Jüdischer National-Kalender 5676.* Vienna: Verlag R. Löwit.

"Richtung soll kommen," *Masken,* Vol. 10, No. 11.

1916

Die jüdische Bewegung. Gesammelte Aufsätze und Ansprachen. Vol. 1, 1900-1914. Berlin: Jüdischer Verlag. (Includes "Jüdische Renaissance" (1900), "Gegenwartsarbeit" (1901), "Feste des Lebens" (1901), "Das Zion der jüdischen Frau" (1901), "Wege zum Zionismus" (1901), "Jüdische Wissenschaft" (1901), "Von jüdischer Kunst" (1902), "Die Schaffende, das Volk und die Bewegung" (1902), "Ein geistiges Zentrum" (1902), "Renaissance und Bewegung" 1. (1903), 2. (1910), "Zionistische Politik" (1904), "Was ist zu tun?" (1904), "Theodor Herzl" (1904), "Herzl und die Historie" (1904), "Die hebräische Sprache" (1910), "Das Land der Juden" (1912), "Er und Wir" (Herzl, 1910), "Das Gestaltende" (1912), "Zwiefache Zukunft" (1912), "Der Augenblick" (1914), "Die Tempelweihe" (1915), "Zum Gedächtnis" (1915).)

Vom Geist des Judentums. Leipzig: Kurt Wolff Verlag.

(editor) *Der Jude; eine Monatsschrift.* Edited by Martin Buber. I-VIII. —Berlin; R. Löwit (Jüdischer Verlag), 1916-1924.

"Von jüdischen Dichtern und Erzählern," *Jüdischer National-Kalender, 5677.* Vienna: Verlag der Jüdischen Zeitung.

"Über Agnon" in *Treue, eine jüdische Sammelschrift,* edited by Leo Hermann. Berlin: Jüdischer Verlag.

1917

"Asketismus und Libertinismus," *Jüdische Rundschau,* Vol. 22, No. 42 (October 19).

"Aus einem Rundschreiben vom Ostern 1914," *Almanach der neuen Jugend auf das Jahr 1917.* Berlin: Verlag der neuen Jugend.

Ereignisse und Begegnungen. Leipzig: Insel-Verlag. (Most of these essays were later included in *Hinweise* (1953).)

"Referat über jüdische Erziehung auf dem Deutschen Zionistischem Delegiertentag, December 1916," *Jüdische Rundschau,* Berlin (January 5). See also "Eine Erklärung," *Jüdische Rundschau* (March 16).

"Sieben Geschichten vom Baalschem," *Jüdischer National-Kalender 5678.* Vienna: Verlag "Jüdische Zeitung". (The sixth story, "Die Sabbatseele" was not included in *Die chassidischen Bücher* (1928).)

Völker, Staaten und Zion. Vienna: R. Löwit Verlag. (A letter to Hermann Cohen and comments on his reply. Later included in *Die Jüdische Bewegung,* Vol. II (1921).)

1918

"Brief über das Wesen der Sprache," der *Mitteilungen des Internationalenen Institutes für Philosophie in Amsterdam,* No. 1 (March). Groningen: Verlag P. Nordhoff.

Mein Weg zum Chassidismus. Erinnerungen. Frankfurt am Main: Rütten & Loening. (Later included in *Hinweise* (1953).)

"Rede bei der Tagung der jüdischen Jugendorganisationen Deutschlands am 5. März 1918," *Mitteilungen des Verbandes der jüdischen Jugendvereine Deutschlands,* Berlin, Heft 2/3 (April/May).

"Schreiben . . ." in *Mededeelingen van het International Instituut voor Wijsbegeerte te Amsterdam:* March. Letter to Mr. Borel published in Hebrew in *Mahut* (March 17, 1917).

1919

Cheruth. Eine Rede über Jugend und Religion. Vienna and Berlin: R. Löwit Verlag, 1919.

"Drei Geschichten von der Menschenliebe," *Der Jude,* Vol. 4, No. 9 (December).

Gemeinschaft, Vol. 2, of *Worte an die Zeit.* Munich: Dreiländer Verlag.

Grundsätze, Vol. 1, of *Worte an die Zeit.* Munich: Dreiländer Verlag.

Der Heilige Weg. Frankfurt am Main: Rütten & Loening.

"Landauer und die Revolution," *Masken, Halbmonatschrift des Duesseldorfer Schauspielhauses,* 14, No. 18/19 (1918/1919), pp. 282-286.

"Nicht was zum Munde eingeht," *Der Jude,* Vol. 4, No. 4 (July).

"Samael," *Der Jude,* Vol. 3, No. 12 (March).

"Die wahre Weisheit," *Der Jude,* Vol. 4, No. 4 (July).

"Zwei Tagebuchstellen. 1. Pescara an einem Augustmorgen (1914). 2. Nach der Heimkehr," *Zeit Echo. Ein Kriegstagebuch der Künstler,* Munich, No. 3.

"Die zweiten Tafeln (Moseslegende)," *Inselalmanach auf das Jahr 1919.* Leipzig: Insel-Verlag.

1920

"Der heimliche Führer (Ansprache über Landauer)," *Die Arbeit,* Berlin (June).

(editor) *Meister Eckharts mystische Schriften,* Gustav Landauer. Veränderte Neuausgabe. Berlin: Karl Schnabel Verlag.

Die Rede, die Lehre, und das Lied. Leipzig: Insel-Verlag. (Includes introductory essays to *Ekstatische Konfessionen, Reden und Gleichnisse des Tschuang-Tse,* and *Kalewala.*)

"Die Wanderschaft des Kinderlosen," Martin Buber, H. H. Cohn. Ch. Z. Klötzel, *Drei Legenden.* Berlin: Jüdischer Verlag.

1921

"Drei Predigten. 1. Das Weinen," *Gabe, Herrn Rabbiner Nobel zum 50. Geburtstag dargebracht,* Frankfurt am Main. (The second and third are included in *Die chassidischen Bücher* (1928).)

Die jüdische Bewegung. Gesammelte Aufsätze und Ansprachen. Vol. 2, 1916-1920. Berlin: Jüdischer Verlag. (Includes "Die Lösung," "Argumente," "Mose," "Völker, Staaten und Zion: I, Begriffe und Wirklichkeit; II, Der Staat und die Menschheit," "Der Wägende," "An die Prager Freunde," "Ein Heldenbuch," "Die Polnischen und Franz Blei," " 'Kulturarbeit'," "Unser Nationalismus," "Vorbemerkung über Franz Werfel," "Ein politischer Faktor," "Der Preis," "Die Eroberung Palästinas," "Jüdisch Leben," "Zion und die Jugend," "Eine unnötige Sorge," "Die Revolution und wir," "Vor der Entscheidung," "In später Stunde," "Anhang: Noten zu 'Völker, Staaten und Zion'.")

"Rede über die politischen Prinzipien der Bewegung auf der 2. Hitachduth Konferenz, Karlsbad, August 1921" in the Yiddish weekly *Volk und Land* (November 18 and 26).

(editor) *Der werdende Mensch* by Gustav Landauer. Potsdam: Gustav Kiepenheuer Verlag.

1922

"Die Aufgabe," *Das werdende Zeitalter.* Vol. 1, No. 2 (April).

"Drama und Theater," *Masken, Zeitschrift für deutsche Theaterkultur* (Düsseldorfer Schauspielhaus), Vol. 8, No. 1, pp. 5ff. (Later included in *Hinweise* (1953).)

Der grosse Maggid und seine Nachfolge. Frankfurt am Main: Rütten & Loening.

"Über den deutschen Aufsatz," *Wilhelm Schneider; Meister des Stils über Sprache und Stillehre.* Leipzig: B. G. Teubner, 1922.

"Vier Gleichnisse des Ferid-ed-din-Attar," *Inselalmanach auf das Jahr 1922.*

1923

"Eine neue Lehre; zwei chassidische Schriftdeutungen," *Der Jude*, Vol. 7, No. 10/11 (January/February).

Ich und Du. Leipzig: Insel-Verlag.

Reden über das Judentum. Frankfurt am Main: Rütten & Loening. (Includes *Drei Reden* (1911), the three talks from *Vom Geist des Judentums* (1916), *Der heilige Weg* (1918), and *Cheruth* (1919), plus an important Foreword.)

"Religion und Gottesherrschaft, Besprechung von Leonhard Ragaz' *Weltreich, Religion und Gottesherrschaft,*" Frankfurter Zeitung, "Literaturblatt," No. 9 (April 27).

Sette discorsi sull'ebraismo, Tradotti di Dante Lattes e Mosè Beilinson con una prefazione del Alessandro Bonucci, Firenize: Israel.

1924

(editor) *Beginnen,* Gustav Landauer. Köln: Marcan-Block-Verlag.

"Brief an Florens Christian Rang" in Florens Christian Rang *Deutsche Bauhütte.* Sannerz: Gemeinschaftsverlag Eberhard Arnold.

"Flucht?," Abendblatt der *Frankfurter Zeitung* (March 21). (Reply to Karl Wilker, *Frankfurter Zeitung* (March 6).)

"Geheimnis einer Einheit" in *Hermann Stehr, sein Werk und seine Welt.* Edited by Wihelm Meridies. Habelschwerdt: Franke Buchhandlung.

Das verborgene Licht. Frankfurt am Main: Rütten & Loening.

"Ein Wort über den Chassidismus," *Theologische Blätter* (Marburg), Vol. 3, Sp. 161.

1925

La leggenda del Baal-scem. Traduzione di Dante Lattes e Mosè Beilinson. Firenze: Israel.

"La Voie," trans. by Bernard Poliakov. *La Revue Juive* (Paris), Vol. 1, No. 6 (November). (Selections from *Reden über das Judentum.*)

"Zwiegespräch," *Insel-Almanach auf das Jahr 1926.* Leipzig: Insel-Verlag.

1926

"Gewalt und Liebe. Drei Verslein," *Das werdende Zeitalter,* Vol. 5, No. 1.

Die Kreatur, a quarterly. Edited by Martin Buber, Joseph Wittig, and Viktor von Weizsäcker. I-III. Berlin: L. Schneider, 1926-1930.

Rede über das Erzieherische. Berlin: Lambert Schneider Verlag.

"Résponse à un Questionnaire," *L'homme aprés la Mort*. Vol. 2 of *Les Cahiers Contemporains*. Editions Montaigne, Paris.
"Zwiegespräch (Kleine legendäre Anekdote nach dem Japanischen) ," *Insel-Almanach auf das Jahr 1926.*

1927

Des Baal-Schem-Tow Unterweisung im Umgang mit Gott. Hellerau: Jakob Hegner Verlag.
"Schlichtung," *Frankfurter Zeitung*, 1. Morgenblatt (October 18, 1924). Reprinted in *Berliner Tageblatt*, Abendausgabe (February 26, 1927) . (On Buddha-translation.)

1928

"Am Tag der Rückschau" (poem dedicated to P[aula] B[uber].) *Jüdische Rundschau*, Berlin (February 7).
Die chassidischen Bücher, Gesamtausgabe. Hellerau: Jakob Hegner Verlag. (Includes *Die Geschichten des Rabbi Nachman, Die Legende des Baal-Schem, Mein Weg zum Chassidismus, Der grosse Maggid und seine Nachfolge,* and *Das verborgene Licht.*)
"Drei Sätze eines religiösen Sozialismus," *Die Neue Wege*, 22, pp. 327ff. (Later included in *Hinweise* (1953).)
"Freiheit und Verantwortung," *Die Brücke*, Untermassfeld (December 24).
"Kraft und Richtung, Klugheit und Weisheit," *Das werdende Zeitalter* (Kohlgrabe bei Vacha), Röhn (April).
"Nach dem Tod," *Münchener Neuesten Nachrichten* (February 8).
"Über die Todesstrafe," in E. M. Mungenast, *Der Mörder und der Staat.* Stuttgart: Walter Hädecke Verlag, page 65.
"Über Rathenau (Briefliche Mitteilung)," in Harry Graf Kesler, *Walther Rathenau, sein Leben und sein Werk.* Berlin-Grünewald: Verlag Hermann Klemm, pp. 89ff., n.
"Über Stefan George," *Literarische Welt*, Berlin (July 13).
"Zuchthaus für männliche Prostitution (Antwort auf eine Rundfrage)," *Das Forum*, Berlin (December).

1929

"Discours sur le judaïsme," (Traduit de l'allemand par J. Krichevsky) , *L'Illustration juive*, Vol. 1, No. 2 (June 25).
(editor) *Gustav Landauer. Sein Lebensgang in Briefen.* Edited in co-operation with Ina Britschgi-Schimmer. 2 Vols. Frankfurt am Main: Rütten & Loening.

"Philosophie und Religiöse Weltanschauung in der Erwachsenenbil-
dung" in *Tagungsbericht des Hohenrodter Bundes*, Vol. 2, Berlin.
"Reden auf der sozialistischen Tagung in Heppenheim: die Begrün-
dung des Sozialismus. Sozialismus und persönliche Lebensgestal-
tung" in *Sozialismus aus dem Glauben. Verhandlungen der sozial-
istischen Tagung in Heppenheim*, Pfingstwoche, 1928. Zürich:
Rotapfel-Verlag, pp. 90ff, 121ff, 217ff.
"Religion und Philosophie," *Europäische Revue* (August), pp. 325-335.
"Über Asien und Europa," *Chinesisch-deutscher Almanach für das
Jahr 1929/1930*. Edited by China-Institut, Frankfurt am Main.
"Ein Wörterbuch der Hebräischen Philosophie. (Besprechung von
Jakob Klatzkins *Thesaurus philosophicus linguae hebraicae*.),"
Frankfurter Zeitung, Literaturblatt (February 24).

1930

"Bemerkungen zu Jesaja," *Monatsschrift für Geschichte und Wissen-
schraft des Judentums*, Vol. 74, Nos. 5/6, 9/10 (May/June, Septem-
ber/October).
Hundert chassidische Geschichten. Berlin: Schocken Verlag.

1931

"Bemerkungen zur Gemeinschaftsidee," *Kommende Gemeinde*, Vol. 3,
No. 2 (July). ("Was uns fehlt; Gedanken zum wirtschaflichen und
sozialen Umbruch".)
"In jüngeren Jahren," in Braun, Harald. *Dichterglaube. Stimmen
religiösen Erlebens*. Berlin-Steglitz: Eckart.
Jewish Mysticism, and the Legends of the Baal-Shem. Translated by
Lucy Cohen. London and Toronto: J. M. Dent & Sons. (Includes
one story, "The New Year's Sermon," not included in the author-
ized translation of *The Legend of the Baal-Shem* by Maurice
Friedman (1955).)
"Religiöse Erziehung," *Das werdende Zeitalter*, Vol. 10, No. 1 (Janu-
ary).
"Verflucht sei der Tag (Jeremia 20, 14-18)," *Der Morgen*, Vol. 6,
No. 6 (February).

1932

"Haus Gottes: Stimmen über den Kunstbau der Zukunft" *Eckart*, Vol.
8, No. 10 (October).
Ich und Du. Reissued. Berlin: Schocken Verlag.

Königtum Gottes. Vol. 1 of *Das Kommende. Untersuchungen der Entstehungsgeschichte des messianischen Glaubens.* Berlin: Schocken Verlag.

"Meta-anthropological Crisis," *Transition.* The Hague: Servire.

Reden über das Judentum. Reissued. Berlin: Schocken Verlag.

Zwiesprache. Berlin: Schocken Verlag.

1933

"Adel" (Zum 60. Geburtstag von Leo Baeck), *Jüdische Rundschau,* Vol. 38, No. 41 (May 21).

"Gespräch um Gott; Bericht über zwei Meinungskämpfe," *Eckart,* Vol. 9, No. 2 (February).

"Le Judaïsme et L'Angoisse Mondiale," *La Revue juive de Genève,* Vol. 1, No. 6 (March).

Kampf um Israel. Reden und Schriften (1921-1932). Berlin: Schocken Verlag. (Includes "Vorrede," "Der dritte Tischfuss" (1926), "Das Judentum und die neue Weltfrage" (1930), "Der Glaube des Judentums" (1929), "Die Brennpunkte der jüdischen Seele," "Nachahmung Gottes" (1926), "Biblisches Führertum," "Weisheit und Tat der Frauen" (1929), " 'Pharisäertum' " (1925), "Bericht und Berichtigung" (1926), "Vertrauen" (1926), "Achad-Haam-Gedenkrede in Berlin" (1927), "Achad-Haam-Gedenkrede in Basel" (1927), "Zwei hebräische Bücher" (1928), "Der wahre Lehrer" (1923), "Der Acker und die Sterne" (1928), "Sache und Person" (1929), "Die Tränen" (1928), "Philon und Cohen" (1928), "Für die Sache der Treue" (1930), "Franz Rosenzweig" (1930), "Der Dichter und die Nation" (1922), "Alfred Mombert" (1922), "Ein Wort über Franz Kafka" (1928), "Greif nach der Welt, Habima!" (1929), "Im Anfang" (1927), "Drei Stationen" (1929), "Nationalismus," "Lebensfrömmigkeit" (1928), "Zion und die Gola" (1932), "Wie kann Gemeinschaft werden?" (1930), "Arbeitsglaube" (1929), "Warum muss der Aufbau Palästinas ein sozialistischer sein?" (1929), "Universität und Volkshochschule," "Volkserziehung als unsere Aufgabe" (1926), "Rede auf dem XIII. Zionistenkongress in Karlsbad" (1922), "Kongressnotizen zur zionistischen Politik" (1921), "Zur Klärung" (1922), "Streiflichter" (1922), "Nachbemerkung" (1922), "Frage und Antwort" (1922), "Die Vertretung" (1923), "Selbstbesinnung" (1926), "Brief an das Aktions-Comité der Zionistischen Weltorganisation" (1928), "Rede auf dem XVI. Zionistenkongress in Basel" (1930), "Jüdisches Nationalheim und nationale Politik in Palästina," "Wann denn?" (1932).)

"Name verpflichtet," *Kulturbund Deutscher Juden Monatsblätter*, Vol. 1, No. 1 (October).

"Die Söhne," *Die Logen-Schwester*, Vol. 6, No. 11 (November 15).

Die Tröstung Israels; aus Jeschajahu, Kapitel 40 bis 55. Mit der Verdeutschung von M. B. und Franz Rosenzweig. Berlin: Schocken = Bücherei des Schocken-Verlags, 1.

"Zur Ethik der politischen Entscheidung," *Politik und Ethik.* Petzen: Versöhnungsbund.

1934

Erzählungen von Engeln, Geistern und Dämonen. Berlin: Schocken Verlag.

"Jiskor; Einleitung zu einem Gedenkbuch," *Jisrael Volk und Land; jüdische Anthologie.* Berlin, Hechaluz, Deutscher Landesverband.

"Die Tugend der Propaganda," *Jüdische Rundschau*, Vol. 39, No. 43 (May 29).

"Über Selbstmord: Antwort auf eine Rundfrage" in Baumann, Karl. *Selbst-Mord und Freitod in sprachlicher und geistesgeschichtlicher Beleuchtung* (Diss. Giessen, 1933), Würzburg-Aumühle: K. Trilsch.

1935

Deutung des Chassidismus. Berlin: Schocken Verlag. (Later included in *Die chassidische Botschaft.*)

Martin Buber. ("The Meaning," "Of Oneness," Ultimate Aims," "The True Foundation," "The Central Myth," "The Only Way," "The Primal Powers") in Lewisohn, Ludwig. *Rebirth; a Book of Modern Jewish Thought.* New York: Harper.

"Vorbemerkung" to Hermann Cohen, *Der Nächste.* Berlin: Schocken Verlag.

1936

"Auf den Ruf hören: Schlusswort im Gespräch Martin Buber-Joachim Prinz," *Israelitisches Familienblatt*, Vol. 38, No. 33 (August 13).

Aus Tiefen rufe ich Dich; dreiundzwanzig Psalmen in der Urschrift mit der Verdeutschung von M. B. Berlin: Schocken, = Bücherei des Schocken-Verlags, 51.

"Die Bibel als Erzähler; Leitwortstil in der Pentateuch-Erzählung," *Morgen*, Vol. 11, Nos. 11, 12 (February, March).

"Erkenntnis tut not," *Almanach des Schocken Verlags auf das Jahr 5696* (1935/36), pp.11-14. Berlin: Schocken Verlag.

Die Frage an den Einzelnen. Berlin: Schocken Verlag.

"Genesisprobleme," *Monatsschrift für Geschichte und Wissenschaft des Judentums* (April 3).

Königtum Gottes. 2nd enlarged edition. Berlin: Schocken Verlag.

"Die Nacht der Gola; drei Midraschim," Trans. by Martin Buber, *Almanach des Schocken-Verlags auf das Jahr 5697.* Berlin: Schocken.

(with Franz Rosenzweig) *Die Schrift und ihre Verdeutschung.* Berlin: Schocken Verlag.

Die Stunde und die Erkenntnis. Reden und Aufsätze, 1933-1935. Berlin: Schocken Verlag. (Includes "Der jüdische Mensch von heute," "Das Erste," "Die Kinder," "Gericht und Erneuerung," "Geschehende Geschichte," "Freiheit und Aufgabe," "Der Jude in der Welt," "Das Haltende," "Worauf es ankommt," "Ein Spruch des Maimuni," "Erkenntnis tut not," "Die Lehre und die Tat," "Die Mächtigkeit des Geistes," "Unser Bildungsziel," "Biblischer Humanismus," "Aufgaben jüdischer Volserziehung," "Jüdische Erwachsenenbildung," "Bildung und Weltanschauung," "Entwürfe und Programme," "Kirche, Staat, Volk, Judentum," "Brief an Ernest Michel," "Offener Brief an Gerhard Kittel," "Zu Gerhard Kittels 'Antwort'.")

Zion als Ziel und Aufgabe. Berlin: Schocken Verlag.

"Zum Einheitscharakter des Jesajabuches," *Der Morgen,* Vol. 12, No. 8 (November).

1937

"Der Chaluz und seine Welt (Aus einer Rede)" *Almanach des Shocken Verlag auf das Jahr 5697 (1936/37),* pp. 87-92. Berlin: Schocken Verlag.

"Dialogues," Traduit de l'allemand par Germain Landier (Réminiscences. La communion dans le silence. La profondeur inexprimable. De penser). *Mesures,* 4 (October 15).

"Gespräche um Gott; Bericht über zwei Meinungskäampfe," *Almanach des Schocken Verlags auf das Jahr 5698.* Berlin: Schocken.

I and Thou. Translation of *Ich und Du* by Ronald Gregor Smith. Edinburgh: T. & T. Clark.

"Offenbarung und Gesetz" (from letters to Franz Rosenzweig), *Almanach des Schocken Verlags auf das Jahr 5697 (1936/37)*, pp. 147-154.

Die Schrift. Translation of the Bible from Hebrew into German in co-operation with Franz Rosenzweig. 15 vols. Berlin: Lambert Schneider and later Schocken Verlag. I. Im Anfang. (1926?). II. Namen. (1926). III. Er rief. (1926). IV. In der Wüste (1927). VI. Jehoschua. (1927). VII. Richter. (1927). VIII. Schamuel. (1928). IX. Könige. (1929). X. Jeschajahu. (1930). XI. Jirmejahu. (1931). XII. Jecheskel. (1932). XIII. Das Buch der Zwölf. (1934). XIV. Das Buch der Preisungen. (1935). XV. Gleichsprüche. (1937?).

1938

"Die Erwählung Israels; eine Befragung der Bibel," in *Almanach des Schocken Verlags auf das Jahr 5699.* Berlin: Schocken.

Die Forderung des Geistes und die geschichtliche Wirklichkeit; Antrittsvorlesung gehalten am 25. April 1938 in der Hebräischen Universität, Jerusalem. Leipzig: Schocken.

"Gegen die Untreue," *Jüdische Rundschau*, Vol. 43, No. 59 (July 26).

Je et Tu. Trans. (from *Ich und Du*) Geneviève Bianquis. Preface by Gaston Bachelard. Paris: Fernand Aubier, Editions Montaigne.

"Keep Faith," *The Palestine Post* (July 18).

Martin Buber und sein Werk. Zu seinem sechzigsten Geburtstag im Februar 1938 überreicht vom Schocken Verlag—Jüdischer Buchverlag. Berlin: Schocken. "Chassidismus"; "Dienst an Israel"; "An das Gleichzeitig"; "Die Bibelarbeit."

"Mitoldot hasheilah 'ma hu haadam'?" (in Hebrew), *Turim* (June 29).

"Ruach Israel bifney hameziut hanochchit" (in Hebrew), *Haaretz* (December 30).

"Tviaat Haruach vehameziut Hahistorit" (in Hebrew) *Harzaat Peticha.* Jerusalem: The Hebrew University.

"Tviaat Haruach vehameziut hanochchit" (in Hebrew), *Mosnayim*, No. 7, Iyyar.

"Die Verwirklichung des Menschen: zur Anthropologie Martin Heideggers" in *Philosofia*, edited by Arthur Liebert, Vol. 3, No. 1-4, Belgrade.

"Wahrt die Treue," *Tirgumim*, Vol. 2, No. 310 (July 26).

Worte an die Jugend. (I. Was ist zu tun? II. Zion und die Jugend. III. Cherut. IV. Wie kann Gemeinschaft werden. V. Warum soll

man lernen? VI. Wann denn? VII. Die Vorurteile der Jugend).
Berlin: Schocken, = Bücherei des Schocken-Verlags, 88.

1939

"Betichut heatid haenoschi ezel Hegel ve Marx," *Davar* (January 20).
"Das Ende der deutsch-jüdischen Symbiose," *Jüdische Welt-Rund-schau*, Vol. 1, No. 1 (March 10).
"Nationale Erziehung," Cernauti: Verlag des "Morgenblatt."
"Pseudo-Simsonismus," in *Jüdische Welt-Rundschau*, Vol. 1, No. 15 (June 23).
(with Judah Magnes) *Two Letters to Gandhi*. (Public letters by Buber and Magnes and the original text of Gandhi's statement about the Jews in *Harijan*, November 26, 1938.) Pamphlets of *The Bond*. Jerusalem: Rubin Mass, April 1939.
"Zur Erzählung von Abraham." *Monatsschrift für Geschichte und Wissenschaft des Judentums*, Vol. 83, (Jan./Dec.)
"Zwei Beiträge zur Klärung des Pazifismus; Botschaft Dr. M. B.s an den Schulungskurs der Internat. Friedens-Akademie, Schloss Greng, 1.-12. August 1939," *Der Aufbau*, Vol. 20, No. 37 (September 15).

1940

"Het Geloof van Israel," trans. L. Alons, in Gerhardus van der Leeuw, *De godsdiensten der wereld*. I. Amsterdam: H. Meulenhoff.
"Neviei Sheker" (in Hebrew), *Lamoed*. Jerusalem.
"Reishitah shel hahassidut" (in Hebrew), *Jahadut Polin*, Tevet and Adar Alef, Jerusalem; also in *Mosnayim*, No. 11, Tamuz and Av.
"Tirgum Hamikra, Kavanato vedrahav" (in Hebrew), *Mosnayim*, No. 10, Kislev/Tev. 5700.

1941

" 'Defaitismus'; zu einer Diskussion," *Mitteilungsblatt der Hitachduth Olej Germania we Olej Austria*, Vol. 5, No. 50 (Dec. 12).
"Elohei Israel veilohei Avot" (in Hebrew), *Zion*, No. 7.
Gog und Magog (in Hebrew), *Davar*, serially (October 23-January 10).
"Goyim veeilohav" (in Hebrew), *Kenesset*, Comments of Israeli writers on Bialik, ed. Jakov Cohen. Tel. Aviv: Dvir Publishing Co.
"Humaniut Ivrit" (in Hebrew), *Hapoel Hazïr*, No. 34 (May 30).
"Sheilat Doro shel Iyov" (in Hebrew), *Mosnayim*, No. 13, Tishri-Heshvan 5702.

1942

"Am umanhig" (in Hebrew), *Mosnayim,* Iyyar 5702.

"Baayat haadam bemishnato shel Heidegger" (in Hebrew), *Sdarim,* Collection of essays by writers of Israel, ed. A. Steimann. Tel Aviv.

"Behamulat hasan'gorim" (in Hebrew), *Mosnayim,* No. 15, Tishri.

"Darkei Hadat bearzeinu (Emet Veemunah)" (in Hebrew), *Machbarot lesifrut,* No. 2 (May).

"Hayesh Koach laruach? Le Mishnatoh shel Max Scheler." (in Hebrew), *Machbarot lesifrut,* No. 1 (September).

"Hayessod hautopi besozialism" (in Hebrew), *Hapoel Hazaïr,* No. 6 (December 24).

"Haruach vehameziut" (in Hebrew), *Machbarot lesifrut.* Tel Aviv.

"Lao-Tse al hashilton" (in Hebrew), *Hapoel Hazaïr,* No. 35 (May 20).

"Lehinui 'Hasozialism hautopisti' " (in Hebrew), *Hapoel Hazaïr,* No. 36 (November 30).

"Raayon hageulah behassidut" (in Hebrew), *Arahim,* Jerusalem: Reuben Mass, Library for Institute for Leaders.

Torat haneviim. Jerusalem: Mosad Bialik.

1943

"Baayat haadam" (in Hebrew), *Machbarot lesifrut,* Tel Aviv.

"Dat uphilosophia" (in Hebrew), *Hagot,* Jerusalem: The Philosophical Society (Hugo Bergmann's 60th Birthday).

"In Theresienstadt," *Mitteilungsblatt,* Vol. 7, No. 21 (May 21).

"Israel bearzo besefer 'Kusari' " (in Hebrew), *Gilyonot,* Nos. 14 & 10, Shevat & Adar A (from *Bein Am learzo*).

"Kropotkin" (in Hebrew), *Hapoel Hazaïr,* June 7.

"Al mahutah shel Hatarbut" (in Hebrew), *Machbarot lesifrut,* No. 2 (November).

"Pirutav shel Raajon" (in Hebrew), (tekes Hajovel letorat Copernicus, The Hebrew University Jerusalem) , *Haaretz* (June 4) .

"Proudhon" (in Hebrew) in *Hapoel Hazaïr* (April 29).

"Zadik ba laaretz (Nachmann mi Bratzlav)" (in Hebrew), *Mosnayim,* No. 17. Tishri.

1944

"Advice to frequenters of libraries," "Books for your vacation" branch Library book news, The New York Public Library, Vol. 21, No. 5 (May).

"Ahavat Elohim veideot haelohut" (al Hermann Cohen) (in Hebrew), *Knesset,* Vol. 8, Tel Aviv: Dvir Co.

"An Chaim Weizmann," *Mitteilungsblatt,* Vol. 8, No. 48 (Dec. 1, 1944).

"Bergson vehaintuiziah" (in Hebrew), Introduction in Part I of *Henri Bergson: Energiah Ruchanit* (Hebrew translation of Bergson's *Creative Evolution),* Tel-Aviv: "L'guulam" (Mosad Bialik).

"Dat umussar behassidut (Bepardeis Hahassidut) " (in Hebrew) , *Amudim,* Nos. 1, 9 & 10 (September 15th and 20th).

"Leinjan *Gog u Magog,"* (in Hebrew), *Haaretz* (December 8).

"Lekach Mi-Sin" (in Hebrew), *Hagalgal,* No. 1 (January 20).

"Mekomo shel Copernicus bephilosophia" in *Nicolai Copernicus* by Sh. Smebasky (lectures at The Hebrew University, May 26). Jerusalem: The Hebrew University Press.

"Marx, Lenin vehithadshut hahevra" (in Hebrew), *Mosnayim,* No. 18, Nisan.

"Social experiments in Jewish Palestine," The *New Palestine,* Vol. 35, No. 1 (October 13).

"Spinoza vehaBaal-Shem-Tov" (in Hebrew), *Machborot lesifrut,* Nos. 3 & 2 (December) (from *Bepardes hahassidut).*

1945

Bfardes hachasidut (in Hebrew), Tel-Aviv: Mosad Bialik through Dvir.

Bein Am learzo (in Hebrew), Jerusalem: Schocken.

"The Crisis and the Truth; a Message," *The Australian Jewish Review,* Vol. 6, No. 7 (September).

Darko shel Adam (meolam hahassidut) (in Hebrew), Jerusalem: Hagalgal and also Mosad Bialik.

"Eternal truths," *The Zionist Record* (New Year annual) November.

For the Sake of Heaven. Trans. (from the German) Ludwig Lewisohn. Philadelphia: The Jewish Publication Society (Trans. of *Gog und Magog)* (1949) .

"Judah Halevi's *Kitab al Kusari,"* *Contemporary Jewish Record,* Vol. 8, No. 3 (June).

Le Message Hassidique. Trans. Phillipe Lavastine (extracts from *Die chassidischen Bücher).* In *Dieu Vivant,* 2.

Moshe (in Hebrew), Jerusalem: Schocken.

"Our Reply," in *Towards Union in Palestine, Essays on Zionism and Jewish-Arab Cooperation.* ed. Martin Buber, Judah L. Magnes, and Ernst Simon. Jerusalem: Ihud Association, pp. 33-36.

"The Philosophical Anthropology of Max Scheler." (Trans. from the German by Ronald Gregor Smith), *Philosophy and Phenomenological Research*, Vol. 6, No. 2 (December).

"To Chaim Weizmann," in *Chaim Weizmann; a Tribute on His Seventieth Birthday*, ed. Paul Goodman. London: V. Gollancz.

"The Beginning of the National Ideal," *Review of Religion*, X (1945-1946), pp. 254-265.

De Legende van den Baalsjém. Trans. R(eine) Colacço Osorio-Swaab.-Deventer, Kluwer.

"The Education of Character" (an address to the National Conference of Palestinian teachers at Tel Aviv in May 1939. Trans. from the German by Ronald Gregor Smith), in *The Mint; a miscellany*, (ed. Geoffrey Grigson), London: Routledge.

"God's Word and Man's Interpretation," *The Palestine Post* (April 8).

Introduction in *Chinese Ghost and Love Stories* (a selection from the Liao Chai stories by P'u Sung-Ling, trans. Rose Quong). New York: Pantheon.

Mamre. Essays in Religion. (Trans. Greta Hort), Melbourne and London: Melbourne University Press & Oxford University Press. All but one of these essays have later been republished in new, authorized translations.)

Moses. Oxford: East West Library.

"Der Ort des Chassidismus in der Religionsgeschichte," *Theologische Zeitschrift* II, 6 (November/December).

Palestine, a bi-national state (M.B., Judah L. Magnes, Moses Smilansky). New York: Ihud. Public hearings before the Anglo-American Committee of Inquiry. Jerusalem (Palestine), March 14, 1946.

"Ragaz veisrael" (in Hebrew), *Baayot*, No. 3 (February).

1947

Arab-Jewish Unity. Testimony before the Anglo-American Inquiry Commission for the Ihud (Union) Association by Judah Magnes and Martin Buber. London: Victor Gollancz Ltd.

Between Man and Man. (Trans. Ronald Gregor Smith), London: Kegan Paul, 1947). (Includes "Dialogue," "The Question to the Single One," "Education," "The Education of Character," and "What Is Man?").

Dialogisches Leben. Gesammelte philosophische und pädagogische Schriften. Zürich: Gregor Müller Verlag. (Includes *Ich und Du*,

Zwiesprache, Die Frage an den Einzelnen, Über das Erzieherische, "Über Charaktererziehung," *Das Problem des Menschen.)*

"Emunah ba-ruach" (in Hebrew, *Haaretz,* (October 31).

Der Knecht Gottes; Schicksal, Aufgabe, Trost. The songs of the servant of the Lord from Jeremiah and Isaiah in the Buber-Rosenzweig translation with introduction and commentary by Henri Friedlaender. -'s Gravenhage: Pulvis Viarum.

Martin Buber, zijn leven en zijn werk; verzameld en bewerkt door Juliette Binger. Ingeleid door W. Banning. -'s Graveland: De Driehoek.

Netivot beutopia (in Hebrew), Tel Aviv: Am Oved. Also in Library of Knowledge.

"Ragaz und 'Israel' " (Address at a memorial for Ragaz in the synagoge Emet Ve-Emuna, Jerusalem), *Neue Wege* XLI, 11 (November).

Tales of the Hasidim, The Early Masters. (Trans. Olga Marx) , New York: Schocken Books.

Ten Rungs, Hasidic Sayings. (Trans. Olga Marx), New York: Schocken Books.

1948

Chinesische Geister- und Liebesgeschichten. Reissued as a volume in the Manesse Bibliothek der Weltliteratur. Zürich: Manesse Verlag.

Hasidism. New York: The Philosophical Library. (All these essays have been retranslated in the authorized translations by Maurice Friedman in *Hasidism and Modern Man* (1958) & *Origin & Meaning of Hasidism* (1960) .)

Israel and the World. Essays in a Time of Crisis. New York: Schocken Books. (Includes "The Faith of Judaism," "The Two Foci of the Jewish Soul," "The Prejudices of Youth," "The Love of God and the Idea of Deity," "Imitatio Dei," "In the Midst of History," "What Are We to Do about the Ten Commandments?," "The Man of Today and the Jewish Bible," "Plato and Isaiah," "False Prophets," "Biblical Leadership," "Teaching and Deed," "Why We Should Study Jewish Sources," "On National Education," "The Jew in the World," "The Power of the Spirit," "The Spirit of Israel and the World of Today," "The Gods of the Nations and God," "Nationalism," "The Land and its Possessors," " 'And If Not Now, When?'," "Hebrew Humanism.")

Moses. Zürich: Gregor Müller.

"November," *Mitteilungsblatt,* Vol. 12, No. 44 (November 5) .

Das Problem des Menschen. Heidelberg: Verlag Lambert Schneider.

Tales of the Hasidim, The Later Masters. (Trans. Olga Marx), New York: Schocken Books.

Der Weg des Menschen, Nach der chassidischen Lehre. Jerusalem: copyright by Martin Buber, printed in the Netherlands by 'Pulvis Viarum' Press.

"Zweierlei Zionismus," *Die Stunde; einmalige Ausgabe.* Jerusalem: (May 28).

1949

"Al hayessod hahinuchi" (in Hebrew), *Sefer Dinaburg,* collected essays (ed. Isaac Baar, Joshua Gutman, & Moshe Shova), Jerusalem: Kiryat Sefer. (translation of *Erziehung*).

"Ein Briefwechsel" (by Karl Thieme) with M. B. in *Rundbrief zur Förderung der Freundschaft zwischen dem alten und dem neuen Gottesvolk—im Geiste der beiden Testamente,* Vol. 2, No. 5/6 (December).

"Eine Erwiderung," *Neue Wege,* Vol. 43, No. 9 (November).

"Erwachsenenbildung" in *Festschrift der Nueva Communidad Israel-ita, 5700-5710.* Buenos-Aires.

Gog und Magog. Eine Chronik, Heidelberg: Verlag Lambert Schneider.

(Interview). (M. Benson: Jérusalem en trêve), *Cahiers sioniens,* Vol. 3, No. 5 (January 1).

"Let us make an end to falsities," *Freeland,* Vol. 5, No. 1 (January/February).

Paths in Utopia. Trans. R. F. C. Hull. London: Routledge & Kegan Paul.

The Prophetic Faith. Trans. (from the Hebrew) Carlyle Witton-Davies. New York: The Macmillan Co.

"Vorwort" in Jacob Burckhardt, *Tarbut Harenaissance beitaliah.*

"Zur Situation der Philosophie," *Library of the Xth International Congress of Philosophy* (Amsterdam, August 11-18, 1948), Vol. I: *Proceedings of the Congress,* p. 317f.

1950

"Bnei Amos" (in Hebrew), *Ner,* No. 1 (April 29).

"Hinuch Mevugarim" (in Hebrew), *Molad,* No. 4, 24/23, Shevat-Adar.

"Hinuch uvehinat Olam" (in Hebrew), *Orot,* ed. by Abraham Levinson. Tel-Aviv: Histadrut haklalit shel haovdim haivriim beeretz Israel.

Die Erzählungen der Chassidim. Manesse-Bibliothek der Weltliteratur. Zürich: Manesse-Verlag.

"Les Dieux des peuples et Dieu; de l'idée nationale chez Krochmal et Dostoïewsky," *Revue de la Pensée Juive 3* (April).

Der Glaube der Propheten. Zürich: Manesse Verlag.

"Gvurat Haruach" (in Hebrew), *Davar,* 25th Jubilee issue.

Hazedek vehaavel al pi Zror mismorei tehillim (in Hebrew). Jerusalem: Magnes Press.

Interview, in *Rundbrief zur Förderung der Freundschaft zwischen dem alten und dem neuen Gottesvolk—im Geiste der beiden Testamente* II, 7 (April).

Israel und Palästina. Zur Geschichte einer Idee. Erasmus Bibliothek, edited by Walter Rüegg. Zürich: Artemis-Verlag.

"Jesus und der Knecht," in *Pro regno, pro sanctuario; een bundel studies en bijdragen van vrienden en vereerders bij de zestigste verjaardag van Prof. Dr. G. van der Leeuw . . . onder redactie van W. J. Kooiman en J. M. van Veen.* Nijkerk, G. F. Callenbach.

"Maase hamlahat Shaul" (in Hebrew), *Tarbiz,* No. 22, Tishri-Tevet.

"Myth in Judaism." Trans. Ralph Manheim. *Commentary,* Vol. 9 (June 1950), pp. 562-566.

"A New Venture in Adult Education," *The Hebrew University of Jerusalem.* Semi-jubilee volume published by The Hebrew University, Jerusalem, April, 1950, pp. 116-120.

Pfade in Utopie. Heidelberg: Verlag Lambert Schneider.

"Remarks on Goethe's Concept of Humanity," *Goethe and the Modern Age* (ed. Arnold Bergstraesser). Chicago: Henry Regnery, pp. 227-233. (Later included in *Pointing the Way* (1957).)

"A Talk with Tagore" in *India and Israel,* Vol. 3, Nos 4/5 (October/ November).

Torat haneviim (in Hebrew), second edition. Jerusalem: Mosad Bialik.

"Über den Kontakt." Aus Jerusalemer pädagogischen Radio-Reden, in *Die Idee einer Schule im Spiegel der Zeit; Festschrift für Paul Geheeb zum 80. Geburtstag und zum 40 jährigen Bestehen der Odenwaldschule.* Heidelberg: L. Schneider.

The Way of Man, According to the Teachings of Hasidism. London: Routledge & Kegan Paul; Chicago: Wilcox & Follett, 1951. (Reprinted in *Hasidism and Modern Man* (1958, Boox IV).)

"Zikron Pegishah" (A Talk with Tagore) (in Hebrew), *Ner* (September 27).

1951

Bücher und Menschen. A four-page booklet privately printed and not sold to the public. St. Gallen: Tschudy-Verlag. Also in *Hinweise* (1953).

"Distance and Relation" (Trans. Ronald Gregor Smith). *The Hibbert Journal* (January), Vol. 49, pp. 105-113.

"Hadussiah bein haelohim vehaadam bamikra" (in Hebrew), *Megilot*, No. 6, Av. (lecture given in French in November 1950 in Paris for the convention for education of European, African, and Australian countries.)

"Heilung aus der Begegnung," *Neue Schweizer Rundschau,* Vol. **19,** No. 6 (October 1951).

"Individual and society," in Brav, Stanley R., *Marriage and the Jewish Tradition; toward a Modern Philosophy of Family Living.* New York, Philosophical Library.

"Judaism and civilization," in *The Present Contribution of Judaism to Civilization* (report of the seventh international and twenty-fifth anniversary Conference (July 12th to July 18th, 1951). London, The World Union for Progressive Judaism.

"Nachtrag zu einem Gespräch," *Die neue Zeitung* (February 21).

"Die Opferung Isaaks," *Frankfurter Hefte,* Vol. **6,** No. **9 (September).**

"Society and the State," *World Review* New Series 27 (May), pp. **5-12.** Also in *Pointing the Way* (1957).

Zwei Glaubensweisen, Zürich: Manesse Verlag, 1950.

Two Types of Faith (Trans. Norman P. Goldhawk). London: Routledge & Kegan Paul; New York: Macmillan Co., 1952; Harper Torchbooks, 1961.

Urdistanz und Beziehung. Heidelberg: Verlag Lambert Schneider. (also published in *Studia Philosophica,* Jahrbuch der Schweizerischen philosophischen Gesellschaft. Vol. 10 (1950) , pp. 7-19.)

"Zum Problem der "Gesinnungsgemeinschaft," in *Robert Weltsch zum 60. Geburtstag; ein Glückwunsch gewidmet von Freuden.* Tel-Aviv—Jerusalem, Privatdruck.

1952

"Abstrakt und Konkret" (additional note to "Hoffnung für diese Stunde" (1952),), *Neue Schweizer Rundschau,* Vol. 20, No. 8 (December), *Merkur,* Vol. 7, No. 1 (January). Also in *Hinweise* (1953).

"Adult Education," *Torah* (Magazine of Natl. Federation of Jewish Men's Clubs of United Synagogue of America), June.

An der Wende. Reden über das Judentum. Köln and Olten: Jakob Hegner Verlag.

At the Turning. Three Addresses on Judaism. New York: Farrar, Straus & Young.

"Bekenntnis des Schriftstellers," *Neue Schweizer Rundschau* N. F. XX, 3 (July) (Zum 75. Geburtstag von Hermann Hesse, 2. Juli 1952).

Bilder von Gut und Böse. Köln und Olten: Jakob Hegner Verlag.

Die chassidische Botschaft. Heidelberg: Verlag Lambert Schneider. (Includes "Spinoza, Sabbatai Zwi und der Baalschem" (1927), "Die Anfänge" (1943), "Der Grundstein" (1943), "Geist und Leib der Bewegung" (1921), "Sinnbildliche und Sakramentale Existenz" (1934), "Gott und die Seele" (1943), "Gottesliebe und Nächstenliebe" (1943), "Der Ort des Chassidismus in der Religionsgeschichte" (1943). The last essay centers on a comparison between Hasidism and Zen Buddhism.)

Eclipse of God. Studies in the Relation between Religion and Philosophy. Trans. Maurice S. Friedman, et al. New York: Harper & Brothers. London: Gollancz, 1953. (Includes "Report on Two Talks," "Religion and Reality," "Religion and Philosophy" (revised), "The Love of God and the Idea of Deity," "Religion and Modern Thinking," "Religion and Ethics," "On the Suspension of the Ethical," "God and the Spirit of Man," "Supplement: Reply to C. G. Jung.")

"Erwiderung an C. G. Jung," *Merkur, Deutsche Zeitschrift für europäisches Denken,* Vol. 6, No. 5 (May).

"Heilung aus der Begegnung," Preface to Hans Trüb, *Heilung aus der Begegnung. Eine Auseinandersetzung mit der Psychologie C. G. Jungs.* (Ed. Ernst Michel and Arie Sborowitz). Stuttgart: Ernst Klett Verlag.

"Hoffnung für diese Stunde," *Merkur,* Vol. 6, No. 8 (August); *Neue Schweizer Rundschau,* Vol. 20, No. 5 (September), pp. 270-278. Also in *Hinweise* (1953).

"Hope for This Hour." Trans. Maurice S. Friedman. Address given in English at Carnegie Hall, New York City, April 6, 1952. *World Review,* December. (Also in *Pointing the Way* (1957).)

Images of Good and Evil. Trans. Michael Bullock. London: Routledge & Kegan Paul.

Israel and Palestine. The History of an Idea. Trans. Stanley Godman. London: East and West Library; New York: Farrar, Straus & Young.

Moses. Heidelberg: Verlag Lambert Schneider.

"On the Suspension of the Ethical." Trans. Maurice S. Friedman. *Moral Principles of Action,* ed. Ruth Nanda Anshen, Vol. VI of Science of Culture Series. New York: Harper & Brothers. (Also in *Eclipse of God* (1952).)

Recht und Unrecht. Deutung einiger Psalmen. Basel: Sammlung Klosterberg, Verlag B. Schwabe.

"Religion und modernes Denken," *Merkur,* Vol. **6,** No. 2 (February), pp. 101-120. (Also in *Gottesfinsternis* (1953).)

Right and Wrong. An Interpretation of Some Psalms. Trans. Ronald Gregor Smith. London: S.C.M. Press Ltd. Also in *Good and Evil* (1953).

"Le Sacrifice d'Isaac." (Traduit de l'allemand par Claire Champollion), *Dieu vivant* **22.**

Zwischen Gesellschaft und Staat. Heidelberg: Verlag Lambert Schneider.

1953

(Auswahl deutscher Verse). in Gerster, Georg. *Trunken von Gedichten; eine Anthologie geliebter deutscher Verse, ausgewählt und kommentiert von* . . . M.B. *(u.a.)* . . . Zürich: Verlag der Arche. (Goethe, Hölderlin, Hoffmannsthal.)

Das echte Gespräch und die Möglichkeiten des Friedens. Speech made by Buber on occasion of receiving the Friedenspreis des Deutschen Buchhandels, Frankfurt am Main, Paulskirche, September 27, 1953. Heidelberg: Lambert Schneider Verlag. Also found as part of *Martin Buber, Friedenspreis des Deutschen Buchhandels,* pp. 33-41, and in *Hinweise* (1953).

"The Cultural role of the Hebrew University," trans. by David Sidorsky. *The Reconstructionist,* Vol. 19, No. 10 (June 26).

Einsichten. Aus den Schriften gesammelt. Wiesbaden: Insel Verlag.

For the Sake of Heaven. Trans. Ludwig Lewisohn. Second edition with new foreword. New York: Harper & Brothers.

"Foreword" to Eric Gutkind, *Community and Environment.* London: Watts.

"Geleitwort," in Strauss, Ludwig. *Wintersaat; ein Buch aus Sätzen.* Zürich: Manesse.

"Geltung und Grenze des politischen Prinzips" in *Gedenkschrift zur Verleihung des Hansischen Goethe-Preises 1951 der gemeinnützigen Stiftung F.V.S. zu Hamburg an M. B., überreicht am 24. Juni 1953.* (Hamburg), pp. 9-20. Also in *Frankfurter Hefte* Vol. 8, No. 9 (September) and *Neue Schweizer Rundschau* N.F. XXI, 5 (September).

Good and Evil. Two Interpretations. New York: Charles Scribner's Sons. (Includes *Right and Wrong* and *Images of Good and Evil.*)

Gottesfinsternis. Zürich: Manesse Verlag. (For contents see *Eclipse of God* (1952).)

"Hasheilah hanisteret" (in Hebrew), *Orot,* No. 2, Elul (from "Bemashber haruach").

"Hassischah haamitit veefscharut leschalom" (in Hebrew), *Davar* (Friedenspreis.)

Hinweise, Gesammelte Essays (1909-1953). Zürich: Manesse Verlag. (Includes "Vorwort," "Bücher un Menschen" (1947), "Leistung und Dasein" (1914), "Der Dämon im Traum" (1914), "Der Altar" (1914), "Bruder Leib" (1914), "Mit einem Monisten" (1914), "Die Lehre vom Tao" (1909), "Das Epos des Zauberers" (1913), "Die Vorurteile der Jugend" (1937), "An das Gleichzeitige" (1914), "Die Forderung des Geistes und die geschichtliche Wirklichkeit" (1938), "Geschehende Geschichte" (1933), "Biblisches Führertum" (1928), "Falsche Propheten" (1941), "Was soll mit den Zehn Geboten geschehen?" (1929), "Mein Weg zum Chassidismus" (1918), "Drama und Theater" (1925), "Das Raumproblem der Bühne" (1913), "Das Reinmenschliche" (1949), "Zu Bergsons Begriff der Intuition" (1943), "Alfred Mombert" (1922), "Moritz Heimann" (1912), "Franz Rosenzweig" (1930), "Erinnerung an einen Tod" (1929), "Drei Sätze eines religiösen Sozialismus" (1928), "Nationalismus" (1921), "Gandhi, die Politik und wir" (1930), "Was ist zu tun?" (1919), "Volk und Führer" (1942), "Hoffnung für diese Stunde" (1952), "Abstrakt und Kongret" (1952), "Geltung und Grenze des politischen Prinzips" (1947).)

"Rede über das Erzieherische," in Flitner, Wilhelm. *Die Erziehung; Pädagogen und Philosophen über die Erziehung und ihre Probleme.* Wiesbaden: Dieterich.

Reden über Erziehung. Heidelberg: Verlag Lambert Schneider. (Includes "Vorwort," "Über das Erzieherische," "Bildung und Weltanschauung," and "Über Charaktererziehung.")

"Sur la mer est ton Chemin" in *Evidences,* Vol. 5, No. 36 (December) (from *Bein Am learzo).*

"Über ein Zusammentreffen und was darauf folgte," *Mitteilungsblatt,* Vol. 21, No. 13/14 (March 30).

"Zwischen Religion und Philosophie" (answer to Hugo Bergmann's criticism of *Eclipse of God), Neue Wege,* Vol. 47, No. 11/12 (November/December), pp. 436-439.

1954

"Aus dem Werk: Über den Zionismus. Wiedergeburt des Dialogs. Eine Bekehrung. Versöhnung. Gott," in Schwerte, Hans; Spengler, Wilhelm. *Denker und Deuter im heutigen Europa: England, Frankreich, Spanien und Portugal, Italien, Osteuropa.* (Martin Buber by Hans Joachim Schoeps). Oldenburg: G. Stalling. Gestalten unserer Zeit, 2.

"Christus, Chassidismus, Gnosis. Einige Bemerkungen" (Reply to an article by Rudolph Pannwitz in *Merkur,* September 1954, *Merkur* (Munich), Vol. 8, No. 80 (October). (Included in translation in *The Origin and Meaning of Hasidism* (1960).)

"Dat umussar" (in Hebrew), *Iyyun,* No. 5.

"Elemente des Zwischenmenschlichen," *Merkur,* February, *Neue Schweizer Rundschau* (Zurich), Neue Folge, Vol. 21, No. 10 (February), pp. 593-608. Also included in *Die Schriften über das dialogische Prinzip* (1954).

"Ewige Feindschaft? Hans Klee and M. B. über das Verhältnis zwischen Juden und Deutschen," *Freiburger Rundbrief,* Vol. 7, No. 25/28 (September).

(in cooperation with Franz Rosenzweig.) *Die fünf Bücher der Weisung. (Die Schrift)* Revised edition. Köln und Olten: Jakob Hegner Verlag.

Godsverduistering; beschouwingen over de betrekking tussen religie en filosofie. Trans. K. H. Kroon Utrecht: E. J. Bijleveld. *(Eclipse of God).*

"Humaniut ivrit—al mahutah shel hatarbut" (in Hebrew), *Machshavot vedeiot,* collected and edited by I. Becker and Sh. Shpan. Tel-Aviv: Yavneh.

"Letters to Franz Rosenzweig on the Law," in Franz Rosenzweig, *On Jewish Education.* Edited by Nahum N. Glatzer. New York: The Noonday Press.

"Mellan Religion Och Filosofi," *Judisk tidskrift,* Vol. 27, No. 1 (January).

(Message), *Pulpit digest,* Vol. 34, No. 194 (June) (Special issue on the hydrogen cobalt bomb). Trans. Maurice Friedman.

"Prophetie, Apokalyptik und die geschichtliche Stunde," *Merkur,* Vol. 8, No. 12 (December). *Neue Schweizer Rundschau* N.F. XXII, 8.

"Samuel und die Lade," in *Essays Presented to Leo Baeck on His Eightieth Birthday.* London: East and West Library. (a chapter from *Der Gesalbte,* the unfinished sequel to *Königtum Gottes,* 1936.)

Die Schriften über das dialogische Prinzip. Heidelberg: Verlag Lambert Schneider. (Includes *Ich und Du, Zwiesprache, Die Frage an den Einzelnen,* "Elemente des Zwischenmenschlichen," and "Nachwort," the last two not previously published in book form, the last an important historical survey published here for the first time.

"Die Wahre Geschichte, zu Kurt Blumenfelds 70. Geburtstag," *Mitteilungsblatt,* Vol. 22, No. 22 (May 28).

Zu einer neuen Verdeutschung der Schrift. Beilage zu dem Werk "Die Fünf Bücher der Weisung" verdeutscht von Martin Buber in Gemeinschaft mit Franz Rosenzweig. Köln and Olten: Jakob Hegner Verlag.

"Zur Klärung," *Mitteilungsblatt,* Vol. 22, No. 23 (June 4).

1955

"Bein adam lehavero" (in Hebrew), *Achsania,* No. 1, Sivan.

Between Man and Man. Trans. Ronald Gregor Smith. Boston: Beacon Paperback.

(in cooperation with Franz Rosenzweig) *Bücher der Geschichte.* Köln and Olten: Jakob Hegner Verlag.

Caminos de Utopía, Tran. J. Rovira Armengol. México: Fondo de Cultura económica. Breviarios del Fondo de Cultura económica, 104.

Eclipse de Dios; estudios sobre las relaciones entre religión y filosofía, Trans. Luis Fabricant. Buenos Aires: Galatea-Nueva Visión, = Ideas de nuestro tempo.

En la encrucijada; tres conferencias sobre el judaismo. (Versión castellana de Luis Fabricant.) Buenos Aires: Sociedad hebraica argentina (*At the Turning.*)

"Epos hakosem" (in Hebrew), "Bechinot," No. 8, Nisan. (Introduction to *Kalevala*), trans. by Shaul Tchernikowsky.

Die Geschicten des Rabbi Nachman. Revised edition. Frankfurt am Main and Hamburg: Fischer Bücherei.

"God and the soul," in Runes, Dagobert D. *Treasury of Philosophy*. New York: Philosophical Library.

"Hoffnung für diese Stunde," *Universitas*, Vol. 10, No. 1 (January).

The Legend of the Baal-Shem. Trans. Maurice S. Friedman. New York: Harper & Brothers. London: East and West Library, 1956.

Die Legende des Baalschem. Revised new edition. Manesse Bibliothek der Weltliteratur. Zürich: Manesse Verlag.

Der Mensch und sein Gebild. Heidelberg: Verlag Lambert Schneider.

"Ein Realist des Geistes," *Ehrfurcht vor dem Leben: Albert Schweitzer. Eine Freundesgabe zu seinem 80. Geburtstag*. Bern: P. Haupt.

"A Realist of the Spirit," trans. Maurice Friedman, in *To Dr. Albert Schweitzer; a Festschrift commemorating his 80th birthday from a few of his friends*. January 14, 1955. Evanston (Ill.), Friends of Albert Schweitzer. (ed. Homer Jack).

Sehertum. Anfang und Ausgang ("Abraham der Seher" and "Prophetie, Apokalyptik und die Geschichtliche Stunde"). Köln: Jakob Hegner.

"Über das Erzieherische," *Pädagogische Blätter*, Vol. 6, No. 13/14 (July).

"Versuch einer Auskunft" in *Wegweiser in der Zeitwende*. Edited by Elga Kern. Munich, Basle: Ernst Reinhardt Verlag. Pp. 264ff.

"We need the Arabs, they need us! Interview with M. B.," *Frontpage*, Vol. 2, No. 3 (January 20).

1956

"Abraham the Seer." Trans. Sophie Meyer. *Judaism*, Vol. 5, No. 4 (Fall).

"Eine Auswahl," *Wort in der Zeit*, Vol. 2, No. 11 (November).

"Character change and social experiment, in Israel," edited by Maurice Friedman, in Davis, Moshe. *Israel, its Role in Civilization*. New York: Seminary Israel Institute.

"Der Chassidismus und der abendländische Mensch," *Merkur*, Vol. 10, No. 10 (October).

"Die Erzählung von Sauls Königswahl," *Vetus Testamentum*, Vol. 6, No. 2 (April).

"Für das Ganze Zeugend," *AJR Information,* Vol. 11, No. 12 (December) (supplement in memory of Leo Baeck . . .).

"Dem Gemeinschaftlichen folgen." *Die Neue Rundschau,* Vol. 67, No. 4 (December).

"Greetings to Dr. Mordecai M. Kaplan," *The Reconstructionist,* Vol. 22, No. 6 (May 4).

"Haadam haboreach" (in Hebrew), *Molad,* No. 14, December. ("Dem Gemeinschaftlichen folgen.")

"Jugend und Religion.—Harmonie mit dem Nächsten. Ein kleiner Auszug," *Einklang* 3 (July).

"Réalité légendaire; le Tsaddik dans sa communauté." (Traduction Yohanan Lavi), in *Renaissance,* Vol. 2, No. 7 (November).

Königtum Gottes. Third revised edition. Heidelberg: Verlag Lambert Schneider.

"Rosenzweig und die Existenz," *Mitteilungsblatt,* Vol. 24, No. 52 (December 28).

The Tales of Rabbi Nachman. Trans. Maurice Friedman. New York: The Horizon Press.

The Writings of Martin Buber. Selected, edited, and introduced by Will Herberg. New York: Meridian Books.

1957

"Distance and Relation." Trans. Ronald Gregor Smith. *Psychiatry,* Vol. 20, No. 2 (May), pp. 97-104. (Later included in *The Knowledge of Man* (1966).)

Eclipse of God. Studies in the Relation between Religion and Philosophy. Trans. Maurice S. Friedman, et al. New York: Harper Torchbooks (paperback).

"Elements of the Interhuman," trans. Ronald Gregor Smith, *Psychiatry,* Vol. 20, No. 2 (May), pp. 105-129. (Later included in *The Knowledge of Man* (1966).)

"Erinnerung," *Die Neue Rundschau,* Vol. 68, No. 4, pp. 575ff.

"Die Erwählung Israels," *Quatember,* Evangelische Jahresbriefe 6, XXI, No. 3, 1956-1957 (June), pp. 136-145.

Fourth William Allen White Memorial Lectures (Introduction by Leslie H. Farber, "Distance and Relation," "Elements of the Interhuman," "Guilt and Guilt-Feelings"). Reprints from *Psychiatry,* 1610 New Hampshire Avenue, N.W., Washington 9, D.C.

Gog und Magog; eine Chronik. Frankfurt a. M.: Fischer, Fischer Bücherei, 174.

"Guilt and Guilt-Feelings," Trans. Maurice Friedman. *Psychiatry,*
Vol. 20, No. 2 (May), pp. 114-129. Also in *Cross Currents,* 1958.
(Later included in *The Knowledge of Man* (1966).)

"Haltet ein!", *Neue Wege,* Vol. 51, No. 6 (August).

"Le Hassidisme et l'homme d'Occident." in *Mélanges de philosophie
et de littérature juives* 1/2; 1956-1957 (Institut international d'-
études hébraïques). Paris: Presses Universitaires de France.

"Hermann Hesses Dienst am Geist," *Neue Deutsche Hefte* No. 37
(August), pp. 387-393.

Moïse. Traduit de l'allemand par Albert Kohn. Paris: Presses Universitaires de France, Sinaï, collection des sources d'Israël.

Pointing the Way: Collected Essays. Trans. and Ed. Maurice S. Friedman. New York: Harper & Brothers; London: Routledge & Kegan
Paul. (Includes most of the essays in *Hinweise* (1953) plus "Heal-
ing through Meeting," "China and Us," "Education and World-
View," "A Letter to Gandhi," "Society and the State," "Prophecy,
Apocalyptic, and the Historical Hour," and "Genuine Dialogue
and the Possibilities of Peace.") Does not include from *Hinweise*
"Das Epos des Zauberers," "Mein Weg zum Chassidismus," "Al-
fred Mombert," "Moritz Heinmann," or the essays published in
Israel and the World.)

"Prophetie et Apocalypse," Traduit par Marthe Robert. *Evidences,*
Vol. 9, No. 68 (December)

"Schuld und Schuldgefühle. (Vorlesung, gehalten an der School for
Psychiatry in Washington im April 1957) ," *Merkur,* Vol. 11, No.
8 (August).

*De Vraag naar de mens; het anthropologisch probleem historisch en
dialogisch ontvouwd.* Trans. I. J. Van Houte - Utrecht: E. J. Bijleveld.

1958

"Aus der Übersetzung der Bibel" (Neviim, Tehillim) in Rudolf
Jockel, *Die Lebenden Religionen.* Berlin and Darmstadt:
Deutsche Buch-Gemeinschaft, C. A. Koch's Verlag Nachf.

"Born of Envy," *Chelsea Review,* Summer.

Das Buch der Preisungen. Köln and Olten: Jakob Hegner.

Bücher der Kündung. Köln and Olten: Jakob Hegner.

"Bücher und Menschen," Neue Wege, February.

"Es Menester Seguir lo Comun al Hombre," in *Entregas de La Licorne.*
Ed. Susanna Soca, printed in Uraguay, 2a Epoca—Vol. 5, No. 11.

For the Sake of Heaven. 2nd Ed. with New Foreword. Trans. Ludwig Lewisohn. New York: Meridian-Books-Jewish Publication Society (paperback).

Gog et Magog. Trans. Hans Loewenson-Lavi. Paris: Gallimard.

Hasidism and Modern Man. Ed. and trans. Maurice Friedman. With an Editor's Introduction. New York: Horizon Press. (Includes "Hasidism and Modern Man," (1957), "My Way to Hasidism," (1918), "The Life of the Hasidim" (from *The Legend of the Baal-Shem,* (1955), *The Way of Man, According to the Teachings of Hasidism* (1950), *The Baal-Shem-Tov's Instruction in Intercourse with God* (1928), and "Love of God and Love of Neighbor" (1943).)

"Hasidism and Modern Man" in *Between East and West.* London: East and West Library.

"Hataamula vehacinuch" (in Hebrew), *Hed hachinuch* (December 31).

I and Thou. Second Edition with important Postscript by the Author. Trans Ronald Gregor Smith. New York: Charles Scribner's Sons.

Ich und Du. Nachworterweiterte. Heidelberg: Verlag Lambert Schneider.

"Il Comando dello spirito e la via attuale d'Israele" in *Israel.* Il Ponte, December.

"Israel and the Command of the Spirit." Trans. Maurice Friedman, *Congress Weekly,* Vol. 25, No. 14 (September 8), p. 10ff.

"It is now High Time" in *London Letter.*

"Kleiner Beitrag" in *Agora. Eine Schriftenreihe,* ed. Manfred Schlösser and Hans-Rolf Ropertz. In association with the Ludwig-Georgs-Gymnasium, Darmstadt and the Verein der Freunde des Ludwig-Georgs Gymnasiums, Vol. 4, No. 11 (November) Darmstadt: Wissenschaftliche Buch Gesellschaft.

Moses. New York: Harper's Torchbook.

Paths in Utopia. Trans. R. F. C. Hull with Introduction by Ephraim Fischoff. Boston: Beacon Paperbacks.

Schuld und Schuldgefühle. Heidelberg: Verlag Lambert Schneider.

"Sur les Récits Hassidiques" in *La Table Ronde,* March.

Tales of Angels, Spirits & Demons. Trans. David Antin and Jerome Rothenberg. New York: Hawk's Well Press.

To Hallow This Life, An Anthology. Ed. with Introduction by Jacob Trapp. New York: Harper & Brothers.

"Der Weg Israels (zur Klärung)" in *Mitteilungsblatt* (October 3).

"What Is Common to All." Trans. Maurice Friedman. *Review of Metaphysics,* Vol. 11, No. 3 (March), pp. 359-379. (Later included in *The Knowledge of Man* (1966).

1959

"Aus erster Hand, ein Gespräch mit Thilo Koch," Nord und West-deutscher Rundfunkverband-Fernsehen-Hamburg-Lokstedt, May 25.

"Ein Beispiel. Zu den Landschaften Leopold Krakauers," *Merkur,* 139, Vol. 13, No. 9 (September), pp. 840ff.

Besod Ssiach (in Hebrew), Jerusalem: Mosad Bialik. (Dialogical writings.)

(editor) Entsiklopedyah Hainochit (in Hebrew) (educational encyclopedia of Jewish and general education. Martin Buber, editor-in-chief.) Jerusalem: Misrad Hahinuk vHatarbut).

"Hebrew Humanism" in Adrienne Koch, *Philosophy for a Time of Crisis.* New York: E. P. Dutton & Co.

"Hoffnung für diese Stunde" in *Reden, die die Welt bewegten.* Ed. Karl Heinrich Peter. Stuttgart: Cotta-Verlag.

I and Thou. 2nd ed. with Postscript by Author added. Trans. Ronald Gregor Smith. Edinburgh: T. & T. Clark.

"I and Thou" in Yervant H. Krikorian and Abraham Edel, Editors, *Contemporary Philosophic Problems. Selected Readings.* New York: The Macmillan Co.

Ik en Gij. Trans. I. J. Van Houte. Utrecht: Erven J. Bijleveld.

Il Principio Dialogico. Trans. Paoli Facchi and Ursula Schnabel. Roma: Edizioni di Communita. *(Die Schriften über das dialogische Prinzip* without the "Nachwort".)

"Israel's Mission and Zion," *Forum, for the Problems of Zionism, Jewry, and the State of Israel,* Vol. 4 (Spring 1959), "Proceedings of the Jerusalem Ideological Conference." Ed. Nathan Rotenstreich, Sulamith Schwartz Nardi, Zalman Shazar. Jerusalem: Publishing Department of the Jewish Agency. Pp. 145ff.

Pfade in Utopia (Japanese translation). Trans. Susuma Hasegawa. Tokyo: Riso-sha Co.

Steeg'n in Utopia (Yiddish Edition) Buenos Aires: Buchgemeinschaft bei de "jiddischer razionalistascher Gesellschaft".

Teudah v-jeud (in Hebrew), Jerusalem: Sifriah Zionit. (first volume of essays on Judaism).

La Vie en Dialogue. Trans. Hans Loewenson-Lavi. Paris: Aubier, Éditions Montaigne.

The Way of Man, According to the Teachings of Hasidism. Foreword by Maurice Friedman. Wallingford, Pennsylvania: Pendle Hill Pamphlet No. 106.

1960

Begegnung. Autobiographische Fragmente. Ed. Paul Arthur Schilpp and Maurice Friedman. Stuttgart: W. Kohlhammer Verlag. (The Autobiographical Fragments from *The Philosophy of Martin Buber* volume of *The Library of Living Philosophers.*)

Brief (Letter) in *Erziehung zur Humanität. Paul Geheeb zum 90. Geburstag.*

"Discours sur la situation des Juifs en Union Soviétique," *La Terre Retrouvée,* September, et *l'Arche,* October.

"Geheimnis einer Einheit, Herman Stehr," *Jahresgabe,* Stuttgart: Brentanoverlag. (Reprint from "Hermann Stehr, sein Werk und seine Welt," 1924).

"Gruss und Willkommen (Begrüssung Theodor Heuss von der hebraischen Universität)" in *Staat und Volk im Werden,* ed. by Theodor Heuss. Munich: Ner-Tamid Verlag.

"Hoffnung für diese Stunde" in *Wo stehen wir heute?* ed. by H. Walter Bähr. Gütersloh: Bertelsmann Verlag.

I and Thou. 2nd Edition with Postscript Added. Trans. Ronald Gregor Smith. New York: Scribner's Paperback.

"Ich und Du" in *Sinn und Sein,* ed. Richard Wisser. Tübingen: Max Niemeyer Verlag. (The Postscript of the 1958 edition).

"Neum al Yehudei Brit-Hamoezot" (in Hebrew), *Chasut,* Hoveret h' (5), Kislev 5721, Sifria Zionite, Bearichat Prof. Rotenstreich and Z. Shazar.

"Neum al Yehudei Brit-Hamoezot" (in Hebrew), *Gesher,* Revuon Lesheilot Hajehaumah (Quarterly Review of the Nation's Problems). Published by the Israel Executive of the World Jewish Congress Editorial Board. 1 Ben Yehuda, Jerusalem Sixth Year (25) 4.

The Origin and Meaning of Hasidism. Ed. and trans. with an Editor's Introduction by Maurice Friedman. New York: Horizon Press. (Includes "The Beginnings" (1943), "The Foundation Stone" (1943), "Spinoza, Sabbatai Zvi and the Baal-Shem" (1927), "Spirit and Body of the Hasidic Movement" (1921), "Symbolic and

Sacramental Existence" (1934), "God and the Soul" (1943), "Redemption" (1947), "The Place of Hasidism in the History of Religion" (1943), "Christ, Hasidism, Gnosis" (1954).)

"Productivity and Existence" (From *Pointing the Way,* trans. Maurice Friedman), in Maurice A. Stein, Arthur J. Vidick, David M. White, editors, *Identity and Anxiety; Survival of the Person in a Mass Society.* Glencoe, Illinois: The Free Press. Pp. 628-632.

The Prophetic Faith. Trans. Carlyle Witton-Davies. New York: Harper's Torchbooks.

Que es el Hombre, 4th ed. Mexico and Buenos Aires: Fondo de Cultura Economica.

"Shtei Pegishot" (in Hebrew), *Molad,* No. 163 (June-July.) ("Zwei Begegnungen")

"Schuld und Schuldgefühle" in *Der leidende Mensch,* Vol. I—*Wege der Forschung.* Darmstadt: Wissenschaftliche Buchgesellschaft.

"Seit ein Gespräch wir sind, Ludwig Strauss zum Gedächtnis" in *Hölderlin-Jahrbuch,* 1958-1960. Vol. 11; Tübingen: J. C. B. Mohr (Paul Siebeck).

"Symbolic and Sacramental Existence in Judaism." Trans. Ralph Manheim. In *Spiritual Disciplines,* Volume IV of *Papers from the Eranos Yearbooks.* Bollingen Series XXX. New York: Pantheon Books, pp. 168-185.

Urdistanz und Beziehung. Second edition. Heidelberg: Lambert Schneider.

"La Via della Communita" in *Tempo Presente* (Gennaio). ("Dem Gemeinschaftliche folgen")

Der Weg des Menschen nach der chassidischen Lehre. Third edition. Heidelberg: Lambert Schneider.

"Das Wort, das gesprochen wird," in *Wort und Wirklichkeit,* Vol. VI of *Gestalt und Gedanke,* Jahrbuch der Bayerischen Akademie der schönen Künste. Munich: R. Oldenburg Verlag.

"Zwei Begegnungen," *Merkur,* No. 148 (June). (Two chapters from the Autobiographical Fragments of this volume.)

1961

Am ve'olam (in Hebrew) ("A People and the World"). Jerusalem: Sifriah Zionit (second volume of essays on Judaism).

Between Man and Man, trans. R. G. Smith. London: Collins, The Fontana Library, paperback edition.

"Books and People" trans. Harry Zohn, *The Jewish Advocate* (Boston).

"Brief an Gandhi" in *Juden, Palästina, Araber*. Munich: Ner-Tamid-Verlag.

"Der Chassidismus und die Krise des abendländischen Menschen," in *Juden, Christen, Deutsche*. Edited by Hans-Jürgen Schultz. Stuttgart: Kreuz-Verlag.

"Dankesrede zum Münchener Kulturpreis" in *München ehrt Martin Buber*. Munich: Ner-Tamid-Verlag.

Eclissi di Dio. Edizioni Communita, Milan. *(Gottesfinsternis)*

"Erinnerung" in *Im Zeichen der Hoffnung*, ed. Erwin de Haar. Munich: Max Huber Verlag.

Good and Evil. Two Interpretations. New York: Scribner's Paperbacks.

"Die Juden in der USSR," in *Die Sowjets und das Judentum*, (Vom Gestern zum Morgen, Zeitgeschichtliche Schriftenreihe), ed. Hans Lamm. Munich and Frankfurt: Ner-Tamid-Verlag.

"Robert Weltsch zum 70. Geburtstag," *Mitteilungsblatt*, June 16.

"Schlussbemerkungen," in *'Die Schrift'—Zum Abschluss ihrer Verdeutschung*. Sonderdruck überreicht vom "Mitteilungsblatt" (MB) des Irgun Olej Merkas Europa. Tel-Aviv: Biaton Publishing Co., pp. 8f.

Tales of the Hasidim, The Early Masters. Trans. Olga Marx. New York: Schocken Books (paperback edition).

Tales of the Hasidim, The Later Masters. Trans. Olga Marx. New York: Schocken Books (paperback edition).

Two Types of Faith. Trans. Norman P. Goldhawk. New York: Harper Torchbooks.

"Wie kann Gemeinschaft werden?" (1930), reprinted in *München ehrt Martin Buber*. Munich: Ner-Tamid-Verlag.

"The Word That Is Spoken." Trans. Maurice Friedman. *Modern Age* (Chicago), Fall, Vol. 5, No. 4. (Later included in *The Knowledge of Man* (1966).)

1962

Logos. Zwei Reden. Heidelberg: Verlag Lambert Schneider. (Includes "Das Wort, das gesprochen wird" and "Dem Gemeinschaftlichen folgen.")

Die Schrift. Translation of the Bible from Hebrew into German by Martin Buber in co-operation with Franz Rosenzweig. Revised edition. 4 vols.: *Die fünf Bücher der Weisung* (1954), *Bücher der*

Kundung (1958), *Die Schriftwerke* (1961). Köln and Olten: Jakob Hegner Verlag.

Die Schriftwerke. Revised edition. Köln and Olten: Jakob Hegner.

The Tales of Rabbi Nachman. Trans. Maurice Friedman. Bloomington, Indiana: Indiana University Press, Midland Books (paperback).

Werke. Erster Band—*Schriften zur Philosophie.* Munich and Heidelberg: Kösel Verlag and Verlag Lambert Schneider. (Includes *Daniel, Ich und Du, Zwiesprache, Die Frage an den Einzelnen, Elemente des Zwischenmenschlichen, Zur Geschichte des dialogischen Prinzips, Urdistanz und Beziehung, Der Mensch und sein Gebild, Das Wort, das gesprochen wird, Dem Gemeinschaftlichen folgen, Schuld und Schuldgefühle, Gottesfinsternis, Betrachtungen zur Beziehung zwischen Religion und Philosophie, Bilder von Gut und Böse, Zwei Glaubensweisen, Reden über Erziehung, Pfade in Utopia, Zwischen Gesellschaft und Staat,* "Die Lehre von Tao," "Die Forderung des Geistes und die geschichtliche Wirklichkeit," "Zu Bergsons Begriff der Intuition," "Gandhi, die Politik und wir," "Geltung und Grenze des politischen Prinzips," "Aus einer philophischen Rechenschaft" (the first section of Buber's responses to critics in the Buber volume of *The Library of Living Philosophers*).

Zur Verdeutschung des letzten Bandes der Schrift. Beilage zu "Die Schriftwerke." Köln & Olten: Jakob Hegner.

1963

"Autobiographische Fragmente" and "Responsa" in *Die Philosophie Martin Bubers (Philosophen des XX. Jahrhunderts).* Eds. Paul Arthur Schilpp and Maurice Friedman. Stuttgart: W. Kohlhammer Verlag.

Elija. Ein Mysterienspiel. Heidelberg: Verlag Lambert Schneider.

Israel and the World. Essays in a Time of Crisis. New York: Schocken Paperbacks (The 1948 original plus "Israel and the Command of the Spirit" (1958), trans. by Maurice Friedman, and "Israel's Mission and Zion" (1957).)

Der Jude und sein Judentum. Gesammelte Aufsätze und Reden. Mit einer Einleitung von Robert Weltsch. Köln: Joseph Melzer Verlag. (Includes I. Reden über das Judentum: Die frühen Reden and An der Wende; II. Die Grundlagen: Der Glaube des Judentums, Die Brennpunkte der jüdischen Seele, Freiheit und Aufgabe,

Der Jude in der Welt, Pharisäertum, Bericht und Berichtigung, Das Judentum und die neue Weltfrage, Das Gestaltende, Im Anfang; III. Wiedergeburt: Regeneration eines Volkstums, Renaissance und Bewegung, Völker, Staaten und Zion, Nationalismus, Zur Geschichte der nationalen Ideen, Jüdisches Nationalheim und nationale Politik in Palästina, Wann denn?, Frage und Antwort, Zweierlei Zionismus, Der Chaluz und seine Welt, Arbeitsglaube, Wie kann Gemeinschaft werden?, Warum muss der Aufbau Palästinas ein sozialistischer sein?, Zion und die Gola; IV. Zur Geschichte des Zionismus: Der Anfang der nationalen Idee, Der Erste der Letzten, Die drängende Stunde, Die Lehre vom Zentrum, Die Erneuerung der Heiligkeit, Ein Träger der Verwirklichung; V. Situationen: Rede auf dem 12. Zionistenkongress, Kongressnotizen zur zionistischen Politik, Selbstbesinnung, Ein politischer Faktor, Die Eroberung Palästinas, Vor der Entscheidung, In später Stunde, Rede auf dem 16. Zionistenkongress, Gegen die Untreue, Pseudo-Simsonismus, Über ein Zusammentreffen und was darauf folgte, Der Weg Israels, Die Sowjets und das Judentum; VI. In der Krisis: Der jüdische Mensch von heute, Kirche, Staat, Volk, Judentum, Die Mächtigkeit des Geistes, Das Erste, Die Kinder, Gericht und Erneuerung, Das Haltende, Worauf es ankommt, Ein Spruch des Maimuni, Erkenntnis tut not, Unser Bildungsziel, Aufgaben jüdischer Volkserziehung, Jüdische Erwachsenenbildung, Entwürfe und Programme, Brief an Ernst Michel, Offener Brief an Gerhard Kittel, Zu Gerhard Kittels Antwort, Brief an Gandhi, Das Ende der deutsch-jüdischen Symbiose, Sie und wir, Schweigen und Schreien; VII. Erziehung und Kulturarbeit: An die Prager Freunde, Die Lehre und die Tat, Kulturarbeit, Volkserziehung als unsere Aufgabe, Universität und Volkshochschule, Jüdisch Leben, Zion und die Jugend, Die Vorurteile der Jugend, Die hebräische Sprache, Hebräischer Humanismus, Warum gelernt werden soll, Grau nach der Welt, Ha-bima!, Drei Stationen; VIII. Gestalten: Vertrauen, Der Wägende, Achad-Haam-Gedenkrede in Berlin, Achad-Haam-Gedenkrede in Basel, Zwei hebräische Bücher, Der wahre Lehrer, Der Acker und die Sterne, Theodor Herzl, Herzl und die Historie, Er und wir, Sache und Person, Herzl vor der Palästina-Karte, Der Dichter und die Nation, Die Tränen, Philon und Cohen, Für die Sache der Treue, Franz Rosenzweig, Rosenzweig und die Existenz.)

Martin Buber. Herausgegeben von Paul Arthur Schilpp und Maurice Friedman. Stuttgart: W. Kohlhammer Verlag. xiv + 660 pp. (The German edition of *The Philosophy of Martin Buber,* Vol. 12 in THE LIBRARY OF LIVING PHILOSOPHERS.) English edition in 1966.

Pointing the Way. Collected Essays. Edited and translated with an Editor's Introduction by Maurice Friedman. New York: Harper Torchbooks (paperback).

Werke. Dritter Band—*Schriften zum Chassidismus.* Munich and Heidelberg: Kösel Verlag and Verlag Lambert Schneider. (Includes *Die Erzählungen der Chassidim, Die chassidische Botschaft, Der Weg des Menschen nach der chassidischen Lehre, Mein Weg zum Chassidismus,* "Der Chassidismus und der abendländische Mensch," "Christus, Chassidismus, Gnosis," *Des Baal-Schem-Tow Unterweisung im Umgang mit Gott,* "Einleitung zu Nachman," "Ein Zaddik kommt ins Land," "Einleitung zu Baal-Schem," *Gog und Magog.*)

1964

"Church, State, Nation, Jewry," trans. by William Hallo with an Introductory Note by Maurice Friedman in *Christianity: Some Non-Christian Appraisals,* edited by David W. McKain with an Introduction by Robert Lawson Slater. New York: McGraw-Hill Paperbacks, pp. 174-188.

Daniel. Dialogues on Realization. Edited and Translated with an Introductory Essay by Maurice Friedman. New York: Holt, Rinehart & Winston, Inc.

"Responsa" in "Martin Buber" Section, conducted, edited, and translated by Maurice Friedman, of *Philosophical Interrogations.* Ed. Sidney and Beatrice Rome. New York: Holt, Rinehart & Winston Inc.

Selections from eighteen of Buber's works in *The Worlds of Existentialism: A Critical Reader.* Edited with Introductions and A Conclusion by Maurice Friedman. New York: Random House. Part I—Forerunners, pp. 42-48; Part II—Phenomenology and Ontology, pp. 105-107; Part III—The Existential Subject, p. 160-167; Part IV—Intersubjectivity, pp. 216-235; Part V—Atheist, Humanist, and Religious Existentialism, pp. 306-318; Part VI—Existentialism and Psychotherapy, pp. 385-396, 485-497; Part VII—Issues and Conclusions, P. 535.

The Way of Man. According to the Teachings of Hasidism. London: Collins Books. Also reprinted in Walter Kaufmann, *Religion from Tolstoy to Camus.* New York: Harper Torchbooks (paperback.

Werke. Zweiter Band—*Schriften zur Bibel.* Munich and Heidelberg: Kösel-Verlag and Verlag Lambert Schneider. (Includes *Moses, Der Glaube der Propheten, Königtum Gottes, Der Gesalbte* [unpublished up till now], "Der Mensch von heute und die jüdische Bibel," "Abraham der Seher," "Was soll mit den zehn Geboten geschehen?," "Biblisches Führertum," "Weisheit und Tat der Frauen," "Prophetie und Apokalyptik," "Falsche Propheten," *Recht und Unrecht. Deutung einiger Psalmen, Biblisches Zeugnis* [from *Israel und Palästina*], "Geschehende Geschichte," "Die Erwählung Israels," "Nachahmung Gottes," "Die Götter der Völker und Gott," "Biblischer Humanismus," *Die Schrift und ihre Verdeutschung:* "Die Sprache der Botschaft," "Über die Wortwahl in einer Verdeutschung der Schrift," "Leitwortstil in der Erzählung des Pentateuchs," "Das Leitwort und der Formtypus der Rede," "Zur Verdeutschung der Preisungen," "Zur Verdeutschung der Gleichsprüche," "Zur Verdeutschung des Buches Ijob (Hiob)," "Zum Abschluss," "Ein Hinweis für Bibelkurse"; *Elija. Ein Mysterienspiel.*

Between Man and Man, new edition with an Introduction by Maurice Friedman, With an Afterword by the Author on "The History of the Dialogical Principle, translated by Maurice Friedman. Translated (except for the Afterword) by Ronald Gregor Smith. New York: Macmillan Paperbacks.

Daniel. Dialogues on Realization. Edited and Translated with an Introductory Essay by Maurice Friedman. New York: McGraw-Hill Paperbacks.

Elijah. A Mystery Play. Selections from Scenes 1, 3, 4, 6, 8, 10, 11, 16, 18, 20, 22, 23. Translated by Maurice Friedman. *Judaism,* Vol. 14, No. 3 (Summer), pp. 260-266.

The Knowledge of Man. Edited with an Introductory Essay by Maurice Friedman. Trans. Maurice Friedman and Ronald Gregor Smith. London: George Allen & Unwin. (Includes "Distance and Relation," "Elements of the Interhuman," "What Is Common to All," "The Word That Is Spoken," "Guilt and Guilt Feelings," "Man and His Image-Work," and "Dialogue between Martin Buber and Carl R. Rogers.")

Nachlese. Heidelberg: Verlag Lambert Schneider. Includes many poems, short tributes, fragments, and essays selected by Buber himself before his death. Previously published in German: "Bekenntnis des Schriftstellers" (1945), "Erinnerung" (1957), "Aus einem Schreiben an das 'Internationale Institut für Philosophie' (Amsterdam)" (1917), "Elijahu" (1903), "Das Wort an Elijahu" (1904), "Aus dem Zyklus 'Geist der Herr'": "Der Jünger" and "Die Magier" (1901), "Gewalt und Liebe" (1926), "Das dämonische Buch" (1924), "Am Tag der Rückschau" (1928), "Geister und Menschen" (1961), "Ein Realist des Geistes" (1955), Über Richard Beer-Hofmann" (1962), "Hermann Hesses Dienst am Geist" (1957), "Authentische Zwiesprachigkeit" (1963), "Seit ein Gespräch wir sind" (1957), "Bemerkungen zur Gemeinschaftsidee" (1931), "Der dritte Tischfuss" (1925), "Erziehen" (1960), "Die Aufgabe" (1922), "Über den Kontakt" (1950), "Stil und Unterricht" (1921), "Ein Beispiel" (1959), "Religion und Gottesherrschaft" (1923), "Fragmente über Offenbarung" (1964), "Gläubiger Humanismus" (1963), "Haus Gottess" (1932), "Religiöse Erziehung" (1930), "Über Religionswissenschaft" (1928), "Philosophische und religiöse Weltanschauung" (1928), "Zur Situation der Philosophie" (1948), "Heilung aus der Begegnung" (1951), "Politik aus dem Glauben" (1933), "Zu zwei Burckhardt-Worten" (1961), "Ein Gespräch mit Tagore" (1950), "China und Wir" (1928), "Über die Todesstrafe" (1928), "Das echte Gespräch und die Möglichkeiten des Friedens" (1953), "Haltet ein!" (1957), "Zur Ethik der politischen Entscheidung" (1932), "Zum Problem der 'Gesinnungsgemeinschaft'" (1951), "Zur Klärung des Pazifismus" (1939), "November" (1948), "Gruss und Willkomm" (1960), "Weltraumfahrt" (1957), "Danksagung" (1958), "Nach dem Tod" (1927). Previously published only in English: "Gemeinschaft und Umwelt" ("Foreword" to Eric Gutkind, *Community and Environment,* 1953), "Über den 'bürgerlichen Ungehorsam'" (In *The Massachusetts Review. A Centenary Gathering for Henry David Thoreau,* 1962), "Nochmals über den 'bürgerlichen Ungehorsam'" (In *A Matter of Life.* Edited by Clara Urquhart. London: Jonathan Cape, 1963.).
Not previously published: "In Heidelberg" (1964), "Weisst du es noch . . .?" (1949), "Erinnerung an Hammarskjöld" (1962), "Über Leo Schestow" (1964), "Chassidut" (1927), "Von der Veredelung der Welt" (1923), "Das Unbewusste" (A translation by

Grete Schaeder of the notes, recorded and edited by Maurice Friedman, of the three seminars on the unconscious that Martin Buber gave for the Washington School of Psychiatry in the spring of 1957. These notes, as yet unpublished in English, form the basis for Maurice Friedman's summary of Buber's teaching on the unconscious in the eighth section of his "Introductory Essay" (Chapter I) to Buber's *The Knowledge of Man* (1965), pp. 33-39.), " 'In zwanzig Jahren' " (1961), "Die Drei" (1960), "Rachman, ein ferner Geist, spricht" (1942), "Danksagung" (1963), "Zuseiten mir" (1964), "Der Fiedler" (1964), "Nachwort" (1965).

1966

Addresses on Judaism. Trans. Eva Jospe. New York: Schocken Books. (Includes translation of *Reden über das Judentum* (1923) and *At the Turning* (1952).

Hasidism and Modern Man. Edited and translated with an Editor's Introduction by Maurice Friedman. New York: Harper Torchbooks. (paperback).

The Kingship of God. Translated by Richard Scheimann. New York: Harper & Row. (*Königtum Gottes*)

The Knowledge of Man. Edited with an Introductory Essay (Chap. I) by Maurice Friedman. Translated by Maurice Friedman and Ronald Gregor Smith. New York: Harper & Row (hardback) and Harper Torchbooks (paperback). (For contents see under 1965.)

The Origin and Meaning of Hasidism. Edited and translated with an Editor's Introduction by Maurice Friedman. New York: Harper Torchbooks (paperback).

INDEX

INDEX

(Arranged by MARVIN KATZ *et al.*)

A

A-perfection, 60f
Aaron, 347
Abraham, 182f, 226, 257, 319, 344, 353
Abraham and Isaac, 363
Abraham stories, 387ff, 393
Abraham, the faith of, 343; the God of, 683
Absolute, the, 152ff, 196; ciphers of the, 357; in the relative, finding the, 198; moral values, 152; as God, which? 295; other, 482f; "absolute person," paradox of the, 228; personality of God, 242; relation to the eternal Thou, 288; reverence for the, 265; value of man, 300
absoluteness, 52
absorption of Jews, 251
abstraction, 135, 257f; philosophical, 207
abstractness of I-It, 279
accountability, 203
acosmism, 121
act, the religious, 300
Acton, Lord, 444
actuality, 55
Adam, 90, 189, 207, 329; Adam's fall, 373
Adler, Alfred, 588
admissions (2) by devotee of I-It knowledge, 293
Aesthetics, 609-628
affectivity, going beyond, 43f
Agag, 31ff
age of the "eclipse of God," our, 318
Agus, Jacob B., 239n
Ahad Ha-am, 18, 555f
Ahaz, 448
Akiba, Rabbi, 684
Albright, W. F., 401
alien thoughts, 421ff
Amalekites, 31
ambivalence of human life, 231

American philosophers ignored by Buber, 270
Ames, Van Meter, 512n
Amos, 218, 386, 391
anamnesis, historical, 219
anarchy, moral, 170
Anointed, the, 371
Anteus, 223
anthropocentrism, 302
anthropological insight, 115
"Anthropology, Buber's Philosophical," essay by Philip Wheelwright, 69-95
anthropology, Buber's philosophical, 171ff, 179; philosophical, 106, 225, 259; theological, 106, 261
anthropomorphic, 88
anthropomorphism, 279, 304
antiquity, 133
"anti-anti-Semitism," 251
anti-Semitism, 250f, 396
antithesis of Judaic faith and Pauline-Johannine teachings, 313ff
Apocalypse, 336, 373
Apocalyptic, contemporary, 326; eschatology of later Judaism, 350; secular, 374
apocalypticism, 347
Apodeixis, 206
Apollo, 219
apostles, theology of the, 312
a priori of relation, 531
Aquinas, St. Thomas, 151, 245, 259, 476
Arabs, 252; peaceful co-existence with, 448
Aristotle, 61, 87, 95, 151, 208f, 219, 222, 259, 261, 268, 439, 444, 476, 649; Aristotle's view of man, 70
art, as symbolic form, 613, 615; contained in nature, 560; criticism, 626f; of living, Buber's new method in the, 249
artist, definition of, 610f; artist's response, 145
artistic experience, metaphysics of, 225

askesis, spiritual, 34
assimilation, attempts at, 341
assumption, Buber's operative, 243
asymmetry, 66f
ataraxia, 79
Athens, 23
at-homeness in the world, 258
Atman, 75
atomic weapons, 604f
atomism, cognitive, 116
atonement, 569
attachment, 126
attitude, non-cognitive, 116; non-conceptual, 116
Auden, W. H., 671
Augustine, St., 208ff, 214, 230, 245, 259, 331, 345, 350, 479, 498, 512, 649f
Aurobindo, Sri, 305, 307
authentic, existence, 171ff, 179, 189; dialogical existence, 200; Judaism as humanism, 341; religious tradition, intrinsic qualities of, 261ff
authenticity, 143f
authority, rejection of all, 274; sacred, 273f
autonomous ethic, 172
autonomy, 534f
avatar, 89; of subjectivity, 150
Avesta, Iranian, 335
awareness, immediacy of, 118
axiology, 75

B

Baader, F. X. von, 203
Baal, 266, 392
Baal-Shem, The Legend of the, 33, 304, 405f, 425, 554f, 634, 636, 735-39
Bach, Johann Sebastian, effect of music of, on Buber, 14f
Baden, Grand Duke of, 23
bad philosophy, 283
Baeck, Leo, 341, 677, 684
Baer, Rabbi Dov, 543
Bakunin, 456
Baldwin, James Mark, 518, 521
Balthasar, H. U. von, 702ff, 712f, 715; essay by, 341-59
Barnabas, the letter of, 342
Baron, Salo, 267f

Barth, Karl, 349
"Bases of Buber's Ethics," essay by Maurice Friedman, 171-200
basis of Buber's doctrine, the ultimate, 296
Bauer, Bruno, 457
Beardsley, Monroe, 609n, 623
beauty, nature of, 621f
becoming, 52
Beer-Hofmann, Richard, 445
Begegnung, 45
"beggar," the lot of the, 700
behaviorist, fallacy, 583; observer, 194
being, 136; as addressed, 533; ground of, 683; "being-itself" (Tillich's), 245; meeting with, 651; the true notion of, 146
belief, two "contradictory" modes of, 353
Benjamin, Rabbi, 432
Berdyaev, Nicolas, 48f, 64f, 512
Bergman, Hugo, 113n, 716f; essay by 297-308
Bergson, Henri, 64, 116, 135ff, 142f, 149n, 225, 228, 250, 348, 476, 511, 518, 643, 659, 703; "the phenomenon," 270; Bergsonian becoming, 143
Berkeleyan subjectivism, 82
Berlin, 23
Bernanos, George, 333
betrayal, 568
"between," 14, 93, 97f, 174, 184, 302, 706f; the double face of, 98
Between Man and Man (Buber's), 258f, 518n, 535, 640-46, 682f, 691n, 721
betweenness, 74, 139ff, 148f, 190
Bewährung, 143, 209
Beziehung, 44f, 69f, 75, 86
bias, Buber's postulative, 128
biased opinion vs. knowledge, 281
Bible, 157ff, 166, 182f, 198, 208ff, 228, 245, 253, 255, 263, 265, 277; Hebrew, 277; interpretation of, 726-31; language of the, 246; Revised Standard, 670-75; translation, Buber's, 204
Biblical, belief, 32; Covenant, 171; criticism, 274; exegesis, 361ff; faith, 189; God a myth, 274; language, 244; law, 378; prophets, 185; trust, 199
Blake, Wm., 644
Bloch, Ernst, 500

Bodhisattva, the myth of, 79
Bohr, Niels, 606
books and men, Buber's attitude towards, 38f
Bradley, G. H., 45
Brahman, 75
Brod, Max, essay by, 319-40
Brownell, Baker, 270f
Brunner, Emil, 514; essay by, 309-18
Brunschvicg, Leon, 43
Buber('s), Martin, biographical data, 1-39; antipathy to missionary activity, 8; childhood convulsion, 9f; death, XX; early contact with philosophers, 11ff; early problem with time, 11f; early schooling, 5f; father's social solicitude, 7; grandfather, 5ff; grandmother (Adele), 4; in Lemberg Gymnasium, 8ff; (early) interest in language(s), 5f; love of theatre, 14; parents separation, 3; stepmother, 5; University-seminar, influence on, 13f; affinity to Kierkegaard, 649f, 652; ambiguous metaphysics, 538f; and Gandhi, 440f; and Moses Hess, 457ff; and Paul's theology of history, 461ff; and philosophy of history, 451-68; and pragmatism, 511-42; and psychotherapy, 577-601; and H. S. Sullivan, 580ff, 585ff; and socialism, 472ff; approach to scriptures, 381; as activist, 404ff; as atypical man, 689; as Bible interpreter, 361-80; as translator, 670ff; as classical author, 629-38; as educator, 543-76; as existentialist, 513ff, 665ff, 685; as Hebrew sage, 296; as idealist, 109; as philosopher, 469-74; as political scientist, 435-47; as problematician, 544; as social philosopher, 437ff; as stylist, 669f; as Zionist, 446-48; as solitary figure, in Jerusalem, 353; attitude to Christianity, a personal confession, 311; attitude to philosophy, 250; attitude to tradition, 250; basic metaphysical assumptions, 539; *beyond* Jewish orthodoxy, liberalism, Synagogue, Zionism, 347f; boundless love for the world, 38, 406; case against philosophy, 259; challenged, 237; chief merit as Bible-interpreter, 277; central question, 666; committment to unargued dialogue, 296;

communicative proximity to Christian, 311; conversations with Catholics and Protestants, 343; contribution to Biblical study, 381ff, 399ff; critics, 238f; critique of religion as feeling, 283; cuts through dichotomy between thought and feeling, 584; debt to Kierkegaard, 261; difference from Cassirer, 74; distinctive teaching, 281; distrust of theology, 246; doctrine at war with epistemology and metaphysics, 282; early (1911) non-belief in divine revelation, 278; estranged from orthodox community, 218; false distinction between philosophic thought and religious tradition, 271; Hasidism, 494; inaugural address (1938), 259; ignores American philosophers, 270; ignores modern critique of revelation, 280; Jewish "Protestant," 210; most basic doctrine, 281; most sustained argument, 258f; on Book of Job, 397; on the Dialogue, 436; on eschatology, 468; on Hasidism, 403ff; on political surplus, 436ff; on public life, 441; operative assumption, 243; philosophical anthropology, 579f; "philosophizing" a series of lapses, 296; philosophy of time, 539; radical challenge, 238; "reduction," 347ff; rejects Kenite theory, 394f; rejects metaphysics, 717; rejects monastic life, 446; rejection of a frozen tradition, 264; religious philosophy, 665-85; seesaws between theology and philosophy of religion, 352; (5) strictures of speculative philosophy, 257ff; thought on art, 609-23; thought on intuition, not a theory, 67; thought springs from reality of dialogue, 294; undisputed literary position in Germany, 341; vs. Hegel's philosophy of history, 455ff; vs. Heidegger, 648f, 667ff; vs. Jaspers, 667ff; vs. Kierkegaard, 483-86, 742; vs. Langer, S., 613ff, 622; vs. Marxist dialectic, 648; vs. G. H. Mead, 527-35; vs. St. Paul's theology of history, 452ff, 459; vs. naturalisms, 539-40; vs. Sartre, 502; vs. Tillich, 246f; writings, key to, 255
Buber's reply to, von Balthasar, 703f, 712f, 715; Diamond, 700; Fackenheim,

691ff; Fox, 699ff, 718-21; Friedman, 710f, 725; M. Kaplan, 744; Fritz Kaufmann, 711f; Levinas, 697, 723; Marcel, 705ff; Muilenburg, 726ff; Rotenstreich, 694-99, 701-05, 712; Taubes, 715, 721, 729ff; Wahl, 715f; Wheelwright, 710

Buber, Solomon (Buber's grandfather), 250

Buddha, 630, 680

Buddhism, 353; Hinayana, 79, 94; Mahayana, 79, 94

Bukovina, 19

Bultmann, Rudolf, 317f, 533

Bunam, Rabbi S., 545, 552, 678

Burdach, Conrad, 261f

C

Calogero, Guido, 94

Calvin, John, 640ff

capitalism, 350, 356

Carlyle, 15

Cartesian, 134; *cogitatio,* 211; dichotomy, 82

case against philosophy, Buber's, 259

Cassirer, Ernst, 73f, 613

casuistry, 358

categorical imperative, 177, 570

Catherine of Genoa, St., 656

Catholic Church, 343; incapable of real dialogue, 343

causality, 74

cause-and person, 18

Celan, Paul, 625, 627

certainty, 181f; none in ethics, 151

Cézanne, Paul, 225f

Chagall, Marc, 615, 678

character, a great, 178f; education, 570; intentional shaping of, 565

charisma, 18f, 164, 218

Cherbonnier, Edmund La B., 246n

Cheruth, Ueber Jugend und Religion (Buber's), 302

children, as potential artists, 559

choice, Aristotelian concept of, 649

choosing and being chosen, 210

chosenness of Jews for sake of all others, 352

Christ, 23, 207, 304, 333, 652, 654; "Christ, Hasidism, Gnosis" (Buber's essay), 306; the cross of, 358; words of, 630f

Christian, community, 382; community, the original, 313; doctrinal tradition, 314; philosophy, the cornerstone of all, 230

Christianity, historical, 314; is impure as a composite, 349; major attack on, 313

Christians, early, 397

Christology, 346

Chuang-tzu, 629

Clairvaux, Bernard of, 233

co-belonging, 46

Cohen, Hermann, 34, 114, 214, 256, 303f, 341, 371, 515, 550, 684

collectivism, 42f; and individualism, dichotomy of, 103

Collingwood, R. G., 616f

collision, head-on, between Judaism and Christianity, 358

commitment, 141; of the artist, 619f; personal, 276

committed openness, 286

Common Faith, A (Dewey's), 269

communication, 279, 285; Jasper's definition of, 668; of the incomprehensible, 689

communication, indirect, 206; severance of, 343

communion, instinct for, 102

communism, 350, 356

Communist Manifesto, 438, 457

Communitarians, Russian, 555

community, 20, 473, 655ff; as a natural creation, 438; meaning of, 656; of tradition, 204; true, 302; vs. society, 437

comparative religion, 312

comprehensibility of the world, 298

conceptualizing, the necessity of theological, 247

concern, moral, 169

concreteness, 118; the gate to reality, 257

confessional theology, 247

Confessions (St. Augustine's), 208ff

conflict between modern thought and Biblical revelation, radical, 273f

confusion, of relative with the Absolute, 183; between religion and philosophy, 58

conscience, 175f, 187f, 569f; a new, 183; as animated by moral teaching, 575; great, 569f

consciousness, 133f; of one's own self, status of, 125f
consecration, 635
consensual validation, 577, 586f
"conservative revolution," history as, 203
constitution, federal (U.S.) , 268
contemporary, history, argument from, 349; spiritual situation, 123
content, critique of, 130
continuity, 742
"continuity," 569
contradiction, inner, 355
contraries, the unity of the, 243
conversation vs. teaching, 693
conversion, 652
"conversion" of M. Buber and of H. S. Sullivan compared, 580f
Cooley, Charles H., 518
cooperative commonwealth, 526
'Copernican Revolution' (Buber's), 309
correlation between language and experience, two-fold, 243
Corrupted by Universals (Brownell's), 271
cosmic, optimism, 702; significance of man's unifying act, 300
cosmogonic myths, 90
cosmology, 540
Courage to Be, The (Tillich's) , 245
covenant, 202, 319, 322, 372f, 396f
creation, 86, 272; continuous, 714; goal of, 176; story of, 367; the, 375ff
creative element in Christianity is Judaic, 345
Creative Evolution (Bergson's), 270
creative milieu, 45
creatives, the, 551
creator God, evil, 334
crisis, man's modern, 260
criteria for God, religion and revelation concepts, 286ff
criterion of knowledge, objective, 239f
criticisms of philosophy of dialogue, 238
critics, Buber's, 238f; higher, 683
Critique of Practical Reason (Kant's), 256
Critique of Pure Reason (Kant's) , 72f
Crito (Plato), 199
Croce, Benedetto, 616

Cullmann, Oscar, 384
cultic celebrations, 402
cultural Zionism, 252
culture(s), 168f
Cusa, Nicolas of, 259
Czartoryski, Prince Adam, 652

D

Daniel (Buber's) , 34, 299
Daniel, Book of, 332; (prophet), 23ff
Dante, Alighieri, 262, 632
Dasein, 495-99, 509
Daube, David, 678f
David, 345
death, 186; being-for, 498
debate between Cohen and Buber, 256
decalogue, 378, 728
decision, 173; crisis of, 658
Declaration of Independence (U.S.) , 268
definition of revelation ends in antinomy, 289f
definitions at fault, 599
Deism, 275f
deity, and history, 441ff; as supreme case of the social category, 531n, 532
Deixis, 206
delusion that scientists do not have values, 591
"Demand of the Spirit and Historical Realty" (Buber's), Key to Buber, 250, 253
Demarcation, the Line of, 571f
demiurge, 208
democracy, genuine, 18
de-personalization, 305
Der Mensch und sein Gebild (Buber's), 145f
Descartes, René, 34, 134, 211, 230, 457, 501, 685
despair, therapeutic, 593ff; of therapist treating schizophrenia, 595ff, 599ff
destiny, divine, 50
detachment, 126
determinism, reconciled with emergence, 522
Deutero-Isaiah, 244, 332, 338f, 346, 358, 382, 384, 397, 402, 460-64, 653, 730
Deuteronomy, 379
devil, 168, 198; redeemable, 725

devotion vs. gnosis, 306ff

Dewey, John, 269, 271, 513ff, 549

dialectic, between God and idea of God, 509f; immanent of K. Mara, 373; inner, 739; of "reconciliation," 344; of "rejection," 344; process, 202

dialectical encounter, 542

dialogic, 86f, 94; character of experience, 243; encounter, immediacy of, 237; life, 535; relations, 239

dialogical, 174f; approach, 92; cosmism, 120; form, 97; knowledge, 293; "dialogical life," 97; method, 93; mutuality, 129; principle, 33, 358; relation, 142; (relationship), 19; relationship (between man and God), 33; return from the dialectic to the, 202; situation, 91, 99, 116, 121f, 129ff

dialogically, 342

dialogicism, situation-bound, 314

dialogue, 22f, 97ff, 117, 129, 141f, 144, 148, 175, 180, 183, 190, 356, 532f, 542, 599f, 662, 666; between the "old" and the "new" covenant, 342; Buber's vs. Socrates', 668; genuine, 706f; genuine vs. therapeutic, 593; human-divine, 285f; "Dialogue in Expectation," 639-64; is unique, 279; must have content, 696f; "dialogue of action," 90; of existence, genuine, 224; of God with man, 697; *Dialogue of History as such,* 354; ontological character of, 240; philosophy of, critique of, 238; philosophy of, and the nature of beauty, 621f; real, 343; reality of, Buber's thoughts spring from, 294; relation not absolute, 660; the basic reality, 199; the God of, 285; the life of, 215, 244, 249; the philosophy of, 171ff, 178, 197; with God only disguised monologue, 277f; with God a form of human self-realization, 278

Diamond, Malcolm L., 700; essay by, 235-47

dia-personal principle, 95

diaspora, 247, 266, 341, 344, 349, 355

dichotomy, the question of, 126f

difference between Buber and Whitehead, 65

Dilthey, Wilhelm, 118f, 203, 250, 511, 643, 702

Dinghaftigkeit, 44

Dion, 253

discourse, two modes of, 235

distance, 357; and relation, 109ff; "Distance and Relation," a Buber essay, 81-85; "distance, the passion of," 80

distancing, 140f, 149f, 174; the process of, 82ff

distortions of reason, existential, 247

distrust of theology (Buber's), 246

divine existence, 62f; limitation of the, 247; message in Jewish tradition, 255; presence, 221; revelation, 698f; unsurpassability, 60

dogma, 353

dogmatic intolerance, R. C's insuperable, 343

dogmatism, 358, 704; spiritual, 145

Dostoyevsky, 333, 456, 578, 677

"Double Truth," denial of, 690

Dread, The Concept of, 650

Dreyfus case, 251

dualism, as flight from real task, 350; incipient, 347

dualisms, 271

duality, 101f, 124; of holiness, 420

Duino Elegies, 225

duration, Bergsonian, 135, 140

Dürer, Albrecht, 560, 647

duty, moral, 152f, 177

"Dying to the world," 601

"each-other," 14

E

Ebner, Ferdinand, 34, 41, 309f, 515

ecclesiastical, biblical research sides with Buber, 345

Eckhart, Meister, 228, 506, 643

eclipse of God, 57f, 289

economic determinism, 260

ecstatic moments vs. routine, 468

ecumenicism, 358

Eden, Garden of, 335, 376

education, 104; character, 549, 563ff; highest form of, 544; subjects of, 557

Edwards, Jonathan, 51, 470

ego, 76; and id, 682f; *ego cogito* (Descartes'), 211f

egoism, 75

egology, 134

Egypt, 353

Ehad, 714

Eheyeh, 230f
Einfühlung, 76f, 142
Einzelne, der, 75f
Eissfeldt, Otto, 388
either-or, 659
Eliezer, Rabbi, 20
Elijah, 332, 389ff, 425
Elimelekh, Rabbi, 413f, 738, 740
Eliot, T. S., 584, 625, 671
Elohim, 218, 221, 228, 323
embraceableness of the world, 298
Emerson, Ralph Waldo, 269
"emotional maturity," 590
emotive language of the Bible, 247
empathy, 117f
Empirical Theology of Henry Nelson Wieman, The, 269
empirical validation, 238
empiricism, radical, 514n
emuna, 189, 198f
Emunah, 216, 230, 314f, 333, 338ff
encounter, 144, 236ff; direct, 276; transforming, 42; with a tree, Buber's, 237, 239; existential, 246; God known in the, 287
engagement, 604
Engels, F., 457
Enlightenment, 342f; the age of, 273
Enoch, 332
entelecheia, 129
epistemological status of I-Thou and I-It, 281
epistemology, Buber critical of traditional, 238; the propaedeutic of knowledge, 134
epoch-conditioning, 349
Epoché, 211
"epochs of habitation," 259; "epochs of homelessness," 259
Eretz Yisrael, 252, 256, 265, 267
Ergreifen, 207
Ergriffensein, 207
Erlebnis, 711f
Erloesung des Alltags, 306
Eros, 130
eschatological actuality, 312
estranged from orthodoxy, Buber, 218
eternal recurrence, 202
Eternal Thou (God), 191f, 241ff, 661, 683, 710, 714
eternity, 13
ethic, "autonomous," 172; of personal relations, 191

ethical, and civic education, 574f; definition of community, 656; responsibility, ontological warrant for, 100f; the suspension of the, 485
ethicising the human sphere, 100
ethics, 717f; and religion, 538; Biblical, 273; Buber's definition of, 172f
Euthyphro (Plato), 179
Eve, 90
evil, 179, 193, 199, 650; on doing, 720f; radical, 568; the nature of, 167f
evolution, 272
évolution créatrice, 228
exegesis of the Bible, 667
exegetical analysis, Buber's penetrating, 313
exile-theology of the Old Testament, 344
existence, authentic, 171ff, 179, 189; authentic dialogical, 200; fulfilment of human, 129; "existence, sacramental," 350f; sacramental, 223; the philosophy of, 142; "existence, uncurtailed," 184
existential, dialectic, reinterpretation of, 658f; distortions of reason, 247; encounter, 246; guilt, 567f; interpretation of faith, 315; nature of man, 261; phenomenology, 208; philosophy, 295; reality, 258; theology, 54
existentialism, 48-68, 310, 455, 458, 475-510; as related to pragmatism, 511-516; religious, 276
existentialist, bias, Buber's, 124; theologians, 318
existentialists, 469; impressive monologues of, 668, 685
Existenz, 358
expediency not moral, 152
experience, 116f, 299ff; "Experience, Great," 298; of faith vs. theology, 690; "experience, the great," 301; the unity of, 101
extreme position on the Jewish religious tradition (Buber's), 267
Ezekiel, 382, 397, 460, 636

F

Fackenheim, Emil L., 691, 692n; essay by, 273-96
fact, the High Priests of, 584; uniqueness of, 389

faith, 27, 187f, 232; and action, 517; Christian type of, 339f; concept of in Hebrew scriptures, 327; Messianic, 368; one great experience of, 689; paradox of, 648; pure unmediated, 347; simple experience of, 107; two kinds of, 269; *Faith, Two Types of,* 311ff, 326f, 333f, 344; Wieman (H. N.) on, 269; without revelation, 275
fallacy, behaviorist, 583
Farber, Leslie H., essay by, 577-601
Fechner, Gustav Theodor, 64, 532
feeling, current romantic attitude toward, 584-585
feelings, 44; role of, 659
Feibush, Rabbi Meshullam, 414
Feiwel, Berthold, 16
Feuerbach, Ludwig, 34, 42, 45, 112ff, 128f, 139, 259, 300, 302, 310, 457, 496, 511, 657
Fichte, Johann Gottlieb, 61, 113n, 506
fictitiousness of reason, ideas, etc., 131
"fidelity," 190
Fiedler, 225
fields of forces, 531
final, answers, none in ethics, 151; cause, 87
finiteness, man's, 202
finitude, historical, 92
Flaubert, Gustave, 323
folk-school, 29
Fox, Marvin, xix, 699f; essay by, 151-70
Franciscans, 732
Frank, Jakob, 634
Frankenstein, 260
freedom, 50, 177, 192, 243, 268; consistent with order, 534; equivalent with responsibility, 535; maximum admissible, 574; and necessity reconciled, 522; the use of, 517
Freeman, Ann, xx
Freeman, Eugene, xx
Freud, Sigmund, 123, 356, 577, 582, 588, 600, 667f, 682, 724
Friedman, Maurice, 136n, 249, 710f; essay by, 171-200
friendship, 191; spiritual, 148
Fromm-Reichmann, 588
frozen tradition, Buber's rejection of a, 264
fulfilment of human existence, 129

fundamentalist and orthodox tendencies, 318
Fürsorge (Heidegger's) , 148
future, always open, 202
futuristic impulse, Israel's, 351

G

Gandhi, Mohandas, K., 440f; Buber's letter to, 265
Gassendi, Pierre, 212
Gaudig, Hugo, 566
Geist, 480
"*Geistesforschung,*" 306
Gemarah, 405
Gemeinschaft, 46, 437
generalization, 257f
generalized other, 521f, 527
Genesis, 89f
genetic fallacy of S. Freud, 582f
Genossenschaft, 70
genuine religion involves possibility of revelation, 284
George, Stefan, 671
German idealistic philosophy, 310
Germans (Nazi) , 164
Geschehen, 144, 146
Gesellschaft, 437
Gestalten, 372
Gestalt psychology, 145f
Geulincx, Arnold, 570
Gewerkschaft, 70
ghetto, 342
Gideon, 319ff, 346, 369ff
Gideonites, 550
Glatzer, Nahum, 728; essay by, 361-380
Glaucon, 152
gnosis, 224, 743
gnostic-hellenistic, 313
gnosticism, Buber's vehemently negative relation to, 306ff
goal and way vs. end and means, 440f
God ('s), 78ff, 85ff, 145, 197; actuality accepted on faith, 293; and becoming, 51f; and creation, 483; and freedom, 50f; and man, 694; and nature, 712; and the genuine moral act, 545; and world, unity of, 486; as Absolute Person, 58f, 242; as abysmal mystery, 62; as *Dasein,* 478; as eternal You (see also I-Thou), 683; as independent existence, 471f;

as love, 531; as not subject to principle of non-contradiction, 509; as relative, 717; as Thou, 85; as Thou, not It, 53ff; as "Thou" not metaphor, 713f; as origin of both nature and spirit, 367; as person, 367, 540; as self-concealing, 244; as self-revealing, 244; as the Thou of man, 227; as Unique and One, 714; being, incomprehensibility of, 272; belief in, 24f; cannot be possessed, 220; choice between, and the Bible, 32; creation, 198; direction to, 179; eclipse of, 289; *God, Eclipse of* (by Buber), 486, 488f, 493f, 499, 715f, 719; encounter with, 422; essence, 61; existence of, denied by G. H. Mead, 541; found in worship and faith, 470ff; hidden, 716, 729; integral to man and history, 690; is dead, 205, 336; known in the encounter, 287; Kingdom of, 340, 344, 375, 379; kingship of, 320; leadership, 339; love of, 662; manifestations, 220; meaning of, 29ff; need for, 27f; not the whole, 484; of Abraham, Isaac, and Jacob, 28, 241, 246, 255; of dialogue, the, 285; of history, 697; of the philosophers, 205, 241, 255; "God of the Philosophers" (Pascal), 28; of the theologians, 241; of theism, transcending the, 245; proof of, 64; relation to Israel, 700; relation to man and world, 403ff; revelation, 79; self-revelation, 315; servant of, 332; service of, 421-24, 443f, 545; service of, in corporality, 411ff; sovereignty, 232; teaching the nature of, 690; "the absolute person," 226f; the grace of 316; the hiding of, 716, 729; the inclusive Thou, 50; the Jewish idea of, 230; *God, The Kingship of,* 319ff; the living, 336; the self-communicating, 315f; the transcendent, 226f; the word of, 644f, 660; to give what is God's to, 435-36; ultimate duties to, 378

Goebbels, Joseph, 445
Goes, Albrecht, 641
Goethe, Johann Wolfgang von, 560, 631, 671, 683
Gog, 740
Golden Mean, doctrine of, 573

Golem, 71
Good and Evil, 537
Good and Evil, Images of (Buber's), 335, 362, 637f, 720
good, deeds of the godless, 718f; on doing, 575; the nature of, 167f, 180
Gordon, A. D., 128, 439, 555
Gospels, 326ff, 678ff
Gottesfinsternis, 357
gottwirklich, 303
grace, 188, 243; moments of, 85
Graham, Billy, 681
"Great character," 570
"Great Conscience," 569f
Grecian urn, 237
Greece, 247, 353
Greek antiquity, 169; Greek-Nietzschean doctrine, 202; philosophy, 133
Gregor of Nyssa, 345
Grosse Maggid und seine Nachfolge, Der, 34, 300
Guardini, Romano, 653
guideposts to life, 209
guilt, 176, 186ff; as preferable to meaninglessness, 597
Günther, Gotthard, 606
Gyges, the ring of, 152

H

Ha-Am, Ahad, 252
"habitation, epoch of," 259
Halevi, Judah, 230, 275
halutz, the, 267
Hamann, Johann Georg, 206, 214, 742
Hammer, Louis Z., essay by, 609-28
Hanslick, Eduard, 623
Harnack, Adolf von, 315, 681
Hartmann, N., 570
Hartshorne, Charles, 531n, 532, 540, 717; essay by, 49-68
Hasidi-c, -m, -sm, 19ff
Hasidic, community, 181, 250, 535; doctrine, 310, 349; essay (Buber's), 182; Great Maggid, 543; ideals of education, 547f; literature, 462, 464ff; man, 544f; message, 204; stories, 310; tradition, 33, 642
Hasidim, in the psalms, 727; *Hasidim, Tales of,* 680
Hasidism, 34, 86, 163, 166f, 171, 217, 223f, 228, 252f, 255, 265f, 277, 304, 312, 322, 324f, 341, 357f, 403ff, 472,

494, 506, 545f, 552, 586, 634-37, 652, 654ff, 666f, 677f, 680f, 683ff, 714, 724, 731-41; compared with Zen, 554; ethics of, 416; in Buber's language, 528; *Hasidism, The Origin and Meaning of*, 633, 635

Haskala, the, 250, 642

Heaven, For the Sake of (Buber's), 65, 68, 308, 320, 424, 426-34, 464, 635, 647, 654ff, 739

Hebraic humanism, 548f

Hebrew, Bible, 277; Bible, unique poetry of, 675; Biblical humanism, 262; economy of text, 675; "Hebrew Humanism" (Buber's), 262; sage, Buber as, 296; University, 250, 259, 310, 543

Hechler, Rev., 23f

Hegel, Georg Wilhelm Friedrich, 47, 58, 61, 112, 131, 151, 207, 228, 260, 336, 354, 451f, 466, 476, 643, 652; as adversary of pragmatists, 528n

Hegelian, dialectic, 204, 260; influence on G. H. Mead, 519; philosophy, 121f

Hegelianism, 511

Heidegger, Martin, 42, 57, 123, 126f, 135f, 141, 147f, 206, 209, 261, 458f, 476, 481, 486f, 489ff, 494-500, 506-09, 512, 647f, 658, 665, 667ff, 677, 685

Heilige Weg, Der (Buber's), 302

Heim, Karl, 42, 309

Hellenism, decline of, 453

Hellenistic Christianity, 314

Hellenizing of faith, 315

henotheism, 218

Heraclitian, becoming, 143; thought, 643f

Heraclitus, 184ff, 510, 691

Herberg, Will, 384n, 582

Herder, Johann Gottfried von, 214

hermeneutical methodology, 381ff, 387, 402

Herschel, Abraham, 87f

Herzl, Theodor, 16ff, 23, 250f, 457n, 543, 555

Herzl, Mrs. Jeannette (mother of Theodor), 16f

Herzlian Zionism, 251

Hesed, 727

Hess, Moses, 457f

Hesse, Hermann, 681

Highest, the, 202, 218

Hindus, 307

Hindu teaching, 184

Hinweise, 206

historical novels, 635

history, as an illusion, 459; "History, In the Midst of," essay by Buber, 89; philosophical interpretation of, 652; ontological affirmation of, 458; redemptive, 646

Hitler, Adolf, 164, 198, 725

Hitlerian, 198

Hocking, W. E., 725n

Hofmannsthal, Hugo von, 203, 633

Hölderlin, J. C. F., 203, 218n, 632, 669, 671

holy, the, and the dangerous, 638; sparks, 736; spirit, sin against the, 37; Holy Yehudi, 740f

"homelessness, epochs of," 259; homelessness, cosmic, 122; social, 122

Homer, 671

homily, is Buber's doctrine a, 280

hope for future, 715

Hopkins, Gerard Manley, 225f

Horace, 17

Hosea, 382, 674f, 730

human, attitude, twofold nature of, 34f; being, becoming a, 590; *Human Community: Its Philosophy for a Time of Crisis* (Brownell's), 271; destiny, ultimate questions of, 235; human-divine dialogue, 285f; existence, fundamental datum of, 43; existence, problematic reality of, 15; freedom, 258; homelessness, 259f; imitation of God's omnipotence, 651; life, ambivalence of, 231; nature, 522, 530; predicament, 132; problematic, the, 71; race, beginnings of, 557; reason, 71f; spirit, 300

Humanism, of G. H. Mead, 526; the goal of, 262

Hume, David, 605f

Humean scepticism, 82

Husserl, Edmund, 72, 134f, 145, 206, 211, 261, 348, 469, 487, 658

Huxley, Aldous, 184

I

"I," 137ff, 278ff

"I am that I am," 201, 230

I and Thou (by Buber), 34f, 41, 49, 53, 172, 181, 190, 192, 223, 235, 243, 402

"I and Thou," essay by Gabriel Marcel, 41-48

Ibsen, H., 442

iconoclasm, 205

idealism, Post-Kantian, 92; the God of religious, 275f

ideas as instruments to get at reality, 270

identity, of nature and supernature in Buber, 350f; philosophy of, 113

ideologies, 444

idolatry, 165

I-hood, 91

Ihud, 448

I-It, attitude, 235ff; attitude of objective detachment, 278ff; relation, 35, 108ff, 137ff, 173, 178, 193ff, 278ff, 323, 471, 476, 490, 492, 507-09, 559f, 575f, 583ff, 592, 603, 605f, 611, 659, 691f, 694f, 704f, 708, 711, 715f, 724, 743; schemata: useful fictions, 57

Iliad and *Odyssey*, German translation of, 671

illumination, 187

Images of Good and Evil (Buber), 172, 651

imagination, mythopoetic, 303

imitatio dei, 86, 88ff

Imitatio Dei (Buber), 544

imperative, categorical, 177

imperturbability, 79

impressionism, Buber's metaphysical, 132

impressionistic trend, 127

inanimate things as Thou, 55f

inauthentic existence, 179

"incapsulated" relationships, 80

incarnation, dogma of, 224, 227

Incarnation, the, 88

inclusion, 117f, 142

"Inclusion," doctrine of, 571

incomprehensibility, of God's being, 272; of the world, 298

indemonstrable, everything philosophical is, 64

independent opposite, 110

India, 271

individual, the, 484, 486

individualism and collectivism, criticized, 721; era of, 42f

inertia, the fanaticism of, 318

influence of philosophy on the religious tradition, 268

infrapersonal, 213

insecurity, philosophical, 151

insight, definition of, 592

instinct, 102

institutional forms of religion, 268

instrumentalism, 270

intellect, limitations of, 516f

intellectus, 81

interaction, mutual, 84

"interhuman," 174; I-Thou relations, 293; relations, 291, 711

interpersonal theory of H. S. Sullivan, 585ff

inter-subjective I-Thou relation, 146f

intersubjectivity, 43f; philosophy of, 42

intolerance, R. C's insuperable dogmatic, 343

intrinsic, moral value, 152; value, 172

intuition, Bergsonian, 136, 144

intuitionism, 115

intuitionist, character of Buber's thinking, 116; strain in Buber, 119

intuitive approach to reality, 239

Iqbal, Mohammed, 64

ir-responsibility, 213

"Is" and the "Ought," 573

Isaac, 182, 257

Isaiah, 253f, 261, 271, 391, 448, 724; vs. Plato, 254

Israel('s), 247, 254, 267, 321, 330, 335f, 338, 340, 361f, 368ff, 538, 546; absolutisms, 356; *Israel and the World* (Buber's), 269; Biblical, 372, 377, 379; boundless loneliness, 355; essence is formal Christology, 354; faith, 312, 400f; state of, 447f; the God of, 88; *Israel und Palästina* (Buber's), 349; universal mission, 352; wandering tribes of, 369

It, 191f, 231; becomes Thou, 659; metaphysical status of, 281; not inferior to Thou, 591

I-Thou, and Josiah Royce, 515n; as noncommunicable, 692; attitude, 236ff; becomes I-It, 689, 692; dialogue a form of knowledge, 282; epistemological status of, 281; language, *sui generis*, 238; nonreversible, 697; relation, 35, 79f, 97, 108ff, 113f, 137ff, 173, 178, 189ff, 215,

278ff, 318, 323, 357, 436, 457, 473, 481-83, 489-94, 502-07, 509f, 527ff, 559f, 575f, 582, 583f, 587ff, 603-07, 610ff, 657-63, 665f, 669, 677, 682, 689, 691f, 694f, 697, 704-11, 723f, 743; without full mutuality, 571f

J

Jacob, 676
Jacob Joseph, Rabbi of Polnoe, 410f
Jacob Yitzchak, the *Zaddik*, 427
Jacobi, Friedrich Heinrich, 206, 214, 657
James, William, 203, 218, 225, 269, 271, 470, 481, 513ff, 538
Jankelevitch, 144
Jansenist doctrine, 210
jargon, of I-Thou, 682
Jaspers, Karl, 227, 229, 321, 343, 479, 481, 482f, 503-09, 512, 647, 652f, 658, 665, 667f, 677, 685
Jeans, Sir James, 88
Jefferson, Thomas, 269
Jeremiah, 346, 382, 397
Jerusalem, 310; new, 374; Jesus' tears over, 359
Jesus, 88, 311, 325, 328-34, 630f, 715; basic doctrine of, 349; and Deutero-Isaiah, 464; of the genuine tradition, 314; of history, message of the, 312; of theology, the, 314; in the Gospels, 679f; the uniqueness of, 312
Jethro, 394f
Jewish, external legalism an abomination for Buber, 347; faith vs. faith in Jesus the Christ, 315; Messianism, 305; nationalism, 251; religious tradition, indispensibility of the, 261; renaissance, 447; responsibility, 255; tradition, 202, 204; scriptures, 381, 401
Jewishness is incommunicable, 355
Jew of Tarsus, 380
Jews, as a community based on a common memory, 264; as scapegoats, 251; "return to their origin," 262f
Job, 220, 226, 345f, 376f, 713; Book of, 329, 508; Job's question to God, 357
John the Baptist, 325f
John, Gospel of, 332
Johnson, Aubrey, 401

Joshua, 372
Journal Metaphysique, 41, 46
Judaic unity of religion and civil society, 349
Judaism('s), 247, 301, 319-40, 666, 684, 700, 714, 744; and Roman Catholic Church the last two witnesses to an absolute mandate from God, 353; Buber "spokesman for," 250; chance, 358; essence dogmatically put forth, 347; in the writings of Buber, 731; is original humanism, 352; Pharisaic, 314; spectre among the nations, 346; "subterranean," 303; talks on (Buber's), 303; the heart of, belief in God, 256; the original moving force in, 218; the religious message of, 312; *Judaism, Three Addresses on* (Buber's) 300
Jüdisch-Christliches Religionsgespräch in 19 Jahrhunderten (Schoeps'), 342
Jung, Carl Gustav, 57, 307, 471, 567, 588, 713; Jung's "religion of pure psychic immanence," 275n
justice, 268
justification by faith, 315, 317

K

Kabbala, 204, 224, 228, 304, 306, 636, 642, 645, 735-40
Kabbalistic, system, 412; tradition, 732-36
Kafka, Franz, 214f, 219f, 337f, 357; Kafka's *Castle,* 577
kairos, 217, 312
Kant, Immanuel, 12, 13, 42, 81ff, 94, 108, 113, 152, 177f, 208f, 214ff, 219, 230, 231, 253, 256, 258f, 276, 442, 470, 494f, 512, 514n-15n, 549, 574, 606; four fundamental questions, 72ff
Kantian, 124; epistemology, 73; ethics, the formalism of, 214; phenomenalism, 663
Kaplan, Mordecai, 744; essay by, 249-72
Kaufmann, Fritz, xix, 711f, 714; essay by, 201-34
Kaufmann, Walter, 741f; essay by, 665-85
Kaufmann, Yehezkel, 371
Kavanah, 217
Kerényi, Carl, essay by, 629-38

key, to Buber's writings, 255; to redeemed human society, Israel holds,
351; to understanding Buber, 250
Kibbutzim, 537, 546ff
Kierkegaard, Soren, 34, 42, 72, 77ff,
120, 143, 148, 180, 182f, 206f, 217,
221, 257, 260f, 270, 276, 310, 331,
445, 469, 471f, 476ff, 482-87, 492,
498, 509, 511ff, 590, 600f, 647, 648ff,
658, 665f, 668, 685, 742; Kierkegaard's "aesthetic" category, 617, 620
King Josiah, 398
kingdom, divine, 377; of God, 340,
350, 379, 715; of love, 538
Klausner, 334
Klein, M., 588
know (to) in Hebrew means to embrace lovingly, 299
knowledge, a third kind of, 292; of
self, 530
Kohn, Hans, 322
Königtum, Gottes, 324, 362, 365n,
368, 399f, 728
Korah story, 365
Kropotkin, Prince, 439
Kuhn, Helmut, essay by, 639-64
Kuk, Abraham Isaac, 544
Kundgebungen, 84

L

Lagarde, Paul Anton de, 218
Landauer, Gustav, 302, 438-40
Langer, Susanne, 613ff
language, as determinate of our con-
cepts, 587; the objectifying, of pos-
itivism, 236; role of, 532f
Lao-tzu, 630
Laplace, Pierre S., 27
Lasalle, Ferdinand, 15
law, Biblical, 378; problem of, 377
laziness, mental, 68
leadership, 20
Lebensphilosophie, 114f, 202, 217, 348
legalism, 358
legislation, social, 165f
Leibhaftigkeit, 83
Leibniz, G. W. F., 529
Leipzig, University of, Buber's attend-
ance of, 14f
Lemberg, 3
Lenin, N., 574
Levinas, E., 723; essay by, 133-50

'libido,' 102
Libido theory, 578
Library of Living Philosophers, 269
Library of Living Theology, 269
Lichtwark, Alfred, 558
limitation of the divine, 247
Lincoln, Abraham, 269
linguistic expression, overcoming of,
696
Lipps, Theodore, 562
listening with the heart, 668
"lived concrete, the," 199
Locke, John, 268, 470
Loeb, Rabbi Moshe, 432, 678, 738
logical possibility, 59
Logos, 6, 247, 661f, 690
loneliness, 588; man's, 121
love, 190f, 713; as anxiety, 583; mean-
ing of, 678; steadfast, 387; to dwell
in, 661
Lowth, Bishop, 385
Ludendorff, General, 18n
Luke, Gospel of, 678ff
Luther, Martin, 78, 317, 331, 640ff,
671
Lvov, 3
lying, 164

M

Mach, E., 605
Machiavelli, Nicolo, 444
Maggid, 419f
Maggid of Mezritch, 407, 733, 738
Magnes, Dr. J. L., 448
Magus, Simon, 717
Maimonides, Moses, 227, 274, 569, 573,
684
"making present," 174f
Malachi, 730
Malebranche, Nicole, 259, 570
Malraux, André, 226, 628
Mammon, 443
man, and God, encounter between,
105; as artist, 609f; as entity, 436;
as God's comrade in the work of
creation, 714; as relatedness, 529-
30; as symbolizing and mythologizing, 73; Buber's language as appropriate to, 586; concrete concept of,
209f; essence of, 42; Greek view of,
631; nature of, 69ff; nullification of,

69; "problematic" to himself, 512; the aim of, 167f; the divinity of, 85; the exemplary, 545; the good, 572; the meaning of to be, 35; the nature of, 695; *Man, The Problem of,* 42; the rationality of, 113; redeemable, 725; twofold nature of, 708; untransformed, 441; vocation of, 225

man's, existential nature, 261; fall, possibility of, 572; modern crisis, 260; uniqueness, 260; volition, 86

Manichaean, 354; "hatred of reality," 49

Manicheeism, 221

mankind, unity of, 551

Mann, Thomas, 213

Mannheim, Karl, 268

Marburg School, 348; University, 256

Marcel, Gabriel, 190, 504f, 512, 618, 705ff; essay by, 41-48

Marcion, 334, 354, 374f, 376

Marcionism, 348

Mariás, Julián, 94

Maritain, Jacques, 617, 620

Mark, Gospel of, 332, 679

marriage, 191; essential meaning of, 484; sacrament of, 78

Martin Buber: The Life of Dialogue (Friedman's), 249

Marx, Karl, 103, 260, 350, 373, 456ff, 511, 668; and Lenin, N., 574; Christian version of, 681

Marxism, 438, 472f, 476; mystique of, 465; dialectic, 648; temptation, 48

Matthew, Gospel of, 358, 678

Mea culpa, 597f

Mead, George Herbert, 513-29, 533-41; and John Dewey, 514; and Wm. James, 514; Mead's failure to account for capacities of the self, 541

meaning, 74

meaning, as mirage, 598

mechanism, 524

Meditationes (Descartes'), 212

meeting, 34, 138f, 144, 147, 209; of man and God, 159; as symmetrical relation, 147; genuine, 196f

Meir, Rabbi, 428

meliorist approach, 446

Mendel, Rabbi Menachem, 425, 429, 678

Mendelssohn, Moses, 341

Mendenhall, George E., 401

Mennicke, Carl, 715

mental laziness, 68

Messiah, 331, 346

Messiahship, ultimate, 305

Messianic, expectancy, the right kind of, 654f; goal, 305

Messianism, 252; as the original idea of Judaism, 459ff; without eschatology, 430

metamorphosis of the religious tradition, 272

metaphysical, impressionism, 132, 704; status of It, 281; status of Thou, 281

metaphysicians, mediaeval and modern, 274

metaphysics, 75, 538f

Meysenbug, Maloida von, 91f

Midrash scholar, 250

Mikhal, Rabbi Yehiel, 733

Mimesis, 208

mind, as symbol using, 521

minimum content of revelation, 287

della Mirandola, Pico, 259

mistrust, 195

Misunderstanding of the Church (Brunner's), 317

Miteinandersein, 135

Mitnaggdim, 680

Mitsein, 657f

Mit-welt, 530

"modernized" religions are not religions at all, 284

modernizing ancient faiths, 275

Moloch, collective, 551

"momemts of supreme meeting," 216

monads, 529

monastic forms, 80

monism, 202; monisms, Asiatic, 356

Monologia (St. Augustine's), 208

"monological," 175

monologue, 599; monologues, disguised, 277f

monotheism, 218f, 257; Biblical, 273

Montague, William P., 64

moral, action by nonbelievers, 700; anarchy, 170; as not equivalent to social, 528, 536; assurance, 160; codes, conventional, and the artist, 619; decisions, making of, 718; ends as social, 526; obligation, 200; obligation, the basis of, 198; decision, complete privacy of each, 161; decision, phenomenology of, 157; order, 170; rules, universally valid, 720; situation, the uniqueness of each, 158; teaching, 575

morality, and religion, 104; and the artist, 561; a struggle, 157; in living community, 168f; linked to God, 159; self-created, 177

Mordecai, Rabbi, 428

Morris, Charles W., 532

Moses, 164, 221, 230, 368, 371f, 379, 392ff, 699

Moses, 319f, 326, 362, 459

Mosheh of Kobryn, Rabbi, 678

motto for Buber's philosophy, 219-20

movement, the, 18

Mowinckel, Sigmund, 401

Muilenberg, James, 726ff; essay by, 381-402

Mumford, Lewis, 270f

Murphy, Arthur, 519

Muschg, Walter, 669

music, analysis of, 622ff

mutualities, two, 105f

mutuality, 129, 192, 236; human, 123; of human relations, 110f; of I-Thou relation, 279; primacy of, 97ff; problem of, 707ff; threshold of, 708

"mysterium," 98

mystery, irreducible, 593

mystic, Buber not a, 297

mystical, approach to world, 299; vitalism, 348

mysticism, 75; a form of pseudo-religion, 284; a grandiose illusion, 283; distinctive nature of Buber's, 298; Jewish, 304; realistic and activistic, 304f; world-negating, 298

myth, cabbalistic, 357; distinction between legend and, 33

mythology, Jewish, 71

N

Nachman, Rabbi of Bratzlav, 417, 636, 652

Nahman of Kossow, 416

Napoleon Bonaparte, 27, 301; as "Gog," 654

narcissism, 582f

"narrow ridge," 205, 232, 246, 249, 266

"National Education" (Buber's essay), 263

national liberation, the desire for, 266

nationalism, 239; as idolatry, 536; identified with the will of God, 445f; justified, 444f; modern secularist, influence of . . . on Jewish life, 268

Natorp, Paul, 207

natural science as I-Thou, 603-07

nature, contact with, 7

negation is ultimate, 59

Neo-Kantianism, 256

Neumann, Karl Eugen, 671

New Testament, 315, 382, 397

Nicolas of Cusa, 482

Niebuhr, Reinhold, 681

Nietzsche, Friedrich, 12f, 42, 80, 107, 140, 260, 336, 476, 481, 487, 500ff, 511, 643, 647, 653, 667, 676ff, 701, 704, 709; Nietzsche's Dionysos, 221

Nirvana (Nibbana), 79f

Noah, 363

nominalists, 207

non-commital objectivity of theory, 206f

non-realization, 299

normative, 173

norms, moral, 178f

nothingness, 652ff

Novalis, 480, 506

novelty, 523

O

objectification, peril of, 48

objective, criterion of knowledge, 239f; knowledge, 135; "objective Spirit" (Hegel), 47

objectivity, impartial, 207; of philosophy, impersonal, 207; the false ideal of, 318; vs. subjectivity, 605f

obligation, the absoluteness of, 152

obscurantism, 276

observer, attitude of, 236

occasionalism, 570; believing, 576

Ockhamites, 207

Odysseus, 631

Oedipus, 637

Old Covenant, the voice of the past, 343

Old Testament, 33, 88, 310, 313, 315ff

Olsen, Regina, 78

omnipotence, 89
omniscience, 51, 54
onlooker, attitude of, 236
ontological, 174; character of dialogue, 240; concepts, 247; reality, 177; problem, Buber's, 107; relevance, difference between factual importance and, 123ff; transpersonal ultimate (God) , 246
ontology, 123ff, 134, 140; of human life, Buber's, 97; of human relations, 119
open system, 499; of G. H. Mead, 524
openness, committed, 286
operationalist description, 194
optimism, Buber's, 120ff
Opus Posthumum (Kant's), 214f
Oracles of Feeling, 584
order, moral, 170
Orexis, 208
Orient, 300
Origen, 345
oscillation, Buber's, 128; on reflection, Buber's, 124
other, the, 10; (God), 105ff
otherness, 82f, 138, 141, 148; "otherness" of God, 357; of the Thou, the radical, 141
Otto, Rudolf, 333
ought, 177, 189f; "ought," the source of, 171
over-againstness, 35ff
overstating his (Buber's) case, 93f

P

pain, 142
Palestine, 266
palimpsest, 364
pantheism, 310; cabbalistic, 358
Panwitz, 353
Paradise story, 376f
paradox, 700f; of human existence, 530; of intense non-belief, 482; of our existence, 298; the language of, 243
paradoxical, expressions, 247; formulations, 244; unity of alternatives, (Buber's), 249
Parmenides, 133f, 141, 230
participant observation, 586
participation, 66, 117f, 345; the law of, 138

party struggles in democracies, 574
Pascal, Blaise, 28, 208, 210f, 255, 260, 331, 479, 498, 578, 742; Pascal's *Pensees*, 544
Pasternak, Boris, 626
Paths in Utopia (Buber's), 350, 439
Paul, Jean, 4
Paul, St., 23, 312, 313, 315ff, 327f, 330f, 334-37, 340, 344, 354, 379, 452f, 506, 641f; Paul's theology, 317; gnostic terminology, 317
Pauline world-view, 314
peace, 166, 268; only as compatible with justice, 713
pedagogical theory, 571
Peirce, Charles Sanders, 61, 68, 514, 532
Pentateuch, 160, 165
perfect, religious meaning of, 60
person, 196f, 611f; -and cause, 18; as psychic system, 578
personal relations, 696
personalistic interpretation of faith, 315
personality, 101, 196, 521ff; as (Kantian) category, 140
Personhaftigkeit, 227
personhood, 82, 85
personnalité, 82
Pestalozzi, 544
Peter, 358f
Pfuetze, Paul, 712; essay by, 511-42
Pharisees, 328, 331, 335f
phenomenological character of Buber's descriptions, 139
phenomenology, 134; Buber's, 103; existential, 208
Philo (Judaeus), 229
philosopher, job of, 436; philosophers as governors, 253
philosophic, thinking and religious tradition, relation between, 269; thinking, the self-corrective character of, 270
philosophical, anthropology, 225, 259, 690, 693; Buber's, 171ff, 179; Buber's doctrine not strictly, 296; "philosophical intuition," (Buber's) , 105; knowledge a third kind of knowledge, 295; theology, 86
philosophy, American, 514ff; bad, 283; deals in abstractions, 292n; of history, Buber's sketch of, 47;

(The) Philosophy of Martin Buber, 269; of religion, 343; of religion, Buber's, 171f; protest and reconstruction within, 513ff

philosophizing, the right kind of, 295

physicalism, misplaced, 230

physics, contemporary, 606f; as a social phenomenon, 607

physicist as philosopher, 606

Picard, Max, 47

Pinchas, Rabbi, 545

pity, the unique value of, 596f

plants, Thou relationship with, 708

Plato, 11, 87, 107, 133f, 141, 152, 184, 207ff, 212f, 219, 221, 253, 259, 261, 271, 439, 448, 457, 508, 649, 685; Plato's *Seventh Letter,* 327; "Plato and Isaiah," Buber's inaugural address, 259

Platonic, 242; ideas, 709; tradition, 230; universal, 180

pluriversum (James's) , 218

poet, as faithful to dialogue, 625f; "beat," 625; genuine, 626

poetry, analysis of, 624ff; definition of, 625

Pointing the Way, 448f, 458n

politics, and morality, 442; as demonic force, 435; utopian, 448f

Politeia (Aristotle), 208

polytheism, 219

Pontius Pilate, 452

positivism, 235f

post-Hegelian, 295

post-Kantian, 295; idealism, 92

postulative, bias, Buber's, 128; nature of Buber's thinking, 132

potential, the absolute infinity of the, 53

potentiality, human, 173

Pound, Ezra, 625

power, 165; vs. reason, 253

practical reason, the primacy of the, 214

pragmatism, 511-42

Prague circle, 323

prayer, 680f; forced, 431; immediacy of, 329

predicament, human, 132

presence, 130, 704

"present, making," 174f

presentness, 173ff, 192, 196

Pre-Socratics, 669

priests, 254

"Primal Present," 216

primal source, 192

principles, of literary translation, 672f; *Principles of the Philosophies of the Future, The,* 42

process philosophies, 197

profane realm, sanctification of, 420

promised land, 448

prophecy, 373, 480f; as apocalyptic, 460ff; Hebrew, 537

Prophet, 364

prophets, 254, 321, 372; of Israel, 715

Prophetic Faith, 272, 319f, 390f, 397f, 459

Protagoras, 270

Protestantism, liberal, 342f

Proudhon, 439, 551

Proust, Marcel, 225f

Psalms, 199

Psalmist, 345

pseudo-religion, 283

psychiatric disorder as failure in meaning, 590

psychiatrist's condescension, 668

psychiatry's debt to H. S. Sullivan, 581

"psychic phenomena," 291

psychoanalytic vocabulary, and character assassination, 598

psychological, categorizations, Buber's rejection of, 240; orientation, 292

psychologist, a scientific, 281

psychologizing God, 303

purity, true, 572

Pygmalion, 559

Q

question, unanswerable, 357

R

radical, challenge, Buber's, 238; evil, 568

Ragaz, Leonhard, 333, 350

Ranke, 680

ratio, 81

rational, consistency (Tillich's), 246; inquiry, 274, 276; inquiry, acceptance of modern principle of, 281f

rationalism, 274, 297f

rationalistic prejudice, Buber's, 308

Read, Herbert, 558

real (defined), 299; existence, 124; person, 535

realism, Buber's, 116, 119

realists, 207

reality, 276, 512; always in a present, 523; concept of, 124f; intuitive approach to, 239; of experienced world, 297; social nature of, 518; "Reality, the Great," 298, 308

realization, 299

Realphantasie, 118, 562

Realpolitik, 322

Realverhältnis zum Seienden, 143

reason, 214; existential distortions of, 247; the right of, 297; vs. power, 253

rebirth, 188; the wheel of, 79

reciprocity, of God and man, 303; vital, 189

reconciliation, 186ff; by the death on the cross, 315

recurrence, eternal, 202

redemption, 301, 305f, 375, 377, 441, 729, 739; a divine-human process, 224; in suffering, 232

Reden über das Judentum (Buber's), 342

Redlichkeit (Buber's), 203

referral of close friend or relative for treatment, 589

reflection, 124f; not equivalent to awareness, 695; position of, 111f

Reformation, 250

Reich, W., 588

reine Beziehung, 215

relatedness, 140; primacy of, 50

relation, as mutuality, 657ff; essential, 97; human-divine, 86; subject-object, 133; three-fold, 536

relationship, 74ff, 215, 694; concept of, 124; genuine and immediate, 441

relativism, the end of all, 353

relativity, as absolute, 54; Buber's supreme metaphysical principle, 49f, 52; of the individual and environment, 524

religion, 296n; and ethics, relation between, 718f; and morality, 104, 700; and the everyday world, 682; "Religion as Reality," (lecture by Buber), 27f; as everything, 26, 222; Buber's ethical basis, 171; genuine, 284; in the United States, 681; of rapture,

Buber rejects, 656; pseudo, 536; worthwhile meaning for, 666

religious, community, the foundation of the, 218; crisis, the contemporary, 265; definition of, 618; existence of man, 742; existentialism, 276; experience, 25f; experience and anthropological philosophy, the unity of, 109; idealism, the God of, 275f; language, Buber's use of, 244; principles, in politics, 440f; renewal, 205; socialists, 311; speculation, highest step of, 213; tradition and philosophic thinking, relation between, 269; tradition, possible attitudes to, 263; truth, 203

Renaissance, 250, 261; modern Jewish, 267

Renouvier, Charles Bernard, 82

Republic, The (Plato's), 152, 199, 254

response to any Thou requires total commitment, 288

responsibility, 141f, 142f, 146f, 167, 173ff, 177, 185, 190, 530n; as focus of dialogue, 100; of man, 533; spiritual, 258; two senses of, 99f

"return to God," 316

revelation, 153ff, 160f, 163, 165, 172, 180ff, 228f, 244, 272, 296n, 377ff; a mixture of the divine and human, 156; a personal, 183; as "hearable" content, 290; attacks on possibility of, 274; Buber's understanding of Biblical belief in, 278; can there be, 277; criteria of, 155f; definition of—ends in antinomy, 289f; divine, 276f, 698; experience—of, 277; existential participation of the Jew in, 345; God's, 273ff; historical, 315; in the Bible, 368; minimum content of, 287; not a code, 158; of God the origin of religious reality, 303; superterrestrial, 227; the human share in it, 699

reverence, the path of, 307; for the absolute, 265

revivalism, 681

"revolution," history as "conservative," 203

revolutions, and the Line of Demarcation, 573f

riddle of the absolute and the relative, solution of the, 63f

ridge, narrow, 205
Right and Wrong, 362, 391
Rilke, Rainer Maria, 215, 221, **223**, 225, 633, 669, 671, 677
risk, moral, 151
Roman Catholic, 310
Romans 4; 11:15, 18, 29; 344, **354**
romanticism, 512
Rosenstock-Huessy, Eugen, 515
Rosenzweig, Franz, 8, 34, 41, 120, 122, 158f, 201, 204, 215, 218, 256, 272, 323, 341, 361, 364f, 385, 514f, 532, 544n, 550, 576, 642, 669-73, 676, 704
Rotenstreich, Nathan, 694ff, 701-04, **712**; essay by, 97-132
Rousseau, Jean Jacques, 268
Royce, Josiah, 514; as transition between absolute idealism and existentialist thought, 515n
R-perfection, 60ff
Ruskin, John, 558

S

Sabbatai Zvi, 634
Sabbatianism, 416f
Sacral Kingship, 401f
sacramental life, **226**
sacramentalism, 358
sacred authority, 273f
sacred scriptures, 680
Sadagora, Galicia, 19, 250
salvation, 255, 260, 266, 272; cross a new way of, 316; messianic-eschatological view of, rejected, 347; universal, 344
Samuel (Bible), 31ff
Samuel-Saul narratives, 389f
Sartre, Jean Paul, 153, 177, 481, 500-02, 509, 512, 647, 649, 658, 665, 677
Satan, 199
Saul, King, 31
sceptical attitude towards philosophical systems, Buber's, 115
Schatz-Uffenheimer, Rivkah, essay by, 403-34
Scheler, Max, 42, 100, 123, 125, 206, 225, 228, 261, 348, 512, 570, 639, 645
Schelling, Friedrich Wilhelm Joseph von, 4, 53, 58, 61, 208, 215, **228**, 276, 511, 667

Schicksal, 202
schizophrenia, 580f, 586ff, 591; as extreme withering of the Thou capacity, 587f; of today's humanity, 219; world of, 663
Schleiermacher, 470, 681
Schmitt, Karl, 442
Schneider, 713
Schneider, Herbert W., essay by, 469-74
Schoeps, Hans Joachim, 329, 342
Scholem, Gershom, 732
Schopenhauer, Arthur, 643, 647
Schopenhauer, Arthur, Kierkegaard's comment on, 513
Schöpfung, 80
Schuenemann, Heinrich, 565
Schuon, Firthjof, 307f
Schweitzer, Albert, 333
science('s) turns Thou into an It, 56; approach to reality, 239f; behavioristic limitation, 57; methodological exclusion, 56
scientific, knowledge, 282; method, intuitive, 390; technology, the age of, 318
scientist, as true mystic of our time, 581
secular behaviorism, 528
security, philosophical, 151
seduction, 165
seelengeschichtlich, 71
Seer of Lublin, 738, 740
Sefirot, the Kabbalistic, 221
Seiende, das, 81, 83
Seiendes, 139
Sein des Seienden (Heidegger), 147
Seinszusammenhang, 83
Selbstständigkeit, 80
self(-), 136f, 173, 189, 521f; acquiring of, 530; and society, 522; absorption, excessive, 239; as a series of dialogues, 585; choice, 650; choice of or loss of, 658; consciousness, presupposition of, 127; enlightenment, 569; fulfillment, 167, 721; in Buber's philosophy vs. Kantian "subject," 534n; knowledge, 530; knowledge of M. Buber, 689; mortification, 423f; other, 527; realization, 189, 197, 695; realization-with-me, 563; rejection, 651; transcendence, 77ff; unification, 650

selfhood, as achievement, 533; Buber's conception of, 74
semantics, 75
sensuality, 112
separateness, man's, 149f
seriousness in life, 681
Sermon on the Mount, 313, 330, 349, 358f
Shakespeare, W., 671
Shaw, Geo. B., 472
shekina, 224, 304, 357, 655, 733, 735
Shema, 219
shift, the great (in Buber's thought), 302f
Shlomo, Rabbi, 735, 740f
Shmelke, Rabbi, 735
Sicily, 253
"Sickness of Time," 122
sickness of our time, 132
Siddhartha, 681
sign, 74
silence, fear of, 594
Silesius, Angelus, 643
smile of Jewish women, 17
Simmel, Georg, 202, 250, 348, 518, 643
Simon, Ernst, 704, 722ff; essay by, 543-76
sin, 315f; as failure to respond to the other, 221
Sinai, Mount, 275, 379
Sinai of the future, 548
singularity, focussed, 75f
"situationless-ness," 184
"situations" vs. "principles," 722
Smith, Adam, 518
Smith, Ronald Gregor, 235
social, democrats, 472f; elite, 552f; legislation, 165f; self, 527n; structure of existence, 530, 532
socialism, 350; classless, 474; utopian, 537
society, and community, 103f; organic interpretation of, 535; unholiness of, 340; vs. community, 437
Socinians, 61
Socinus, 54, 64
Socrates, 94, 270
Söderblom, Bishop, 333
Soliloquia (St. Augustine's), 208
solipsist, 82
solipsistic predicament, 119
solitude, 38; man's sense of, 71
"Some Problems in Buber's Moral

Philosophy," essay by Marvin Fox, 151-70
Sophist, the, 134
Sophists, 270
Sophocles, 671
soul, whole, 720, 724
source, the theocracy of the, 349
sovereignty, God's, 232
space-time, objective, 236
spectator, 141; position of, 111
Spinoza, Baruch de, 59, 227, 231, 246, 480; the God of, 246
Spinozistic philosophy, 121f
spirit, and world, 38; become word, 709
spiritual conception of U.S.A. "without benefit of clergy," 269; "spiritual elite," 724; "spiritual monasticism," 81; "spiritual" themes, 148
spontaneity, 191; as response, 710; social, 436
stages of selfhood, 533
state, as compulsion, 574
Stein, Edith, 229
Steiner, Rudolf, 306f, 716
Stirner, Max, 75f, 270, 504f, 509
Stoic *ataraxia*, 575
Stravinsky, Igor, 612, 623
subject, autonomous, 135; -object antithesis, 309f; -object problem, the vanishing of the, 135; -object relation, 133f
"subjectivism" in Buber, 744
success, 19
suffering, 232; servant, 372, 399; the mystery of, 342
Sufis, the, 732
Sullivan, Harry S., 580f
Sumeria, 353
super-human personality, 105
supernatural, 197, 273f
"supernature," a misleading concept, 712
superterrestrial revelation, 227
suprapersonal, the, 221
Symposium (Plato's), 87, 219
Systematic Theology (Tillich's), 244f
Szondi, Dr., 550

T

taboos, 567f
Tales of the Hasidim, 223
Talmud, 336, 569

Tannaites, 374

Taoism, 353

Taoist teaching, 184f

Taubes, Jacob, 715, 721, 729f; essay by, 451-68

teacher, role of, 717f

"teaching," the, 629ff; practical vs. theoretical pedagogy, 543

temperament, Buber's early revolutionary, 203

temporal life, division of, 25

Ten Commandments, 570f

tenderness, definition of, 583

terminology, Buber's vacillation in, 116

Teshuvah, 655

Thales, 457

theism, traditional problem of, 242

theologians, 60f; existentialist, 318

theological, anthropology, 261, 744; conceptualizing, the necessity of, 247; implications of dialogue, 241ff; truth, no objective criterion of, 241

theologies of Paul and John, 313

theology, 241ff, 703; apologetic, 247; Christian, 304; confessional, 247; Theology of the New Testament (Bultmann's), 317f

theory, romantic devaluation of, 592

therapy, 588

things, relationship with, 145

thinking, as internalized conversation, 522; "thinking, the new," 201

third kind of knowledge, 292

Thomas, St., 331

Thomists, 665

Thou, 106ff, 137ff, 191, 216, 231, 278ff, 296n; as a priori, 138; as innate, 138; epistemological question of the, 107f; eternal, 661; Thou-I relation (Buber's), 10; into It, 659; meeting with the eternal, 154; metaphysical status of, 281; of the faithful vs. the human Thou, 660

thouhood, 74

Tillich, Paul, comparison with, 244ff, 647, 683, 715

Timaeus (Plato), 208

time, in G. H. Mead's philosophy, 522ff; the irreversibility of lived, 186; sickness of our, 122, 132

Toennies, Ferdinand, 437, 655

Tolstoy, Count Leo N., 224, 555

Torah, 163, 204, 209, 222, 331, 364, 372, 378f; levels of reading of, 418ff

Torczyner, Harry, 670, 674-76

Tower of Babel, 386

tradition, authentic religious, intrinsic qualities of, 261ff; Buber's rejection of a frozen, 264; community of, 204; Jewish, 202, 204; the Judaeo-Christian, 86, 88; metamorphosis of the religious, 272

tragedy, in presence of, 17

transcendence, act of, 144; divine, 229

"Transcendental Relativity," 54f, 63f, 68

"Transference," 589f

transformation of the world, 715

translation of great books, 670-77

transpersonal, 213

transtheistic position, Buber avoids the, 245

treatment, necessity of recovery from, 591

Tree of Knowledge, 376f

Trietsch, Davis, 16

Trimurti, the Indian, 221

troth-truth, 204

true, being of a person, 604; purity, 572

Trueb, Hans, 567

trust, 193ff, 566, 589; ethics of, 104

truth as attitude, inquiry, struggle, 143; is commitment, 141; as hierarchy, 516; Truth As Meeting (Brunner's), 317; participation as the essence of, 515; principle of, 131; religious, 203

truthfulness, 589

truths, unimportant and most important, 516

Tur-Sinai, Harry, 670

twofold, nature of everything, 298; pattern of Jewish existence, 355

Two Types of Faith (Buber's), 269

U

übertäubt isolation, 42

"ultimatum," 343

Umfassung, 142, 148

Umkehr, 209

Umwelt, 83, 187, 488

unconditionality of the spirit vs. conditionality of a situation, 441

undiscussible, discuss the, 53

unification, Buber's doctrine of, 300
unifying process, 299
unique and particular, related to the "general," 689
uniqueness, 173ff; Israel's, 352ff; of each moral decision, 158
United States, 268
unity, 301; deed, and the future, 538; essential for faith, 347; in duality, 215f; of the contraries, 243
universal and particular, harmonization of, by G. H. Mead, 534; "Universal Judaism" (Cohen's), 257
universalism, 207
Upanishads, 681
Urdistanz, 357f
Ursprung, 343
Usener, 218
utopia, 351; paths of, 356
"Utopian Zionism" (Buber's), 257
Uzziah, King, 254

V

Valéry, Paul, 612
validation, empirical, 238
values, discovered, 153; eternal, 536, 567, 720; intrinsic, 172
valuing, 173
Vedantist, 185
Verbunden(heit), 141f, 149
Vergegenwaertigung, personale, 117
Vergegnung, 4
Verhältnis, 69, 86
Verherrlichung, 226
Verstehen, 119
vicariously suffering servant, 316
Vico, Giambattista, 47
Vienna, 3; University of, 250; University of, Buber's attendance in, 13
violence, the evil of, 165
vocation of man, 225
voice of God, in a criminal, 720
volcanic hour, 123
voluntarism, of Wm. James, 514

W

Wahl, Jean, 713; essay by, 475-510
war(s), 24; Jewish-Arab, 547
Ward, James, 64
Warren, Robt. Penn, 625
Wartenburg, Paul Yorck von, 217n

"We," 103f, 184ff
weapons, atomic, 604f
Weber, Max, 18, 369, 382
Weizsäcker, Carl F. von, essay by, 603-07
Weizsäcker, Viktor von, 645
Welt, 187
Weltanschauung, 28
Welthaftigkeit, 80
Weltsch, Robert, essay by, 435-47
Weltweiser, Buber as, 222
Werfel, Franz, 207
Westöstliche Divan (Goethe's), 223
Wheelwright, Philip, 710; essay by, 69-95
Whitehead, Alfred North, 49, 58, 64f, 197, 532, 540
whole being, 118
wholeness, 173ff
Wie erlangt man Erkenntnisse hoeherer Welten? (Steiner's), 307
Wieman, Henry Nelson, 269
Wilson, Woodrow, 269
wisdom, Buber's, 68
"wishful thinking" as substitute for truth, 589
Wittig, Joseph, 645
Wolf, Rabbi Ze'er, 415
Word and the Spiritual Realities, The (Ebner's), 309
Word of God, 228, 383, 644f, 690
world, meaning of, 28; and spirit, 38; -embracing, 299; -immanence, 35f
World War I, 302; prediction of, 23ff
Wundt, Wilhelm, 518

Y

Yahweh, 85, 218, 221, 228f, 315, 320ff, 387, 392ff, 399ff, 459, 462, 467; "Yahweh, Servant of," 358
Yehudi, 65, 426-33; and Jesus of Nazareth, 464f; Holy, 654ff, 715, 740f
Yeshaya, Rabbi, 429, 431
Yitzhak, Rabbi, 735

Z

Zaddik, the, 19ff, 404, 408, 417ff, 634, 636, 684f, 734
Zaddikim, 467, 733
Zalman, Rabbi Shneur, 680
Zarathustra, 676, 701
Zechariah, 372

Zeitgeist, 41
Zen Buddhism, 298, 301, 554, 732
Zeus, 87
Zion, 704f
Zionism, 261, 266f, 439, 446ff, 457, 473, 544, 547f, 555, 563; political, 353

Zionist, Congress, 16; movement, 250f
Zoroastrianism, 353
zu-gedacht, 202
Zusya, Rabbi, 738
Zwischen, philosophy of the, 42f, 139, 146, 148
Zwischenmenschliche, das, 174